Assessment in Higher Education

Higher Education Policy Series
Edited by Maurice Kogan

Higher education is now the subject of far reaching and rapid policy change. This series will be of value to those who have to manage that change, as well as to consumers and evaluators of higher education in the UK and elsewhere. It offers information and analysis of new developments in a concise and usable form. It also provides reflective accounts of the impacts of higher education policy. Higher education administrators, governors and policy makers will use it, as well as students and specialists in education policy.

Maurice Kogan is Professor of Government and Social Administration at Brunel University and Joint Director of the Centre for the Evaluation of Public Policy and Practice.

The Idea of a University
Edited by David Smith and Anne Karin Langslow
ISBN 1 85302 728 6 pb
ISBN 1 85302 727 8 hb
Higher Education Policy Series 51

Changing Relationships Between Higher Education and The State
Mary Henkel and Brenda Little
ISBN 1 85302 645 X pb
ISBN 1 85302 644 1 hb
Higher Education Policy Series 45

Higher Education in a Post-Binary Era
National Reforms and Institutional Responses
Edited by David Teather
ISBN 1 85302 425 2 pb
ISBN 1 85302 535 6 hb
Higher Education Policy Series 38

Innovation and Adaptation in European Higher Education
The Changing Conditions of Advanced Teaching and Learning in Europe
Edited by Claudius Gellert
ISBN 1 85302 628 X pb
ISBN 1 85302 535 6 hb
Higher Education Policy Series 22

Reforming Higher Education
Maurice Kogan and Stephen Hanney
ISBN 1 85302 715 4 pb
Higher Education Policy Series 50

Transforming Universities
Changing Patterns of Governance Structure
and Learning in Swedish Higher Education
Marianne Bauer, Susan Marton, Berit Askling and Ference Marton
ISBN 1 85302 675 1 pb
Higher Education Policy Series 48

Towards a New Model of Governance for Universities?
A Comparative View
Edited by Dietmar Braun and François-Xavier Merrien
ISBN 1 85302 773 1 pb
Higher Education Policy Series 53

Higher Education Policy Series 56

Assessment in Higher Education

Student Learning, Teaching, Programmes and Institutions

John Heywood

Foreword by Thomas Angelo

Jessica Kingsley Publishers
London and Philadelphia

The right of John Heywood to be identified as author of this work has been asserted by him in accordance with the Copyright, Designs and Patents Act 1988.

First published in the United Kingdom in 2000 by
Jessica Kingsley Publishers Ltd,
116 Pentonville Road,
London N1 9JB, England

and

325 Chestnut Street,
Philadelphia
PA 19106, USA

www.jkp.com

© Copyright 2000 John Heywood

Library of Congress Cataloging in Publication Data
Heywood, John, 1930–
    Assessment in higher education / John Heywood.
        p.   cm. -- (Higher education policy : 56)
    Includes bibliographical references and index.
    ISBN 1 85302-831-2 (alk. paper)
    1. Universities and colleges--Examinations. 2. College teaching-
    -Evaluation. 3. Education, Higher--Evaluation. 4. Education,
    Higher--Aims and objectives. I. Title.   II. Series : Higher
    education policy series : 56
    LB2366.H49   1999   99-41630
    378.1'664--dc21   CIP

British Library Cataloguing in Publication Data
Heywood, John, 1930–
    Assessment in higher education. – (Higher education policy; 56)
    1. Grading and marking (Students) 2. Education, Higher –
    Evaluation 3. Educational accountability
    I. Title
    378.1'664
    ISBN 1 85302 831 2

Printed and Bound in Great Britain by
Athenaeum Press, Gateshead, Tyne and Wear

Contents

For Georgine Loaker and the Faculty of Alverno College who have promoted Assessment As Learning, and my mentors John Cowan, George Carter and Deryk Kelly.

Foreword

Assessment has come to mean so many different and sometimes conflicting things in higher education that responding usefully to that range in a single volume would have seemed an impossible task. Therefore, I'm very pleased to report that, in *Assessment in Higher Education*, Professor John Heywood has succeeded in realizing that daunting challenge.

This is a work of exceptional breadth and depth, exemplifying what Ernest L. Boyer, in *Scholarship Reconsidered* (1990) referred to as the scholarship of integration. Boyer defined integration as 'serious, disciplined work that seeks to interpret, draw together, and bring new insight to bear on original research' (p.18). Professor Heywood has done just that in identifying, synthesizing, and bringing his insights and experience to bear on research from a vast array of topics, disciplines and sources. The topics illuminated range from classroom feedback to policy issues, from validity concerns to vocational education, and from retention studies to reflective thinking. The disciplinary literatures represented include cognitive science, many and various branches of psychology, measurement and evaluation, instructional science, and higher education – but also medicine, engineering, and the physical sciences. The range of institutions and national systems drawn on is similarly vast. Professor Heywood provides readers a great service not only in reviewing relevant research and practice from across the English-speaking world – and often beyond it – but also in 'translating' and explaining the import of those findings to the various constituencies. As one example, he takes care throughout to deal with common misconceptions that US academics have about assessment practices in the UK and vice versa. If this is not the first truly international book on assessment in higher education, it is certainly the most comprehensive and useful.

Assessment in Higher Education also shows impressive depth in its treatment of assessment as a field of inquiry. In their recent *Assessment Essentials*, Palomba and Banta define assessment as '... the systematic collection, review, and use of information about educational programs for the purpose of improving student learning and development' (1999, p.4). Central to this model is the belief that our assumptions about learning outcomes should be empirically tested and that our claims should be based in evidence. Throughout this book, which goes well beyond the 'essentials,' Heywood maintains a clear, consistent focus on the profound importance of assessment for understanding and improving student learning and development, without slighting questions of accountability and quality assurance at programme and institutional levels.

In additon to the *scholarship of integration*, this volume embodies the *scholarship of application*, about which Boyer wrote:

> The third element, the *application* of knowledge, moves toward engagement as the scholar asks, 'How can knowledge be responsibly applied to consequential problems? How can it be helpful to individuals as well as institutions?' And further,

'Can social problems themselves define an agenda for scholarly investigation?'. (1990, p.21)

Precisely because Professor Heywood has kept a focus on the practical as well as intellectual needs of his audiences, *Assessment in Higher Education* will be of much use to academics, administrators, and policymakers interested in designing, implementing, and applying the results of assessment. In sum, the careful reader will find a wealth of knowledge, insight, resources, and practical guidelines in this volume.

Thomas Angelo,
The SNL Assessment Center School for New Learning,
De Paul University

Preface

In the western world, during the last 15 years, there has been an enormous increase in interest in 'assessment' in higher education. In the United States, in the mid-1980, the American Association for Higher Education initiated an assessment forum that has since caused a wide-ranging debate at its annual conferences. In the United Kingdom in the early 1990s the funding agencies began to focus on the 'quality assessment' of higher education, and a Quality Assurance Agency was established.

Unfortunately, as the assessment movement has grown so the term has acquired many meanings. On the one hand, it has been applied to the assessment of student learning, while on the other hand it has been applied to the assessment of institutions, programmes and teaching. It is often used as a substitute for evaluation. A new vocabulary has emerged, and the purposes of the first two chapters are to describe this vocabulary, and to suggest an integrated model of the assessment-curriculum-learning-teaching process.

Whether it is the assessment of student learning or the effectiveness of institutions or programmes or teachers in achieving that learning the process of assessment is the same. It requires a declaration of purpose that is open to evaluation, methods for achieving that purpose, and assessment techniques that reliably and validly check that the purposes are being achieved – and if not, why not. Illustrations throughout the book show that simplistic evaluations often produce misleading information, and that the design of assessment techniques that validly assess student learning is neither a routine nor simple matter.

It is now well understood, as it was not before, that assessment has a powerful influence on student learning. However, it is not so well understood that institutional structures and procedures have an equally profound influence on teaching and learning, and the way learning is assessed. Often changes are made in structures and procedures that pay scant attention to either the cognitive and personal development of students or to the ways in which they learn. A general consideration of this point is made in Chapter 3 and it is illustrated from time to time throughout the text. The term 'assessment' is applied to the assessment of teachers by their peers and the possibilities and limitations of this process are discussed. Many agencies require that institutions obtain student ratings of the teaching they receive, as well as data from alumni. Problems and practice in the interpretation of such data and the uses to which such data may be put are discussed in Chapter 4. The rating of teaching, however, gives but a limited view of the experience received by students in higher education institutions. If we are to understand the factors which influence attrition and retention then it is necessary to assess the experience students have of higher education in general. Chapter 5, therefore, considers some of the studies and instruments used to evaluate the experience of higher education.

These early chapters show repeatedly that in circumstances of increasing diversity teachers will need to know much more about the qualities which students bring to their courses if the design of assessment and instruction is to be effective. Factors relating to temperament, teaching and testing are considered in Chapter 6, and cognitive personal development in Chapter 7. The way the strategies and styles students bring to their learning are influenced by assessment and instruction is discussed in Chapter 9. This chapter is preceded by discussion of concept learning and the implications that this has for the design of the curriculum and assessment. Some techniques for assessing the level of understanding during class work are considered.

The remaining chapters consider developments in the techniques of assessment and the desire to improve the quality of the assessments made. Chapter 10 rehearses the problem of reliability in the grading of assessments and the calculation of final grades. It also considers issues relating to the comparability of standards as between the programmes offered by institutions and between them. Chapters 11 and 12 discuss techniques that have been used to make assessment more valid including portfolios. These chapters range from the assessment of essays through orals, practicals, simulations, and projects to problem based learning. Very often these new techniques require more time from assessors than has been the case in the past, and in consequence it will be necessary for curriculum designers to evaluate the benefit–costs of the technique proposed. The advantages and disadvantages of objective tests, and aspects of their design, are considered in Chapter 13 based on classical test theory. That discussion is preceded by a brief review of the role of structured and short-answer questions in assessment. Chapter 14 concludes with a description of developments in peer and self-assessment as teachers strive to develop reflective practice.

From whichever perspective assessment is viewed, all avenues lead to the conclusion that for learning to be enhanced a multiple-strategy approach to assessment and instruction is required. This has implications for structures and procedures at all levels, namely the institution, the programme, the department, and the classroom.

John Heywood

Acknowledgements

I am deeply grateful to Professor John Cowan (formerly of The Open University in Scotland and Visiting Professor at the University of Salford) and Dr Peter Knight (University of Lancaster) who read all the drafts, made numerous valuable suggestions, and encouraged its completion. While I have not responded to all their points I hope they will welcome the finished product.

This work builds on three others produced in the last 20 years. During their production I received advice, help and in particular encouragement from numerous colleagues and friends. I would like to give a special thank you to Mr Lester Parker (Department of Education and Employment, Sheffield) who acted as my critical friend in the work leading up to this book. Among those in the UK who have encouraged my work and to whom I owe a debt of gratitude I would like to mention Sir Charles Carter who started it all off, Professor Clive Church (University of Kent), the late Mr 'Bill' Humble (British Steel Corporation), Dr Gerry Forrest (Joint Matriculation Board), Mr Denis Monk (Middlesex Polytechnic), Dr Bob Oxtoby (Bolton Institute of Higher Education), Dr Michael Youngman (University of Nottingham), and Professor Mantz Yorke (Liverpool John Moore's University). In the United States I have received help and encouragement, for which I am most grateful, from Dr Clifford Adelman (US Department of Education), Dr Tom Angelo (DePaul University, Chicago), Dr Jill Bogard (Librarian, The American Council on Education), Dr Richard Culver (SUNY, Binghamton), Drs Georgine Loacker, Marcia Mentokowski, Dr Glen Rogers and numerous colleagues and students of Alverno College and Dr T. Marchese (American Association for Higher Education). Finally, in Ireland, I am grateful to Dr Seamus McGuinness and the late Denstone Murphy for their support when we worked together on assessment in school education.

Chapter 1

Assessment in Higher Education
Clarifying Issues and Terms

Summary

The developments in assessment theory and practice during the last decade have been accompanied by inconsistency in the application of terms. Confusion abounds and this has been compounded by the importation of business terms, in particular those related to quality and its management in industry. A major purpose of the first three chapters is to unravel this confusion so as to clarify the issues involved. In this chapter attention is given to the debate which has taken place about the concept of validity particularly as it relates to testing. This issue is taken up again in Chapter 3 with reference to the assessment of institutions and programmes. Problems of reliability are considered in Chapter 10. The move to outcomes based curriculum is recorded, and the concept of curriculum integrated assessment introduced. Assessment is defined as a multidimensional process for judging individuals and institutions in action. In so far as individuals are concerned, it is important that everyone involved in the production of a curriculum, including policy makers, should understand the role that assessment plays in learning. For this reason they should have a defensible theory of learning.

Judgement: the case for assessment

Teachers at all levels of education sit in judgement of both themselves and their students, and therefore assess the daily lives of themselves and those whom they teach. Some school teachers loathe making formal assessments of their pupils, preferring to leave this to public examinations set by others than themselves; yet even they make judgements about their pupils. Making judgements is part of life whether the ones made are right or wrong, valid and reliable or not.

Consider for a moment the judgements that have to be made when cooking. As Nicolas Freeling, the cook-cum-crime writer reminds us, you cannot give definite times or exact quantities because nothing is ever quite the same from one week to the next.

> Even things like flour or potatoes fluctuate in the quantity of water they hold, a piece of meat a week old from one butcher is not at all like another piece eleven days old from another butcher, and sorry, but the success of a dish is not following the book. It's having done the dish often enough to get it right. (Freeling, 1991)

We might add that it is not simply a matter of trial and error, for good cooks learn to distinguish between the different meats and potatoes given them to cook. These are skills in assessment. Judging when a turkey is cooked is a skill based on learning. Cooks have also to develop skills in taste if they are to judge the state of something that is being cooked. We too, develop ideas of quality based on visual and taste perceptions.

Although such decisions are only exceptionally matters of life and death, every time we drive an automobile we make judgements which might affect the life and cause the death of other people let alone ourselves. One of the general skills we use in both cooking and car driving is 'estimation'. It is used in several dimensions, as for example, when estimating the time required to cook a cake (taste/time, sight /time) or, the time required to overtake another vehicle (sight/time, time/distance). It is complicated by judgements of the relative speed of any oncoming vehicle that must also to be taken into account. In cooking it is often necessary to estimate the quantities of material required and this is sometimes a complex judgement because of the uncertainties involved in the behaviour of the 'ingredients' in the environment. Many judgements we make are estimates. When goods are purchased estimates of life and reliability are made. We want to be relatively certain that a machine will be reliable and not malfunction repeatedly. Nevertheless, such judgements are made within a framework of uncertainty and many require a high level of risk as for example when purchasing a new automobile or buying a house. In the case of the former, while we might know how an engine works, in practice few of us have the up-to-date practical knowledge to judge the potential performance capabilities of a vehicle. Similarly, in respect of the latter, we use another generic skill to predict that a house will provide our family with a suitable living environment, but we can be by no means certain that it will.

Given the significance of risk in everyday life it is important to ask if the curriculum should be designed to help us to develop risk-taking (coping) skills. If it is objected that estimation is learnt in mathematics, or the braking properties of automobiles in science, then the transferability from the textbook explanation to action in life needs to be tested. There is, for example, little evidence that in real life situations car drivers understand the significance of braking distance.

If these points have been laboured it is because assessment and assessing is a generic skill that is used regularly in daily life. It may, as in the case of these examples, be of things, or of people, or of the institutions in which they work. Gossip is by and large a series of statements about other people that by implication are judgemental. More formal judgements are made about people at work. Independently of any statutory tests or examinations teachers continually appraise their students. In all these circumstances, therefore, it is surprising that assessment should have become the afterthought of the educational process. It is equally surprising that some teachers should resent the attempts to make formal assessment more central in the educational process however difficult such assessment may be; but that is what has been happening the world over in both school and higher education systems.

This new era has been introduced largely without reference to the terminology of traditional psychometric testing and this has confused matters because it has brought with it a new language some terms of which substitute for others that have been traditionally used. Worse still, the term 'assessment' is used in a variety of ways. It will be appreciated that this argument has nothing to do with the role of assessment in the determination of standards. It is simply saying that assessment is a complex generic skill in use in everyday life and that most students would probably benefit from assessment above and beyond having their facts and homework marked. So far teachers have gone only a little way along this path. Many now take the view that assessment drives learning and design their assessments to have a positive influence on learning. Many also now accept that the development of skill in self-assessment is valuable; but the idea that there should be formal training in assessment within school and higher education programmes is seldom debated. At the same time it is evident that some parents, politicians and teachers have accepted the axiom that since assessment drives learning the curriculum ought to be assessment-led. Unfortunately excessive zeal can lead to excessive assessment and impede rather than enhance the learning–teaching process. Notwithstanding the good intentions of those involved in such policies such excesses display illiteracy in assessment and its functions and limitations to the possible and potential. In contrast, teachers' anxieties about assessment are too often focused on the limitations of assessment and its perceived potential to harm some children and students rather than on the beneficial effects it could have on learning. Effective assessment depends on assessors having a sub-stantial knowledge of human development and learning, and this is the reason for the inclusion of Chapters 7, 8 and 9.

Each of the following sections acts as an introduction to more detailed discussion in later chapters. This chapter begins with a brief discussion of the way in which assessment is being used in higher education. Its purpose, along with Chapter 2, is therefore to describe recent developments in the vocabulary of assessment and its practices, and to relate them more generally to the curriculum and instruction in higher education.

The use of the term 'assessment' in higher education

Assessment is a relatively new word in the context of general education. Traditionally terms like testing (tests), examining (examinations) and grading (grades) were used. However, early in the 1970s the term assessment came to be generally associated with these activities. Before that the term assessment seems to have been associated with individuals and it was sometimes specifically associated with judgements about children who had specific learning and/ or, other needs.

By 1986 Hartle (1986) had distinguished five functions of assessment in use in American higher education.[1] At that time he concluded that:

---

1   (1) Mandated requirements to evaluate students and/or academic programmes. This explains the use of the term assessment in programme reviews (e.g. pass rates of examinations as indicators of performance).

(2) To assess the value-added of a programme in education (e.g. studies of the relationship between 'A' level grades or SAT (Scholastic Aptitude Test) scores and degree performances).

What assessment appears to have become in higher education is a catch-all phrase that refers to a wide range of efforts to improve educational quality. This tendency to use one concept to refer to a handful of different (if related) things means that there are few shared meanings and little agreement about the nature, purpose or content of appropriate public policies. Nonetheless, upgrading the educational quality of higher education – often in the name of assessment – will be a growing interest of state policy makers and an increasingly important challenge to educators in the next decade. (Hartle, 1986).

And this has turned out to be the case. During the intervening years, the term has come to be used in higher education in the following ways. First, and at one end of the spectrum, it is used as a substitute for the term 'evaluation' which is not entirely helpful since we often want to 'evaluate (rather than assess) the reliability and validity of assessments'. Second, it is used in respect of institutions and their mission. It is a measure of the effectiveness with which they achieve their goals. It is an assessment which accrediting agencies use, thus accreditation is a form of appraisal (Karelis, 1996). Third, it is used of programmes. Fourth, in this context it also implies the assessment of staff as they teach. These two developments in programme and institutional assessment will be discussed in Chapter 3. Finally, and most importantly, it is used to describe the assessment of student learning, and that is the prime focus of this book.

Admissions procedures (standards) and school learning

For politicians assessment is about standards on the one hand and value for money on the other. The most significant indicator of performance is the assessment made of students by tests and examinations. Parents make other judgements, as for example the performance of schools in getting students into Ivy League universities. In the UK it is argued that if parents know how schools are ranked this will make schools more competitive and improve standards. Thus both the main political parties agree that the 'A' level results (the examination used for selection to universities in the UK) of every school should be published, and this they have done irrespective of the environment in which schools work. The results for the independent (fee paying schools) are also published. Admission to university is what Culver and Sackman (1988) describe as a marker event in a person's life, and admissions policies are in consequence matters of political as well as personal debate. They can have a huge 'backwash' effect on the schools' curriculum and teaching, as the Report of the

(3) Use of standardized tests to measure general or specialized knowledge and skills (e.g. the content and skills tested by 'A' level of the General Certificate of Education. In the US the ACT and SAT and programmes like the College Outcome Measures Project. In the UK the statutory tests which children at the ages of 7, 11, 14 and 16 have to take).

(4) Decision making for the purpose of rewarding institutions for student performance on established criteria.

(5) The measurement of changes in student attitudes and values.

Committee on the Form and Function of the Intermediate Certificate Examination in Ireland showed (ICE, 1974). Admissions policies and the transition to university will be considered in more detail in Chapters 4 and 5.

In these circumstances there are pressures for good results and unless the examinations (tests) and grading systems are designed to enhance learning their backwash effect can be limiting on learning – if not positively harmful. It is for this reason that so many educators have been critical of examinations and tests (Holt, 1964). In the United States, as Eisner has pointed out, the chase for good scores in the Scholastic Aptitude Test (SAT) influences both curriculum and student learning. If it is believed that more work in mathematics will bring students higher scores in the mathematics section of the test then they will study maths at the expense of other courses (Eisner, 1979).

In the United States there has been a drive to establish national standards for secondary education: these are essentially statements of expected outcomes. In teacher education where standards and assessment are seen as a vehicle for change (Diez, 1998) standards are related outcomes assessment (see Chapter 2). An example of a teacher education programme is shown in Figure 1.1 (Nelms and Thomas, 1998). The British notion of standards in schools is somewhat different and much concerned with the comparability of grades awarded by different examining boards, and within the national curriculum standard setting for multiple levels of competence (Boyle and Christie, 1996).

Examinations, quizzes and coursework (continuous) assessment

As indicated previously the term 'assessment' is used in several different connotations. Unfortunately so are the terms 'test' and 'examination'. In the United Kingdom and countries of the old commonwealth the term 'examination' is familiar. At school level there are examinations set by teachers and public examinations. The school examinations will mirror the public examinations so that pupils will learn how to respond to the public examinations. The important examinations which universities use for entry are taken between the ages of 17 and 18. School teachers will also set tests from time to time. Such tests are like the 'quizzes' which American teachers in higher education regularly set their classes. Although this is not a regular practice in UK higher education the setting of substantial exercises such as essays and projects is. This is called coursework assessment and that is how the term assessment came into the higher education vocabulary in the UK. One classification of coursework assessment is shown in Figure 1.2. It shows there has been little consistency in the way coursework is implemented or in the purposes it serves. The terms continuous assessment and coursework assessment have no meaning in the US because teachers normally test students at regular intervals during their courses and derive grades from those tests. Some teachers set what are called 'comprehensive examinations' at the end of their courses that use techniques other than multiple- choice questions.

The term examination is usually reserved for written examinations which are set at the end of the year although in the last decade there have been many changes in the timing of such examinations during the academic year. For example, many universities now follow a two-semester system and courses have to be completed and assessed within the semester. While this has had profound implications for examining, its implications for student learning were not debated. This issue will be considered in more detail in Chapter 5. It should also be noted that by 1969 many teachers were experimenting with different kinds of examining technique (CVCP, 1969), and as will be shown in later chapters some have stood the test of time. In America much use is made of standardized tests.

Standardized tests and norms

A standardized test is one that has uniform procedures for its administration and scoring. The purposes of such tests are to minimize errors due to variations in test procedures, and to enable comparison of data over time and across groups participating at the same time. Test norms are prepared for this purpose as well as for scoring. A norm is established for a particular group by testing a representative sample of that population. Very often this is done for an age or an occupational group, the average score of the group being taken as the norm. Such tests will usually have better quality items and higher reliabilities than teacher-made tests of the same type. Among the best known standardized tests relevant to higher education are the ACT (American College Testing Program), the SAT (Scholastic Aptitude Test of the Educational Testing Service) which are used for criteria for college entrance, and the GRE's (Graduate Record Examinations) used for admission to graduate school. Standardized tests are not used in the UK where the grade of the final examination serves as the criteria for admission to graduate study (see Chapter 10).

The problem of gender bias, and bias against minorities and socio-economic classes in the construction of tests has occupied test designers in the United States for many years. These were accompanied by more general criticisms of the SAT (e.g. Crouse and Trusheim, 1988). More generally, Berliner and Biddle (1995) have responded to criticisms that national performance as measured by the SAT has declined, by arguing, that since the SAT is mainly used by students interested in going to college, its aggregate scores should not be used to judge national performance as a whole: moreover, students from minority homes are now obtaining higher average scores. It has become an issue in the UK (Gipps and Murphy, 1994). In so far as the design of tests is concerned the Educational Testing Service has issued guidelines (ETS, 1980, 1986). One of the reasons for the move to authentic assessment was to avoid such bias. An investigation in the Rochester New York School System found that while inequities persisted alternative assessments have the potential to diminish such inequities but that care has to be taken in their design (Supovitz and Brennan, 1997).

The Teacher Education Program Outcomes come from the knowledge base that has been approved for the Middle-Level Education degree. The outcomes are written to address what graduates should know and be able to do upon completion of the program.

1. **Diagnoses Learning Needs**. The graduate uses a variety of assessment techniques and utilizes appropriate technologies to gather information about students and integrates this information to determine learners' strengths and areas to be developed.
2. **Plans or Student Learning**. The graduate integrates knowledge of discipline content, the nature of the learners, learning theories, instructional strategies, and state/local curriculum guides to plan instruction.
3. **Facilitates Student Learning**. The graduate implements plans with flexibility and is guided by knowledge of discipline content, the nature of the learners, learning theories, and instructional strategies.
4. **Demonstrates Appropriate Knowledge**. The graduate has general knowledge across a broad spectrum of liberal arts and sciences and posses discipline-specific knowledge at a level appropriate for the chosen teaching field.
5. **Fosters Student Well-Being to Support Learning**. The graduate interacts with students, school colleagues, parents, and agencies in the larger community to foster student well-being and learning.
6. **Assumes the Role of Professional Educator**. The graduate acts in accordance with the structure, standards, and responsibilities of the profession and recognizes the role of the school in supporting a democratic society.

Figure 1.1. Teacher Education Program Outcomes at Clayton State University College (V.C. Nelms and M.G. Thomas (1998). 'Assessment: A Process'. In Diez (1998). (Reproduced by kind permission of the authors.)

Psychometric testing

Few teachers either in school or higher education have much knowledge of psychometric testing and most are not, therefore, familiar with its terminology except for the terms 'reliability' and 'validity' and these may not be used by them in the ways defined by psychometricians.

Some school teachers and student medical advisers who are trained as counsellors may be trained to administer and interpret tests. In Ireland, for example, the Differential Aptitude Test (DAT), locally normed, is widely used by counsellors who are trained teachers. In higher education in many countries teachers have been trained to use the Myers-Briggs Type Indicator and other useful instruments (see Chapter 9).

The Differential Aptitude Test is a battery of eight tests. These cover verbal reasoning, numerical ability, abstract reasoning, clerical speed and accuracy, mechanical reasoning, space relations, spelling and language usage. The objective format is used (i.e. requiring single answer responses – see Chapter 12), as is the case with most psychometric tests. The value of such a test is that it produces a profile of strengths and weaknesses. In this test persons with high scores on verbal reasoning tend to have above average scores on the other seven tests (Cronbach, 1984; Kline, 1993).

The ACT, DAT and SAT are group tests. That is to say they meet the requirements for testing large groups of people. The best known test of intelligence, the Stanford-Binet, is also a group test. There are, however, tests designed to be administered to individuals to measure cognitive abilities. The best known is probably due to Wechsler. One of his tests (WAIS – Wechsler Adult Intelligence Scale) measures the cognitive abilities of adults; others measure pre-school and primary school intell-

---

(a) **Cumulative assessment**. A proportion of the mark in a three (or four) year course is arrived at from scores achieved during the first and second years. The proportion of marks allowed for the first year is usually smaller than that for the second, e.g.

First year	12% = 100% of year
Second year	24% = 100% of year
Third year	64% = 100% of year
	100% of total

The marks may be achieved by combinations of coursework assessment and examinations, or examinations alone. For purposes of certification they could be equated to 100%.

(B) **Diagnostic coursework**. An early assessment of student performance to determine those in difficulty and the nature of the difficulties.

(C) **Informal coursework assessment**. Most tutors make a judgement about the qualities of their students while a course is in progress. Such judgements are often used to moderate the marks given to candidates in the final meeting of examiners with the external assessor. Students are not informed about such procedures.

(D) **Formal coursework assessment**. The characteristics of such systems are that the students know how coursework will contribute to their final mark. There are several systems (the terminology is my own).

Fixed percentage schemes; In such schemes coursework is formally assessed and the proportion of marks awarded for continuous assessment seems to remain constant and impose such restrictions on departments. The proportions awarded depend on the value ascribed by individual departments to coursework assessment.

Positive moderation schemes. These are schemes in which coursework is formally assessed but the result is only used to raise a candidate's final mark.

Formal requirement schemes. These are those which require satisfactory performance in coursework before a person can either obtain a final degree or sit final examinations. The scheme adopted depends very much on department (or faculty) objectives in initiating coursework assessment procedures. Broadly speaking, there are two categories which might usefully be described as **supplementary** and **complementary** in terms of the information sought by the examiners about a candidate:

In schemes which provide **supplementary** information the examiners hold that the coursework assessment is measuring the same abilities (qualities) as the written examination. It is therefore a check on the written examination and, as such, is used as a means of moderating the final mark.

Coursework assessment which provides **complementary** information to the examination is thought to measure different qualities to those measured in written papers.

N.B. When the inquiry on which these terms were derived the terms **formative** and **summative** were not in the vocabulary of assessment. Most marks were obtained for summative purposes.

Figure 1.2 Some types of coursework which have been used in the UK

igence as well as in the age range 6 to 16 (the Wechsler Intelligence Scale for Children). A verbal scale measures a person's understanding of verbally expressed concepts as well as their ability to respond orally. The sub-scales include verbal arithmetic problems. A performance scale, which includes picture completion, picture arrangement, block design and object assembly, measures the ability to solve problems involving the manipulation of objects and materials.

The Wechsler tests are intelligence tests and they provide Intelligence Quotients (IQ) for overall, verbal and non-verbal performances (Cronbach, 1984; Kline, 1993). In Britain the British Psychological Society has sponsored the development of a British Ability Scale.

Recent developments in testing require that teachers in higher education have a thorough understanding of the concepts of reliability and validity. In the following section problems associated with validity are considered. Those relating to reliability are discussed in Chapter 10. The equations for reliability are given in the glossary.

The reliability and validity of assessments

The issues about the reliability and validity of psychometric tests, standardized tests and examinations in higher education have been well understood for many years (e.g. Cronbach, 1971; Hartog and Rhodes, 1935, 1936; Milton, Pollio and Eison, 1986). However, these terms apply equally to the assessments that are made of institutions and programmes (Nichols, 1991). For example, how valid and reliable are the assessments made in accreditation programmes, more especially the self-assessments? The fact that Erwin (1997) among others can suggest that there is considerable scepticism and continuing controversy about accreditation in North America indicates that there is need to examine the reliability and validity of the practices adopted. In the UK, Ashcroft and Palacio (1996) guide educators through a series of questions which would enable them to establish the validity of their practices.

The problem of reliability if not well understood by teachers is well explored. It will be considered in relation to standards in Chapter 10. A key question is whether a test can be valid if it has low reliability. Until recently, apart from Cattell, the view has been taken that high test reliability is required for norm referenced tests if the test is to be valid (Cattell and Kline, 1977). Of course a reliable test may not be valid. Reliability is a necessary but not sufficient cause for validity. Any departure from the purely objective (one correct answer) will introduce some degree of unreliability, but it is up to those who use the tests to determine the degree of tolerance they are prepared to allow.

It is only in recent years that much more attention has been paid to validity. This is the result in part of the move toward outcomes assessment, in part to the development of criterion referenced approaches to its measurement and its consequences for psychometrics, and in part to a general debate about the philosophy of assessment at both school and higher education levels (e.g. AERA *et al.*, 1985; Alverno, 1994; Brown and Knight, 1994; Gipps, 1994; Messick, 1994).

Validity is the extent to which assessment measures what it is supposed to measure and is therefore directly related to accountability which checks that agreed objectives have been obtained. In so far as assessments in general, and tests in particular have been concerned, validity has at least the following dimensions (see Wigdor and Garner, 1982).

- *Face Validity* The extent to which an assessment appears to be measuring the variable it is intended to test (for example visual inspection of the items or questions in comparison with the declared objectives; do they, for instance, measure analysis?).

- *Content Validity* The extent to which a test measures the content (or skill) which it is supposed to measure.

- *Predictive Validity* The extent to which an assessment predicts future performance (for example degree grades as a predictor of work performance). Criterion Validity is similar (see below).

- *Criterion Validity* Comparison of an assessment designed to evaluate performance in a task with an alternative evaluation (e.g. a test designed to predict bus driver performance compared with actual observations by a skilled judge). It predicts what an individual or a group with particular scores on a test will perform on the criterion measure that will have been chosen to be close to the issue of interest. Cronbach (1971) uses the term *concurrent* to describe this type of validity (see also Kline, 1993).

- *Construct Validity* The extent to which an assessment measures the content (aptitude, attitude, skill) it is intended to assess, and predicts results on other measures of content, aptitude, attitude, and skill as hypothesized. It is based on evidence that bears on the interpretation of the meaning of test scores. Wigdor and Garner (1982) write that it 'is scientific dialogue about the degree to which an inference that a test measures an underlying trait or hypothesised construct is supported by logical and scientific analysis' (see also Kline, 1993).

We cannot necessarily conclude that a test measures what it appears to measure (face validity), with any confidence whatsoever. Cattell and Warburton (1967) have shown that in selection face validity is likely to be a disadvantage and is not related to true validity. This is a considerable problem in the assessment of teaching and will have to be taken very seriously in the assessment of the performance of university educators.

Predictive validity and criterion validity are similar dimensions. In the United States colleges in higher education require students to obtain certain scores on the ACT and SAT for admission. They assume that students with these scores will be able to cope with university studies. Some take the view that this is a not altogether safe assumption and use high school grades as well. Similarly in the UK with the so-called 'A' level examination with the exception that this subject-based examination is also used as an indicator of potential in particular subjects.

The final degree grade is the criterion against which the predictions are judged. Complaints by industrialists that universities do not produce the students they want would have to be justified by different criteria, and for this the 'A' level examination might not be valid (i.e. as a predictor). This is a particularly contentious issue at the present time when the Engineering Council wants to raise the grades at 'A' level of those aspiring to become professional engineers (Levy, 1997). If the course content and methods were changed this might alter the predictive validity of 'A' level in these circumstances, if the university examinations remained the same.

It will be seen that the determination of these forms of validity depends on a statistical correlation. In the case of the 'A' level examination in England, the relatively small correlations that have been obtained between 'A' level performance and final degree grade have been the subject of much controversy. Why, it is argued, undertake such detailed study in a few subjects at school if they are not satisfactory predictors of performance when the students could have a broader education in a wider range of subjects? This particular issue is a matter of continuing debate. Nevertheless it is a good predictor of whether or not a student will obtain a degree. Chapman (1996a, see also 1996b) found significant positive correlation for eight subjects over a 21-year period. However, the strength of the relationship varied between subjects. The relationship also varied at department level. Some departments with high entry qualifications produced below average proportions of good degrees. From a political point of view the 'A' level became the gold-standard of education and this was justified in so far as it is the best predictor available. So far, there has been no change in this view. The arguments are compelling for if drop-out and time-in university (retention) rates are taken as a criterion then the English university system of education must be one of the most efficient in the world. Most conventional students have in the past completed their courses in the normal period of three years from the age of eighteen. It remains to be seen how, with the diversification of the system, the large numbers of non- traditionally qualified students will respond. Is there a simple linear rule which says that the greater the number of students in a system the greater the drop-out rate?

Forrest (1991) has suggested that as, in the future, the 'A' level will no longer be the examination taken by the majority of students, the equivalent of the American SAT be developed, i.e. a British Scholastic Aptitude Test (SAT).

Strictly speaking, a test has concurrent validity if it correlates highly with another test administered at the same time to a large and representative sample. As Kline (1993) has pointed out, this raises the question of how big a correlation it has to be for a test to be considered to have concurrent validity. He argued that where there are benchmark tests (there are very few in psychology) that a correlation of 0.75 might be expected. In practice moderate correlations of 0.4 or 0.5 may be expected. Although this is unsatisfactory, when they are considered together with other evidence they become part of the construct validity of the test. For this reason, Kline argues, concurrent validity studies are best regarded as aspects of construct validity.

Construct validity is the most comprehensive validity even though there is some controversy about its meaning and function. Wigdor and Garner (1982) say that it 'involves a process of research which is intended to illuminate the characteristics of ability by establishing a relationship between a measurement procedure (e.g. a test) and an observed underlying trait'. They give the example of leadership that has been the basis of particular ability tests. It will be seen that the term construct is synonymous with concept. Kline (1993) writes, 'In the sciences constructs are frequently the object of investigation or study but are only useful when they can be precisely defined. A good example of a construct is the notion of species.'

In regard to testing, 'intelligence' is such a construct. Construct validity calls on us to set up hypotheses in relation to the construct – in this case 'intelligence' – and to evaluate them. Kline mentions the correlation with other intelligence tests (concurrent and predictive validity), the relationship with academic performance, occupational groups and social class. He points out that in exposing the test to a number of hypotheses it is important to establish what the test does not measure.

The last word on construct validity might be left to Cronbach (1980) who said: 'The justification (of a test) is never complete and will be more compelling to some people than to others', and this will apply as much to the students in our classes as it does to our colleagues. 'There is always more to justification than the presentation of empirical evidence. The evidence must be embedded in logical argument', which may take into account the findings of other research.

Cronbach (1980) went on to describe validation as a 'rhetorical process' in which:

A defender of the interpretation tries to spell out an argument compatible with what most of his hearers believe. The defender of an alternate solution does the same. Who ever accepts either conclusion acts as if the statements in argument describe reality. Some links in any responsible argument rest on substantial evidence and are widely believed, and some links are debatable. The listener has considerable choice.

Gipps (1994) points out that test developers have traditionally only provided evidence of one or two types of validity. However, within the last decade test developers have argued that validity is a unitary concept in which construct plays the unifying role (Gipps, 1994). Messick (1989), who has played a leading role in the debate wrote that 'Validity is an integrated evaluative judgement of the degree to which empirical evidence and theoretical rationales support the adequacy and appropriateness of inferences and actions based on test scores or other modes of assessment'.

Which leads Gipps (1994) to point out that this takes the definition of validity beyond that of measuring what a test measures. It becomes an assessment of the evidence available to support test interpretation and potential consequences of test use, points which had been taken up by Ridgeway and Passey (1992 – see below). This takes us into the realm of personal, institutional, and society goals, and in terms of the quality assessment of higher education, the process itself. The questions which Furneaux (1962) raised about university examinations (see Chapter 2) related both to the validity of examination papers (i.e. of the questions) and the procedures used to determine who failed, who passed, and who should re-sit. The questions that lead to a position on construct validity asked by Messick (1992), and quoted by Gipps (1994), cover these and other items relating to scoring, bias, interpretation and fairness. Nevertheless the problem of the validity of examinations and assessments at the operational level in higher education of the teacher as assessment designer or selector of tests remains. For which reason the limited view of validity as taken in the textbooks remains relevant.

At the broader level Ridgeway and Passey (1992), who have been particularly concerned with assessment in mathematics, have argued that there is too little concern with conceptual issues about the uses to which tests are put. This was and is a matter of concern for teachers involved in the national curriculum in England and Wales. Among other things is the fear of payment by results. To help clarify these issues Ridgeway and Passey proposed five more dimensions of validity. These are:

- *Ideological Validity* which refers to the educational, moral philosophical and political values that are implied by use of any particular assessment scheme.

- *Generative Validity* which refers to the changes in behaviour which occur because a particular set of measures in use (e.g. using tests of arithmetic to assess a school's relative standing in mathematics is likely to drive the curriculum towards basic skills, and away from conceptual understanding). Generative validity is knowable in principle, but can only be determined after a particular set of measures has been adopted.

- *Tentative Generative Validity* which refers to decisions about what measures to adopt and should be governed by judgements about the likely generative validity of different measures, and one's personal judgements of their long term value to the educational process. Tentative generative validity (TGV) identifies likely directions of change and their inherent value. (It follows that a measure can have as many TGVs as there are raters.)

- *The Corruption Coefficient* (CC) measures the extent to which scores can be raised on a particular measure without changing the phenomena which the measures are supposed to relate to (e.g. coursework scores can be improved by teacher input, without benefiting the student's understanding).

- *Stick and Carrot Validity* assesses the extent to which an assessment system can be used to control the education system.

It will be seen that they are entirely consistent with arguments for a systems approach to assessment, curriculum design and teaching as advocated in earlier paragraphs.

In their view, 'if student learning is to be enhanced, one must first achieve a consensus on appropriate ideological validity, then ensure that measures are chosen with high TGV and low CC. It is also necessary to ensure that stick and carrot validity, when it is high, is used for beneficial rather than negative purposes.'

At the beginning of the decade the concept of validity began to be re-examined (Messick, 1994), particularly as a result of the interest in outcomes-based assessment, and the need to consider the implications for systems which integrated student and institutional assessment across the curriculum. Rogers (1994) said of this particular dimension:

> First, in performance-based curricula, student performance is often supported by feedback, which confounds measurement. Nonetheless students and faculty learn much more from performance assessments than just about the ability that is the measurement focus of individual assessments. For example, students learn what it means to perform, use feedback, and transfer performances across contexts; faculty learn how their teaching is connected to student learning. In contrast, measurement assumes that student abilities can be assessed and reported uni-dimensionally.

This argument leads to the concept of *experiential validation* of the curriculum which is the student's observation that he/she has grown in some valued ability (or abilities) through his/her learning experiences (Mentkowski and associates, 2000).

This view presents a substantial challenge to traditional concepts of validation and has implications for the concept of validity. Thus:

> In rethinking validity, assessment practitioners must recognize that an individual's performance is often unique. Even in the same broad context, students create different ways to perform. Even when well- specified 'similar' complex performance tasks challenge measurement of unitary constructs. Still, with multidimensional performances assessors can give meaningful feedback to students because it is relevant to future performance on the job, in the community, and in further educational pursuits. (Rogers, 1994)

Threats to validity

The title of this section is taken from a paper by Crooks, Kane and Cohen (1996) who, while welcoming the broadening and unifying of the concept of validity, argue that it is difficult to work with in practice. This may have the effect of continuing the neglect of validity in the quality monitoring of assessments that has characterized research over the decades. They argue that it is necessary to develop new approaches that focus on the key issues of validation. They propose that any system of assessment may be viewed as a chain linked to the student. Any weakness in one link will weaken the chain as a whole. An alternative description would simply be to describe it as a system and to note that if the linkages in the system are not made the system cannot function. The eight links in their chain chart the familiar process of assessment. Their point is that validity comprehends the links, although depending on the type of assessment some links may be more important than other links. Each link may be 'stressed' (*threatened*) with consequences for the chain. The eight links are listed below and examples of threats are given in parentheses after each definition (they give many more in their paper).

1. Administration of assessment tasks to the student. (assessment anxiety)

2. Scoring of the student's performances on the tasks. (inappropriate scoring)

3. Aggregation of the scores on individual tasks to produce one or more combined scores. (inappropriate weights given to different aspects of performance)

4. Generalization from the particular tasks included in a combined score to the whole domain of similar tasks. (too few tasks)

5. Extrapolation from the assessed domain (4) to a target domain containing all the tasks relevant to the proposed interpretation. (parts of the target domain given too little weight)

6. Evaluation of the student's performance, forming judgements. (poor grasp of assessment information and its limitations)

7. Decision on actions to be taken in the light of the judgements. (inappropriate standards)

8. Impact on the student and other participants arising from the assessment processes, interpretations, and decisions. (positive consequences not achieved)

To take the last point, they note that actions arising from assessment decisions may have negative consequences which can be of profound significance for the student. They can reduce motivation and increase anxiety; they can reduce self-esteem; they can induce students to focus on recall at the expense of higher order skills and so on. Clearly this is a useful list for designers of assessment. They argue that validation will be easier if it is planned for in the design stage. In this way validity becomes a major component in any quality audit. Other aspects of validity as they relate to quality are discussed in Chapter 2. In the meantime this chapter concludes with a discussion of other issues in the terminology of assessment, the curriculum and testing.

Ability, achievement and aptitude

Just as with assessment, so too the terms 'ability', 'achievement' and 'aptitude' have acquired several meanings depending on the context in which they are used. As if to complicate matters the items (questions) in tests used to measure both ability and aptitude are often identical. We used to 'label' students as being of high or low ability; now we talk about them as being of high or low achievement. The term ability had become associated with intelligence and intelligence had been thought to be a fixed capacity. Thus the ability (intelligence) of a person determined their attainment and such measures were used to predict potential (for a comprehensive discussion of the IQ debate see Mackintosh, 1998). At one and the same time school tests and, in particular, public examinations predicted potential and measured attainment. But these tests and examinations measured a particular kind of potential, that is, the capability to undertake academic study. They did not represent the totality of a person's achievement or the range of aptitudes they might possess. Schools, it was argued, ought to present to future employers the range of a student's capabilities or achievements and as such take into account extra-curricula attainments. Students should be provided with a record of their overall achievement. Thus it was more correct to talk of a student's achievements and not their abilities, and work began in the UK and Ireland on Records of Achievement and in England and Wales the Employment Department sponsored a National Record of Achievement for use in higher education.

The term aptitude does not seem to be used much outside of professional circles except perhaps in everyday usage in discussions about students. Both 'achievement' and aptitude tests measure developed ability. They differ in respect of the purpose they wish to accomplish. Achievement tests are intended to obtain measurements of what a person can do at a particular time: they are measures of attainment. Aptitude tests are intended to predict what a person is likely to be able to do as a result of subsequent education and training: hence, the Scholastic Aptitude Test. The National Research Councils' Committee on Ability Testing suggested that is useful to think of 'aptitude' and 'achievement' tests as falling along a continuum.

> Tests at one end of the aptitude-achievement continuum can be distinguished from those at the other end primarily in terms of purpose. For example, a test for mechanical aptitude would be included in a battery of tests for selecting among applicants for pilot training since Knowledge of mechanical aptitude would be included in knowledge of mechanical principles has been found to be related to success in flying. A similar test would be given at the end of a course in mechanics as an achievement test to measure what was learned on the course. (Wigdor and Garner 1982)

The two ends of the continuum can be distinguished by the degree to which the tests depend on prior knowledge (Anastasi, 1980). Thus questions on an achievement test, as for example the 'A' levels mentioned above, are designed to test that the requirements (knowledge and skill) of the course (syllabus) have been covered. In this case the syllabus is clearly specified. However, the knowledge required for an aptitude test would not be so clearly specified. For example, as it becomes necessary to change jobs employers might use aptitude tests to find out how the range of a person's experience has contributed to that person's potential to fulfil the requirements of the task they have in mind. One might predict that aptitude tests will be increasingly used by employers as technology changes the nature of work.

Cronbach, following McClelland *et al.* (1958), defines ability as 'a response subject to voluntary control'. Notice, he says, that we define ability tests in terms of what the tester is trying to learn rather than describing the test itself (Cronbach, 1971). He argues that since most of the terms have no well-established definition there is no need to define the terms formally. Thus measures of general mental ability are those, like the British Scale of Abilities referred to above, which are valuable in any kind of thinking and learning. Tests that seek to measure specialized abilities such as clerical speed and accuracy, mechanical reasoning and manual dexterity are often referred to as measures of special or specific abilities. Educators concerned with the design of the curriculum use the term more generously. Thus communication skills, problem solving skills and other domain related criteria are sometimes called abilities.

It is necessary to insist that tests only measure the ability as it is found at the moment of testing. They do not indicate how the testees acquired that level of performance or portray a fixed or inherent capacity in the individual. Moreover they provide only indirect measures from which abilities must be inferred.

Tests of ability may focus on knowledge, reasoning and other specific skills depending on the test. The British Ability Scales claimed to measure five major 'mental processes': Reasoning; Spatial Imagery; Perceptual Matching; Short-term Memory; and Retrieval and Application of Knowledge. It will be seen that these are quite different from the abilities associated with studying a subject, as for example history, although the possession of such 'generic' abilities would, it is argued, contribute to the acquisition of the specific abilities associated with history. Thus the term ability is also partially defined by the context in which it is used. This particular usage has come into higher education through the work of Alverno College. The ability-based curriculum employed at Alverno sets out to develop through the subjects studied eight abilities (communication; analysis; problem solving; making value judgements and independent decisions; social interaction; responsibility for the environment; understanding of the world; aesthetic response) (Alverno, 1994). These have also been called competences and capabilities (see Chapters 2 and 14).

So long as one is aware of the context in which the terms are used there should be little difficulty in interpretation. Since ideas about intelligence have been so influential in parental and political attitudes toward the organization of the curriculum, it is important that those involved in educational management and policy making as well as teachers, should have a considered view of the nature of intelligence and ability.

Formative and summative assessment

Unlike some of the other assessment language the terms formative and summative seem to have been readily adopted by the higher education fraternity. The term summative applies to those terminating examinations which grade students either at the end of a course or at the end of their period of study. Many summative examinations provide the students with no feedback as to how they have performed. Formative assessments are made as the student progresses through courses and the years of study. They will always be diagnostic in that the feedback will show students and their teachers how they are doing. However, some formative assessments might also contribute to the mark which the students obtain at the end of their programme. This is particularly true of coursework in the UK and Ireland (see Figure 1.2). At the same time continuous or coursework assessment (both terms are used in the UK) is formative if the marks are fed back to the student soon after the work has been handed in. (That is, provided it does not have to be handed in at the time of a terminal examination.)

Cowan and George (1997) and Cowan (1998) extend the concept of formative assessment (they use the term 'evaluation') to embrace the teacher. It is the means by which the teacher finds out about the learning and teaching experience during teaching and learning activities of various kinds. It verges on action research where the teacher treats his/her class as a laboratory for research (Cross, 1986).

Among the assessment techniques they used were concept mapping and protocols. Other suggestions that they make are the use of end-of-year letters in which your students tell you about their experiences with you as a teacher. In a slightly different way they can be asked to write a letter of advice to next year's students about what to expect and how to cope. Formative assessment predicates that the teacher is prepared to learn about learning, for which reason considerable attention is paid to the nature of learning in later chapters.

In a remarkable and major innovation the curriculum at Alverno College (see Chapters 2 and 14) merges the formative with the summative so that the needs of the learners are supported in a dynamic way.

Convergent and divergent assessments

Pryor and Torrance (1997) have distinguished between convergent and divergent assessments. In the former the teacher undertakes repeated summative assessments; it corresponds to supplementary coursework in Figure 1.2. However, this does not imply a behaviourist view of education and tick lists of 'can do' statements. It does imply an analysis of essays and other activities from the perspective of the requirements of the curriculum. The student is a recipient of marks that would be fed back during the course. In contrast, divergent assessment does not involve much planning; its intention is to analyse the interaction between the learner and the curriculum from the perspective of the learner and the teacher. It produces a descriptive rather than a judgemental evaluation, and it seems to correspond to the complementary category of coursework in Figure 1.2.

Curriculum integrated assessment

One model that may be inspected is that of Alverno College (see Chapters 2 and 14). At that college, the formative and the summative are merged so that the needs of the learners for development in the cognitive and affective domains are supported in a dynamic way; the learners pursue the goals of the curriculum. These goals focus on development and the acquisition of eight generic 'abilities'. The teaching in each subject area is designed to support these goals and aid the students to integrate their learning through experiential learning. They call this 'curriculum integrated assessment' (Rogers, 1994). But the curriculum can also be described as being 'assessment led' since, in its pursuit the assessments are designed to enhance learning, and guide the learner's path of development (Alverno, 1994). This approach stems from the now well accepted view that assessments can impede or enhance learning. In this case the objective is to enhance learning.

Curriculum, content, course, programme and syllabus

These terms can only be understood in the context and culture in which they are given. Whereas the term curriculum is commonly used to describe the educational programme of a school it is seldom used in higher education in the UK and books with curriculum in higher education in the title are rare. Gaff and Ratcliff (1996) is a major exception. However, books are written about the aims of higher education and these have a bearing on the curriculum (e.g. Barnett, 1990).

One reason for this state of affairs is undoubtedly established practice. In the UK students come to study a subject, e.g. history, physics. If they have to take other subjects they will do so because they are relevant to the main subject being taken, e.g. maths as a necessary requirement for physics; Russian as a necessary requirement to study Russian politics. Most subjects are taken to honours level and it is possible to take two subjects although many tutors advise against this because teachers seem to expect as much from the students as they do in a single honours course. In contrast in Ireland at the University of Dublin the pattern outside of professional courses is for many students to take a two- subject honours degree.

In the British context the emphasis on specialist study almost precludes debate about the curriculum, whereas the wide-ranging general education programmes in the United States would seem to leave a door open for a thorough debate about the curriculum and what should be taught, received and negotiated. A major issue in both countries is the extent to which the curriculum should be consumer dominated, and to what extent it should be based on received wisdom, notwithstanding market forces.

Some colleges in the US require their students to take a set of 'core' subjects. In the Enterprise in Higher Education Initiative in the UK, the drive was to try to ensure that each subject provided for the development of core skills and competencies required for industry, alongside the acquisition of knowledge. In the US the Department of Labor promoted the SCANS curriculum in high schools. This showed how the competencies required at work could be taught across the subjects of the conventional curriculum (SCANS, 1992). There is much interest in these issues in the technology departments of American universities. In the UK the acquisition of work experience during vacations that can be formally assessed is also encouraged.

It has been said that it is much more difficult to establish an integrated inter-disciplinary course in the UK than in the US. Traditionally departments teach a subject: work that cuts across more than one department is difficult to organise.

Unlike in America the term faculty is seldom used to describe academic teachers. In the UK and Ireland a faculty is an organization of more or less cognate departments (e.g. faculty of law, faculty of science). The senior officer of a faculty is the Dean who in the older universities is usually elected for a short period (e.g. three years). Not all universities have faculties. Some may have Boards of Studies that bring together specific subjects. The term school is sometimes used instead of a faculty, or it may exist within or outside the faculty system (e.g. school of education). Very often complex organizations emerge and they may well function against innovation. It is commonly said that universities are very conservative.

The terms 'course' and 'subject' are used interchangeably. A course for a degree corresponds to a programme. The term course may also be used to describe a unit or module within a programme. A syllabus is a statement of content and like the term course it may apply to the programme or a unit within that programme.

Generally teachers are recruited to teach particular courses within a programme and to undertake research in that area. They are specialists and many would refuse to teach cognate topics within the programme outside their specialization. It is easy to see that this can lead to lack of flexibility and make it difficult for departments to change.

In sum, university organization has evolved in such a way as to make change at all levels (curriculum, programme and course) difficult to accomplish. There is little doubt that this conservatism has contributed to the rise in the assessment movement at institutional level and the pressures on accreditation agencies to use their powers to force change.

The assessment of attitudes, dispositions, interests and other traits (entering characteristics)

Independently of social origins, teachers at all levels of education have found that it is useful to know more about their students than prior measures of achievement. For example, study habit inventories have been found to be valuable to both teachers and students in higher education. In both higher and secondary education teachers have found certain personality tests to be a useful aid in the design of instruction as well as in the understanding of their students. Other teachers have found that inventories which seek to establish the learning styles of their students also help in these respects notwithstanding questions of validity and reliability of some of the instruments that have been used (Heywood, 1989a; Kline, 1983, 1993). Other chapters will consider these issues in more detail.

In particular such data needs to be available to the teacher at the beginning of the course. Any understanding of the effect of institutional processes on student learning requires multiple measures that embrace the domains of intellect and personality. More has to be known about the students than their academic achievement.

Assessment and student learning

In this text the view is taken that since students learn in part to be assessed that their learning should be assessment-led in the most positive meaning of the phrase. As Loacker and her colleagues remind us:

> Though the word assessment did not emerge from classroom or campus, it derives from an idea important to educators – that of sitting down beside or together (from the Latin *ad* and *sedere*). In the seventeenth century an assessor was 'one who sits beside or together' or 'who shares another's position'. Early uses of the word focused primarily on determining the worth or value of something in monetary terms, but underlying those uses was the idea of expert judgement made on the basis of careful observation. 'Assessment' was thus a word destined for the tongues of education – whether of humanists or scientists. (Loacker, Cromwell and O'Brien, 1986)

It follows that assessment is a multidimensional process of judging the individual in action. Because assessment is the principle guarantor of quality assurance in education, it is important that politicians, parents (particularly those involved in the management of educational institutions),and teachers understand the factors which govern the quality of the assessment techniques used, as well as the role that assessment plays in learning and instruction. For this reason they should have a defensible theory of learning. Testing is not a simple matter, as the chapters that follow will show.

Chapter 2

Toward Multiple Strategy Assessment

Summary

In this chapter other dimensions of terminology taken up include, objectives, outcomes and behaviour; competence and capability and criterion referenced testing; authentic assessment and coursework and performance based assessment. These are included because the first purpose of this chapter is to describe how the so-called 'objectives' movement developed into what is now called outcomes or performance based assessment. For this reason the first part of the chapter is semi-historical. The chapter's second purpose is to demonstrate how the 'objectives' approach necessarily implies a multiple-strategy approach to assessment. Unfortunately, the term multiple-strategy assessment that seems to have been coined at about the same time in the UK and the USA has slightly different meanings in these two countries: these are discussed. Examples of the multiple assessment of student learning in the UK and the USA are given. Practical difficulties in the way of developing multiple-strategy assessment are discussed. Both the objectives and multiple-strategy assessment models imply a systems approach to the design implementation and evaluation of the curriculum, learning and assessment process. These models have profound implications for the role of the teacher in the learning, instruction, assessment dimension of his/her role in higher education.

Introduction

In 1962 W.D. Furneaux published what has become a seminal paper on the psychologist and the university (Furneaux, 1962). In it he discussed data obtained from an analysis of examination results for first and second year students of mechanical engineering at one of Britain's premier universities.

At the time the students were taking a three-year programme. Selection procedures would have ensured that they were highly able as measured by their prior performance. In the university programme their performance was assessed by examinations taken at the end of each of the three years of the course. The examinations taken at the end of years 1 and 2 were hurdles. Failure in them would mean that the student would either have to repeat the year, or leave. In the first year the students took five written papers. In the second year the students took eight written papers. If the marks obtained in each of the years are correlated, information can be obtained about the effectiveness of the first year examinations as a predictor of success in the second year.

Inspection showed little evidence of high correlations between the papers set in the two years. For example, applied electricity and applied heat had much higher correlations with second year mathematics than did first year mathematics! All of the correlations of engineering drawing with second year papers were low: all but one of them were below 0.35. The correlations for coursework were somewhat higher. All in all no close links between associated pairs of paper in years 1 and 2 were found.

Furneaux also analysed the structure of the first year examination using a factor analytic technique. The analysis showed one large and two small factors. The large factor accounted for 76 per cent of the variance in mathematics, and 69 per cent, 84 per cent, 72 per cent and 78 per cent of it in the remaining papers. However, it only contributed 48 per cent and 36 per cent to engineering drawing and coursework marks. Furneaux had concluded on the basis of the correlation analysis that each of the examinations was measuring some kind of examination passing ability. Now, as a result of the factorial analysis, he suggested that the first factor was closely related to a generalized ability to pass examinations. He suggested that the marks of examiners could account for more than 30 per cent of the differences between candidates in some kinds of examination although it would not account for 52 per cent of the coursework variance. In these circumstances tutors gain relatively little information from coursework and engineering drawing relative to performance in the second year. Apart from inconsistency in marking, the determinants of coursework are different from those in other papers.

The correlation analysis led Furneaux to pose three questions to the college authorities. These were:

1. What is the appropriate criterion for a first year pass? Suppose a candidate fails mathematics, given these results, is it justifiable to exclude her/him from the next year when a pass in applied electricity is a better prediction of performance in second year mathematics than mathematics itself?

2. If engineering drawing has very little to do with performance in later years why include it in the performance requirements for this stage?

3. Suppose a candidate obtains a good average mark for year 1, in spite of failing (say) three papers. Is it reasonable to make him /her repeat the whole of the first year's work, while another candidate who obtains a lower average mark but has no failures is allowed to proceed to the second year?

These apply equally to procedures in other subjects. Of course departments have wrestled with these problems over the years and come to a variety of solutions. For example, it may be argued that a modular structure designed to enable a student to take courses at different levels simultaneously, would overcome these problems. However, some tutors argue that this, in effect, is lowering standards. But this begs the question; What is a standard anyway? (see Chapter 10).

Furneaux did not explore other possible interpretations of this examination passing factor. However, one possible explanation is that with the exception of mathematics all the examinations were in the applications of physics, and required the application of mathematical techniques to the solution of a problem which only had a 'single' solution. Thus what mattered was the ability to correctly interpret the question so as to choose the correct technique: all these examinations might be measuring mathematical ability as opposed to the understanding of physics. It is, as subsequent work has shown, possible for students to solve application problems correctly without understanding the science (e.g. Price quoted by Heywood, 1974).

If this is the case then another question arises. It is: What is the point of having a large number of written papers to test the same skill? There is no reason to believe that this kind of problem does not apply to subjects other than the sciences and technologies, as for example, in the humanities.

At the time when these questions were put, engineering and science departments in universities were being criticized for not producing graduates with the qualities that industry said it required. Therefore, the question was asked, should some attempt be made to test these other qualities? Answers to this question may have necessitated changes in the structure of programmes and teaching. As it was, this question remained largely unanswered. Nearly 30 years later a government-sponsored project, the Enterprise in Higher Education Initiative, posed the same questions! Some have argued that the degree result should be presented as a profile so that the performance of the candidate in a variety of cognitive skills may be displayed.

To arrive at answers to these questions it is necessary to be clear about what the aims and objectives or, in today's jargon, outcomes of the course, should be. At the time of Furneaux's report the idea of defining the objectives of courses had only just begun to reach the UK from America. Two years later, in 1964, the two volumes of *The Taxonomy of Educational Objectives* were published for the first time in the UK and while it stimulated a considerable debate at school level it failed, by and large, to trigger a similar debate in the university sector as it then was.

The taxonomy of educational objectives

The Taxonomy of Educational Objectives was published in two volumes. The first, which is much more widely cited, was devoted to the cognitive domain. It is commonly known as Bloom's Taxonomy after the senior author. The second was devoted to the affective domain. Its lead author was David Krathwohl. There has been some criticism of the use of the term taxonomy because it does not meet the requirements that a taxonomy would have to meet, say, in biology (Furst, 1994, citing R.M. Travers, 1980, and others), and that the objectives cannot be expressed in a taxonomy in any case.

The idea of *The Taxonomy* emerged from a meeting of college and university examiners who 'believed that some common framework used by all college and university examiners could do much to promote the exchange of test materials and ideas for testing.... After considerable discussion, there was agreement that the framework might be best obtained through a system of classifying the goals of the educational process using objectives' (Bloom 1994).

The cognitive domain was chosen to be published first because not only was it central to test development but 'it was also the domain in which most of the work in curriculum development had taken place and where the clearest definitions of objectives as *descriptions of student behaviour* were to be found' (Bloom, 1994; my italics). The principal categories of the cognitive domain are shown in Figure 2.1. These are sub-divided in great detail and from the sub-categories statements are derived which state what a person will be able to do in each category as a result of the learning they have done.

The committee which developed *The Taxonomy* agreed that it should try to avoid value judgements about objectives and behaviours and that neutrality should be maintained in respect of educational philosophies and principles. In this way a wide range of objectives would be included from different educational orientations. However, criticisms from British educational philosophers (Hirst, 1974; Ormell, 1974; Pring, 1971; Sockett, 1971) suggested that it did not meet these criteria. They argued that *The Taxonomy* was based on inadequate epistemology. As Furst (1994) said, 'they believed it provoked questions rather than answered them about the nature and structure of educational objectives.' He freely admits that the committee, of which he was a member, paid little attention to the philosophical dimension.

Instead they placed much of the burden of defining educational goals and cognitive levels upon test items, the correct response to which was taken as necessary evidence of the attainment at issue. Thus the authors took as the only viable alternative the operational definition in which the intended student behaviour was implicit (Wilhoyte, 1965). They did recognize, however, that operational definition was not sufficient; one also had to know or assume the nature of the students' educational experience.

1. **Knowledge**
   Knowledge of specifics
   Knowledge of terminology
   Knowledge of specific facts
   Knowledge of ways and means of dealing with specifics
   Knowledge of conventions
   Knowledge of trends and sequences
   Knowledge of classifications and categories
   Knowledge of criteria
   Knowledge of methodology
   Knowledge of universals and abstractions in a field
   Knowledge of principles and generalizations
   Knowledge of theories and structures
2. **Comprehension**
   Translation
   Interpretation
   Extrapolation
3. **Application**
4. **Analysis**
   Analysis of elements
   Analysis of relationships
   Analysis of organizational principles
5. **Synthesis**
   Production of a unique communication
   Production of a plan, or proposed set of operations
   Derivation of a set of abstract relations
6. **Evaluation**
   Judgements in terms of internal evidence
   Judgements in terms of external criteria

Figure 2.1 **The Taxonomy of Educational Objectives:** *An outline of the major categories in the cognitive domain.*

The problem arose from the fact that the committee had chosen Ralph Tyler's definition of an educational objective. For him, an educational objective represented a change in behaviour in ways of acting, thinking and feeling.

> A behavioural objective expresses what a person will be able to do. It is action oriented. At the end of a class or course a student will be able to *define...*, *discriminate between...*, *identify...*, etc.

The committee used the term behavioural in a broad sense. It is, wrote Furst (1994) a broad concept rather than the usual (overt) behavioural one, because it includes covert as well as overt states. It is this that creates the philosophical difficulty because tests measure something that is overt, hence the need to know or assume the nature of the students' educational experience. Many criticisms of *The Taxonomy* were made on behaviourist grounds. There was an unwillingness to accept the broad use intended by the committee. Had the authors been behaviourist then *The Taxonomy* would have produced a curriculum based on drill and practice.

As will be shown in later chapters the need to have a multidimensional knowledge (i.e. not simply test scores), of where and who the students are educationally is of paramount importance in designing courses and curriculum. In the meantime the authors foreshadowed what has come to be known as outcomes-based assessment since they declared that:

> The Taxonomy is designed to be a classification of the student behaviors which represent the *intended outcomes* of the educational process. It is assumed that essentially the same classes of behavior may be observed in the usual range of subject-matter content of different levels of education(elementary, high school, college), and in different schools. Thus a single set of classifications should be applicable in all these circumstance.
>
> What we are classifying is the intended behaviors of students – the ways in which individuals are to think, act or feel, as a result of participating in some unit of instruction. (Only such of those intended behaviors as are related to mental acts of thinking are included in the part of the Taxonomy developed in the handbook for the cognitive domain.)
>
> It is recognized that the *actual behaviors* of the students after they have completed the unit of instruction may differ in degree as well as kind from the intended behavior specified by the objectives. That is the effects of instruction may be such that the students do not learn a given skill to any degree.
>
> We initially limited ourselves to those objectives referred to as knowledge, intellectual abilities, and intellectual skills. (This area, which we named the cognitive domain, may also be described as including the behavior; remembering; reasoning, problem solving; concept formation, and to a limited extent creative thinking.)

There is still much confusion about outcomes. For example, one assessment specialist went so far as to propose that objectives were used by course designers whereas specifications of learning outcomes were made by teachers (Otter, 1991). However, it was possible to show that the statements of learning outcomes in that report differed little from the kind of statements of behavioural objectives in *The Taxonomy*. This muddle may in part be put down to emotional reactions to the use of the term behaviour. In the end it seems that those who used the term outcomes have won the day and the term outcomes-based assessment is commonly used and educators are encouraged to think in terms of educational outcomes. These, depending on context, may go beyond the assessment of student learning and take into account student attrition and retention rates. In a report of The National Postsecondary Education Cooperative (NEPC, 1977) outcome is used to 'refer to those education-related consequences of students' post secondary experience'. That organization describes a taxonomy which 'is restricted to those outcomes that are typically intended outcomes of some post-secondary education experience and within the power of postsecondary institutions to shape to educational advantage through programmatic or policy interventions'.

The situation has become more confused in teacher education in the US where outcomes have become linked to standards and quality assurance. In Missouri general objectives are called quality indicators. For example, 'the preservice teacher understands how students learn to develop, and provides learning opportunites that support the intellectual, social, and personal development of all students.' The performance indicators associated with this aim are that 'The preservice teacher knows and identifies child/adolescent development: strengthens prior knowledge with new ideas: encourages student responsibility: knows theories of learning' (MoSTEP, 1998). The teacher education programme is expected to have as its objectives and outcomes these performance indicators although neither the term objective nor outcome is used. Rather they are performance standards for education professionals. Any hope of developing a common language would seem to be doomed.

Nevertheless, in respect of student learning, Eisner (1979) reminded us, that as well as intended outcomes (or what ever term is used) all classroom activities, and all courses, have unintended outcomes. Sometimes they may enhance learning and at other times they may impede learning. Thus in evaluating whether or not the objectives have been obtained the teacher needs to know what was actually learnt and whether it was worth while. Indeed the evaluation may lead the teacher to change her/his objectives in a future lecture (seminar, etc.) or course.

Expressive outcomes

Unlike the authors of *The Taxonomy* Eisner also made a distinction between behavioural objectives and problem solving. He conceded that problem solving was an objective. When he used the term outcome he did so to distinguish between pre-formulated goals and what actually happened. He argued that while there was a case for pre-formulated goals there were many teaching activities for which we did not pre-formulate specific goals. We undertook them in anticipation that something would happen, even though we could not specify what (as for example in business games and case studies). We do not think much beyond the data, even though we could predict from the ample criteria at our disposal. What we do is to evaluate retrospectively what happened against these criteria. From this he deduces that teachers should be able to plan activities which do not have any specific objectives. This leads him to express the view of many educationalists, who would say with him that:

Expressive activities precede rather than follow expressive outcomes. The tack to be taken with respect to the generation of expressive outcomes is to create activities which are seminal; what one is seeking is to have the students engage in activities that are sufficiently rich to allow for a wide, productive range of valuable outcomes. If behavioural objectives constitute the algorithms of the curriculum, expressive activities and outcomes constitute their heuristics. (Eisner, 1979)

This statement will surely be met with approval by teachers in the arts and humanities. There are, however, two difficulties with it. The first you might argue is a quibble. It is that even to establish a strategy which will allow things to emerge is to formulate a goal in the expressive domain in which the cognitive and affective are merged. My second objection is that all too often such statements can be used as an excuse for not planning teaching. A great deal of research has been done which shows that students rate many lectures poorly. Often this is related to poor planning and lack of understanding of student learning. To follow Eisner properly demands both an understanding of how students learn, and how to plan classroom activities which takes that into account.

The classes of the cognitive domain

The Taxonomy was eventually published in the US in 1956. It revealed the six major classes of: Knowledge, Comprehension, Application, Analysis, Synthesis and Evaluation shown in Figure 2.1.

The knowledge category is concerned with those things that can be remembered. They arranged the sub-classes of behaviour in this category from the specific and concrete to the more abstract. It was the category of knowledge which caused many of the epistemological difficulties which British philosophers had. Sockett (1971), for example, wrote, '"remembering" is unintelligible just as a psychological process (even if we lay aside its counterpart – "forgetting") for we remember *something*, cases of remembering are cases of being *right* about what was or is the case. We cannot posit remembering in any sense apart from content. If remembering is thought of as

---

The principal sub-categories of comprehension are:

1. Translation
2. Interpretation
3. Extrapolation

The category of translation is developed as follows:

Comprehension is evidenced by the care of accuracy with which the communication is paraphrased or rendered from one language or form of communication to another. Translation is judged on the basis of faithfulness and accuracy, that is, on the extent to which the material in the original communication is preserved, although the form of the communication has been altered. The ability to understand non-literal statements (metaphor, symbolism, irony, exaggeration).

Skill in translating mathematical verbal material into symbolic statements and vice-versa.

Figure 2.2. Illustrating the category of comprehension in more detail.

content- free we have an empty concept which could not even be part of an educational objective' (quoted by Furst, 1994). Each of the other classes of *The Taxonomy* were divided into sub-classes. Those for comprehension are given in Figure 2.2.

In the category of application the authors showed how the problem- solving process is stimulated by having to apply knowledge. This was in part intended to help the reader differentiate between comprehension and application although it is also showed that *The Taxonomy* was intended to cover problem-solving (Anderson and Sosniak, 1994a). Similar diagrammatic explanations may be provided for the classes of analysis, synthesis and evaluation. Evaluation has sometimes been called judgement since, 'it is defined as the making of judgements about the value, for some purpose, of ideas, works, solutions, methods, material etc. It involves the use of criteria as well as standards for appraising the extent to which particulars are accurate, effective, economical or satisfying' (Anderson and Sosniak, 1994b).

Each of the classes and their sub-behaviours was accompanied by test items, most of which were of the 'objective type'. This had the advantage of demonstrating that objective items could be used with effect in most subjects, and second that they could be designed to test more than remembering (see Chapter 13).

The affective domain

The work on the affective domain was completed some time afterwards (Krathwohl, Bloom and Mersia, 1964). It was not received with anything like the fervour given to the cognitive domain. Apart from foreign criticism that it was 'too American' there was no 'readiness' for it at the time. It was in the the late 1980s when the movement for the assessment of transferable skills developed.

At that time Kaplan's (1978) useful but relatively unknown illustration of the affective domain would have been very helpful because it gave acceptable examples of what it was all about (Figure 2.3).

In the case of law Petter (1982), also illustrated by Imrie (1995), has shown how law schools cannot achieve their objectives without taking into account the affective domain. The two are entwined. The same applied to the Enterprise in Higher Education Initiative in the UK which encouraged the development of personal transferable skills within courses (Heywood, 1994).

Although Krathwohl and Stewart undertook some work on the psychomotor domain it was left to Harrow (1972) to produce a substantive study of this area (see also Simpson, 1966). Krathwohl and Stewart had attempted to create an integration between the affective and psychomotor domains (Krathwohl 1994). Harrow's taxonomy had as its main categories, *reflex movements, basic fundamental movements, perceptual abilities, physical consistency, skilled movements, and non-discursive communication.*

Alverno College is one of the few institutions of higher education to appreciate the importance of the affective domain in education for personal growth (Mentkowski, 1988). This domain 'contrasts sharply with the cognitive in that the cognitive has to do with growth and development of intellectual skills and abilities. Although it is an

- 1. Awareness

1. Listens to others
2. Receives others as co-workers
3. Listens to advice
4. Verbally pays attention to alternative points of view on a given issue
5. Refers to subgroup(s) (social, intellectual, sex, race, etc.)

6. Acknowledges some aesthetic factor in the classroom (clothng, furniture, design, arrangement, art)
7. Aware of feelings of others (introvert, extravert, anxiety, hostility, sensitivity)
8. Recognizes own bias as a bias
9. Recognizes other bias as a bias

- 1.20 Willingness to Receive

10. Seeks agreement from another
11. Seeks responsibility
12. Seeks information from another
13. Pursues another way of doing something

14. Seeks materials
15. Asks another to examine aesthetic factor in classroom
16. Inquires how another feels about event or subject

- 2.00 Responding

- 2.10 Acquiescence in Responding

17. Complies with existing regulations (rules)
18. Complies to a suggestion or directive
19. Offers materials on request
20. Gives opinion when requested

21. Responds to a question
22. Takes responsibility when offered
23. Remains passive when a response is indicated
24. Actively rejects direction(s) or suggestion(s)

- 3.00 Valuing

- 3.10 Preference for a Value

25. Seeks the value of another
26. Defends value of another
27. Clearly expresses a value
28. Defends own value

29. Openly defends the right of another to possess value
30. Tries to convince another to accept a value
31. Agrees with value of another
32. Disagrees with the value of another

- 4.00 Organization

- 4.10 Conceptualization of a Value

33. Makes deductions from abstractions
34. Makes judgements (implies evaluation)

35. Compares own value to that of another
36. Attempts to identify the characteristics of a value or value system

- 4.20 Organization of a Value System

37. Compares and weighs alternatives
38. Shows relationship of one value to another

39. Ties a specific value into a system of values
40. Synthesizes two or more values into one value

- 5.00 Characterization by a value or value complex

- 5.10 Generalized set

41. Revises judgements based on evidence
42. Bases judgements on consideration of more than one proposal

43. Makes judgements in light of situational context

- 5.20 Characterization

Figure 2.3 Kaplan's taxonomy of affective behaviour for the classroom.

over-simplification, it may be said that the cognitive has to do with the mind, WITH THINKING, while the affective has to do with the emotions, with FEELING. This is not to say that the two domains do not overlap, because they do. In fact, in some respects, it is almost impossible to distinguish between the two' (Alverno College, correspondence with J. Heywood).

The Alverno faculty also appreciated that if they were to be successful in both domains they would have to encourage what is now called *active learning* that is, learning other than that obtained through classroom lectures and seminars. It would have to be more student- centred and activity based. (see also McGill and Beatty, 1992 for a discussion of action learning).

Related to action learning Steinaker and Bell (1969) produced a taxonomy of experiential learning. This had categories for, *exposure* (seeing, hearing, reacting recognizing), *participation, identification* (classifying, explaining, experimenting, writing, drawing), *internalization* (generalizing, comparing, contrasting and transferring), and *dissemination*.

Other criticisms of *The Taxonomy* (cognitive domain)

Some criticisms of *The Taxonomy* have already been mentioned. They and others have been debated by Anderson and Sosniak (1994b) and their co-authors. The purpose of this section is to discuss some of the practical difficulties which emerged, and to indicate some of the ideas which followed without laying claim to linearity between cause and effect.

The aims of education

There is no doubt that this approach to determining the goals of education showed many statements of aims to be innocuous in terms of the process they were supposed to stimulate. Many were pious platitudes (Jevons, 1972). At the same time *The Taxonomy* undermined the language that university teachers used to express their goals. However inadequate such statements were, to exclude them from discussion about the objectives of education was to remove an important determinant in the motivation driving university faculty to teach. There was a tendency among those promoting the objectives approach to dismiss such statements out of hand. This was reciprocated by the teaching fraternity, or at least by those who had heard of it, and so there was no sector-wide debate about the value of *The Taxonomy* and the objectives approach. As will be shown in the next chapter, such statements can be of considerable value, for example when they arise from naive criticisms of higher education such as are regularly portrayed in the media. Provided they are not pious platitudes they are important because they enshrine the values which invigorate systems.

Dressel (1971, 1976) was vociferous in his criticism of *The Taxonomy*. He felt that it completely underestimated the role of values in human behaviour. An education which ignores this dimension at the expense of the cognitive fails.

> The values themselves no matter how well stated, do not resolve conflicts which will yield, if at all, only through intellectual efforts directed by value concerns and conducted in full awareness of the fact that value-free intellectual exchange is an ideal unachievable by man and probably undesirable. (Dressel, pp.00).

However, these are not reasons for not stating objectives if by this we mean a full awareness of our own position and the goals we hope to achieve. When subject specialists seek to clarify their own position and methods they necessarily make statements from which definitions of the learning skills required for the pursuit of understanding in their particular subject can be derived (Figure 2.4 shows an example in history). The trouble is that so often we assume that we and our students know where we are going. We have also assumed that our students acquire the range of skills inherent in such statements of the aims of higher education as, for example, those in the American reports on excellence in higher education or in *The Idea of a University* (Newman 1852, 1947). Unfortunately there is plenty of evidence to suggest we do not achieve these cherished ideals (see next chapter). If nothing else happened, the publication of *The Taxonomy* created a climate in which many teachers were forced to think about what it was they were trying to do, and some found great stimulation from trying to achieve their aims through its application to their courses.

Assimilation and Synthesis

You already know that history requires a lot of reading. At university the book lists are much longer and the library much bigger. You will need to learn how to understand, sort and make you own (i.e. to assimilate and synthesize) large amounts of complex and often conflicting information and argument. For this you may need to speed up your reading. It is not usually most sensible to try to read every book from cover to cover! Besides there is no time. So you must learn how to get what you need quickly out of a great many books and articles.

You must also consider how to take notes, from books and articles you read, from lectures, and from seminars. You need to decide how to store the information you acquire.

Criticism

At pre-university level most people learn opinions of other historians. Now you are required to have opinions of you own. But writing history is not just a matter of expressing opinion; valid opinions must be based on reliable evidence.

So you must learn to evaluate the evidence on which the interpretations of other historians are based. You will need to examine it in detail and consider whether it is reliable and relevant. This may require a great deal of specialized reading. Part of this task to discover how historians reach their conclusions and how these conclusions can be judged.

Analysis

History is not merely telling a story; it involves discussing problems about the past.

You will need to learn to analyse the problems that you meet; separating them into their component parts and examining the evidence about each part.

You can then reassemble the problem in the analytical framework you have devised. This involves manipulating concepts, handling complex information and needs considerable clarity of thought and logical argument.

This may be difficult but when you succeed you will have produced an historical interpretation of your own, rather than borrowing one second-hand from some 'expert', as at 'A' level.

Interpretation

Good historians need imagination and lateral thinking to develop new ways of looking at the past and interpreting the evidence. Probably the most important quality of all in a good historian is a passionate curiosity. Provided that you always respect your evidence you should try to develop the confidence to attempt new interpretations.

Discussion in groups is a valuable place to practise this. In a group you can try out new ideas on your fellow students and your tutor; they will tell you whether they think the evidence supports you.

Expression

However imaginative your interpretation and however logical you analysis, you will not succeed as a historian unless you can share your ideas, both on paper and orally. You need to polish your expression to make it as clear and precise as possible.

You should concentrate on your written sytle, noting carefully where your readers (usually your tutor) have not understood you and asking yourself why not.

Take every chance to speak in tutorials, seminars and discussions, trying to develop a clear and logical delivery.

Everyone agrees that a history degree is hard work. We hope this advice has shown you why it is also very much worthwhile. You already have many of the skills and intellectual qualities discussed here, otherwise you would not be at university, but they can certainly be improved upon and matured.

Set yourself targets and aim for improvements. You will find that you are enjoying the subject more and more and that soon you will be able to make a contribution of your own.

Figure 2.4 From Introduction to History (1991) University of Durham (a pamphlet written for students, cited in Heywood 1994)

The hierarchical nature of The Taxonomy

A fundamental principle of *The Taxonomy* is that the categories are hierarchical. Learning and thinking are cumulative and hierarchical. A learner must have know-ledge before they can comprehend and so on through the classes. The face validity of this argument is strong. Unfortunately, as Krathwohl points out, there has only been one major study that has looked at the structure of *The Taxonomy*. It was due to Kropp and Stoker (1966), and its results were ambivalent. According to Krathwohl that is the position today 'yet, even without definitive data that indicate how the structure should be changed modifications have been suggested'.

Gagné who produced a taxonomy that has many similarities with the Bloom Taxonomy, also considered the issue from the perspective of the transfer of learning. In the Bloom Taxonomy the hierarchical principle suggests that transfer is vertically ordered (i.e. one transfers from comprehension to application and so on) although the authors clearly state that evaluation can occur in any category. In the 1977 edition of *The Conditions of Learning*, Gagné gives an example of an item in *The Taxonomy* which assesses horizontal transfer (Rohwer and Sloan, 1994).

Perhaps the most serious criticism came from Ormell (1974) who found that some of the demands for knowledge were more complex than those for analysis and evaluation.

Lower and higher order thinking skills (HOTS)

Bloom (1994) suggested that one reason for the phenomenal use of *The Taxonomy* was that it filled a void. Teachers could now establish what students were learning. 'As they did so, they became aware that too much emphasis was being placed on the lowest level of *The Taxonomy* – "knowledge." Frequently as much as 90 per cent of the instructional time was spent at this level'.

Without wishing to draw causal or linear historical relationships, it is useful to note that some members of the critical thinking movement began to develop their own taxonomies. There is little doubt that they were strongly influenced by *The Taxonomy*. However, in addition to adding items, they apparently also disagreed with its classes. A distinction came to be made between knowledge and comprehension and Higher Order Thinking Skills (HOTS). Much of the debate in higher education about teaching and learning centres on the meaning, teaching and assessment of such skills (Baird, 1988; McPeck, 1981; Powers and Enright, 1987). Imrie's RECAP model followed this pattern. He divided the taxonomy into two tiers. At the first level, object-ives state the minimum essentials which students should achieve. These may be tested by short answer and multiple-choice questions. Students can be tested for mastery. He calls the second level which comprises analysis, synthesis and evaluation problem-solving skills. These objectives focus on skills important in problem solving. They can be tested by essays, case study questions, and use norm- or criterion-referenced assessments (Imrie, 1984, 1995). One problem with the use of problem solving skills, as will be shown in Chapter 7 is that some cognitive development theorists hold that these are Piagetian skills and not the highest level that can be obtained (i.e. reflective judgement). Crooks (1988) cited by Imrie (1995) also uses the term critical thinking to encompass these skills.

The SOLO Taxonomy (Biggs and Collis, 1982) attempts to link the forms of know-ledge with development. There are five modes of learning which many similarities with Piagetian development stages (see Chapter 7). These are Sensori-motor, ikonic, concrete-symbolic, formal and post-formal. The forms of knowledge related to these are tacit, intuitive, declarative, theoretical and meta theoretical. There are five structural levels (hierarchically ordered) in a learning cycle that is repeated in each of the forms. Both Gibbs (1992) and Ramsden (1992) have described these levels in terms of the type of answers a person might give to a question. In this way it might be related to degree levels. Following Gibbs' description the levels are:

1. Pre-structural. A stage of ignorance where the learner has no knowledge of the question.

2. Unistructural. Where the learner is able to give an answer that contains one correct feature.

3. Multistructural. Where the answer contains a check list of items.

4. Relational. The answer integrates the items into an integrated whole.

5. Extended abstract. The answer is related to the more general body of knowledge.

Imrie (1995) argues that the attempts to link these to levels to degree grades is problematic. In this respect it is of interest to note Iliffe's model for marking essays cited in Chapter 11. The SOLO taxonomy is also of interest because there is conceptual overlap with the deep and surface learning strategies discussed in Chapter 9 (Entwistle and Entwistle, 1992; Ramsden, 1992) in that (3) may correspond to surface learning, and (4) and (5) to deep learning.

The categories

Although many teachers continued to apply the term 'higher order thinking' to those classes other than knowledge and comprehension, the critical thinking movement perceived different categories even though many of the sub-abilities corresponded with those found in *The Taxonomy*. One of the attractions for practitioners was undoubtedly the introduction of a category of problem solving. This, after all, was what they (scientists in particular) were trying to teach. Similarly those in the humanities could value a category of critical thinking.

Collier's list of categories (Figure 2.5) which were developed for teaching theology is attractive, and would seem to apply to many areas of higher education. When it was published it was accompanied by a detailed discussion of the teaching methods appropriate to the achievement of each domain (Collier, 1989).

---

1. Basic Knowledge
2. Comprehension of subject discipline
3. Self-directed learning
4. Communication skills
5. Application to new situations
6. Analysing an argument
7. Invention
8. Assessing quality

Figure 2.5 The main categories of K.G. Collier's objectives for teaching and learning in higher education.

There were subject areas which, the authors of *The Taxonomy* acknowledged, would require alternative categories. In technical drawing, for example, there was a need for technique and Visualization (Heywood, 1984). In engineering science at 'A' level in the UK, in addition to technique, a category for originality was introduced in practical work. The sub-abilities in these categories could be associated with items in the different classes of *The Taxonomy*. In other words, particular sub-abilities could apply as much to one class or another, which suggested that *The Taxonomy* was not strictly a Taxonomy. It also confirmed Ormell's point that some items in the knowledge category were at a difficulty above that of some items in later classes (Carter, Heywood and Kelly, 1986).

Rohwer and Sloane (1994) consider that had the committee had available to it the cognitive developmental model described by Case (1985) that it would have related the educational objectives to the developmental capabilities of students. But this would require that the knowledge domains be changed to include causal reasoning, verbal reasoning, mathematical reasoning, scientific reasoning and social reasoning. According to Case 'how' students learn remains constant across the stages of development but the strategies they use to learn change with the type of problem to be solved. Thus, it is an imperative that assessors of student learning should have knowledge of human development (Chapter 7). Rowher and Sloan also consider that if recent developments in cognitive science are taken into account that a different taxonomy would have to be created for each domain of learning.

In so far as assessment is concerned those working in developmental psychology and cognitive science would take the view that student knowledge can only be assessed by tasks that require a substantial amount of work accompanied by detailed explanation. Multiple-choice tests would, therefore, be of little use in these circumstances, and it is this axiom which lends support to the so-called 'authentic' test movement.

Rowher and Sloane also consider the effect that Gagné could have had on *The Taxonomy* but his work on capability, competence and performance is important in its own right.

Gagné: Capability, competence and performance

Gagné whose initial studies published in 1965 were based on a neo-behaviourist perspective had, by 1975, moved to an information processing model to explain his instructional model, that at the same time became more refined. His taxonomy had many similarities with the Bloom model. In the early work learning was perceived to develop from the simple to the complex in eight steps. These began with Pavlovian learning, moved through chaining to the learning of concepts, and thence to the learning of principles and finally problem solving. Gagné published illustrations of lectures designed against this model, and many students and teachers found it useful to plan their lessons in this way (Heywood, 1982).

By the mid-1970s Gagné had reconsidered the intellectual skills required for instruction (Gagné 1965, 1977). At the lowest level of complexity were discriminations. These were a prerequisite for learning concrete concepts. Next in the sequence were rules and defined concepts, followed by higher order rules and problem solving. From the point of view of the assessment movement each of these is a capability. So a concept is the capability an individual has 'to identify a stimulus as a member of a class having some characteristic in common, even though such stimuli may otherwise differ from each markedly' (Gagné, Briggs and Wager, 1992).

- Gagné identified five kinds of learning ability that he called:
- intellectual skill
- cognitive strategy
- verbal information
- motor skill
- attitude.

Each of these calls forth a performance. Gagné *et al.* (1992) give, as an example of intellectual skill appropriate to higher education, the prediction of the effects of a currency devaluation. Verbal information is very similar to Bloom's category of knowledge: it is the information which we are able to state: it is sometimes called declarative knowledge.

Information of this kind is necessary for learning. Motor skills encompass a variety of performances ranging from writing to using machines. Attitudes belong to the affective domain, and in this sense there is a similarity with the affective domain of *The Taxonomy*. They are learned capabilities, and they involve the making of choices. They are subject independent.

Gagné, Briggs and Wager argue that each of these learned capabilities 'require a different set of learning conditions for their efficient learning'. This has profound implications for the design of the curriculum and instruction in higher education. Assessment require the learners to demonstrate performances – hence, the idea of *performance based assessment*.

Capability

Rohwer and Sloane (1994) considered that had the authors of *The Taxonomy* had access to Gagné's system they would have found a degree of correspondence which was such as not to merit any change. However, They might have included the category of cognitive strategies. Gagné and his co-authors attribute the idea of cognitive strategies to Bruner, Goodnow and Austin (1956). Cognitive strategies are used by individuals to 'get to the heart of the matter'. Once a strategy has been learnt it can be used to solve new problems. Diagnosis in engineering and medicine requires a 'working back' strategy that once learnt can be applied to new situations. This is a definition of capability but it is narrow when compared with its more generally understood sense in higher education. In the UK, Higher Education for Capability takes its definition from a recommendation by the Royal Society of Arts to describe a programme in which it was hoped to encourage universities and colleges to develop capabilities required for the world of work.

> Young people ... acquire knowledge of particular subjects, but are not equipped to use knowledge in ways which are relevant to the world outside the education system. This imbalance is harmful to individuals, to industry, and to society. A

well-balanced education should, of course, embrace analysis and the acquisition of knowledge. But it must also include the exercise of creative skills, the competence to undertake and complete tasks, and the ability to cope with everyday life; and also doing these things in cooperation with others. (RSA, 1989)

Stephenson and Yorke (1998) have recently described some of the projects that have been undertaken in this programme.

Competence and performance

A similar programme sponsored by the Employment Department used the term competence in relation to occupational task. The Department states that: 'By competent we mean performing at the standards expected of an employee doing the same job' (Mitchell, 1987) (see Chapter 11). If one is able to accomplish a task then one is competent in that task. In some jobs, as for example an airline pilot or a surgeon, the employee is required to have a minimum competency in a wide range of tasks. Thus in order for a person to be employed in those jobs they require some certification of competency. For this reason there is interest in competency based learning and assessment and this has extended to teaching as well as, perhaps surprisingly, to liberal education.

Gonczi (1994) distinguishes between three conceptions of competency. In the first a competence is considered to be a group of behaviours which enable an 'atomised' task to be completed. The specification of such tasks must be transparent, and there can be no disagreement about the construct of the task. 'In effect the task becomes the competency.' It is not concerned with the connections between the tasks. Standards relating to competences defined in this way have been developed in Australia and Britain (see Chapters 5 and 11).

The system of National Vocational Qualifications promoted by the British government for persons at work is based on what a person can do at work. In this sense achievement is declared as a competence. These competences are related to standards.

A vocational qualification as a statement of competence should incorporate the assessment of skills to specified standards, relevant knowledge and understanding, and the ability to use skills and apply knowledge and understanding in the performance of relevant tasks. (ED, 1986)

Gonczi (1994) argues than when such an approach is used for the development of professional skills it is inadequate, since among other things, 'it ignores the complexity of performance in the real world and ignores the role of professional judgement in intelligent performance'.

One of the problems of competency based teacher education as it was introduced in the United States (see Houston, 1980) was that written tests could not possibly indicate the competency of a person to teach. It did not ensure there was a connection between knowledge acquired and capability to perform the task. In consequence there has been a search for other ways to evaluate teacher competence, and in the United States these involve alternative assessments using portfolios (see Chapter 12). It has also been argued that such programmes de-professionalise teaching and other public service occupations by their technical and reductionist approach to knowledge and values which involves the preparation of long lists of narrowly defined competencies (Hyland, 1996).

Medical educators do not assume that only those things that are defined are the only elements of competence. McGaghie *et al.* (1978) wrote:

> The competencies are many and multi-faceted. They may also be ambiguous and tied to local custom and constraints of time, finance and human resources. Nevertheless, a competency based curriculum in any setting assumes that the many roles and functions involved in a doctor's work can be defined and clearly expressed. It does not imply that the things defined are the only elements of competence, but rather that those which can be defined represent the critical point of departure in curriculum development. Careful delineation of these components of medical practice is the first and most critical step in designing a competency based curriculum.

This view clearly meets Gonczi's requirement that it should take into account the complexity of the task and allow for the development of professional responsibility. Nevertheless matters are not that simple for as McGuire (1993) notes the topic abounds with semantic confusion and prior to that spelling, for there is even disagreement about the form of the plural. Should it be *competences* or *competencies*? My computer programme responds to the latter not the former. McGuire (and this writer) have pointed out that any response to a test is a performance. McGuire argues that the use of the term performance in the test context is a naive disregard of plain English. We are not concerned with performance *per se*; 'rather we are concerned about the conclusions we can draw and the predictions we can make on the basis of that performance'. And this is a high inference activity.

Others working in the medical field have tried to distinguish between competence and performance. For Norman (1985), competence described what a person was capable of doing, whereas performance was what one does in practice. Mast and Davis (1994) considered that the distinction used by psychometricians avoided the confusion inherent in these terms. In the psychometric setting competence is a theoretical construct: it is not observable. In contrast performance is observable. Performance measures, like any test, are influenced by the environment in which they are set. They are not pure measures of competence that is inferred from performance.

Miller (1990), another medical educator, defines competence assessment as the measurement of an examinee's ability to use his/her knowledge. This includes such things as acquiring information, analysing and interpreting data, and the ability to manage patient problems (Mast and Davis, 1994).

Gonczi (1994) draws attention to another movement that developed during the last 20 years. This approach considered that there were generic intellectual skills which should be developed as the means for the transfer of learning, as for example, critical thinking. He argues that there is no evidence that such generic competences actually exist and finds support for this in the substantive literature on critical thinking (e.g. Norris, 1992), and investigations of the differences between experts and novices (e.g. Chapter 9). The data, he suggests, show that high levels of competence are domain specific. He argues that the notion of competence is 'relational'.

It brings together disparate things – abilities of individuals (deriving from combinations of attributes) and the tasks needed to be performed in particular situations. Thus competence is conceived of as a complex structuring of attributes needed for intelligent performance in specific situations. This approach has been called the 'integrated' or holistic approach to competence. (Norris, 1992)

Generic competences are placed in the knowledge context of the problems to be solved. This is exemplified by the model of the examination in engineering science described below, and the profile of a general practitioner described in Chapter 11. This approach to defining professional competence has been adopted by the professions in Australia. Given the context of this section, it is of interest that *The Taxonomy of Educational Objectives* has had a considerable influence on medical education. For example The Royal Australian College of General Practitioners proposed the following weightings, subject to a major review every five years:

1. Cognitive skills (66% – divided into recall of knowledge 14%, interpretative skills 18% and, problem solving 34%).

2. Affective (interpersonal) skills – 26 per cent.

3. Psychomotor (manual and perceptual) skills – 8 per cent (Marshall, 1993).

In terms of the expectations we have of professional people and our ability to enter into dialogue with them this approach leads to a 'closed' rather than an 'open' system of education. A liberal education cannot be achieved unless a serious attempt is made to develop generic competences in such a way that we are brought to understand how others in different occupations use these competences. How else is an understanding of value positions to be obtained, and more to the point, how can dialogue be entered into without that capability?

Fleming (1992) offers a partial way out of this difficulty with the concept of *meta-competence*. This idea is derived from the medieval disputation which 'complemented the repetition of taught content with a sense of flexibility, of criticism and potential for change. The fixity of written knowledge ultimately supported the flux of the argument out of which was known, and what could be done with that knowledge would often emerge as susceptible to further development.' Within the medieval disputation Fleming sees the presence of *meta-competence*. He argues that the specific knack which experts have is the ability to reflect on their competences and to manipulate them in solving problems. The knowledge they have is that which enables them to understand the competence itself. Thus 'developing meta-competence is about lining subject specific knowledge with the particular competences that should be practised by the learner.' He concludes that this can be achieved by particular approaches to learning and instruction. He does not, nor did his remit require it of him, consider the specific problem of the professions although it is clearly relevant. In so far as liberal education is concerned the curriculum of Alverno College would seem to meet his aim especially as self-assessment is built into the learning-instruction process.

This curriculum first caught the attention of the wider world in the mid-1980s. Among those who drew attention to it was the President of Harvard (Bok, 1986). At that time interest focused on the principle of assessment-led learning which like those who developed the engineering science examination, they proposed. The College began with the idea that working women, as part of their liberal education, required a number of generic abilities (see Figure 2.6).

Once they had identified these abilities they asked the question: 'How can we tell how far along a student is to developing these abilities?' The answer to this question led them to assessment. In its turn it led them to a new approach to assessment quite unlike anything that had been done before. Each subject was required to contribute to the students' development in the abilities as well as to teach the knowledge component associated with that subject. Since they are committed to assessment outside of the classroom an Assessment Center administers faculty designed assessments that are broader than single course ones. It is supported by a full-time staff, and several hundred volunteer assessors from the outside community, including industry and commerce. They are trained for the task and provide 'interpretative feedback' to the students throughout each year. At the same time the classroom teacher is considered to be the most important assessor of the student's development.

> If learning is to be *integrative/experiential*, assessment must judge *performance*. If learning is to be characterized by *self-awareness*, assessment must include *self-assessment* as well as *expected outcomes* and *developmental criteria* that are public. If learning is to be *active/interactive*, assessment must include *feedback* and elements of *externality* as well as *performance*. If learning is to be *developmental*, assessment must be *cumulative* and *expansive*. Finally, if learning is to be *transferable*, assessment must be *multiple in mode and context*. (Alverno, 1994)

By *integration* is meant the ability 'to continually create new wholes out of multiple parts'. It would differ from *synthesis* in *The Taxonomy of Educational Objectives* in so far as *synthesis* is confined to a single subject. Integration brings knowledge from a variety of different perspectives. *Feedback* is considered to be important and provides the matter for reflection and growth. It is related to *externality* in that if the abilities are to be *transferable* some assessment must be made at a distance from the classroom. Hence the need for an assessment centre. Within this concept of externality they attach considerable importance to self-assessment. Cumulative assessment shows how the students progress or regress and student portfolios are used to plot this journey (see also Chapter 14).

At the College all students are required to develop skill in each of the abilities listed in Figure 2.6. These were first called competences but they changed to abilities to avoid comparison with teacher education competences as listed in the 1970s which they perceived to be narrow and inhibitive of learning. Each subject area is required to contribute to the development of these skills so that the student is assessed in both knowledge and ability (as defined here). Each of the abilities is divided into 6 levels along which the student has to develop. Students are required to develop to level 4 in each of the abilities during their first two years, and in their major studies to take this development further to level 6. An important goal of this curriculum is that the students should be able to integrate these abilities when solving the practical problems they are likely to face in later life because the solutions to such problems are unlikely to depend on the application of a single ability. Examples of this approach will be found

Ability Domain 1: Develop communications ability (effectively send and respond to communications for varied audiences and purposes)
Level 1   Identify own strengths and weaknesses as communicator
Level 2   Show analytic approach to effective communicating
Level 3   Communicate effectively
Level 4   Communicate effectively making relationships out of explicit frameworks from at least three major areas of knowledge
Level 5   Communicate effectively, with application of communications theory
Level 6   Communicate with habitual effectiveness and application of theory, through co-ordinated use of different media that represents contemporary technological advancement in the communications field.
These to be developed in writing, speaking, listening, using media quantified data, and the computer.

Ability Domain 2: Develop analytical capabilities
Level 1   Show observational skills
Level 2   Draw reasonable inferences from observations
Level 3   Perceive and make relationships
Level 4   Analyse structure and organization
Level 5   Establish ability to employ frameworks from area of concentration or support area discipline in order to analyse
Level 6   Master ability to employ independently the frameworks from area of concentration or support area discipline in order to analyse

Ability Domain 3: Develop workable problem-solving skill
Level 1   Identify the process, assumptions, and limitations involved in problem-solving approaches
Level 2   Recognize, analyse and state a problem to be solved
Level 3   Apply a problem-solving process to a problem
Level 4   Compare processes and evaluate own approach in solving problems
Level 5   Design and implement a process for resolving a problem which requires collaboration with others
Level 6   Demonstrate facility in solving problems in a variety of situations

Ability Domain 4: Develop facility in making value judgements and independent decisions
Level 1   Identify own values
Level 2   Infer and analyse values in artistic and humanistic works
Level 3   Relate values to scientific and technological developments
Level 4   Engage in valuing in decision-making in multiple contexts
Level 5   Analyse and formulate the value foundation/framework of a specific area of knowledge, in its theory and practice
Level 6   Apply own theory of value and the value foundation of an area of knowledge in a professional context

Ability Domain 5: Develop facility for social interaction
Level 1   Identify own interaction behaviours utilized in a group problem-solving situation
Level 2   Analyse behaviour of others within two theoretical frameworks
Level 3   Evaluate behaviour of self within two theoretical frameworks
Level 4   Demonstrate effective social interaction behaviour in a variety of situations and circumstances
Level 5   Demonstrate effective interpersonal and intergroup behaviours in cross-cultural interactions
Level 6   Facilitate effective interpersonal and intergroup relationships in one's professional situation

Ability Domain 6: Develop responsibility for the environment
Level 1   Perceive and describe the complex relationships within the environment
Level 2   Observe and explain how the behaviour of individuals and groups have an impact on the environment
Level 3   Observe and explain how the environment has an impact on the behaviour of individuals and groups
Level 4   Respond holistically to environmental issues and evaluate the responses of others
Level 5   Respond holistically to environmental problems and independently develop responsible alternative solutions
Level 6   Select and rigorously support a responsible solution to an environmental problem with an implementation strategy

Ability Domain 7: Develop awareness and understanding of the world in which the individual lives
Level 1   Demonstrate awareness, perception and knowledge of observable events in the contemporary world
Level 2   Analyse contemporary events in their historical context
Level 3   Analyse interrelationships of contemporary events and conditions
Level 4   Demonstrate understanding of the word as a global unit for analysing the impact of events of one society upon another
Level 5   Demonstrate understanding of professional responsibility in the contemporary world
Level 6   Take personal position regarding implications of contemporary events

Ability Domain 8: Develop aesthetic responsiveness to the arts
Level 1   Express response to selected arts in terms of their formal elements and personal background
Level 2   Distinguish among artistic forms in terms of their elements and personal response to selected art works
Level 3   Relate artistic works to the contexts from which they emerge
Level 4   Make and defend judgements about the quality of selected artistic expressions
Level 5   Choose and discuss artistic works which reflect personal vision of what it means to be human
Level 6   Demonstrate the impact of the arts on your life to this point and project their role in your personal future

Figure 2.6 The Alverno Abilities and their levels. (Reproduced by kind permission of Dr. G. Loacker and Alverno College Productions, Milwaukee.) (Following definitions given previously, I have introduced the term domain into the competence category titles.)

in the colleges evaluation studies of its programmes which seem to suggest that it has had some success in achieving this goal (Mentkowski and associates, 2000). This has implications for the grading of the assessments made as well as the method of reporting (see also Chapters 12 and 14).

> A student does not receive grades as a result of assessments. The validations she receives when she has successfully completed an assessment indicate that she has met the detailed, rigorous requirements set by the college. The record of courses taken, completed validations and a detailed profile of the student's strengths and accomplishments become part of the student's permanent records. (Alverno, 1994)

From the beginning they set out to evaluate what they were doing and established an institute for this purpose. The first major reports from this institute appeared in the 1980s. Of these No. 3 (Mentkowski and Doherty, 1983) which sought to establish the validity of their abilities in respect of the students' later careers, is probably of most interest. It inspired the college to carry on.

Competency or performance-based learning is related to the idea of mastery. In a strict mastery system the learner has to demonstrate they can perform a task before they move on to the next task (Bloom 1976). In higher education Keller's (1968) scheme of personalized instruction is based on the mastery concept (Blair, 1977; Imrie *et al.*, 1980; Vaughan, 1982). The Alverno scheme seeks mastery through cognitive and affective development and this is far from a strictly behaviourist interpretation of competence.

Authentic assessment and coursework

Related to the idea of competency and performance-based learning is the concept of authentic assessment. Fischer and King (1995) define this as 'an inclusive term for alternative assessment methods' (i.e. to traditional norm and criterion referenced tests) 'that examine students' ability to solve problems or perform tasks that closely re-semble authentic situations.' The British National Vocational Qualifications (NVQs) discussed in Chapters 5 and 11 would be categorized as authentic assessments by some authors. That is to say, they are assessments of the work that individuals actually do.

Terwilliger (1997) has attributed the term to American author Wiggins (Wiggins, 1989, 1993). In the UK it was used by Torrance who authored a book on authentic assessment in which no reference is made to Wiggins (Torrance, 1995). It is not in common use in British higher education as it is in the US. This is in spite of the fact that, as described by Wiggins, evidence of authentic practice in public examinations can be traced back to the 1960s. It would apply in particular to the assessment of projects (Heywood, 1977a). The 'authentic' movement has been much associated with the promotion of assessment using portfolios.

In the United States the idea of authentic assessment derived from criticisms of traditional methods of testing in schools. Those who were seeking to reform schooling argued that the assessment of achievement should be designed to reflect more precisely complex 'real life' and real life problems than is possible with objective tests (multiple-choice questions).

Terwilliger (1997) has taken issue with the proponents of this view, not because traditional testing is not open to criticism, but because the term 'authentic' implies that such assessments are superior to more conventional tests. Indeed in the UK some proponents of the NVQ approach take this view, and they defend it on the ground that the performances involved have high validity (see Chapter 11). However, whereas much research has been done on the validity of NVQs, Terwilliger suggests that in respect of authentic assessment this is not the case in the United States. Its advocates 'rarely present data, evidential or consequential in support of the validity of "authentic" assessments'.

In respect of mathematics Lesh and Lamon (1992) define authentic mathematical activities as those which involve real mathematics; realistic situations; questions or issues that might actually occur in real-life situations; and realistic tolls and resources. Terwilliger points out that this definition is circular because authentic is made synonymous with the terms real, realistic, and real-life situations. As he, and others, have pointed out, what is 'real' to one person is not necessarily 'real' to another; indeed, it might be unrealistic. There is also the problem in mathematics that some real-life situations may require very long questions, which may create difficulties for some students. It is by no means clear that the applications of mathematics render the learning of mathematics more easy than when it is taught in its 'pure' form using symbols (Heywood, 1976). It is clear that 'real mathematics' as defined here is restricted to certain applied situations and not the 'real life' mathematics done by mathematicians!

Terwilliger argues that the claim that authentic assessments are superior to conventional forms of assessment is based on face validity, that is, if it looks right it must be right; but it is easy to show with the aid of psychometric tests that this is very often not the case.

The claim that authentic assessment necessarily encourages higher order thinking is dismissed by Terwilliger. He assumes from the examples of project work given by Wiggins that the role of knowledge in assessment is down-graded. There are, he argues, ample empirical data which show the central role of knowledge in many domains of human understanding (e.g. Chi, Glaser and Farr, 1988). He quotes Hirsch (1987) thus:

> The polarisation of educationists into facts-people versus skills-people has no basis in reason. Facts and skills are inseparable [as are values]. There is no insurmountable reason why those who advocate the teaching of higher order skills and those who advocate the teaching of common traditional content should not join forces. No philosophical or practical value prevents them from doing so, and all who consider mature literacy to be a paramount aim of education will wish them to do so.

This is the position taken by this writer. It implies a multiple strategy approach to assessment as will be outlined below. It seems clear that the complementary course-work that accompanies some courses in the UK straddles the categories of authentic and performance-based assessments as a function of the type of rubric used (e.g. Figure 1.2).

Domain and level	Method
Cognitive domain	
Knowledge	Lecture, programmed instruction, drill and practice
Comprehension	Lecture, modularized instruction, programmed instruction
Application	Discussion, simulations and games, CAI, modularized instruction, field experience, laboratory
Analysis	Discussion, independent/group projects, simulations, field experience, role-playing, laboratory
Synthesis	Independent/group projects, field experience, role-playing, laboratory
Evaluation	Independent/group projects, field experience, laboratory
Affective domain	
Receiving	Lecture discussion, modularized instruction, field experience
Responding	Discussion, simulations, modularized instruction, role-playing, field experience
Organization	Discussion, independent/group projects, field experience
Characterization by a Value	Independent projects, field experience
Psychomotor domain	
Perception	Demonstration(lecture), drill and practice
Set	Demonstration, drill and practice
Guided response	Peer teaching, games, role-playing, field experience, drill and practice
Mechanism	Games, playing, field experience, drill and practice
Complex overt response	Games, field experience
Adaption	Independent projects
Originality	Independent projects, field experience

Figure 2.7 Matching objective domain and level of learning to appropriate methods of instruction (from Weston and Cranton, 1986). (Reproduced by kind permission of the Editor of the Journal of Higher Education (first in Heywood, 1989a). (1986 by the Ohio State University Press. All rights reserved).

Knowledge
What was the heart rate?
Where is the primary lesion?

Comprehension
When would you use that type of hernia repair?
Why is the fracture in the same place it was before?

Application
Your are watching the patient and she falls. What would you do?
Here is a lady with no vibratory sensation. What problem does this pose?

Analysis
What are the most significant aspects of this patient's story?
That is a curious bit of information. How do you explain it?
How would you divide that information into other ways of looking at

Synthesis
How would you summarize this?
What are your conclusions?

Evaluation
Why is that information pertinent?
How valid is this patient's story?

Figure 2.8. Examples of medical faculty questions according to the six levels of The Taxonomy of Educational Objectives.

The Taxonomy and instruction

Although little research has been done on the relationship between *The Taxonomy* and instruction, several models have been proposed. Of interest to higher education is one proposed by Weston and Cranton (1986) which is shown in Figure 2.7.

The impact of *The Taxonomy*

There is no doubt that *The Taxonomy* had a major impact on educational thinking although, it seems that it is the second part, rather than the theoretical framework with which educators are most familiar (Anderson and Sosniak, 1994b). Summaries of the classes and sub-abilities were widely publicized. Word of *The Taxonomy* was brought to Britain by several distinguished educationalists. Among them was R.A.C. Oliver who pioneered a syllabus-free examination at the Advanced level of the General Certificate of Education in General Studies which used *The Taxonomy* for a framework. Subsequently its sponsor the Joint Matriculation Board required all of its subject committees to state their aims and objectives and indicate the proportion of marks allocated to each category in their Advanced level examinations. An account of *The Taxonomy*'s influence on one subject committee which led to the idea of multiple-strategy assessment is given in the next section.

Although *The Taxonomy* did not have the pervasive effect on higher education that its originators may have wished, it was taken up by some college and university teachers, particularly in the areas of engineering, science and medicine (Hubbard and Clemens, 1961; Miller, 1961 (see Figure 2.8). It was used to argue the case for the adoption of multiple-choice testing in the foundation year at the University of Keele (Iliffe, 1966). Some teachers still use it, especially in the United States (Fincher, 1985). In addition to its influence in English-speaking countries it has stimulated research in continental Europe and the Middle East (Lewy and Bathory, 1994), and Asia (Bom Mo Chung, 1994).

Perhaps the most important legacy that *The Taxonomy* has left is the movement for outcomes-based assessment and learning. It has forced teachers to be precise about what it is they want to do. As I have argued elsewhere, many of the published outcomes when extracted from their subject content will be found in similar if not identical form in *The Taxonomy*. Nordvall and Braxton (1996) have argued that to focus on outcomes as a measure of the value added alone is flawed and that the focus of some assessment activities should be shifted to the process. They see the levels of *The Taxonomy* being used to do this and imply a multiple strategy approach to assessment and instruction.

This approach depends on the willingness of teachers to use a variety of methods of instruction because the same method of teaching is unlikely to meet all the objectives that it is desired should be obtained. Or, to put it another way, each educational objective will be achieved by a preferred method of instruction that is deliberately designed to ensure that that objective is achieved. This approach also implies a much more sophisticated approach to the planning of classes and courses.

Beyond education Humble showed how *The Taxonomy* could be used to analyse the jobs of managers and supervisors in a large company. He appreciated many years before it became fashionable that the affective domain was of equal importance in the evaluation of jobs, and the subsequent training for such jobs. His analysis is described in full in Heywood (1970, 1989a).

Bloom (1994) concludes that one of the 'primary reactions to *The Taxonomy* was a shift from a concern about teachers' actions to a concern for what students learned from these actions.' This is certainly the direction that the assessment movement in the United States took when it began, and has led to its concern with outcomes and authentic assessment. Bloom also argued that its value was as a prototype. By 1971 he and his colleagues had enough material to show it had been related to many subject areas, and in 1971 this information was given in the *Handbook of Formative and Summative Evaluation of Student Learning* (Bloom, Hastings and Madaus, 1971).

The Taxonomy did convince many teachers of the need to define aims and objectives. It did not however convince them of the need to have a learning theory that they could defend if their assessments were to have a positive effect on learning. This study is as much about the need for such theories as it is about the practice of assessment. Bloom hoped that *The Taxonomy* would encourage teachers to help students learn to apply their knowledge. If they can deal with problems with which they are unfamiliar this will guard against rote learning and ready-made solutions. The implications for assessment are clear. Yet, in spite of this principle we still hear of school and university examinations that students perceive to require primarily the recall of knowledge.

Toward a revised *Taxonomy*

Since 1995 a group (which includes Krathwohl, one of the authors of the original *Taxonomy*) has been meeting to revise the original and incorporate conceptual changes which have taken place since 1956 (Anderson, 1996). At the time of writing Anderson said that the revised version was far from complete. However, Anderson felt able to provide some of the flavour as it affected the domains and testing.

The group now draws a distinction between two types of knowledge. The first is the ability to recall, which is how it was used in the original classification. This ability is a cognitive process. But there was also an emphasis on what is to be recalled, that is, content. So in the new edition the process knowledge dimension will come under the heading 'remember'. The second dimension will consist of the major categories of knowledge. This makes possible a matrix in which each cognitive process can be related to each type of knowledge (e.g. recall of methods, application of methods). In statements of objectives the verb will correspond with the cognitive process and the noun will correspond with content.

The group also makes an important gesture to those teachers, especially in higher education, who believe that such categories are restrictive. They use terms like 'knowing' and 'understanding', and for many teachers the domain of knowledge in the original taxonomy was rather clinical and detached from the emotional context in which knowledge is generated. However, this will be rectified to some extent in the proposed revision. The group following, Krathwohl (1985) and Carroll (1985), distinguish between knowledge that is strategic/motivational and knowledge that is social/cultural. The first takes into account the point that although knowing is idiosyncratic, being derived from our unique experiences, it is nevertheless a legitimate educational goal. Sometimes collective knowings become accepted knowledge. Since we have to learn to know, this category comprehends the meta-cognitive processes and learning strategies used in learning. The social/cultural dimension 'reflects our appreciation of the cultural specificity of knowledge'.

While the authors retain the principle of increasing complexity, which seems self-evident, they have reserved their judgement on the principle of cumulative hierarchical structure. They argue that there will be conditions when a cumulative hierarchy is present. This will depend on the problem to be solved or the domain of knowledge under consideration. Some academic disciplines may require different cognitive processes and, together with the structure of the domain, they will determine whether a cumulative hierarchy is formed (see Hirschfeld and Gelman, 1994 for a cognitive science perspective).

The group also takes a different view of problem-solving. It is now argued that problem-solving uses several processes. In solving problems learners have to reflect on their actions, evaluate what they do and adjust if necessary. 'It is meta-cognition that most clearly differentiates problem-solving from application.'

In respect of assessment, the new version will recommend to test designers that they need take into account 'tasks, responses, scoring rules and procedures, and interpretation-in terms of the cognitive processes and knowledge being assessed'. In this way, it would appear that they move toward the concept of multiple-strategy assessment (Heywood, 1989a).

Toward multiple-strategy assessment

The term 'multiple-objective examination' was coined by Heywood (1977a) to describe a type of comprehensive examination whose sub-tests focused on well-defined knowledge and skill domains. It derived from investigations in assessment in engineering science, history, geography and mathematics (Carter, Heywood and Kelly, 1986; Heywood, McGuinness and Murphy, 1980). In the 1986 report it was defined as multiple-strategy assessment and latterly the phrase (term) has incorporated instruction and learning. The term had a somewhat different meaning to the way in which it was to be used in the United States, as will be explained

The term had its origins in Furneaux's criticisms of engineering examinations. It will be recalled that they had identified one large factor that suggested they were all measuring the same thing. This seemed to be a waste of examining time. It should have been possible to have a variety of tests which would test objectives, as well as give satisfaction to industrialists that attempts were being made to produce the kind of graduates they required. The investigators had been given the opportunity to design a new examination in engineering science at the Advanced level. This examination would be equivalent to many examinations taken at the end of the Freshman year in many universities. It was taken at the end of two years' study (about 200 hours of class contact time, and was intended to be the equivalent of physics in order to be accepted as an entry examination to university departments of engineering. Traditionally the physics examination consisted of two three-hour written papers and a laboratory practical. There was, therefore, six hours of examination time available. The Board responsible for the examination agreed that the laboratory practical could be replaced by coursework assessed throughout the two years. The new examination now comprised five sub-tests. Knowledge of Principles (etc.), that is the first category of *The Taxonomy* was tested by various forms of multiple-choice question in one sub-test lasting one hour. Engineering Comprehension was tested by asking the candidates to read an article from an engineering journal and answer questions on it. This sub-test also lasted for an hour. The third hour was taken up by a Design and Planning Exercise. This was intended to replicate the project planning, specification, and design. This was also of one hour's duration. It was thought that there should be a high correlation between this paper and the practical coursework.

The second three-hour paper was taken up by one section for long answers and another section for short answers that tested the application of the principles of engineering science to practical problems and some of these were related to a social and economic context. These may be regarded as different sub-tests because of the time-allowance factor.

The coursework required the students to undertake a number of investigations of approximately 12 hours duration and a project of 50 hours duration. The assessment schedules for coursework were criterion- referenced.

It was predicted that factorial analysis would reveal that each of these sub-tests would yield a specific factor that was particular to that sub-test. Repeated factorial analysis over a period of years suggested that this was the case (Carter *et al.*, 1986). This is what is meant by multiple-strategy assessment.

An attempt was made to replicate this concept in experimental examinations in history and mathematics with a younger age group (+15 years) that is, to design a series of sub-tests that would test different objectives. The evidence supported this general approach to the design of public examinations (Heywood *et al.*, 1980; Resnick and Goulden, 1987). It was argued that comprehensive (multiple- strategy) examinations whose sub-tests focus on well-defined domains should help teachers break the mould of traditional thinking about assessment (Heywood, 1989a), as well as help them develop higher order thinking skills. A multiple-strategy approach to assessment was required.

In 1986 National Governors Association in the United States also introduced the idea of multiple-strategy assessment. They said:

Assessment of undergraduate learning and college quality needs, at minimum, to include data about student skills, abilities and cognitive learning: substantive knowledge of individual students at various points in their undergraduate career: instructional approaches used by faculty; and educational curricula. Because the nature of undergraduate education requires many skills and cognitive abilities be acquired and developed, colleges and universities should use a number of assessment approaches and techniques. An assessment program that uses multiple measures of student learning will more accurately and fairly depict a student's knowledge and abilities, regardless of background or status. Instead of limiting education access, assessment may actually provide incentives to ensure that unprepared students receive proper counselling, placement and academic assist-

ance needed to perform in college and to graduate in a reasonable amount of time.
(NGA, 1986)

The differences between the two approaches arise from organizational structure and
management of examinations and testing in institutions in the UK and US. In the UK
although an Academic Council of some sort certifies the awards made by a department it seldom interferes in the work of departments unless there are clear grounds for
so doing. Departments take responsibility for organizing the examinations and
assessments on which awards are based. Each subject will have its own Court of
Examiners advised by an external examiner, although there will be a university wide
system for appeals. At the present time it would be unheard of for the university to
arrange for all its students to be tested separately from the departments' examinations
on specified outcomes. However, as Nichols (1991) makes clear, this is one of the
intentions of the NGA. Such measures would include attitudinal surveys of institutional effectiveness, cognitive development, and behavioural change and performance.
At the same time departments are not excused from having to define outcomes which
according to Rogers in Nichols (1991) should focus on student learning and the
improvement of teaching and learning.

In the UK while student evaluations of courses are expected, institutions do not
have active policies to assess cognitive skills independently of the examination and
assessment policies of particular subjects. Work has been done on the development of
instruments which would evaluate the experience students have of university (see
Chapter 4). This is not to say, or to argue that there may not be a case for
institution-wide policies in respect of particular areas, as for example, the development of generic inter-personal skills.

In the US it is not uncommon for universities to have offices for institutional
research for the purpose of monitoring how well an institution achieves its goals. Such
offices may well carry out independent testing of the students (for example, see
Chapters 4 and 5 for the details of the Alverno College Office of Educational Research
Longitudinal survey).

Multiple-strategy assessment implies a variety of measures consistent with the
goals of the university as well as the subject, because simple achievement tests by
themselves do not tell us about the quality of the educational process. Other measures
have to be used by teachers and institutions to evaluate the quality of the process and
the progress of students. Thus multiple-strategy assessments vary as a function of the
organizational level at which they are implemented. Those that Carter *et al.* (1986)
described were for assessment of student learning outcomes. In the conditions in
which they were developed the designers had a level playing ground because not only
were the teachers interested but they had to teach and assess for the public
examination. Moreover, the eight sections of syllabus were covered by the same
examination. In the university each of these sections would be a separate subject and
examined separately by the educators who taught the course. Therefore, to introduce
a comprehensive examination of this type would require an immense change in
attitude by the whole department to assessment and teaching since there would have
to be an integration of their activities, and they would have to work as team. Such a
change could not be brought about without the active leadership of those responsible

for the department. This would have to be supported with the authority of the agencies from whom accreditation is sought (see Chapter 3) As Carter and his colleagues make clear, they were fortunate enough to have a product champion (Heywood, Carter and Kelly, 1997). This is not to say that the individual teacher who is responsible for the assessment of the courses he/she teaches, cannot develop some simple form of multiple-strategy assessment; but as Ashcroft and Palacio (1996) warn, before embarking on such a course the educator should carefully weigh up the cost – benefits of so doing. The most important cost is likely to be the time factor (see Chapter 11).

There is, therefore, much more to assessment than the measurement of achievement, and much more to the measurement of achievement than traditional achievement tests imply. If achievement is to be adequately assessed then multiple measures will be required and this will not come cheaply if it is to be done properly.

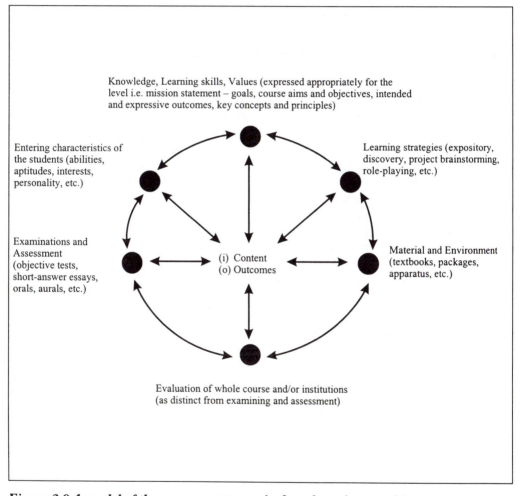

Knowledge, Learning skills, Values (expressed appropriately for the level i.e. mission statement – goals, course aims and objectives, intended and expressive outcomes, key concepts and principles)

Entering characteristics of the students (abilities, aptitudes, interests, personality, etc.)

Learning strategies (expository, discovery, project brainstorming, role-playing, etc.)

Examinations and Assessment (objective tests, short-answer essays, orals, aurals, etc.)

(i) Content
(o) Outcomes

Material and Environment (textbooks, packages, apparatus, etc.)

Evaluation of whole course and/or institutions (as distinct from examining and assessment)

Figure 2.9 A model of the assessment-curriculum-learning-teaching process.

The curriculum-assessment-instruction-learning process

In the argument that follows readers should feel free to substitute outcomes for objectives. They should also note that the model includes the key concepts that are to be covered under the heading of aims and objectives. Those which it is finally agreed to teach as a result of the curriculum design process form the essential components of the syllabus. The model (Figure 2.9) represents the phases of design as well as the phases of implementation for both result from the same complex process. There are, of course, other ways to present this information as I have shown elsewhere (Heywood, 1989a) but they do not show the impact of the curriculum process on the syllabus.

It is clear that if objectives are to be achieved and feedback introduced, instructional procedures will be changed until they meet the required objectives. Assessment is therefore an integral part of curriculum and instructional design. When it determines whether the students are achieving the required goals it also indicates whether changes in instruction ought to be made. Assessment should not be, as it so often is, an afterthought of the educational process. In this respect it is significant that in a survey reported by El-Khawas (1986) the largest area of agreement among baccalaureate colleges was for linking assessment to instructional improvement, which is the major theme of this book.

The model shown in Figure 2.9 is based on the fundamental proposition that whether the focus is the design of the curriculum, an assessment procedure, or even the evaluation of an institution, the starting point is the same, i.e. the understanding and expression of what we are trying to do. Today that is summarized in a statement of aims and objectives (outcomes). Whether it is at the level of the programme, a topic specific course or a classroom session they derive from the mission statement of the institution which in its turn is responsible for the resources and organizational structure which will bring about these ends (see Chapter 3).

From previous arguments it is axiomatic that for each assessment or instructional objective that has to be obtained, there will be methods of testing or instruction which are more appropriate than others. For example, if it is proposed that students will be able to evaluate critically historical sources, an assessment in history will have to provide a variety of sources which the student will have to evaluate against set questions in a given period of time. If they are to learn to do this they will have to be given a variety of sources and shown how to use these sources and this takes time. If the objectives of assessment are to be met then instruction has to be designed to meet those objectives.

The importance of evaluation is that it will show whether the face validity judgements made while designing the curriculum hold or not. Things are seldom what they seem to be. For example, it was found that teachers in the engineering science programme assumed that if students had implemented a 50-hour design and make project that they could answer a written one-hour question on planning and design without any specific instruction. This turned out not to be the case and a specific note of guidance had to be issued to the teachers. Similar problems occurred with the experimental examinations in Ireland in history and mathematics. The teachers set a sub-test in problem-solving in mathematics that they claimed was a key objective. However, very poor results were obtained and once again it was found that the teachers were not showing their pupils how to deal with such problems (Heywood *et al.*, 1980). Thus an objective is more likely to be obtained when the instructional strategies (including materials) are designed to obtain that objective

This is not to deny that there will be many unintended and expressive learning outcomes to any educational experience (Eisner, 1979). One of the unintended outcomes of the evaluation of the engineering science coursework was that it became clear that the project design written paper was measuring a different skill from that used in actual projects that underlines the importance of continuous evaluation (Heywood, 1997b).

Nevertheless, notwithstanding either the need for expressive outcomes or the unintended consequences of planning there must be a focus which necessarily implies an objectives approach, since all learning requires organization, structure and meaning in the formal situation. While much learning is informal, and while students may already have attained the goals we wish them to obtain it is nevertheless the case that learning is enhanced in situations where both the learner and teacher are clear about what they wish to achieve. Thus the understanding of 'learning' which is the central goal of formal education must contribute to the selection of 'objectives' and determination of classroom structures. As Furst (1958) argued 'every instructor must have a defensible theory of learning', and this must take into account the entering characteristics of the students (e.g. aptitudes, interests, general background) for they could be in a position where the instructional sequence is too easy or too hard. By this he means a theory based on an evaluation of research and not one that has been tacitly assumed.

Few policy makers, industrialists, parents or teachers seem to grasp this issue. For example, if students are to be able to 'transfer' what they have learnt to new learning they have to have understood the concepts and principles that they have been taught. Often this is not the case (see Chapter 9). If these higher order skills are to be developed then, often, more time is required than is currently allowed for real as opposed to notional assent to be given. This is why the syllabus (which is taken to be a listing of what is to be learnt) is in the middle of the diagram (Figure 2.9). It is the sum of the times taken by the various activities designed to meet the objectives that all concerned with the curriculum agree are essential. The syllabus contains the screened list of key concepts only.

From the above it will be seen that the process of curriculum, instructional design and assessment are the same. Moreover, it is a complex activity. While it is convenient to begin with aims and objectives, any discussion of these must, at one and the same time, consider the learning experiences (strategies) necessary to bring the students from where they are (entering characteristics) to where they should be (objectives), as well as the most appropriate mode of assessment, and the essential knowledge required. This approach to curriculum design and assessment places the syllabus as the final outcome of the first phase of the procedure for design and implementation.

It is notoriously difficult for diagrams of this kind to show the dynamic nature of the process because the second phase is implementation. Their implementation may produce outcomes other than those anticipated at which stage decisions have to be made about the original objectives, i.e. whether to change them or whether to change the instruction to obtain the original objectives. So in response to a criticism by Loacker (private communication), the centre of the diagram shows the end of the second phase, i.e. outcomes, since they also result from a complex interaction between the same parameters. This is not to argue that knowledge is unimportant; it is to place knowledge in the perspective of the essential concepts and principles necessary for understanding and autonomous learning. By definition the curriculum is the formalization of what is to be learnt (learning). It creates the essential balance between product and process.

To summarize

1. Curriculum design, assessment and instruction begin at the same point, that is the understanding and expression of what it is we are trying to do.

2. For each general objective there will be appropriate methods of testing.

3. Specific learning strategies will be required if the objectives are to be successfully obtained.

4. The combination of all these elements may lead to a substantial reorganization of the syllabus.

An integrated approach of this kind has implications for both the role of the teacher, the institution and the assessment of quality (see for example Nordvall and Braxton, 1996, and the Quality Assurance Agency's *Guidelines for Quality Assurance in the UK*).

Chapter 3

Assessment and Accountability
Institutions and Programmes

Summary

This chapter is primarily about assessment and accountability and the accreditation of programmes. It begins with a brief discussion of accountability.

In recent years the term assessment has come to be related to the evaluation of educational institutions and their programmes. However much one might wish to divorce academic assessment of student learning from assessment of institutions and programmes, this cannot be done without prejudice to the problems which assessment creates. Assessment is as much concerned with the experience of the institution, the effects of grades on subsequent careers, and the effects of instruction on learning as it is with technique. Fortunately, the same model may be applied to the institution as well as to assessment and learning. To do so requires that the institution has a clear idea of its aims (mission) for it is the extent to which it achieves its aims that is the primary measure of accountability.

Subsequently the term quality was introduced into the dialogue but with little fundamental appraisal about what quality is (Harvey and Knight, 1996). Quality assessment focused on the delivery of academic programmes, and a search began for performance indicators with which to measure quality. The discussion on validity begun in Chapter 1 is extended in respect of these institutional measures.

There is a danger that institutions become overburdened by the sheer volume of data they are supposed to collect, and that they will not make effective use of the data they have. They should choose a small number of indicators that will help them focus on key issues. Part of the problem is that many of those who demand such indicators have little understanding of the complexity of the institutional process. Those concerned with institutional effectiveness need, in particular, to understand how institutional structures can enhance or impede learning.

Accreditation programmes have also come in for a lot of criticism in the United States. A particular concern is that some of them demand so many outcomes that the process may become trivialized. For change to take place institutions need to have a wholehearted commitment to the process as something they themselves require internally. Without this, change is unlikely to take place. Some aspects of accreditation and institutional evaluation are considered and in particular the value of mission statements.

Since accountability begins in the classroom, problems of measuring teaching effectiveness, especially by peers, are discussed. It is argued that university teachers need to be trained (see also Chapter 14).

Assessment as accountability in higher education

It is not part of the purpose of this chapter to enter into any detailed discussion of the issues relating to accountability. This has been done often and well and in respect of all sectors of education (Astin, 1974: Kogan, 1986). Accountability has many dimensions and many persons to serve. There are many stakeholders, and trying to meet the demands of all of them could lead to contradictions in policy.

As for teachers, they exercise accountability toward their institution, parents and their students. The view taken here is that front-line accountability is in the classroom. The key question for institutions is how with the resources they have can they better serve student learning. Accountability should be a determination of whether agreed objectives have been achieved, and the action to be taken, if any, if they are not.

The assessment of institutions

One has to admit that the drive for institutional assessment, and the greater transparency of institutional practices, has come from outside the institutions of higher education, in response to a political demand for public accountability.

At the same time this has been useful for institutions because it enables them to focus on key issues when funding is relatively static or declining in periods when there is increasing demand for higher education. In some universities it seems to have given the senior administration more power than they had before to get some things done within their institutions. The position varies as between the western industrialized nations. The United States, for example, moved to a mass system of higher education relatively quickly in the twentieth century, whereas it was only in the last decade of the century that Britain took considerable steps to move in the same direction. Much the same could be said of Australia. Nevertheless there existed in the public sectors of both these countries embryo systems of public accountability since colleges in that sector had, as in the United States, to obtain approval of their degree programmes. In some states, as for example Virginia, the state took a lead role in rethinking the way in which the curriculum was delivered to meet specific markets and to modify its design in order to accelerate student progress (Ewell, 1997).

In the United States accreditation has been defined as 'the process of recognizing educational institutions and the various programmes they offer for performance, integrity and quality which entitles them to the confidence of the educational community and the public' (*Journal of Higher Education*, 1979). It is undertaken by voluntary and professional associations who themselves through the Council on Post- Secondary Education evaluate and co-ordinate their processes (Nichols, 1991). In the process of accreditation institutions are required to subject themselves to self-study and self-evaluation. Church and Murray (1983) argued that the stress on self-scrutiny strikes a balance between institutional autonomy and public accountability. And accreditation tends to show not that programmes are comparable but that they have reached a minimum standard. A decade later, procedures for the assessment of programmes in the United Kingdom were to lay great stress on self- assessment.

In the United Kingdom the universities although funded by the state were not considered to be part of the public sector since they enjoyed relative protection from the state and received their funds via a University Grants Committee. The institutions in the public sector were oriented to the provision of technological, technical and craft education and their equivalents in the commercial sector of industry. They received their funds via local authorities who actively governed them. In 1956 ten of these institutions were promoted to College of Advanced Technology status. They were allowed to offer diploma courses for award by a National Council for Technological Awards who initiated a process of validation to ensure that the standards offered were comparable with those of a university degree (Davis, 1980; Church and Murray, 1983; Heywood, 1969). Subsequently, in 1966, these colleges became universities. At the same time 30 more institutions in this sector were given polytechnic status with the right to offer courses for degrees offered by a Council for National Academic Awards which took over and developed the work of the National Council for Technological Awards (Silver, 1990). By the early 1980s substantial experience had been gained of validation and there was an emerging debate. One authority concluded that 'while there are some differences in emphasis and operation, accreditation cannot be seen as something wholly divorced from validation'(Church and Murray, 1983).

Accreditation and validation are *propter hoc* activities. From a mass of data and visits to an institution an accrediting agency decides whether an institution is capable of offering the programmes that it wants to offer at the level stated. If approval is given it is granted for a limited period of time (e.g. five years) at the end of which it seeks renewal. In granting approval a whole range of factors are taken into account: these include various indicators of past performance, programme details, resource provision human and physical, library provision, etc. There are many similarities with accreditation in the United States. In the United Kingdom *post hoc* judgements of quality, in terms of the standards met by programmes, are made by external examiners in respect of the examinations which students sit. The validation agency had the right to see their reports. In the present situation these have to be made available to the subject review panel (see below). At the present time, as in the US, there is considerable interest in outcomes based indicators of performance.

While all these developments were taking place, the professional associations in Britain which granted degree equivalent qualifications by virtue of Royal Charters, also provided a validation service for use by departments in universities and colleges (Heywood, 1983). Since membership of these institutions is almost a *sine qua non* for graduates, departments would deem it foolish not to ensure the programmes they offered met the requirements of these associations.

One of the problems that departments offering professional courses have to face is that they have been required to prepare submissions to several different organizations each of which require slightly different information. This position causes an immense amount of work (Fitzgerald, 1994; Heywood, 1983; Yorke, 1996). Serious attempts are being made to alleviate this situation. At the same time an enormous amount of work is required to complete data on performance indicators. Again the position is no different in the US. Yorke (1996) points out that the European Union may wish to establish a framework for professional body recognition throughout Europe as part of its employment policies which allow for the free movement of workers between states. (At present the situation is somewhat analagous to that existing for school teachers in the US where the development of a national qualification may eventually allow teachers to move between states with ease.)

In the mid-1980s, calls were made by the National Governors Association in the US for multiple-strategy approaches to the assessment of higher education (NGA, 1986). As indicated in Chapter 2 this broadened the use of the term assessment to include programme and institutional assessment.

Harvey and Knight (1996) have pointed out that these and similar developments in Australia, Denmark, the Netherlands and the United States were undertaken without any fundamental appraisal of what quality is. Too often 'quality assessment and assurance processes have started by determining how quality is to be assessed or reviewed rather than by asking what it is to be assessed'. This point is no better illustrated than by the definitions adopted in relation to quality in the United Kingdom shown in Figure 3.1. Harvey and Knight argue that the failure to analyse quality can lead to impressive contradictions in policy.

Quality Assurance encompasses all the policies, systems and processes directed to ensuring maintenance and enhancement of the quality of educational provision in higher education.

Quality Control relates to the arrangements (procedures, standards and organization) within higher education institutions which verify that teaching and assessment are carried out in a satisfactory manner. Quality control would include the external examiner systems and is usually *post hoc*.

Quality Audit is the process of ensuring that the quality control arrangements in an institution are satisfactory and effective. In practice, prime responsibility for quality audit lies individually within institutions, and it extends to most aspects of quality assurance in an institution including staff development and curriculum design.

Quality Assessment is the process of external evaluation of the actual provision of education. The process of external assessment by peers of actual provision in particular subjects is by scrutiny of institutional documentation and student work; direct observation; interview; and by reference to performance indicators such as completion rates.

Figure 3.1 Terms relating to quality in higher education used by the funding councils in the United Kingdom.

We begin with developments in the UK in the 1980s. Both the Council for National Academic Awards and Committee of Vice- Chancellors and Principals investigated performance indicators (CVCP, 1985; CDP, 1987; PCFC, 1990). Substantial work was also done in Canada, and in America many states have made it a legislative requirement that higher education institutions make public their performance as indicated by numerous dimensions (see Figure 3.2) (CAPIOA 1993; Cave, Hanney and Kogan, 1988; Johnes and Taylor, 1990; Ewell, 1993, 1996; NCES, 1997; SSPEI, 1991). At the same time the universities in the United Kingdom were the subject of reports on their management (CVCP, 1985). Substantial studies were also done in Australia (Linke, 1991), and Kells (1993) had summarized developments in 12 countries for the OECD.

By the end of the 1980s the Total Quality Management (TQM) movement in industry invaded higher education, and a great amount of work was done in the United States to reconcile these ideas with work in the institutions of higher education. (Doherty, 1993; Lewis and Smith, 1994). In Britain some institutions set their criteria by British Standards (i.e. of the British Standards Institution) for quality. Some agreed definitions of quality, quality assurance and quality control are given in Figure 3.1 and indicators were linked to programme quality (Yorke, 1991, 1996, 1998).

In 1992, after the polytechnics had been incorporated into the university sector, the arrangements for funding the universities were changed and they were brought under the control of separate funding councils for England, Scotland and Wales. These councils were required to establish Quality Assessment Committees to advise them on the allocation of funding. In response, the Higher Education Institutions through the Committee of Vice-Chancellors and Principals established a Higher Education Quality Council and one of its early powers was to establish an Academic Audit Unit to check that quality assurance systems in universities were adequate and functioning (HEQC, 1994). The Higher Education Funding Councils introduced quality assessment which focused on the delivery of academic programmes. Yorke (1996) reports that both the audit and assessment exercises have found the 'potential of performance indicators to supply supportive evidence to institutional self-studies and to the documents supplied to the panels of assessors.'

If the value-added concept of quality is used it may have unintended consequences for policy if the policy makers have other notions of quality which are more consistent with their beliefs. Value-added is the extent to which an institution enhances the knowledge and skills which students bring to their studies. Therefore a high quality institution is one which greatly enhances that knowledge and those skills. Thus while 'Oxbridge' and the 'Ivy League' produce relatively able and some exceptional students they may not enhance their value very much since they select the most able students in the population in the first place (Harvey and Knight, 1996; Herrnstein and Murray, 1994; Nordvall and Braxton, 1996). For example, in 1997 the UK Minister for Higher Education proposed that the relatively large and extra annual sum of money used to support the colleges of universities of Oxford and Cambridge be withdrawn. This brought forth howls of protest from the Oxbridge dominated press in which traditional notions of quality were used to defend the payment. Such notions are, as Harvey and Knight (1996) point out, 'based on the assumption that the distinctiveness and inaccessibility of an 'Oxbridge' (Ivy League) education is itself quality'. However, this traditional notion of quality does not even define quality and its myth based on exclusivity is the mainstay of social institutions such as government, the fashion industry and Harrod's. As Jacobi, Astin and Ayala (1987) point out, reputation can also influence resource allocation; the more prestigious institutions have greater access to resources as the example shows. No change was made!

Carter points out that a simple measure of the correlation between the scores of admission tests (e.g. ACT and SAT scores – in his case the English 'A' level scores) and final performance in university examinations, must by its nature be an inadequate measure of value-added, because it smooths out much data that contributes to academic performance. Single scores do not fully describe how the performance of total populations vary. In consequence they can, in terms of the value-added component, provide misleading information (Carter and Heywood, 1991). In the United States Nordvall and Braxton (1996) draw a similar picture. When the value-added approach is based on outcomes measured by standardized tests it suffers from the fact that the relationship between test content and curriculum content is often weak. In respect of the ACT Comp test (see Chapter 5) which is used to assess general education, this is put as low as 30 per cent in respect of the number of items used in the test (Pike, 1989). Nordvall and Braxton in common with some other commentators consider that standardized tests have limited potential when it comes to the assessment of outcomes in higher order thinking.

Any measure of value-added would have to take into account drop-out rates. If these are low a weak correlation coefficient does not necessarily imply that the system is inefficient. All it suggests is that on the one hand some persons do not do so well in their final performances as might have been predicted from their entry results, whereas on the other hand others do better. It does not imply a large rate of failure and therefore, inefficiency.

Similarly, it is equally necessary to know if there continues to be a differential between the rates of drop-out among subjects of the curriculum, and how these relate to the grades awarded. For instance in the past it seems as though drop-out rates may have been greater in those subjects which awarded more top grades (Heywood, 1971).

Carter (Carter and Heywood, 1991) described a model which would explain how the 'A' level examination at admission which is approximately normally distributed (Forrest and Whittaker; 1983, see Chapter 10) is transformed into an approximately normal distribution at output. The model was tested on two cohorts of electrical engineering students graduating in successive years. The results showed that the overall trend is for the lower end of the input mark spectrum to be upward shifted in performance. The mid range of the input mark spectrum is less shifted (perhaps even static with improved statistics), and the upper range of the input mark spectrum is downwardly shifted. In all cases initial populations on any mark interval are broadened towards the output.

In so far as engineering students are concerned this would confirm Marsh's (Marsh, 1987) suggestion that students with a low input mark would have a considerable chance of success if they were given an appropriate educational experience. More generally, and applied to the 'Oxbridge' example, because these universities demand high entry grades, and since their degree grades are distributed across the spectrum, this data suggests that in general, their students' marks are more likely to go down than up, which in simplistic terms gives a negative coefficient of value-added.

On these grounds it could be argued that the Oxbridge colleges do not merit these extra funds since the value these colleges add is likely to be relatively small compared with an institution which brings up the relatively weak to an upper second or first class level.

Even so, we are still left with defining value in the first place. In the same debate the concept of 'excellence' was also used to justify payment. Those institutions that take the best students, and are provided with the best resources, are necessarily excellent and need to be supported for that reason. As Harvey and Knight (1996) argue 'excellence' is an elitist concept in as much as it sees quality as only possibly attainable in limited circumstances. This is not to argue against elitist institutions, it is to argue that the application of alternative value-added measures to their work might show them to be capable of maintaining excellence without additional funding. This example is a profound illustration of Harvey and Knight's point that in order to use measures of quality we need to understand what we mean by quality.

1. Mission Focus
   - (a) expenditure of funds to achieve institutional mission
   - (b) curricula offered to achieve mission
   - (c) approval of mission statement
   - (d) adoption of a strategic plan to support the mission statement.
   - (e) attainment of the goods of the strategic plan

2. Quality of the Faculty
   - (a) academic and other credentials of professors and instructors
   - (b) performance review system for faculty to include student and peer evaluations
   - (c) post-tenure review for tenured faculty
   - (d) compensation of faculty
   - (e) availability of faculty to students outside the classroom
   - (f) community and public service activities of faculty for which no extra compensation is paid

3. Instructional Quality.
   - (a) class sizes and student/teacher ratios
   - (b) number of credit hours taught by faculty
   - (c) ratio of full-time faculty as compared to other full-time employees
   - (d) accreditation of degree-granting programs
   - (e) institutional emphasis on quality teacher education and reform.

4. Institutional Cooperation and Collaboration
   - (a) sharing and use of technology, equipment, supplies and source matter experts within the institution, with
   - (b) other institutions and with the business community
   - (c) cooperation and collaboration with private industry

5. Administrative Efficiency
   - (a) percentage of administrative costs as compared to academic costs
   - (b) use of best management practices elimination of unjustified duplication of and waste in administrative and academic programs
   - (d) amount of general overhead costs

6. Entrance Requirements
   - (a) SAT and ACT scores of student body
   - (b) high school class standing, grade point averages and activities of student body
   - (c) post secondary and non-academic achievements of student body
   - (d) priority on enrolling in-state residents

7. Graduates' achievements
   - (a) graduation rate
   - (b) employment rate for graduates
   - (c) employer feedback on graduates who were employed or not employed
   - (d) scores of graduates on post-graduate professional, graduate or employment related examinations and certification tests
   - (e) number of graduates who continued their education
   - (f) credit hours earned of graduates

8. User Friendliness of Institution
   - (a) transferability of credits to and from institution
   - (b) continuing education programs for graduates and others
   - (c) accessibility of the institution to all the citizens of the State

9. Research Funding
   - (a) financial support for reform in teacher education
   - (b) amount of public and private sector grants.

Figure 3.2 The state of South Carolina determined that the critical success of the mission of higher education could be determined by the performance indicators listed above in relation to the 9 critical success areas shown(1996). (For commentaries from higher education see **The Xchange,** *1997: for another example, that of Winoma State University, see Martin, 1996.)*

Choosing and using performance indicators

There are many possible performance indicators. One American study reported as many as 410 of organizational effectiveness (Krakower, 1985) some of which Yorke (1996) considers to be dubious and others he considered to go beyond the bounds of practicality. South Carolina, as Figure 3.2 shows, selected 37. Some may regard these as too many. Yorke, who reviewed progress in America, is of the opinion that the full implications of the federal drive to encourage states to legislate for performance indicators has yet to be felt. Even so, institutional researchers such as Ewell have routinely collected performance data for many years to help with institutional management, funding bids and accreditation. Yorke's point is supported by American documentation (Gaither, 1995, 1996). One college, Babson, believes that higher education is missing the opportunity to link outcomes with mission, vision, and strategic goals and the processes that deliver them which inhibits improvement (Engelkemeyer, 1998).

Care has to be taken in selecting appropriate indicators; this means being clear about the purposes for which they are to be used. But as Yorke makes clear such research as has been done highlights the fact that many indicators are not particularly robust when it comes to their application. He gives 'value-added' as an example. A key technical issue relates to the bases on which value-added is calculated. All methods depend on certain value judgements.

Some indicators can be dangerously naive particularly when they are used to compare one institution with another. For example in the UK *The Times* publishes an annual league table of universities based on a number of criteria. However, research by Johnes and Taylor (1990) shows that when non-completion rates, degree results and first destination of graduates are analysed having taken into account variations in 'input' the remaining variation was very small as between the institutions. It will be noticed that these three variables are related to the outcomes of teaching. Since the variations may be accounted for by institutional diversity, simple league tables of the kind published by *The Times* could be said to be perverse particularly as they do not take the quality of teaching into account. The picture is further complicated by the fact that they do not take into account grade deflation/inflation, and Carter has shown how complicated the relationship is between input and output grade measures (Carter and Heywood, 1991).

The seriousness with which indicators are taken in the UK is demonstrated by the Research Assessment Exercise that is undertaken every five years. In this exercise, publications of staff working in particular subject areas are rated by their peers on a five-point scale. This is then used by the Funding Council as a major part of the equation leading to the grant awarded to state-funded institutions. Moreover this information is made public in the newspapers and provides yet another signal with which the public can judge universities. Yorke reports that such research as has been done in Australia (Murphy *et al.* 1994) and the UK (JPIWG, 1994a) shows that such indicators used should vary with the subject area concerned. Using Australian data Murphy (1998) has shown how 'benchmarking' as practiced in industry (Camp, 1989) can be applied to the evaluation of the quality of papers submitted in the research assessment exercise.

None of this is to argue against the use of performance indicators. Institutions should be transparent, and clearly their self-satisfaction in the past has led to pressures for openness. Indeed as the report from Babson College shows they may remove impediments to change. While different indicators may be used at different levels in the system there has to be a relationship between them which connects them to the overall mission of the institution as it functions as a sub-system within higher education, and as higher education functions as a sub-system of society. For example, drop-out (retention) rates matter at all levels and these may vary as between subjects. A systems approach is required at each level for indicators to have meaning in terms of action/non-action required at institution, subject organization (e.g. faculty, department, school), and programme and subject teaching levels.

Yorke (1998) reviewed the use of performance indicators relating to student development in the UK. The paper is presented in such a way that the data relating to other countries may be substituted for UK data. He considered five indicators. These are student entry and exit performance, and related the indicator of 'value-added'; teaching quality (also touching on the related indicator of staff quality); retention and completion; and placement in employment. In each case he asks: *Whose interest?* before considering the validity and reliability of the indicators as well as their side effects. In each case there are problems with the validity, and he shows convincingly how data relating to retention and completion can be subject to misinterpretation although data in this area can be obtained that are highly reliable. He argues that some indicators are more 'trustworthy' than others. Trustworthiness is a function of the level at which they are being used. Since indicators provide information of varying degrees of fuzziness indicator data should 'be evaluated and acted upon at the "lowest" level possible, and "higher" levels (should) audit whether the data have been obtained and acted upon in an appropriate manner. Some matters are capable of being dealt with by individual members of staff (such as, feedback on teaching sessions), whereas others have to be referred upwards, such as the provision of computer work stations.'

Other dimensions of validity in respect of institutional and other assessments

Lester Parker of the Employment Department in the UK, in an internal memorandum (quoted by Heywood, 1994) extends the concepts of validity discussed in Chapter 1 to embrace quality assurance at the institutional level. Validity should embrace quality assurance, credibility, cost effectiveness and evaluation which Parker calls enabling. He writes:

Quality assurance is about ensuring that there is an effective mechanism for ensuring the maintenance of standards. A quality assurance mechanism should,

(a) address both the design and application of the assessment, especially the need to obtain sufficient evidence without introducing unnecessary demands for the candidate (institution)

(b) facilitate consistency of judgement between assessors

(c)   be practical to maintain

(d)   address the above key aspects as appropriate to the purpose of the assessment.

Quality assurance therefore requires that assessment should be both valid and reliable. Parker continues:

Validity is enhanced if,

(a)   There is agreement about what is being assessed and why. (Descriptions of purpose, abilities etc. should be unambiguous, and with appropriate detail.)

(b)   The criteria, upon which evidence is judged as sufficient, are explicit, unambiguous, critical to the purpose of the assessment and consistently applied.

(c)   The assessment process itself facilitates or allows the candidate (institution) to respond in such a way as to provide an accurate reflection of the candidate (institution) in relation to the purpose of the assessment.

(d)   The assessment does not inadvertently place demands on the candidate that are irrelevant to the purpose of the assessment.

A credible assessment is one which is accepted and valued by the assessors and users of the assessment. Thus credibility is enhanced if,

(a)   Assessors and users have confidence in the quality assurance applied to the assessment.

(b)   Assessors and users are confident about the validity of the assessment.

(c)   Assessment methods are easily understood.

(d)   A range of assessment approaches are employed together.

(e)   The expected behaviours covered by the assessment are realistic for the individuals in question.

(f)   Those aspects which are to be assessed are technically, politically and ethically defensible subjects for assessment.

Cost-effectiveness is about striking the right balance between assessment precision and the investment (time and money) in assessment. Cost-effectiveness is more likely to be enhanced if alternative levels of investment are considered against the expected assessment precision. In general, greater precision costs extra. Thus cost efficiency is about operating the assessment effectively with minimum costs. It is likely to be enhanced if,

(a)   planning and control of assessment is efficient

(b)   assessment is simple rather than complex to operate, however in one sense simplicity can be viewed as cost inefficient. This occurs when assessment become monolithic and everybody is treated the same regardless of their individual requirement.

Knight points out that the calculation of cost-effectiveness involves large value judgements. He asks: What is a fair cost for a given effectiveness, assuming that effectiveness can be fairly specified and accurately measured (private communication).

Parker also included a characteristic which he called 'enabling'. Traditionally this concept has been called 'diagnostic' in test manuals. It assumes that treatment is at hand, and many would argue that this is seldom the case in education. Parker asks the question: 'Does a test which is set for enabling (diagnostic) purposes achieve that goal?' In this conceptual framework this component of validity can only be measured over a long period of time. It is a component of system validity just as the notion of transparency is. The latter arises from the fact that students persistently claim that they do not understand what is required and this often in spite of the best efforts of teachers to explain the rubrics in printed word.

Transparency refers to the extent that there is openness and a shared understanding concerning:

(a) what is to be assessed

(b) when assessment takes place

(c) how assessment is to be undertaken

(d) what the consequences and outcomes will be.

Parker describes enabling as a characteristic about whether the assessment provides insight that increases the possibility of positive change either in the person assessed or in the provision of learning opportunities. Thus the enabling power of assessment is enhanced if:

(a) it distinguishes clearly between desired and undesired performance or practice

(b) that which is to be assessed is made explicit and is valued by the provider of learning opportunities and the learner

(c) the results of assessment are communicated to the learner clearly, sensitively and at appropriate intervals.

For some purposes, e.g. formative assessment, the enabling power of assessment is critical; while for others, e.g. assessment for a national award, it is of secondary importance.

The complex process of institutional evaluation

Yorke (1991) found it difficult to convey all the information in one diagram. Whatever one does it tends to be simplified: neither do diagrams illustrate the dynamic nature of institutional activities, actions and lack of action. For this reason Figure 3.3 is presented in the form of a circle. The inner major circle is the open/closed sub-system of the institution. It is surrounded by the higher education system of which it is a sub-system. Another circle, for example, might show the education sub-system, but these links would seem to be better shown in another diagram.

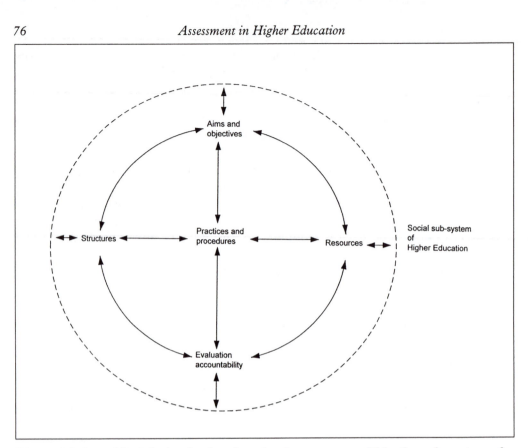

Figure 3.3 A model of the institutional evaluation process within the sub-system of higher education.

In Figure 3.3 the dotted outer circle is the socio-cultural system representing the agencies and factors that impinge on the measurement of institutional effectiveness as demonstrated by its practices and procedures.

Society requires a variety of measures. Politicians need to have some view of the 'effectiveness' of universities, which is not the same as 'efficiency'; unfortunately the two are often confused. For example, a high drop-out rate may not mean inefficiency; it may mean that a subject is particularly good at 'cooling out', that is, sifting out potential failures: that it does so early is good for both the student and the subject (Clarke, 1960). For those who don't take or pass the tests it might be that in any event their experience of higher education was beneficial. This example serves as a reminder of the limitations of quantitative measures intended to provide an understanding of the benefits of higher education to the individual. Qualitative studies may well be more likely to yield information than this of value. The public require to be assured that such studies are undertaken.

There are of course indicators which can tell if political decisions are being enacted, as for example in the affirmative action programmes in the United States relating both to the admission of students and the employment of staff. At the same time some findings may require much more detailed study before the indicators can be understood, and that should be one of the purposes of indicators, i.e. to signal the need for further study. For example, in the United States Haberman (1988) reported that women earn higher grades than men in all subjects in both high school and college, yet they only receive 32 per cent of the merit scholarships. He puts this down to the fact that in the norm referenced Scholastic Aptitude Test and American College Test women do not do as well as men in the mathematics and verbal tests although the difference between them in the verbal test is not great. He argued that these tests should not be used as the mechanism for rating scholarships because they do not predict subsequent achievement as well as high school grades. Yorke (1991) illustrates this complexity as well as the need for the sub-systems to interlink like a nest of tables (my analogy) the smallest being the student learning experience and largest representing Society. Unlike Figure 3.3 Yorke's model does not, however, show the aims and objectives. These are implicit. In this exhibit the communication lines indicate the complexity with which the different elements in the sub-system interact. They convey feedback and this brings about responses in the elements. The importance of evaluation cannot be underestimated however unpleasant the findings might turn out to be. For example in the UK it will be important to evaluate the effects of the introduction of fees in 1998 on the admission of students since it is argued that it will prevent poorer students from wishing to enter university. In America finance has been shown to be an important factor in student retention (Cabrera *et al.*, 1992).

An important aspect of evaluation is to 'screen' aims (and in consequence indicators) to ensure that institutions as well as their sub-systems are not pursuing contradictory goals (see below). It is essential to indicate the effect of the structures on the sub-systems of student learning and research and this is achieved by placing these in a circle that surrounds both systems. Structures may also impede adaptation. For example, a hierarchically ordered institution in which 'commands' flow down and 'information' is transmitted upwards may find it difficult to adapt to participatory learning which some 'customers' may demand in the future (e.g. independent study) (Burns and Stalker, 1961).

As originally conceived Figure 3.3 was a model of the institution evaluation process. Equally it expresses the idea of the institution as a learning system since all the lines of communication are also lines of feedback and they indicate the success with which an institution is achieving its goals. Since institutions have to adapt they have to learn, and the same factors that enhance or impede learning at the classroom level will also enhance or impede learning at the institutional level (Heywood, 1989b).

In spite of the fact that universities are considered to be very conservative they have had throughout the western world, to adapt to many changes imposed on them by the socio-political systems in which they function. The systems of higher education have been relatively 'open' to social pressures exerted through governments driven by a socio-technical economic imperative. In particular they have been forced to adapt to increased numbers of students without any consequential increase in funding. They have also been forced to adapt to more rigorous systems of quality control. Change has been assisted, some may say forced, by the number of persons in authority in the sub-systems who have been prepared to support such change without much debate.

Internally it has also been new-knowledge driven (e.g. the introduction of new subjects, the need for syllabus change).

One of the most remarkable changes in Britain has been the recent and rapid acceptance of semesters and modular programmes by more than half the universities. These might lead to a credit based system along American lines. There has also been pressure to give course equivalents in terms of European Transfer Units. Nevertheless there are many in management, research, and teaching who have resisted change and whose local systems have remained relatively closed. Some teachers believe that these changes are just a response to the latest educational vogue. Unfortunately there is much to favour that view, for much change has been undertaken without reference to its effects on student learning.

However, the demand for accountability and the requirement that universities are assessed has forced the language of quality on them, and irrespective of the quality of their management systems all have to respond to these public demands. Unfortunately the perceptions of what these demands should be sometimes differs between the legislature and the body academic. Keller (1996) writing of the American tussle says:

> Both the states and the colleges and universities, however, are ambivalent about what higher education should be doing. Both want research that helps cure diseases, suggests better social policies, contributes to new business and new products (and raises a university's prestiges), and both want to mollify the growing legions of parents, law makers and media commentators, and students who feel that undergraduate teaching has worsened, and that few institutions bother to employ the considerable research available about how to improve undergraduate learning. So the question has become what kind of outcome measures are appropriate? Some seem obviously justified, even easy to gather. Others, like the measurement of how much students have learned in their four years of baccalaureate study, seem very difficult, like trying to measure how much and what state legislators have learned after one term in office.

Nevertheless educators are right to remain cautious because change is often a mixed blessing and seldom do change agents, like governments, want to evaluate the effect of the changes they induce. Being cautious, however, is not a case for the *status quo*. Academics have to demonstrate that their views are based on a firm understanding of student learning as it is understood in the research literature.

Accreditation and institutional effectiveness: toward the quality assessment of higher education

As has been indicated there has been a long history, institutional as well as professional, of accreditation in the United States and many organizations are involved in accreditation. The external critique of higher education has forced the accrediting agencies to look at their work, for as Erwin (1997) reports: 'The US accreditation system is under threat of demise because of the lack of credible information in the accreditation review process. In the past over-reliance was evident on using the amount of resources, such as library books, or percentage of staff with doctorates as measures of educational quality. Lately, the peer review process is under question, with doubt over the objectivity and worth of observations. Opinions have less priority over hard data about quality.'

He points out that in a number of countries quality assurance programmes have been developed that have similar characteristics. First, there is a separate monitoring and coordinating agency; second, the process begins with self-assessment (evaluation) and is followed by peer review; third the results are made public; and, fourth the results are supposed to influence decision making in institutions (Westerheijden and van Hught, 1995, cited by Erwin, 1997). As Erwin points out, whether it is Australia, Britain, Denmark, France or the Netherlands, just as in the United States there is strong reliance on the information produced by individual institutions and the departments within them. It should not pass without remark that the exercise of gathering together the information required by those undertaking the review is very substantial.

Erwin is of the opinion that the practice of stating clearly what is to be learned has been more commonplace in the UK (at least in what used to be called the public sector of higher education where the accrediting agency demanded such statements) than the US. It is evident, however, that there is a strong move in the US to state programme objectives (learning outcomes). He considers that 'objectives about knowledge, skills such as technology, and developmental characteristics should provide a clear direction for teaching, for programme assessment, and for the public who wish to understand more about education'. He argues that while educators are familiar with knowledge and skills they have little knowledge of developmental characteristics. This is not surprising for, as yet, few university teachers have been trained. There is evidence that when they become involved in research on their own instruction they find the kind of knowledge provided to teachers, adjusted for context, invaluable (Angelo and Cross, 1993; Heywood, Sharp and Hides 1999; Mentkowski and associates, 2000). At the very least discussion of assessment has to embrace knowledge, skills, developmental characteristics and values from which there can be no escape. It cannot be about the techniques of assessment alone.

In response to criticisms of accreditation in the United States the federal government recognized the Council on Post Secondary Accreditation (COPA). It also gave the Secretary for Education the right to determine whether an accrediting agency assessed that an 'educational institution or program maintains clearly specified objectives consistent with its mission': and, determine 'that institutions or programs document the educational achievements of their students in verifiable and consistent ways' (i.e. methods of assessment) 'and other data': and, assess 'the extent to which institutions or programs systematically apply the information obtained (through assessment methods and information about graduate school placement, job placement rates, licensing examination results, employer evaluations and other recognised measures)' (quoted by Nichols, 1991).

Outcomes assessment

In respect of general education COPA has codified practice and in 1986 issued a report in which it recommended that programs 'sharpen statements of admission and

objectives to identify intended educational outcomes', and 'develop additional effective means of assessing learning outcomes and results' (Nichols, 1991).

One effect of these drives was to cause institutions of higher education in the US to
develop offices (institutes, units) for the evaluation of their own effectiveness. The
Southern Association of Colleges and Schools uses the term 'institutional effectiveness' instead of 'outcomes assessment'. Nichols reports that one of the reasons
advanced by COPA for this choice of terms was that, 'member institutions felt that the
term "outcomes" had become jargon laden and had acquired undesirable connotations of "measuring everything that moves", and to indicate that the concept
described was broader than that of assessment solely within an institution's academic
departments.'

These are views with which this author concurs. There is no better way to kill a
concept than to break it down into hundreds of micro parts and try to measure them.
The English Educator Ted Wragg once wrote an article about the use of worksheets by
teachers that was headed 'Death by 1000 Worksheets'. In this context it is easy to
substitute 'outcomes!'

Stein (1996), commenting on the experience of the State of Missouri's Performance Reporting/Funding programme, says that:

> The tendency to design massive data systems about performance is supported by
> those who want to ensure that everything of value is measured; the meaningful use
> of such systems to inform policy discussions is limited. A small number of indica-
> tors helps to focus discussion; support is gained for changing the way higher
> education communicates to external constituencies. The inclination to perfect per-
> formance reporting systems through refinement works against the creation of a
> functional data base. Performance reporting requires stability in the number, con-
> cept and measurement definitions of indicators used for a meaningful database to
> emerge. (See also comment in Chapter 2 on recent requirements by the Missouri
> State to determine the standards of teacher education.)

Institutional effectiveness.

There are, however, other major reasons why Nichols and his colleagues used the term
institutional effectiveness in the title of their handbook. These were, that:

> Whilst student outcomes assessment should be the central and most visible focus
> of the assessment movement, the longer-term success of the movement is
> contingent upon its integration and support at the institutional level on each
> campus. In addition, the term institutional effectiveness is more descriptive and
> inclusive of the identification of institutional and departmental programmatic
> intentions than is the term outcomes assessment (Nichols, 1991.)

The importance of the commitment of the institution to the evaluation of institutional
effectiveness and the implementation of assessment measures which may be
non-traditional in a particular context cannot be over-emphasized. Without such
support change will be difficult if not impossible.

In this context, and since there are well understood premises for bringing about
change, it is surprising to read that:

In the early years, Missouri's targeted audience for performance reporting and per-formance funding was external to the institutions, i.e. legislators and the Missouri public. This approach more easily permits institutions to engage in a compliance model, with little internalization of the value of such initiatives. More recently students, faculty and the administrators have become an important audience incl-uded as stakeholders. Emphasizing both internal and external audiences increases ownership of the process and the program. (Stein, 1996)

Unfortunately, initiatives in this direction are likely to fail unless the stakeholders recognize that their starting points may differ from each other. Thus as Karelis (1996) points out:

> The very notion that public bodies involved with education, such as the US De-partment of Education, might convey questions and concerns to academic leaders, therefore strike many of these leaders not just as tiresome but as shocking, as a re-versal of the natural order.

Their 'guardian' role was being questioned.

Different perspectives on quality lead to confusion

One of the problems in Britain in the 1960s and 1970s was that management and the trade unions were often at odds with each other because they spoke with different 'languages' that had different ethical foundations (Heywood, 1989b). The same can be said of the discussions between academics and those arguing for business models in the pursuit of academic quality assurance. As Loveluck (1995) points out there are two different ethical systems involved and some of the elements in them are irrecon-cilable. Thus the attempt to impose a consumerist model on a guardian model was bound to end in confusion. He cites the response to the first quality assessment exercise in support of this view. There was confusion about the meaning of quality, of which there were at least six possible definitions, and this confusion was perpetrated 'in disregard of the ethical considerations involved in the determination of the appropriate concept of quality and its implementation in both national strategy and corporate policy'.

Quality issues, argues Loveluck, can never be value free. Following R.M. Green, the Director of the Ethics Institute at Dartmouth College's School of Business Admin-istration (Green, 1994), he suggests the following steps for solving ethical questions posed by quality:

1. Specify the conduct under question as a moral rule.

2. Identify all the stakeholders who are directly or indirectly affected by this rule.

3. Put yourself in the shoes of each of the stakeholders.

4. Considering their interests determine how each stakeholder would benefit or be harmed by this conduct now and in the foreseeable future.

5. Identify all who would be affected if this moral rule prevailed.

6.   Weigh both the immediate effects on this conduct and its impact as a
      moral rule, considering such matters as quantity, duration and likelihood
      of benefits and disadvantages involved.

7.   Decide on balance, whether you would be prepared to see this moral rule
      as operational. If not, then the conduct is wrong. If so, then the conduct
      is morally right.

Loveluck, like Davidow and Malone (1992) who have described the substantial
changes being made in organizational structures, see the empowerment demanded at
all levels of the 'virtual organization' as a useful analogy. In organizations where
management has to trust employees, there is also a need to define and maintain high
ethical standards. The implications for higher education and its management both of
institutions and within institutions are obvious.

A collegial approach to quality assessment

Support for a collegial approach to quality assurance is to be found in several writings
(Smyth, 1989; Warren Piper, 1993). Barnett (1994) points out that collegiality has
been lost as management has become centralized. However, Watson, Hallett and
Diamond (1995) have described how at Victoria University of Technology in
Melbourne the management of the institution tried to harness the collegial culture of
the institution to improve quality in academic programmes through sponsorship of
five projects. These were mandated from the top but integrated through bottom-up
initiatives. There was a reference group of academics to guide and support the teams,
and in addition there was a technical reference group. Each project also had a
reference group to support its activities. The authors consider that the project
approach had been valuable and had helped this new institution begin to develop a
collegial culture. They argue that:

> Collegiality is not based on rigid quantification of outcomes but on shared values,
> cooperation and collaboration, It should ideally be part of a proactive process con-
> cerned with building lateral, multidisciplinary collegial relationships. To survive
> quality assurance must be concerned with promoting rather than restricting inno-
> vation in the complex diversity of the university environment. Participation of staff
> at the policy making level is critical for identifying and assessing the strengths,
> weaknesses and opportunities for continual improvement in the education system.

It is possible that in some areas of academic work it will be easier to obtain institutional
commitment than in other areas. For example in respect of information technology
Hall and White (1997) have shown how essential university commitment and
practical support was necessary for the introduction and development of multi-media
approaches across the university. Laycock (1997) has described how a scheme for
quality improvement in learning and teaching was introduced across a university and
received considerable commitment in its first stages. Both of these projects were
undertaken in the UK. If the Australian academic commentator Candy (1997) is
correct the pressures on the higher education system will remain and institutions will
have to become more flexible than they have been in the past.

Mission statements

Nichols (1991) and his colleague describe a four-year plan for implementing an assessment programme for institutional effectiveness. They consider that the development of an Expanded Statement of Institutional Purpose is the most important stage in its development. Their approach is very similar to that described previously. The components of this stage are first a description of the institution's mission, and second the determination of institutional goals that will meet that mission.

The mission statement begins with brief statement of the institution's history and is followed by an equally brief statement of its philosophy. The second part of the statement describes the type of students enrolled, and the geographic area served. The third component shows how the faculty should contribute to these ends. Finally, the academic environment or organizational climate is described.

Writing mission statements has become a commonplace activity. Some are quite short and some are innocuous – leading nowhere (Jevons, 1972; Rae, 1998). A mission statement should provide for drive and be sufficiently unambiguous to allow for a more specific interpretation of aims at the institutional and departmental levels. A mission statement is analogous with the cartoon an artist draws before beginning to paint. It is there to be worked on and developed. Yost (1991) suggests that the kind of questions which lead to a mission statement are of the 'Should we? Can We? What will be the consequence of?' As the goals become more specific so the questions change to the how much? From these emerge the goals of the institution as well as the procedures for determining them.

Inspection of these approaches and more recent literature (e.g. Banta *et al.*, 1996) suggests that the emphasis of the US federal government on mission statements may have precluded a more fundamental debate about the aims of higher education. The same is true of the UK. Detailed studies such as those by Barnett (1990) seem to have received little consideration outside of that part of the community engaged in research in higher education *per se*. Yet there is surely a need for a fundamental reappraisal of the aims of higher education which examines the purposes of higher education in the twenty-first century.

Screening the aims of higher education

Yost (1991) who describes how an 'Expanded Statement of Institutional Purpose' can be developed makes no mention of screening, i.e. the process by which aims are ranked for their significance and contradictions between them removed using the philosophy, sociology and psychology of education (Furst, 1958). However, at the policy making level, the Council of the National Postsecondary Education Coopserative (NEPC, 1977) suggests criteria for the selection of outcomes against three levels of screening. They say that 'Conceptual criteria involve philosophical and/or political considerations. They can be thought of as a set of issues relating to the question "Why should this outcome be included in the data set under development?" Methodological criteria involve technical issues of measurement availability, and data collection design.' They distinguish between three levels or 'screens' at which questions should be asked to determine the value of an outcome. At the first screen are questions about relevance, utility and applicability of the outcomes related to a policy issue. At the second screen there are questions about its interpretability, credibility, and fairness. At the third screen the questions are about methodological issues including, scope, availability, measureability and cost. They ask 'How sound is the information likely to be?'

The case of industry and higher education

It is not without justification that governments have tried to force the institutions of higher education to take notice of what industrialists have to say about the skills of the graduates they have to employ. Universities and colleges are conservative institutions and not prone to radical change. This is not to say that they do not change for it is abundantly clear that they do: but such changes that are made are made within the parameters that stem from their tradition. Thus when pressed to adopt a semester system universities in the UK fitted it into the three-term system rather than follow the two-semester system operated by many institutions in the US where the break between the semesters is made at Christmas. At the same time it is by no means clear that industrialists have legitimacy in this area, or for that matter, would want it (Heywood, 1969).

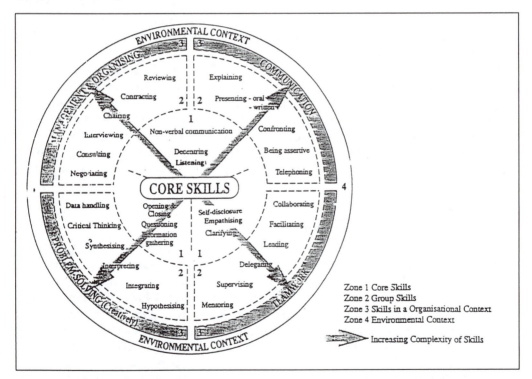

Figure 3.4 The Transferable Personal Skills Developmental Model of the University of Sheffield's Personal Skills Unit (from Heywood, (1994) and reproduced by kind permission of the Director).

Obtained from questions about the nature of intelligence, academic intelligence, and unintelligence put to experts in research on intelligence and lay persons by R.H. Sternberg and his colleagues. Among the findings was the fact that research workers considered motivation to be an important function of intelligence whereas lay persons stressed interpersonal competence in a social context. In Sternberg (1985a).

1. Practical problem solving ability; reasons logically and well identifies connections among ideas, sees all aspects of a problem, keeps an open mind, responds to others' ideas, sizes up situations well, gets to the heart of problem, interprets information accurately, makes good decisions, goes to original sources of basic information, poses problems in an optimal way, is a good source of ideas, perceives implied assumptions and conclusions, listens to all sides of an argument, and deals with problems resourcefully.

2. Verbal ability; speaks clearly and articulately, is verbally fluent, converses well, is knowledgeable about particular field, studies hard, reads with high comprehension, reads widely, deals affectively with people, writes without difficulty, sets times aside for reading, displays a good vocabulary, accepts norms and tries new things.

3. Social competence: accepts others for what they are, admits mistakes, displays interest in the world at large, is on time for appointments, has social conscience, thinks before speaking and doing, displays curiosity, does not make snap judgement, assesses well the relevance of information to a problem at hand, is sensitive to other people's needs and desires, is frank and honest with self and others, and displays interest in the immediate environment.

Figure 3.5 Abilities which contribute to intelligence.

Cardinal Newman's Statement of the Aims of University Education. Discourse VII on Knowledge and Professional Skill. In Newman, 1947.

But a University is the great ordinary means to a great but ordinary end: it aims at raising the intellectual tone of society, at cultivating the public mind, at purifying the national taste, at supplying true principles to popular enthusiasm and fixed aims to popular aspiration, at giving enlargement and sobriety to the ideas of the age, at facilitating the exercise of political power, and refining the intercourse of private life. It is the education which gives a man a clear conscious view of his own opinions and judgements, a truth in developing them. It teaches him to see things as they are, to go right to the point, to disentangle a skein of thought, to detect what is sophisticate and to discard what is irrelevant. It prepares him to fill any post with credit and to master any subject with facility. It shows him how to accommodate himself to others, how to throw himself into their state of mind, how to bring before them his own, how to influence them, how to come to an understanding with them, how to bear with them. He is at home in any society, he has common ground with every class; he knows when to speak and when to be silent; he is able to converse, he is able to listen; he can ask a question pertinently and gain a lesson seasonably, when he has nothing to impart himself; he is ever ready, yet never in the way; he is a pleasant companion and a comrade you can depend on; he knows when to be serious and when to trifle and he has a sure tact which enables him to trifle with gracefulness and to be serious with effect. He has the repose of a mind which lives in itself, which lives in the world and which has resources for its happiness at home when it cannot go abroad. He has a gift which serves him in public and supports him in retirement, without which good fortune is but vulgar and which failure and disappointment have a charm. The art which tends to make a man all this, is in the object which it pursues as useful as the art of wealth or the art of health, though it is less susceptible of method and less tangible, less certain, less complete in its results.

Figure 3.6 Cardinal Newman's statement of the aims of university education.
Discourse VII on knowledge and professional skill. In Newman (1947 edition).

However, the professions do insist that account is taken of what the products from professional courses will have to do. It is for this reason that in engineering surveys of alumni are made. But as Youngman *et al.* (1978) pointed out the problem with such surveys is that they are based on opinion rather than the jobs actually done. Moreover, while they may reveal a new knowledge base they may neglect the skills in the job to be done. Also, in so far as an institution is concerned, they relate to a specific subject and not to the whole curriculum. An institution wants to know if there are specific generic skills that should be developed across the curriculum. Alverno College took the view that there were and designed its curriculum to assist with the development of those abilities (see Figure 2.6). The British Employment Department thought there were such generic skills and gave them the term 'transferable'. Many of the skills sought belonged to the realm of the 'personal'. The Employment Department established an Enterprise in Higher Education Initiative to encourage universities to take a whole curriculum approach to their development.

The Employment Department supported the view of industry and commerce that graduates, irrespective of subject, lacked attitudes and skills that would enable them to participate successfully in commercial and industrial ventures. However, when this view is scrutinized it seems that universities should be accused of not providing a liberal education which gives a broad general view of life rather than providing for specific needs of industry (e.g. Barnett, 1990; Newman, 1852/1947).

For example, one study of 10,000 job advertisements in quality British newspapers revealed that 59 per cent of the advertisements for graduates contained explicit reference to required personal skills. Of the remainder, a further 15 per cent could be inferred to require such characteristics. Of the 32 significant characteristics that were isolated 20 were considered to be genuine transferable skills. They collated into four generic categories of: communication, teamwork, problem solving (creativity), and management and organizing, as shown in Figure 3.4 (Green, 1990). For an example of its application to library work see Levy and Usherwood 1991).

Of course these are not dimensions of personality (indeed the relationship between personality and performance with these skills is complex) but they coincide with the skills Sternberg (1985a) found that experts in intelligence and lay people considered to be the parameters of intelligent behaviour as shown in Figure 3.5.

Sternberg defined intelligence as a 'mental activity directed toward purposive adaptation to, and selection and shaping of, real world environments relevant to one's life' (Sternberg, 1985b). Clearly such intelligence transcends the cognitive and affective domains, and its acquisition depends as much on the development of personal transferable skills as it does on the cognitive. Equally it must depend on a high level of emotional intelligence for it is through such intelligence that personality contributes to performance (Golman, 1996). Sternberg, and latterly Perkins (1995) claim that intelligence can be taught. Clearly, if it can then it has to embrace both domains. It is equally clear that Newman, who is often cited in support of liberal education, believed this to be the case, as inspection of Figure 3.6 shows. The research undertaken by the Office of Educational Research at Alverno College shows quite clearly the value of a broad general education to professional work. Especially when the curriculum is geared to the pursuit of the eight generic abilities outlined in Figure

2.6, and their integration through experiential education (Mentkowski and associates, 2000).

Heywood (1994) argued that documents which had been published to show the skills wanted by graduates such as those prepared by the Employment Department's REAL working party (cited in full in Heywood, 1994), and the Massachusetts Institute of Technology (Dertouzos, Lester and Solow, 1989) showed that a broad general education of the kind required to meet Newman's ideal was required. Without enterprise learning education was not truly liberal. As Bridges (1992, 1996) argues 'enterprise education should be understood not as replacing the aspirations of liberal education but rather as supporting or extending them.' Ross, Parry and Cohen (1993), who wrote about the implications of enterprise for the Philosophy Department at the University of Leeds, considered that the Employment Department was 'trying to achieve is a restoration of the values of university education which were prevalent during the Scottish enlightenment, when philosophy was central to the curriculum, and other disciplines were taught in a distinctly philosophical way.'

Evidently there are lessons for universities, industry and commerce and assessment specialists. Universities are challenged to establish they provide a liberal education; it may be argued, in particular in the UK that they do not. Industry is challenged to make effective use of the liberally educated graduates they say they need. Assessment specialists are reminded that if they seek change they must work with the language of education for, as this example shows, a detailed analysis of the complaints of industrialists has surprising outcomes.

The quality assessment of higher education (subject area review)

In the UK the quality assessment of education by outside agencies is now established practice. These assessments are undertaken subject by subject, and the process is now called 'subject review'. As in North America the exercise is heavily dependent on self-assessment. In England, the quality assessment of education, now called the 'subject area review', is the responsibility of the Quality Assurance Agency for Higher Education. Each subject area in each institution is reviewed periodically. At present the intervals are of five-year's duration. Prior to peer review, a self-assessment exercise is undertaken by the provider of the subject area. This is wide ranging, and in addition to statements of aims and objectives it has to include data on student progression and achievement (QAA, 1997).

A peer review attempts to establish the extent to which the student learning experience and student achievement in each of six aspects of the provision meet the stated objectives. These six aspects of the provision are:

1. Curriculum design, content and organization.
2. Teaching, learning and assessment.
3. Student progression and achievement.
4. Student support and guidance.

5. Learning resources.

6. Quality management and enhancement.

The peer review provides a graded profile of the assessors' evaluation of the extent to which the declared institutional and departmental objectives are perceived to have been obtained. Each of the six aspects is assessed on a four-point scale in ascending order of merit. An excellent department could, therefore, be awarded 24 points although the agency continues to deplore the cumulation of points from totally different judgements. A subject area that has all the aspects graded at two or more is reported as quality approved. The range for quality approval is, therefore, 12–24. It will be interesting to see if, as the system progresses, reviewers use the whole range.

During the visit the review team:

*   scrutinizes institutional and course documents, reviews and reports including external examiners reports

*   samples student work (examination scripts, coursework, projects, artefacts, dissertations etc.)

*   directly observes various forms of teaching and learning being carried during the visit

*   meets with academic, administrative and support staff

*   meets with students, former students and where appropriate employers

*   examines the provision of learning resources.

Considerable guidance is provided by the Quality Assurance Agency as to how the information should be presented.

This approach has been developed to cope with an existing system of higher education. While statements about the learning experience might appear to be educationally sound they will inevitably be shallow. This is because neither they nor their colleagues whom they are reviewing have received any substantial education and training in teaching and learning. Most of them will possess only naive models of teaching and learning. The introduction of compulsory training in Britain might change attitudes and knowledge but it will depend very much on what the training is perceived to be. The Australian Committee of Vice-Chancellors evidently feel they know what good teaching is, which implies that both assessors and teachers have a good idea of what effective teaching is. The Committee in its Guidelines for Effective University Teaching (April 1993) said in respect of student learning, that effective university teachers should:

*   provide students with opportunities to be involved in the structuring of their own learning experiences, and encourage them to take control of their own learning

*   develop students' confidence by setting assignments which are challenging and relevant to subject aims, and by providing constructive and timely feedback

- develop students' analytical and critical thinking skills by demonstrating these skills, and providing students with tasks appropriate to the development of these skills

- provide learning experiences that will enable students to develop both individual initiative and skills needed to work cooperatively with their peers

- assist in the development of students' communication skills by providing opportunities for oral, graphic and written presentations and for feedback on their performance

- encourage and enable students to evaluate their own and each other's work critically

- make time available for giving advice to and for supervizing individual students.

The Committee also stated further criteria for effective university teaching in the areas of teaching and assessment, and subject management. The relationship between teaching and programme outcomes or statements of institutional effectiveness should be evident from this example. However, it is unlikely that any one teacher, in what is a relatively short period of time, could accommodate all these dimensions. Their accommodation would require the contribution of everyone in the department and would require a departmental plan for their implementation. The document takes up this issue in detail and concludes with a section on the institutional valuing of teaching. The five requirements relevant to this text other than those listed are:

1. Select for a range of assessment methods for each subject, a combination of methods which meets the criteria of validity, fairness, and appropriateness for subject goals, and specify these clearly.

2. Select content, skills and learning experiences in the subjects they design or teach which will foster students' intellectual and personal growth, and meet the requirements of the relevant profession.

3. Express subject aims and objectives in the context of what students should expect to gain from their overall experience..

4. Organize subject content coherently and at a level appropriate to the student group and level of study.

5. Review regularly the content and focus of a subject, make revisions as required, and reflect critically upon their own teaching using feedback from a variety of sources to ascertain to what extent they are being successful in helping students realize their own as well as subject aims.

These are, of course, written expressions of the curriculum-assessment-instruction-learning models discussed in Chapter 1. They illustrate the general move in the western industrialized nations to demand outcomes (performance) assessment.

Any system of peer review is open to question, and just as the external examiner system has come in for criticism (see Chapter 5) so too will peer review come under scrutiny. It has received considerable criticism in the US (Erwin, 1997). Skolnik (1989) criticized the method of programme review undertaken by the Ontario Council on Graduate Studies. A connoisseur model is used. A committee of experts conducts the appraisal of graduate study programmes. Skolnik considers it to be a 'self perpetuating elite that represents the *status quo* and gives dominant weight to the academic values and perspectives of the sciences'. The effect of the science model is to promote quantity of publication at the expense of quality especially in the humanities where he argues creative scholarship is inhibited. He draws attention to a conspiracy with journal editors who govern what is acceptable. He argues for the decentralization of the appraisal process and for multiple centres of connoisseurship so that other approaches to scholarship can be recognized. This is the system in the UK at the undergraduate level but there is no evidence that it is any less restrictive since the elites simply appear to become subject-based and the conservative view of criteria supported by journal editors continues irrespectively of the discipline.

It is too early to say if the revisions that have been made, and continue to be made, will gain the wholehearted support of educators. At the same time there is much to defend and it should cause educators to think about what they are doing.

The peer review of teaching

The peer review of teaching has come in for some scrutiny more especially since it has been argued that such review is to be preferred to student ratings of teaching. Marsh and Dunkin (1992) have summarized research on the validity of classroom observation in higher education, and their conclusions would question the practice of sending untrained observers into classrooms for a single visit.

It has been reported that peer ratings which have not been made in the classroom correlate substantially with student evaluations of teaching. Marsh and Dunkin, however, suggest that this may be because peers have obtained their evidence from students. In so far as observation is concerned several studies have failed to yield a reasonable correlation between peer and student ratings. However, two studies have found moderate correlations between instructor self- evaluations and student ratings. One study found that peer observation may affect the classroom performance of the teacher. This is sometimes found when student teachers are being supervised during their classroom practice, and this effect may be enhanced when the supervisor has both an advisory and an assessment role

In the context of the UK the question arises as to whether peers external to the department can make any better judgements. It should be noted that in US teacher education many teacher educators consider that supervisors who do not have a particular knowledge of subject content can be trained to make valid observations. Marsh and Dunkin (1992) who also reviewed research on the training of observers, found that the ratings of specially trained observers frequently correlated positively with student ratings, teaching effectiveness, and student achievement at school level. Dunkin and Barnes (1986) found the same to be true at tertiary level. They describe an experiment by Murray (1983) in which he trained observers to rate the frequency occurrence of specific teaching behaviours among 54 university teachers who had been rated in previous courses as high, medium and low in student evaluations. The correlation between two sets of observational reports *per* rater was found to be 0.32. However, the average response across all the reports for each instructor was found to be 0.77. The observations differentiated significantly between the three groups of teachers. From the data it was concluded that instructors who were rated differently by the students exhibited teaching behaviours which confirmed the ratings.

On the basis of the available data Marsh and Dunkin (1992) concluded that it would be possible to train peers to estimate the frequency of specific behaviours. At the same time, they noted, that it was not surprising that the correlation between two peer visitors judging a single lecture was low. A single visit by a lone examiner to a classroom is thus inherently unfair. Moreover Marsh and Dunkin note that because specific teaching behaviours can be observed there is no guarantee that they are important.

Murray (1980) found peer ratings (compared to student evaluations) to be less sensitive, reliable and valid: more threatening and disruptive of faculty morale, and more affected by non-instructional factors like research productivity. Marsh and Dunkin (1992) conclude 'that the use of peer evaluations of university teaching for personnel decisions is unwarranted'. Nevertheless some investigators have concluded that while peer-observation might be useful in formative evaluation it should not be used for summative purposes.

Peer review and the effectiveness of teaching

One of the problems with peer review is the fact that teachers are likely to differ among themselves as to what constitutes effective teaching. The model they adopt is unlikely to have been influenced by educational research, and will in all likelihood be influenced by the type of subject they teach. Such models are also likely to influence the approaches they take to the assessment of student learning.

Abrami, d'Appollonia and Rosenfield (1994) analyse three definitions of effective teaching. They call them product, process, and process-product. The product model defines effective teaching in terms of positive changes brought about in the cognitive, affective, and where applicable, psychomotor domains. Effective teaching is measured by the products or outcomes of teaching. Models of this kind are very popular at the moment.

The weakness of such models in the assessment of effective teaching is that there are no necessary correlations between the outcomes. Abrami and his colleagues note that increased knowledge of facts does not guarantee an increase in higher order thinking skills. Another criticism is that there need be no causal relationship between the number of products affected and teaching effectiveness. Such models do not explain how student beliefs about learning influence their achievements. From the point of view of teaching effectiveness in higher education this is untenable.

The value of outcomes assessments for students is that they can provide statements of what learners can do irrespective of the preceding educational experience. It is this philosophy which underpins the system of national vocational qualifications in the UK. It implicitly accepts that a student can come to an outcome in a variety of ways.

Another problem is that faculty very often disagree about the products that should be measured. Many question the assumption that they can be measured. Again to use an example from Abrami and his colleagues, a scientist who believes that students should know the range of concepts in her/his subject may well take a poor view of instruction which is designed to help a student discover a few fundamental principles. Such views are not confined to scientists. There are considerable debates across the curriculum about what to teach and how teach it: nowhere is this more true than in teacher education!

In contrast, the process view of teaching effectiveness is concerned with the acts and activities of teaching rather than its consequences for outcomes. Peer review based on this model would examine the preparation of course outlines, activities and objectives, and the delivery methods associated with them. This approach would include ratings of lecture organization, the enthusiasm with which they are delivered, and the rapport which teachers have with their students.

There are several problems with this model and not least with the meaning of the terms used. Abrami and his colleagues point out the ambiguities in terms like *instructor clarity*. They note that such terms contain constructs which are both additive and hierarchical. The pacing of instruction by a science teacher who believes that students should know a lot of concepts will be different from that of a teacher who believes that students should be led to discover a few fundamental principles.

Abrami and his colleagues draw attention to the fact that the term 'effective teaching' is underpinned by the value judgement that effective teaching can be measured. Some acts will constitute effective teaching and others will not. A poor teacher would not enact those acts considered to be effective. There are, as we know, many factors beyond the control of the teacher that may influence both the process and products of instruction.

Koon and Murray (1995) point out that measures of teaching performance often fail to take into account important measures that are likely to influence teaching. Among these are faculty workload which embraces such things as the number of courses taught, the number of new courses taught, workload per course including preparation, research load, number of students supervised, and special administrative duties.

In my experience and that of many of my colleagues there can be considerable variations in the weighting of these factors among faculty in the same department. If these are not taken into account, there is a strong argument that judgements about colleagues will be 'unfair'. There is also a case to be made for independent assessors without specialist knowledge in the field to act as arbiters of personnel decisions since there is much evidence that peers can be prejudiced. These assessors would sit on panels concerned with personnel decisions and have access to this type of data.

While these models highlight factors that may account for some of the differences in judgements between peers they also highlight problems in the design of student evaluation rating schedules. These will be considered in Chapter 4.

Education for teaching in higher education

As indicated previously the subject review exercise in the UK is in addition to the Research Assessment Exercise. Both are made public. Writing of the American situation Astin (1994) said that a:

> Critical but poorly understood issue in the 'teaching versus research' controversy is the method of assessment used to evaluate faculty for hiring promotion and tenure. Assessment of research and scholarship almost always relies primarily on an examination of the creative products of the faculty member, whereas assessment of teaching focuses instead on superficial process variables (syllabi, student evaluations of classroom performance, and less frequently-direct observations of classroom behaviour). Teaching is hardly ever assessed in terms of its products (student learning and development). In a sense, this would be like attempting to assess a professor's research by looking in her office, watching her in a library or a laboratory, or observing how she sits in front of a word processor.

It is difficult to see how one can go beyond this in the absence of a thorough knowledge of how students learn, on the part of both the assessors and teachers; and this will require substantial training (Heywood, 1995). In Britain such training is to be made compulsory. But, as is well understood in teacher education, pre-service training by itself will avail of nothing unless the teacher is supported in the teaching environment and allowed to develop as a teacher by the team with which that teacher works. This means that the teacher will have to change his/her role in a number of ways, and some of these will reduce the privacy of the teaching activity.

One way forward, which has been shown to be promising, is that advocated by Cross (1986) who has argued that teachers should consider their classrooms to be laboratories for research, the term research being interpreted some what differently to the classical scientific view of research (Cross and Steadman, 1996). Together with Angelo and Steadman, she has worked with numerous teachers, and through them demonstrated how this might be done effectively (Angelo and Cross, 1993). Bennett, Foreman-Peck and Higgins (1996) in the UK produced a most useful short work on *Researching into Teaching Methods* although they make no mention of this work by Cross and her colleagues. The goals which Cross and her colleagues have for teachers may satisfy the needs for teacher assessment if teachers are encouraged to keep portfolios.

In this respect, Astin (1994) was enthused by Shulman (1992) who believed that teaching should be assessed by portfolios. The portfolio is the basis of the assessment undertaken for the certification of university teachers in the UK by SEDA. Quite a lot of work has been done on teaching portfolios in the US which has been brought together by the American Association for Higher Education (Edgerton, Hutchings and Quinlan, 1991; Wright and Knight, 1999). Those who advocate their use believe that they transform 'the process of assessing teaching into a kind of scholarly research enterprise, in which the faculty member engages in a continuous process of assessing and documenting what is going on in the classroom'.

The kind of information that can be kept in portfolios includes the planning of courses and details individual contact sessions. At the same time, they can show how these activities relate to the objectives of the general programme; assessment, tests and examinations with an evaluation of the marking; samples of student work including responses to examination papers showing the effects (if any) on subsequent course design; video or audio tapes possibly with comments by colleagues, and ratings and comments from students.

Perhaps if teachers in higher education had been prepared to do this and receive training a long while ago, the enormous bureaucracy that has been established to assess the quality of education might have been unecessary, except for an audit to determine that these things are done, and well done.

Chapter 4

The Assessment of Teaching by Students and Alumni

Summary

Policy makers seem to believe that student evaluations of teaching (SET) are the best measure of teaching effectiveness. This chapter reviews the substantial body of research on SETs that examined their use in personnel and pedagogical decisions. It should be noted that there is no agreed definition of instructional effectiveness.

Three schools of thought have emerged. One considers teaching effectiveness to be multi-trait and requiring a substantial inventory for its measurement. A second considers that summative decisions of teaching effectiveness should be based on global ratings requiring relatively short questionnaires. The third argues that the dynamics of the classroom have to be taken into account. This would require some form of ethnographic study.

Various criticisms of SETs are considered. Research suggests that provided they are well designed they are both reliable and valid but they should be interpreted with caution. A major concern is the perception students have that little notice is taken of their ratings. There is some evidence to support this view. A Code of Practice for their use completes this section.

Since the experience of teaching is different to the experience of programmes and college more generally research on the Course Experience Questionnaire (CEQ) is summarized. Among the conclusions that illustrate the value of such questionnaires is the finding that those who teach a major course of study reflect what is happening in that subject area more generally across institutions. Thus, when institutions are compared the comparisons should be within fields.

An alternative to the CEQ is discussed because it considers other aspects of the student experience. The chapter ends with a discussion of the value of alumni studies. It is concluded that although relatively simple enquiries are of value the results need to be interpreted with caution.

The student experience of teaching as assessed by rating scales

Administrators and policy makers have encouraged student evaluations of teaching (SETs). The evaluation of the reliability and validity of these scales has led to prolific research, and there have been some 2000 entries (articles and papers) recorded under this heading. It is said to be the most researched topic in higher education. Many of these have reported high quality research and several meta-analyses have been undertaken. Doubtless this interest is in part due to the fears that some faculty have that the judgements of students might be unreliable and biased. They would argue that such judgements should not influence promotion decisions.

Apart from their use by administrators for personnel decisions they have three other functions. These are to provide (i) faculty with diagnostic feedback about their teaching with a view to course improvement, (ii) students with information that will enable them to select courses and teachers, and (iii) a vehicle for research on teaching which will provide information about how teachers behave, and what they do (Marsh and Dunkin, 1992).

These instruments are widely used in Australia, Canada and the United States, and it is in these countries that most of the research has been done. They are beginning to be used in the UK.

The dimensions of student rating scales

Marsh and Dunkin (1992) argue strongly that student evaluations of teaching effectiveness (SETs) are multidimensional, and they maintain that the SEEQ which Marsh (1987) developed, not only responds to these dimensions, but that this is supported by empirical and logical analysis. They also show how the nine factors derived from their analyses are supported by principles of learning described by Fincher (1985) and Mackie (1981). Inspection of these learning principles shows that many of them correspond to the factors derived by Marsh and his co-workers. These factors are.

i   *Learning/Value.* Items in this category would seek answers to questions such as: Do students consider their learning to have been of value? Has their interest in the subject matter improved as a result of the course?

ii   *Instructor enthusiasm.* Items in this category would seek answers to such questions as: Was the student's interest in the course aroused by the teacher's enthusiasm? Was the student motivated to learn by the instructor?

iii *Organization/Clarity.* Items in this category would ask whether the organization and structure of teaching and the course enhance or impede learning.

iv   *Group interaction.* Items in this category would relate to the extent of the interaction between students and the tutor, and as facilitated by the tutor between members of the group.

v   *Individual rapport.* Items in this category would seek to establish the extent of contact the students had with their tutors, and the guidance available.

vi   *Breadth of coverage.* Items in this category would seek to establish if the students found the teaching meaningful, and how well they believed they could generalize the knowledge obtained.

vii *Examinations and grading*. Items in this category would seek to establish if the students felt the procedures for assessment were relevant and fair, and if there was feedback, and the consequences of that feedback for students.

viii *Assignments/readings*. Items in this category would seek to establish if the assignments and readings enhance or impede learning.

ix   *Workload/difficulty*. Items in this category would seek to establish if the workload and perceived difficulty enhanced or impeded learning.

Tutors are unlikely to have much difficulty with these categories. They are all matters of both formal and informal discussion among colleagues. One might expect teacher-designed rating scales to cover them in one way or another. One would also expect they would include global items that ask students to rate the overall effectiveness of the course and instruction.

The use of rating scales in personnel decisions

Consideration of the use of rating scales in personnel decisions has led to a considerable debate between Abrami and Marsh and their colleagues. Its essence is displayed in two review papers they have written which together cover the topic (Abrami, d'Appollonia and Rosenfield, 1994; Marsh and Dunkin, 1992). They were also the subject of a critical review by Feldman at the American Educational Research Association's meeting in 1995 (Feldman, 1998). An important part of this critique is devoted to the dependence- independence dimension of student rating (i.e. the extent to which student ratings are influenced by their peers). The discussion that follows while taking his remarks into account is built around the framework of the debate between Abrami and Marsh and their colleagues. The report by Marsh is a more extended review than that by Abrami although there is considerable overlap between the two. They are not the last word on this matter as a paper by Koon and Murray (1995) shows. As in the case of other reports the starting point of the reviews is papers by Cohen (1980, 1981), and Feldman (1976a and others). In 1988 Feldman concluded that it was important to demonstrate that students were accurate, consistent and unbiased assessors, for that is what they are when they rate. The rating forms had also to show they could cope with different pedagogical methods, and take account of innovation. It also had to be shown that the different rating forms included items that would assess the same teaching qualities (Abrami, d'Appollonia and Rosenfield, 1994). Marsh and Dunkin (1992) reported that the reliability of student ratings is not a contested issue and that the stability of ratings over time and their consistency compare with the best designed objective tests. Given the psychometric setting in which such studies are set it is of more than passing interest to know that some of the data from earlier studies has been re-analysed in these reviews. For the reader not versed in the ways of factor and multivariate analysis Dunkin and Barnes (1986) provide an introduction to the findings of investigations that met specified criteria which may be more palatable. Much of what Dunkin and Barnes said remains relevant as the two reviews show.

In so far as personnel decisions are concerned Abrami and his colleagues take the view that the assessors should be concerned with the global judgements of students and not with specific items. Much of the paper by Abrami, d'Appollonia and Rosenfield is devoted to an analysis of earlier studies. It leads them to the view that there is a general factor which describes teaching effectiveness. This is in contrast to Marsh who finds the experience of teaching is multidimensional.

The literature that they analysed showed no consensus of what constitutes instructional effectiveness as perceived by students. Although student ratings were factored, with the exception of Marsh (1991) no attempt had been made to compare one with another. Therefore, they analysed 17 multi-section validity studies that contained either complete factor matrices or correlation matrices. From an aggregate correlation matrix they obtained four factors the first of which accounted for nearly 63 per cent of the variance. Each of the other factors accounted for approximately 3 or 4 per cent of the variance. Therefore, they concluded that there was a 'common' structure to instructional effectiveness.

The global items were loaded highly on the first two factors: 'it remains our opinion that the best alternative to averaging across specific items is to base summative decisions of teaching effectiveness on global ratings.' Support for this opinion came from Cashin and Downey (1992). As a result of an analysis of ratings in 20,000 classses in 105 institutions, they found that global items accounted for more than 50 per cent of the variance, and on this basis recommended that short rating schedules should be used for summative evaluations. Subject specific schedules for the purpose of teaching improvement would necessarily be longer, and be used only in a formative framework.

Abrami and his colleagues warn that not all specific items predict student achievement, as for the example rating of class difficulty. Overall there seems to be substantial agreement with the view that there is a 'modest positive relationship between global ratings of instruction and instructor-produced student learning of lower academic skills (e.g. knowledge of basic facts, simple comprehension, etc.).' Much less is known about the validity of ratings as predictors of other outcomes of student instruction (Abrami, d'Appollonia and Rosenfield, 1994).

The pedagogical dimension

Abrami, d'Appolonia and Rosenfield give an example of a matrix which lists the content to be learned on one axis, and the depth at which it was learned in terms of the categories of the Bloom Taxonomy on the other. Students have to make the ratings on a five-point scale with the possibility of 'not applicable'. An instructor would have to declare at the beginning of the course the levels the students would be expected to attain. These would have to be related to the time allowed for each element in the matrix. In this respect, it also shows how student evaluations can be used for research on the relationship between objectives and instructional methods used to obtain them, as well as into the curriculum and its ability to cope with key concepts. Such research presupposes that correlations can be obtained with valid measures of achievement.

Abrami, d'Appollonia and Cohen (1990) argued that rating schedules should contain items that are relevant to the instructional situation (i.e. the learning milieu). For example, an item about the friendliness of teachers will be much less relevant in a large class than it would be in a small class. Rapport will necessarily be different in the two situations. The need for instructionally specific items arises, in particular, in innovative teaching situations. Such investigations would have to take into account the fact that sometimes students can resist innovation and this could lead to poor teacher ratings.

At a time when pedagogical evaluations are being pressed upon teachers in higher education it would be wise for faculty to take into account the findings of Smith and Cranton (1992). They found that student perceptions of the amount of improvement required in four dimensions of teaching differed significantly across levels of instruction and class size. They were led to suggest that:

1.   A faculty member seeking to improve his/her instruction should not assume that all of the items are of equal importance when seeking to make changes.

2.   Faculty who seek to compare themselves with others would in all probability be making a mistake.

3.   Data from student ratings should not be used for comparisons among faculty or across courses without consideration of the instructional settings.

The relevance of these axioms to administrators should be self-evident. Even so, some subject specific data have to be taken with caution. I have asked students to tell me which is the best sequence with which to complete certain coursework activities. I have then implemented their ideas in the next course only to find them rejected by the new students. Feldman (1998) draws attention to an investigation by Miller, Wilkes and Cheetham (1993) who had a similar experience. They found that the cognitive style of the student population shifted substantially from year to year. Changes introduced were not necessarily appropriate for the group that followed. In my case, it did not void other data contained in my specific subject questionnaires that indicated whether or not I was achieving my first and second order objectives.

Amin (1993) who made a study of student ratings at the University of Yaounde in the Cameroon concluded that the most important criterion of course and teacher evaluation was the overall rating of the course. The most important factors explaining the variation in ratings were the overall organization of the course, its influence and interest, the effectiveness with which the subject matter was conveyed, and the teacher's rapport with students. He argued that his findings suggest that it is more meaningful to talk of course evaluation rather than teacher evaluation.

Bennett *et al.*(1995), on the basis that the pursuit of feedback from formal questionnaires can be hampered if the process is too time consuming for staff and students, developed and trialled a short instrument (HELPA) which could be analysed quickly by computer: the nine criteria related to behaviour in class. The tutor could obtain rapid feedback (10 minutes per 100 students). Comparisons were made on a year-on-year basis and examples are given of how a lecturer was helped to adjust his performance to the restraints imposed by the department.

Kerridge and Mathews (1998) report a study in the UK among students of marketing whose ratings of modules were analysed against individual grade results, admission entry criteria, gender and academic level. A few significant correlations were found. They were in the parameter of academic level, and indicated student needs rather than the perceived quality of staff output.

Fox (1999) and his colleagues at the University of Salford have criticized the current literature for paying insufficient attention to practical problems of implementation and interpretation. Because of such problems a questionnaire based on mean class scores using a five-point scale has been replaced by an 'analysis of comments' approach. This was due to the fact that there had been a considerable response from students to the enhanced comments section in the original questionnaire.

Apart from basic data, e.g. recording module title and date, this questionnaire contained four items. These were a seven-point scale on the degree of satisfaction with the module; a seven-point scale in response to the statement *I would recommend this module to a friend who was interested in the course*; a comment on the three aspects of the course you like; and, a comment on the three aspects which you dislike.

A very positive response to the first cycle of the questionnaire was received from most departments. Faculty did not find the questionnaires difficult to analyse. Fox (1999) compares and contrasts the use of the two questionnaires by two groups of business students. These demonstrate just how difficult the 'traditional' form is to interpret. Although the new global questionnaire was by no means perfect all the comments could be understood and the absence of certain comments was reassuring. The frequency with which comments appear is an indicator of feeling on any one matter. The number of comments averaged 42 per student. Fox gives examples of low frequency comments on factual issues that could not be dismissed lightly. He concludes that the initial experience is of much greater clarity and flexibility, and considers that these findings support those who advocate the use of comments (e.g., Tiberius *et al.*, 1989; Yorke, 1996).

Mention should be made of a novel approach to student evaluations used in Australia by McKenzie, Sheely and Trigwell (1998). They asked students in an architecture degree course to pictorially represent their impression of the preceding year. The resulting illustrations, some of which are shown, included self-portraits, cartoons, metaphorical images and diagrammatic representations, as for example, flow charts. The investigators show how they concluded that such drawings provide valuable information for course evaluation.

In sum it seems that short questionnaires using global items can be used reliably and validly for personnel decisions. Longer and more specific ratings can be used in formative evaluation. In any event care has to be taken with the design of items.

Problems in the design of items

Abrami and his colleagues (Abrami, d'Appollonia and Rosenfield 1994) write:

> Consider the following item from a student rating form: 'rate the extent to which your instructor motivated you to learn'. Does this item ask you to describe an instructional process or an instructional product? The item does not ask students to judge instructor preparation or delivery but the consequences of its teaching. It is, therefore, not a measure of a teaching process. But is it an accurate indirect assessment of an instructional product? It is accurate only to the extent that student self-report of motivation reflects student persistence at learning, the intensity of student effort, student choice of tasks to be learned, etc. Rating forms often include items that ask students to assess the success of instructors at encouraging them to learn but seldom include items that assess specific behaviours associated with that motivation.
>
> Similarly, rating forms do not often contain items that ask students to assess an instructors impact on specific cognitive and meta-cognitive achievements. Instead rating forms more frequently ask students to rate 'How much have you learned in this course compared with others?'

Their example of how this might be done has been given above.

Teacher hostility toward student ratings

Anecdotal evidence suggests that many teachers have been hostile toward student evaluation. This may be due to fear that ratings would be used in personnel decisions. Chief among the criticisms is that ratings are unreliable and invalid. Are students uniform in their assessments of instructors? Are the results of ratings consistent over time? Are the ratings free from the influence of bias? etc. Teachers are quick to criticize items, and not without good reason.

There have been few empirical studies of the attitudes of those who are the subject of the ratings. One study of over some 400 faculty at a private suburban university in the north-east of the United States focused on how useful faculty members found each question in a course and teacher evaluation form. It also obtained their attitudes to the usefulness of student ratings and information about their use in personnel decisions. Schmelkin, Spencer and Gellman (1997) who conducted the inquiry found that the attitudes of faculty were generally positive toward student evaluations. In respect of formative evaluation, that is the use made of them, the most helpful was found to be feedback information on faculty interaction with students. This was followed by feedback on grading practices, global ratings of instructor and course, and structured issues related to the course. Overall the findings of this study supported Marsh's view that the ratings are multidimensional and that students differentiate their ratings along several dimensions. However, they found discrepancies between staff and student interpretations (obtained in another inquiry) of interaction. While faculty had reported that the feedback on interaction was useful students had reported infrequent interactive behaviour. They felt that one of the reasons for this discrepancy was the fact that faculty were not given much, if any, guidance on how to interpret student feedback. (See also section 'Improving teaching effectiveness' below). This is consistent with other research which showed that many users were not sufficiently knowledgeable to be able to interpret the findings.

In respect of gender, a study of a large population believed to be representative of the US as a whole, found that female students did not report 'interacting informally with faculty after class' as often as male students. Neither did they interact with faculty as much on research projects as males. Drew and Work (1998) felt that although the 'chilly climate' for women in college reported by Sandler, Silverberg and Hall (1996) was not present this particular matter was a cause for concern. The instrument used by Drew and Work was the *College Student Experiences Questionnaire* (Pace, 1990).

Newport (1996) in a trenchant criticism of the use of ratings for personnel decisions argues that students are unqualified to make ratings. To reinforce the point he uses research from teacher education which suggests that novice teachers are equally unqualified, and reminds his readers that in any event there is no agreed answer to the question: 'What is good teaching?' If there were, institutions would be able to develop and use a common questionnaire. He forgets that what is being measured is experience, and if bias is controlled experience is a perfectly valid measure. However, it will be the more impressive if outcomes are taken into account (see below), and if administrators understand just how complex the experience of higher education is.

Newport (1996) was unable to find any studies which looked at the differences and quality of ratings as between students who obtained A's and B's and those with D's and F's. It is an important point and such research ought to be done but in a more detailed context that establishes why the low achievers obtained the results they did. In the paragraphs that follow some of these issues are considered.

Bias

A major criticism of student ratings is that they are subject to bias (i.e. aspects of evaluation unrelated to the intrinsic characteristics of teaching). Factors affecting bias include qualities that are beyond the control of the teacher, as for example, academic discipline, age, gender, race and personality of the instructor. While bias has not been rigorously defined there have been a number of investigations in these areas. Generally, while the effects of bias on student ratings have tended to be small there are several that merit discussion. Three will be considered here. These are the effects of teacher expressiveness on ratings, beliefs about the effect of ratings on teacher evaluation of student performance, and possible positive effects of poor instruction on student learning. The potential of expressiveness (acting) to influence instruction is known as the *Dr Fox Effect* (see below).

In this respect it is important to be able to distinguish between 'bias' and 'fairness'. Thus, Marsh and Dunkin (1992) point out that according to this definition the effects of grading leniency whereby students give better than deserved ratings to teachers who give them high grades is not bias because this is in the control of the teacher. 'If variable X legitimately influences the effectiveness of instruction and this influence is validly represented in SETs, then the influence of X should not be interpreted as bias. For example, prior subject interest apparently affects teaching effectiveness in a way that is accurately reflected in SETs. It may not, however, be 'fair' to compare ratings in courses that differ substantially in prior subject interest for personnel decisions unless the influence is removed using statistical control or appropriately constructed norm groups'.

The effect of class size on bias has been investigated by Chau (1997) using a simulation methodology which tested the sensitivity of an SET scale to three hypothesized instructors rated as excellent, poor and average. In the ideal scenario without confounding factors it was found that the SET statistics distinguished between the instructors. However, once confounding factors were introduced it was found that even mild levels of random response from students significantly distort SET statistics based on average scores, and that the class size and random response factors interact. Decisions are compromised if class averages are used alone and those responsible for decision making need to use class medians and standard deviations in order to interpret the data.

In the UK a study of class size and student performance was undertaken at one university. Over a period of ten years some 5000 modules and 250,000 grades were examined. The investigators found that students perform less well in large classes. Students in the larger classes stood significantly lower chances of getting good grades. Wide variations between subject areas were found in respect of this relationship. Paradoxically the expansion in this university leading to larger classes did not lead to a reduction in overall performance. The investigators speculate as to why this might be and argue that other changes at the university have probably masked the effects of class size. Among them might be changing patterns of assessment (Gibbs, Lucas and Simonite, 1996). It is important to remember that class size is but one variable in the situation.

Self-serving bias

This is the familiar syndrome where individuals take credit for their successes and blame others for their failures. It is an everyday experience. This syndrome predicts that students who do badly or worse than expected will blame their teachers and rate them at lower levels than they deserve. Gigliotti and Buchtel (1990) found no consistent evidence to support this thesis although they did find that class average grades were related to ratings of 'personal fit' (e.g. usefulness of course). But Marsh and Dunkin (1992) argue that this result and others do not rule out grading leniency effects which may operate simultaneously. However, support for the idea that grading leniency produces some bias is weak, and in any event, its size is likely to be small.

Related to this is the possibility that some students might award high ratings in the expectation of, in return, receiving high grades. Another related scenario is that teachers who expect low course and examination marks will buy high effectiveness ratings by lowering standards (i.e. raising marks). Because teachers who expect average or above average examination marks are unlikely to take such action the overall effect on grades will be to skew the distribution of the course average examination marks. The average marks will be curtailed and this effect will be accompanied by a low standard deviation. Fox (1994) who examined this effect among 500 students in accounting and business at the University of Salford found no evidence of such 'bunching'. A mildly negative relationship was found between student approval and examination performance.

Deviant teachers

Murray (1983) reported that several of the teachers in his study who received high overall effectiveness ratings did not exhibit normal or predicted patterns of classroom behaviours. They were 'deviants'. In these circumstances, if fixed weightings for the dimensions of classroom teaching which correlated significantly with student ratings are used for promotion decisions, these 'deviants' would be penalized. If committees weight teaching decisions on a case-by-case basis then ratings of teaching have not helped the system to become more objective, and it will trundle on as in the past, the subject of bias and prejudice (Hildebrand, 1972; Skolnik, 1989).

The outcomes insufficiency effect

Koon and Murray (1995) draw attention to an effect where some students, for whom a course is of low priority or who do not have much time to spend on additional study, might grade a teacher rated as highly effective by other students, more highly than would be warranted by the outcomes achieved. Similarly, poor teaching could stimulate the students to work harder in order to compensate for this poverty of teaching. In these circumstances the student is forced to pay much more attention to the text, and may have to seek help from peers. Koon and Murray (1995) argue that instructor ratings would tend to be more valid than outcome measures in respect of teaching performance when the insufficiency effects are uncontrolled.

The Dr Fox Effect, content and assessment

One of the most interesting phenomena associated with teaching delivery is the *Dr Fox Effect*. This relates to the skill of the lecturer in seducing favourable evaluations from students. In the original experiment which draws attention to the problem Dr Myron L. Fox was the name given to an actor who lectured educationalists and graduate students in an enthusiastic manner. The lecture he gave was designed to have little educational value. In spite of this his audience rated him highly. While the experiment had many methodological weaknesses it was used by critics to damn student evaluation schedules.

Attempts were made by Ware and Williams (1980) to remedy some of these defects in another study. They concluded that differences in expressiveness consistently explained more of the variance in student evaluation ratings then did differences in content. Their data was re-analysed by Marsh and Ware (Marsh and Dunkin, 1992) who found that when the students were informed before the lecture that they would be tested on the materials in the lecture, and that they would be rewarded on the basis of the number of examination questions answered correctly, the *Dr Fox Effect* was not supported. Expressiveness manipulation only affected ratings of instructor enthusiasm. Other research also found that in the absence of external incentives the expressiveness of the instructor had more impact on all rating factors.

A meta-analysis undertaken by Abrami, Leventhal and Perry (1982) found that expressiveness manipulations had a substantial impact on student ratings but only a small impact on achievement. Fortunately, given the purposes of teaching, content manipulations while having little effect on the ratings have a substantial effect on achievement.

Effects of prior information and feedback on test performance

These experiments are entirely consistent with the view that examinations drive learning. This point is further reinforced by research by Perry (1991) and associates. They wished to investigate how instructor expressiveness varied with the students' perceived ability (control) to influence achievement test scores. Perceived control is the ability to predict and influence events especially those associated with academic achievement. For example, a teacher who gives students broad information about what might appear in an examination paper is enabling them to exert some degree of control over their subsequent performance. Perry and associates showed that perceived control is not stable and can be altered by the type of feedback given on responses to multiple choice tests. This suggests that the way prior information is given is of considerable importance and may influence student behaviour differentially. Instructor expressiveness does not influence the achievement test score of students who have low perceived control, whereas it increases the achievement test scores of other students (Marsh and Dunkin, 1992).

Student dependence-independence and personality

Feldman (1998) draws attention to the dynamics of the classroom and argues that it may affect the consistency of ratings. If there is strong agreement among students about a programme this is likely to enhance the consistency of the ratings. However, if there are competing groups and each group promotes its view of the teacher than there is likely to be less consistency among the ratings. Classroom dynamics of this kind, can only be discovered by participant observation or some other form of ethnographic study. Such observations would take into account the effects of gender and minority groupings as well as the effects of isolation – deliberate or imposed.

Some dimensions of personality have been shown to influence approaches to learning (Abouserie, 1995; see also Chapter 7). If students were to project their deficiencies on to the teaching (teacher) this might affect the ratings they give. An evaluation of the importance of 'background' variables in SETs led the University of Queensland to revise its 'all purpose' rating schedule into two instruments: 'teaching feedback' and 'subject evaluation'. Academics are actively encouraged to use the *Approaches to Studying Questionnaire* (Timpson and Andrew, 1997; see also Chapter 7).

The importance of outcomes

Koon and Murray (1995) pointed out that there are a number of 'outcome' factors which influence student ratings that would explain the large amount of unexplained between-teacher variation which remains in teacher ratings (Cohen, 1987). They argued that between- teacher variation in mean student ratings should correlate with a comprehensive set of student outcome measures. (e.g. critical thinking, problem finding and problem solving, synthesizing). They also argued that factors such as career perceptions and motivation were equally important and would explain more of variation in overall effectiveness ratings than student achievement. In their multi-section multi-year study they tested this hypothesis and in particular considered long- and short-term motivation alongside achievement test results. A 10-item teacher evaluation questionnaire and a 12-item course evaluation questionnaire were administered together with a final examination. Within the course evaluation questionnaire items were included to obtain student assessment of their short- and long-term motivation. The short-term measure was indicated by the amount of study time devoted to the course per week Advanced course registrations in the same area as the course were taken to be indicative of long-term motivation.

The instructor designed achievement test had been constructed so that 25 per cent of the items tested the higher levels of thinking described by the Bloom Taxonomy. Their analysis (the result of several regressions) led to the conclusion that when student outcomes other than post-course tests are included in the analysis, the variation due to the objective test of learning is reduced. Other outcomes, in this case motivation, account for some of the variance. They conclude that multiple measures of outcomes should be taken into account when evaluating the validity of student ratings. It should be noted that having given details of the test they do not analyse the two parts separately, which is to be regretted.

Improving teaching effectiveness

There have been a few studies that have attempted to determine the value of student ratings in influencing teacher effectiveness. A survey of seven North American universities yielded a high positive response to questions that asked if SETs had led to improved teaching. But what was meant by 'improvement'? In Australia Dunkin (1990) found that self-perceived teaching was negatively related to the use of SETs. Thus able teachers might not have seen any use for them whereas poor teachers might use them in the hope that their teaching would improve. There are two ideas that are worth consideration.

First L'Hommedieu, Menges and Brinko (1990) in a meta-study considered three kinds of feedback from student to teacher. These were written (printed summaries of the data), personal (face-to-face) with some discussion, and consultative. They found that the effects of written feedback were small but positive, while written feedback augmented by consultation had a more substantive effect.

Wilson (1986) experimented with a particular form of consultation in which a consultant was used. He administered a 24-item SET. Together with teachers who had received distinguished teaching awards, he designed a teaching package for each item. Volunteer participants indicated on the basis of SETs and their own self-evaluations items where they had need of assistance. These were discussed briefly in a first session with a consultant. Just before they were about to teach the course again they met the consultant for a more substantial session. During this discussion they discussed from three to five items which had been rated poorly and perceived to be in need of treatment. At that time the teacher was given appropriate information from the teaching packages which the consultant thought would help improve teaching in these areas. As soon as possible after the meeting the consultant sent a written resume of the meeting to the teacher. During the term that followed the consultant checked with the teacher to see how he/she was responding. Wilson found that this led to an improvement in the targeted items, and he concluded that SETs without consultation are unlikely to lead to improved teaching.

All of these findings are about teaching in the absence of any formal training, and most scales are rating traditional models of teaching in which self-administered formative evaluation is present.

> In the traditional view teaching consists primarily of the transmission of inform-ation by the teacher to the student. According to this model the teacher's effectiveness as a sender is directly proportional to the teacher's possession and proper application of specific, definable skills or techniques (strengths), and inversely proportional to the amount of interference caused by specific definable flaws in the teacher's techniques (weaknesses). Feedback from students would than serve the function of making the teacher aware of his or her strengths and weaknesses, and thereby helping him or her to exploit those strengths and eliminate those weaknesses. (Tiberius *et al.*, 1989)

Student perceptions and expectations will also have been influenced by these models, albeit 'unconsciously'. Innovative teaching requires changes in student behaviour as well as changes in their expectations, if judgements about, say, teachers as facilitators and not information givers are to be 'fair'. Students will not be 'conditioned' to the perspective taken by Tiberius and his colleagues (1989).

> We, however, believe that teaching is a much more interactive process. Teacher and student join together to form a teaching-learning alliance – they agree (sometimes explicitly, but most often implicitly) to work together toward common educational objectives. The stronger the alliance, the more effective the teaching. The strength of the alliance is based on those conditions which establish and sustain any cooper-ative relationship: mutual respect, understanding and willingness to negotiate.

It follows that in such circumstances a student would feel able to talk directly to their teachers about their teaching. Clearly this ought to be the case with relatively small groups. Tiberius *et al.* (1989) undertook a comparative study of different methods of rating within the clinical setting of medical education (i.e. feedback given from ratings only, and feedback from ratings and student group discussion). A control group received no feedback while the study was in progress. The teachers also rated themselves. The feedback from the rating scales alone had little impact on teaching. However, the group discussion technique in which Tiberius took the chair had a considerable effect on teaching. He uses the term 'dramatic'. He and his colleagues explain this result by the fact that improvement in teaching arises from the teacher–learning alliance. And in their study the more highly rated teachers were those who were judged by the students as possessing the greater number of interpersonal (relational) attributes. Those teachers who were considered to be uncommitted were poorly rated. One can see why this should be in clinical settings involving small groups. Some teachers said that enthusiastic and knowledgeable students brought out the best in them. In many respects these results are similar to those found in school education, and it is surprising that there is no mention of, for example, the work of Good and Brophy (1973).

Group discussion is undoubtedly one way of changing students' expectations. In management development and other programmes it is common practice to begin a course with a discussion which enables the students to indicate what they hope to get from it, and for the teacher to outline his/her objectives in order to try to match expectations. Such discussion would influence the construction of the rating scale to be used at the end of the course and it might be modified during the meeting.

Chapple and Murphy (1996) considered that there had been too much reliance on course evaluation questionnaires and proposed that a nominal group technique should be used. This is a structured activity designed to facilitate group based decision making (Partington, 1992). It is a single session conducted by a group leader. In this investigation the groups ranged from 10 to 23 persons and the duration was between one and half and two hours.

The leader put to the group two questions: How might the course be strengthened? What are the strengths of the course? The students were then asked to consider their answers to these questions in silence, and at the same time to write down their responses. In the next stage each individual had to present their ideas succinctly. The investigators found that the effectiveness of this phase diminished with group size. They now recommend a group of between 6 and 8 persons. The number of items generated in their groups ranged from 7 to 25.

In the next stage a general discussion leads to a clarification of the ideas as well as indications of agreement and disagreement. Finally, each participant votes on the five items that were of most significance for them, and ranks them in order of importance.

Chapple and Murphy point out that the nominal group technique is only valid if the items collected are representative of the whole group. It can also be time consuming so it has to be done when the majority of students are accessible. The group leader was found to have a significant effect on the collection of data. Some students did not participate openly or truthfully when the course leader took charge of the group. On the other hand neutral arbitrators often did not understand the points made. Eventually the student groups provided their own leader. Some students found the structure of the groups too rigid.

It was found that this technique generated issues that were of immediate concern to the students, and that these concerns might change as the course progressed. Early feelings of discontent might not re-emerge at the end of term session. It was also found that the responses tended to be inconsistent and to ignore curriculum content. The latter would not be surprising in situations where the curriculum is 'received'. Students would expect the content to be the considered wisdom of the profession, in this case Nursing; what mattered to them was the organization and presentation of teaching and learning.

Notwithstanding these and other difficulties with the technique Chapple and Murphy conclude that it is useful but that it may be more effective in identifying individual rather than consensus concerns, and reactions to recent processes of learning rather than overall course content.

There are several reports of the use of focus groups in the student evaluation process. Provided that they are only one component of the process, they have the advantage of being able to select the participants. Gowdy (1996) describes how the evaluation committee in his college agreed to the selection of students who were bright, perceptive and articulate. They had to agree to participate. By selecting the right time of the day (breakfast) he obtained 100 per cent attendance and a high level of participation.

Shannon, Twale and Hancock (1996) focused on how academics acquired and made use of feedback at an American university. They found that those who had received some training in pedagogical methods gathered feedback about their teaching more than teachers who had received no such training. Teachers from colleges of education and liberal arts departments used more methods than those in mathematics and science who did least to modify their instruction. Anecdotal evidence suggests that this pattern might be repeated elsewhere outside of the United States.

Feldman's view that participant observation and other forms of ethnographic study would lead to an understanding of the dynamics at work in classrooms could also lead to changes in teaching. Such studies are rare although they have been done (e.g. Heywood and Montagu-Pollock, 1977).

Finally, in the near future in the UK, it will be possible to look at the differences between trained, and experienced but untrained teachers with SETs. The results should be revealing but they will depend in no small way on the model of teaching and learning that the trainers use as the basis of their programme.

Student attitudes

Marlin (1987) points out that while there have been numerous studies of the validity and reliability of student rating scales there have only been a few studies of the perceptions which students have of the process. This led him to study the perceptions of economics students at all levels of study in two roughly comparable university schools. He found that while students believed that existing procedures were adequate for the evaluation of teachers, and that there was no need to falsify ratings, that students believed that they would have little effect on the careers of faculty. They perceived that the ratings were a mechanism to let off 'student steam'. There is, therefore, a belief among many students that faculty only pay lip service to the ratings. Unfortunately, this often seems to be the case, and, if it is, why bother with the ratings in the first place? If they are acted on then students need to know. To quote from Marlin, 'As one student put it, "why don't you tell us what is done with the forms? Who reads them? What do they do after they read them? These sheets are useless without seeing what the results are? No one ever tells us. They are a great idea if they are followed up properly".' These are fundamental questions which require answers.

Emotional state and age

Wachtel (1998) has pointed out that there is very little research that looks at the emotional state of students when they make their ratings. He only found one study in his survey which suggested that the more hostile and anxious the students were at the end of the term (semester) when the ratings were made the more likely they were to give lower ratings. This would effect the validity of the rating. He could not find any studies that corroborated this work. He also drew attention to the fact that there were no recent studies of the effects of age on ratings.

Rating scales and questionnaires

It has been shown that, within the traditional climate of university teaching, short rating scales can be used, and that overall ratings are both reliable and valid. It has also been argued that within specific areas such scales may need to be content driven. It is, therefore, important to be clear about the purposes of the scale. If they are to be used for personnel decisions then global ratings would seem to be best when they are supported by a relatively small number of specific items. Furthermore, such items should be related to course outcomes that go beyond achievement test data. These models seem to work well in traditional environments where learning is conceived to be essentially the transmission of information. There is a challenge to test designers to design instruments which take into account higher order thinking skills, and this has implications for teaching and learning since it may put the teacher in a more facilitative role.

Where small groups are involved discussion is likely to have more successful outcomes than questionnaires. When the curriculum/ syllabus has been changed questionnaires and other methods of assessment may have to be used to elicit student learning, this to include understanding of how they learn (e.g. Tomlinson and Towell, 1999). Thus the more learning is understood the more complex the roles of both teachers and students become. This point is well illustrated in the forthcoming study of the Alverno College curriculum (Mentkowski and associates, 2000). In these circumstances traditional ratings are likely to be inadequate but students will have to come to a realization of how they themselves learn if the ratings are to be changed to respond to these new circumstances. As yet this is not a formal part of the higher education process.

It will be clear that student ratings of teaching effectiveness are only partial assessments of the experience of higher education. It is also clear that the rating scales are based on certain assumptions about the nature of 'teaching'. As such they might inhibit instructors from seeking out other, and more effective ways of influencing student learning for the better. It is equally evident that they are open to abuse by administrators and policy makers, so it is important that faculty and administrators should be well versed with the findings of this extensive research.

Toward a code of practice

As a result of a comparative study of the value of student ratings in France, Germany, the Netherlands and the UK, Husbands and Fosh (1993) (who wrote before the review discussed above was completed), concluded that some of the biases that had not been considered might be specific to particular countries. They believed that some factors would always bias the ways in which students rate teaching. But as with Newport's objections these can be overcome by taking into account outcomes. However, they made the point that if student evaluations were not used in a rudimentary way their results would go against natural justice. In this respect Hall and Fitzgerald (1995) developed a code of practice for the Association of University Staff of New Zealand. These principles were:

1. Student evaluation should be used, but not in isolation, for summative evaluation.

2. Those entrusted with the task of making tenure, promotion and similar decisions should be skilled in interpreting and drawing together the different sources of information.

3. Evaluations of teaching should be based on a representative range of a person's teaching.

4. Evaluation instruments should be based on a representative range of a person's teaching.

5. Evaluation instruments should clearly state the purpose of the evaluation and indicate whether the forms will be returned to the lecturer(s).

6. Students should be able to provide a valid judgement in respect of each item.

7. The results of an evaluation of a teacher's performance should be based, as far as possible on his/her own merits: that is, the instrument should not incorporate items which reflect the performance of others teaching the course.

8. The administration of a summative evaluation questionnaire should follow standardized procedures which safeguard the validity and reliability of the information obtained.

9. Guidelines should be provided for ensuring that evaluations are administered at a time that will maximize the validity of the information obtained.

10. Evaluation procedures should protect the identity of individual students.

11. Clear guidelines must be given as to who may initiate an evaluation and for what purpose. If someone other than the staff member concerned initiates an evaluation, the staff member concerned must be fully consulted.

12. Clear rules governing the confidentiality of evaluation information and reports should be specified.

13. Guidelines should be provided to assist teachers to interpret the results of an evaluation report: appropriate training and resources should be available in the event of an unfavourable evaluation.

14. Provision should exist for allowing a teacher to set aside an evaluation where there is evidence that the results are invalid.

15. Provision should exist for regularly reviewing an institution's evaluation procedures: that is, the evaluation system itself should be regularly evaluated.

16. Clear guidelines should be provided by the university in respect of the use of student evaluations for disciplinary procedures. Evaluations collected for reasons such as promotion, probation and formative development should not be used in disciplinary contexts.

Performance indicators using student ratings

The Course Experience Questionnaire

Student ratings when used as performance indicators are not aimed at individual teachers. They have as their aim 'the collection of information about programmes of study and the academic units responsible for teaching these programmes' (Ramsden, 1991). The Course Experience Questionnaire developed by Ramsden for this purpose was trialled at the request of the Australian Performance Indicators Research Project (Linke, 1991).

Since 1992 the CEQ(30) has been distributed to all Australian university graduates within a few months of course completion. From 1993 a shortened version of the instrument has been used with 23 instead of 30 items (CEQ(23)). It is being used as a standard national summative instrument to measure perceptions that students have of their assessment, curriculum and instruction. These are regarded as key determinants in the approaches which students take to their learning (Wilson, Lizzio and Ramsden, 1997).

The rationale for the CEQ has its origins in work carried out in the UK by Ramsden and Entwistle (1981). Using a Course Perceptions Questionnaire which they had developed they found that when departments provided good teaching, set clear goals and standards, allowed freedom in learning, were open to students, and set appropriate work loads, then students were more likely to learn effectively. Confirmatory studies showed that the relation between teaching quality and student learning was functional (Ramsden and Entwistle, 1981)

Ramsden (1991) concluded that these and other studies (Biggs, 1990) demonstrated the importance of teaching methods which encourage student autonomy, cooperative behaviour and enterprise. It followed that the Course Experience Questionnaire should evaluate these dimensions together with assessment. Ramsden and Entwistle had found that minimalist approaches to learning were adopted when teaching was narrowly focused on examinations such as to cause rote learning. The CEQ included five scales. These were: good teaching, clear goals, appropriate work load, appropriate assessment, and emphasis on independence. In respect of the latter the defining item was 'students here are given a lot of choice in the work they have to do'.

More than 3000 students from 13 institutions completed the scales. Some of these institutions had become universities after 1987. As between the pre-1987 universities and the post-1987 institutions no difference was found in the levels of ratings given by the students: one sector's students did not give higher ratings than those in the other sector. The students were all in final year programmes, and they indicated to the investigators what their major subject or main course was. This produced responses from ten areas of study making comparisons in eight areas possible. Most of the responses could be linked to small and large academic units. Their data was supplemented with data from a survey of a thousand or so students in accounting departments which had incorporated some of their items (Matthews, Brown and Jackson, 1990).

Academics in these institutions were also asked to rate themselves against similar items in the CEQ. The pattern of results was similar to those reported by Marsh (1987). In all the fields of study the academics gave themselves higher ratings than the students but the level awarded corresponded to those of the students. Those giving themselves low scores were, as academic units, given low scores by their students. There was, however, a large discrepancy between the engineers and their students. (Other investigations suggest that this might not be uncommon among this group (see Seymour and Hewitt, 1997)). However, 10 per cent of the variance in the Good Teaching scale in the CEQ was explained by field of study.

The results suggest that those who teach the major course of study reflect what is happening in that subject area more generally across institutions. Thus, when institutions are compared the comparisons should be made within fields. The scales that gave the best discriminations were Good Teaching, Clear Goals and Appropriate Work Load. However, in the social sciences Appropriate Assessment produced considerable differences. The CEQ showed that there were statistically significant differences between institutions. It also showed that it could discriminate between academic units at the extremes of the distribution. Because there were recurring differences between disciplines within fields of study (e.g. social sciences including sociology and psychology) lower levels of aggregation are to be preferred. If the larger unit is used data need to be interpreted with caution.

Wilson, Lizzio and Ramsden (1997) suggest that not much confidence can be put in three independent evaluations because of the small size of their samples although they broadly confirmed the factor structure of CEQ(30).

In response to the demand in both Australia and Britain that courses should help with the development of transferable generic skills (see Chapter 3) a six-item scale to measure these skills was developed. This could be added to CEQ(30) becoming CEQ(36). It was also incorporated within CEQ(23) which retained the strongest loading items from Ramsden's 1991 analysis of CEQ(30). The schedules are described in full in Wilson, Lizzio and Ramsden (1997).

A substantive multidisciplinary study was undertaken to obtain, among other things, new data on the construct validity of these items, and to establish the reliability and validity of the generic scale. The data confirmed that both forms were reliable instruments.

In response to a criticism by Richardson (1994) the discriminant validity of the instrument was examined. It was found that it could distinguish between programmes in medicine and psychology (see Chapter 12). In so far as a relationship between CEQ ratings and course outcomes was concerned a positive association was found between scores of the CEQ and the measures of learning outcome, i.e. satisfaction, academic achievement and learning outcomes.

Overall, the authors argue that the study demonstrates the validity of the instrument as a performance indicator in Australia. However, they warn against the temptation for university administrators 'to engage in simplistic cross-institutional rankings of relative merit'. They tabulate the uses and misuses of CEQ. They consider that it is well suited for work in the UK and cite its use at Oxford Brookes University (Gibbs and Lucas, 1995) as an example. Ramsden considers that

> Information about change or stability in students' perception over time is much more important than data from any one administration. In fact, evidence of how a course or department has responded to student evaluation data – the capacity of its teachers to learn from their mistakes – might be regarded as one of the most important indexes of its educational effectiveness.

An alternative approach

Ramsden's suggestion that the CEQ could be used in the UK was rejected by Yorke (1996) in respect of its use in the quality assessment exercises. He argued that it was not possible at one and the same time to satisfy the requirement for an indicator that can be used across the whole sector of higher education without sacrificing the aim of diversity among institutions and programmes. He also argued that the CEQ had a number of technical limitations. Among these were its limited coverage – a fact which Ramsden acknowledges. There are no items in the questionnaire relating to curriculum content or to practical work in laboratories and studios. Neither are there items relating to facilities and off-campus work. Looked at from the UK perspective of the quality assessment exercises Yorke expressed concern that student perception data would not be sufficiently robust for comparisons that might be used for the allocation of resources.

Yorke is particularly critical of the good teaching and independence scales. There is only one item in the good teaching scale which relates to a specific teaching skill. Judgement of a programme on the basis of freedom of choice is dubious. Cowan (private communication) asked what is the possibility that both teachers and students are equally ignorant of sound criteria to apply?

There are always constraints on students. This is particularly true of students pursuing professional recognition. They have to satisfy minimum requirements set by their professional bodies. Yorke considers that there are also constraints that influence the practice of assessment. While it is true that course regulations define the assessment framework, and variation in the framework would naturally raise questions about the validity and equitability of the assessment, it is not necessarily true that course regulations are sound. As Ramsden says, they can lead to teaching and assessment approaches which cause either deep or surface learning (see Chapter

8).The problem lies surely with the category of independence and not in the desirability of collecting perceptions about assessment and curriculum.

Like any questionnaire the CEQ is open to criticism and Yorke identifies flaws in some of the items. For example, some of the items attempt to measure two things. He is also critical of the instruments used by Ramsden to obtain concurrent validity. Following common practice Ramsden does this by cross-referencing the perceptions with data from other instruments. What is problematic is the choice of instruments. In this case one of those used by Ramsden was the Approaches to Studying Inventory (Entwistle and Ramsden, 1983) but as Yorke points out that inventory is about approaches to learning and not the perceptions of students, which seems to invalidate its use in these circumstances.

Yorke accepts that the CEQ can discriminate between organizational units, and that although it has limited coverage and requires further development 'it has considerable value as an instrument for the gathering of data for internal cycles of evaluation and enhancement, where the local context can be taken into account'. This would seem to be congruent with the view expressed by Wilson, Lizzio and Ramsden (1997) and outlined above who also in response argue that in a survey of students across all years at one Australian university, satisfaction with facilities was a much weaker predictor of overall student satisfaction than the current scales of the CEQ.

Yorke's comments were made in the context of a project on performance indicators begun by the Council for National Academic awards and completed for the Higher Education Quality Council (Yorke, 1996). A major aim of the project was to develop questionnaires that would focus on the experience of students in the participating institutions. They were all 1992 universities. For the usual reasons that questionnaires can involve a large number of students who can respond anonymously as well as for the reason that, with caution, data can be compared over time, a questionnaire approach was adopted. Two questionnaires were developed. These were called *broad brush* and *fine brush*. The *fine brush* arose from the view that any dissatisfaction expressed in the *broad brush* instrument could be explored in more detail in the *fine brush* instrument. The areas covered in the fine brush instruments were

Academic aspects (version A):

Lectures (11 items)

Working in groups (16 items)

Working independently (8 items)

Work experience placement (12 items)

Tutorial Support (8 items)

Assessment (12 items)

Organisation of the Programme (11 items).

Institutional Services (version B):

Library service (17 items)

General computing services (13 items)

Housing accommodation (4 items)

Catering (15 items)

Other student support services.

Joining the Institution (version B):

Application (13 items)

Enrolment and registration (7 items)

Choosing to come to this institution (7 items)

Unfortunately the *fine brush* study was developed later and work on it was limited, and it was not subjected to the same psychometric treatment as the broad brush instrument. Thus while the items were evaluated for face validity and coverage no assessment of the reliability of the instrument was made. Two versions – A and B – were produced of each instrument.

---

1. How clear to you are the aims of your programme?
2. How stimulating is your programme?
3. To what extent is your programme helping you to develop skills relevant to a variety of life-situations?
4. How satisfied are you with the amount of choice within your programme?
5. How satisfied are you with the way in which the components (modules/units) of your programme fit together?
6. To what extent do you feel that you belong to an academic section (department/school) within the institution?
7. How committed to the students are the staff teaching your programme?
8. To what extent is your programme encouraging your personal development?
9. How adequate for your needs is the provision of guidance regarding academic choices within your programme?
10 How heavy is the workload on your programme?
11. To what extent does the teaching on your programme encourage you to participate actively?
12. To what extent is your programme helping you to develop subject-specific skills?
13. How much of a problem is caused for you by the way in which your programme's assessment (assignments, etc.) are scheduled?
14. To what extent is your programme helping you to develop your ability to work with others?
15. How informative is the feedback you receive on your assignments?
16. How satisfied are you with the speed of return of your assignments?
17. To what extent is your programme helping you to develop skills in working independently?
18. How well do you understand what the assessments (assignments, examinations) on your programme expect of you?

How do you rate the following?

19. The programme information received on enrolment this year.
20. The programme information received during this year.
21. The teaching on your programme.
22. The day-to-day organization of your programme.
23. The teaching rooms for the programme.
24. The availability of library materials.
25. The computing facilities.
26. The facilities within the institution for working on your own.
27. The catering facilities.

Please respond to any of the next three questions ONLY IF THEY APPLY to your circumstances

28. How do you rate the facilities for practical activities on your programme?
29. How satisfied were you with your placement in a work environment?
30. How satisfied are you with the institution's support services?

To what extent would you recommend your programme to your friends?

Figure 4.1 Version A of Yorke's Broad Brush Questionnaire.
(Reproduced by kind permission of M. Yorke from *Indicators of Programme Quality*. Higher Education Quality Council.)

The face validity of the sections (as opposed to the items) in the fine brush questionnaire is self-evident. The investigators found that they were generally acceptable to students although some students felt they were too long. They reported that the sub-questionnaire that asked students what they gained from higher education proved unsatisfactory. Essentially this question was about the value-added of the higher education experience. An alternative approach would need to be developed for this dimension.

The *broad brush* questionnaire was, however, tested for both reliability and validity. Comparing it with Ramsden's CEQ Yorke notes that while it has a wider coverage than the CEQ it is less psychometrically correct because the items in the *broad brush* questionnaire are substantially independent of each other. This means that there are 29 single item sub-scales each of which has to be tested for reliability. The items in version A are shown in Figure 4.1. A matrix of the items produced few significant correlations. Therefore it is the item-by-item analysis which assumes importance in such questionnaires. These items will generally have been chosen in this way to achieve particular objectives. In Yorke's case the individual item stabilities were found to lie in the range 0.71 to 0.90 having been determined by testing and re-testing the schedule on a small group of students over a period of two weeks.

Yorke searched for an underlying structure. Of the six factors yielded, only one, 'personal fulfilment', accounted for any large slice of the variance (31.7%). He suggested that the *a priori* determination of composite groups might be as useful as a factorial analysis, and he invited his readers to produce their composites from the items. In the event neither method was found to be entirely satisfactory. The members of his project team were divided over the use of composites. Some thought that summary data of this kind could be useful while others thought that it would smooth out the key information that resided in the individual items. Yorke wrote:

> This polarisation reflects the tension inherent in the use of indicators – whether they are being used to assist developmental activity at a programme level, or to provide management (and possibly external bodies) with performance scores. The polarisation is not simply Manichean: there are shades of grey between the two extremes, but it is important within an institution for all concerned in the collection and use of information to share an understanding of (and, one would hope, agreement upon) the different ways in which it is expected to support the institutions functioning.

Having got such data what does an institution do about it particularly if it is negative? In the first place a number of items relate to organizational functions which can be corrected. The same is true of some of the academic items. A teacher can be cajoled into allowing more time for questions, or helped to give more structure to her/his lectures. Teachers can be trained to work with groups and so on. But there are certain items the understanding of which requires a more substantive knowledge of student learning. For example, a person's perception that the assignment load is too heavy may be at odds with what others in the group say. This raises the problem for the tutor as to whether the matter should be pursued with the individual concerned. If it is a general issue then the matter can be resolved. If it has to be pursued with the individual then the tutor may well require a more comprehensive understanding of learning.

The reactions of alumni

Some institutions have attempted to obtain the views of alumni who have not been involved in any form of longitudinal study. There have also been surveys of large and small groups of professionals. In some cases, such as Hutton and Gerstl's (1969) survey of mechanical engineers in the UK, the results had some impact on the curriculum demands made by the profession. Such surveys are increasingly held to be valuable in ascertaining the quality of education offered by institutions. The quality assessment of education in the UK (subject review) takes note of attempts by departments to obtain the views of their graduates. The research evidence supports this approach. Two studies that support the case are summarized in the following paragraphs.

In Canada Donald and Denison (1996) explored the role of broad indicators in the evaluation of undergraduate education by alumni. They were particularly concerned with the level of satisfaction experienced by former students. Citing Astin (1993) they noted that student satisfaction is frequently overlooked in contemporary discussions of higher education outcomes.

They make the point that satisfaction may well change in the first two or three years after graduation because during this period the graduates will be testing the value of their qualifications in the labour market. Referring to Clarke *et al.* (1986) they draw attention to the fact that during this period graduates will gain insights into the education they received. In consequence they will be able to highlight its strengths and weaknesses (Graham and Cockriel, 1990). In sum, retrospective evaluations that relate the undergraduate experience of alumni to their subsequent employment are of considerable value to those concerned with education. They designed a simple questionnaire that asked for responses to a limited number of Likert type scale items. Two open-ended items were included. These were (i) 'What features of your education at X would you have judged to have been most meaningful to your subsequent graduation?' and (ii) 'What advice would you care to offer the university based on your subsequent experience?'

The items distinguished between broad indicators at the level of the institution and programme. Their survey was conducted among graduates from five major programmes. Although the response rate was small (12% = 356) they deemed it satisfactory for their purposes. They have much to say about the methodological issues surrounding their study. However, it is the results of the indicators relating to the quality of teaching and its value in preparing them for employment that are of concern here. About half the sample reported that the quality of teaching was high. Only 12 per cent thought that it was 'low'. A greater proportion of the most recent graduates thought the quality of teaching was low. (Do they become more sanguine with age?). The really interesting feature of the response is that most of the 'low' respondents blamed institutional pressures. For example:

The inherent reward system for the professors leans heavily towards research and grants. The unfortunate result is a steady decline in the quality of classroom lectures and teaching in general. It would be useful to review the criteria for evaluating professor performance and increasingly emphasize teaching skills.

As Donald and Denison point out, it is unlikely that insights of this kind could be obtained from undergraduate ratings. Similarly, the value of improving themselves generally, and the opportunity to acquire in-depth knowledge in an academic discipline which were frequently reported appear often in the literature in student outcomes but not in the literature on course ratings and programme review. Yet students may well take these factors into account when they rate teachers and courses.

The respondents' remarks also highlighted the difference between academic and professional needs with suggestions for more provision in the areas of communication skill, interpersonal skill and knowledge of business.

Donald and Denison included an open-ended question at the end of their scale which asked the graduates to describe what features of their education they judged to have been most meaningful to them subsequent to their graduation? The most frequently mentioned feature was the 'ability to think'. Donald and Denison suggest that this finding highlights a discrepancy between the frames of reference of graduates and university decision makers. 'Where the latter focused on traditional administrative distinctions between teaching, program and student life, alumni focused more on learning and developmental outcomes.' This supports the views of Koon and Murray (1995) discussed earlier. These graduates also blurred the distinction between formal class and informal out-of-class learning. This further illustrates the complexity of the higher education process and the need to take the kind of systems approaches to its study advocated by Pascarrela and Terenzini (1991). These are particularly well illustrated by the longitudinal studies undertaken on the large scale by Astin (1997a) and on the small scale at Alverno College (Mentkowski and associates (2000); see also Mentkowski and Doherty, 1983). The complexity of these approaches and some of their outcomes are briefly described in the next chapter.

The need for focused studies: a cautionary tale

In the UK a number of surveys of graduates working in professional fields have been undertaken which focus on specific issues. For example, Lee (1969) hypothesized that when graduate mechanical engineers reviewed their education they would give poor ratings to traditional laboratory work. He expected them to want more project work and that was not fashionable in the period preceding the survey. He felt this would be the case for projects likely to be more related to what they had to do in industry. To his surprise a survey of some 500 graduates show they valued traditional laboratory work. On further investigation he found that the reason for this response was that laboratory work was the only time in the course that they came near to obtaining an identity as an engineer! The main corpus of their programmes had been mathematics and applied science.

However, two survey studies of alumni urge caution in interpreting the results. One found that alumni who are satisfied with their jobs are more likely to report being satisfied with their education than those who were not. Dissatisfaction with pay had a significant effect on the ratings by women (Pike, 1994). Another which examined medical graduates found that there were significant differences between the responses of those in primary practice and those in hospital medicine about the relative importance of different subjects in the curriculum (Clack, 1994).

An important criticism of alumni studies that concentrate on the relationship between education and unemployment is that they neglect that most important aim of liberal education that is to prepare students for life in society. Therefore, ratings by students and alumni need to be treated with caution, not because they may be biased, but because they may not be getting at the truth. Institutions need, from time to time to encourage in-depth studies of their programmes and processes (e.g. Jahoda, 1964; Marris, 1964; Mentkowski and associates). At the same time there is a substantial case for keeping in touch with alumni by means of relatively simple measures.

Success, failure and satisfaction are brought about by complex processes which require academics to have much more understanding about the nature of student learning than they have had in the past. This complexity is examined in more detail in Chapter 5.

Notes

1. Three research designs have been use to study student ratings (see Abrami, d'Appollonia and Rosenfield, 1994). Laboratory designs have been used to examine the causal relationships between instructional processes and particular products. Abrami *et al.* are very critical of laboratory studies for a number of reasons, among them that they failed to represent actual differences between instructors in the field. They felt that they could be used to explain why ratings and achievement are related by establishing which instructional strategies causally affect the products of instruction.

The second procedure is called multi-section validation. In these studies the validity criterion is the mean section performance. Koon and Murray (1995) describe a multi-year multi-section validity experiment. First year psychology students were assigned to sections. The mean final year high school grade was computed for the students in each class section. No significant differences were found within any year. Each class section used the same textbook and was tested with the same final examination. Each class filled out the same teacher rating questionnaire, and the same course evaluation questionnaire. Each instructor contributed items to a pool, and the final examinations that were set in December and April were assembled by the course co-ordinator. The other instructors did not see the examination until it was set. Within the course evaluation schedule students were asked to rate their own learning, and to estimate the weekly amount of time they had spent studying for the course. This was used as a measure of their short-term motivation. The number of teachers involved was 36. Each taught the two-semester introductory course at least once in each of two years. The study was conducted in each of four years, hence the multi-year structure.

There are a number of criticisms of multi-section designs. One is that the sample size of the course sections is inevitably small. Another is that the variance in achievement scores is almost always attributable to a student variable such as ability. It is also argued that other criteria other than objectively scored tests should be explored. Koon and Murray (1995) try to do this (see Marsh and Dunkin, 1992).

The third design that is favoured by Marsh is Multitrait-Multimethod (MTMM) analysis. In these studies the multiple traits are the student rating factors. These are assessed by multiple methods, that is, SETs and instructor self-evaluations. The analysis begins with a correlation matrix of the two. There is considerable debate between Marsh and Dunkin (1992), and Abrami *et al.* (1994) about the relative merits of these approaches. The reader is referred to Koon and Murray for a simplified account of some of this debate.

Chapter 5

Assessing the Experience of Higher Education
Pre-entry through College

Summary

Following on from Chapter 4 the first purpose of this chapter is to show just how complex the assessment of the experience of higher education is in order to illustrate the problems involved in arriving at satisfactory indicators of performance. Not least among them are those associated with the particular definitions of attrition and retention used.

The chapter begins with a description of Astin's Input- Environment-Outcome model. This is followed by a description of Chickering's seven vectors that influence the student experience. Some of the results of Pascarella and Terenzini's review of research in the US are detailed. Recent research on attrition in the UK is summarized.

Astin challenges the view that performance indicators should be based on simple industrial models. He considers the better analogy to be with medicine. Astin points out that outcome measures by themselves have little to say about institutional performance unless they are related to the input-characteristics of students. Consideration is, therefore, given to admissions policies. It is pointed out that as the number of non-traditional applicants increases different policies will have to be applied, and in particular means will have to be found to bridge the vocational divide. In terms of assessment at entry the new General National Vocational Education Qualifications (GNVQs) in the UK are described together with the American College Testing Programs Work Keys. Reports of bridging courses in engineering in the UK suggest that university tutors have found it necessary to change both their assessment and instructional strategies to accommodate this new type of student.

As systems of higher education become more diverse it may be necessary to provide foundation courses that are general and not tied to specific subjects so as ensure non-traditional students can make an informed choice.

Chickering pointed out the need for clarity of institutional objectives and for internal consistency in policies, practices and activities. He also argued for curricular flexibility, variety in instructional styles and modes, greater student involvement in learning, and learning oriented assessment. This view is supported by other research.

Among the other findings reported are those which highlight the importance of social and academic integration, commitment to learning goals as well as to the institution. An important factor in the decision to continue is the effect that experience of an institution has on participants. External factors may also influence that decision. In so far as integration is concerned, at the micro-level of institutional life, the classroom and the department, this can be enhanced or impeded by faculty in their personal response to students, assessment practices, and the organization and presentation of their courses; in short the management of learning.

Astin's I-E-O model

Astin calls his framework for the analysis of student outcomes the Input-Environment-Outcome (I-E-O) model. Inputs refer to the characteristics that the students have when they enter the institution (entering characteristics). Environment relates to all those factors in college that impinge on the student experience: policies, programmes, academics, peers, and organizational structure. Outcomes are the result of that experience. Thus the effects of college are established by comparing the input and output characteristics, and in so doing accounting for the process. It is a substantial jump from obtaining college experience through student course evaluation questionnaires. At first sight this would be seem to be an industrial model but Astin is at pains to argue that it is not.

Performance indicators, industry, policy making and higher education

A major issue between academics and policy makers has been the objection of academics to performance indicators based on simple industrial models. Academics argue that educational institutions cannot be compared with factories. Whereas the inputs into a manufacturing process are specified to have the same characteristics and be in all respects identical, the inputs to college, the students, have a variety of different characteristics to which the manufacturing process – the college organisation – has to respond in a variety of ways. While this might be the theory the practice is very often the reverse, for the canons of institutions and their sub-systems are often very rigid. This is not to deny the view that industrial models may be inappropriate for the assessment of the student experience of college.

Astin (1994) rejected the industrial model at the outset of his investigations of the impact of college on outcomes:

> Graduates of college are clearly not produced in this way. Their personal characteristics at the time of graduation may, to be sure, have been influenced by the college experience, but their physical and psychological make up depends heavily on background and environmental factors largely independent of the institution. Students, in other words, are fully functioning organisms before they get to college; the purpose of our education is presumably, to enhance the students' functioning, or to develop the talent of its students.

Astin considers that the better analogy is with medicine that has as its goal the condition of the patient. Colleges, in the same way, arrange educational programmes that are relevant to the student. Like patients, some students will benefit from the treatment and others will not. Therefore, Astin argues, 'a critical ingredient in the assessment of college impact it to measure the change in the characteristics of students over time'. This principle, with the caveat that student change should not be associated with institutional impact, governed his approach to the study of outcomes.

> In many ways, assessing the impact of educational programs is analagous (i.e. with medicine where the essential aspect of an effective treatment is that it changes the prognosis). People will continue to grow and develop (from input to outcome) regardless of whether or where they attend college, and because human behaviour tends to be consistent over time, it is possible to predict (prognosticate) from current information (input) what a person will be like at some later time (outcome). High achievers in secondary school (input), for example, tend to be high achievers in college (outcome). But we can make a better prediction as to whether this high achiever in high school will also be a high achiever in college if we have more input information on the student's ability, motivation and family background. The basic issue, then is whether attending a given college or being exposed to a particular type of environment changes the prediction of how the student will develop.

It would be nice for all concerned if Astin's example of the high achieving student maintaining that high achievement approximated to the truth. Yet, in England, where it is well understood that the correlations between grades obtained in examinations at input and the grades obtained in final examinations at output can be low, the examinations used for selection at input have been 'safe' predictors of success at some final grade or another, for drop-out and failure rates have been relatively low in many subjects in the past. Nevertheless, some important questions remain. Why, for example, do some high achievers get lower grades than expected, and why do some low achievers (relative to the criteria for selection) get higher grades than predicted? Also, why are drop-out rates from some subject areas greater than those in other areas? Neither the method of obtaining answers to these questions, or the answers prove to be simple, as the sections which follow will show. They will serve to reinforce the view that performance indicators, if they are to be used, should be developed and employed with a 'medical' rather than an 'industrial' model in mind.

Astin's Taxonomy

This taxonomy was developed so as to take account of a wide range of possible outcomes.

Therefore, its first dimension took into account both intellective (cognitive) and non-intellective (affective) factors. This is entirely in keeping with Newman's view of the purposes of higher education (Newman, 1852, 1947) or, what is sometimes called the development of the whole person. The non-intellective factors include student attitudes, values, self-concept (esteem), aspirations and everyday behaviour. Whereas in the past the term intellective would be taken to mean higher order mental processes such as reasoning and logic, recently a distinction has been made between knowledge acquisition and what is perceived to be a failure in higher education to develop higher order thinking skills.

Astin makes the point that the non-intellective dimensions can be evaluated by self-administered questionnaires, whereas the evaluation of the cognitive is much more difficult.

The second dimension relates to the type of data to be collected. Astin distinguishes between two types of data, the *behavioural* and the *psychological*. Behavioural data is derived from observable activities, for example personal habits in the affective domain and career development in the intellective domain. Psychological data relate to the internal states of an individual. For example, in the affective domain the attitudes, values and self-concept that an individual has, and in the intellective domain the knowledge and critical thinking skills possessed by that person.

Astin also considers the temporal dimension of college life to be important. While colleges typically look for long-term benefits students may perceive them to be too remote and of little benefit. 'Most professors and staff, if they focus at all on student outcomes, limit their attention to outcomes that can be assessed while the student is enrolled.' Thus, Astin focused on what could be observed during the four years of college life.

Chickering's seven vectors

The complexity of the task of measuring the impact of college on students is also illustrated by Chickering's (1969) seven vectors that influence student development. As students progress through college they continually apprehend more complexity as they grow along each of seven vectors. However, growth along these vectors requires stimulation and this is one of the functions of college education. The titles of the vectors are reasonably self-explanatory. The first is achieving competence. If we do not feel competent our development may be impeded and our psychological disposition might be such as to compel us to withdraw. Pascarella and Terenzini (1991) quote Chickering as saying that, on reflection, he should have given intellectual competence and interpersonal competence more attention.

British academics have by and large only concerned themselves with intellectual competence: failure has more often than not been associated with lack of intelligence, a problem for the student and not the institution. It is only recently that they have been driven to consider the importance of inter-personal and intra-personal competence, and what is now termed emotional intelligence in success and failure. As was shown in Chapter 3 these skills are considered to be important for employability. For this reason Chickering's second vector, the management of the emotions, is of importance. Here the task is to develop an increasing capacity to implement passion and commitment accompanied by an increasing capacity to implement them through intelligent behaviour.

One of the problems that some highly intelligent people have is that they are unable to manage their emotions (Goleman, 1996). The consequences of this for examination performance are discussed in Chapter 6.

Chickering's third vector is developing autonomy. Autonomy in learning has come to be encouraged as a major aim of education, policy makers say they value it highly, but I suspect that it is for the somewhat unworthy motive of overcoming shortages of resources in educational institutions. It is a term whose definition is fraught with difficulty. As defined by Chickering it is 'the independence of maturity' which requires the person to recognize the necessity for interdependence. Indeed, in the article cited by Pascarella and Terenzini, Chickering considers that this vector might have been called 'interdependence'. It is worth noting that lack of confidence sometimes leads individuals to spurn interdependence.

The fourth factor establishing identity is in keeping with Erickson's theory of human development. Change in this vector is fostered by growth in the first three vectors and its development facilitates developments along the remaining three vectors. These are *freeing interpersonal relationships* (vector 5), developing purpose (vector 6), and developing integrity (vector 7). Chickering has said of the last vector that it would now have to take into account the work of Perry (1970) and Kohlberg (1971) (see Chapter 7). To respond to some critics it would also have to give a more substantial account of intellectual development.

In so far as the assessment of institutional effectiveness is concerned, Chickering drew attention to the need for clarity of institutional objectives and the internal consistency of policies, practices and activities. He also argued that curricular flexibility, variety in instructional styles and modes, student participation in learning, and learning-oriented evaluation promote impact. Reference to all of these can be found in semi-official and official literature but whether substance is wanted by those who promote policy is another matter. Chickering also considered that institutional size, residence, faculty and administration and peers and friends contributed to the impact that college has.

If these are the factors that impact on the experience of higher education, then they may be regarded as key factors on which indicators of performance should be built. It would appear that the course experience questionnaires should try to meet these criteria.

Causal models of the college experience

The models of the factors influencing the educational experience developed in the 1960s and 1970s were primarily sociological in orientation although they can be a given a psychological (developmental) dimension quite readily. They are, therefore about the functioning of the internal sub-systems within higher education institutions, and those external to the institution that have a bearing on its functioning.

Viewed from this perspective the fundamental unit in the system is the role. Students and teachers are the basic role players when the focus is on academic learning. Descriptive models of the student sub-system show that the student's role-set is overlapped by numerous other role-sets which may have an influence on student behaviour directly or indirectly. Significant among them are the family and school system, the academic and social systems within college as well as other external systems which impinge on the life of the college. An attempt was made to investigate the structure and function of sandwich (cooperative) courses using a model of this kind. The attitudes and experience of students were obtained from groups at each level in the system (i.e. high school, in each year of university study, and after graduation). These were related to the views of those responsible for teaching (in high school and college), work experience, programmes (in colleges and accreditation authorities), and those responsible for policy in education and industry (Heywood, 1969, 1989a). One of the questions considered in that study which continues to be discussed in the UK is the relevance of prior experience of work before entering university for those traditional students who would normally go straight to college.

From the perspective of the present discussion it had many similarities with Tinto's (1975, 1987) model developed to study the process of attrition in the United States (also an issue in the UK in the 1960s, Heywood 1971; Miller 1970). The six parameters of Tinto's model were pre-entry attributes (or entering characteristics as they are sometimes called), goals and commitments, institutional experiences, their effect on goals and commitments, and outcomes (i.e. decisions leading to departure. Both of the models assume that as students move through school and colleges they pass through a plurality of social systems in which they play different roles. In this journey they continually evaluate their goals and commitments.

Since the more satisfying the experience the more likely they are to stay, Herzberg's (1959) approach to the study of motivation in organizations might be a useful approach for the study of the higher education experience. Herzberg distinguished between satisfiers, elements that increase job satisfaction; and dissatisfiers or hygiene factors that diminish job satisfaction. The five satisfiers were achievement, recognition, work itself, responsibility and, advancement. The dissatisfiers were the organizations policy and administration, supervision, salary, interpersonal relations supervisors and working conditions. The reader will have no difficulty in placing these in an educational context, and Elton (1996) has applied it to the higher education context and suggested ways in which assessment is likely to enhance motivation. But he reminds faculty that students have the right to determine their own motivational priorities

From Tinto's perspective the more a person integrates into the system the more they are likely to stay. Social and academic integration occurs when the student comes to share the normative attitudes and values of peers and behaves as required in the formal and informal structures of the institution.

Braxton, Sullivan and Johnson (1997) having undertaken a review of the empirical evidence for Tinto's theory came to the conclusion that it needed revision. Nevertheless two of Tinto's core hypotheses were confirmed from the data collected from single resident institutions. These were the greater the level of social integration, the greater the level of subsequent commitment to the institution, and the greater the level of subsequent commitment to the institution, the greater the likelihood of student persistence in college. They did not find similar support in commuter colleges. In spite of these findings, Braxton and his colleagues suggest that the theory provides an organizing framework for research in individual universities and colleges. For example, Terenzini and Wright (1987) used Tinto's model to study students' reports of academic skill acquisition. Pascarella and Terenzini (1991) draw attention to the similarities between Astin's (1985) concept of 'involvement' and Pace's (1984) 'quality of effort'.

There are also similarities between Tinto's student integration model and Bean's (1980) student attrition model. Bean assumes that the student's attitudes which shaped her/his behavioural intentions to leave or persist are themselves shaped by the effects of the student's experience of the institution on her/his beliefs. Whereas Tinto's model does not take into account external factors in shaping perceptions, commitments, and preferences, Bean's model does. In respect of grades Tinto's model considers academic achievement to be an indicator of integration whereas Bean considers academic achievement as measured by grades to be an outcome variable resulting from socio-psychological processes. The reality is, surely, that it is a bit of both, a view that would seem to be supported by Cabrera.

He and his colleagues (Cabrera *et al.*, 1992) undertook an empirical study in a university in the United States to evaluate the two models. They decided that both theories were correct in so far as persistence was found to be the result of a complex set of interactions between personal and institutional factors. They considered Tinto's model to be more robust because the study confirmed 70 per cent of the model's hypotheses whereas only 40 per cent of Bean's were confirmed. However, they found that Bean's 'proposition of the role that factors external to the institution play on the college persistence process is far more complex and comprehensive than the one portrayed by the Student Integration Model'. They concluded that while there was some overlap between the two models they were complementary, and that the importance of the Student Attribution Model was that it highlighted the role of external factors.

In Britain the move to full-time higher education began in the 1960s when it was found that the attrition from part-time vocational and professional courses was very large (Crowther, 1959). Studies showed that attrition was due to many causes in which non-academic factors played an important role. This is likely to be the case in any system where study is prolonged.

Weidman (1989) has also described a model in which non-college reference groups (peers, employers, community organizations) are considered to be of considerable importance. An important feature of his model is that it considers that parents continue to have a socializing role even when their children are away from home.

In 1985 Pascarella proposed the general causal model in which growth in college is a function of the direct and indirect influence of the five variables. These were student background, pre-college traits; structural organizational characteristics of institutions; interaction with agents of socialization; institutional environment; quality of student effort, and learning and cognitive development. Subsequently, he and Terenzini applied this to Tinto's theory of withdrawal by taking into account the student's commitment to goals on the one hand, and on the other hand institutional commitment as the student moves through the freshman year. In this model the organizational climate is shaped by the characteristics which the students bring to college as well as to organizational features such as the department, size, selectivity and residence. These create the conditions for socialization on the campus. Taken together they influence the quality of effort.

Both Pascarella and Weidman acknowledge the hierarchical nature of the organization and its influence on student growth and development. However, there are several methodological problems in the analysis of data. Ethington (1997) gives several examples including the disaggregation of higher order variables to the individual level (i.e. institutional level variables to predict outcomes at the level of individuals.

In all these models the entry characteristics of the students are considered to be of considerable importance. The predispositions which students bring to the college experience may have a considerable bearing on their behaviour. In the American system, outside of professional courses, they may limit the perception that a student has of how to change from a dissatisfying situation to a more satisfying pattern of studies. For this reason considerable importance is attached to counselling.

In Britain where large numbers of students are now entering with non-traditional qualifications, problems may be created for universities as these students establish new identities and envisage the possibility of career change. If this is the case, much more attention will have to be paid to entering characteristics other than examination results than has been done in the past. It also highlights the importance of learning contracts if universities are to pursue their traditional aims in respect of what might be called 'high culture'.

Pascarella and Terenzini (1991), who have reviewed these models, admit that they have many similarities. They agree that sociological models pay less attention to the psycho-dynamics of the student experience, that is to the cognitive and emotional readiness for change: 'each of the two generic approaches to the study of change among college students has much to offer the other'. For which reason they argue that attention to student traits should be expanded beyond those relating to background characteristics and demographic factors.

From the perspective of this book it is important to be reminded of the fact that the focus is on the assessment of learning, and how institutional, departmental and course arrangements, peers and tutors impact on student learning within the cultural framework in which they function. In this respect the forthcoming study of Alverno College is of considerable importance because that college's curriculum is assessment-led (Mentkowski and associates, 2000). Its key features are described in Chapters 2 and 14. In relation to this particular section their causal analysis extends beyond college to graduation after five years. During college, change is measured during the first two years. In the full longitudinal study data werw obtained from an individual on each of four occasions. The Human Potential measures used included Sentence Completion Test based on Loevinger' theory of ego development; Measure of Intellectual Development based on Perry's theory of intellectual development (see Chapter 7); The Defining Issues Test as a measure of moral development (see Chapter 7); Critical Thinking Appraisal (see Watson and Glaser, Chapter 7); Test of Cognitive Development (see Piaget, Chapter 7); Test of Thematic Analysis intended to measure the kind of ability developed in liberal education, Picture story exercise to measure tendencies in habitual modes of thinking, and the Moral Judgement Interview (see Chapter 7). This data was also obtained from interviews and questionnaires. Performance data was obtained from alumnae who gave detailed accounts of how they performed in each of six specific situations (Behavioural Event Interview). These details have been given to show how evaluation of programmes requires a variety of measures if the complexity of the student learning experience is to be understood.

The Pascarella and Terenzini review

How College Affects Students (1991) is a very full and systematic analysis of the literature in which Pascarella and Terenzini attempt to establish the affects of college on students as measured by the changes they undergo in eight areas of human behaviour. These were (i) development of verbal, quantitative, and subject matter competence; (ii) cognitive skills and intellectual growth; (iii) identity, self concept, and self-esteem; (iv) relating to others and the external world; (v) attitudes and values; (vi) moral development; (vii) educational attainment; and (viii) career choice and development. They also evaluated the economic benefits of attending college, and the quality of life after college.

They analysed nearly 3000 studies related to the effects of the college experience that had been completed in the United States over a 20-year period. Their synthesis was based mainly on studies of traditional four-year college students in the age range 18 to 22 years, many of whom lived on campus.

Many of Pascarella and Terenzini's findings are consistent with two studies conducted by Bowen (1977), and Feldman and Newcomb (1969) as well as those from Mentkowski and associates (see above). They confirm, what is generally assumed by academics at least, that the college years are a time of change on a broad front. Once the effects of maturation are disentangled then:

> Students not only make statistically significant gains in factual knowledge and in a range of general skills; they also change on a broad array of value, attitudinal, psycho-social and moral dimensions. There is some modest tendency for change in intellectual skills to be larger in magnitude than in other areas, but the evidence is quite consistent in indicating that the changes coincident with the college years extend substantially beyond cognitive growth. Thus, the change that occurs during the college years does not appear to be concentrated in a few isolated areas. Rather, the research portrays the college student as changing in an integrated way, with change in any one area appearing to part of a mutually reinforcing network or pattern of change in other areas.

Pascarella and Terenzini have little to say about the role of assessment in student learning which is in contrast to Britain where much work has highlighted the role of assessment in directly determining strategies for learning (see Chapter 9). Thus, while it might be expected that students acquire specific knowledge, as is the case with the American studies, it is by no means clear that they will have developed their higher order thinking skills. Given the concern that students no longer bring to university skills in writing and speaking at a level appropriate for university study, the finding that American students develop a range of intellectual competences that can be related to the experience of college is important. This is because, 'the individual becomes a better learner'. By popular consent that is what societies want in tomorrow's world, individuals who can learn, for learning is the essence of adaptability. Pascarella and Terenzini argue that the effect of college on development cannot be explained by maturation or by differences between those who attend and those who do not attend college.

Consistent with other studies they found that the more students involve themselves in learning and instruction the greater the acquisition of content and cognitive development. There are also gains in tolerance, independence intellectual disposition, and reflective judgement. But if such involvement is to be promoted, Pascarella and Terenzini argue, tutors require an awareness of students' cognitive and developmental status so that they can devise learning experiences that begin where the students are at. This has considerable implications for the design of assessment as well as for the structure of courses. Braxton *et al.* (1996) in a study of first-time freshmen found that both academic and social integration were positively influenced when expectations for academic and career development were met. Social integration was positively influenced by expectations for opportunities for social development. However, decisions to remain in college are only indirectly affected by collegial atmosphere and academic and career development.

Pascarella *et al.* (1996) have examined the development of internal locus of attribution among first-year students in a limited study of two-year and four-year institutions not necessarily representative of US higher education as a whole. Nevertheless policy makers have a major interest in this research since one of the goals of higher education is that students should take responsibility for their learning. Locus of control may facilitate learning in new situations and, therefore, help a person to become more adaptable. As might be expected, a whole variety of influences assist the development of the internal locus of attribution. Pascarella *et al.* confirmed their 1991 proposition that the impact of college is the 'cumulative result of a set of inter-related experiences sustained over an extended period of time rather than the result of any specific experience'. They also found that freshman students in 'two year' institutions developed in the direction of internal attribution more than their opposite numbers in four-year institutions. One reason for this might be different kinds of teaching in the two-year colleges. Three teacher behaviours were identified as having a positive impact on attribution. These were teacher organization and preparation, teacher instructional skill and clarity, and teacher support (see Chapter 6). However, they conclude that no single experience will be an important determinant for all students. The impact of involvement on performance is complex as several studies show (e.g. Grayson, 1997). Thus, an institution which seeks to provide a liberal education should make provision for a variety of academic and non-academic experiences.

This was Newman's view. Thus, measures of the effect of higher education have to go beyond college experience questionnaires and tests to encompass such things as moral development as is the case with the Alverno study. In the British Isles there is no tradition of such measurements but if the effects of college are to be understood they will have to be made. The question is whether or not such testing should be the norm.

Astin's longitudinal studies

Like Pascarella and Terenzini's review Astin's studies often make difficult reading for someone unfamiliar with the American scene. Astin undertook two major longitudinal studies of students as they passed from entry to output. The commentary which follows is based on Astin (1997a). Taken together his investigations involved some 500,000 students and 1300 institutions. In the second study freshman data for the year 1985 were compared with output data for 1989–1900. The methodology used was similar to that of the first study (Astin, 1977). Some additional items in the environmental measures were included. In all there were 192 measures of the undergraduate environmental experience (e.g. type of university, large, small, independent, religious affiliation, curriculum structure, faculty, methods of teaching). An additional 57 items measured student involvement (e.g. place of residence, with faculty, with peers, major field of study); 142 variables described input characteristics (e.g., ACT, SAT scores, pre-tests on possible outcome measures, personal characteristics); and 85 measures of outcome (e.g. achievement, cognitive and affective development, beliefs and values).

Clearly it is beyond the scope of this text to give a fair summary of all the 82 analyses. Therefore, attention is drawn to those factors that seem to have a direct bearing on retention, and indirectly bear on the assessment of student learning. Astin's most important finding was:

> That the student's peer group is the single most potent-source of influence on growth and development during the undergraduate years, and in so far as the affective development of students are concerned students' values, beliefs, and aspirations tend to change in the direction of the dominant values, beliefs and aspirations of the peer group.

This finding has much to say to policy makers and academics who wish to 'condition' the curriculum to produce more graduates in this or that area. Science and technology in the UK are a case in point. It is also another challenge to those in the British Isles and elsewhere who are encouraging diversification within higher education institutions since, if Astin is correct then diversification may operate against the development of within-study peer groups that can mutually assist the journey through higher education.

Astin believes that the pedagogical problems facing public institutions of higher education in the United States arise from dilemmas they have when they try to serve multiple functions simultaneously. He argues that this can best be understood from the historical context in which American university education developed. The British 'college' was the proto-typical model. It had the primary commitment of educating undergraduates and generated a strong sense of community.

> This study has shown, once again, that this traditional model of undergraduate education leads to favourable educational results across a broad spectrum of cognitive and affective outcomes and in most areas of student satisfaction. Perhaps most important, however, is the finding that institutional structure, as such, is not a key ingredient; rather, it is the kinds of peer groups and faculty environments that tend to emerge under these different structures.

Attempts to reproduce colleges in the 1964 British universities have not been met with rapturous applause, but this may be because they were involved neither in the selection nor teaching of students which is what differentiated them from the Oxbridge colleges. Nevertheless, as Astin argues, there are examples of large institutions in the US trying to develop communities. At Ohio University a questionnaire to assess the level of involvement which freshmen have has been used with some success to identify those who are not involved and who may be at risk. A variety of strategies were used to create involvement. They led to a 10 per cent reduction in drop-outs (Williford and Moden, 1996). Many universities have taken freshman initiatives and there have been a series of international conferences on this topic.

It has to be remembered that Astin is referring to general education programmes. He makes no comments about major dominated programmes that were rare in his studies. However, it is difficult to believe that students in such programmes would not benefit from mixing with peers who work in other subject areas. It would seem that studies of student perceptions of involvement in institutions in the British Isles would be rewarding. They might even contradict Astin's findings. Astin (1997b) shows how comparison of actual and expected rates enables an institution to measure how it is performing in relation to its student input characteristics. Some may be performing above average and others below average. This is an important reminder that outcome measures by themselves have little to say about institutional performance. There is, as Carter and Heywood (1991) showed, a need to relate input to output and to understand the process that leads to the outcomes. This is why the Alverno model is so important. The students are required to develop abilities to a certain level. These are to all intent and purposes outcomes. However, as indicated previously, not only does the institution monitor the process by which they are achieved, it engages its students in the process through self-assessment. Moreover, its monitoring is extended to detailed studies of how its graduates use the education received in their daily lives and work (Mentkowski, Much and Giencke-Holl, 1983; Mentkowski and associates, 2000). In a collegial system of this kind student rating forms should be irrelevant.

In Astin's study, as might be expected, two-thirds of the students with high school grade averages of A- and above could expect to complete their course within four years. Those entering with high school average grade of C- or less had only a one in five chance of finishing in four years. However, this may be as much to do with the institution as it is with the student. Retention was found to be positively related to residential experience, involvement with peers and faculty, and the humanities orientation of the faculty. It was negatively affected by institution size, working full-time, working part-time off campus and commuting. If ever Newman's practices at the Catholic University of Dublin, as well as when he was a tutor at Oriel (Oxford) required vindication, Astin's study provides it. The study also demonstrates that 'time devoted to studying and homework, tutoring, cooperative learning, independent research projects, giving class presentations, taking essay exams, and having class papers critiqued by professors' was associated with favourable student outcomes. On the negative side, taking multiple-choice exams, watching television, working full-time, and commuting were among the factors that led to an increase in the drop-out rate. But his findings would not support the traditional mode of British examining by essays solely at the end of each academic year.

Non-completion (attrition, leakage and retention)
Science, maths and engineering

Astin's findings in respect of engineering are of particular interest because they have been reinforced by the results of an investigation by Seymour and Hewitt (1997).

Astin found that the climate characterizing the typical institution with a strong emphasis on engineering is not ideal for student learning and personal development. Irrespective of the leanings of an institution Seymour and Hewitt infer that at the departmental level science and maths students are equally disadvantaged in these respects.

Most American university undergraduate curriculum programmes follow a 'distributional' approach, 'in which general education requirements are satisfied by an approved list of courses organized into broad curricular groupings' (Astin, 1997a). Engineering, in contrast, is major dominated. It follows a four-year programme and its general format is similar to engineering programmes in Australia and the British Isles. American students may also follow focused studies in science and mathematics. A key difference between such programmes and those in Britain, as mentioned previously, is that students can easily change to another subject. Such a change represents a loss to the discipline but not to higher education. It is a 'leakage' from the discipline. Seymour and Hewitt's (1997) review of attrition and retention in science, mathematics, and engineering (SME) shows not only that leakage from these subjects is increasing but that there has been a continuing decline in enrolment in these subject areas. 'Between 1966 and 1989, freshman interest in mathematics fell by four fifths. The sharpest and most recent decline in enrolment occurred in engineering and computer science (from 12% in 1982 to 8.6% in 1988)'. Other studies document similar declines in enrolment for advanced science, maths, and engineering.

By far the most important problem, at least from the perspective of a department concerned, is that in Seymour and Hewitt's study between 40 and 60 per cent of the students with higher than average abilities had switched course within two years of taking their first college science or maths classes. This problem was not marginal since it affected the white male majority on most if not all campuses.

The most common reasons for switching arose from the students' response to a set of problems experienced by both switching and non-switching students alike which related to the structure of the educational experience and the culture of the discipline as reflected by the practice and attitudes of the faculty. Many teachers, it was reported, simply did not care about teaching.

Seymour and Hewitt describe a group of engineering and science students who were more pulled than pushed out of the system. They included able and multi-talented students who 'would have stayed had the teaching been more stimulated and the curricular more imaginative'. They were ambivalent about switching but were in the end pulled out by the poverty of the educational experience they received.

In contrast, there was a group who were pushed out rather than pulled. This group felt they were adequately prepared, and had wanted to study courses in this area because of personal interest. While these students would have preferred to study science and technology, poor teaching and the weeding out process pushed them out of these subject areas. These were the 'most angry, regretful, and frustrated' of all the students interviewed. At the same time there were also students whom Seymour and Hewitt interviewed for whom switching was appropriate.

At the heart of the issue is the culture of professionalism existing in SME. It creates particular notions of standards that must be met, and the system is designed to weed-out students who cannot immediately meet these standards. At the locus of the culture is the weed-out system. In these circumstances it is easy to blame everything for the leakage except the pedagogical methods employed by the faculty. Students may be blamed because they are inadequate, and cannot face the academic challenge promoted by these subjects; schools may be blamed for not sending forward their brightest students, and in any case, the problem is not serious because that is what we are here to do. Thus, the problem is rationalized and marginalized so that it is not seen to be of significance.

Seymour and Hewitt show quite clearly that ability is not the problem. Even so the problem can be rationalized again. Size of classes may be the cause, poor tutorial abilities of teaching assistants may be blamed, and others may be held responsible for the inadequacy of laboratory and computer facilities. But Seymour and Hewitt consider these to be non-problems and found no evidence in support of them. Also, they show that students reject faculty as role models. They find many faculty unapproachable or unavailable for discussion of either academic or career planning concerns.

The students also considered the curriculum to be over-packed and overloaded. Of particular concern to the focus of this book are: (1) those students who experienced conceptual difficulty, and who when this was not addressed, experienced a fall in confidence in learning leading to 'reduced class attendance, falling grades and despair'; (2) harsh competitive grading systems reduced the potential for collaborative learning strategies which many students view as critical to good understanding of the material, and to a deeper appreciation of concepts and their application (which reinforces Astin's point about the importance of the peer group); and (3) that the curve-grading systems used reflect 'disdain for the worth or potential of most under-classes'. They perceive that the system is designed to drive a high number of students away.

Adelman (1998), however, shows that credit requirements (as indicators of 'work load') in engineering are not much higher than in other fields. He agrees that the perception of overload is one of the major factors influencing students to leave engineering. Even if the overload factor is not true it may still be possible that pedagogy and curriculum encourage particular approaches to learning that are not conducive to understanding. Factors such as this will not be yielded by either the kind of survey completed by Adelman or the ethnographic approach adopted by Seymour and Hewitt. Both have value but in these circumstances the actual programmes need to be evaluated *in situ*.

It should be a matter of concern that the women who leave engineering courses possess higher grades than the men who leave. These women do so because of a higher degree of academic disatisfaction (Adelman, 1998). However, as Adelman points out, their original choice of major may have been less intrinsic than that of men. There is a lot more besides but that is not the province of this book.

A Canadian study of persistence in physics found that one of the differences between those who stayed and those who withdrew was the differing perceptions that the two groups had of skills in and knowledge of physics. Those who withdrew were characterized by low attendance and differences in view with faculty about the amount of study time required (Vazquez-Abad, Winer and Derome, 1997).

All these findings are consistent with Astin's on attrition. Seymour and Hewitt believe that it will be extremely difficult to make faculty accept that attrition is anything but a marginal issue, or to attend to curriculum reform in which these issues are central. 'Even to begin so fundamental a debate requires a willingness to explore the body of knowledge about how people learn that has largely been developed by faculty who are not members of SME departments'. Seymour and Hewitt would be even more depressed to know that the efforts of engineering educators who have faced up to these issues have been largely ignored by the profession (Heywood, 1995). It is to be hoped that the new curricular being developed in the engineering coalitions will solve these problems. A not dissimilar situation might be found in many departments in other countries.

Failure in German medical schools

In Germany admission to medical schools is regulated by law: 45 per cent of places are awarded on the basis of the secondary school leaving certificate (Abitur) and a Test for Medical Studies (TMS); 10 per cent are awarded on the basis of the TMS result alone; 20 per cent are awarded on the basis of the length of time the applicants had to wait for a place; 15 per cent are awarded on the basis of an interview conducted by faculty; and the remaining 10 per cent are awarded to special cases (e.g., hardship, foreigners). A study by Trost, Klieme and Nauels (1998) showed large differences between the groups in respect of performance in the First Medical examination. The highest pass rates (80%) were among the first group. Had the students been admitted at random only a 48 per cent pass rate would have been achieved. Pass rates of 49 per cent and 45 per cent respectively, were achieved by those admitted by interview, or on the basis of waiting time. A total of 28,000 students were involved in the study. The authors suggested that the interview, which was unstructured, might be improved.

Non-completion studies in Britain

Wastage, as it was originally called, has not been of great interest to British academics. As indicated previously, it has been treated rather like the faculty in Seymour and Hewitt's study as something that is marginal. This is illustrated by the fact that until 1998 there had been no major discussions of drop-out since 1971 when the spring issue of *Universities Quarterly* was devoted to the topic. Even then most of the concern was with the predictive relationship between entry qualifications and final outcome. Overall wastage rates of between 11 and 14 per cent were recorded, and, as in the United States, most of the withdrawal occurred in the first year of the programme. The rates varied as between the subjects, greater rates being recorded in engineering and technology sandwich courses. The relatively low rate was evidently a function of the highly selective enrolment to universities. As with the selective universities in the United States, there was a link between socio-economic status, enrolment and performance (Astin, 1997a; Opacic, 1994). The present picture seems to be very much the same. Similar differentials between the subjects were reported by McGivney (1996) (cited by Ozga and Sukhnandan, 1998). The majority of students seem to withdraw early in the programme. In Ozga's study they had done so by the end of January in their first year (Ozga and Sukhnandan, 1998; Yorke, 1998). Yorke (1998) was surprised by the fact that many of those who left transferred to other institutions; half of those who had withdrawn in his study re-entered higher education. Similar data were not available in 1971.

Now about half of all UK students are non-conventional in the sense of not having entered university direct from school with 'A' level examinations. This is particularly true of the 1992 universities who have contributed greatly to the widening of access to higher education. This has meant that many students have entered the system with non-traditional entry qualifications. In these circumstances it might be expected that the relationship between entry qualification and outcome might change. If it is assumed that in the past the students came from the top-end of the bell-shaped curve of academic achievement then as access broadens many universities will have to cope with a wider range of ability than they have in the past. Further, if it is assumed that the pedagogy (teaching and assessment) was matched to level of ability, then it might be expected that if institutions do not change their pedagogy, drop-out rates might increase. This would seem to be the case in the US. It is, therefore, important to establish if this is the case in the UK and elsewhere.

At the same time as access to the universities increased (partly by doubling the number of universities) policy makers encouraged universities to adopt semester structures similar to those in the United States as well as to design courses in modular form. Although the system is dominated by the major and double major, the modular system has made some programmes more flexible, in so far as student perceptions are concerned. At the same time, credit accumulation systems have been developed which enable transfer between and within institutions. Yorke (1998) suggests that students are using this new flexibility.

One of the consequences of these changes is that it is now much more difficult to measure drop-out, it is much more difficult to define, and movement between courses and institutions is more difficult to measure. Difficulties are also created for students who leave the system and return at a later date. Yorke *et al.* (1998) have pointed out that the definition used will depend on the person or organization who wants the data. It is, however, significant that the term non-completion is now used in preference to either wastage or drop out. The major reason for interest in non-completion is the 'apparent' cost to the system. Yorke puts it at £91 million or roughly 3 per cent of expenditure. He estimates the cost of withdrawal due to academic failure at £32 million. The data on which these estimates were based was obtained from one institute of higher education, three 1992 universities, and two traditional (red brick) universities. All these institutions were in the north-west of England and accounted for 7.5 per cent of the total full-time and cooperative student population.

The term 'apparent' cost was used because it is implied that withdrawal for whatever reason is a waste. However, it is now understood that there may be an element of value-added to a person's educational experience irrespective of withdrawal for whatever reason. Crosier and Woodrow (1997) point out that some of the reasons for non-completion may lie to some extent outside of the student (cited by Yorke, 1998). Some time spent in higher education does seem to lead to a gain in knowledge and skill, as the American studies show, and this must be to the advantage of the student and society (Blundell *et al.*, 1997 cited by Yorke)

Yorke draws a distinction between non-completion and withdrawal. 'The former subsumes both voluntary and involuntary causes, whereas the latter should subsume only voluntary causes'. A Canadian study makes another distinction between instit-ution-initiated withdrawal and student-initiated withdrawal. Poor performance leads the institution to seek withdrawal whereas such things as stress, family circumstances lead to student-initiated withdrawal (Johnson and Buck, 1995).

While the full programme non-completion rate has some advantages over other measures, in that it can answer questions about the proportion of students failing to qualify, it has several disadvantages. Important among them is the fact that it does not delineate the various causes of non-completion. An alternative definition is the proportion of study units in which a group of students does not pass assessment. That has the advantage, Yorke suggests, of eliminating most of the non-academic reasons for withdrawal. The problem is that some could contribute to failure.

If the academic reasons for failure are added to the proportion of third-class degrees awarded, it may be argued, as Seymour and Hewitt have for SME in the US that, academic departments generally in the UK need to reflect on their pedagogical approaches. In the UK standards are set against curved grading systems (see Chapter 10) and in England a third-class grade is really a statement to the effect that a student has an incomplete grasp of the subject (see Chapter 11). Given that students come from the higher end of the achieving spectrum this cannot be regarded as satisfactory. As Yorke reminds us, 'It is appropriate to recall that teaching is not necessarily followed by good learning.'

One response to the problem of withdrawal in Britain has been to suggest that entry qualifications should be increased. However, a study at the University of Lancaster concluded that this might not be the most appropriate way of reducing wastage (Johnes, 1990). In parallel with Yorke's project which was concerned with non-completion within the system, a detailed study of non-completion in a campus university was completed by Ozga and Sukhnandan (1998). They make a distinction between mature and conventional students. They found that the process of non-completion was quite different for the mature students: they withdraw primarily for external reasons. This is consistent with the concept of multiple causation put forward in the 1950s to account for the substantial losses from part-time further education (Crowther, 1959). Ozga and Sukhnandan found that mature students are more likely to complete in arts and social science courses and least likely to complete in science and mathematics. They suggest, in keeping with Seymour and Hewitt (1997) that 'it is possible that the assumptions of academic staff about the incompatibility in this group may have inhibited the effective use of strategies for their retention'. Knight (private communication) points out that many 18-year-olds drift into higher education and make little effort at choosing courses or institutions. As we saw, commitment is an important factor in the causal models discussed above.

In so far as the conventional non-completers were concerned they left because of lack of preparedness, and incompatibility. Compatibility is defined as the degree-of-match between the student's expectations of university life – both academic and social

– and the reality. Mature students who had strong levels of compatability had information about institutions and courses that was reliable and detailed. Their expectations were often fulfilled. In contrast, conventional students who found they were incompatible with university lacked information and had often made choices for reactive reasons (e.g. it had not been their first choice of institution, or they had had to take the subject which was going). This is consistent with Hewitt's finding some 20 years earlier that arts students showing a vocational interest tended to be more successful than those who did not (Hewitt, 1971). Yorke also found that conventional students, predominantly middle class, tend to be less enchanted than others with the choices they make.

Both reports conclude that there needs to be better advice at school level. They also suggest there is scope for institutions to make clear to students what it is they are offering. Ozga and Sukhnandan argue that the factors acting on non-completers almost predicted withdrawal. 'They were poorly prepared for entering HE, and their additional lack of focus on where and what they wanted to study combined to produce institutional incompatability'.

They also draw attention to weaknesses on the institutional side, and in particular to the lack of early monitoring and intervention by academic departments, although they regard a decision to leave as being positive if it is made within 20 weeks.

One of the problems preventing early attention to retention by departments was the reliance on assessment. Some withdrawals departed early and before assessment. Only one department in the campus survey recognized that academic and personal problems were inter-related, 'however, that department also expressed concern about "getting in too deep"'. This raises questions about how much tutors should know about their students and how they learn, as well as issues about the tutor's relationship with counselling and other services. Whereas such services are highly regarded in the US they are not in the UK other, perhaps, than in the Open University. Academics as well as students have little understanding of their functions. Such attitudes may well have to change as the proportion of adults in the system expands.

In contrast with North America

A study by Eppler and Harty (1997) considered the differences between traditional and non-traditional students in relation to achievement motivation and academic performance. They found that both groups rated themselves higher on learning goals (e.g. effort, persistence) than on performance goals (e.g. grades, mistakes). Older students who had taken a year or more away from college had a stronger commitment to learning than the younger students. The older students endorsed learning goals while the younger endorsed performance goals. The older students were more intrinsically motivated. The least successful students were low on both dimensions. In Howard and Henney's (1998) study non-traditional students of both genders were more likely to enter into classroom discussion than male (traditional) students.

More generally, the cultural and educational contexts in which the two systems function, differ considerably. Worldwide there are of course considerable similarities between professional courses, and there is considerable exchange among the research workers in these disciplines. In medical education there is a considerable exchange of information about pedagogy and assessment. Nevertheless there are some interesting points of comparison and there is no reason why the two systems should not learn from each other. However, as between the American and British systems there is one key difference. The latter has been dominated by a highly selective process in schools in which pupils begin to determine their careers as early as the age of 15. It is therefore, no surprise that students who are highly focused should tend to be more successful in their studies than those who are not. However, highly focused students do not always have the ability to succeed. Interest and motivation are not sufficient guarantors of success. To use Adelman's term the secondary school provides a curriculum momentum and as Marshall (1939) points out this comes early in the British system. In both the American and British studies there are recommendations that schools should do more to help their students. There is also an obligation on universities, for if students do not know that they don't know, then universities need to have some way of enabling students to find out. Adelman (1998) points out that this happens in every field. Universities may need to have a general foundation curricula designed so that the student can make such choices. In Britain the foundation year at Keele University was of such a kind but did not meet with favour because of its four-year duration. As the correlation between jobs and the curriculum studied weakens so the need for a broad approach will strengthen. Even within the professional subjects there is scope for radical change in the beginning semesters (Adelman, 1998). It is also of no mean interest to find that in the US attending more than one institution is not a drag on degree completion – for anyone (Adelman, 1998).

Another feature of the UK studies is the difficulty in plotting the paths of students. In the US where there is extensive data Adelman (1998) has undertaken the first national tracking study of students in any undergraduate discipline (engineering) and shown how it could be used with any discipline.

It is somewhat alarming to note that problems of lack of focus, the need for early warning systems and for counselling were all discussed in the 1960s in Britain. That they have still to receive general attention is some measure of how much and how far the attitudes of academics have to change. As the student body changes so these problems are likely to multiply if the American experience is anything to go by. As in America these studies highlight the significance of the institutional context in which withdrawal takes place, and it is possible to infer that student involvement needs to begin at once, for lack of involvement may well enhance feelings of incompatibility and insecurity.

Planning for discontinuity with traditional students

The transition from school to university may be as traumatic for some students as the transfer from primary to secondary school is for others. Some authorities think it is more so (Bey, 1961). Derricott (1985) argued that the discontinuity between primary (elementary) and secondary education ought to be planned. The same argument applies to the discontinuity between secondary and tertiary education as it applies to the transition from school or college to work. It is more easy to plan for the latter because work experience can be obtained during formal learning in one way or another. The curriculum can also include practices which allow for the development of key skills in the 'people' and 'personal' domains (Heywood, 1994). It is much less easy to create links between schools and college because of the large number of schools involved. Colleges can provide open days, they can interview applicants if numbers are small: however, all that glitters is not gold. They cannot demonstrate what the experience (formal and informal) of college will be like.

In these circumstances, it is all very well for universities to exhort the schools to better prepare their students without taking cognizance of the demands they make on students through their admission requirements. They are more likely to make an impact on prior learning through these requirements than they are by any other method. The situation is no different in the US (Barry, 1982; Wiggins, 1993). Eisner (1979) makes the point that students believe that more work in mathematics will lead to higher scores on the SAT; often they fail to enrol on courses that genuinely suit their interests and attitudes. Many schools have created specific courses to help students acquire good scores with these tests. And why shouldn't they follow this route when it is known that achievement in college (course taking) and performance on college entrance examinations is closely related (Alexander and Pallas, 1984; Noble and McNabb, 1989). In these circumstances the role of the American College Test (ACT), and Scholastic Aptitude Test (SAT) in selection must be questionable.

Answers to the questions about what and how students should learn require some knowledge of learning, and as indicated previously this is a matter which universities have often failed to attend. An important question which has to be answered is what information is likely to be of use in making a judgement about whether the talent (gifts) a student brings will be compatible with what the student seeks. In all these dimensions assessment in its several facets has a major role to play.

Admission requirements

Traditional students in the UK are required to pass a number of subjects at the Advanced level of the General Certificate of Education. The grade level achieved determines the number of points considered as a basis for university entry. Students apply through a central admissions process to university departments at the end of the year prior to admission in the following September. The application document has to be about student potential rather than student achievement. It indicates the grades they are expected to get. It also gives the grades they obtained in an examination at the age of 16. They are provisionally accepted on the basis of this information. If they are accepted they are told what grades they must obtain in order to be actually accepted. While this description is somewhat oversimplified it shows the importance of subject and grade. In Scotland while the situation may be similar for less able students, the more able will have accumulated their credits for university entrance in the penultimate year of their school studies. In the UK departments especially those in the sciences will generally require mathematics and a science subject related to the subject to be studied at university (e.g. physics for engineering). Languages will require the language followed to have been pursued at school except when they are not taught in most schools (e.g. Chinese and Russian). The position is less clear cut in the humanities and social studies. Some economists prefer their students not to have read economics at school. What matters in these circumstances is that the applicants are told what is expected of them. The higher the status of the institution the greater will be the demands. In Ireland the subjects tend to be less important; while there may be subject requirements it is the total number of points collected from public examinations that matters.

A large-scale study by the American College Testing Program (ACT) confirmed Wigdor and Garner's (1982) view that admission in the US is a complex process. McNabb (1990), its author, was surprised to find that in spite of the fact that institutions and their students spent large sums of money on standardized tests many continue to rely heavily on local placement tests. In his opinion they did not take full advantage of the potential offered by standardized tests. He also found that the majority of institutions had made changes in their placement practices. The most selective institutions made the least number of changes. These changes represented a high level of dissatisfaction with existing practices. This national survey included institutions that used the Scholastic Aptitude Test (SAT). There were a number of schools that used neither of these tests for placement.

School reports

In the UK schools' reports have always been treated with a degree of scepticism although Crum and Parikh (1983) found one university where variables like application, reliability and intelligence had a dominant role in determining degree performance. One way round this problem is for the universities to make use of Records of Achievement (see 'Profiles', Chapter 11). Higgins (1994) points out that the central admissions form asks for a lot of the information that would go into a record of achievement. A major problem is the opportunity-cost to admissions tutors of using such Records in the selection process. Higgins, however, was concerned that when students apply to university they have not completed their studies. Their real achievements should be measured after they have taken their examinations. He makes suggestions as to how the admissions process might be changed so that it is based on achievement rather than potential.

An American analysis supported the use of prediction models which used both ACT results and high school grades rather than ACT scores of high school grades alone (Ang and Noble, 1993; Noble, 1991). The high school grade information schedule asks information about courses taken or planned, grades obtained, and an interest inventory. The information is machine scorable.

It is interesting to note the experience in England in these respects. In the mid-1960s the Committee of Vice-Chancellors and Principals designed an equivalent to the SAT, called the Test of Academic Aptitude. It was hoped that it might be a better predictor than the 'A' level GCE, but this was not found to be the case (Choppin, 1973). It seems that this is because the 'A' level is in a subject that most students are going to learn at college. The additional knowledge which students have over their American counterparts gives college teachers different starting points at entry. Given the broader curriculum offered by American colleges, it is perhaps surprising that standardized tests of academic aptitude do not produce a correlation which is much better than high school GPA. Another surprising feature of the English correlation studies was that the General Studies 'A' level examination, the design of which had been greatly influenced by the Bloom *Taxonomy*, was found to be a relatively good predictor of academic performance in universities. Forrest (1991) suggested that in view of the changing intake to universities, a test such as the Test of Academic Aptitude which could be set to all applicants irrespective of background was to be preferred.

It should be noted that in the British context the question papers are retained by the students, even those that use objective items. This means that there is a considerable backwash on the system. Because the questions tend to follow cyclic patterns question spotting by both teachers and students alike becomes an art form. Therefore, the style of question determines both instruction and learning. If examinations call primarily for regurgitation of knowledge, then that is what the examiners will get. If, on the other hand, the questions search for problem solving and critical thinking skills then teaching and learning will focus on them.

Wiggins (1993) takes up some of these points in respect of the North American system. Few students, he says, are prepared for admission. This is undoubtedly true of state schools in England in respect of admissions to Oxbrige (i.e. high status universities). The public (fee paying) schools set out to prepare their students for the process, although they have the advantage that most of them are boarding. State schools have to answer the question why it is that that two or three public day schools do so well in the Oxbridge stakes. If Oxbridge is really concerned about the lack of interest by students in state schools then it will have to go out into these schools and show teachers what is wanted and actively help them prepare the students for these institutions.

Wiggins uses a freshman examination in European history to illustrate what is required in America. The questions have many similarities with 'A' level papers. He points out that they require rigorous and creative analysis. Because multiple-choice questions reward regurgitation they prevent students from acquiring the skills necessary for survival in their first year. He says few students have the skills to meet the expectations of assessors when they set questions like: 'What is the single invention the world would be better off without and why? Describe a risk and the impact it has had on your life. What does your room say about you?'

Wiggins also draws attention to an exemplar booklet published by the Carleton School District, Ottawa, which shows the students the scoring rubrics, analysis of the descriptors used, and their meaning. It also provides examples of student responses that have been marked and thoroughly analysed.

Just as industry wishes that university graduates were better prepared for work, and helps achieve this goal through work experience, there is no reason why universities should not help students prepare for university while they are at school. The preparation of booklets like those written by Carleton School District might prove to be a very salutary task for tutors.

Bridging the gap for non-traditional students

There has been a substantial increase in the number of non- traditional students amounting to as much as 50 per cent of the enrolment in some UK universities. Such students are normally over the age of 23 and are likely to have had experience of work as well as study for other qualifications. Some will have virtually no formal academic qualifications.

Some of the pre-1992 British universities and all of the 1992 universities had experience of dealing with reasonable numbers who had qualifications other than 'A' level in the general area of their study. In particular there were Ordinary (ONC/OND) and Higher National certificates and Diplomas in science and engineering subjects whose students had or were also working in industry. The Colleges of Advanced Technology accepted both 'A' Level and ONC students. It was found that students with a good ONC did better than those with two 'A' levels, and nearly as well as those with three (Heywood, 1971). A common interpretation of this fact was that while ONC students had the advantage of experience in industry together with a knowledge of engineering, they lacked the academic approach of 'A' level and some knowledge deficits in mathematics and physics. These colleges encouraged their faculty to make some compensation for this in the early stages of their programmes in order to bring the two groups into compatibility with each other.

More recently, with changes in the National Certificate and Diploma regulations, those studying in technician programmes in colleges of further education with two years full-time education in them have, providing they obtained good awards, been able to transfer to honours degree courses of two years duration in some universities (commonly known as 2+2 courses). Sharp and Culver (1996) describe one of these programmes. They had the same problems that their predecessors had of integrating the vocational into the academic. The requirements for the technician course in the feeder colleges were for a curriculum based on continuous assessment. This was in contrast to the university where the main method of assessment was formal written examinations set at the end of the academic year. They reported that the students found it difficult to perform at higher levels of intellectual functioning (i.e. analysis and synthesis). To try to remedy this defect the tutor introduced cooperative learning strategies with the aid of a colleague who had had experience with this type of tuition. Their paper reports that the first results were encouraging. McDowell (1995) has reported similar problems in other bridging courses in engineering.

At Napier University in Scotland, where they had substantial financial support, new materials were developed for the whole programme, and in particular two generic modules on 'effective learning', and 'information sources' were designed. A variety of assessment procedures were used, and the generic modules were assessed by port-folio. The formal subjects were assessed under examination conditions (Anderson and Percival, 1997).

Bridging the academic–vocational divide

From General National Vocational Qualifications (GNVQs) to applied 'A' levels

Having developed a national system of vocational qualifications (NVQs) (see Chapter 11 for a detailed description) the British government introduced General National Vocational Qualifications (GNVQs; in Scotland GSVQs) to bridge the academic-vocational divide. They 'should cover broad occupational areas, and offer opportunities to develop knowledge and understanding, and to gain appreciation of how to apply them at work' (NCVQ, 1991). The government intended that they could be used for university entry and an advanced GNVQ programme set at level 3 would correspond to an advanced level of the General Certificate Education programme. Specifically foundation level GNVQs would be equivalent to four General Certificate of Secondary Education Certificates (GCSE) awarded with grades between D and G; intermediate level GNVQs would correspond to four and five GCSEs awarded with grades A to C; and, advanced GNVQs correspond to two GCE 'A' levels (grades unspecified).

There is no direct subject equivalence. The advanced GNVQ is intended to be equivalent to two 'A' levels. Neither is there an equivalent grading system. Whereas there are five grades for 'A' level (A–E) the GNVQs are awarded at three levels: pass, merit and distinction.

The number of students in GNVQ schemes has expanded enormously and in 1996 it was reported that 30,000 would be seeking places in higher education. This, it was expected, would create problems for selectors since they would not be well versed in judging the potential of advanced GNVQ candidates more especially as they would have been assessed by non-traditional methods.

Unlike the syllabuses of the advanced level examinations there are only a few advanced GNVQs available in such areas as art and design, business, information technology, performing arts, entertainment business, manufacturing and science. UCAS, the organization which administers the admission of students to universities, is quick to note that they are not narrowly aligned but relate to broad areas of study (UCAS, 1996). In this respect there is some similarity with the focused curriculum in some American high schools.

UCAS characterizes GNVQs as providing general education in a vocational context and in this sense they seem to have communality with the American work keys programme described below. An advanced GNVQ is made up of 12 vocational units (eight mandatory and four optional), and three core skills of communication, application of number and information technology. The course is intended to be as challenging as a two 'A' level course. The core skills units are stated at five levels of increasing difficulty and students have to achieve level 3 in all three core skill areas.

Except where written tests are inappropriate tests are set for seven out of eight mandatory units; they are set and examined by external examiners. Worries have been expressed about the standards of these tests and UCAS reports that their 'rigour is being further tightened'. They are not differentiated, which is a further matter of concern. Differentiation rests with other assessment processes undertaken during the student's course (e.g. activities, projects, assignments). These are put together in a portfolio which 'is a weighty document containing a great deal of evidence'. Completion of the portfolio and the unit texts give the candidate an overall pass (see Chapter 12).

To obtain a merit or distinction the candidate has to produce high quality work (outcomes) and show particular strengths in the process skills of planning, information seeking and handling and evaluation. These bear on the student's capability 'to reflect upon a learning strategy, use and evaluate source materials effectively and continuously review his/her progress throughout the particular project'. The outcome assessment is based on the synthesis of knowledge presented, the skills and understanding shown and the use of concepts and knowledge in the programme area. A study by Coles (1998) of the differences and similarities between 'A' levels and the GNVQs suggested that from the perspective of users neither qualification achieved the range required. In respect of assessment he suggested that there needed to be a stronger emphasis on practical work and the design of questions that tested analysis and application. Knight, Helsby and Saunders (1998) argue that advanced GNVQs are hybrids. They are too educationally led to offer a vocational qualification, and too vocationally led to allow students to introduce students to critical academic engagement.

Work Keys: a development of SCANS in the US

SCANS is an acronym for the Secretary of the US Department of Labor's Commission on Achieving Necessary Skills (SCANS, 1992). Work Keys (1995) has been developed by the American College Testing Program (ACT, 1997) to be compatible with the SCANS assessments. It came into full use in schools and businesses during 1995 and details of the pilot studies are already available. Its purpose is to help measure the workplace skills identified by SCANS (Figure 5.1). It is, therefore, intimately related to the curriculum and not independent of it. Work Keys offers workplace assessments in reading for information, applied mathematics, listening and writing, teamwork, locating information, applied technology, motivation, observing, speaking and learning. These assessments are offered at one of five levels and because they measure competency they are criterion referenced. The idea is that jobs should be profiled so that the job profile can be compared with the individual's performance profile. It can, therefore, be used for selection or diagnosis at work. It is also intended that high schools use job profiling in consultation with employers to establish the levels of competency that students should have to obtain jobs.

The curriculum is tied to the requirements for job and career enhancement rather than for general education. It will value learning by doing (also valued in Britain at this level in vocational education) and applied instruction. Thus rather than using literature as the basis of writing students would be taught to write business letters, memorandums and reports. In general the SCANS committee would argue that those skills should be taught in the high school curriculum in addition to literature. A performance-based portfolio is provided for individuals so they can demonstrate their attainments at work (see Chapter 12). This is similar to the national records provided with NVQs (see Chapter 11).

WORKPLACE COMPETENCES: Effective workers can productively use:

Resources – They know how to allocate time, money, materials, space and staff.

Interpersonal skills – They can work in teams, teach others, serve customers, lead, negotiate and work well with people from culturally diverse backgrounds.

Information – They can acquire and evaluate data, organize and maintain files, interpret and communicate, and use computers to process information.

Systems – They understand social, organizational, and technological systems; they can monitor and correct performance; and they can design or improve systems.

Technology – They can select equipment and tools, apply technology to specific tasks and maintain and ' troubleshoot equipment.

FOUNDATION SKILLS – Competent workers in the high-performance workplace need:

Basic Skills – reading, writing, arithmetic and mathematics, speaking and listening.

Thinking Skills – the ability to learn, to reason, to think creatively, to make decisions, and to solve problems.

Personal Qualities – individual responsibility, self-esteem and self-management, sociability, and integrity.

Figure 5.1. The SCANS (Secretary's Commission on Achieving Necessary Skills)
Competencies and Foundation Skills for workplace know-how. Learning a Living:
A Blueprint for High Performance. US Department of Labor, Washington, DC
(1992).

The Work Keys assessment tests are each of one hour's duration. The results are sent to the individual, explain the scores obtained, and give detailed instructions on how that individual might improve his/her scores.

Other non-traditional students

Even with the alternative GNVQ system in the UK there will still be a number of students whose qualification and/or experience will promote difficulties for academically oriented departments. This will be true of any system of mass higher education. In some universities in Britain foundation courses in specific subject areas and other access courses are being run for such students. Even so teachers wished they knew more about these students before they started the course. In order to determine the knowledge of such students some tutors give them multiple-choice tests in which a number of the questions have been culled from 'A' level examination papers.

As American studies show (Forrest, 1982) the earlier the orientation and the more continuing guidance that non-traditional students receive the more likely they are to survive and prosper. While this is an axiom that applies to any group that is non-traditional within a specific context this particular group is likely to be of above average achievement although many of its members may have had difficulty with written examinations in the past. They may, also, like traditional students, experience psychological difficulties with both teaching and assessment in the early period of their programmes.

Success or failure depends on the student's ability to bridge successfully the gap between school or work and university study. Students still have to negotiate their programmes, and assessment and teaching may have a considerable influence on their learning. It is insufficient to only pay attention to the initial stages of programmes, as the study of pathology of assessment in the next chapter shows.

Conclusions

The principal purposes of this chapter were to demonstrate the complexity of the educational experience, and to argue that outcome measures by themselves have little to say about institutional performance unless they are related to the input characteristics of the students. These have to take into account prior experience both in the academic and work spheres, and institutions have to bridge the gap to formal academic study for the many non-conventional students who are entering higher education in increasing numbers.

Among the factors that influence the experience of higher education are the ways in which students involve themselves and integrate into institutional life. At the micro-level of institutional life, the classroom and the department, this can be enhanced or impeded by faculty in their personal response to students, assessment practices, and the organization and presentation of their courses; in short, the management of learning. As the next four chapters will demonstrate, learning and teaching are complex activities.

Chapter 6

Temperament
Teaching and Testing

Summary and Introduction

This chapter follows on from Chapter 5, in which it was established that most attrition occurs in the first year of programmes. Pathological factors influencing dispositions toward learning and testing are examined; they may or may not be of a minor kind. Most students are likely to experience some stress, which may be at a low level or at a high level. Indeed some stress would be appear to be essential for learning. A few students experience severe psychological difficulty.

The transition from school or work is a major discontinuity in life. To some extent it can be planned. There is a danger that the onus to prepare students is put on schools, but there is much that can be done in institutions of higher education to alleviate stress. Whereas it may be thought that stress results from examinations, this is not always the case. The climate in which students learn can be as much a cause of stress as anything else. This climate and its attendant changes stem from the classroom, through the department or school, to the institution. The studies reported here support the views put forward by Astin (1997a) and Malleson (1965) that the role model for institutions that wish to alleviate stress and promote positive behaviour toward learning is the traditional college. How to bring about the support and involvement which will assure success is the major problem facing universities.

The climate of the classroom is greatly influenced by the structure and pedagogy of the course, and much of what happens in the classroom can contribute to anxiety and stress. However, the studies reported testify to the enormous variability in human nature, and to the fact that individuals respond in different ways to what they perceive is happening to them.

In this chapter the concern is primarily with aspects of temperament as they relate to the assessment hurdles erected by the institution. In this respect it is necessary to distinguish between course anxiety and test anxiety. Research on test anxiety reveals that while it is a weak predictor of academic performance there is, it seems, a relation between type of test item set and anxiety (high/ low) type. In some circumstances students perform better under stress. Different temperament types also appear to be better served by different types of assessment and teaching situations. Clinical evaluations of students in difficulty also lead to the view that courses are best designed to include a variety of assessment techniques. Clinicians warn that variety is not a panacea of success, and may bring with it different kinds of stress. Too much variety in some courses may lead to confusion and be inhibitive of learning.

Just as research on test anxiety reveals the need for multiple- strategy approaches to assessment, so too does research on teaching and course structure lead to the view that variety is required in teaching. However, variety should not be undertaken for its own sake, whether it is of assessment or of teaching. It should be implemented in response to the objectives the course is designed to obtain. This may necessitate the redesign of the course.

At the level of the institution, procedures and course structures may also create anxiety, particularly in highly specialized systems where change is made difficult. Institutions should aim to create what in some medical schools is called 'well-being'. They should act to prevent rather than cure.

The transition to college and student difficulties

Transition to higher education comes for many at a time when the adolescent is changing into adulthood. It is a time for changing identities and identity conflict may be a source of study difficulty. It is a time when, to quote Malleson (1965) people 'experiment with identities themselves ... they are experimental changes of personality which feel very total at the time'. It is a period of turbulence and, as Malleson says, it requires both the understanding and the help of the university and society at large to define the role of the student.

It has been a common understanding among tutors that many students not only find it difficult to manage their finances in the first semester but that they also have difficulty in managing their time. It is distressing to find that Thomson and Falchikov (1998) find this still to be the case, and that so little seems to have been done about it.

When Malleson wrote he argued, as has Astin (1997a), that the residential university might help students to adapt to their role because its circumscribed community enabled a person to more easily understand the role of a student. 'It is indeed one of the disturbing aspects of modern university life that society at large is rather tepid toward the student image and, in consequence, the student himself is trying to avoid the appellation.'

> The student must be able to experiment with the identity of an educated, cultured adult. Adolescents get identities through other people: they emulate, they model themselves, they put-off and on the identities of others and, in particular, the adults around them. This I believe, is the peculiar importance of the teacher, particularly the university teacher. If he is to do his job really well, he has somehow got to make his personality available for his students to try it on for themselves.

Is this perspective any different 20 years on? It is certainly consistent with Chickering's (1969) comments on the experience of higher education in the US. For many tutors the 'making of their personalities available to their students' would be a tremendously difficult task. It may involve some in changing their perceptions of the role tutors should have. Apart from the implications of teaching implicit in this view is the idea that not only should students be able to experiment with different curricula but with different tutors as well.

Other North American studies come to similar conclusions to those from the UK (Whitman, Spendlove and Clark, 1984). Following the Yerkes-Dodson Law (1904), they suggest that individuals in low and high stress learn the least, and those under moderate stress learn the most. This will be examined in more detail in the sections on test anxiety and temperament.

Course anxiety

To begin with the first year, it is clear from the attrition/retention studies that academic pressures on students in this period are a threat. This seems to be as true of non-English-speaking countries as it is of Australia, the US and the UK. An investigation at the Free University of Brussels concluded that its findings were consistent with previous studies in the English-speaking world. Mid-term perform-ance was strongly related to examination grades, academic self-esteem, expectations and efficacy of study, in that order of importance (Van Overwalle, 1989).

Thomson and Falchikov (1998) report high levels of stress among first-year students at Napier University in Scotland. They suggest that it might be due to the perceptions that the students have of overload due to assessment. They suggest also that it might be due to a mismatch between a student's desire to study at a deep level (see Chapter 9) and the overload that may cause them to study superficially.

Boyle and Combs (1971) found that the complexity of the material to be learned, together with fear of failure, combine to produce stresses for which coping strategies are required. They point out that bright students from high school no longer stand out in university, and this may produce a stressful challenge. A decrease in self-esteem might lead to depression and anxiety. One American study which supported earlier and similar findings showed that self-concept variables strongly moderate personality and learning style dimensions (Geisler-Brenstein, Schmack and Hetherington, 1996). In a study of 675 second-year students at University College, Cardiff, it was found that both academic and life stress were negatively correlated with self-esteem. Those with high self-esteem were less stressed than those with low self-esteem (Abouserie, 1994).

Silver (1968) reported that some law students who were not ranked at the top of the class stopped trying because their best efforts went unrewarded. Another study suggested that students who show insights in class participation may stop particip-ating if they find their performance in examinations is only average (Turow, 1977). Stress from the pressure of examination grades can also lead to poor study habits.

Stevens (1973) argued that stress arising from the pressures in law school may cause undesirable social effects. It may lead to a decrease in helping others, individual differences among students may not be recognized, and there might be an increase in aggression. Cobb (1976) considered that students require social support in order to mediate stress, otherwise these social effects may indirectly diminish a student's performance.

At least two studies in the United States report that the psycho- social state of first-year students at the end of their year in medical school is worse than when they began (Von Almen *et al.*, 1991; Parkeson, Broadhead and Tse, 1990). The invest-igation at Duke University showed that at the end of the year the health status of women was worse than that for men. Parkeson *et al.* reported that the most marked change was in respect of depressive symptoms. They also found that strong ties were positively related to better health and life satisfaction. Medical schools and the study of medicine are, of course, somewhat exceptional when compared with conventional studies in university.

Loneliness is another factor that might contribute to stress. At the universities of Haifa and Jerusalem males were found to be significantly higher in loneliness than females, but that females were significantly higher in depression than males (Wiseman, Guttfreund and Lurie, 1995). Fisher (1994) suggested that homesickness might be a salient factor.

These findings lend support to the thinking of Astin (1997a) and Malleson (1965) on the importance of the collegiate life and involvement. Studies of the kind undertaken by Riding and Wright (1995) at the University of Birmingham into cognitive style, personal characteristics and harmony in student flats among male and females could be of considerable importance in understanding how universities can provide for the socialization and involvement of students. The problems of achieving this with students in urban non-residential universities are likely to be considerable, as one American study shows (Schweitzer, 1996). Over half the respondents were unaware of the services available to them.

One problem experienced by law students in some American colleges that might heighten stress is that many received little feedback about their progress until after the first semester examinations. In an effort to alleviate the lack of feedback students may resort to 'bogus feedback', and so alleviate anxiety. Those who do well in ungraded writing seminars may 'believe' they will rank high in class (Ellinwood, Mayerson and Paul, 1983). There is no reason to suppose that this does not happen in other subjects: experience would suggest that it does. Feedback which helps a person improve their performance is likely to enhance learning; in this sense, computerized objective tests used for formative assessment have the advantage of providing instant feedback (Zakrzewski and Bull, 1998).

Pascarella and Terenzini (1991) have drawn attention to the attributional dimension of motivation. If students attribute their problems to external causes, and do no not perceive themselves to be in control of the situation their problems may increase. Therefore, there is a need to have their perceived control and self-efficacy restored. Pascarella and Terenzini report that attributional retraining has been shown to enhance achievement and cite Perry and Penner (1989; 1990) to this effect.

It is now fairly well understood that computers create anxiety for some students. This is sometimes linked to attitudes towards computers. Kernan and Howard (1990) found that the two should be treated as separate constructs. Fortunately, the predictive validity of the computer anxiety scale was found to be low.

It is clear from the above that course anxiety is a complex phenomenon. It is also clear that much can be done to alleviate the problem.

Focus: the short- and long-term goals of students and achievement

Several studies were reported in Chapter 5 which suggested that if students lack focus this might put them at risk. Focus and motivation would seem to be related. In an investigation of the dynamics of success and failure among students of the University of Birmingham, Wankowski (1969; 1973) related Eysenck's measure of neuroticism to the long- and short-term goals which students had. He asked the students for three types of information, in response to open-ended requests. These were,

1. Short-range goals: name your vocational objectives, including plans for using your degree qualification.

2. Reasons for entering university: state your two most important reasons for coming to university.

3. Long-range goals: state your most strongly anticipated goals within the next ten years.

He found that male high achievers with clear goals tended toward stability, as did female high achievers with less clear goals. On the introversion/extraversion dimension, however, he also found that male high achievers with less clear goals tended toward introversion and the low achievers with less clear goals toward extraversion. He was led to the view that goal orientation might be associated with personality dimensions. Success is, therefore, a function of having definite goals, made up one's own mind to go to university, an interest in studies, and little difficulty with study. Wankowski felt that much of the 'problem of wastage is largely the problem of teaching'.

Using the Omnibus Personality Inventory, Elton and Rose (1966) found a significant difference between engineering students on the dimension of intellectual disposition. Strangely, an absence of high intellectual interests was found among the persisters. These results led them to suggest that the faculty might consider a second experimental programme with the objective of developing new avenues of professional competence for the 25 per cent who withdraw. In another report they argued that student-leaving is a result of maladjustment and directed hostility, which is consistent with recent findings of Seymour and Hewitt (1997).

Following on from Becker, Greer and Hughes (1968) study of student life which had shown that students develop different perspectives to their work as a function of their perceptions of grading, Milton *et al.* (1986) began their ten year study to assess student attitudes and beliefs about grades. Like Wankowski, the parameters were goal-oriented. In this case it was hypothesized that within colleges there were two groups of students who could be defined as learning- and grade-oriented. The former would view the classroom as a place in which the information gained was valuable both personally and professionally; the latter would think of college as a place that graded and tested them and had to be suffered as a necessary evil.

An instrument was devised which would produce data against a fourfold typology of student orientation. These were:

1. A group of students with both high learning and high grade orientations (HighLO/High GO).

2. A group of students with high learning but low grade orientations (High LO/Low GO).

3. A group of students with low learning but high grade orientations (Low LO/High GO).

4. A group of students with low learning and low grade orientations (Low LO/Low GO).

It was administered to many college and university students along with the Alpert and Haber Anxiety Scale, the Brown and Holtzman Study Habit Inventory, the Sixteen Personality Factor Questionnaire, the Levenson IPC Scales, and the Myers-Briggs Type Indicator.

Of these groups, the Low LO/Low GO were the most difficult to identify. They were found to be high in tension, frustration and introversion, but reported levels in the middle range of test anxiety and average skills. The students whom college teachers would be likely to consider ideal were in the High LO/Low GO group. Capable of abstract reasoning, they showed self-motivation, inner- directedness and interest in intellectual matters. They acknowledged responsibility for their own actions in determining success and failure, and employed the most effective study methods. Anxiety facilitates their performance. They are in contrast to the High LO/High GO students, who had the highest level of debilitating test anxiety and lowest scores on abstract reasoning. They were rather extraverted with a tough-minded approach to ideas and situations. Finally, the Low LO/High GO are distinguished by their personality traits, which included a strong desire to do the right thing and to act in conventional ways. They reported the lowest levels of facilitating test anxiety, and showed a consistent pattern of low scores on study habits and academic attitude dimensions.

Although Milton and his colleagues found that they could distinguish students in all four categories, some features of their analysis are surprising. Taken as composite groups, high-learning, and grade- oriented students had similar perceptions of many of the purposes of grades. Two areas where they differed were those concerned with cheating and dropping classes. Grade-oriented students are likely to cheat and drop courses if they think that they are going to get poor grades. This lack of difference between the groups puzzled the investigators and led them to suggest that the patterns measured by their instrument represented the different approaches which students adopt to help them in their learning in classroom situations. High GO students, they argued:

> find themselves in an uncertain world – the world of higher education – and look to external supports to evaluate how well or poorly they are doing. They are uncertain young people, and powerful others, such as parents, teachers and future employers, as well as public symbols such as grades, all provide a structure within which these students can at least find some comfort and possibly some satisfaction.

> We feel that a student may be grade oriented not because he or she necessarily wants to be, but because such an orientation is a plausible and situationally effective way of dealing with the traditional classroom environment as well as with early post college endeavours. In many instances an instructor's classroom policies and procedures make such an orientation seem both logical and reasonable for the student.

It follows, they argued, that this group of students should have teachers who are not grade-oriented but emphasize and look for learning. They need not only to be given help with study skills, but to search out answers to the question, 'Why study?' which will take them beyond 'getting a job' to the meaning that education has for them. Nowadays, such teachers would be described as those who promote 'deep learning'.

A weakness of the Milton study is that it does not relate the student profiles to performance. We might predict, in keeping with previous studies of motivation, that the correlations between groups and performance will be relatively low except for the Low LO/Low GO group which, it seems, is the most problematic.

As long ago as 1961 Christian Bey had suggested that students could be distinguished by their dispositions to academic life, of which he identified three – the academic, the intellectual and the social. Academics worked hard to obtain good records; intellectuals strove to broaden their understanding and increase their power of reflection, while socials wanted, among other things, to be respected, liked and admired or loved by people. In Britain, Taylor (Gibbs *et al.*, 1984) investigated student orientations at Surrey University, and concluded that there were four main types. She called them vocational, academic, personal and social. The difference between the US and UK typologies might be expected, for in Britain all courses are, as we have seen, to some extent vocational or professional. She was led as a result of her interviews to suggest that the first three types could each be divided into two sub-categories defined by interest. Intrinsic interest categorized a student who is interested in the course for its own sake, whereas extrinsic interest characterized a student who was pursuing the course as a means to an end. In Taylor's classification the intrinsically academically oriented person follows intellectual interests, whereas the extrinsically and academically oriented one is concerned with academic progress and grades. An intrinsic student with a personal orientation is concerned with broadening or self- improvement, whereas the extrinsically motivated person in this category would look for proof of capability.

These studies with their different orientations toward college life provide explanations for student behaviour which teachers often dismiss as low motivation or, for that matter, low ability. An understanding of these orientations is of considerable importance if teachers are to improve the overall effectiveness of their courses as well as the advice they give students. However, such studies do not account for the wide variety of situations that affect students daily, some of which substantially deflect them from their studies. While these orientations may represent dominant types, I have observed that persons who, from a relatively young age, have persisted with intellectual activities can, during their college career, suddenly find the social life so rewarding that it completely disrupts their studies. The severe conflict of goals that occurs is not necessarily recognized immediately by them, as they rationalize their model of normality to justify their conflicting circumstances.

In the preceding sections the tendency has been to look at extremes from the perspective of the teacher who has to help students. It has not meant to imply that learning is best done under 'no-stress' conditions. Students, and indeed people in general, need to be stretched if they are to go beyond where they are (Dember, 1965), for which reason the tasks which they are set need to force them to make the small jump which is necessary for them to learn. Learning is an 'energetic' exercise which involves stress, tension and anxiety.

Adult learning

As has been shown, the many more mature students entering university are also likely to be affected by course organization (Ozga and Sukhnandan, 1998). Indeed, if as is the case with short courses, the course is not seen to be achieving their goals, frustration may set in to the detriment of assessment (FitzGibbon and Heywood, 1986). Goal achievement for them is likely to rank high in their needs and it is not surprising that Taylor found Open University students could be not classified along the extrinsic/intrinsic dimension described above.

Lam (1978) was led to distinguish between three types of anxiety among a small sample of adults attending professional courses in education. These related to course structure, the inter-personal process, and the evaluation outcomes. They are not at odds with factors influencing many young students in their first year. Lam wrote:

> Emergent factors for reduced anxiety about evaluation outcomes include food, reading materials, classmate sociability, occupation, and satisfaction with the instructors. The importance of formal feedback about learners' performance in the course in relation to reduced anxiety about evaluative endurance in the second period of the learning process, and its disappearance at the last period of the learning process, seem to suggest that once adults are assured of their ability to perform well, their self-confidence is reestablished. It was also found that this did not require continued encouragement from the instructor in the last critical stage of learning. On the other hand, the perceived understanding of the course content through assigned reading materials, and the perceived acceptance by fellow learners were vital in reducing anxiety about evaluative outcomes. In line with the previous observation, this seems to suggest that the sources of adult self-confidence in performance had shifted from the formal assessment to their own perceived abilities and rapport with classmates.

The whole process indicates the need for clarity of objectives, and this applies where a large amount of work is required over a long period of time. Objectives that are perceived to be realistic will ease tension and enhance learning. These findings indicate that once adults are assured of their ability to perform well they become confident, and this surely applies to young students. They also indicate the importance of viewing coursework, not as an adjunct in assessment, but as part of the total assessment-instruction process (i.e. multiple-strategy assessment). More generally any assessment, of whatever age group, cannot be valid unless the students know their goals and specified objectives and outcomes.

Student difficulties: the psychologically disturbed

The medical evidence suggests that the majority of students overcome the difficulties of transition fairly readily and reasonably quickly. It is worth remembering that most of us find the first stages of a new job difficult. Many students have study problems in this period, and it is for this reason that some tutors have adapted records of achievement for student and tutor evaluation of personal and intellectual development. There is, however, a group of students which, in any intake, will be seriously psychologically disturbed. Malleson considers that these psychological impediments have their heaviest effect during the second half of the first academic year. He goes on to say that 'this is not when we see them'. Neither is he surprised by this because at this stage neither the student nor his/her teachers may be aware of the extent to which he or she is experiencing difficulties with their studies.

Linke (cited by Malleson, 1965) argues that it is important to distinguish between study difficulties and examination difficulties, even though the same student experiences both. Study difficulty may arise when the student sees himself or herself as an inefficient worker.

Student health physicians have identified two kinds of study difficulty that they have termed primary and secondary. This framework is supported by much of the evidence from the US that has been outlined above (Whitman, Spendlove and Clark, 1984). Four types of primary study difficulty have been identified. They are:

1. Obsessional slowing with ritual. The student never gets started on his/her studying while making enormous preparations.

2. Poor study habits with general disorganization. The student has a more hysterical personality. Work is never organized efficiently.

3. Retention and recall difficulties. The student is a hard worker who is never able to retain the material he/she has studied.

4. Product difficulties. The student is afraid of being criticized and this prevents him/her from writing essays, preparing these, etc.

Malleson thought tutors might recognize these syndromes during the second year of study. In these cases the student's work is interfered with directly, whereas work is only interfered with incidentally in secondary study difficulty. While the latter may be due to a neurotic condition, it is just as likely to be due to some normal stress that preoccupies the student for the time being. Mental energies are redirected away from study in this condition.

In regard to primary study difficulty Malleson points out that patterns of secondary hostility can grow up between an academic tutor and the student. He writes:

> University teachers do not warm to the 'poor' student in the same way they do to the 'good' one. The student with psychological studying difficulty, being perhaps more than ever in need of support from staff, feels that they treat him coldly; indeed

he may even feel that they are 'gunning' for him. He reacts defensively, and an antagonism can quickly develop. Effecting a rapprochement in this situation is one of the most useful jobs a student health physician can do.

In Malleson's view, and those of student physicians in general, primary study difficulties are most appropriately treated by counselling and psychotherapy.

Obtaining knowledge from students: personal profiles

In these circumstances what knowledge of students, beyond that of their abilities, should tutors have, and what should their relationship with student physicians be? At the very least, tutors should have a basic knowledge of the factors that cause both examination and study difficulty. On the one hand they require a much greater knowledge of the psychological make-up of their students, and on the other they may require training in supportive conversational and therapeutic skills. Should personal development profiles be expected of students, and can they be made of value to both students and their teachers? There is a need to examine how personal development profiles can contribute to this understanding of needs as well as the easier disclosure by students of their difficulties (see Chapter 11 for further discussion).

Other problems following the first year

While the importance of the first year's contribution to retention should not be understated, it should be remembered, as Malleson makes clear above, that study difficulties can be observed in later years. Abouserie (1994), in the study reported earlier, found among second-year students that examination and examination results were the highest causes of stress among students, followed by too much to do and the amount to learn respectively.

There may be a problem of commitment in the second year. In the case of medical students the pressures to study for long hours and do well in examinations may, in those courses where there is no patient contact, cause them to reconsider their commitment to become doctors. Of peculiar difficulty to medical students in their second year is hyperchondriasis, which is a state where the students may come to believe they catch every disease they study (Bojar, 1971). It would not be surprising to find this happening more generally among students. The second year may, after the stress of the first, be considered to be a time of relaxation.

The third year brings students back to the issue of identity. In the case of medicine, depending on the programme, it may be the beginning of the application of theory to practice. Gainsbauer and Mizner (1980) draw attention to that most intense of experiences, when students come into contact with dying and death.

There can, of course, also be difficulties with examinations and assessment in every year of every course, and it is to this dimension we now turn.

Examination difficulties

Apart from the specific problem of test anxiety which is dealt with in more detail in the next section, clinicians have identified a number of syndromes relating to examinations. According to Malleson (1965), about 10 per cent of students in the UK seek the help of student medical services because of difficulties with examinations. He identified the three syndromes shown in Figure 6.1. These can be easily related to the types identified by Janis (1982a; 1982b cited by Whitman, Spendlove and Clark, 1984). First, there are some students who are hyper-vigilant. They become excessively alert to stressful situations, and this results in panic. A student who becomes hyper- vigilant might not have the ability to integrate ideas in any meaningful way. During the examination, the student rushes through the paper in order to rid himself/herself of the stressful situation. This 'premature closure' diminishes the student's problem solving capabilities.

One of the interesting problems that the physician faces is that of delay. Does the physician advise the student to take the examination at a later date or not? Such evidence as there is suggests that where poor students are concerned they may not be helped by a delay. It has also been suggested that students who fail, regardless of intellectual aptitude, become hostile as a result.

Another pioneer of British student health, Ryle, listed three types of students who get themselves into difficulty (Ryle and Lungi, 1968):

(1) Psychiatrically disturbed, academically adequate students with good performance test scores and high N (neuroticism) scores on the Eysenck Personality Inventory.

(2) Psychiatrically disturbed, academically failing students who tend to do well on performance test scores except for a stress/gain measure which is significantly low.

(3) Psychiatrically well, academically failing students who tend to do badly on performance tests but show high stress gain; they tend to be stable extraverts.

Group (1) students appear to be disorganized by stress, while Group (3) students need to be put under pressure in order to make use of their capacities to the full. The former require security and treatment. They might benefit from a tutorial approach that, if tutors were able to recognize the two types, might create problems of organization, and promote a not inconsiderable challenge to teachers.

Ryle (1969) who was one of the first to draw attention to the effect of the examining system on students, said that any alternative system is likely to produce its own crop of casualties and its own varieties of stress. The solution, he said:

> seems to be to introduce a far greater flexibility and variety into the methods of testing used, so that individuals handicapped under one set of conditions have the opportunity to show their powers in a different testing situation. One cannot make an individual selection of students simply in terms of those who will succeed in one particular form of examination: each university must therefore endeavour to provide for students of widely differing temperaments the opportunity to give the best possible account of themselves. In practice, this could be achieved by relying upon a range of assessments for each subject being examined. Some weight could be given to coursework, without necessarily going as far as the American system of course credits. Formal examinations during and at the end of the course could

include project work, dissertation and extended essays to a greater extent, so that memory and speed would be less crucial to success than they are in the present standard 3-hour feats of memory, endurance, and (to be generous) synthetic thinking ability. However, even the fairest method of assessment will still produce stress, because students have a human desire to do well and have a human fear of failure.

Many of these things have happened, but not necessarily coherently. When the research on test anxiety and personality is examined it, like the medical evidence, supports the concept of multiple-strategy assessment.

Test anxiety

Investigations of test anxiety are difficult to carry out. Although there have been one or two attempts to study the conduct of undergraduates during a test, the majority of studies have relied on self- report inventories. Such items are often of the form:

While I may (or may not) be nervous before taking an exam, once I start, I seem to forget to be nervous	I always forget	I am always nervous during an exam
When I am poorly prepared for an exam or test, I get to be upset, and do less well than even my restricted knowledge should allow	This never happens to me	This practically always happens to me
The more important the examination, the less well I seem to do	Always	Never

These items are taken from Alpert and Haber's (1960) inventory. The idea behind such inventories is to distinguish between students who have a low test and those who have high test anxiety. Does one group perform better in examinations than another? Can their performance be related to temperament?

One study made of students during a test required them to respond to questions immediately after the test paper had been read for the first time, halfway through the test, and about ten minutes before completion. The purpose was to assess their 'internal dialogues' from ratings that they gave to a checklist of 18 positive and 19 negative thoughts. Another scale was used to rate their subjective states, i.e. totally calm to anxious and panicked.

The results were consistent with other studies. The low test anxiety students had more positive than negative thoughts than the high test anxiety ones. It was also shown that the 'dialogues' became more negative as the level of anxiety increased (Galassi *et al.*, 1981). In this experiment the low test anxiety students achieved higher test grades and experienced fewer bodily sensations which could be associated with arousal. They also predicted that they would have a successful performance, and felt that if the test is fair they would do well. Because of these feelings they were able to concentrate on the task at hand.

Physiological responses to test anxiety have been investigated many times (Hollandsworth *et al.*, 1979; Holroyd and Appel, 1980). One interesting finding which relates to the above-mentioned study was that the students with low test anxiety did

1. *Pre-examination Strain*

Here it is only necessary to note the occurrence of two different presenting types: those that are over-working and getting overtly anxious and hyper-excitable, and those that are heavy and torpid, who cannot get down to study and who feel numbed and discouraged. For these examination cases, in contra-distinction to the cases of primary study difficulty, drug treatment and strong supportive therapy over the critical period of the examination are of the greatest value. The time factors, let alone the pressures of anxiety, forbid any thorough psychotherapeutic approach.

2. *Examination Panic*

These are the cases of students who start their papers, but get increasingly anxious or exhausted and finally leave the examination room. Sometimes they actually faint or have nose-bleeds, sometimes they are overcome by headache or by migraine, but for most, it is just an increasing and finally overwhelming feeling of nervousness, tension and despair, with an incapacity to remember things they previously knew. The great majority of these students have already suffered from a long period of mounting pre-examination strain with anxiety, though as a rule have not come for treatment. Since one sees these cases very much at the last moment (they are often hustled over to the student health centre), there is not usually a great deal one can do. A few, however, do respond to very firm surrogative handling - not to say bullying. Giving a cup of tea and two methyl pentonyl capsules, or even intravenous methedrine, then accompanying them back to the examination room, or obtaining permission for them to carry on with invigilation in the student health centre itself, is sometimes successful. Sometimes it is not.

3. *True Examination Phobia*

This is comparatively rare but interesting condition. The student is often an efficient studier, and basically a healthy chap, measured by ordinary social and personal standard, but has an intense irrational fear of examinations of a kind that can only be called phobic; it compares truly to the way that people have phobias about heights, cats or spiders. Sometimes these poor people are so terrified by the examination that they cannot get up the steps of the examination hall but turn and flee as they come within sight of the building.

Figure 6.1 Malleson's descriptions of three types of examination difficulty.
(From Malleson 1965)

not respond to low levels of physiological arousal. They were moderately to highly aroused during testing but this, they said, facilitated their performance. Spielberger (1966), whose studies are among the most often reported, found that although high anxiety had no effect on the performance of low-ability students, it tended to facilitate the performance of the very brightest students in the middle of the range.

From the counselling perspective these findings are of some interest. They suggest that rather than train anxious types to relax they should persuade them to redirect the internal energies which they use up in test anxiety in directions which would help them facilitate their performance. This implies that the counsellors should explore with such students the problems which they might have in learning.

We should not condemn counselling exercises that encourage relaxation or, for that matter, discourage teachers from demonstrating them to classes. Teachers simply have to recognize that it is a matter of choice as to whether the exercises are used or not. They could try to demonstrate the value of imagery through its use as an introduction at the beginning of seminars and/ or lectures. Some students will laugh; others will take it seriously. It has proved a very successful learning aid in schools (Heywood, 1996). If it is done near to exam time it might be very helpful, as might a demonstration of the clenched fist technique (Stanton, 1988). Many universities, through their student services, provide information about the medical nature of anxiety (e.g. through distribution of pamphlets of the American Psychiatric Association), as well as approaches to the relief of stress during study and testing (e.g. The Open University in Scotland; McDonald and Hogg, undated).

Students should note that teachers are increasingly coming under stress (Heames and Cox, 1997) and that shared activities might be helpful to both.

An attempt at stress management in a medical school taught the students in six one-and-a-half-hour sessions over three weeks self- relaxation skills, schedule planning, priority setting, leisure-time planning, and cognitive modification techniques. In comparison with a control group, the experimental group showed improvement on a variety of measures which included knowledge about stress, self- support inventory scores (assessing stressing symptoms and life style), personal ratings of stressful situations, and their daily activity schedule (Kelly, 1982). (Techniques for managing the stress of engineering students have also been suggested by Pinsky and Wiegel (1983) of Iowa State University).

It seems that the type of items used in tests (examinations), as well as the skills they purport to evaluate, relate to anxiety. Spielberger (1966), for example, also found that high-anxiety students obtained superior test scores on a learning recall test when relatively few errors of recall were possible. In contrast, low-anxiety subjects obtained superior test scores when relatively more errors in recall were possible. Among his other findings were that low-anxiety students performed better than high-anxiety ones. Four times as many high- anxiety students failed as those of low anxiety. Perhaps the most important finding from the point of view of learning was that in learning concepts (see Chapter 9) high-anxiety/high-intelligence students perform better than low-anxiety/high-intelligence ones. At the same time, high-anxiety/low-intelligence students performed not so well than low-anxiety/low-ability subjects.

The performance of high test-anxiety students shows just how difficult the problem of test structure is. Early results from the Test Anxiety Inventory showed that this group of students performs best when it is not threatened with evaluation and faced with a difficult or challenging task.

At first sight, it might be assumed that assessment of a project would be an excellent substitute for a test for this group of students. It should stimulate interest and at the same time provide a challenge. It might also remove the threat from the situation. Unfortunately, in other studies it has been shown that this type of student does badly on essay and short-answer questions, whereas they do well on multiple- choice ones. This suggests that they might have difficulty with projects, an inference that is supported by the fact that the students from whom these data were obtained did badly in a take-home examination. The explanation offered by the investigators for this performance was based on an information-processing model of cognitive activity. In this model information is encoded, stored, organized and retrieved as required. A test demands the retrieval of information, and if a student's knowledge is inadequate because of problems in the encoding and retrieval of information, then he or she will not be able to perform well in an examination. The students in this study reported problems in learning material throughout the course, difficulties in picking out points in reading assignments, and generally in encoding information at a superficial level (Benjamin *et al.*, 1981). That this might be the case with regard to project work is indirectly supported by work on projects in engineering reported in Chapter 12.

Without this level of understanding the subject there can be no interest, and if there was interest it may well have been deflated by the difficulty level of the task. The initial task for a counsellor assisting students in this situation would be to try to establish if there was both interest and aptitude on which further understanding could be developed. It may be that training in study skills could help. Hidden within the findings of this study is the idea that tests should be designed to focus on study skills. For example, comprehension tests could be designed to focus on the essential points in an article (see Chapters 11 and 12). Other questions could be designed to elucidate concepts, the understanding of which is so often an impediment to learning.

Barger (1982) gave increased information to students about the questions likely to be set. In one format used in his classes in the University of Nebraska, a previous test was issued with the information that the same content would be tested, but by different questions. Another format gave the students the opportunity to be tested in the same course during two consecutive sessions. The findings suggested that while increased information reduced anxiety, it did not necessarily improve test perform-ance. In Britain essay question spotting by students can have disastrous consequences if there is no specific advice. Szafran (1981) reported that test anxiety was reduced among sociology students at the University of Nebraska when several days before the test they were given as a study guide a pool of questions from which the actual test was to be taken. Prior notice questions and open book examinations may reduce anxiety for some students (see note at the end of the chapter for a discussion of these techniques). As Sambell and McDowell (1998) have shown, the hidden curriculum of assessment is profound. How students react to different modes of assessment is a

1. Concerns are relevant to the situation and appropriate actions are taken	Worry about the assessment to be given by the assessors and have fears of a negative assessment
2. Focuses on the problem in hand	Focus on the self
3. Task-oriented	Task-avoidant
4. Believe they are actors who have to respond to the situation in which they find themselves	Believe they are observers who respond to stable personal dispositions
5. Have behavioural, problem-solving cognitions	Have static cognitions
6. Are active in nature	Are inactive and their behaviour is constrained
7. Believe that they are able to perform the actions necessary to achieve the desired consequences	Do not believe that they are self-efficacious and in consequence do not believe they can perform the actions necessary to achieve the desired consequences
8. Have cognitions which they can vary from situation to situation	Have cognitions which are global, stereotyped and restricted in range
9. Direct their physiological arousal as an energy with which to meet the demands of the test	Feel physiological arousal as distress with which they become preoccupied
10. Use imagery – i.e., mentally rehearse problem-solving strategies	Use visual imagery to view themselves from the perspective of an assessor who is evaluating them negatively

Figure 6.2 Some characteristics of low and high test anxiety persons.
(From Wine, 1982)

function of their motivation and orientation. As an example they report the response of two students to a multiple-choice test. One saw it as threatening while the other used it for guidance and feedback. Clearly assessors can help students by the guidance they given.

The relative importance attached by students to different examinations and their effects on anxiety were investigated among medical students taking examinations in medical psychology and physiology at the University of Barcelona. It was found that the different levels of anxiety induced by these examinations were related to the importance attached to the examination, and this was negatively correlated with the importance attributed to chance in marking (Pablo *et al.*, 1990).

Teachers and counsellors are often in contact with students whom they think are anxious. One assumption that they may make is that high- and low-test anxiety students are simply two ends of a continuum. It seems they are not. Wine (1982), who analysed many studies of test anxiety, showed that the two groups differed from each other qualitatively. Some of the dimensions that characterize the two groups are shown in Figure 6.2.

Wine was also among a number of authorities to point out that the assumption made in earlier studies that test anxiety was simply a state of emotional arousal was without foundation. As we have seen, the cognitions are involved, and without their involvement it would not be possible to train for a redirection of energy; all that would be possible would be training in relaxation. It is clear from her evaluations that students should be able to be helped to redirect their energies. Briefly, she concluded that the person with high test anxiety was likely to respond to evaluative testing conditions with ruminative self-worry. During examinations such persons oscillate between worrying about their worries and the task in hand. She called this the direction attention hypothesis, which she believed to be closely related to the dimension of worry–emotionality proposed by Morris and Liebert (1969). Wine concluded from all the evidence that:

1. Highly test-anxious individuals tend to be generally self-preoccupied but negatively so. When asked to describe themselves with pencil and paper measures they do so in terms of self-devaluation.

2. When examinees are evaluated during their tasks more non-relevant thoughts are reported by those examinees with high anxiety than those with low.

3. High test anxiety individuals are more likely to attribute   responsibility to themselves for task failure and to set themselves low levels of aspiration when the test performance does not differ.

Marton, Hounsell and Entwistle (1984) postulated that learners either follow a deep or surface approach to learning. Marton reported that what mattered in the experimental situation he used with students was their experience of the situation. If they felt threatened and anxious they adopted a surface approach, whereas if they were relaxed and interested and not anxious they adopted a deep approach to the task (see Chapter 9). Of course, some students may be just 'apathetic', and still others may adopt a strategic approach to meeting course requirements (Kneale, 1997). Interest and the promotion of interest through the test task may, therefore, have considerable implications for the level of test anxiety induced (see also Thomson and Falchikov, 1998).

It is found that females score more highly on measures of test anxiety than males, although the correlations with Grade-Point- Average are relatively small (Christenson, 1979). Just to add to the complexity, Grade-Point-Average has been found to be significantly negatively correlated with scores on the test anxiety instruments mentioned above, and this relates also to course grades and aptitude tests.

At Oxford and Cambridge women have, in general, received lower degree classifications than males. One reason for this might be that they record significantly higher levels of anxiety than males, and that this is specifically related to examination and grading. Short-term anxiety and examination anxiety levels increased nearer the examination (Martin, 1997).

While test anxiety is only a weak predictor of academic performance, it has been found that desensitization from anxiety, coupled with training in study and learning skills, can improve academic performance (see below). Tooth, Tonge and McManus (1989) found that while pre-clinical medical students suffered increases in stress and anxiety, anxiety levels were not of themselves the cause of poor performance. They attributed this to deficiencies in study and learning skills. Research on coping skills has not produced definitive results, although one study suggested that defence mechanisms may have a debilitating effect in that while they may reduce anxiety they may also distort the situation by diverting the student's attention away from the task at hand (Gur and Sackheim, 1979).

American studies indicate that intelligence and motivation are the most important factors in test performance, but motivation is a complex concept. It is a reminder that some students, particularly high-achieving ones, like competition. There is some evidence to suggest that test anxiety may have most influence on students in the middle range of ability. Taking all this research together, what attitudes should the teacher take?

There are, it seems, specific things which can be done with tests. Because we shall always be faced with complex groups of students the least we can do is to ensure limited variety in the test procedures that students take. This applies generally to curricular strategies. For example, at the University of Newcastle in Australia it was decided that, rather than adopt medical or psychological treatment for students who were unable to cope, curricular strategies, assessment procedures, marking, feedback and timing should be changed. This had the effect of increasing student satisfaction toward the course (Feletti and Neame, 1981).

A significant minority of final-year students at the University of Keele found their examinations to cause moderate to high levels of stress. Most of the students in this investigation argued that the terminal examination should be replaced by a variety of assessments distributed across the final year (Sloboda, 1990) which is in keeping with earlier findings of Ryle (1969).

An Australian study showed that in medical examinations student levels of anxiety are not stable and predictable from one examination to another, which implies that examination anxiety is not necessarily a consistent response to a specific and recurring situation (Kidson and Hornblow, 1982). It also confirms the view that training (counselling) may be possible. Therefore the lesson overall would seem to be as significant for the counselling role as it is for the course designer. The problem of coursework and its assessment and anxiety due to course structure are considered again in later sections of this chapter.

Nevo and Sfez (1985) designed a questionnaire which will help test designers to take into account examinees' feelings and attitudes towards tests. The Examinees' Feedback Questionnaire was used with a national examination for university entrance in Israel, which consisted of five multiple-choice tests (general knowledge, figural reasoning, mathematical reasoning, analytical thinking, and English). The questionnaire was completed immediately after the examination. The results, while not bias free, led to changes in the administration of examinations. One effect of the evaluation questionnaire was to make examinees feel that someone cares. Such questionnaires can reduce post-examination stress.

Given the limitations of psychological instruments, it is not surprising that other approaches to temperament should reveal other dimensions. A good example of this is the work of Furneaux (1962), who investigated introversion/extraversion and neuroticism among students of engineering in Britain.

Temperament and performance

In the seminal study by Furneaux (1962) referred to in Chapter 2, measures were also made of introversion/extraversion and neuroticism among his small sample of high achieving mechanical engineering students. He sought to answer the question: Were those who were tense, excitable and highly strung likely to perform better than those who were phlegmatic, relaxed and apparently well-adjusted? Or, put another way: Does the level of neuroticism influence performance? It might be predicted that extraverts would not do so well as introverts for, apart from anything else, introverts tend to be bookish and academic studies have as their goal the development of bookish traits. Introverts work hard to be reliable and accurate, but in the extreme they take so much time at the task that they might do badly in examinations. In contrast, extraverts might do an examination quickly, but this is likely to be at the expense of reliability.

Furneaux categorized the students into four groups: stable-extraverts, neurotic-extraverts, stable-introverts and neurotic-introverts. The group most likely to fail university examinations was found to be the stable-extraverts followed by (but at some distance numerically) the neurotic-extraverts. In this particular study the neurotic-introverts did best.

Another simple test was administered to these students to measure intellectual speed, and it was found that among the stable-extraverts those who were slowest tended to obtain low examination marks. In most American studies of test anxiety a negative relationship has been found with intelligence, but it has been suggested that this could have been due to the particular tests used, since under the pressure of time their stress-inducing effects might contaminate the outcomes.

Furneaux explained the performance of the students in his sample in terms of the Yerkes-Dodson principle, which was derived from studies of the behaviour of rats. It was shown that rats who were hungry would make their way through a maze to find food more quickly than when they were replete. However, it was also found that if the drive that the rats exhibited reached too high a level, performance would decline. There is an optimal drive level for each task to be performed. Above this, performance falls off. The Yerkes-Dodson principle states that the optimal drive level is high for simple tasks but is reduced as the complexity of the task is increased. This means that high drive can soon go over the optimum level for complex tasks.

Given that people who easily enter into states of high drive are likely to obtain high examination scores then, Furneaux argued, it is this group which is likely to obtain high examination scores. Similarly, persons who have an extraverted disposition but who at the same time have a low drive level will do badly in examinations. If these tendencies are related to the intellectual qualities of the examinees then an introvert with high drive will be able to compensate for relatively poor intellectual qualities whereas, in contrast, good intellectual qualities may compensate for extroversion and low drive.

Furneaux found that the more neurotic students did badly in the engineering drawing paper. Those who were stable did better. This, he argued, was because the task was so complex that optimum drive occurred at a low level. He found that the most common cause of failure was poor-quality drawing, which was of a kind that might be due to disturbing influences. Discussion with the examiner led him to the view that supra-optimal drive might have occurred, because there was some evidence of excessive sweating, lack of coordination, and faulty judgement.

There are lessons for teachers in this study. These are, that teachers should be clear that the key objectives for a course are sought and that the examination is designed to obtain those objectives. Moreover, those objectives should take into account the temperament of the students. Furneaux showed that when the examination in engineering drawing changed, so did performance – for the better. The grade that had depended on the quality of the drawing presented was changed so as to respond to assessment of the ability to interpret and convey information using graphical methods. It is likely (although we are not told) that the students were more interested in this than they were in perfectionist drawing. Moreover, the skill performance required would correspond more to the skill requirements of the written examination. It was also observed that the students in the less stable groups improved their performance.

Another study relates to what psychologists call Type A personalities. Type A persons are extremely competitive and achievement oriented. They are prone to heart attacks. They have a sense of time urgency and find it difficult to relax. They are dismissive of incompetence. Although outwardly self-confident, they may be troubled with doubt. Type A personalities are subject to one kind of stress, but there are also those who are characterized by lack of self-confidence, anxiety and a tendency to be overloaded with responsibility.

In this study Kagan and Fasan (1988) also found that lack of self-confidence was positively related to examination scores. They suggested that this may be explained by motivation (which would be in keeping with the Yerkes-Dodson Principle) or study skills. A person who feels overloaded may not be able to apply him/herself to study, whereas those lacking in self-confidence may have found some extra motivation with which to apply themselves. This is consistent with the view that some stress may enhance performance.

A key finding was that the relationships between stress and academic performance could be attributed to variables other than academic aptitude. However, the correlations between preferred class climate and achievement were strongly related to aptitude. For example, classes in which there was little or no interaction were preferred by those with a high verbal ability. Perhaps, suggest Kagan and Fasan, they believed that social interaction would mitigate the rigour of the course.

In summation, anxious and overburdened students preferred highly structured teacher-centred courses. The relationship between this and Furneaux's study is the attention this study pays to classroom climate. It is not simply a matter, as Kagan and Fasan (1988) suggest, of making more effort to generate more discussion through challenging questions which require abstract and divergent thinking, but of planning courses so that variety is a function of the objectives to be achieved.

There is more to it than this, and Kagan and Fasan's point should not be dismissed lightly, because such instruction is needed; yet many teachers feel incompetent to lead such discussions (Nunn, 1996). Why should they be, when many students do not value discussion? Fassinger (1995) suggests that the problem has been looked at from the wrong angle because the approach has been to explore the teacher's role in interaction, rather than the climate of the classroom to which individual students and groups contribute. As a result of a study of the interactions in class between students and male and female teachers, she came to the conclusion that the teacher's interpersonal style was not directly related to class participation. Rather, the climate stemmed from course design. Thus class activities which create positive emotional climates are likely to foster interaction.

Changes of culture (and this example is a change of culture because the majority of students either don't participate in discussions or feel that discussions are not worthwhile) require confidence to be developed in the new approach. Thus Fassinger suggests that semesters should begin with seminars in which students are facilitated to help each other to develop confidence. Teachers could also ask students to list behaviours that build or diminish confidence. Small group discussions would enable students to develop empathy with each other. In this way, insecurities may be overcome.

Teachers may allow positive contributions in class to affect grades positively, and they can arrange the room so that it can facilitate instruction. Group assignments or partnerships may bring about a positive emotional climate in the classroom, although as Freeman and Sharp (1999) have shown, the selection of persons to fill the groups may be more difficult than Fassinger supposes.

These studies show that teachers need to have skill in the planning of courses that take classroom climate into account as well as skill in the performance of the strategies most likely to achieve the objectives. There is a need also to encourage students to respond for students are equally wary of change.

Discussion

Stress and anxiety

It is clear that stress is a complicated phenomenon. Most of us require some stress to cause us to learn. Stress may function extrinsically or intrinsically. It seems we are better motivated if we are driven intrinsically. The drive to do well in an examination may arise from an intrinsic achievement motive that is independent or partly independent of the subject content. Some persons who function with low levels of anxiety do not perform as well as some with high levels as, for example, the history students in Kagan and Fasan's (1988) study. In sum, individuals vary in their response to stress. Given this to be the case, it could be argued that institutions need not have any regard for the problem. Indeed the British approach to wastage, as is evident in the Dearing Report (1997) is sanguine on the matter, to the point that it is hardly raised because, compared with other countries, the system is highly efficient, with relatively small attrition rates.

Institutional behaviour

Course loading

There is evidence to suggest that the achievement of some students may be diminished because of the perceptions they have of the climate in which they are learning. For example, while there may be a group of students who perceive themselves to be overloaded, those who do not complain may nevertheless be overloaded in such a way that it dictates the learning strategies they use. It is for this reason that loading (e.g. amount of assessment, tuition, expected homework) is an important factor in the design of courses. Thus the institution can do things which can improve the learning for all students, both at the level of course structure and the implementation of instruction.

Course structure

In Britain there has been a move to adopt semesters and modular patterns of courses, similar to that in the United States. This move has taken place without any attempt to evaluate the merits of the one-year three-term system in which most of the courses ran throughout the year. This was accompanied by the assessment of course work during the year, and terminal examinations at the end of the year. The semester system was adapted around the three-term system. Instead of running from September to Christmas and January to May the semester begins in October and runs through December, the Christmas holiday and for a few weeks more, during which time examinations are taken. The next semester begins and often students receive no feedback about their results until much later. Anxiety may be caused by lack of feedback.

If the experience of the introduction of coursework assessment in the 1960s and 1970s is anything to go by, the introduction of modular systems may increase the pressures on students unless this is anticipated and organization-wide planning undertaken for its prevention.

Semester systems in which examinations are set at the end of each semester will also redistribute the pressures on both staff and students. It is difficult to predict how this will affect the psychological dispositions of students but, given the immediacy of examinations at the end of the first semester, the effects which Malleson noted will emerge earlier, and may, as in the past, not be detected until it is too late.

Ozga and Sukhnandan (1998) pointed out that students who left before the first 22 weeks were over were more likely to try to return in one way or another than those who left after that period. This brings us back to the purposes of the 'weeding out process'. Is it intended to be ruthless and negative, or is it intended to be constructive and allow students to sort themselves out? The curriculum response to such questions would be profound, but it comes up against the culture that binds so much of our behaviour. The British system is subject major dominated and specialist. A positive approach to 'cooling out' would demand a broad curriculum in the first year which is not yet 'plausible' in the English context. Yet the Dearing Committee envisaged that there would be continuing change in higher education. If the research on anxiety is taken into account it would seem to indicate a phase of general education before any specialist study is begun.

Modules and assessment

As indicated above, modular structures redistribute stress for both students and teachers. In a single module system, the teacher in Britain has been expected to complete a course in 15 weeks which traditionally would have been completed in 30 weeks. This necessitates substantial changes in teaching and the requirements for assessment can introduce rigidities and reduce the flexibility required for multiple strategy assessment and instruction. It may also reduce the time for the development of skill in reflective thinking.

Coursework

The medical evidence confirms the importance that other investigators have attached to the first year. It follows a major discontinuity in the young adolescent's development and may be as important as the early years of a child's life to that development. In the past, it has been widely held that all that is necessary is the provision of a few lectures on note taking and study habits. The accumulated evidence suggests that much more is required. In this context coursework assessment is probably more important in the first year than in later years, and particularly for below average students. If such students do not understand what their tutors are trying to achieve at this stage, then some may never really acquire higher order thinking skills or deep levels of understanding. Coursework should help them perceive and develop new skills and, in particular, the capacity for reflective thought. It should also help students from falling behind. The fact that most attrition occurs in the first year reinforces the need for diagnostic coursework. It may require new approaches to course design; it may also require non-traditional approaches to assessment and learning (e.g. in the development of the capacity for reflection, see Chapter 14), and these may require the participation of the student's peers.

Taken together, these may require teachers to 'do' somewhat less than they anticipate. To put it more constructively, they may have to redesign their courses from scratch, and this will involve them in the scrutiny of their aims and objectives in the light of what is known about learning and assessment.

Study courses

Study courses are frequently recommended and there are many reports of such programmes in secondary schools and tertiary education.

Study courses in high school and transition

Hadwin and Winne (1996) draw attention to work by Matt, Pechersky and Cervantes (1991), which shows that those study strategies which are used by college students differ considerably from those used in high school. This might account for some of the difficulties that such students have during the freshman year.

Study skills programmes

One solution to these problems has been the development of study skills programmes (e.g. Ramsden and Entwistle, 1981; Zeller and Wells, 1990). Tait and Entwistle (1996) have recently described a new project in which a revised version of the Approaches to Study Inventory has been used in conjunction with a computer based package to help both staff and students improve study skills. In America, a Learning Disabilities Questionnaire has been developed which, it is thought, might screen students at intake. The items dealt with such things as word pronunciation, comprehending mathematical problems, formulating summaries, spelling, slow reading rate, finishing timed-tests and note taking (Glenn *et al.*, 1997).

Hadwin and Winne (1996), in a rather depressing study, have reviewed empirical investigations of the value of such courses. They wanted to identify learning tactics that had been empirically demonstrated to be effective. They reviewed 566 articles on the topic, of which only 52 were found to meet the criteria they had established for evaluation. Even then, only 16 fully met their criteria.

One of the reasons for this limited choice was their definition of study strategy. This term refers to occasions when students define their own short-term (local) goals and overall (global) goals for studying and select and coordinate alternative study habits they expect will be helpful in achieving those goals. When students additionally monitor their studying and adapt tactics as they observe the contribution each makes to learning, they are 'self-regulating' (Winne, 1995).

The aim of study strategy workshops is to help students become self-regulating. Therefore they have to learn the primary tactics of deep processing, and acquire a collection of individual tactics from which they can learn to make strategic choices. Students should not be taught rigid tasks, but how to adapt. They found some empirical support for concept mapping, self-questioning, and monitoring time spent studying. Their general conclusion is that students should not be taught discrete tactics which are dissociated from normal courses. They should be equipped to learn in a variety of contexts, and for this they need to be taught about local goals and alternative ways of achieving them. If such training is blended into their normal courses they will learn to develop a range of adaptive strategies. They need to be genuinely involved in self-regulation, framing goals, selecting tactics, and adapting tactics. Finally, Hadwin and Winne point out the need for students to have feedback from their peers and tutors about the effectiveness of their tactics.

Thomson and Falchikov (1998) argue that generic skill training courses might help some students better manage their time in terms of its value to their approach to studying. They, along with many others recognize that these recommendations have profound implications for the design of courses, assessment and instruction, as well as for the training of teachers.

Conclusion

The studies reported here support the views of Astin (1997a) and Malleson (1965), who pointed out the importance of a collegiate climate in providing the social support which students need if they are to become involved which, in Astin's study is an important key to success. They fully justify Newman's assertions about the value of collegiate life, made some 150 years ago. How to bring this about is the major challenge facing large and often commuter based urban universities.

At the University of California Los Angeles, where a 'well-being' committee was established to involve students in a whole range of activities designed to enhance social and emotional well-being in order to prevent emotional impairment, prevention is considered to be better than the cure (Coombs and Virshup, 1994; Passnau and Stoessel, 1994).

'Well-being' for its faculty and students should be a major goal of higher education institutions. More than anything else it is likely to ensure value-added quality. To achieve well-being teachers will have to have much more understanding of learning and cognitive and personal development than they have had in the past. The following three chapters indicate what that understanding should be. The first (Chapter 7) considers cognitive development.

Notes on open-book and prior-notice examinations

Open-book examinations

One method that has been suggested that might reduce stress by reducing the amount of factual data to be recalled is to allow the candidates to bring their books into the examination. It has also been suggested that students are less prone to cheating. Michaels and Kieran (1973) summarized the results of literature evaluation as follows:

- No change, or slight increase in achievement resulted when open-book examinations are administered
- Students liked open-book examinations better. The possible reason is that they were less anxious.
- Better study preparation resulted when open-book examinations were used.
- Different abilities were tested in the open-book examination. Students were not tested on memory only but on reasoning.

- Slight increase in validity, variance, and reliability values were found in open-book examinations over closed-book set examinations.

In their own study of high school students they found some evidence to suggest that open-book settings could create an environment in which there was an optimal level of stress. In the mathematics open-book examination that they set they found evidence that the open-book examination could increase achievement as measured by test scores in areas such as knowledge and comprehension.

Some science and mathematics examinations include table and formulae and so avoid recall which, if it is at fault, causes an unnecessarily wrong answer. Gibbs, Habeshaw and Habeshaw (1986) have reported instances where students have access to computers during their one-day final examinations. There is great scope for computer access during examinations and it may be a means of setting challenging problems. Examination designers may have to rethink the structures of such tests and be prepared to move away from conventional formats (e.g. completing the test within two or three hours).

Open-book examinations in English literature at GCE 'A' level have been set by the Joint Matriculation Board. These showed that the effectiveness with which the candidates used this facility was related to their ability. The most able improved their performance, while some of the least able used the texts very little and wasted time paging ineffectively through them. The teachers involved generally considered that the prospect of open-book examinations would improve the quality of work through-out the course.

The main cognitive benefit to be expected from open-book examinations would seem to be the raising of the level of skills tested. By eliminating knowledge items from the material to be examined more time is left for more testing items. Weak students are likely to need help in preparing to make the most use of such examinations (Boniface, 1985). In order to reduce search-time Trigwell (1987) suggested that students prepare crib-cards. The objection to this is that the students will already be familiar with what they know (Wood, 1993). But Trigwell said that even though much of the information in the cards would be relevant to answering questions with which the candidates were unfamiliar they nevertheless found them difficult to answer. Too much information could confuse the candidates. It is, therefore, important to be clear about the objectives which the additional information is meant to achieve.

Prior-notice examinations

A prior-notice examination is one which the questions, or a group of questions from which the actual examination will be set, are given out sometime before the examination is set. Another approach is to give the candidates a specified time in which to submit the answers. Gibbs *et al.* (1986) define this type of paper by the amount of time required for completion, e.g. 168 hours (or one week). The advantages claimed for this type of examination, in addition to the elimination of memorization and question spotting, are reduction in anxiety, higher-quality answers and the testing of something worthwhile. It is quite likely that some students would be anxious during the week. Gibbs *et al.* (1986) note that this technique could be open to plagiarism. In English

Literature this technique might encourage creative writing or skill in reviewing books under time pressure (Brockbank, 1968).

Cameron and Heywood (1995) described how on two occasions graduates in a teacher-training course were allowed to opt either for a prior-notice or a traditional three-hour examination. On the second occasion a list of six questions was given to those students who chose the prior-notice condition. They were given two to do and there was no choice. After the first test the 'rumour' got around that taking a prior-notice examination was more difficult and it caused a much smaller group to volunteer for the second. As far as was possible, the unseen and seen questions were designed to test the same content and skills. It was found that there was no statistically significant difference between the groups. It might be objected that the groups were self-selecting. However, if the aim is to reduce anxiety among those students who perceive themselves to be anxious then self-selection would be the better approach. The major objections are that the 'unseen' group could decode the examination and that the papers may not have been totally equivalent. They were difficult to design.

In another experiment with undergraduates in the same department it was found that when the examination questions were selected from a group of prior-notice questions that the students prepared model answers which were not always correct!

Another approach reported by Edwards (1984) and used in examinations in systems analysis at both undergraduate and graduate levels, included a question on a case study which was distributed before the examination. It contained the solution, and the question was set to obtain criticisms of the solution and suggestions for improvement.

Chapter 7

From Formal Operations to Reflective Judgement

Summary

This chapter begins by advancing yet another comment on the causes of retention, and proceeds to the sections on learning and assessment which are pursued in this and the chapters that follow.

One reason why students fail their examinations might be because they are not at Piaget's level of formal operations. The chapter starts, therefore, with a brief description of Piaget's theory of cognitive development. It is related to the concept of critical thinking. Difficulties in defining critical thinking are described and attempts to measure it considered: criticisms of the critical thinking movement related to the nature of the tests which impose a structure on the respondents that does not allow them to demonstrate how they would cope with perplexing situations. These tests and tests of Piagetian formal reasoning essentially assess performance with puzzles for which there is a definitive answer.

Cognitive developmental psychologists have now begun to examine adult development. In respect of higher education, they consider that there are stages beyond formal reasoning through which the student must go to be able to exercise the reflective judgement that is required to consider perplexing situations. Three models of development are discussed. These are due to Fischer, Perry and King, and Kitchener. Finally, given the context of liberal education which aims at both the cognitive and moral development, Kohlberg's model of moral development is considered.

Research and practice indicate that assessment, instruction and course structure designed in response to these theories can have a positive impact on student performance. The implications of these theories for assessment and instruction is profound.

Cognitive development: Piaget

The idea of development is well understood in school education. The theories of Jean Piaget have had a profound influence on teaching, in primary schools in particular, even if their interpretation has often been naive. Piaget argued that children's development takes place through a number of invariant sensori-motor and concrete-operational stages en route to a final capability in what he termed 'formal operations'.

The stages are invariant because a child must pass through one stage in order to advance to the next (Crain, 1992). They are also qualitatively different. It is only in the final stage that it is abstract and hypothetical. Piaget recognized that children could be at different stages in different areas of reasoning. He gave the name *decalage* to these irregularities. The lower stages do not disappear but they become integrated into a more comprehensive range of possibilities. Anyone who has arrived at the stage of formal operations can also think in 'concrete' terms. The evidence suggests adults use 'concrete' operational thinking more than they do 'formal' operational thinking.

Piaget held that knowledge was a process; thus, to know something was to act on the thing that is to be known. In order to adapt to the world the child acquires schema which are generalized by repetition in similar or analogous situations. Thus, adaptation is made possible by '*assimilation*', that is, matching the events in the environment to the mental patterns that the child has already developed. This process requires the child to revise these patterns in order to obtain a better fit with the environment: it is called '*accommodation*'. Piaget used the concept of '*equilibration*' to describe the conflicts usually experienced by the learner as their existing world-model is challenged. Such conflicts should, if we don't give up, motivate us to formulate new hypotheses and ideas (Crain, 1992). '*Equilibration*' is the final state in achieving a resolution of the changes required to move from one stage to the another.

Piaget held that children have to be actively involved in learning so as to construct knowledge. This supported the proponents of discovery learning. The idea that a learner, in order to adapt, has to move from one state of equilibrium to another lends support to the idea of cognitive conflict in which dissonance is induced, thereby creating the need for a new equilibrium. However, such conflict can have serious consequences for learning when the dissonance is with deeply held values as might happen in a politics class (Marshall, 1980). Knight (private communication) suggested that the important problem to be faced in higher education is that dissonance is often not recognized, and when it is, it is often ignored, e.g. Galileo. Conflict can be introduced relatively simply, and have positive effects as Coelho and Sere (1998) demonstrate. Through confronting students in this age range (14–17) with 'measurement variability' during a physics experiment, they led students to consider important questions which they would not otherwise have considered. McElwee (1993) has found with university students studying physics within a home economics course that the effects of conflict may not be lasting.

Piaget's theory has been much researched and many difficulties have emerged (for summaries see Crain, 1992; Burman, 1994). One of the most important criticisms came from outside empirical research. Matthews (1980) argued, contrary to some interpretations of Piagetian theory, that young children are capable of raising all the fundamental questions of philosophy, but within the context of their own language and frameworks of operation

The term 'formal operations' is associated with the use of terms such as abstract reasoning, critical thinking. In Piagetian theory it is the application of scientific reasoning to problem solving. It is not surprising, therefore, that much of the research on Piaget has been done in the fields of mathematics and science. Some of these researches have been designed to establish at what Piagetian level children are at in school (Adey and Shayer, 1994; Shayer and Adey, 1981), and at what level students should be in order to solve certain scientific problems (Monk, 1990).

Studies in the US in the 1960s and 1970s suggested that the majority of American freshmen students had not reached the stage of formal operations when they entered university Blanc, De Buhr and Martin, 1982; Renner and Lawson, 1973), and that many adults could not perform the abstract tasks suggested by Piaget (Horn and Donaldson, 1976). It was found that students were greatly helped if they possessed skill in spatial- visualization (Cinquepalmi, Fogli-Muciaccia and Picciarelli, 1983).

Collinge (1994) suggests that some of the results, which were obtained in science, may be an artefact of test design. He found that children's (11-year-olds) scientific ability is often underestimated because of their inability to recognize a variable as a variable, or to differentiate which variables are significant. Many children will manipulate variables if they can be recognized, but they need training in order to do this. Thus the problem of formal operations may well originate in school and the particular way it approaches education in science, and this has implications for the design of assessment and instruction during the first session of university study. These results highlight the importance of the 'flow' between school and college and the importance of university departments, not only of understanding what goes on in schools, but of engaging with them in studies of what is happening.

In their synthesis of evidence on the effectiveness of institutional interventions to develop formal reasoning Pascarella and Terenzini (1991) illustrated one particular approach which consistently caused positive effects. It was an 'inquiry' or 'learning cycle' approach, devised by Karplus (1974). In order to move students from the concrete to the formal, students participate in a laboratory where they work with practical materials. This stage is called exploration. They draw ideas and concepts from this exploration. This is the stage of invention. In the final stage the students generalize or apply the concept. This is called the stage of discovery.

The critical thinking movement in higher education

Criticisms of student learning were not confined to the lack of formal operations in the US. A considerable body of opinion felt that students were not able to think critically. One way in which this concern was expressed was through the view that students were being caused to think mainly at the lower levels of the Bloom Taxonomy, accompanied by demands that students should be taught higher order thinking skills (HOTS). It was suggested that courses in critical thinking should be established. Although this 'movement' (for want of a better word) took place in the United States, some of the issues it raises relate to any system of higher education which is moving from an elite to a mass system of participation. The general thrust of the debate, including discussion of the meaning of critical thinking, will be found in *The Generalizability of Critical Thinking*, edited by S.P. Norris (1992); but as Lewis and Smith (1993) wrote, little progress has been made in clearing up this 'intellectual swamp'. In that book Ennis assumes critical thinking to *be reasonable reflective thinking focused on deciding what we believe or do*. However, this definition approximates to what is being discussed in higher education about reflective practice in higher education. It involves judgement and therefore self-assessment (see Chapter 14).

While agreeing that *The Taxonomy of Educational Objectives* is a useful point of entry into the field, it was criticized because it was not strictly hierarchical, and because it was too vague (Ennis, 1981, 1983). Given his example of 'what do you assess when you test the ability to analyse?' this criticism seems to be unfair, since the authors elaborated the broad categories with the aid of sub-categories. However, Ennis argued that the analysis of a political situation and the analysis of a chemical substance do not have anything in common. But is that so? Aren't the authors arguing that the same mental processes are undergone when anything is subject to their definition of analysis? It seems that the examples of test questions they give are quite specific. A more significant criticism is that the categories do not fit our understanding of creative learning, by which is meant the ability to do things with what we have learned. Thus, to say that we are developing problem solving, critical thinking (reasoning, if you like) and creative skills accord more with what we want to do. Even so, there is an obligation on us to say what we mean by these skills. All too often in teaching we say we are developing problem solving or critical thinking skills without defining what we mean, and face validity inspection of students' work associated with our teaching may well suggest that we have not moved far from information giving.

Ennis (1992) distinguished between an infusion and an immersion approach to critical thinking. In respect of the former, he means critical thinking instruction within subject matter teaching, in which the student is helped to think critically 'and in which general principles of critical thinking dispositions and abilities are made explicit'. Proponents of this approach include Glaser (1984), Resnick (1987) and Swartz (1987). In contrast, it is also held that one learns to think critically if one becomes immersed in the subject. There is no need to make the principles of critical thinking explicit (McPeck (1981). Many teachers in schools and higher education take this view.

Related to this is the issue of generalizability or transfer. How, for example, do we learn skills that will enable us to think critically about the situations we face in everyday life? Is this something we learn independently of our education? Would an infusion (i.e. specific training) help? Does it occur because of an immersion in a subject(s)? Or, more probably, is it a combination of all three? This is a large and contested issue.

One way of approaching this issue is to look at it from the perspective of learning and to ask if by using an infusion approach to critical thinking, problem solving and decision making, learning is enhanced? Such an approach embraces critical thinking and problem solving as being the same thing. It sees the issue as semantic in that sometimes those teaching in the humanities regard themselves as critical thinkers, whereas some technologists consider themselves to be problem solvers. Both would seem to use similar heuristics and these heuristics differ little from models of problem solving. So there is a problem as to whether problem solving and critical thinking are the same things. Decision making also uses a similar heuristic, but is action oriented. Whichever one is used people (teachers) in general also use the term 'reasoning', and this term has now reappeared in psychology textbooks.

There is probably one axiom over which there will be no disagreement and that is that all disciplines involve both higher and lower level thinking. Lewis and Smith (1993) consider that higher order thinking is demonstrated by the fact that it adds to the store of knowledge. Another way of looking at the problem is to recognize that we often scan information without understanding it in (what we call) 'depth'. Indeed, when we find study difficult we may give up because we feel we don't have the mental capacity to go into it in 'depth'. We may put this down to any number of reasons, ranging from lack of interest to lack of ability. We observe of both ourselves and others that outside our spheres of competence none of us are very good at reasoning, and even in our areas of competence we often appear to lose arguments because we have not thought things through (Perkins, 1995). At the very least, we can see the value of training in reasoning or logic. Thus, analysis of the components of reasoning, that is higher order thinking, as a curriculum study would seem to make eminent sense.

As a result of this kind of thinking, elaborate lists of what it was students would be able to do emerged. For example, by 1985, Gubbins had compiled an extensive matrix of 60 critical thinking skills distributed among the categories of problem solving, decision making, inferences, divergent thinking skills, evaluative thinking skills and philosophy and reasoning (Sternberg, 1985b). Other profiles were being developed at the same time in higher education, and Figure 7.1 shows one from the faculty of some 30 or more institutions working in the field of the arts and the humanities (Cromwell, 1986). They also produced one in psychology (Halonen, 1986), and this concern to develop profiles of the critical thinker continues. No wonder there is confusion.

A teacher may want to compile his/her own list. For example, Underbakke, Borg and Peterson (1993) were concerned to evaluate the research which could form a knowledge base for teaching higher order thinking, based on the view that it manipulates information so as to produce certain outcomes. Thus 'higher order thinking, accordingly, consists of ways of handling content: to learn to think more effectively is to learn more effective ways of dealing with information.' Therefore, they say in the classroom, provision has to be made for the following types of experiences:

1. Hypothesizing and Testing: Conceiving connections among variables of a problem, and formulating and verifying these connections.

2. Assessing Arguments: Identifying and solving problems that require evaluation of arguments.

3. Solving Interpersonal Problems: Analysing issues and interpersonal problems and engaging in discussions leading to their satisfactory resolution.

4. Problematic Thinking: Resolving uncertainties when information is only partial.

5. Developing and Maintaining Flexibility and Student Awareness: Keeping options open, evolving novel approaches to problem solution, and becoming aware of procedures and thought processes involved in solving problems.

Foundational Knowledge, abilities and attitudes.
The critical thinker:
1. Asks significant and pertinent questions and states problems with specificity. Arrives at solutions through hypothesis, inquiry, analysis, and interpretations.
2. Assesses statements, insights and arguments according to the knowledge and skills provided by formal and informal logic and by the principles of aesthetic judgement.
3. Derives meaning through an educated perception, whether propositional, systematic, or intuitive.
4. Formulates propositions or judgements in terms of clearly defined sets of criteria.
5. Strives to acquire knowledge of the various disciplines, knowing that such knowledge is a necessary, though not sufficient, condition for critical thinking.
6. Understands the different modes of thought appropriate to the various disciplines. Can apply these modes of thought to other disciplines and to life.
7. Is aware of the context or setting in which judgements are made, and of the practical consequences and values involved.
8. Thinks about the world through theories, assessing these theories and their contexts to determine the validity of their claims to knowledge of reality.
9. Seeks and expects to find different meanings simultaneously present in a work or event. Is intrigued and curious about phenomena others might avoid, disavow, or ignore.
10. Recognizes and accepts contradiction and ambiguity, understanding that they are an integral part of thought and creativity.
11. Constructs and interprets reality with a holistic and dialectical perspective. Sees the interconnectedness within a system and between systems.
12. Is aware of the problematical and ambiguous character of reality. Understands that language and knowledge are already interpretations of phenomena.
13. Tolerates ambiguity, yet can assume a committed position.
14. Is aware of the limitations of knowledge and figures epistemological humility.

Knowledge, abilities and attitudes related to self-awareness
The critical thinker,
1. Demonstrates capacity for continuing intellectual development and lifelong learning. Sees the development of critical thinking as an aim and as a process of self-assessment and correction.
2. Recognizes own intellectual potential and limitations in dealing with different tasks. Constantly evaluates the limitations and strives to develop the potential.
3. Extends the range of experience by educating the self in a variety of realms meaning.
4. Recognizes the style of one's own thought in its creative potential as well as boundaries. Is willing to explore the style of others to augment one's own perception.
5. Treats one's own thinking with dignity.
6. Can apply insights from cultures other than one's own.
7. Is self-directed, with the courage to criticize both society and self.
8. Assumes responsibility for thought and action by being able and willing to explore their meaning and consequences.
9. Demonstrates commitment to a specific world view, while having the capacity to understand and accept others. Is open to the interchange of ideas and to the possibility of changing one's own views.
10. Finds joy in the activity of thinking critically.

Knowledge, abilities and attitudes related to the social dimension to critical thinking
The critical thinker,
1. Is aware of the development and production of knowledge and critical thinking as historical and social process of cooperation among human beings. Knows that thought and knowledge have relevance and meaning only in a social context.
2. Is aware that critical thinking is a social process, and so actively seeks critique from others to increase both self-awareness and understanding of society.
3. Enters willingly into the give and take of critical discussion. Is ready to be called upon to justify and defend thoughts and actions, and is willing to call upon others to do the same.
4. Is sensitive to audience, taking seriously the task of communicating with others. Listens carefully and is able to express thoughts clearly, to argue cogently and appropriately, and to edit sensibly.
5. Examines the assumptions and validity of every communication. Is committed to reflection about the assumptions that guide our construction and interpretation reality.
6. Goes beyond own interests of own particular culture to understand other interests and points of view and to foster, when appropriate, synthesized ecumenical views.
7. Uses knowledge and skills to intervene and support critical and intelligent positions on controversial issues facing the community. Is specifically committed to defend or promote those individuals and social relations that will guarantee the possibility of continuous development of critical thinking in any human being.

Figure 7.1 Profile of the critical thinker in the arts and humanities.
(Reproduced by kind permission of Cromwell 1986)

From the above it seems that while there may be confusion over the definition of critical thinking, philosophers and psychologists have derived a set of skills (abilities) and categories that may have been instrumental in developing an outcomes approach to the assessment of critical thinking. An institution might wish to use such lists for the description of student performance outcomes.

Lewis and Smith (1993) ssuggest that a broader term is required which includes problem solving, critical thinking and decision making. They propose that higher order thinking is an all-encompassing term. By this they mean 'the thinking that occurs when a person takes new information and information stored in memory and interrelates and/or rearranges and extends this information to achieve a purpose or find possible answers in perplexing situations.' The key difference is the addition of perplexing situations. They acknowledge that it derives both from the insights of psychology and the notion of critical thinking as an evaluative act.

The measurement of critical thinking

In European countries and English-speaking countries whose universities operate British type degree programmes critical thinking (however defined) would be considered to be an important goal of education and, as such, measured by the examination questions and assessments set. That such measurements are problematic has not really been assimilated into the systems functioning in the British Isles in most cases of assessment in higher education.

By contrast in the United States a number of tests have been designed to measure what purports to be critical thinking for evaluative purposes. The most used of these tests is *The Watson-Glaser Critical Thinking Appraisal Manual* (Watson and Glaser, 1964).

Evaluation of that test by several investigators, including King and Kitchener (1994), concludes that it 'reflects a combination of well and ill-structured problems'. However, when the tasks are examined against the mode of response required, King and Kitchener note, that although the tasks appear to be ill-structured, the response options 'reframe the response into one that is well structured'. In consequence, the value of the test as a test of critical thinking is severely limited. This is the basis of their criticism of both this and the *Cornell Critical Thinking Test* devised by Ennis. Many academics on the other side of the Atlantic would take the view that it is impossible to test critical thinking with multiple choice questions, but Ennis (1993) has vigorously defended the use of multiple-choice questions in his test.

Pascarella and Terenzini (1991), who reviewed various measures of critical thinking and investigations, concluded that college, but not necessarily via the formal curriculum, had a net positive influence on critical thinking. It could not be explained away by other factors such as aptitude and socio-economic status. 'It appears to enhance one's ability to weigh evidence, to determine the validity of data-based generalizations or conclusions, and to distinguish between strong and weak arguments'.

Such tests do not measure reasoning about ill-structured or 'perplexing problems', as Lewis called them. Most of the problems in life that we face on a daily basis are ill-structured. It is the capability to resolve such problems that King and Kitchener called reflective judgement. They argue that these tests assess Piagetian formal reasoning, and that reflective judgement requires development beyond formal operations, hence the idea of post-formal reasoning which encompasses the work of Fischer, Perry and King and Kitchener, discussed in the next three sections.

Fischer's skill theory

Fischer's skill theory is an attempt to resolve the paradox where most investigations show that most adults cannot perform complex tasks, yet common experience suggests they can think in sophisticated ways about abstract concepts.

Fischer argues that these contradictory findings may be explained by a theory that considers cognitive development to be a function of the collaboration that a person has with his/her environment. Fischer calls this collaborative framework 'skills theory'. The contradictory findings of research are explained in this theory by the systematic variations in an individual's levels of performance. Individuals routinely function below their highest capacity in ordinary environmental conditions, but in environments which optimize performance they demonstrate high levels of performance (Fischer, Kenny and Pipp, 1990).

New levels of competence which enable adolescents and young adults to understand abstract concepts are acquired yet most of their behaviour does not suggest they have made cognitive advances. One criterion that suggests a change in cognitive developmental level is a sudden alteration in performance during a limited age period. Fischer calls this a 'spurt'. In this theory the change from one cognitive developmental level to another is characterized by a cluster of 'spurts' in performance. 'The spurts do not all occur at exactly the same age, nor do they take exactly the same form. Adolescents do not suddenly metamorphose on their fifteenth birthday. Instead, the change is relatively rapid, occupying a small interval of time.'

Individuals will only operate at their optimal levels when they practise skills in familiar domains and receive environmental support for high level performance. According to Fischer, most conditions will produce slow, gradual, continuous improvement, rather than sudden improvements in performance.

Unlike stage theory, which holds that children pass through the same stages of development, skill theory argues that the steps which individuals take to attain a skill vary considerably as between one individual and the next, as a function of both the environment and the individual. Because of these variations it will be difficult to find any two children who spontaneously follow the same steps in any domain. At the same time the theory states that irrespective of the path taken all skills pass through the same developmental levels. All skill acquisitions involve the same group of transformation rules. Fischer and his colleagues point out that their postulates are similar to that taken by many information-processing theorists, namely that 'the same fundamental acquisition processes occur in development, learning, and problem solving at all ages'. Instruction and assessment should, therefore, be designed to take account of these different needs. This theory has considerable implications for the design of modular systems and the pacing of assessment and learning within them.

Fischer argues that both theory and data suggest that cognitive development continues into adulthood, and this is the experience of students in university education. They acquire abilities which help them to deal with abstractions and inter-relationships in increasingly complex ways.

From the educational perspective, since an individual must actively construct every new skill, not only must the skill be practised but the educational environment must induce and support the behaviours that comprise the skill. Thus if transferable skills are to be developed they must be practised throughout a person's educational programme, irrespective of the structure of that programme.

> Even when students have the capacity to function at a certain level, they cannot be expected to do so easily or automatically. They need times for both constructing the needed skills and environmental support to stimulate and guide the construction (Fischer *et al.*, 1990).

Fischer's model suggests there is something beyond the Piagetian stage of formal operations and much interest is now focused on the higher stages of human development among adults. In addition to the view that development does not culminate in adolescence it is argued that there are other domains of development, including the affective and moral, as well as other forms of cognition which contribute to mature intelligence. For example, it is now asked if growth in adulthood occurs through distinct stages? Not everyone agrees that development is necessarily hierarchical or, for example, that formal operations are universal (Alexander and Langer, 1990).

In 1970 Perry published a post-Piagetian model directly related to higher education that was based on studies of students at Harvard and Radcliffe. It has proved of considerable interest and is used as a basis for the design of curriculum and instruction.

Post-formal reasoning: Perry

Broadly speaking, according to Perry's theory, the attitudes we hold and the concepts and values with which they are associated depend on the stage of development we are at. There are nine such stages and they relate to the curriculum and instruction in so far as together they reinforce the stage we are at, or help us move forward to another stage. He argues that much teaching tends to reinforce the earlier stages.

In the first stages the students come to the university expecting to be told the truth, that is, that which is right and that which is wrong. Subject-based knowledge is absolute. Things are right or wrong, or true or false. Thus in Stage 1 all problems are seen to have right answers and authority must be followed so it is that the best teachers provide the right answers. By Stage 3 it is apparent that authority is 'seeking the right answers' and only in the future will we know the right answer. Perry calls these first three stages 'dualism'. From dualism the student moves into a phase of scepticism, for now it is clear that not only does the authority not have the right answers but everyone, including the student, has the right to hold his or her own opinions, and some of these can be supported by evidence. Thus, by Stage 5, some answers are found to be better than others and everything has to be considered in its context. It is a stage of relativism. The student begins to perceive that good choices are possible and that commitments have to be entered into. By Stage 9 (acting on commitment) decisions are made with relative ease, a sense of identity and personal style is obtained and one is now able to take responsibility for one's own actions.

Like Fischer, Perry found that growth occurred in spurts that were followed by periods of stabilization that would seem to indicate equilibrium in the Piagetian sense. Culver and Sackman (1988) borrowed a term from Levinson (1978) to describe these growth experiences. They called them 'marker events'. A marker event has the following characteristics. It:

- is a significant event which influences an individual's development
- results in a change or expansion of the personal belief system
- provides new insight and, frequently, a change in priorities
- serves as an anchor for new learning and long-term memory recall
- usually involves a concrete experience and reflective observation
- can be positive or negative
- can be forced but can be programmed.

Culver and Sackman evidently think that the event begins in the practical and that it is reflection on what happens which leads to abstraction or formal reasoning. (In so far as positive learning is concerned, the story of Archimedes' experiment made such a profound impression on me when I was young that I have always called such occasions 'Eureka' events). These descriptions are also consistent with Lonergan's (1954) philosophy of insight. They come as a result of mental activity, and may not come when an instructor desires. Indeed, they may come well after a course is over.

Culver and Sackman argue that learning activities which have high levels of marker potential will involve the learner in activity-based learning. This is consistent with the views of such distinguished scholars as Bruner and James in the US and Mascall in the UK, who believe that the learner (novice) has to try to experiment with what it is like to become the expert. If one wants to be a theologian, one has to behave as a theologian.

In Culver's case it was that if one wants to be an engineer, then the teachers have to provide opportunities for one to behave as an engineer. He and his colleagues used the Perry model as the basis for several course designs (Culver and Hackos, 1982; Culver and Olds, 1986; Pavelich and Moore, 1996).

Pavelich and Moore (1996) explain how at the Colorado School of Mines most undergraduates complete project courses in six of their eight semesters, beginning in the first semester of their freshman year. In these courses the students work in teams to solve an open-ended problem provided by a government or industrial agency. They point out that college educators have difficulty in teaching open-ended problem solving for the reason that freshmen, sophomores and many seniors do not understand these problems as a professional does. Many freshmen, for example, do not understand why evidence has to be used to justify a decision. Sophomore and seniors see no need to devise alternative solutions. Faculty at the School of Mines have found it helpful to understand the problem in terms of Perry's model and to approach the acquisition of professional understanding through courses designed to be responsive to the levels of the model.

In order to test the theory they chose to interview rather than to use either of the two instruments that had been developed for this purpose (Moore, 1988). They thought that a limited number of interview questions would ensure that there would be few questions about the meaning of the data. They were aware that there was only a moderate correlation between interviews and the schedules (Baxter-Magdola, 1987; Culver *et al.*, 1994). Interviews generally gave higher ratings.

The interviewer's focus was placed on the thinking processes that lead to a conclusion and the ways students justified their points of view. The interviews were video-taped, and independent raters evaluated them for Perry positions. Over 40 students were interviewed in each of the freshmen and senior years and nearly that number in the sophomore. The statistical data show significant differences between the freshmen and the late sophomores, and these differences increase when freshmen are compared with the late seniors. On the Perry positions, the freshmen average position on a continuum was 3.27, the sophomores was 3.71, and the seniors was 4.28. Over one-quarter of the seniors tested above 5. From the school's point of view these students were in an excellent position to enter the profession. However, what of the students who were rated below position on the scale, for some of these were found to struggle with decision making in their profession? Some of them acknowledged 'the multitude of possible answers to an open-ended problem in their profession, but see themselves as having no responsibility for a legitimate input, into deciding the direction of the problem's solution'. Their answer to the question as to how one operates when there are multiple demands on a design is, 'You tell me what to optimize and I'll optimize it for you'. They really see themselves as technicians awaiting the decisions of others.

As a result of these studies the faculty at the school considered that, rather than change the curriculum, they should refine their teaching methods and balance challenge with support. While exposing students to the vagaries of knowledge and requiring them to deal with them, faculty would help the students deal with the discontinuity between the students' perceptions and those of their teachers. The faculty would have been aware of Baxter-Magolda's work, in which she showed that students operating at the high levels of the Perry position preferred a working relationship with faculty akin to that of colleagues, whereas those at the lowest levels preferred a more distant, yet positive, relationship.

This paper, although about engineering, may be read by anyone unfamiliar with the subject. The quotations from the interviews illustrate quite clearly the meanings of the Perry positions. However, it does raise a number of questions one of which arises from the fact that it is a cross-sectional study. Such studies assume that what happens in each of the years is constant. They also assume the maturation observed is a function of the course. Some factor needs to be allowed for that part of maturation that is not influenced by college. This applies particularly to longitudinal scores. It is not safe to assume that change scores are reliable, and it is necessary to make allowance for that in their interpretation. Pascarella and Terenzini (1991), who drew attention to this problem, also note that 'change' and 'development' have different meanings. A change from time A to time B simply implies two different conditions that are not necessarily predictable. Development implies ordered, predictable and hierarchical shifts in behaviour. Observed changes do not necessarily imply ordered growth.

Quite clearly Pavelich and Moore had as their aim the development of professionalism. It is important, therefore, to know how this relates to the aptitude, age and achievements of the students.

One study which did correct for aptitude, prior achievement and age was at Alverno College. That investigation comprised both cross-sectional and longitudinal studies. One measure designed to measure development on the Perry continuum was used. To study how effective students were at considering all aspects of a controversial issue they used an *Analysis of Argument* test developed by Stewart (1977). (See also Winter, McClelland and Stewart, 1981). Both of these instruments covered aspects of the stated aims of Alverno College. The *Measure of Intellectual Development* developed by Knefelkamp (1974) for determining the Perry continuum requires the respondent to write three short essays. The scoring is based on the nature and origin of knowledge displayed and the responsibility taken for decision making. Somewhat less positive results were reported than in other studies. In the cross-sectional analysis seniors were found to be higher than freshmen on two of the essays whereas, in the longitudinal study, while there was an increase in one essay there was a decrease in one of the others. In the *Analysis of Argument* instrument the respondents have to attack and defend a complex issue. Separate scores are given for the arguments for and the arguments against. In the Alverno study of the seniors in the cross-sectional study, statistically significant differences in scores were obtained on the defence score but not on the attack, although there were changes in the right direction (Mentkowski and Strait, 1983; Mentkowski and associates, 2000).

In the British Isles teachers would be totally unused to having an institutional test of the institutions goals in this way. Some would claim, especially in the Humanities, that the essay questions they set are intended to test these characteristics. Whether they do or not is a matter of conjecture, because there have been no independent studies of scripts which might give a more objective judgement. It would seem clear that studies using tests of this kind, adapted to the culture, would be of value in establishing the effectiveness of traditional modes of examining which continue to be used.

Kloss (1994) who is a university teacher of English, explained how he has taught with the Perry scheme over a period of ten years. He derives four conclusions from his experience. These are,

> (1) that the best subject matter within my discipline to challenge dualistic students and stimulate such movement is fiction and poetry, especially the latter, since it provides more possibilities for ambiguity, varied interpretations, and multiple perspectives, three of the challenges that constrain adoption of multiplicity and relativism; (2) that small group work used frequently fosters and reinforces the exchange and importance of multiple perspectives; (3) that free guided discussion – with the students talking 80–90 percent of the time nurtures growth because it diminishes the instructor's authoritative role and increases reliance on peers' perspectives and contributions to creating knowledge; and (4) that expectations need be kept high that students can achieve understanding, and that without exception

they be both encouraged and constrained to substantiate opinions, ideas, and hypotheses with evidence. (Kloss, 1994)

Of particular interest in this context are his remarks on classroom assessment, questioning, and modules. For classroom assessment he used the one-minute paper advocated by Angelo and Cross (1993). During the first few weeks the students were asked to say (on an index card) how things were going. The responses show how the students' thinking is changing, and he records how they begin to change after a month or so. In order to devise questions for assessment, he exposed his criteria to the students, together with a set of sample questions and, through discussion, character-ized the differences in the nature of questions. He recommends that, if it is possible, sample answers be provided to enhance the discussion. He suggests that students can be further involved if they attempt to answer questions when in groups. His second point is that he had to learn to talk less and listen more, and to accompany this with fewer questions so as to engage the students more actively.

Kloss found that the challenges helped his freshmen to move from dualism to multiplicity within the period of a module of semester length. Because students want to retreat from new ways of thinking, he also found that it was better to nudge than to shove. This affirms the view that student development is a gradual process, and cannot necessarily be accomplished by one teacher alone in one module. Attention has to be paid to the totality of the student's experience.

Post formal reasoning: the reflective judgement model

King and Kitchener's (1994) reflective judgement model has been relatively well rehearsed. In many respects it is similar to the Perry scheme. Like Perry, it assumes that as individuals develop, so they become more able to evaluate the claims of knowledge and both to advocate and support their points of view about controversial issues. 'The ability to make reflective judgements is the ultimate outcome of this progression.' To arrive at this destination the learner passes through seven stages, each of which has its own assumptions and logic. The stages develop from the relatively simple to the complex, each with a different strategy for solving ill-structured problems. Thus each stage has its own view of knowledge and concept of justification. Reflective thinking takes place in stages 6 and 7. 'True reflective thinking pre-supposes that individuals hold epistemic assumptions that allow them to understand and accept real uncertainty.' It is only when they engage with ill-structured or novel problems that they engage in reflective thinking as defined by King and Kitchener.

The outline of the stages in this model is shown in Figure 7.2, King and Kitchener found that their model complemented Fischer's model. In the Reflective Judgement a spurt marks the emergence of a new stage. The skill levels in the Fischer model correspond directly to the stages in the Reflective Judgement model. According to Pascarella and Terenzini (1991), Rodgers (1989) considers that the first three stages coincide with Perry's, but differences appear on the framework at position 4. However, he was not able to conclude whether they are distinct theories or simply the clarification of Perry by King and Kitchener. A colleague who saw an earlier summary I had written, which included the tabulation in Figure 7.2 responded 'pure Perry'.

Stage 1	Knowing is limited to single concrete observations: what a person observes is true.
Stage 2	Two categories for knowing: right answers and wrong answers. Good authorities have knowledge; bad authorities lack knowledge.
Stage 3	In some areas, knowledge is certain and authorities have that knowledge. In other areas, knowledge is temporarily uncertain. Only personal beliefs can be known.
Stage 4	Concept that knowledge is unknown is several specific cases leads to the abstract generalization that knowledge is uncertain.
Stage 5	Knowledge is uncertain and must be understood within a context; thus justification is context specific.
Stage 6	Knowledge is uncertain but constructed by comparing evidence and opinion on different sides of an issue or across contexts.
Stage 7	Knowledge is the outcome of a process of reasonable inquiry. This view is equivalent to a general principle that is consistent across domains.

Figure 7.2 Reflective judgement stage of the King and Kitchener model. (Adapted from King and Kitchener, 1994)

Characteristic assumptions of stage 3. Reasoning
Knowledge is absolutely certain in some areas and temporarily uncertain in other areas.
Beliefs are justified according to the word of an authority in areas of certainty and according to what "feels right" in areas of uncertainty.
Evidence can neither be evaluated nor used to reason to conclusions.
Opinions and beliefs cannot be distinguished from factual evidence.

Instructional goals for students
Learn to use evidence in reasoning to a point of view.
Learn to view their own experiences as one potential source of information but not as the only valid source.

Promoting reflective thinking – stage 6. Reasoning

Characteristic assumptions of stage 6. Reasoning
Knowledge is uncertain and must be understood in relationship to context and evidence.
Some points of view may be tentatively judged as better than others.
Evidence on different points of view can be compared and evaluated as a basis for justification.

Instructional goals for students
Learn to construct one's own point of view and to see that point of view as open to re-evaluation and revision in light of new evidence.
Learn that though knowledge must be constructed, strong conclusions are epistemologically justifiable.

Figure 7.3 Promoting reflective thinking in the King and Kitchener model – stages 3 and 6. Reasoning. (Adapted from King and Kitchener, 1994)

King and Kitchener do not respond directly to Rodgers except by inference. They argue that the decisions that students make when they are in a relativistic frame of reference should reflect a level of cognitive development beyond relativism. In the Perry model, the student remains within the relativistic frame and has to make an act of faith in reaching a commitment. The purpose of the Reflective Judgement Model is to deal with the form and nature of judgements made in the relativistic framework. Individuals, it is held, hold epistemological positions beyond relativism. Whatever else one may say, such a position would seem to be more satisfying.

King and Kitchener have much to say about teaching in higher education and high school and they take a broad view of who may be a teacher and what teaching is. According to their test – The Reflective Judgement Interview (see below) – first year college students in the United States lie in the range stage 3 to stage 4. Seniors were found to be around stage 5. Thus, they argue that many seniors are at a loss when they are asked to defend answers to ill-structured problems. They argue that if reflective thinking is to be developed, teachers should:

- show respect for students regardless of the developmental levels they may exhibit
- understand that students differ in the assumptions they make about knowledge
- familiarize students with ill-structured problems within the teacher's area of expertise
- create multiple opportunities for students to examine different points of view
- informally assess (i.e. from student journals, assignments, etc.) assumptions about knowledge and how beliefs should be justified
- acknowledge that students work within a developmental range of stages and set expectations accordingly challenge students to engage in new ways to thinking while providing them with support, and recognize that challenges can be emotional as well as cognitive. At the same time recognize that students differ both in their perceptions of ill-structured problems and their responses to particular learning environments.

More generally, King and Kitchener argue that the campus environment should foster thoughtful analysis of issues throughout the campus and they suggest how student affairs strategies can promote reflective thinking. This is, of course, no different to the views held by Newman, or those who defend collegiate universities.

The differences between stage 3 and stage 6 from a teaching perspective are shown in Figure 7.3. It will be appreciated that since these could apply at any level of education they would have to be developed to describe the requirements of a particular level (e.g. college, high school).

The *Reflective Judgement Interview* (RJI), which is the instrument used to detect the stage at which a student is, has been found to have high inter-rater reliability to specific subject domains. The interview is structured with standard probe questions, each with a specific purpose. Thus two questions, that will clearly elicit a level of development and are of direct relevance in today's media governed society, are (1) How is it possible that experts in the field have such different views about this subject? and (2) How is it possible that experts in the field disagree about the subject?

Examiners working in the tradition of the honours degree essay type examination will recognize at once the potential of such questions when they are set against some controversial and ill- structured issue. It further raises the question as to whether the value-added of a programme should be measured by a content (syllabus) free examination along these lines. In England the Joint Matriculation Board's Advanced Level Examination in General Studies was an attempt to do something similar, although its structure could be directly attributed to the Bloom *Taxonomy*.

More generally, in so far as the experience of higher education is concerned, a group of individuals who did not attend college were compared for reflective judgement with a group who did attend college, in a longitudinal study. Although both groups showed an increase in reflective judgement, the group who attended college showed significant gains (King and Kitchener, 1994).

Wood (1997) has carried out a major secondary analysis of claims regarding the *Reflective Judgement Interview*. He notes that while many of the conclusions about the instrument were consistent across studies there were some conflicting patterns in the conclusions because researchers had failed to 'consider plausible alternative explanations that a reasonable sceptic might raise'. He criticizes researchers for not investigating the statistical procedures used in terms of what may and may not be concluded before beginning an investigation. There is nothing new in this criticism of replicatory research but it needs to be restated.

Although smaller more selective colleges appear to do better on reflective judgement than public institutions this may be due to selectivity in admissions in the smaller institutions. In so far as performance and expertise is concerned it seems that differences between graduate student samples as a function of area of study are more pronounced at lower levels of study. Wood draws attention to an unpublished study by DeBord (1993) which found that graduate students in psychology scored significantly higher on RJI when topics dealt with ill-structured psychological dilemmas as opposed to the usual dilemma topics. There is a need to investigate whether the lower scores obtained by natural science/mathematics graduate students on the RJI would be improved if ill-strucured topics in these subjects were included in the interview. Wood suggests that sampling of more general cognitive outcomes should have a definite content area in order to control for the discipline and intra-individual differences.

These findings clearly have relevance to those who intend to investigate the effects of the curriculum on the development of generic skills thought to be independent of content in such higher education systems as the UK.

Wood found that the psychometric properties of the RJI were promising. However, the design of college outcome measures using the instrument should take into account general verbal ability, educational attainment and area of study. Astin (see Chapter 5) would surely argue that account has to be taken of the whole process. Wood suggests that the next step is to design a more efficient and easily scored measure to assess reflective judgement. Wood's analysis found among other things that differences between the samples were more pronounced at lower levels of educational attainment than at higher levels. He notes that this is consistent with the view that performance on the RJI is dependent on verbal ability (which is a necessary but not sufficient condition for high scores).

Pascarella and Terenzini (1991) in their evaluation of within college effects, drew attention to the fact that the magnitude of instructional and curricular effects on general cognitive skills tends to be smaller than the overall effects of college experience. This, they suggest, may be due to the fact that development follows the gradual spurt-consideration cycles of the kind suggested by Fischer and King and Kitchener. In an earlier paper Kitchener (1983) had pointed out that no single instructional or curricular experience over a limited period is likely to have the impact on development that a carefully constructed set of cumulative experiences over a long period of time is likely to have. Clearly that was the view taken by the Colorado School of Mines in the design of their programme (Pavelich and Moore, 1996). King and Kitchener (1994), when discussing the list of things which teachers and institutions can do, assume 'that teaching students to think reflectively is an institutional goal that is best met when it is built into the whole curriculum – and co-curriculum – of the college'. They do not, however, believe there is one best way of teaching reflective thinking, and provide a list of resources ranging across the arts and sciences (King, 1992).

At the very least the model, irrespective of the RJI, provides criteria against which teachers can design their course. The interview may provide ideas for question design. In Britain little attention has been given to the detail of reflective judgement yet reflective judgement has become a major aim of higher education and needs to be thought about in some detail. King and Kitchener's work can serve as a major resource for constructive debate. In this respect it is strange to find that while Schon's (1983) ideas on reflective practice have had some impact in Britain that King and Kitchener (1994) have nothing to say about his work when, surely, there is some relationship (see Chapter 14).

Developmental models pose a considerable challenge to education. For example, in modular courses set at two different levels, the one supposedly higher than the other, it is conceivable that the design of instruction is such that both assume the same level of development and, in consequence, little development takes place. If it is correct that the development of reflective thinking skills should take place in subjects, does the compression of subjects into a 12–15 week period instead of 24–30 weeks inhibit curriculum designs for growth? The Pavelich and Moore study (1996) indicated that they need not, but it demanded an integrated course over four years in which there were radical departures from traditional methods of teaching. Similar questions apply to the conduct and methods of assessment.

There are other and very profound approaches to the development of reflective practice – in America for example the qualitative approach fostered by Angelo and Cross (1993). At this stage the reader may like to turn to Chapter 14 where their work is discussed again together with Cowan's (1998) profound autobiography on developing skill in reflective practice.

Kohlberg: liberal education and moral judgement

In the countries of the Western world there remains a tacit presumption among many that there is a moral purpose in education. As expressed by persons such as Newman, this is the essence of liberal education. It has to do with preparation for life which involves political, social and ethical questions (see Chapter 3). Even though curricula have become fragmented and specialist, those who criticize developments in higher education in Britain often call upon Newman, even though they misinterpret him, to support their ideas (e.g. *The Times*, Leader, 10 August 1998). By and large though, in Britain, those who write about morality in higher education seem to be scarce on the ground (e.g. Collier, 1993). Collier (1997) is of special interest because he writes about the role of institutions as moral agents, both in respect of the faculty they manage and the students they teach.

There is, by contrast, much more interest *per se* in the United States in liberal education and, in consequence, with personal and moral development. Thus an important component of Pascarella and Terenzini's analysis of the effects of higher education is a synthesis of the large number of investigations which have tried to establish whether changes in moral reasoning capabilities take place as a result of the college experience.

Consideration of the Perry scheme shows that it contains an ethical dimension as well as a cognitive one. However, most work has been stimulated by Kohlberg's theory of moral development. Kohlberg's scheme is shown in Figure 7.4 (Kohlberg and

---

1. *Stage 0. Pre-moral stage*

2. *Pre-conventional level*
   Stage 1   The punishment and obedience orientation.
   Stage 2   The instrumental relativist orientation. (Right action consists of that which instrumentally satisfies one's own needs and occasionally the needs of others.)

3. *Conventional level*
   Stage 3   Interpersonal concordance ... good behaviour is that which pleases or helps others and is approved by them ...
   Stage 4   Law and order orientation ... right behaviour consists of doing one's duty, showing respect for authority and maintaining the given social order for its own sake.

4. *Post-conventional, autonomous, or principled level*
   Stage 5   Social contract legalistic orientation ... right action tends to be defined in terms of general individual rights and in terms of standards which have been critically examined and agreed upon by the whole society ...
   Stage 6   The universal ethical principal orientation. Right is defined by the decision of conscience in accord with self-chosen ethical principles appealing to logical comprehensiveness, universality and consistency.

At this level there is a clear effort to define moral values and principles which have validity and application apart from the authority of the groups or persons holding these principles and from the individuals' own identification with these groups.

Figure 7.4 Kohlberg's stages of moral development simplified (Reproduced by kind permission of the late Professor Lawrence Kohlberg first in Heywood (1989a)).

Turiel, 1971). From an interview study of children and adolescents Kohlberg deduced that there were six levels of moral development within three categories.

In its earliest formulation, stage 0 (pre-moral stage) was listed as the first of four levels. At the first stage the individual thinks that what is right is what they are told is right. At the next level they begin to conform to the norms of society, and in the third and final category they begin to think about what is good for society and their guiding principles are those of social justice. The theory is concerned with moral thinking, not moral action, although Kohlberg believed there should be some correlation between the two and that at the higher stages of development behaviour is more predictable and consistent (Kohlberg and Turiel, 1971 and Kohlberg *et al.* 1975).

Kohlberg (1975) did not believe that his stages were either the product of maturation or of socialization. Rather they arose from the child's thinking about moral problems. Our ideas change and develop as they come to be challenged by those with whom we interact. From the educational point of view we can arrange for role playing opportunities to help children see one another's points of view.

Like Piaget, Kohlberg believed that the levels were invariant; they always unfolded in that sequence. Moreover, the levels are general patterns of thought; at the same time they were not lost as the individual moved through the stages. Finally, this stage sequence is universal; it applies in any culture independently of the specific beliefs of the culture, a view which brought some criticism (Baumrind, 1978). Inspection of the levels does suggest they are specific to Western liberal morals.

Towards the end of his life Kohlberg proposed a seventh level. He regarded it as a 'soft' stage. It describes a position where things are viewed, not so much from the standpoint of the individual, but from the universe as a whole (Kohlberg and Ryncarz, 1990). The research reviewed by Pascarella and Terenzini was based on the six level model and the instruments designed to determine levels of moral development.

There were, of course, several criticisms of the theory, one of which will be considered here. This came from Gilligan (1982). She pointed out that Kohlberg's stages were derived from interviews with males and that this introduced a male orientation. Gilligan and also Lyons (1983) argued that in contrast to man's notion of morality as 'having a reason', the woman's sense of morality is a type of 'consciousness' which produces a sensitivity towards others. Caring predominates. These distinctive ways of making moral choices lie in a continuum and are not dichotomous. It might be expected that if there are sex differences that women would score differently from men and that, in this case, their scores would be lower, as was the case. Rest (1983) however, believes the extent of the sex difference has been overstated, but this would not nullify the general hypothesis.

Both Kohlberg (1990) and Gilligan (Gilligan, Murphy and Tappan, 1990) have begun to consider post-adolescent moral development. Crain (1992) envisages the possibility that there are two lines of moral thought, one focusing on logic, justice and social organization, and the other on care that could become integrated within adult years. One could also envisage the possibility that people will switch between the two as a function of the situation in which they find themselves. Thus, Gilligan *et al.* (1990) argue that 'reason must be reunited with relationship thereby making feelings inseparable from human thought'. As Lonergan (1972) wrote, 'knowledge alone is not enough and, while everyone has some measure of moral feeling for, as the saying is, there is honour among thieves, still moral feelings have to be cultivated, enlightened, strengthened, refined, criticised and pruned of oddities.'

Moran (1984) has contributed a substantial critique of the theories of Piaget and Kohlberg from the perspective of religious development. He argues that moral development does not just end in a stage. It must continue throughout life: the educational journey does not end until death.

Measuring the Kohlberg levels

Two instruments have been developed to determine levels of moral development. One uses interview techniques (*The Moral Judgement Interview*), and the other pencil and paper responses (*The Defining Issues Test*). Most of the investigations have used the *Defining Issues Test* for the reason of ease of administration among relatively large samples. Both are based on the evaluation of moral dilemmas with which the respondents are presented. The evaluation is given in response to standardized questions. In the pencil and paper test there are 12 issue statements which indicate ways in which respondents in stages 2 and 3 might respond. A five-point scale assesses the importance the respondent attaches to the statement in making decisions about each dilemma. The inter-rater reliabilities of the *Moral Judgement Interview* have been found to be high. Test/re-test correlations of above 0.9 have been found. The reliabilities of the pencil and paper test have been found to be in the region of 0.8.

Pascarella and Terenzini (1991) argue that since there is a general liberalization of personality and value structures which can be associated with the experience of college, it is reasonable to suppose that increases in principled moral reasoning would accompany that experience. They found impressive support for this view, although it was not possible to indicate the magnitude of the gains. This does not worry them greatly, because the gains indicate a major re-orientation of thinking. Like the gains reported in the Alverno study for the Perry levels, most seem to be made in the first and second years of college. This is perhaps not surprising because students move rapidly from adolescence into adulthood, and this is a time of personal challenge and conflict. Investigations with the *Defining Issues Test* have produced more consistent results that positively relate development in moral reasoning to the experience of college than has the *Moral Judgement Interview*.

These particular studies do not yield information about a person's understanding of the factors that lead them to change; and they do not specifically examine the role of the institution or staff, or peer group, or the environment outside the classroom, in influencing moral values. Collier (1997) puts the question thus:

> How may the actual behaviour of the heads, with their senior colleagues, influence the habits of behaviour or students? I speak of 'habits of behaviour' because I am not concerned with an overt conformity to particular moral precepts, but with moral values in the sense of 'enduring dispositions towards particular forms of behaviour'.

Collier was particularly concerned with those values – such as integrity – which sustain the probity of life. In this respect, it is worrying that a medical school should report that the educational experience inhibited rather than facilitated the development of moral judgement (Self, Baldwin and Wolinsky, 1992).

Collier (1993) is of the opinion that provision for the teaching of values should be made within the curriculum. Their goal would be to prepare students to think critically about value questions and subjective perceptions. In order to explore and analyse value issues students have to become personally involved in the morality of human situations if the existential dimension necessary for such study is to be secured. Collier had organized courses to meet these goals at Bede College of the University of Durham. Like Collier, Penn (1990) argued that the moral dilemma model should be taught in tandem with cognitive skills of logic, role taking and justice as, by itself, it is an ineffective way of achieving moral reasoning.

Schlaefli, Rest and Thoma (1985) analysed 55 studies of specific interventions. These interventions were peer discussion of moral dilemmas, personal development programmes involving some experimental activity and self-reflection within academic courses, where value issues arise from the study of the discipline, and short-term interventions which look at specific issues (e.g. Does moral education improve moral judgement?).

The analysis found that discussion of moral dilemmas and personal development programmes had the strongest effects. Academic courses were not very effective, and the short-term interventions least effective, which is rather alarming if one of the purposes of higher education is to develop people who characteristically exercise moral reasoning in their everyday work and life. Pascarella and Terenzini conclude that 'the key role of college in fostering principled moral reasoning may therefore lie in providing a range of intellectual, cultural and social experiences from which a range of different students might potentially benefit.' This finding provides more support for the collegiate model advocated by Astin as well as a multiple strategy approach to assessment and learning.

Conclusion

It is generally agreed that the purpose of higher education is the development of people who are capable of reflective thought and judgement. Recent advances in developmental psychology cast doubt on whether these goals are achieved. Perry showed that much assessment and teaching inhibits these goals. King and Kitchener's model helps make explicit, as do other discussions of critical thinking, what has been tacitly assumed to be reflective judgement. These models provide criteria against which the work of departments and teachers can be judged. In order to obtain these goals substantial changes in course structure and methods of teaching and assessment may have to be made. When institutions and their programmes are evaluated against models of development appropriate to higher education they are often found to be wanting. While attendance at institutions of higher education would seem to have positive effects on development in the cognitive and moral spheres, much more can be done at the course, teaching and assessment levels to enhance that experience. Courses, teaching, tutoring and assessment need to be structured so as to challenge and support students simultaneously as they move forward in a gradual development fired by spurts which move them from one slope on the learning curve to the next. To develop reflective practice, teachers as well as their students have to become reflective practitioners. The implications of this for assessment are discussed in Chapter 14.

Chapter 8

Learning Concepts

Summary

For the purpose of this chapter learning is taken to be that process by which experience of the world and thought develops new concepts and reorganizes old concepts and concept frameworks (or scaffolds).

Learning is both a necessary and contingent activity. It is something we cannot avoid. Mostly it happens informally in response to our environment. Education formalizes learning; thus a requirement of effective teaching is that the tutor has to have some knowledge of learning, and the way in which assessment may or may not influence learning. The aim of this chapter is to draw attention to some aspects of learning relevant to these issues.

Because learning is a complex activity, no one perspective (theory) suffices for its understanding. Several theories have been proposed; each has its advocates and has achieved some popularity, as for example, the information-processing model. This chapter focuses first on the process of perception and how we grasp the meaning of an idea and fit it into the existing set of ideas that we can connect with it (apperception). Some educationalists call this schema theory, which is the historical tradition of Allport (1955); Bartlett (1932, 1958); and more particularly in higher education Abercrombie (1960) and Hesseling (1966). Attention is drawn to the ease with which we are deceived, and how the perceptions of the teacher and student can be at such variance as to cause dissonance in learning. The implications of perceptual learning for the curriculum and teaching are discussed.

Many students find the learning of concepts difficult and many misperceptions are held which impede learning. Strategies for helping the learning of concepts include the introduction of cognitive conflict. In order to evaluate the understanding students have of concepts teachers can benefit from the regular use of classroom assessments. The *one minute paper* is a valuable technique in this respect. It is found that students often need more time to learn concepts than is allowed The difficulties many students have in understanding concepts once again illustrates the need for teachers to have a knowledge of learning that extends to exploring how their students learn. This may be facilitated through think aloud techniques and concept mapping. Assessment cannot be considered in isolation of an understanding of student learning. The chapter ends with a brief discussion of 'key' concepts as an aid to curriculum design.

Learning and perception

Much of our learning, if not all, begins with sense perception. We receive information through sight, sound and touch. Consider for a moment the room in which you are reading this book, assuming you are in a room. A cursory glance shows that there is a huge amount of information to be obtained from the artefacts in the room as well as its structure. It is possible that you will not be able to put a name to all the objects or patterns you see. In some way you are able to dredge from the mind something which enables you to say 'that is a chair'. The fact that you can do this is why 'computer' or 'information processing' models of learning are so popular. It seems sensible to presuppose that the mind has a storehouse of information ordered in elementary bytes which can be commanded to find the byte associated with what you see. The mechanism that makes the association is easily related to information processing. Be that as it may, the issue for our present purpose is how we construct this storehouse of information.

Before the days of the computer psychologists had proposed that the mind acquires elementary *schema* which becomes incorporated into frames of reference against which we can make our associations. These elements of knowledge have been variously called *schema, schemata, categories* and *frames of reference*. Allport described such categories as accessible clusters of associated ideas in the mind which serve as a frame of reference for fresh perceptual samples of immediate modes of behaviour.

Champagne, Gunstone and Klopfer (1983) distinguished between *micro-* and *macroschema*. The former is a mental structure that guides the analysis and interpretation of an identifiable class of phenomena. A *microschema* generally incorporates concepts, propositions, and more or less integrated networks of these two elements. The latter is a mental structure which encompasses several *microschema*.

In one of the earliest and seminal tests on learning in higher education Abercrombie (1960) described how students in medicine and architecture perceived and learnt about the objects in their environment. For example she described how medical students perceived X-rays and showed that there was no guarantee that they would perceive them in the same way. We are, it seems, easily deceived. So how is it we learn and how are we deceived?

The need to sample information

We cannot help listening, seeing and touching. We take very little notice of most of what we hear, touch and see. Some things stimulate us to want to know more and when they do, formal learning begins. For the most part we dismiss what we hear, touch and see. If we did not we would go mad. Consider the journey to work. We have of necessity to sample. This sampling will be affected by our prior experience. However, our focus might be blurred because of something that has happened in our immediate past. Experience affects our performance in two ways. Immediately, as an emotion, and collectively as the accumulation and affirmation of schema. This assembly itself has been the subject of sampling, and any sampling is necessarily biased (or prejudiced). Sometimes the sampling is imposed on us, as for example in conventional teaching: we are provided with knowledge in that environment. Sometimes, however, our interests and actions determine the sampling we make, as for example in project-based learning. In this perspective not everything is socially learned or constructed: we can and do make our own constructions.

Because we have to sample and because so much learning is a function of our personal and environmental history we are necessarily biased or prejudiced. We acquire dispositions toward things and events. Our value dispositions begin to be formed when we are very young, and they pervade our future actions. One study that illustrates this point was by Duff and Cotgrove (1982) who found that when compared with students from economics, engineering and management, students of social science were 'anti-industry'. The investigators argued that students' choice and career were a function of their experience in early adolescence. In the 1990s many investigations were undertaken in science and technology to understand the perceptions which students had of these subjects. This was because they failed to attract a sufficient number of qualified students. These studies have extended across the age range, gender, type of school and country (e.g. Kent and Towse, 1997; Palmer, 1997; Woodward and Woodward, 1998).

Perception at the micro level of the classroom is equally problematic. Student understanding of what has been said may not conform with the teacher's understanding of what he/she has imparted. This may be due to any one of a number reasons not least among them the perception that the students have of the teacher. For example, at one American college a course evaluation showed that while female instructors were given higher formal ratings than men, they were also expected to offer greater inter-personal support because they were perceived as warmer and more potent individuals. This finding was considered by Bennett (1982) to arise from culturally conditioned gender stereotypes and is an excellent example of the prior conditioning of experience.

Perceptual learning and the curriculum

It follows from the above that a liberal education should make us aware of how we learn, even if only to understand how we become prejudiced, and to reflect on those prejudices. That, after all, is the purpose of reflective practice. But, it may be argued, the more we understand about learning the more likely we are to develop powers of critical thought, which is a major goal of higher education. Nowhere is this more of an imperative than in our dealings with the media, particularly in response to editors and producers who have their own hidden agendas. Television can easily deceive and its subliminal effects go unnoticed. It is a characteristic of the educated person that they will not rely on one source of information. That, by itself is, however, insufficient, and we need to be shown how television deceives, and to realise that viewing and interpreting the media are skills (e.g. Bagelley *et al.*, 1980), and we need to have those skills tested. This will necessarily involve us in understanding our perceptual processes.

Various approaches have been adopted to confront us with the problems of perceptual learning (e.g. in business studies, Dinkelspiel, 1972; generally, Hesseling, 1966; at the Open University, Cowan, 1998; teacher education, Heywood, 1982; and general education, Rollers *et al.* 1972). Very often dissonance is used to change our perceptions. Hesseling (1966) calls it a *chocs des opinions*, a phrase which would seem to be self-explanatory. Others have called it 'cognitive challenge' or 'cognitive conflict' (see below). It inevitably involves students in active learning, and may use instructional strategies such as brainstorming, role playing, and other forms of group work planned for the occasion. They will involve the student in an encounter with new and unexplained phenomena that demonstrate the inadequacy of our previous experience to explain, and if it is a problem to solve. This creates a conflict with our previous experience which if the issue is to be permanently resolved has to be internalized if it is to become a guide to new thinking (Rollers *et al.*, 1972).

Sometimes such courses can be a cause for anxiety for tutors who, having changed their roles, either do not get an instant return or find their goals are not being met. Rollers and his colleagues, for example, found their students did not answer their own personal questions. So they introduced a project to give some structure to the course because 'it enabled the student to gain comprehension and control over his present capabilities and some perspective on his present value'.

Students cannot, it seems, be left on their own to develop structures unless they are clear that this is what they are expected to do. It is unfortunate that 'satisfaction with courses' may be related to perception of their structure (Kozma, 1982), but this is what we should expect from perceptual learning theory. Students have to be trained to cope with unstructured situations.

The use of cognitive conflict to change perceptions is discussed again later. Of course not everything we learn is biased (i.e. in the sense of being prejudicial). It may simply involve different understandings. Different environments use words in different ways. Dialects emerge and communication between different social groups can be made difficult. English is becoming the lingua franca. However, English usage throughout the world suffers from many cultural variations

Reading and oral comprehension are the basis of most learning and require the selection of schematic knowledge which fits the material to be comprehended. Thus, prior knowledge is important. If the necessary knowledge structures are not available in the mind it follows that reading comprehension will be difficult. Thus, in higher education students need to have sufficient prior knowledge if they are to understand difficult texts or deal with unfamiliar material. Just as for entering students (see Chapter 5) the teacher has to establish what the student knows and teach accordingly, so it is with every course (Ausubel, 1968). Henry (1990) reports concern in the United States with the failure of many 17-year-olds to become adept readers, particularly of primary source materials. Among his suggestions were for reading to be used as a means for providing background information. In many respects such reading would have the characteristics of an advanced organizer. Other strategies include interdisciplinary programmes, and survey courses in the classics.

Criticism of American education came to a head in the popular and controversial publications of 1987, notably in the work of Bloom and Hirsch. Hirsch (1987) described in his *Cultural Literacy* some 5000 essential names, phrases, dates and concepts that he thought every American should know. In the UK, some years earlier, Richmond (1963) had attempted a similar task, and tested students on his view of what that knowledge should be. From the point of view of this context, *Cultural*

Literacy was schema driven. The items that Hirsch uses to describe schema are concepts and he builds up concept trees and principles to show their importance in understanding language. Moreover, he attaches the same functions to schema that others have given to concepts, i.e. that they aid us to store knowledge in a retrievable form so that it can be applied rapidly and efficiently. Hirsch draws attention to the fact that we cannot model how we use schema in any detached way but that we use different types of schema. Some are static pictures (for example, birds), but there are also procedural schema related to occasions about birds on which the memory draws. Some schema are directly available to the mind while others are in the recess of the mind and take a long time to retrieve. Thus general information about birds is at a deeper level than specific information about birds, which is most often used.

What these specifics might be is a matter of debate. In England what school children should read has been a matter of heated controversy. Experience would suggest that this matter is not simple. It seems evident that we need both a wide general knowledge and to be able to study in depth. More generally, and simply put, schema theory leads to a view that in order to be able to communicate effectively students require a broad general education which will enable them to pursue the topics of the moment in depth with critical understanding. This requires that students are able to understand the concepts in use and the interpretations to which they are put. Such learning is problematic.

Concepts and their characteristics

At the level of the curriculum and instruction concepts serve as the basic building blocks for the knowledge scaffolds or frames of reference we construct. For the practical purpose of teaching the terms concept and schema are to all intent and purpose interchangeable. Concepts create the structure of content (knowledge): without content there can be no learning.

A concept is a class of stimuli that have common characteristics (De Cecco and Crawford, 1974; Howard, 1987). 'A concept is something in a person's head that allows her/him to place stimuli in or out of category' (Anglin, 1977 quoted by Howard). The functions of concepts are, therefore, to help us to reduce the complexity of the environment. We identify objects in the world around us, and with these build up networks (map, trees) of concepts with which to examine this world and appraise the new knowledge which 'comes' at us all the time. Concepts are identified by their attributes (colour, form, size) and each of these attributes can vary. The colour of an object is inadequately described by its primary feature. These variations describe the value of the attribute, and some attributes are more dominant than others. When the attributes and values are added together a conjunctive concept is produced (for example, car as compared with motorcycle or bicycle). Disjunctive concepts are produced when attributes and values are substituted one for another. Many relational concepts (for example, distance, time) are equally difficult to comprehend (De Cecco and Crawford, 1974; Howard, 1987).

Conjunctive concepts are the most used. It is in higher education that disjunctive and relational concepts are likely to be in common use. Ericksen (1984), records how in *Zen and the Art of Motor Cycle Maintenance: an inquiry into values*, the author, Persig (1974),

> Steadily evolved the concept of quality from a set of attributes of a satisfactory term paper – such as unity, vividness, authority, economy, sensitivity, clarity, emphasis, suspense, brilliance, precision, proportion, depth and so on to the point where quality ended up as a philosophy of life.

At this stage a high level of abstraction is reached, and this is the essential problem in higher education; the higher the level of abstraction, the more difficult it is to define a concepts boundaries. In consequence many concepts are fuzzy (e.g. democracy), and it is in handling them that high level skill in analysis is required. It is the ability to analyse and then synthesize complex concepts which distinguishes the able learner from the less able learner who is only able to describe at the level of comprehension.

Student teachers who have graduated from university often do not understand the concepts they have supposedly learnt in their courses, or what they 'understand' in examination conditions. Moreover they have difficulty in understanding the need to design their teaching around concepts (Heywood, 1997a). Support for this finding is found in studies of science learning at college level. For example, in the final assessment of 23 third-year Australian undergraduates taking a course in evolutionary theory and the philosophy of biology, 16 were failed by all three authors of the questions – a zoologist, an educator and a philosopher. Brown and Caton (1983) could not find evidence of a critical understanding of the concept of natural selection. The students regarded it as a dogma: they also had difficulty in understanding the significance of refutable propositions in science. In an earlier study in England (Brumby, 1979) only 18 per cent of first-year undergraduates were able to apply this concept to common environmental problems, in spite of the fact that they had GCE 'A' level in biology. The authors of the former study concluded that the students' problems were due to a specialization in biology which lacked theoretical underpinning, while the latter suggested that discussion of the wider issues of the evolution debate increased the problems students had in understanding the fundamental concept of natural selection. In another study, by Prosser (1979) of Griffith University, an attempt was made to isolate the major instructional and prerequisite concepts of part of a short physics course taught to first-year biology students for the purpose of determining the intellectual level at which these concepts were defined. A task analysis was performed on a set of instructional objectives which showed that the concepts were too abstract for many students. Prosser suggested that such courses should be arranged so that less formal reasoning would be required, or that the central focus of science courses should be intellectual development. A similar study among freshman chemistry students in three institutions in Australia and the United States concluded that students may not only need to learn concepts but also the language of chemistry (Hill *et al.*, 1980).

Gilbert and colleagues (1982) suggested that one of five things happen to learners when they are learning concepts:

1. The learners' concepts remain unchanged although a technical language is adopted.

2. The learners' concepts remain unchanged but the concepts and propositions taught are retained for examination purposes.

3. The learners are confused such that presented concepts and propositions reinforce incorrect or naive interpretive frameworks.

4. The concepts and propositions taught are assimilated into appropriate interpretive frameworks but not transferred to others.

5. The concepts and propositions taught are correctly understood and so modify all interpretive frameworks.

There is a continuing flow of evidence to confirm that students have difficulty in learning concepts in higher education.

Misconceptions in learning concepts

Reference has already been made to the difficulties that we have in learning concepts. The problem is not ameliorated by age. In two papers Clement (1981, 1982) described the preconceptions which students had of concepts in an introductory mechanics course. In the first paper he explains how freshman engineering students used formulae correctly but had only a weak understanding of the physical situation. Previously Price (cited by Heywood, 1974), had shown the same thing to happen with 'A' level students in Britain who were studying engineering science. In Clement's paper students confused the concepts of acceleration and speed, and showed little understanding of the qualitative conceptions of how charged particles affect each other.

Clement describes how he evaluated the effects of a physics course and found that many students had a stable alternative view of the relationship between force and acceleration which is 'conceptually primitive', and is highly resistant to change. Galileo apparently experienced the same thing with his students (Drake, 1974). Clement also tested sophomore, junior and senior engineering majors enrolled in an upper level engineering course and found that while the scores were somewhat higher 'an alarmingly high number of students still gave wrong answers of the same kind' on the very basic problems set.

By that time others had reported similar misconceptions. Among them Driver (1973, 1983) had shown that these misconceptions are acquired at very early ages. Since then there have been numerous studies in the sciences of the preconceptions which students have (McElwee, 1995), and such studies continue to this day (e.g. Marques and Thompson, 1997; Trumper and Gorsky, 1997). One concerned itself with the difficulties which students experience when they are required to transfer science concepts to practical technology projects in school (Levinson, Murphy and McCormick, 1997).

The theory generated to explain the persistence of these misconceptions suggested that it was because knowledge is constructed (Driver and Bell, 1986; Steffe and Gale, 1995). It was a relativistic epistemology which has in the last few years come in for criticism from realists within the scientific world, and theologians in the tradition of moderate realism (Matthews, 1994; Matthews, 1997; Bishop and Carpenter, 1993). It is no part of the purpose of this discussion to become involved in that debate. It is, however, important to draw attention to the implications that this view has for the role of the teacher and learning. It is a view that rejects the transmission (*tabula rasa*) mode of learning because human beings do not receive knowledge – they construct or create it. Therefore, students should be put in positions where they actively learn and are not recipients of knowledge. In these circumstances the teacher becomes a facilitator of knowledge who provides the experiences which the student will use to construct meanings.

Of course we do not have to have a sophisticated theory of knowledge to believe that we learn from experience through reflection and action. This is the basis of the Kolb theory described in the next chapter. It is not surprising that a series of books on effective learning and teaching in higher education should have been built around that idea of active learning and its assessment (e.g. Baume and Baume, 1992; Brown and Pendelbury, 1992). A derivative, action learning, is used by McGill and Beaty (1992) to describe the Kolb cycle in a group situation in which the participants in a 'set' each take forward an important issue in which they receive the support of other members of the group (see also Cowan, 1998).

Whatever view of knowledge we take it is clear that the students' mind cannot be regarded as a blank state. It contains prior knowledge and this knowledge is problematic. Newly acquired concepts, to quote Clement (1982) 'must displace or be remolded from stable intuitive concepts,' and an 'awareness of such preconceptions should allow the development of new instructional strategies that take student's beliefs into account and that foster a deeper level of understanding than is currently the norm.'

The persistence of misconceptions – resistance to change

Misconceptions occur in all walks of life. They are not simply a problem in the learning of mathematics and science. It is particularly true of student learning. Students may allow misconceptions to remain because they believe that the expert knowledge of their teachers is not intended to be understood at this stage (Brophy, 1987). We have all experienced students who believe that the first day of college is the start of new learning experience and not the continuation of previous experience (Meyer, 1993). Maybe we have unconsciously reinforced that view through the attitudes we have brought to our teaching. For this reason we need to know where our students are at and to make clear to them that the reason for a prior knowledge test is to ensure continuity of learning.

Meyer (1993) has drawn attention to the fact that students (indeed all of us) actively use strategies that will prevent understanding. Depending on how they learn so they respond to questions put in texts. Anderson and Roth (1989) found that where students thought the most important material was in the textbook then that material was regurgitated. Others who valued vocabulary filled their answers with terminology, and those who relied on their own knowledge made little use of the knowledge given in lectures. We have also experience of the students who strive to return what they believe the lecturers want. In my own case this has produced long and unwanted quotes from some of my writings.

Mathematicians will be aware of students who always use the same heuristic to solve problems irrespective of whether it is appropriate or not, Luchins (1942) called this 'set mechanization'. Various techniques have been suggested to change students' awareness. Thinking-aloud techniques also help teachers to understand how students learn. Meyer (1993) has suggested that students might teach students in small groups. She suggests that in an economics course students might be asked to 'Explain the gross national product in terms your grandmother would understand'. This helps students to organize their thoughts and reorganize them as a function of the discussion which follows.

In the paragraphs that follow some of the strategies which deal with the learning of concepts will be considered.

The structuring of learning

The fact that students have misconceptions and that this is widespread, puts an onus on teachers to respond to this problem in their teaching. At its simplest it means that lectures and classes must be carefully planned. There is a substantial body of knowledge about the sequencing of knowledge and the teaching of concepts at school level (De Cecco and Crawford, 1974; Howard, 1987; Heywood, 1997). There is no reason why this does not apply in higher education in respect of substantive concepts. There are ways of sequencing examples and non-examples, and such things as analogies and metaphors. These apply equally in the humanities as well as in the sciences (Cowan, 1998; Dunleavy, 1986; Howard, 1987). As has been indicated in earlier chapters students' concepts of learning and the nature and structure of the discipline also play a part in their approach to the subject of study.

Time required for learning concepts

There is a tendency among teachers to design extensive syllabuses and then to cover that syllabus at great speed because it is too large. This will mean that some students may be disadvantaged. If teachers are to ensure that concepts are learnt they may have to slow down and reorganize the structure of their programme. Stearns (1994) described a '1-2-3-4' process for handling the learning of complex concepts. These steps are (1) lecture, (2) individual learning, (3) small group learning, and (4) large group learning. Steps 2, 3 and 4 revolve around carefully constructed case studies that allow students to apply and discuss these concepts. This is one of the principles of the Harvard Business School's case method approach (Barnes, Christensen and Hansen, 1994). In the second step the students read the case study and answer the questions to the best of their ability. This is done as homework and the students have to come prepared to discuss their answers in a small group there to come to an agreement about the right answers that may require negotiation and voting. It is not sufficient for the students to record their answers without explanation. Furthermore teachers should not answer substantive questions. In the final session a delegate from each group presents their answers. The large group is facilitated by 'why' questions. Many tutors will have managed teaching in this way and will not find it strange. Others will find they have to take on a facilitative role. Stearns began his cycles just before the end of a lecture when the instructions were given. Step 4 is included because although small groups typically create better solutions than individuals there can be pressures within the group which lead to poor solutions (Janis, 1972). Whole group discussion allows clarification of responses and all are able to hear alternative solutions. Stearns makes the point that the tutor can also learn about the thought processes that led to the solution advanced.

Teachers often underestimate the time required for teaching a concept for understanding: the example above illustrates this point. However, there is a consensus that learning that has, perhaps slowly, built a good understanding, is remembered long after that which is crammed in the pursuit of 'breadth' is forgotten. This will have implications for the structure of the syllabus.

Cognitive challenge (conflict)

Mention has already been made of the potential of cognitive conflict to change perceptions.

Although the introduction of cognitive conflict into a class is relatively simple (Rosenshine and Meister, 1992), not every teacher may feel able to use such strategies, as McElwee (1995) found out. He wanted teachers to introduce cognitive conflict in classes where students had misperceptions about the process of boiling water.

McElwee's study, which was undertaken with junior high school students in the US and UK and with undergraduates in home economics who required some knowledge of science, showed that the number of misconceptions could be reduced. It also showed that some teaching of abstract theory could increase the number of misconceptions. In formal teaching, where scientific ideas were clearly taught but the misconceptions were not taken into account, the misconceptions persisted. McElwee considered that some misconceptions were more easily changed than others, and that other methods of teaching would have to be investigated. (McElwee, 1993, 1995).

Rosenshine and Meister (1992) suggest, as do many teachers, that students might be challenged by asking them to undertake a task which they are unlikely to be able to complete on their own which is set in such a way as to stimulate and not reduce motivation. Schoenfield (1985) found that this approach prepared students in mathematics to respond to a new heuristic. When they became skilled at applying a strategy, further new heuristics would be introduced. Assessment tasks focused on the student's ability to discriminate between strategies, and to select the one most appropriate for the solution of the problem.

Some form of cognitive conflict is likely to be necessary with freshmen because if they are at Perry's lower levels of cognitive development they are likely to want the teacher to tell them what to believe. This will be challenging for the teacher because, as Duit (1995) notes, the students may not see the conflict even when it is presented clearly. Sometimes dissonance may inhibit learning.

Value dispositions and cognitive dissonance

It seems that in certain circumstances conflicts between the values of the teacher and those held by the student can impede learning. In this respect the dispositions of students and their value systems are important. Dissonance may arise when students have a different conception of the nature of the subject to those of their tutor or, when they have different conceptions of learning to their tutor, or have different values to their tutor.

Watkins (1982) in Australia obtained evidence which suggested that the different academic environments in the various faculties might attract and satisfy students of different personality types. Another study, by Long (1976) in the US, found that conservative and liberal students viewed academic subjects differently and did not use the same dimensions when describing academic subjects. The costs of a 'poor' choice could be great if the values which a student brings to the class are in conflict with those of the teachers and such dissonance can be an impediment to learning. It is a problem that has worried teachers in the humanities because they believe that such conflicts might lead students to evaluate their courses poorly.

If, for example, a first-year student is introduced to cognitively complex material about a value system that is foreign to him or her, as might occur in political science, learning may be impeded or resisted. A student's consistent like or dislike for an instructor occurs when:

- the student likes the instructor, and agrees cognitively and affectively with the message given by him or her, as it is understood
- the student dislikes the instructor and disagrees affectively with the message from him or her, as it is understood.

Learning may take place in either case, for, as Marshall (1980) has pointed out, consistency is sometimes maintained because the student imposes his or her own understanding on the message so as to comport with the feelings he or she has about the instructor.

The more difficult the problem, the more likely is inconsistency or cognitive or affective dissonance (Canter and Meisels, 1971; Marshall, 1980). While the student may like the teacher in the beginning, what are perceived as untenable views on the teacher's part may cause him or her to change the understanding of the instructor's message and perhaps to dislike the instructor. Cognitive dissonance as Festinger (1957) called this phenomenon, is particularly likely and acute when the level of cognition required is difficult and the conclusions run counter to the student's disposition.

Hesseling (1966) called this mode of thinking, in which 'truth' is confused with desire – or in which there is a fusion of subjective and objective – 'autism'. Such autism, he maintained, always interferes with logical thinking. In this sense, our experience is prejudiced, and we are not free and unbiased to engage in 'open' interplay with our experience. We have to learn that there are likely to be discrepancies between our perception and the actuality of the incoming data. Of more importance is the fact that our previous experience contributes to these discrepancies. It is in this sense that an individual's experience may impede learning.

A major concern is that students who are affected by dissonance will return poor assessments to their teachers. However, a study among a large group of students concluded that cognitive dissonance is a weak framework for understanding course evaluations. What mattered more than the recruitment of interested teachers was the building and reinforcement of reputations for teaching interested classes (Granzin and Painter, 1976). Marshall (1980), in his investigation mentioned above, found among a group of students taking politics some who changed position away from those of the instructor and yet learnt. At the same time, their post-course ratings of the instructor went down. He put this down to good instruction.

Nevertheless, as Marshall indicates, such good instructors might have to put up with lower performance ratings. What matters in all evaluation is the objectives that are perceived by both teacher and student to have been achieved. But as Knight (private communication) points out, in 'high stakes' situations it would be professional suicide to do anything which would lower ratings, hence the importance of ensuring that those responsible for personnel decisions have a thorough understanding of the problems associated with student ratings outlined in Chapter 4.

Teaching scaffolds for developing higher-level cognitive strategies

The term scaffold has been used so far to describe mental structures that facilitate higher level learning. It is also used to describe instructional procedures that enable students to bridge the gap between their present situation and their intended goal (Paris, Wixson and Palinscar, 1986; Rosenshine and Meister, 1992). For example, using questions to prompt a student response during a dialogue is a cognitive strategy and students can be helped to employ it themselves. At the other end of the spectrum is group work that obliges a student to explain, elaborate and in particular to defend their position to others. All of these may be assessed both in the written form as well as by the observation of behaviour groups.

Similarly, assessment criteria can be turned into checklists so that the student can assess their own course work before it is submitted for assessment. Rinehart, Stahl and Erickson (1986) (cited by Rosenshine and Meister, 1992) required their students to use the following questions about précis which they had to write.

- Have I found the overall idea that the passage is about?
- Have I found the most important information that tells me more about the overall idea?
- Have I used any information that is not directly about the main idea?
- Have I used any information more than once?

The rubrics developed for assessment can easily be translated into such checklists as will be evident from the examples in Chapters 11 and 12.

There is some support for the view that students who are trained in self-questioning will do better than those who are not (Hadwin and Winne, 1996; Spires, 1993). Think-aloud techniques (see below) and cue-cards may be provided to help students develop skill in self- questioning (Wong and Jones, 1982). As previously suggested, discordant views can be introduced to prevent good techniques from becoming self-confirming. Ultimately the goal of higher education is to move from reliance on the lecturer to self-responsibility for learning. Thus, when using scaffolds to develop strategies the prompts have to be withdrawn so that the students can use them on their own. Whether students will use checklists or remember them is not an issue. They will be aware of the relative quality of their work when compared with their previous performance.

Although much of the work summarized by Rosenshine and Meister (1992) was in the areas of reading comprehension and mathematics the strategies reported have application in all areas.

Cooperative learning and syndicates

During the last decade teachers in higher education have begun to take more interest in forms of collaborative learning. Group work has as a prime function the clarification of ideas (concepts) and structured controversy is a form of cognitive conflict used to change misconceptions especially in science. Education in this perspective is viewed as collaboration, conversation and reacculturation. It would include peer tutoring (Bruffee, 1995). Once again it is based on the philosophy of active learning as is cooperative learning which has been pursued in higher education by Johnson, Johnson and Smith (1991). It is a systematic, rather than a random approach to group learning. It is based on the constructivist paradigm that students construct their knowledge in an active way while working cooperatively with classmates. This is in no way different to Newman who held that one of the best ways of learning was from one's peers. It is held that people are more likely to voice and defend their ideas and challenge others in small groups. A constructivist philosophy would not seem to be necessary to hold and pursue that view.

The key difference between cooperative learning and group work is that the cooperation between students is structured, and seeks individual accountability and the development of social skills. Individual accountability is achieved through the assessment of the performance of each individual in the group, and for this reason it is necessary for the members of the group to know who needs more assistance in completing the assignment, and that they cannot 'hitch-hike' on the work of others. Johnson and Johnson attach considerable importance to the group process. Groups process their functioning at the end of a session when they answer two questions: (1) What is something each member did that was helpful to the group? (2) What is something each member could do to make the group even better tomorrow? Such questions are the basis of reflective judgement. Johnson *et al.* (1991) argue that one of the most powerful ways to use formal cooperative learning groups is through the use of structured academic controversies. This, they say, promotes higher level learning, deep level understanding and long-term retention of what is learnt. Clearly cooperative learning is a technique that should develop the personal transferable skills which industry believe graduates should have. In the UK in the 1970s a group led by Collier experimented with syndicate methods which were evidently very similar to cooperative learning, and Collier records that his first experiment was conducted at

Temple University in the United States. 'The heart of the technique is the intensive debate within the syndicates', which he argues does not prevent individuals from developing their own distinctive opinions (Collier, 1983). He was particularly concerned with the value dimension in teacher education.

Group work in many institutions of higher education has not been systematized in the way of either cooperative learning or syndicates. Often the groups are randomly selected, and this can lead to conflict and a failure to learn. In this respect Freeman and Sharp (1999) have shown how the personality structure of groups can inhibit or enhance their learning.

Assessing how students learn

The assessment of prior learning

As indicated above, it is axiomatic that teachers need to know what their students already know. In certain circumstances a department as a whole may need to know what their new intake knows especially when it comprises traditional and non-traditional students. As indicated in Chapter 5 this problem is being experienced by many universities in the UK especially where they are having to run foundation courses to bridge the gap between what is known and what is required to be known for the university course proper. An objective test will reveal knowledge deficits although it may not reveal misperceptions unless the items have been designed to produce such data.

Angelo and Cross (1993) provide suggestions as to how misconceptions and pre-conceptions might be assessed. Among examples from the sciences and humanities they cite the experience of a history tutor who gave her students five minutes to answer three questions already known. At the end of the five minutes she shuffled the papers and handed them back so that each student had someone else's paper. They then shared their answers and found that the range of answers to the first two questions was considerable. The third question asked, 'What significant achievements had been made by the people who lived in the Americas before 1491?' She declined to give the answers. Instead she put a fourth question on the board, 'Where did you get those three answers'? At the end of the session the students knew their knowledge of pre-Columbian America was shaky. This was followed up by a library research assignment in which they had to double- check their answers. The students found there were no generally accepted answers.

Angelo and Cross consider that exercises of this kind relate to the following teaching goals:

- the development of the ability to distinguish between fact and opinion
- the acquisition of the facts and terms related to the subject
- the learning of concepts and theories in the subject
- the development of an openness to new ideas
- the cultivation of an active commitment to honesty.

Although questioning is widely used by teachers it is seldom thought through. This technique and others described by Angelo and Cross show how questions can be designed to achieve key goals.

Teachers also need to know whether their teaching is being effective. Many teachers have found it useful to ask their students questions like, 'What was the most important thing you learnt in this class?' and 'What important question remains unanswered?' Sometimes quite unexpected answers emerge. Angelo and Cross call these questions *minute papers*. They suggest they are probably most useful at the end of lectures and lecture/discussions. They argue that among other goals such papers help students develop the ability to synthesize and integrate information and ideas as well as to think holistically, and to see the whole as well as the parts.

The use of such papers may help students with the development of other learning techniques such as concentration and listening. Angelo and Cross demonstrate, with many examples, the value of simple classroom assessment to the teacher in understanding what is going on his/her classes.

Think aloud protocols

The idea of protocols comes from Simon who has been particularly interested in what distinguishes the expert from the novice. This has now become a relatively well-used technique for finding out about student learning and the problems they experience and was subsequently described in detail by Ericcson and Simon (1984) They may be written or recorded. For example, Cowan (1983) asked students to record their thinking as they undertook a problem-solving task. He found that undergraduates, faced with sketches that, for example, illustrated problems relating to the loading of beams that are not attached to given values and dimensions, rely on the quantitative methods taught in class to solve the problems. This they do by attaching number or symbols to the diagrams. Few develop qualitative strategies based on past experience. Even practising engineers tend to favour one overworked qualitative strategy. This confirmed Clement's (1981) finding and it also demonstrated set-mechanization. Cowan developed a self-study package to overcome this problem by encouraging development of qualitative understanding. He reported a significant increase in text scores.

Other studies in statistics and maths have used think-aloud protocols to try to find out how undergraduates solve problems, which allow researchers to analyse student strategies in terms of the errors made (Allwood and Montgomery, 1979). An American study in the area of mechanics found that the novice tended to solve the problems by assembling individual equations, while the expert solved them using a process of successive refinements (Larkin and Reif, 1979). Protocols may be of particular value in the evaluation of different approaches to computer assisted instruction, as for example in Spanish (Fernandez Prieto and Marsh, 1999). Another approach that will be discussed in the next section is to get students to draw concept maps.

As for any questionnaire, care has to be taken in the design of the questionnaire as questions can easily be misunderstood (Low, 1995). There are two approaches. In the first the observer notes the talk aloud and 'summarizes back'. In the second the observer records, transcribes and then analyses.

Think aloud techniques can be used as teaching aids to help students generate questions, clarify difficult statements and concepts, and summarize important infor- mation. They can also help forward thinking. They may help students acquire responsibility for their own learning. Meyer (1993) uses them to help students evaluate their performance in examinations. She asks students to think through the problem aloud, and responds only if the student hesitates or contemplates an unspoken thought. Even if the question is a multiple-choice item, she asks the student to evaluate each alternative aloud. She points out that while this may reveal misinter- pretations about what is required, it facilitates beliefs about what is not an acceptable answer.

Concept mapping

Concept mapping has been used by students to record, and to develop learning, by lecturers to assemble content, and by student and tutor for formative evaluation. Concept maps may be used to describe many relationships other than those of the key concepts of a curriculum described earlier. They come in all shapes and sizes. Hyerle (1996) distinguishes between eight types of thinking map. A circle map helps define words or things in context and presents points of view. Bubble maps describe emotional, sensory and logical qualities. For example, at their centre in a circle might be a heroic person, and from the centre other circles describe the characteristics of the hero. Tree maps, as evident from previous examples show relationships between main ideas and supporting details. Block schematic diagrams are examples of flow maps. Maps of the London tube or the Washington (DC) metro are flow maps. Flow maps may show causes and effects as well as predict outcomes. Maps may also be used to form analogies or metaphors. Sometimes they look like the main support of a spider's web.

Danserau and Newbern (1997) call bubble maps 'node maps'. The nodes contain the central ideas. The links go to other nodes surrounding the central node and show relationships between the nodes. The nodes are linked together via the central node and lead to a key concept. One of the examples where they give good communication is characterized by easy to illustrate complex relationships, less work clutter, easy to remember, and easy to navigate.

It is evident that maps of this kind are similar to mind maps and graphic organizers. Within the context of this chapter concept maps may be used to analyse a concept. Figure 8.1 shows an analysis of a liar in order to help you answer the question 'What kind of a liar are you?' Moreira (1985), the author of this map, also gave examples of student generated concept trees which could be used to study misconceptions as well as meaningful knowledge. They can be very useful in establishing prior knowledge.

Danserau has also used maps as a guide to lectures either by means of a handout or overhead transparency. Once students are trained they can generate their own maps, and if they wish, they can replace conventional notes with such maps. (McCagg and Dansereau, 1990). Czuckry and Danserau (1998) argue that a team mapping project can replace the traditional term paper. Students in an introductory psychology course

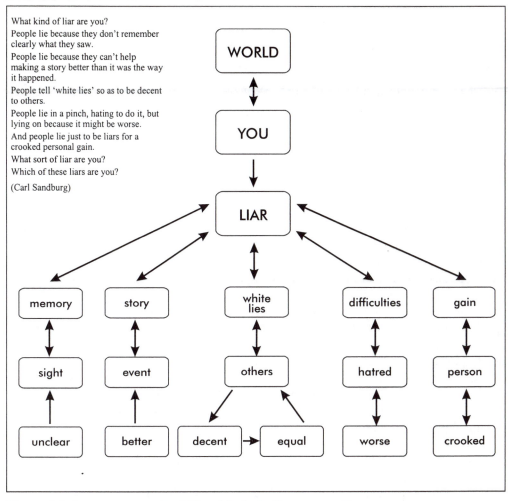

Figure 8.1 A concept map for 'What kind of a liar are you?'
(Reproduced by kind permission of M. Moreira first in Heywood, J. (1989a) from Moreira (1985).

and a memory cognition course completed a team mapping exercise. They were then asked to compare the mapping assignment to their perceptions of traditional writing assignments. The students preferred the mapping assignment, and they found it more interesting. They believed it involved them in more learning.

Danserau has used mapping to enhance communication between drug abuse counsellors and their clients. 'It seems to be helping; a series of controlled studies has shown that heroin and cocaine addicted clients exposed to mapping versus standard counselling treatment are more likely to stay drug-free during and following treatment' (Danserau and Newbern, 1997).

Sharp, Harb and Terry (1997) have drawn attention to the value of concept maps in planning writing as have other investigators. Angelo and Cross (1993) considered that the goals of concept mapping are to develop the ability to:

- draw reasonable inferences from observations
- synthesize and integrate information and ideas
- think holistically: to see the whole as well as the parts
- learn concepts and theories in the subject
- understand the perspectives and values of the subject
- acquire an openness to new ideas
- think for oneself.

The second objective in that list is a reminder that concept maps can have a major role in the design development and evaluation of interdisciplinary courses and projects.

Hadwin and Winne (1996) had difficulty in finding evaluation studies of concept mapping. Only four met their rigorous criteria. They offered the tentative conclusion that concept mapping could help students to study but that its success would be affected by the context in which the students were studying. When a course required deep as opposed to surface learning concept mapping was likely to be successful. The benefits of concept mapping emerge as students persist. The more students persist the more they are likely to benefit. And, as is the case with so many strategies, students with low content knowledge might feel insecure when asked to map concepts. For students to learn any study strategy, and in particular concept mapping, it needs to be blended into the course.

Hadwin and Winne (1996) did not refer to Okebukola's (1992) study of Nigerian students (pre-degree) who had experienced cooperative and individualistic exper- iences of concept mapping over a six-month period. He found that, in solving three biological problems, that this group was significantly more successful than a control group which had not experienced such training.

Irrespective of these findings it is clear that tutors can evaluate student learning from concept maps. Such maps need not be of the formal kind described in the reports described above. They may be in the form of sketches rather than line diagrams of one kind or another; for example, Fordyce (1991), in a pilot study with a colleague in which he explored the macro-schema of mechanical stress. He wanted to find out both what his colleague felt and what he would be likely to discover from the undergraduate concept maps, so he obtained a map from the expert that could be compared with those obtained from the students. The maps produced by the expert and the students were nothing like traditional concept maps. On the left-hand side of the expert's map was the use of stress: on the right-hand side the relationship between stress and strain was described. The link between stress and strain was not seen as simple. (I draw attention to this observation because student misconceptions might think the link is simple – see above). The mapping and accompanying audio recording took 25 minutes.

A preliminary workshop was given to all students to exemplify what Fordyce was looking for. Then, during the first part of the term the students became familiar with the mechanisms; they became their own researchers. The questions they had to answer in this process of discovery were:

1. What are the features of the theme for you?

2. How do you hold the features (as an equation, as a voice, as a picture of an equation written down, as some form of graphical representation, or as a real situation)?

3. What is the meaning of the feature for you? And how do you interpret what you have justified)?

4. What is the nature of the link between the features for you, if any?

Of the several findings one is of particular interest. As the map was constructed an element which Fordyce called the 'core' emerged. This was the area of the map the respondent felt most confident about. With first-year students this related to work they had done before entry to the undergraduate programme, e.g. in stress and strain the expressions for stress and strain formed the core. 'Where new material was defined this did not form the core in terms of confidence; here aspects or features of the map were known about and memorized but they had not been accommodated in the core.' At this stage, in today's parlance, they had not been internalized and were not owned.

As well as eliciting data about the levels of confidence possessed by the students the exercise also illuminated their difficulties and showed the teacher where they had to go. The 'novice' engineers maps had recognizable components of the 'experts' map but their maps were at different levels of abstraction. First-year students had no datum values with which to judge their answers.

Because the level of confidence was found to be important this study highlights the importance of the affective component in cognitive thinking. This dimension is a neglected aspect of teaching in the sciences yet, it seems that it is *personal justification* which provides the feeling of confidence in a topic area.

This study confirms the view put previously that knowledge structures require time and experience to develop. They cannot be hassled. Further, it supports the contention that teaching should be governed by an understanding of student learning. Teachers should avoid imposing their structures on those of beginning students. In so far as first-year students are concerned Fordyce felt that 'it would be reasonable to expect only simple "first level" models in relation to a confident "unified scientific outcome" where it exists'.

Curriculum design and key concepts

Once time is allowed for the learning of concepts something has to be dropped from course content. This means reorganizing the curriculum around the key concepts thought to be most important. The idea of 'key concepts' is due to Taba and Freeman (1964). She defined them as procedural devices to help teachers in the selection and organization of content. They are, therefore, ''objectives,' and as such are important for curriculum design because they create the learning strategy requirement and thus the time requirement and therefore the syllabus. They may also be regarded as themes

Perception:	The individual's assimilation and modification of data presented by the environment through the senses.
Learning:	The process by which experience develops new and reorganizes previous concepts and patterns of behaviour.
Activity:	Any process through which an individual engages in living.
Communication:	The effective transmission and reception of relevant information.
Design:	A process in which problems are formulated, analysed, solutions planned, treated, tested and the outcomes evaluated.
Management:	Direction and control over self and/or others.
The individual:	A human being with unique needs and potential for adaptation and control of self and environment.

Figure 8.2 Key concepts in a course for occupational therapy

that pervade the whole curriculum, as the example in Figure 8.2 for an occupational therapy curriculum shows.

The way the key concepts of a subject link together is likely to differ between the subjects of the curriculum. This point is illustrated by Donald's (1982) work in the United States. She investigated 16 college courses, 11 of which used concepts in a linear hierarchy. The most important concept was the most inclusive one. In all but one of the courses the key concept had the pre-ordinate role. In physics, for example, the whole of the course was built around the concept of 'wave shapes' (Figure 8.3). The branches of the tree go from the more important to the less important aspects. The key concepts in science are tightly structured whereas those in the social sciences are loosely structured, with certain key concepts acting as pivots or organizers.

The design of interdisciplinary and integrated programmes is greatly facilitated by the use of key concepts. Seven are used to integrate the programme in geography, history and social studies shown in Figure 8.4. These provide an integrating theme, even though the subjects retain the distinctive nature of their disciplines. Although they are at a high level of abstraction and overarch the disciplines, they do not possess a special epistemological status, and if they were to do so they could impose on the students an idiosyncratic structuring of ideas which is not merited.

It will be appreciated that the mere formulation and presentation of a concept does not resolve the problem because decisions have to be made about how to teach each key concept, that will demand an understanding of student learning. Understanding learning can be helped by think aloud strategies and concept mapping.

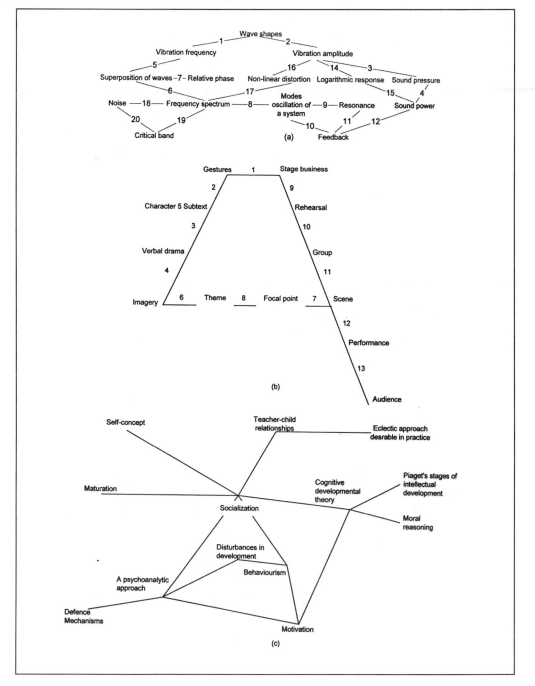

Figure 8.3 Key concept structure in (a) Physics, (b) English and (c) Developmental Psychology.
(from Donald (1982)first reproduced in Heywood (1989a) by kind permission of the author and the editors of the *Journal of Higher Education*).

1. Communication:	The significant movement of individuals, groups or resources or the significant transmission of information.
2. Power:	The purposive exercise of power over individuals and society's resources.
3. Values and beliefs:	The conscious or unconscious systems by which individuals and societies organize their response to natural social and supernatural circumstances.
4. Conflict/consensus:	The ways in which individuals and groups adjust their behaviour to natural and social circumstances.
5. Similarity/difference:	Classification of phenomena according to relevant criteria.
6. Continuity/change:	Distinction of phenomena along this essentially historical dimension.
7. Causality:	The notion that change in a state of affairs can be attributed to the phenomena preceeding.

Figure 8.4 Key concepts for an integrated programme in history, geography and the social sciences. Although relevant at any level of interpretation these particular concepts were applied to the development of a programme for 8–13-year-olds.
(Reproduced by kind permission of W.A.L. Blyth and his colleagues Blyth *et al.*, 1973 at the University of Liverpool)

Conclusion

The learning of concepts has been shown to be more problematic than is sometimes thought. Misconceptions are easily acquired. Teachers need to assess student understanding continually so that misconceptions may be avoided. There are a number of techniques at their disposal for this purpose. Teachers may find they have to change their methods of instruction and in particular slow the pace of delivery. This is likely to have implications for the structure of the curriculum. The design of the curriculum around essential 'key' concepts should help the teacher focus on what matters. The problem of learning concepts is further complicated by the learning dispositions which students bring with them. This problem is discussed in the next chapter.

Chapter 9

Learning Strategies and Learning Styles

Summary

This chapter is about what the students bring to learning in the form of their dispositions to learn and their learning styles. In the first part of the chapter discussion focuses on holist/serialist strategies, and in particular on deep/ surface/strategic and apathetic strategies. Institutions, departments and teachers can have a powerful influence on the strategies that students adopt. Learning is shown to be a complex activity dependent in no small measure on the interaction between type of instruction, course structure and the perceptions of students as well as their dispositions. Assessment is shown to have a powerful influence on the learning strategies that students adopt.

Among the talents which students bring with them are dispositions toward the way they organize, remember and think about new knowledge (Messick and associates, 1976). These different styles of conceptualization and patterning of activities may be the most important characteristics of an individual (Tyler, 1978). These cognitive or learning styles are thought to play an important part in learning and studying. The arguments put forward in the case of some of these styles are discussed here. Of these one of the most debated is that of convergent versus divergent thinking. Another that has been much discussed is that of field dependence/ independence.

Some styles derive from a particular theory of learning. One, with its associated inventory which has proved to be very attractive to teachers is the Kolb Theory of Learning Styles (Kolb, 1984). More recently, a similar theory to Kolb's has been developed by Honey and Mumford (1992). Assessment and instruction may be designed around the features of these models.

Attempts have been made to relate personality and style, and a popular instrument among teachers for obtaining these dimensions of human behaviour is the Myers-Briggs Type Indicator. Like the extraversion/introversion-neuroticism test developed by Eysenck, it is a derivative of Jungian personality theory. It is discussed at the end of this chapter.

The instruments used to measure strategies and styles can help teachers better understand their students' learning within the context of their teaching. The implications for the design of assessment and instruction are profound. All avenues lead to the same conclusion, namely, that teachers should expose their students to a variety of carefully planned assessment and instructional techniques (learning experiences) if optimal learning is to be achieved.

Learning strategies

Holistic and serialist learning strategies

These terms are now part of common usage. They originate with the work of Pask and his colleagues. During the 1960s he, Lewis and Scott had suggested that learning strategies, teaching strategies and plans of action can be differentiated by type (Pask, 1988). Their concept of style is based on what they call conversation theory. Conversations are behaviours that may be observed in the form of understandings. Within conversation theory, *understanding* includes the relationship between the topics discussed but also the ability to apply that relationship to new situations. We may have conversations with ourselves which can be in the form of gestures or mediated through a computer interface.

An *entailment mesh* is a network or map of topics which has neither direction nor hierarchy. Paths on the map that are marked to show specific conceptual events are negotiated by *learning or teaching strategies*. Examples of such events are learning about a topic or understanding it in relation to other topics. In contrast to a *strategy* a *style* is a disposition to adopt one class of learning strategy or one class of teaching strategy in the conversations which are usually verbal but may be in laboratory experience. The problem is to whom does the style belong. Individuals are only partly autonomous because they are open to exchange of information with others. Pask thinks that if styles are characteristic of people then it is probable that they characterize people in context. In academic learning they adopt a strategy as a personal style. Thus in a situation of formal examinations and the serialization of tuition they will be biased to a serialist style, whereas in subjects like architecture and art a holistic bias can be detected. These holist and serialist learning strategies are mirrored by similar teaching strategies. Holists prefer global predicates and relations of topics whereas serialists prefer step by step approaches to learning. Teaching preferences along these lines are readily identifiable. They suggest strongly that strategic mismatches between potentially effective learning styles and teaching strategy can impede learning. Later studies suggested that matched performance is better than mismatched performance. They also revealed different types of serialists and holists. There are those serialists who move step by step; they do not proceed to the next thing to be learnt until they have mastered the present. There are also serialists who learn by rote; they follow a well-defined and narrow route and may do well in examinations which demand memory skills (cited in Pask, 1988).

Pask distinguished between redundant and irredundant holists. Both focus on the global and predicate rules but the redundant holist learns better with minimally specified rules. Some holists prefer analogies and generalizations that provide contrasts and similarities *within* the material. Whereas there is another type of holist who likes to discover or invent these analogies and generalizations between the topics. Pask argues that while this is one of the most productive ways of learning neither, the serialist or holist is at an advantage since learning involves both discovery and invention as well as integration of both local and global rules. He noted that whatever the problem some persons use the same strategies which, if they are holist, would be mismatched in academic environments where a serialist style is the dominant approach. However, Pask also reported that some persons are more flexible and versatile than others in their response to changing contexts, a fact which relates to that aim of education which is to learn to be adaptable in life's situations.

Pask used the terms *improvidence* and *globe trotting* for learners who relied on one process at the expense of the other. Serialists show *improvident* behaviour because they are likely to miss important relationships between ideas whereas *globe trotters* rely on holism and build up views quickly that do not contain the evidence to support the conclusions reached. This would seem to have implications for the way examiners approach the marking of essays (see Chapter 11).

A slight variation of these ideas is to be found in Svensson's (1976) distinction between *holistic* and *atomistic* approaches to learning. The former tries to understand the text as a whole whereas the atomistic learner is not orientated to the meaning of the text as a whole but toward the sequence and details (Marton, 1988).

Studies of reading have found the three styles of global, analytic and synthetic learner. In a global approach reliance is placed on prior contextual knowledge. An analytic reader is oriented to the detail of word identification and meaning, thus relying on the information in the material rather than on prior knowledge. The synthetic style integrates in progression the other two strategies (see Kirby, 1988). Most people are able to switch between styles as a function of the situation in which they find themselves. For example academics, who are skilled readers, are unlikely to engage in the global strategy of processing, but to quote 'if academics were assessed on the basis of their performance in situations related to problems with their automobile or with their home life, much more global processing would be observed.'

The theory offered by Pask would seem to support a multiple- strategy approach to assessment and teaching. While individuals may well switch strategies as a result of context, the 'normal' contexts in which they work may cause such a press that they find it difficult to, if not resent, changing tack. If a goal of higher education is to develop flexibility then individuals have to be able to call on a wide range of learning strategies.

Deep and surface approaches to learning

The idea of depth and surface approaches to learning comes from work by Marton and Säljö (1976; 1984) and Svensson (1976) in Sweden. It was further developed in the UK (Gibbs, 1981; Marton, Hounsell and Entwistle, 1984; Ramsden, 1984) and Australia (Biggs, 1987; Kirby, 1988). Most of these studies have been done with students in higher education. Marton and Säljö in their study were led to distinguish between deep and surface approaches to understanding or, as it is sometimes phrased 'search for meaning'. They also found a holistic/atomistic dimension of the kind described above that related to the way the students organized the information given. In the Marton and Säljö experiment the students were asked to read a text and told they would be questioned on its context and how they tackled the task.

Several methods were used. In one of them, a text was given to students to read after which they were asked to recount it, answer questions on the content, describe how they had read it, and how they went about remembering its content. On the second occasion they were asked to recall as much as they could of the text. A second revised and enlarged text was given next and the procedure repeated. In another investigation a split-group technique was used with independent halves. On the first occasion one half were given questions in advance on particular points in the text while the other half received no guidance. For the second occasion half the group were given instruction as to how they should read while the others were given no instructions. A free recall was requested, and questions were asked about the text immediately after reading and after 65 and 85 days. Students in similar subject studies who were not in the experiment were also interviewed. An examination was also set. Further variations in technique were used and questionnaires and interviews administered. The samples were 30 first-year students in education and 29 in political science and economics. Marton and Säljö concluded that

> The students who did not get 'the point' failed to do so simply because they were not looking for it. The main difference which was found was whether the students focused on the text itself or on what the text was about, the author's intention, the main point, the conclusion to be drawn.

Marton suggests that the strategies they found, apart from anything else, are indicative of different perceptions of what is wanted in learning in higher education. For some, 'learning is through the discourse and for others learning is the discourse.' Those who adopt the former strategy get involved in the activity while those who take the latter view allow learning to 'happen' to them. It is this second group who are *surface* learners who pay but superficial attention to the text, who are passive, who do not reflect and who do not appreciate that understanding involves effort.

What we would appear to see is the traditional distinction between active and passive learning that is intrinsically understood by academics even if not explained when they talk about study in depth. Learning through discourse is exactly how Newman (1947 edition) described the effects of university education in *The Idea of a University.*

This investigative technique is open to criticism, for the phenomenology on which it is based is a form of empiricism. By itself it cannot say if and when the levels of consciousness are raised by the 'surface group'. Or does it imply that they are never raised by persons in this group? It might also be objected that the technique depends on reading and therefore neglects reflective thought. Nevertheless, it has shown the care, for example, with which examination questions should be designed and it has also produced other research that supports this general thesis. For example, in Australia studies among senior-year students have suggested that deep-level students were more likely to perceive their course as encouraging independence in both attitudes and approach to learning, and as not being overburdening (Watkins, 1981).

During the late 1970s Entwistle (1988) began an extensive programme to extend the work he had begun on motivation (Entwistle and Wilson, 1977). He and his colleagues wished to confirm Marton's conclusion that the outcome of learning was related to the approach to learning. In their factorial analysis they found two factors were related to deep approaches to study. One described a student who would concentrate on relating ideas without examining the evidence in detail. The other placed reliance on factual detail but was not accompanied by a clear overview. Few students, it seemed, were capable of undertaking all the processes demanded by a fully deep approach.

Entwistle and Ramsden's (1983) UK study of their *Approaches to Study Inventory* yielded four factors which were called orientation to studying. The first factor was called the *meaning orientation*: it had high loadings on the deep approach and it was associated with comprehension learning and intrinsic orientation. By contrast, the second factor, the *reproducing orientation*, was highly loaded on the *surface* approach, operation learning and improvidence. These were associated with fear of failure and extrinsic motivation. This was illustrated by Kember *et al.* (1995) who, using Biggs Study Process Questionnaire, found that surface approaches correlated with high attendance in class and long hours of study time. The former was explained by a need to have the lecturers explain the course: the latter by the inefficiency of the surface approach which led to poor grades.

The other factors were labelled *non-academic orientation* and *achieving orientation*. The former was related to disorganized approaches to study, and the latter to *strategic approaches* to study, extrinsic and achievement motivations.

In their pilot study Entwistle, Hanley and Ratcliffe (1979) had identified a *strategic* approach to learning in which students try to 'manipulate the assessment procedures to their own advantage by a careful marrying of their efforts to the reward system as they perceive it.'

Another investigation of a small sample of nursing tutors, primary, secondary and further education teachers studying for a part-time degree found that the majority of all categories adopted a strategic approach. However, when the learning environment was changed *deep* approaches to learning were fostered. The females were found to tackle details first rather than the overall picture. The males were equally divided in their approach (Sutherland, 1995).

Kneale (1997) reported concern among British universities that there was a worrying increase in such *strategically* motivated students; 40 per cent of departments responding in their survey, most of them in the old universities, expressed such worries. Although their numbers are small many have high entry qualifications, suggesting that they would be capable of a high level qualification. They can have a demotivating effect on other students. But if the assessment is valid why shouldn't students seek to satisfy its demands? Cassidy (1999) using the ASSIST inventory (Tait and Entwistle, 1996) found among health science students following a research methods course that academic achievement was positively correlated with a *strategic* learning approach and negatively correlated with an *apathetic* learning approach. This confirmed previous research by Busato *et al.* (1998) and Eachus and Cassidy (1997a, 1997b). He concluded that a *strategic* learning approach is associated with belief in one's capabilities and actual academic performance having found positive correlations between internal locus of control and *deep* and *strategic* study approaches, as well as between internal locus of control and self-confidence, and self-confidence and *deep* and *strategic* study approaches. He also concluded that the adoption of a surface or apathetic approach and a belief in external factors, such as luck and powerful others, leads to weaker beliefs in one's own proficiency and weaker academic performance. Because deep learning was neither associated with academic achievement nor the research methods course he concluded (following Lyddy, 1998) that in later education the student's emphasis is on performance rather than learning.

The ASSIST (Approaches and Study Skills Inventory for Students) developed by Tait and Entwistle (1996) is a 38-item inventory and has four scales which measure the deep, surface, strategic and apathetic (lack of direction and interest) approaches to learning and academic aptitude (i.e. academic self-confidence). Prior to that Entwistle had suggested a 30-item inventory based on the best psychometric items. This has proved attractive to some investigators. Richardson (1994) suggested that the ASI could be abbreviated by focusing on the eight sub-scales that had been consistently identified with meaning orientation and reproducing orientation across the different academic disciplines studied by Entwistle and Ramsden (1983). His inventory required 32 items. He used it to investigate the different approaches to learning taken by mature and non-mature students (Richardson, 1995). From two small samples he found that mature students scored significantly higher on meaning orientation than non-mature students. They also tended to produce lower scores on reproducing orientation. He noted that their persistence and subsequent attainment was at least as good as non-mature students. Richardson argued that these inventories should be used with care because the integrity of some of the scales had not been confirmed. He also concluded that basic study orientations may be interpreted as a function of the cultural context in which they are measured (i.e. they are given different meanings by the respondents).

Entwistle's shortened inventory was used by Abouserie (1995) together with *The Inventory of Learning Processes* devised by Schmeck (1993). This inventory has scales for *deep processing, elaborative processing, fact retention* and *methodical study*. These were paralleled with a self-esteem scale, and a scale for achievement motivation. She found that achievement motivation contributed positively to scores on meaning orientation and methodical study among education students at the University of Wales. She suggested that personality variables in general and self-esteem in particular influence approaches to studying. This would be consistent with those investigations that have found a relationship between personality and performance.

Entwistle believes that the way instructions are interpreted is an important factor in determining the approach adopted. They create an intention to learn in a certain way that determines the level of processing. His colleague, Wilson (1981) queried this emphasis on intention, and argued that it is the conception of what learning involves which is one of the most important factors affecting the approach the student adopts. He argued that the approach learners take will depend upon several factors:

> First, is likely to be the difficulty of the subject matter: some texts can be skimmed over while others can only be understood by systematically setting out the arguments, evidence and conclusions. Second, is the interest and importance of the text: a 'set' book will receive a closer look than supplementary reading, but especially if its subject matter appeals to the student. Third, maybe the student's natural preference of reading in a particular way; the studies so far reported have not really clarified whether there are in fact basic differences in approach or whether the approaches actually used reflect the fourth factor, viz. the student's conception of what it takes to learn complex subject matter.

Both of these interpretations lend support to those who, in the 1960s, introduced new and multiple approaches to assessment with the view of positively influencing learning. Perhaps the most important questions that arise are:

1. Are all students able to both surface and deep study? (Are these strategies or substantive dispositions?)

2. What implications does this have for teaching?

3. What implications does this have for the institution?

Ramsden (1988) argues that it is clear that individual students display variability in their approaches to learning. He had previously reported that students could adopt both *surface* and *depth* approaches (Ramsden, 1984). Student expectations are a powerful influence on the style they adopt. Thus, the perceptions that students have of assessment even at the end of an exercise will dictate their approach even if that is not the approach which is called for (Marton and Säljö, 1984). As we know from perceptual learning theory, prior experience of similar tasks is a powerful influence on subsequent performance (see Chapter 8). Ramsden (1988) considers that the evidence for consistency in approach over time is persuasive. However, he argues that consistency is not the same as fixity and orientations to study may be changed in response to teaching, assessment, and the curriculum. As the example, above, of the *strategic* student shows departments can have a big influence on the strategies used by the students (see below and Ramsden and Entwistle, 1981).

But the matter is complicated, for *deep* approaches to learning may not result in good grades unless they are accompanied by sufficient work, but the accompanying coursework should not overload the students (Kember *et al.*, 1995). Another investigation among medical students in which two learning style inventories were used, while supporting the distinction between *surface* and *deep* learning, obtained little correlation between learning styles and academic performance (Leiden, Crosby and Follmer, 1990). Ramsden notes that as between the different subjects of the curriculum the types and timing of the approaches required will vary. Scientists undertake different tasks to those studying in the humanities.

The perceptions that students have of effective teachers seem to be similar to those held by students of school teachers, not least among them of the teachers who take time to respond to their pupils. Departments in particular and institutions in general convey images to students, not only of what is expected of them, but of what they can expect of their tutors. These pictures are not always happy ones. Ramsden (1988) takes up the issue of strategies versus style and points out that they have been confused in summaries of research on deep and surface learning. Styles are bipolar but each has positive aspects. Following Messick's definition, styles are stable and persistent characteristics of the individual. But approaches can change. So how does one help students learn strategies within the confinements of their style? Ramsden answers this question by reference to Pask's learning style model. Because the *holist* and *serialist* styles can be conceptualized as contextually dependent then, depending on the circumstances, learners would use differing mixtures of comprehension and operation learning. It is possible to have a dual conception of these types of learning as being consistent and variable. Thus Ramsden argues that both styles and strategies (approaches) 'need to be seen as consistent and context dependent'.

The importance of context is illustrated by several studies. For example, an investigation by Fogarty and Taylor (1997) in which 500 students of mature age returning to study were administered the short form of Entwistle's (1981) *Approaches to Study Inventory* found that *deep* or *surface* orientations may be positive or negative depending on the learning context and subject area. In this study the predictive validity of the *Inventory* had been tested against mathematics, but the deep orientation was found to be unrelated to academic progression in mathematics. However, high scores on the *surface* orientation were associated with poor academic performance.

In another study Hargreaves (1996), at the Queensland Institute of Technology, used the Study Process Questionnaire (SPQ) developed by Biggs, the *Course Experience Questionnaire* (CEQ) and the *Learning Styles Inventory* (LSI). The CEQ showed that good memory is not sufficient to pass examinations. It also showed that assessment was controlling approaches to learning. The SPQ showed that there was a significant proportion of surface learners. However, Hargreaves reported that a significant proportion of them could change their strategy as a function of the teaching techniques experienced.

Fyfe (1996) and Sadler-Smith (1996) have suggested that there is a curvilinear relationship between age and approaches to learning. At the extreme ends of the curve learners demonstrate deeper approaches to learning. Mature business studies students were found to have deeper approaches to learning than younger students. Sadler-Smith explained this with the suggestion that the deeper approaches to learning found among students over the age of 23 years might be due to breaks in their formal education. James (1997) investigated the effect of work experience during a degree course on learning strategies. His study was conducted with students in environment related courses and confirmed the findings of Fyfe and Sadler-Smith. However, he cautions that there is considerable variation among the students at each age level, and that 'teachers in higher education need to guard against making assumptions about individuals from the generality of the population'. Individual capacities and context limit the extent to which individuals can pursue study in depth.

Sadler-Smith (1996) also found that there was a significant difference between male and female business studies students in that the males perceived themselves as adopting a deep approach in contrast to the females. Among mature students returning to study after several years absence Fogarty and Taylor (1997) found that broad learning orientations could be distinguished and that while the *deep* orientation was unrelated to progression in mathematics *surface* orientation was related to poor academic performance. Hargreaves (1996) suggests that lecturers need to change their teaching paradigm from one where the lecturers stand outside the student learning context, to one where the lecturers are closely involved in the learning context. Courses and assessments would have to be designed which demand students use a variety of approaches, and then recognize that they do so.

Learning in school and higher education

In his attempt to draw conclusions from these various studies of deep and surface learning Schmeck draws attention to a number of points that have a bearing on school education. First (my ordering), is Marton's finding that university students in physics and economics can pass in economics and science and yet have no basic understanding of the concepts and principles of these subjects. They acquire large bodies of knowledge without acquiring the understanding required by these concepts and principles. At the same time:

> we have adults who do not see it as their function to reflect, form opinions, evaluate, disagree, oppose, challenge, conceptualise, or integrate information in meaningful ways. We have adults who plod along without thought until, at roughly 10 year intervals, they have what has come to be popularly known as the 'mid-life crisis' – permitting themselves for one brief period to ask 'what does it all mean?'

Schmeck's solution lies primarily in the design of examinations and classroom tests; he advocated that questions should be set which integrate knowledge. This is in keeping with Heywood (1977a; 1989a) who sees the prime function of a terminal examination as integrating knowledge. Students have to be encouraged to make a perceptual shift. Taken together all of this work leads to the view that it all begins in elementary school, for it seems that by the time students reach high school the semblances of deep and surface approaches have emerged (see also Bennett *et al.*, 1984) There are, therefore, signs that orientations hev emerged in high school which would influence student expectations of what to expect from university which will not easily be changed, especially by simple 'short study' courses (Selmes, 1985). Schools can encourage deep learning, and in a sample of Scottish and Hungarian students (mixed sex) Entwistle and Kozeki (1985) found that school attainment correlated with intrinsic motivation and the deep approach. As Richardson (1994) points out, care needs to be taken when interpreting cross- cultural studies.

Following arguments by McCarthy and Schmeck (1988), Schmeck considers that cognitive style may have its origins explained by the possibility that some children have to 'prove' themselves if their self-esteem is inadequate. In order to establish conditional worth within the classroom context of achievement and competition they learn to 'crack the code' with analytic skills. If a student clings to this way of doing things then they will continue to approach things in this way and develop a high level of analytic cognitive style and not move beyond this to Kirby's (1988) level of thinking in synthesis.

In contrast, a person who does not crack the code will be left at the global stage, become field dependent and continue to be childlike and undirected and, within the context of study, have low esteem reinforced. Schmeck relates this to parenting and not merely schools. Early parenting can influence the dependence/independence continuum as well as the locus of control. This view is supported by Elkind (1988), and more recently by Rutter and Smith (1995). Geisler-Brenstein, Schmeck and Hetherington (1996) have affirmed the proposition that self-concept variables strongly moderate relationships among personality and learning style dimensions. Thus, teachers should encourage creative self-expression and help students to realize that self-expression has to precede self-improvement on the grounds that 'you can't change who you are if you don't know who you are! Much of this can be achieved by relatively simple changes in teaching.

Learning styles
Introduction

We all have preferred ways of organizing what we see and think about (Messick and associates, 1976) or different styles of conceptualization and patterning of activities which may be the most important characteristics of an individual in respect of learning (Tyler, 1978). These cognitive or, as they are more commonly called, learning styles, have been shown to be related to learning and studying. Although numerous learning styles have been proposed (Grasha, 1984) only a few will be considered in this chapter, the purpose of which is to consider if an appreciation of learning styles can be used to enhance the design of learning, and to consider the implications for assessment.

Based on the view that no one theory embraces everything Grasha takes an eclectic view and considers that all theories should be examined for their potential in teaching. This is the approach taken in this book. Teachers have to search for what works for them and the students of their subject, and it has to be a continuing search and evaluation of theories as they are generated. So what are these theories and how may they be of use to teachers?

Convergent and divergent thinking styles

Probably the best known cognitive styles are those described on the continuum of convergent–divergent thinking. Divergent thinkers are commonly described as creative. These descriptions originate with Guilford's (1954) study of the intellect. The Guilford model assumes that creativity and intelligence are different things and that creativity is as important as intelligence. Convergent thinkers tend to concentrate on test questions which require a single answer, whereas divergent thinkers do not like the confines of conventional tests; they are more at home in generating many solutions. It is said that they perform well in activities like brainstorming. Divergence is associated with creativity, which for some is contentious.

Hudson (1966), using tests for convergent and divergent thinking in the UK, found that those who were studying arts (humanities) subjects were much more creative than those who studied science. This led to a furore at the 'political' level, because lack of divergence among scientists might have been a contributory factor to Britain's poor industrial performance and caused an investigation of the problem by the Council of Engineering Institutions (Gregory, 1972).

One of the problems with the tests used by Hudson was that they were of the pencil and paper variety. Scientific creativity is difficult to measure with such tests. Guilford considered that effective thinking resulted from the sequential use of convergent and divergent processes. In Britain Whitfield (1975) showed models of the engineering process which illustrated this point. In general, it is held that there has to be a balance between convergent and divergent thinking. Freeman, McComiskey and Buttle

(1968) found that balance between convergence and divergence was an important predictor of academic performance among students of electrical engineering.

Recently Hartley and Greggs (1997) and Hartley (1998) divided students by subject into four categories. They completed four tests with the purpose of replicating Hudson's study with university students. The categories were those taking arts, arts and social sciences, social sciences and the sciences. Taken as a continuum they found only weak support for the view that divergent capability would decline in the direction of science. However, when four categories were collapsed into two there was a significant difference between those studying the arts and those studying science.

Convergent and divergent thinking styles are an integral part of Kolb's theory as will be shown in subsequent paragraphs.

Field-dependence and field-independence

Many factors come together to influence our perception (see Chapter 9). Cognitive or learning styles may also be described as the particular mode of perception which an individual brings to the understanding of his or her world. In the United States Witkin (1976) (Witkin and Goodenough, 1981) suggested that individual dispositions toward perception of their environment lie on a continuum, the polar ends of which he called field-dependent and field-independent. Those who are field-dependent look at the world in a global way, while those who are field-independent would see it analytically. The reactions of the field-dependent person to people, places and events are undifferentiated and complex. In contrast, the events (objects) in the environment are not associated with the background of that environment by the person who is field-independent. The relationship between these ideas and those that have just been described will be self-evident.

Using the embedded figures test (Witkin *et al.*, 1971), which was developed to test for field-dependence and independence as well as other tests, Zocolliti and Oltman (1976) described an investigation which set out to examine the relationships between these two dimensions and the right and left brains as they were understood at the time. They were not able to confirm that the two dimensions were related to one side of the brain in particular although they concluded that the field-independence–dependence dimension was probably related to the degree of segregation of functioning between the two hemispheres. In another study, Sigman and Oltman (1976) came to the conclusion that the two dimensions were characteristic perceptual strategies, each of which could be adaptive in certain conditions.

The embedded figures test is the only inventory for the evaluation of learning styles that does not depend on verbal statements. The field-dependence–independence dimension has been shown to be slightly related to verbal ability but unrelated to overall academic achievement (Witkin *et al.*, 1977). Several investigators, (Witkin, 1976), have claimed that an individual's location on the continuum between the two poles contributes to academic choice, success and vocational preference. Field-dependent persons require their learning to have more structure, direction and feedback than field-independent ones, who tend to dislike collaborative learning, for instance. This would explain the everyday experience of teachers who find that some students who do not like group work are nevertheless good at analytical academic work. Tyler (1978) has pointed out that the same may apply to teachers in higher education, and this would account for the liking that some teachers have for lectures and others for group discussion.

Collinge (1994) in his study of scientific thinking briefly discussed in Chapter 7 argued that the field-dependent–independent dimension would indicate who was and who was not capable of isolating significant variables. Subjects who were field-dependent would be unable to do such tasks. Of the two possibilities open to Collinge to counter this difficulty – training in the perceptual dimension of field independence and cognitive restructuring – he chose the latter because perceptual training had not been found to be successful. He argued and demonstrated that cognitive restructuring was a prerequisite to being able to perceive and manipulate variables in science. Field-independence helps to develop skills in 'careful comparison, reorganisation and restructuring information, isolation of the particular from the general, and disembedding of confounding and overlapping information'. Seventeen activities designed to promote cognitive restructuring were developed and administered to an experimental group. The Group Embedded Figures test was used in combination with a Science Reasoning task, and significant increases in field-independence and science skills were recorded. Field- independence was found to be a factor in the application of formal operations, and cognitive restructuring was found to increase skill. 'Any activity that develops this type of careful observation is developing scientific thinking.'

One study has gone so far as to suggest that the Embedded Figures Test measures cognitive ability rather than cognitive style (Highhouse and Doverspike, 1987). Related to the field-dependent–independent dimension is the capacity to perceive spatial relations.

Spatial ability

In 1964 MacFarlane Smith generated a controversial thesis that argued that the shortage of qualified engineers and scientists in Britain was due to the fact that the grammar schools of the time did not emphasize teaching in subjects that would help to develop the spatial and mechanical abilities essential for performance in technology. Incidentally, mathematical ability was held to be different from numerical ability and to depend on spatial ability. A variety of test data was adduced to support this thesis. The biographical data of persons such as Einstein was also used to defend the argument.

It had already been suggested by Zangwill (1961) that the left and right hemisphere dominances of the brain were related to the 'symbolic' and the 'visuo-spatial' respectively. By 1967 it seemed to be understood that the right hemisphere is largely concerned with integrating data from our senses not only to orient us in space but also to enable us to integrate our external perceptions (Warrington *et al.*, 1966).

In 1969 a striking demonstration of the different functions of the two hemispheres of the brain came from Sperry, Gazzaniga and Bogen (1969). They had surgically divided the organ that connected the two hemispheres as a treatment for intractable epilepsy. They found among eight patients that their right hands were able to write normally but were not able to copy a geometrical figure, whereas with the left hand they were able to copy the figure. From this they argued that the two sides of the brain performed different functions. Bogen was led to believe that the individual with two intact hemispheres had the capacity for two distinct modes of thought. Propositional thought was lateralized in one hemisphere and appositional thought was the specialization of the other. MacFarlane Smith (1964) assumed that the verbal/numerical abilities (which were associated with analogical reasoning) depended on the left hemisphere, and that the capacity for relational thinking depended on the right.

It is now known that hemispheric asymmetry is somewhat more complicated than this, and as yet no comprehensive model is available (Hellige, 1993). At the same time Hellige argues that the data shows that hemispheric asymmetries do exist and influence behaviour. Moreover, in the rather simplistic terms of the educationalist there is no reason not to take the view that the curriculum encourages some mechanisms of the brain and underutilizes others. This view has encouraged several recent tracts on 'whole brain education'.

It is now understood that the right hemisphere is dominant for processing global aspects of visual stimuli, whereas the left hemisphere is dominant for processing local detail (Hellige, 1993). Visual-spatial processing is important for work in several professions including engineering, medicine and science. Thus, tests of spatial ability are likely to be of use to tutors who have to deal with freshman studies. For example, Rochford (1989) reported a study at the University of Capetown which found that one of the reasons for underachievement in freshman courses in engineering drawing, astronomy and chemistry was that they were handicapped by lack of skill in three-dimensional perceptual learning. Over a four-year period it was found that one-sixth of engineering students entering engineering had spatial learning deficiencies which were associated with significant underachievement. For example, students perceived depth and distance differently in photographs and equivalent line diagrams of molecular structures. From the perspective of examinations they concluded that: 'some students may be partially or temporarily disadvantaged by visual presentation in textbooks, or in examination papers, of pictures of molecules either in photographic form alone or through the medium of line drawings alone.' Because spatial skills could be acquired within an appropriately designed course, such tests should not be used for selection on their own. They reported other experiments in training in geometric spatial programmes which had improved scores in organic chemistry (Lord, 1985) in support of their argument.

Hsi, Linn and Bell (1997) studied engineers who used spatial reasoning in industry. Having identified the strategies employed, they designed a specific programme of instruction which was integrated into an engineering graphics course where there was a high failure rate. It enabled the students to make significant progress in spatial reasoning. Spatial reasoning, as might be expected, was a significant predictor of course grade. The intervention also reduced gender differences to an insignificant level by the time of the post-tests.

There is considerable evidence that students in the biological sciences have difficulty in perceiving the 3D structure of molecular configuration. This is evident in schools when relatively advanced level students are required to visualize how the diagrams should change to represent the effects of a rotating structure (Shubbar,

1990). Not surprisingly, it is found that third-level students have similar difficulties (Freeman and Thomas, 1999). Clearly, computer associated training may help the development of this capability. However, as Freeman and Thomas warn, the student must use divergent thinking and heuristic approaches as well as the convergent thinking dictated by algorithmic processes. If a programme demands too much convergent thinking, then it may inhibit the development of the strategies required for 3D literacy. This has implications for the method of assessment used in computer modelling courses.

The Myers-Briggs Type Indicator

The Myers-Briggs Type Indicator (MBTI) is a measure of both personality and style. Teachers have found the inventory to be of use in understanding classroom behaviour, and the design of instruction. Moreover, training courses for those who wish to administer the test are readily available. It is based on Jungian typology and describes 16 personality categories (types) into which individuals fall. It is criticized because it is difficult to obtain factor analytic data from it which will show that it has validity (i.e. that individuals really fall into these types. However, Kline (1993) considered that it merited an entry in his handbook because it is widely used in personnel testing. It has the disadvantage that we can all too readily see ourselves and others in the descriptors like those suggested by Kiersey and Bates (1979) and we can easily begin to type each other with the letters assigned to the test parameters. As Kline says,

> The critical question is whether the MBTI does classify individuals into these types or not. If it does we might still ask to what extent these types resemble those suggested by Jung. Even if they did not, however, it might still be the case that the typology is valuable for selection or vocational guidance.

At the very least it can serve as an indicator of individual differences in a classroom even if they are not strictly the types proposed. Moreover, the literature that it has spawned can help teachers reflect on themselves and their attitudes toward their students as well as doing the same for their students (e.g. Kiersey and Bates, 1979; Silver and Hanson, 1995).

Jung called the total personality the psyche. It is a complex network of interacting systems. The primary ones are the ego, the personal unconscious and the collective unconscious. There are also two primary attitudes and four basic functions. Together they constitute separate but related parts of the psyche. It is from these that the typologies referred to above derive. The basic dispositions are introversion and extraversion. According to Jung the conscious introvert is an extravert in his/her unconscious and vice versa (Engler, 1979).

The four basic functions are ways of orienting experience and perceiving the world. To quote Jung, 'These four functional types correspond to the *obvious* means by which consciousness obtains its orientation and experience.' (Engler, 1979). Thus *sensation* results from our sensing of the world through our senses to see what exists. *Feeling* is the activity of valuing and judging the world and tells you whether it is agreeable. *Intuition* is perception about the world via the unconscious, and our *thinking* gives meaning and understanding to the world we inhabit and tells us what it is. *Sensing* and intuition involve our immediate experiences and almost contrary to everyday usage of *feeling* it and thinking defined by Jung as rational functions since they require acts of judgement. At the same time the functions are grouped in opposite pairs (i.e. *thinking/feeling* and *sensing/intuition*) and one function is dominant in each pair. According to Jung 'these four functional types correspond to the *obvious* [my italics] means by which consciousness obtains its orientation.' Thus a person who is dominant in *thinking* may have submerged the *feeling* function. Similarly with *sensing* and *intuition*. For example the person with high intellectual powers may have submerged the intuitive function. Those functions that are underdeveloped have the power to influence life and it is from them that strange moods and symptoms emerge. The actualized self requires a synthesis of these four functions. Clearly individuals have to reconcile many contradictions in their personalities and neurosis arises when the reconciliation of these contradictions becomes difficult.

The Myers-Briggs Type Indicator pairs the perception and thinking functions for the purpose of assessing personality and produces four types thus:

Sensing + Thinking – ST

Sensing + Feeling – SF

Intuition + Feeling – NF

Intuition + Thinking – NT

One of the reasons why it appeals to personnel selectors is that each of the above types is said to indicate career preferences e.g.

ST – applied science, business, etc.

SF – patient care, community service, etc.

NF – behavioural science, literature and art, etc.

NT – physical science, research and management, etc.

Of course, professional groups are likely to have all four types in them and teaching is no exception. Since all of us are learners we will want to learn according to our preferred type. Silver and Hanson (1995) have shown how teaching and learning may be classified against these psychological types. For example, teachers who are empathizers are SF; instructional managers are ST; theoreticians are NT, and facilitators are NF; friendly learners are SF; practical learners are ST; intellectual learners are NT and imaginative learners are NF. Similarly, one may classify the press of learning environments (e.g. organization, and competition v-discovery – ST v. NT); the emphasis of instructional strategies (e.g. research v-self-expression NT v. NF); teaching strategies (e.g. group investigations v-programmed instruction SF v. ST) and evaluation and assessment procedures (e.g. objective tests v-essay ST v. NT).

Whatever the validity of their instrument the theory when applied to education shows just how complex teaching and learning is and just how far removed it is from that stereotype of teaching as 'chalk and talk'. Teachers have to live with and design for diversity in teaching and learning.

The potential of the MBTI as an aid to instructional and assessment design is demonstrated by a practising teacher of business studies (Rutsohn, 1978). He taught in a business education seminar programme and examined the idea that personality plays an important part in the determination of a student's responsiveness to a particular learning technique. Admittedly, the sample was very small, but the ability of the instrument together with other assessments to provide profiles is evidently powerful.

In this class (for which there was no textbook) the majority of the learning resulted from group interaction. The students were not told that they were the participating in a research project. It was based on the following design:

1.   Students took the Myers-Briggs Type Indicator.

2.   At the end of each class they recorded their beliefs about their learning for that particular class.

3.   The instructor recorded the behavioural pattern of each student during the classroom period.

During the course four different instructional strategies were used. These were an unstructured seminar, an assigned structure, an assigned structure with assigned group leaders, and the instructor as group leader. In an assigned structure the group was provided with rules of order. They were assigned to a particular group and the leaders emerged informally. Each group was given the opportunity to present and defend their findings in front of the whole class. The instructor actively participated by asking questions after the group had presented their positions, summarized the class consensus, and commented on the problems. When the instructor acted as group leader the class formed one large group and the instructor was very directive. Rutsohn drew up profiles of personality versus students preference for class type and observed behaviour. For example, a student labelled by the Myers-Briggs Type Indicator as introverted, intuitive, feeling and perceptive was profiled for Assigned Group with Emerging Leadership as follows: 'Did not feel that this technique was satisfactory. His major criticism was the lack of monitoring and guidance in the specific areas for discussion. An inordinate amount of time was spent on irrelevant ideas. This severely limited the time to concentrate on the solving of the problem.'

Contrast this with another student profiled for the Assigned Group with Emerging Leadership who was classified as extraverted, sensing, thinking and judging. This student found the learning experience: 'Quite rewarding. The involvement factor was quite high and the group interaction most rewarding.' This individual preferred a structure which was informal and lacking an assigned leader.

The four profiles described by Rutsohn are summarized in Table 9.1. Even within a very small sample it shows that there is no one instructional technique that will suffice. Rutsohn suggests that in selecting a learning technique the instructor could benefit from a profile of the class personality. This would enable the teacher to better organize instruction. Perhaps it would be necessary to try several techniques during the course in order to reach all the personalities in the class.

Table 9.1 Relationships between personality type, instructional strategy and leadership role in a business studies class. (Adapted in Heywood, 1989a, from Rutsohn, 1978)

Personality type	Unstructured learning experience	Assigned group emerging leadership	Assigned group, assigned leader	Instructor as group leader
Extraverted, sensing, thinking, judging	Excellent learning experience	Quite rewarding	Good learning experience. Restrictive structure	Perceived as valid learning experience
Introverted, sensing, thinking, perceptive	Perceived as fruitful	Responded positively	Learning experience minimal	Best technique
Extraverted, intuitive, feeling, perceptive	Viewed quite favourably	Did not like structure as a learning technique	Satisfactory * learning but believed group too small	Best of all structures
Introverted, intuitive, feeling, perceptive	Completely unsatisfactory	Not satisfactory	Excellent learning experience	Excellent learning experience

*This person was elected group leader.

In another study the learning styles of both staff and students in a US College of Business showed that staff were more likely to teach in an intuitive manner whereas students wanted to learn in a sensing style. The level of congruency was found to be related to academic performance, and student evaluations were significant, while differences in course grades which did not fall in the expected directions were not (Cooper and Miller, 1991).

The MBTI has also been used in the evaluation of innovative courses. At the University of Salford in the UK the MBTI was used as a diagnostic instrument in a bridging course. Its intention was to help non-traditional students gain an understanding of their natural learning styles and to develop more effective learning strategies. Compared with traditional entry students it was found that the non-traditional students in the innovative bridging course had high levels of extraversion and feeling. On the Perry Scale the students in this course were at slightly lower levels than conventional students. Another test showed that they tended to converge on the problem rather than explore other possibilities (Culver *et al.*, 1994). Clearly, information of the kind yielded by the MBTI and the other instruments is of value to those planning and implementing the course. This study illustrates the influence of prior knowledge on learning, the need for tutors to know what that knowledge is, and the practical value of meta- cognitive awareness of learners (see also Moran, 1991).

In the US a longitudinal investigation of students in a chemical engineering course taught in an innovative way compared the profiles of the students on the course with performance. The MBTI showed that in the freshman year of the innovative course the intuitors earned higher grades than the sensors and the thinkers outperformed the feelers, and the judgers outperformed the perceivers. The introverts had a slightly better GPA than the extraverts, but the extraverts subsequently turned in a better performance than the introverts which was contrary to expectations. More sensors than intuitors rated the experimental course which emphasized applications over theory as more instructive than other more traditionally courses they had attended. While it was not possible statistically to demonstrate whether the students in the experimental group obtained greater mastery of curriculum content, the authors conclude that an instructor who integrates theory with practice can expect positive results (Felder, 1995; Felder, Felder and Dietz, 1997). Rosati (1997) from a seven-year longitudinal study of Canadian engineering students found that success for the weaker students in their first year was more probable if they were type ITJ and that graduation within four years is correlated with INTJ types. The findings of both the UK and US studies support the concept of multiple-strategy approaches to assessment and instruction.

FitzGibbon (1994) used a development of the MBTI by Kiersey and Bates (1984) to evaluate journals made by student teachers (see Chapter 14). Their analysis forms four temperament categories out of the 16 types. Very briefly, the first type labelled SJ exists primarily to be useful to the social units they belong to. The second type SP wants to be free above all; they are impulsive, and can become restless and move if too many ties are acquired. The third type NT is fascinated by power. They are the most critical self-intelligence, and are reluctant to accept without question. The fourth type NF pursues the goal of becoming, their search is circular, and thus perpetual.

Kolb's theory of learning

Kolb's (1984) experiential theory of learning is illustrated in Figure 9.1. It proposes that the learning of concepts is undertaken in cycles which involve four processes. First comes a specific experience that causes the learner to want to know more about that experience. For that to happen the learner has to reflect on that experience from as many viewpoints as possible. From this reflection the learner draws conclusions and uses them finally to influence decision making or take action. A different style of learning is required for each activity. It will be apparent, for example, that the cycle draws the learner into a form of reflective practice (see Chapter 14). The axes represent the available information or abstraction contained in the experience (y axes) and, the processing of information through reflection or action on the conclusions drawn (x axes). At the centre the student is a receiver but as the student moves between the stages on the perimeter of the cycle he/she is an actor (Svinicki and Dixon, 1987).

Kolb's theory holds that we have a predisposition to think in a style associated with one of these activities. Thus in any group of people one is likely to find persons with different learning dispositions or styles. This is consistent with all the other theories. If correct the implications for teaching and learning are profound.

It is argued that different types of learner require different treatments. Thus if a teacher wishes to teach a concept or a principle he/she should teach it in four different ways since each class is likely to be made up of different kinds of learner (i.e. with respect to style). It will be argued below that each learner should become conversant with the styles that are not their own. Teaching and assessment in this way will ensure

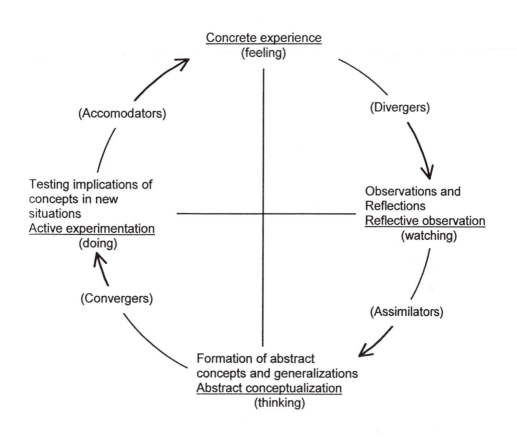

Figure 9.1 An adaptation of Kolb's experiential learning model based on FitzGibbon (1987) and Stice (1987).

that that happens (Svinicki and Dixon, 1987). There is some evidence that styles can change in response to task in higher education (see Nulty and Barrett below). Finally, teachers are likely to teach the methods that suit their own style, and it will require some effort to adapt to this approach to teaching (Heywood, 1997c). Following FitzGibbon (1987) the four styles are:

1. Convergers: Their dominant learning styles are abstract conceptualization and active experimentation. It is the mode of learning which has often been associated with the classroom and caused by traditional assessment. People with this style do best in tests where the problems require single solutions. Not very emotional, they tend to prefer things to people. Convergence

relates to that part of problem solving which is related to the selection of a solution and the evaluation of the consequences of the solution.

2.   Divergers: These are the opposite to convergers. Both terms come from the early research in creativity, and Kolb cites Hudson's study in particular. Divergers are best in the situation of concrete experience and reflective observation. They like to 'imagine' and generate ideas. They are emotional and relate well to people, and do not perform as well in tests which demand single solutions. Divergence relates to that part of the problem-solving process which identifies differences (problems) and compares goals with reality.

3.   Assimilators: Their dominant learning skills are abstract conceptualization and reflective observation. They are not so much concerned with people as with abstract concepts. They are interested in the precise and logical development of theory rather than with its application. Kolb describes them as pure rather than applied scientists. Assimilation relates to the solution of problems and the considerations of alternative solutions in the problem-solving process.

4.   Accommodators: These are the opposite of the assimilators. Their dominant learning strengths are concrete experience and active experimentation. They like doing things and want to devise and implement experiments. Such individuals take more risks than those with the other learning styles. Kolb says 'we have labelled this style "accommodator" because he tends to excel in those situations where he must adapt himself to specific immediate circumstances'. Such individuals are at ease with people, although they are relatively impatient. Accommodation relates to the choice of goal(s) and the execution of solutions in problem-solving. It will be seen that in the cycle the first quadrant is concerned primarily with divergent and accommodative thinking, the second primarily with assimilation, the third primarily with convergent thinking and the fourth primarily with accommodation.

Following Stice (1987) the stage of concrete experience with which the cycle begins is a stage of 'feeling'. The learner has to become sensitive to feelings and people. In the second stage they watch. They have to be patient and objective in order to analyse. Careful observation is required before a judgement is made. In the third stage feelings are replaced by thinking. Logic is invoked, theories are proposed and, finally, they are acted upon when the learner becomes a doer.

FitzGibbon (1987) has shown how the Kolb cycle can be applied to the supervision of classroom practice. In the course with which FitzGibbon is associated the graduate student teachers are seen on five occasions during their teaching practice. Each of these is assessed: one at least will be by another supervisor. After the lesson there is a conference between the supervisor and the student. A written evaluation of the supervision of teaching practice using Kolb's model would have considerable advantages to both the teacher and student. The relationship to learning type is given in Figure 9.2. FitzGibbon does not comment on the problem of assessment. It might be assumed from this model that there would be personal growth, in which case the five

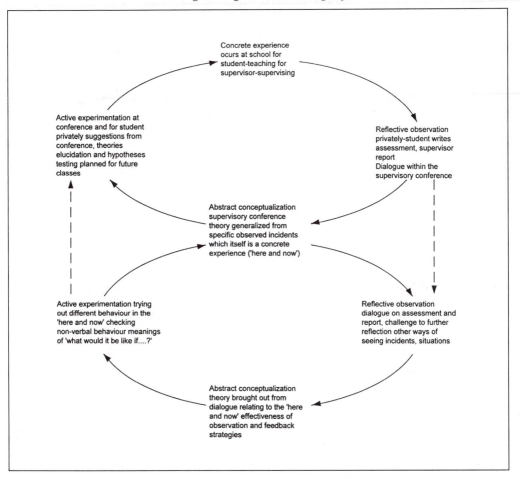

Figure 9.2 Kolb's experiential model of learning applied to the classroom supervisor of trainee teachers. (Reproduced by kind permission of A. FitzGibbon and the editor of the European Journal of Teacher Education.)

assessments could not be given equal weight. Competency based rather than graded assessment would seem to be more appropriate.

Kolb and his colleagues devised a self-assessment inventory to measure the preferred learning styles of individuals (The Learning Styles Inventory), which has been substantially revised. Using the original version with 800 persons for whom they had undergraduate data only, they found that those who had studied business were accommodators. Nursing and engineering undergraduates were convergers; history, political science, English and psychology students were divergers; and economics, and those studying mathematics, sociology, chemistry and physics were assimilators. They came to the conclusion that different subjects required or encouraged/developed different styles of learning. Svinicki and Dixon (1987) have shown how this might be translated into practice. Kolb argued that undergraduate education was a major factor influencing style while at the same time recognizing that his results might be due to the academic process of selection. Our interest here is that divergers and accommodators could be disadvantaged by some traditional techniques of assessment and teaching.

Kolb related his learning styles to problem-solving. His model shows quite clearly that all four skills are required in the solution of problems. In this respect it is consistent with Whitfield's (1975) finding on creativity in industry. There is, however, a difficulty with this thesis, for if a person selects a field which is consistent with their natural learning style they may try to mould their subsequent work to fit that style rather than allow the job to force them to learn other styles. For example, Plovnick (1971) found that the major style in physics education was convergent. Ten years later, studies at Rutgers University by Enyeart, Baker and Vanharlingen (1980) found that deductive logical ability contributed more to achievement in an introductory college physics course than inductive logical ability. Plovnick predicted that those undergraduates who were divergers would be uncertain of physics with a career, and this was found to be true. The assumption here is that graduates entering careers in physics will find that jobs in physics require convergence. However, if Whitfield is correct they will have to function at some time or another in all four modes of learning.

An interesting feature of research in problem solving is the fact reported by several authorities that, once taught a method of problem solving, students use the same technique to solve all others. This 'problem set', as Luchins (1942) calls it, is extremely limiting and can prevent effective transfer. As will be shown in the next chapter experience can both inhibit and enhance learning. The same may be true of learning styles (Thomas and Bain, 1982).

Svinicki and Dixon agree with Kolb that there are fundamental differences in the nature of the disciplines, and because of these differences the discipline itself can circumscribe an instructor's choice of learning activities. They demonstrate how the application of the model might work in pharmacy, history, public policy, architecture, engineering and psychology. (See also Stice, 1987, for a complete example in engineering.)

Using the Learning Styles Inventory together with an outcomes measure Nulty and Barrett (1996) found that during the first third of their studies student respondents in Australia adopted learning styles that were similar to each other irrespective of the main discipline studied. However, in the third year the learning styles appeared to be related to the discipline that was the principal focus of their study. Notwithstanding difficulties with the representativeness of their sample the data led Nulty and Barrett to suggest that the problems faced by teachers of first-year students may be qualitatively different from those found by teachers of more senior students.

> In each discipline, teachers may need to adopt behaviours which accommodate the nature of the students' learning styles. In addition, teachers (and students) may benefit by doing this in such a way the students learn to converge on the learning style which more closely reflects the epistemological concerns of whichever discipline is in question.

There is a danger here that such a requirement would be at the expense of the everyday generic requirement that individuals should be able to adapt style to task.

Loacker and her colleagues (1984) report on the Alverno experience with Kolb's LSI thus:

> The identification of experiential validation of knowledge and theory as a significant cause of learning relates to the student's awareness of learning as a process of experiencing, reflecting, forming new concepts, and testing one's judgements and abilities in action... At entrance students showed a marked preference for 'concrete experience' over abstract conceptualization' and for 'reflective observation' over 'active experimentation'. Eventually students showed that they had come to rely equally on concrete and abstract models and to use a similar flexibility in choosing either reflective or active approaches.

The curriculum at Alverno would seem to help students meet Whitfield's (1975) criteria for work and enable them to function in the style merited by the occasion (Mentkowski and associates, 2000).

Severiens and Ten Dam (1994) evaluated 26 Kolb studies for gender differences and found that men were more likely to prefer abstract conceptualization than women, which seems to fit the picture of women's ways of knowing described by Belenky *et al.*, 1986).

Kolb modified the first editions of his inventory because of evaluation research that proved to be non-supportive. The second instrument has also been criticized for lack of reliability and stability (Sims *et al.*, 1986). Highhouse and Doverspike (1987) have tested its construct validity by correlating it with field-independence, field- dependence and the Vocational Preference Inventory (Holland, 1978). They concluded that it measured preferences rather more than cognitive style.

Nevertheless, as the studies by Loacker (1984), FitzGibbon (1994), and Heywood (1997c) show, independently of what it actually measures this, inventory can be used by teachers to better understand their students and to design their courses. This latter point is particularly well illustrated by Svinicki and Dixon (1987) who relate the many different types of instructional activity to the components of the cycle most likely to support that method. Concrete experience may include laboratories, observations, primary text reading, simulations/games, field work, films, readings, problems and examples. Reflective observation may be achieved through journals and logs, brainstorming and discussion, thought and rhetorical questions. Abstract conceptualization may be assisted by lectures, papers, model building, projects and analogies. Active experimentation is assisted by any activity which involves the student such as simulations, role playing, case studies, projects, field work and homework. And, active experimentation may trigger off the cycle again.

Cowan *et al.* (1994) consider that it may not always be desirable to enter the Kolb cycle at the top (concrete experience). If you are going to test out a theory, then you would begin with the theory, and 'prepare to test it out in your own situation, carry that through into the reality of everyday experience, and then reflect on what that tells you about the relevance and usefulness of the theory, and how you might modify it to suit your own needs and constraints'. Cowan (1998) uses this position to describe a model which overcomes a major criticism of the Kolb model to the effect that life would become very boring if learning were to become a series of Kolb cycles. His model rotates through experience, reflection, generalization, testing and back to experience. He points out that we should beware of the assumption of linear progress round the cycle.

> I have found that learners may take one particular experience, and hence assemble a fragment of a generalization. They may then return to another particular experience, reflecting and again partially generalizing. And, so they go on, oscillating between the two perhaps four or five times, before eventually being ready (or being prompted) to move on to the next stage.

An interesting feature of an adaptation of the Kolb model by McCarthy (1990) shows that it can be used for learning systems design. Each quadrant can be divided into principal, teacher and student perspectives. Quadrant one is devoted to the question 'What?' Quadrant two becomes 'Why?' Quadrant three becomes 'How does this work?' and Quadrant four 'If'. These questions are addressed to the principal, the teacher and the student in turn and their roles change as a function of the question type. For example, in Quadrant three the student is a user of content and skill, the teacher becomes the coach and the principal the facilitator of resources. Perhaps the most important feature of the system is that the students can be taught to use the system for themselves. Thus Weber and Weber (1990) used McCarthy's 4 Mat wheel to show students how to write their oral reports. It is interesting to note that the students generated a model very similar to those generated by Svnicki and Dixon (1987).

Using Cognitive Style Analysis (Riding, 1991, 1996), Riding and Staley (1998) examined the cognitive styles of male and female students in a business studies course in England. They were particularly interested in the self-perceptions that the students had of themselves in relation to their performance and cognitive style. The dimensions were wholist/analytic (i.e. the extent to which individuals process information in wholes or parts), and verbal/imagery (the extent to which individuals represent information verbally or in mental images). Among the findings were that in respect of the wholist/academic style students underestimated their performance on subjects which did not match their style and overestimated them on those that did. The opposite was found to be true of the verbal/imagery style. When there was a style/subject mismatch students overestimated their performance, and underestimated it when they were matched. Riding and Staley argue that students have to develop a self-awareness of their style so that they can understand its appropriateness for the particular subject they are studying. They will then be in a position to view a mismatch as a challenge to find alternative strategies. They give the example of verbalizers who change pictorial information in a book to words, and imagers who could change words into illustrations (Riding, 1996). This study is an important reminder that there are dimensions to learning styles other than those defined by the Kolb model, and that other dimensions have to be taken into account in the planning of learning and its implementation.

In the UK Honey and Mumford (1992) have also developed a model that has many similarities with Kolb. They call their styles Activists, Reflectors, Theorists and Pragmatists. Here is their description of the Activist.

> Activists involve themselves fully and without bias in new experiences. They enjoy the here and now and are happy to be dominated by immediate experiences. They are open-minded, not sceptical, and this tends to make them enthusiasts about

anything new. Their philosophy is: 'I'll try anything once'. Their days are filled with activity. They tackle problems by brainstorming. As soon as the excitement from one activity has died down they are busy looking for the next. They tend to thrive on the challenge of new experiences but are bored with implementation and longer-term consolidation. They are gregarious people constantly involving themselves with others but, in doing so, they seek to centre all activities around themselves.

Honey and Mumford have also developed an inventory for classifying persons into these styles which, unlike the other inventories previously mentioned, is cheap to obtain and easy to administer. There is also no professional requirement for training. Apart from the problem of cost the question arises as to the value of these inventories for teachers and teaching.

Assessment: Matching instruction to teaching

Clearly instructors cannot match their own teaching style to a class where styles are mixed. It is equally clear that students should be encouraged to function in styles other than their natural bent. As Grasha (1984) says, 'In building an environment compatible with a preferred learning style, one may miss an opportunity for significant learning.' Therefore the onus is on the instructor to vary the strategies they use and to vary the demands they make on students. This was brought about by action research. Kember and Gow (1994) have found the same to be true of higher education. In relation to deep/surface orientation it was discovered that there was a relationship between lecturers' orientations to teaching and the quality of student learning. They also advocate an action research model to bring about change.

Action research of the kind promoted by Heywood (1997a, 1997c) involved the teacher trainees finding out their own learning style and obtaining the learning styles of their students, either from a learning styles inventory or an assessment based on the students' work. These were then related to assessment after a structured lesson(s) to meet the Kolb requirements had been given. To meet this requirement the idea that the concept or principle to be learnt had to be repeated in four different ways had to be abandoned, otherwise there would be no possibility of determining whether or not the different strategies made a difference or not. Thus the lesson had to be designed so that there was a progression with new knowledge emerging in each quadrant. These projects were found to help the student teachers obtain a better understanding of their pupils. There is no reason why instruction in higher education should not be designed in this way.

As the population in universities becomes increasingly diverse the lecturer will benefit if he/she has some indication, however crude, of the learning dispositions of his/her students. The real challenge is to design assessments that will tap the dispositions of students in each of the four quadrants. In this respect Sharp, Harb and Terry (1997) have described how they designed a *Writing Across the Curriculum* programme based on the Kolb model, and they describe in some detail how it was matched to a variety of assessments. They suggest, among other ideas, that assimilators might be comfortable with free writing for comprehension and analysis, and with micro-themes that are small amounts of writing preceded by large amounts of thinking. Convergers will respond to short answers to problems so that the sheets can be used for further study. Accommodators like answering 'what if' problems. Divergers like to express their views to others, so peer reviews of papers may be helpful. However, as Cowan (private communication), points out a balance has to be achieved between shaping assessment to the learner and validly testing learning priorities. All of which supports the need for multiple-strategy assessments within courses. Sharp *et al.* (1997) show this can be achieved with ease.

Variety does not necessarily mean variety within a single session, as is clear from the programme of Sharp *et al.* (1997). A Kolb programme may be spread over a series of classes. Neither should a teacher try to vary the pattern of instruction for the sake of variety. Rather the methods used should be determined by the objectives of instruction taking into account the learning needs of the students.

There is an advantage to the students if the teacher discusses with the students the purpose of the learning styles inventory because it can help them develop meta-cognitive awareness of where they are at and the influence of prior knowledge on the learning now demanded of them (Moran, 1991).

One of the advantages of a carefully designed programme where variety is partially in response to different learning styles is that it forces both teacher and learner to adapt. It can, therefore, help promote learner adaptability, and that is currently held to be an important goal of higher education (Hayes and Allinson, 1996).

Student isolation is often found to be a contributing factor in levels of dissatisfaction and low completion rates. One remedy is to build up relationships between supervisors and students on an individualized basis. It has been suggested that in such 'close' relationships the cognitive styles should be matched (Armstrong, Allinson and Hayes, 1997). Given Riding and Staley's (1998) findings there is the possibility that students could be lulled into a false sense of security and overestimate their capability. As Riding and Staley (1998) argue, eventually students should be helped to develop self-awareness of their own style and shown strategies which will help them move from one style to another as required by the subject material.

Naturalistic approaches to learning styles

Grasha (1990) became disenchanted with the inventory approach to evaluating student learning styles. He turned to qualitative approaches that were grounded in the everyday experiences of students. These included direct observations of student behaviour, in-depth interviews, the analysis of self-directed learning projects, and the analysis of the guiding metaphors students used when describing the teaching–learning process. He borrowed an idea from Mann *et al.* (1970) for his method of observation. He records that Mann gave descriptions of the following styles – compliant, anxious-dependent, discouraged worker, independent, hero, attention seeker, silent student and sniper. A hero, for example, is intelligent, creative, involved, introspective, struggling to establish identity, and rebellious, ambivalent towards teacher, erratic in performance! Grasha designed a course that would cater for these underlying orientations. It underpinned Mann's typologies which were dependent, independent and cooperative. In-depth interviews were based on Perry's approach and his findings were consistent with Perry and King and Kitchener (See Chapter 7).

When Cowan analysed learning projects with the aid of a modified Learning Projects Check List (Toppins, 1987), he found that his students were as self-directed as adult learners, which was to contradict findings by Tough (1979). Subsequently he made one-third of a student's course grade depend on a learning project designed by the student which is broadly related to course content.

Grasha points out that one of the essential differences between creative and less creative problem solvers is the use they make of metaphor. Metaphors help us to organize our thoughts and guide our actions. He set out to establish the metaphors that his students had about the teaching–learning process. This procedure also doubled as a course evaluation that gave him valuable insights into student perceptions. He concluded that the qualitative data provide a depth of insight not found with traditional measures. At the same time during a workshop he found that while many preferred the naturalistic approach, 40 per cent of the students preferred the more traditional instruments. He suggested that this might be a distinction between those who like making intuitive judgements and those who like an orderly thought process.

Conclusion

Traditional assessment differentiates between individual students. For teachers without any knowledge of the social psychology of learning and assessment, the differences between students will, in all probability, be put down to ability or lack of it. The extensive research that has been done on approaches to learning shows that the orientation learners adopt is greatly influenced by assessment, instruction and the approach taken to the structure and delivery of the curriculum, and the standards set. Much that is done in universities and colleges to achieve the goal of critical and reflective thinkers is counter-productive. Assessment systems drive learning, and often cause *surface* approaches to learning. These are, as developmental theory shows often reinforced by the modes instruction used. As Chapter 14 will show, the encouragement of deep reflective learning requires different approaches to assessment and instruction.

Research on learning styles provides some valuable insights into some approaches that might be taken to instruction and assessment. It also shows other ways in which teachers can come to understand their students and the way they learn in their classes. All of the above suggests that teachers should expose their students to a variety of carefully designed assessment and instructional techniques (learning experiences) designed to obtain the objectives they wish to achieve. The remaining chapters in this book consider the advantages and disadvantages of a range of assessment techniques. They begin with a discussion of standards.

Chapter 10

Standards

Introduction

Standards are the benchmarks against which we rate ideas. A novel may be described as being above or below the standard usually set by a particular novelist. A piece of clothing may be sub-standard. Standards are inextricably related to quality. An implicit language governs our use of the term. Thus we understand that a Volkswagen 'Beetle' is not sub-standard by comparison with a Cadillac or Rolls-Royce. Sub-standard can only be applied in this case to the particular class, and quality can only be judged in terms of automobiles of the same category. Setting benchmarks, as is the case with automobiles, is complex. No one would say that a performance which gains a grade point average of B (or two one in the British system) is sub-standard to a GPA of A (or a First). It is said to be of a lower standard.

Traditionally in higher education standards have been defined by 'letters' or 'numbers' related to a percentage score given to a candidate for an assessment or aggregate of assessments. The aggregation of assessments produces the overall or final grade. In the traditional view, for standards to be accepted they should not vary from year to year or from course to course. If the number of persons obtaining a particular standard goes up year on year it is possible to argue that there has been grade inflation. It is equally possible to argue that the performance of students has improved. Similarly, if the proportion of candidates performing at a particular standard (level) is reduced year on year, then it is possible to argue that there has been grade deflation, but it is equally plausible to argue that the quality of performance is lower than it was in previous years.

Whether or not there has been grade inflation or grade deflation depends on the reliability of the marks of examiners and their internal consistency as well as the ways in which they are combined. It will depend on their validity in so far as an examiner perceives herself or himself to be marking the same qualities. For a single written examination paper in which an examinee responds to several questions, each question will have to be perceived by the students to be of the same level of difficulty as the other questions in the paper. It should cause a similar level of mental activity.

All in all, examining is a complex activity. It would be simplified if the marks of examiners were reliable and valid. It would also be simplified if the same methods of aggregation were used to arrive at overall grades. Quality assurance would be enhanced if it could be argued that all subjects produce grades that are of the same standard. Unfortunately this is not the case. The marks of examiners are found to be unreliable and their tests may not be valid. One of the reasons why objective tests are used so much in the United States is that they are highly reliable although they may not be valid.

In Britain the external examiner system has been regarded as the guarantor of quality, but as the system has diversified the external examiner approach has been found wanting. It is proposed that external examiners and professors should be trained and fora developed for the discussion of ideas and problems. However, attempts by those responsible for quality assurance in the UK to define *graduateness* and *thresholds* (benchmarks), have so far, only revealed how complex the problem is.

The common and misleading stereotypes of North American and British testing are that objective testing dominates the former, and the essay (or their problem solving equivalents in the sciences) dominates the latter. Neither tells the whole truth because essay tests are set in the US, and in the UK much use is made of substantive coursework assessments (e.g. lengthy essays and projects).

In both cases there is awareness among teachers of the limitations of the particular system in use. In consequence an assessment movement has developed in which the emphasis is on producing authentic or valid assessments. In both systems there is a move to derive scores and grades from performance based outcomes, but they are not without problems.

It can be concluded that all avenues lead to the view that if the processes of examining and assessment are to be improved more explicit statement of criteria showing how these should influence learning will have to be made. This chapter is primarily about how standards are determined in traditional systems and the principles that should underpin their determination. The systems and their participants will be found wanting. Because the final grades which students receive have a powerful bearing on their subsequent careers, it is appropriate to begin this chapter with a discussion of problems that have emerged in the award of grades. This highlights the importance of the marks of individual examiners and the methods of aggregation used.

Differential grading between subjects and the comparability of qualifications

Parents want the best for their children. Therefore, they will encourage them to take those qualifications that will qualify them for those institutions that are perceived in turn to get them into the best jobs. In the UK this has encouraged those institutions which perceive themselves to have low status to seek parity of esteem with institutions having higher status. Thus, in the 1960s ten technological institutions awarding a diploma which was said to be equivalent to a university degree sought and gained university status (Heywood, 1969). Later in 1992, most of those institutions awarding degrees of the Council for National Academic Awards also obtained university status and the right to award their own degrees.

In Britain National Targets for Education and Training depend heavily on the 'supposed equivalents of different qualifications' (Robinson, 1997). There is, therefore, considerable concern with the equivalence of qualifications. Indeed Robinson

(1997) points out 'a common theme running through educational policy in Britain is the perceived need to establish parity of esteem between the "academic" and the "general" route through post-compulsory education and training and the "vocational route".' As we have seen at the practical level this has caused some universities to provide bridging courses for non-traditional students. But while policy may be challenging existing hierarchies in society (Dearing, 1997, and Chapter 11) less sanguine analyses suggest they will continue (Ainley, 1994). Such debate is relatively unknown in the United States where institutions are clear about whether they are primarily teaching based or research based.

Irrespective of these policy and philosophical approaches to the development of qualifications in the UK there has been a long-standing concern with the proportions of classified degrees awarded as between the different subjects. As long ago as 1967 the National Union of Students reported that 14 per cent of graduates in mathematics received a first class honours degree whereas only 4 per cent received a first-class in history. This has been found to be a persistent trend (Dearing, 1997). Even if the relative proportions changed similar questions would remain, and to a large extent remain unanswered. For example, why in 1993/94 did the University of Cambridge award first-class honours degrees to 24 per cent of its students which was 10 per cent more than those awarded by any other university? No one knows the answer to this question.

The National Union of Students did not discuss the relative qualities of students. Could it be that the students entering history were not the same standard as those taking mathematics? Was there a substantial weeding out of students in mathematics so that only the best remained? When we enquire further we find out that the drop-outs from the 'sciences' are more numerous than those from the 'arts'. So an 'arts' student is more likely to get a degree than a 'science' student. We could go further and ask if the fact that arts subjects produce fewer firsts than science subjects means that, contrary to popular myth, science subjects are easier to study than arts subjects?

In spite of the difficulty of obtaining answers to such questions a curriculum study at Stanford University showed the value of longitudinal studies of course transcripts. A 15-year study found little difference in mean grades among the natural science, social sciences and humanities when class size differences were taken into account (Boli, Katchadourian and Mahoney, 1988).

In Britain the Graduate Standards Programme (GSP, 1997a) which was established 'to develop definitions of "threshold" and mechanisms for providing assurance about their achievement', taking into account recent developments in higher education, succeeded in showing just how difficult this task is. At the same time its analysis showed how some improvements could be made in the system. One of the focuses of this chapter will be on the external examiner system which the programme thought could be improved.

It might be supposed that the grades awarded would relate to some minimum standards of attainment (threshold) and course coverage (whatever that might mean). However, the programme came to the conclusion that 'assessment of undergraduate degrees is not carried out in terms of anything that can be identified as "threshold" standards'. It might also be supposed that there exist simple definitions of what a graduate with first-class honours or a grade point average of 4.5 should be able to do. They don't. The programme sought to define 'graduateness' but concluded that, 'at present, it is not, sufficiently robust a concept to define the nature of a UK first degree or to offer a threshold standard for all degrees' (GSP, 1997b).

In sum, irrespective of the system of higher education, very little is known about the comparability of qualifications. What *is* known is very much the function of myths which assume that the qualifications of Ivy League institutions will be better than those of other institutions (e.g. Ellis, 1995; Herrnstein and Murray, 1994). While this may be the case, and independently of whether or not this is a desirable or an undesirable state of affairs, it is not proven. Murphy (1996) points out that in spite of the British obsession with comparability, little or no notice was taken by the higher education establishment of the studies of comparability between subjects offered by the same matriculation board, and between the same subject offered by different boards (Boyle and Christie, 1996). Yorke *et al.* (1998) made no reference to that work in their study of the bench marking of academic standards.

Until recently academics in the UK have argued that the system is protected by the external examiner system. It does, so it is argued, maintain comparability between degrees of different institutions. Unfortunately, in other asides, academics have wanted to have their cake and eat it, because they are often heard to say 'but of course the degree in history (or whatever) from institution X is better than those from institution Y'. Such statements are implicit criticisms of a system set up to maintain comparability of standards.

But as Knight (private communication) points out, the question remains as to whether standards can be defined in general terms. The attempts to define outcomes described in Chapters 11 and 12 imply that they have to be defined with reference to the curriculum.

External examining

The term 'external examining' has several meanings. Although its use has extended over 300 years in the United States the examples cited show more congruence with what happens in the British school system than they do with what happens in universities following the British approach. For example, at Swarthmore College the system that has been in operation since the 1930s has as its purpose the certification of the one-third of undergraduates seeking honours. In their junior year the students undertake a plan of study which is negotiated. The external examiners set and mark terminal examinations in the field (Jones, 1933; Milton and Edgerley, 1976). This is the method of examining that is used for most of the subjects in the advanced level of the General Certificate of Education in England with the exception that the syllabus is also set by the matriculation board. In order to cope with several thousand papers which have to be scored in each subject the three or four examiners responsible for examining are supported by a number of assistants. The task of the examiners is to obtain comparability of marking among the assistants and to arrive at a common standard.

It seems that there is some confusion in the US about how examining is undertaken in the UK. Hartle (1986) writes that, 'Unlike British or European Institutions, our certification of student achievement is done by the same teacher who teaches the student.' On the contrary, this is what usually happens in British Institutions, with the caveat that the examination paper before it is set, and the marked answers of the final examinations are subject to the scrutiny of an external examiner within the context of the framework agreed by all the teachers contributing to the course (i.e. all modules or units in the final year). In modules or units that are taught by more than one teacher the team will agree the assessment and examining strategies. There are many variations in practice. In my own department the overall strategy (i.e. the number and timing of assessments, and the weightings to be applied to each assessment) is determined by the department. The assessments that determine the final overall grade are scrutinized by the external examiner. If a course (e.g. Philosophy of Education) is taught by a single tutor, that tutor, subject to the aforementioned remarks, designs the examinations and/or assessments for that course and also marks them. The external examiner is provided with a sample of all the papers so that at the examiners' meeting which determines the grades he is in a position to comment on the standards and fairness of the marking. In particular the external assessor is expected to help in making the decisions about borderline candidates. Subsequently he/she submits a report on the 'standard' of the qualification to the university and makes recommendations if necessary. In this system (which until recently was not semester-ized) only the final year's work is presented for scrutiny. Work undertaken in each of the preceding years is set and examined by the teachers. Students are required to pass in the work of each year before they can proceed to the next year. They may have to sit supplemental examinations in subjects that they may have failed.

Within the past decade not only has a mass system of higher education been developed in Britain but it has become modularized and semesterized as in the United States. (The Graduate Standards Programme (GSP, 1997b) reports that a unitized framework has been adopted by about 25 per cent of the universities while 65 per cent have adopted a modular framework. In the latter, the blocks of learning are of more or less equal size and separately assessed as in the American system. In the former, existing courses have been restructured into a number of units which may or may not be of uniform size or be independently assessed.)

Modular systems are extremely complex since apart from being separately assessed the modules may be available to several different programmes leading to different degree qualifications. They need to be scrutinized for fairness as well as the learning they are likely to create (Brown and Knight, 1994; Kneale, 1997). Such complexity has important consequences for the work of external examiners (Silver, 1996: Warren Piper, 1994). The Graduate Standards Programme concluded that modular structures bring 'disparate disciplinary cultures into juxtaposition with one another and require the combination and calibration of students' performances across the boundaries of these disciplines – where no common language exists'. In consequence the external examiners' task is made exceedingly difficult.

In this respect it is interesting to note that the Registration Council for Secondary Teachers in Ireland looks at the degree of cognateness that a module has with the principal course of study. It should also be noted that in the teacher diploma described in parts of this chapter there are tensions between the academic subject specialists who come from a wide range of disciplines as well as with those responsible for teaching methods. Some of these differences are reconciled through agreement to standardize marks. Others are understood and seldom appreciated, and so are the cause of excessive frustration.

In spite of these criticisms of the external examiner system there has been interest in it in the United States. Fong (1987) who reviewed the arguments for and against external examining, drew attention to a project initiated by the Association of American Colleges which involved 18 institutions of varying size, in the evaluation of the work of external examiners in a variety of educational settings. Most of these institutions assessed their students by a combination of written comprehensive and oral examinations. Some used a thesis as a substitute for a written paper.

Fong considered the external examiner system has considerable advantages. Instructors have two goals for their classes. First, they want to invest a class with knowledge and skills that will enable each student to be competent in the subject of study. Second, they seek to maximize the abilities of individual students. Instructors seek a floor to student achievement, the pass/fail line, and above that to distinguish whether degrees of achievement are excellent, good or merely satisfactory. Instruction in the classroom is guided both by criterion and selection-referenced considerations. Unlike commercial examinations, external examiners themselves, who are most frequently instructors at other institutions, are experienced in balancing these two goals of evaluation. An external's sense of what constitutes adequacy and excellence may differ from the host faculty's but the discussion and negotiation of these standards is precisely where the perspective of the outsider becomes valuable.

Academics in the UK would undoubtedly have acquiesced in these views. Nevertheless, the Committee of Vice-Chancellors and Principals were concerned about academic standards and they issued a report which included a code of practice for external examiners (Reynolds, 1986). In a section on the purposes and functions they said that it is neither possible nor desirable to establish a uniform external examiner system across all institutions and applicable to all subjects. But exceptions and reservations have deliberately been omitted in the interest of a clear statement of widely applicable guidelines.

> The purposes of the external examiner system are to ensure, firstly that degrees awarded in similar subjects are comparable in standard in different universities in the United Kingdom, though their content does of course vary; and, secondly, that the assessment system is fair and is fairly operated in the classification of students.

In order to achieve these purposes external examiners need to be able (a) to participate in assessment processes for the award of degrees; (b) to arbitrate or adjudicate in problem cases; (c) to comment and give advice on course content, balance and structure of degree schemes, and on assessment processes.

The last codicil is of some importance since it recommended what for many academics would be an extension of the role of the external examiner. For some this was unwelcome. At the same time the document spelt out the rights of external examiners. These included the right to see:

all degree examination scripts. In those cases where it is agreed that the inviting department should make a selection of scripts to be sent to an external examiner, the principles of such selection should be agreed in advance.

any work that contributes to the assessment and the degree classification. In some cases it may be agreed that the department should make a selection of such work to be sent to the external examiner, the principles for such selection being agreed in advance.

The Committee recommended that:

The views of an external examiner must be particularly influential in the case of disagreement on the mark to be awarded for a particular unit of assessment, or on the final classification to be derived from an array of marks of a particular candidate at the examiners' meeting.

And that:

External examiners should be encouraged to comment on the assessment process and the schemes of marking and classification. In some subjects participation in the devising of such schemes is essential.

The principles outlined in the document were generally adopted throughout the university system (CVCP, 1987). Nevertheless, in 1994 Warren Piper, in his profound study of examining in Britain, concluded:

Despite the problems of managing large teams of examiners, each with their own area of responsibility, frequently no steps are taken to help them maintain consistent standards. Marking guides are used in fewer than half the courses. Statistical treatment of marks is so rare that one is forced to consider the possibility that many examiners are blind to some of the problems of combining marks from different examiners assessing varied tasks. Completely blind double marking is not universal. Most external examiners make adjustments at the margin rather than seeking to re-calibrate wayward ranges of marks. It is the technical aspects of marking which are reported as troublesome. Marking is overwhelmingly normative and a heavy reliance is placed on examiners' memories.

There is no reason to suppose that this situation in respect of the technical aspects of marking differs in other countries. Warren Piper went on to say that the judgements of external examiners are 'largely informed by a pertinent body of theoretical knowledge about the processes involved in examination'. It is a skilled craft and not an expert occupation. No wonder it has been suggested that it should be abolished (AAU, 1992; CNAA, 1992). Elton, a distinguished Professor of Higher Education quoted by Warren Piper, felt that it was an expensive cosmetic and should be abolished.

The giving of university status to the polytechnics in 1992 with their wide-ranging backgrounds and activities, caused Reynolds, the author of the 1986 report, to question whether it was feasible to ever maintain comparable standards when comparability rested on such shaky foundations (Reynolds, 1990). Barnett (1992) has long argued that diversity will create differential standards, and that in consequence differential standards should be accepted. In Australia, where the British tradition has strongly influenced the development of higher education, similar questions have been asked about the external examiner system. In spite of the interest shown in the external examiner system in the US, the North American system is characterized by differentiation and this is acceptable to the public.

Warren Piper argued that if the identity of academics was defined by the job they do rather than by the subject they taught, then they might be open to professional training in the art and science of teaching and examining. Since he reported in 1994, the training of new university teachers in the UK has become mandatory, and the expansion of higher education into a mass and diverse system has forced the Higher Education Quality Council to reconsider the issue of standards (GSP, 1997a). Among its recommendations is that the system of external examining should be strengthened; new fora in which examiners may review their practice and calibrate standards should be established, and for increased training and development opportunities for internal assessors and examiners. In the sections which follow the theoretical knowledge which examiners should have is discussed.

Marks: absolute or relative

Error is inherent in any type of test, be it essay, objective or, for that matter, oral. The three main types of error are 'time error' due to short time changes in the candidate's performance, marker errors due to inconsistencies in marking and discrepancies in marking, and paper content errors which are demonstrated by differences between the results of supposedly similar papers. Thus any mark includes an error and it is customary to calculate the standard error of a mark (see Glossary). For example, the standard error of a score in a multiple-choice test of between 90 and 109 items is 5.

The more items a test contains the more reliable it is likely to be. A test of, say, ten multiple-choice items is not likely to be very reliable.

The standard error is likely to be more for an essay examination scored out of 100. This has considerable implications for candidates at the borderline of a grade. Figure 10.1 illustrates this problem in respect of the type of classification used in the British system. In this illustration the mark which defines the differences between the two divisions of second class honours is 60. A candidate with a mark of 59 may merit a true mark as much as 64 or as little as 54 (for the sake of argument). It is clear that the correct way to express a mark is the stated mark plus or minus the error e.g. 35+/- 3.

McVey (McVey 1976a, 1976b) in a series of studies in the Department of Electrical and Electronic Engineering at the University of Surrey, involved his colleagues in the determination of the standard error of their papers and the error due to the content of the paper. He was interested in the levels of both inter-marker and inter-examination reliability. He asked his colleagues to design two papers instead of the usual one that the students would sit. Each of the papers was to be of the same standard and to cover the same area of syllabus. They were vetted by the committee that looked at all the papers set in the examination. The two papers were set at intervals of between one and four days to the same group of candidates in place of those that they usually sat. He relied on paid student volunteers to take the two examinations necessary for his experiment: 578 scripts were marked by 11 pairs of examiners. Of the differences in marks obtained between the examiners, 52 per cent were of 10 marks or less, 18 per cent exceeded 20 marks, and 5 per cent exceeded 30. He found the standard error to be 7.64 marks, which, he thought, given the limitations of the experiment, was an underestimate, and this in a subject that is supposedly more objective than subjects in the humanities.

In a subsequent experiment he tried to distinguish between marker error and error due to the content of the paper (McVey, 1976b). The two are interrelated, and paper error must contribute to marker error, especially in circumstances where ambiguous questions are set. In essay or problem solving papers where the number of questions to be answered is small, the content of the syllabus that is likely to be covered may be small compared with what had to be studied by the student. Therefore a student who has 'spotted' (predicted) the questions on the paper correctly may be at an advantage compared with one who has not. A paper should be equitable. McVey concluded that paper-content error is greater than marker error. James (1977) who replicated the experiment and obtained similar results was able to administrate the examinations as a normal part of the course. Both of these studies suffered from the defect of small samples. However, those essay questions that I have designed, and subsequently judged to be poor, seriously affected my marking.

In boards of examiners applying the British system much time is spent debating the merits of candidates at the borderlines. As Warren Piper (1994) reported this is often done in the absence of any knowledge of the standard error. Examiners are often observed to take up entrenched positions. Knowledge of the standard error should at the very least make them give a mark firmly in the band to which they believe the candidate belongs in the first instance. Thus if they believe a candidate to be worth a 2.2 then it is better to give the candidate 57 and not 59. Marks are not absolutes and a mark at 59 should leave room for negotiation but the examiners should be aware that that is the intention.

Next consider the candidate at the borderline whose answers are scored by a second assessor. In relation to Figure 10.1 one marker might give candidate A 59 and another marker 61; similarly, candidate B might be given 34 by one marker and 36 by another. Which are the correct marks? There is no answer to that question. Now consider candidate C at the 50 per cent level who is a candidate for our secondary teacher's diploma. If that student gets 51 he or she will earn an additional annual salary increment throughout his or her teaching career; if 49 is awarded, this increment is lost. It is in such circumstances that the external examiner is asked to adjudicate.

The problem of justice is accentuated by the fact that it is reasonable to hypothesize that, a month or so later, these examiners might reverse their marks. It is for this reason that the notion of continuous assessment, in which a series of marks is collected over the period of an academic year, might prove, when averaged, to be a more accurate assessment of the candidate. In the North American system teachers often administer a number of short tests during the period of a course. These issues are discussed in more detail in the next section.

[The reader might like to turn at this point to the later section on grade intervals and selection since the intervals between grades affect the interpretation of standard error and the marks of examiners.]

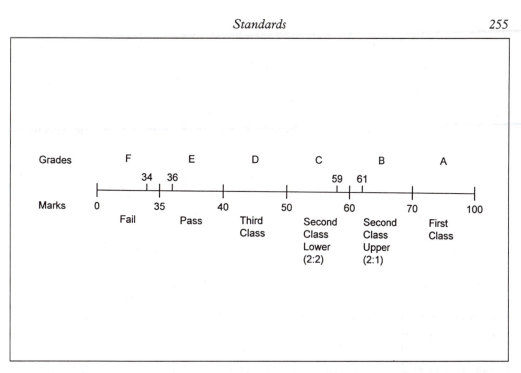

Figure 10.1 Example of a grading scale for an examination with total marks of 100 to show the problem faced by examiners at the borderlines in institutions of higher education in the UK. At the University of Dublin where a uniform system of marking is used throughout the university the following equivalences with the North American system apply. Equivalent grade A = 66%+ , and then A- = 63–65%; B+ = 61–62%; B= 58–60%; B- = 55–57%; C+ =52–54%; C= 48–51%; C- = 45–47%; D= 40–44% and F = 0–39% (University of Dublin, Trinity College, Prospectus for Visiting Students 1999/2000).

The reliability of the marks of examiners

It has been understood since 1908 (Meyer, 1908) in the United States and 1935 in Britain that the marks of examiners are highly variable. Starch and Elliott (1912, 1913a, 1913b) showed that the marking of test papers in English, history and mathematics was highly variable when they were marked against a 100 point scale. Not only were different marks recorded for the same candidate when scored by two different teachers, but even the same teacher accredited different marks to the same candidate when that teacher re-marked the paper.

In Britain Hartog and Rhodes (1935) obtained similar results from studies of Chemistry, English, French, History and Latin examinations. They concluded that the marks of examiners were unreliable. Reliability (or consistency, as Wiseman preferred to call it) is the measure of the extent to which a test or examination gives consistent results with repeated applications. This is the reliability of the test in time. It has been generally understood that a test cannot be valid unless it is reliable although this axiom has been questioned in recent years especially in relation to criterion related testing. Both reliability and validity are generally determined by correlational analyses. Hartog and Rhodes (1935, 1936) not only drew attention to the lack of correlation between the marks of two examiners rating the same papers but to the fact that they were likely to produce two different distributions. This point is illustrated in Figure 10.2 (see Chapter 1 and the Glossary for definitions of reliability and validity).

One of the problems in the interpretation of reliability data is that analysts tend to concentrate on the disagreements between examiners rather than the extent of agreement. Vernon (1965) was impressed by the latter when he evaluated Hartog and Rhodes study, for they showed important public examinations at matriculation and university honours level were marked consistently. For example the median disagreement between any two examiners was not more than 3 per cent. He felt that this figure probably represented the standard error of the mark, but he accepted that some marks might be very much greater. He went on to say

> Nevertheless, this study deserves to be taken very seriously, since it indicates that many less thorough examinations are deplorably unreliable; that in the absence of a scheme of instruction drawn up and applied by experienced examiners much worse discrepancies may arise; that when the average and dispersion marks are not standardized, gross differences may appear in the proportions of credits, passes and fails, etc., which are awarded, and that even a percentage error may make all the difference between a pass and a fail, or a first and a second class.

Vernon's remarks are supported by the fact that very high reliabilities have been found between markers in GCE and other public examinations at school level (Murphy, 1982; Wilmot and Nuttall, 1974). However, markers in these examinations receive considerable guidance which university markers do not. Investigations of university marking such as those by McVey and James suggest that Vernon was somewhat sanguine. Wilson (1986) found that the magnitude of error in forecasting was somewhat larger than the forecasters (economics teachers) might have expected. He said it seemed that some teachers accepted uncritically those outcomes which were expected but search for 'reasons' to explain those which were not. However, where a teacher is only responsible for small groups on a year-on-year basis then their knowledge of their students may lead to more reliable marking. Equally it could be prejudiced.

Wilmot quoted by Cresswell (1986a) found that one of the main reasons for disagreement between examiners about marking was that they made random but straightforward mistakes, such as misreading graphs, overlooking points in answers, etc. This was certainly the experience of the moderators of engineering science at the GCE Advanced level (Carter, Heywood and Kelly, 1986).

It is clear that marks are not absolute and that the design of questions and their marking needs to be rigorous. We cannot afford to be sanguine about our marking, neither can we afford to treat the setting of papers with indifference. It is for reasons such as these that much attention is being given to criterion and semi-criterion referenced assessments.

The potential for error in examinations has implications for the way in which marks are combined from different examination papers to arrive at a single score (grade). This is especially so with modular systems. It also has implications for the number of grade intervals that are used. Since the former relates to the responsibility of examiners and the latter to examining authorities, issues relating to the combination of examiners marks are considered first. There is some repetition of the previous discussion, because both problems arise from the relative unreliability of marks.

The perceptions of examiners and the combination of their marks

We have seen that the marks of examiners for the same set of answers can vary, but the shapes of the mark distributions between examiners are also subject to considerable variation. It also seems that the behaviours of examiners tend to persist with time. That is, a person who tends to mark low will tend to do so in subsequent examinations and vice versa. Teachers in their role as examiners tend to adopt certain dispositions toward marking which arise from their beliefs about the purposes of examinations which in turn define their frames of reference. Thorndike and Hagen (1977) described three such frames of reference. They called them Perfection, Peer and Potential and they relate to the standard against which a grade is given, i.e. 'absolute norm', 'relative performance', and 'change in performance during the term'. One American study has shown that instructors using peer or perfection models tend to give lower grades than teachers who use a potential for growth model (Geisinger, 1980).

Thus between different examiners in the same faculty (subject) there may be considerable differences in their mark distributions. To be fair to students action needs to be taken to correct these misalignments which are due to variability in the marking of papers and not to differences in either the qualities (objectives/outcomes) tested or the individual performance of the students. The significance of this issue may perhaps be brought home by consideration of the marks on a school report of the kind that was issued by many British schools in the past. We should expect to do no less for our students in higher education than is done for our children in secondary school. The argument applies equally to the compilation of a Grade-Point-Average.

Suppose now that all the teachers who teach a particular class produce different distributions: then any summation of these marks will be unfair to the students. The unfairness of such reports is immediately apparent. For example, in Figure 10.2 a mark from Teacher A of 60 per cent is an excellent one, whereas from Teacher B it is only a little above average, assuming that the subjects are of equal difficulty and the students had the same range of abilities and similar motivation towards the learning tasks. Marks on a report are comparatively meaningless without additional information, for which reason some schools also give the average mark in each subject; not that this is entirely helpful because we still do not know how the individual teachers distribute their marks. Even if we did know this it would be entirely wrong to add the marks of different distributions (either within a subject or among subject(s)). Figure 10.3 shows how this can reorder the rankings from distributions which are approximately the same. In all cases in this rather extreme example the candidates obtain the same marks in subjects A and B. However, in Figure 10.3(a) the range of marks for subject C is 40–60 with a spread of 20, whereas in Figure 10.3(b) subject C is marked in such a way that it is given a spread of 60 with a range 20–80. Figure 10.3 (c) shows how when the marks from examiners for two other subjects are introduced the ranking

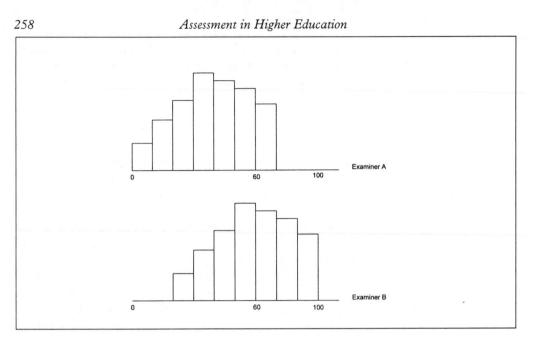

Figure 10.2 Hypothetical distributions of marks for the same group of students in the same subject due to different examiners in an institution of higher education in the UK.

(a)

Student	A	Subjects B	C	Total	Rank Order
1	58	62	40	160	1
2	68	42	45	155	2
3	60	40	50	150	3
4	31	59	55	145	4
5	48	32	60	140	5

(b)

1	58	62	20	140	5
2	68	42	35	145	4
3	60	40	50	150	3
4	31	59	65	155	2
5	48	32	80	160	1

(c)

Student	A	B	Subjects C	D	E	Total
1	58	62	20	40	70	250
2	68	42	35	25	60	250
3	60	40	50	40	60	250
4	31	59	65	35	60	250
5	48	32	80	60	30	250

Figure 10.3 Hypothetical example of rank-orders arising from different distributions of marks.

in exhibit 10.3 (b) is changed. All the candidates now obtain the same result. It is important to remember that changes in the average mark do not alter the ranking; it is the combination of marks that lie within different dispersions.

Dalziel (1998) analysed the marks of a 17 component assessment of 1039 first-year students in psychology at the University of Sydney in four different ways. These simulations were a function of the qualitative as well as the quantitative assumptions which examiners can make. It is a reminder that examiners do make qualitative judgements even if they are hidden, and that these influence the marks candidates receive. All of his systems were shown to be tenuous in determining final marks.

> Without the evidence that the variables involved are quantitative, any number of potential systems for producing marks and grades are equally valid (and, potentially, equally wrong, in the sense that they do not represent anything quantitative in the first place). Hence a student may score one mark or grade under one assessment system, but may receive quite a different mark or grade under another system, and the critical determining factor in which mark or grade is received is not just the student's academic performance but also the assumptions of the assessment system used by the course administrator.

There are no simple solutions to these problems. Dalziel suggests that examiners might discontinue using numbers at all but, as he points out, this might create great uncertainty among examiners and administrators. He also suggests that qualitative categories which are ordered but not numbered would seem to come near to a criterion referenced system. Of more importance is the point that since most procedures are relatively arbitrary students should be informed at the beginning of their course about the mechanisms in use. It might then be possible to involve the students in the decision-making process.

Standardization

Some teachers advocate a technique that standardizes marks in that they are all brought to the same mean and standard deviation while at the same time preserving each markers' distinctions within his/her scores. The term *scaling* is often used instead of standardization in this context.

We do this in my own department with the assessments for our diploma course for graduates intending to be secondary school teachers (Cameron, 1984). As a general finding our examinations are always marked a little more severely than the coursework which constitutes a considerable component of the final work. Whereas, each written examination is scored by an individual examiner, the coursework may be scored by several. Nevertheless, the mean scores are consistent, but within each year and within each form of assessment there can be considerable differences in the mark distributions of the examiners. The coursework was, with one exception, set mainly in the methodology of the subjects that the student teacher intends to teach. There were nine subject areas. Each was the responsibility of a different teacher/examiner. In one year the highest subject average was 71.5 (SD = 1.6) and the lowest 58.4 (SD = 7.6). The groups were relatively small. However, it meant that only the very highest in the second subject could approach the lowest of the first. Such a poor comparative performance is hardly likely in practice. While we obtain considerable marker consistency from year to year we experience variations as between the markers, and for this reason we scale or standardize our marks by bringing them to the same mean and standard deviation

One of the difficulties of this system is that the student cannot predict from raw scores what grade he/she is likely to get. In universities where students are allowed to know the grades (but not marks) they receive in individual subjects this can lead to difficulties because the only marks that individual teachers have are the raw scores. Since the assessor can only convert these to a grade a student's expectations (having averaged his/her grades) may not be met when the marks are standardized. This can and has led to appeals. One of the problems is that individual examiners might award more honours marks than they are in a position to justify. For example, in one particular year when 54 per cent of the candidates would have been awarded honours after standardization, prior to standardization the assessors had awarded 63 per cent honours marks for written examinations, 81 per cent honours marks for teaching practice, 91 per cent honours marks in teaching methods assignments, and 98 per cent honours marks in dissertations. The use of raw scores would have led to grade inflation and almost all of the candidates would have received honours.

One way round the problem of standardization is to ask the institution to agree that when marks are standardized tutors should be instructed not to give students their raw marks. It is easy to see that in modularized semester systems this may not be popular. In our case it was expected that student teachers should familiarize themselves with these problems as part of their preparation for teaching, and lectures were provided on this aspect of assessment.

As indicated there was a small but consistent difference between the marks awarded for coursework and those for the written examinations. This is in keeping with trends reported elsewhere. When there is a large difference between the two there is a substantial case for standardization if the coursework is measuring the same quality. If it is not, there may be a case for letting the marks stand (see below). However, if the effects are such as to cause grade inflation then at the very least those marks would have to be weighted. Clearly this again could be a problem in modular systems. Kneale (1997) reports that in some modular systems students can fail 40+ credits yet still graduate with honours. She also found that there were considerable variations in the penalties applied for failure in a module. Clearly if there is to be comparability there would have to be a common set of rules which would apply within and across institutions.

An advantage of standardization in modular structures where students can choose between subjects is that they do not have to worry about the folklore that is handed down about the relative severity of particular examiners. They can take a course that is perceived to be interesting but tough without worrying about the assessor's severity, in the knowledge that the marks will be related to those of other examiners. There remains a grade boundary issue and problems will arise when the scores come from criterion related marking. At The Royal Melbourne Institute of Technology University in Australia another approach was developed to take into account non-homogeneity among students as well as other variations (Brown, 1998). Its author points out that traditional approaches assume homogeneity among the student population, and that all courses are of the same difficulty. But course groups may comprise traditional and non-traditional students some of whom may be at an advantage over others in the class. It could happen that the brightest students attend an elective and raise the mean score of that course. Is it fair to lower that mean when it might reflect true performance? Similarly, a teacher may inspire a group to perform well above average. Should they be penalised? Brown (1998) described a statistical procedure that had been implemented successfully to address the problem of the variation in average outcome due to non-homogeneity and unreasonable variation in the assessment process. His technique makes use of confidence limits to compare population and sample means.

In order to predict the expected class mean score with respect to population mean an average performance index is calculated. This takes into account biases in class statistics, as for example, those caused by double degree students with a year's more experience than single degree students mixed in the same class. (This index is the ratio of the average of all the students' results divided by the population's results across all subjects.) The expected result for any group of known students can be calculated by taking the average Performance Indices of this group and multiplying by the known population mean. When necessary the result can be subjected to non-linear scaling.

Relatively simple databases are required for the system Brown described. It was applied to 37 subjects (modules) in his department. In the light of developments in modularization the evaluation of techniques such as this will assume increasing importance.

A valid objection to the method of standardization that I have described for my department is that coursework, especially teaching practice, is unlikely to be developing the same qualities as the subjects requiring written examinations (Isaacs and Imrie, 1980). It may also be argued that the questions within a written paper might test different outcomes. The same kind of thing may happen in a language course where verbal fluency and literacy understanding are different qualities tested on different occasions. Students may perform substantially better in the latter than in the former. Scaling may then prove an unjustifiable smoothing. This effect would be particularly important in multiple-strategy approaches to assessment and learning. However, as the case for scaling disappears, so does the case for a single mark. It is for this reason that there has been so much interest in profiling (see Chapter 11).

Tognolini and Andrich (1995) suggest that procedures such as we have used where marks are being aggregated from subjects (topics) which may be measuring different things should be called *equating*. They show that at the University of Western Australia first-year subjects varied in difficulty. In some subjects it was easier to obtain higher grades than in others. The transformation procedure proposed takes this into account by using measures of achievement/ability rather than aggregates. It is based on latent trait test theory (see Chapter 13 for references).

It will be understood from this discussion that students who concentrate their efforts in areas of high marks will benefit from the raw scores whereas the reverse will be true for students in low scoring areas, i.e. they will benefit from standardization. When the marks of examiners are consistently close there is perhaps little need for standardization. It does, however, ensure fairness, and it may have deflationary effect on the number of honours awarded as the example given above demonstrates. It might be expected that universities offering the same award with roughly similar student populations would award approximately similar distributions if their degrees are to be considered comparable. The question which examiners have to answer is, do their marks represent demonstrated achievement, expressed in assessment criteria, or do they represent numbers to be manipulated on the basis of assumptions about what the distributions ought to be?

Reconciling inter-collegiate differences in specific subjects

As indicated earlier there is a mythology in all countries about which universities and departments within them are 'best'. Even within the external examiner system that is supposed to protect standards one first-class honours degree is said to be better than another. Given the freedom of universities to set and teach their own subjects it would seem almost impossible to arrive at an objective judgement about the merits of different degrees. The recommendations of the Graduate Standards Programme (GSP, 1997a) go some way to helping with its recommendations for training and assessment for external examiners. This would open the way for comparability studies of the kind undertaken by the matriculation boards (Forrest and Shoesmith, 1986; Jones and Ratcliffe, 1996).

Of particular relevance to this discussion is a report by Smith (1978) for the Joint Matriculation Board (now the Northern Examination and Assessment Board). In that report he describes the different kinds of moderation used to establish the standards of internal assessments made in schools which contributed to some or all of a grade for an award. When schools assess their own students some means of moderation is required to ensure they are operating to the same standard as those parts of the subjects which are assessed by the board. Sometimes the moderation is undertaken by external assessors (e.g. Carter, Heywood and Kelly, 1986), and sometimes where there is an externally set written paper it can be undertaken statistically.

> This involves a comparison of the marks for the internally assessed component (or components) with the marks awarded in a component (or components) of the external examination which is being used as the moderating instrument. The internally assessed marks of the group of candidates in a school are adjusted if the evidence derived from the external criterion suggests that adjustments are necessary (Smith, 1986)

Much of this report is devoted to an explanation of two methods of statistical moderation using the results of GCE advanced level examination in biology. Of particular interest is the way it handles small groups since some argue that scaling should not be undertaken with small groups (Brown, Bull and Pendelbury, 1997). In higher education a nationally normed objective test could be used as a calibrating instrument for a particular subject. The objection to doing this is that it would require and perhaps create a national curriculum. However, in some professional subjects there is already a core curriculum and the Graduate Standards Programme reported that some of those working in professional programmes saw merit in the use of shared programmes of assessment in parts or in stages of their programmes (GSP, 1997b). As long ago as 1974 Carter and Lee showed that there were few differences in content in first-year electrical engineering programmes. They saw no reason why first-year students should not sit a nationally set objective examination. It should be possible to design a reasonably long test so as to enable choice of section (content). The statistical properties of an objective test make it ideal for this purpose (see Chapter 13). The Graduate Standards Programme Reports suggest that external tests like the GRE and GMAT in North America, which are set in objective format, might be a way of clarifying degree standards and thresholds.

Elton (1998) is of the opinion that degree programmes have become so diversified that the concept of a common standard is problematic. He suggested that it might be possible to establish a threshold level that might be sufficiently similar for all degree courses, but this would not be accomplished without difficulty. He noted that if degree classes are substituted and profiles introduced, a change which he felt was pedagogically desirable, that it would not be possible to aggregate performance in one overall grade. This would not invalidate the need for examining to become more professional, and he argued that examiners should develop the skill of educational connoiseurship advocated by Eisner (see Chapter 14).

On the broad front of the whole examination in a subject it is likely that cross-moderation studies may be more rewarding especially if examiners can also meet at the time the examinations are being designed so as to discuss their aims and objectives and be involved in the process. Support for such an approach will be found in the findings of the comparability studies undertaken by the matriculation boards in England. Forrest and Shoesmith (1986) write:

> Cross-moderation methodology is particularly attractive, for it involves the very people who influence most of the critical decisions which are made after each examination: their experiences of reading and discussing scripts of different provenances are in their minds when those decisions are taken. In contrast, it has proved surprisingly difficult to design research studies which will result in conclusions of a quantitative kind capable of being translated into action at grading meetings.

Unfortunately it would seem that there is a long way to go before such studies are feasible in higher education. In respect of the UK the Graduate Standards Programme (GPS, 1997b) concluded:

> that the use of a common language across subjects and institutions does not necessarily mean that academics are employing a common model of assessment in which the cut-offs are the same. The common vocabulary reflects administrative need for a cross-subject (and cross-institution) grading system that allows for comparison of quite distinct and different types of substantive judgement. There is no attempt to ensure, that, for example, student work regarded as grade one (if one uses a grade scale from one to five for arguments sake) in classics is in fact sufficiently similar to that accorded a grade one, in say, chemistry. The process of making such equations is conceptually separate from the process of determining what actually are the substantive judgements that describe particular levels.

The programme did not take into account the large body of work that has been undertaken in recent years on the relative standards of the GCE 'A' level by independent investigators (e.g. FitzGibbon, Tymms and Vincent, 1994), as well as official investigations within the system (e.g. Jones, 1997). Like them Jones of the Northern Examination and Assessment Board (the successor of the Joint Matriculation Board), as a result of a new study of standards at 'A' level, concluded that by themselves statistical methods are not enough. He was less sanguine than Forrest and Shoesmith and wrote that 'Making definitive statements about comparative standards is notoriously difficult, even if cross-moderation methodology is employed and particularly when those syllabuses embody different designs, content and approaches to assessment.' Although it may be argued that this is not applicable to universities with so diverse curricula, it would seem to be in line with the thinking of the Graduate Standards Programme. Such thinking ought not to be used to preclude such studies since they will undoubtedly gain insights into the assessment process irrespective of the system being investigated.

Differential subject performance and the problem of comparability

Unfortunately, scaling will not resolve the differences in marks that arise between subjects. As long ago as 1967 the National Union of Students (NUS, 1967) pointed out that there were substantial differences in the percentage of first-class honours degrees awarded between the arts and science subjects. More were awarded in the sciences and the NUS found it difficult to believe that this was due to the fact that students in arts subjects were of poorer quality. To illustrate their point, Figure 10.4 shows the distribution of marks between four subjects in the first-year examinations of a university. The last subject is mathematics. It is, of course possible that in mathematics where marking is fairly objective, this distribution is real and shows two groups of students with different qualities.

As we have seen, one of the problems is the perception that markers have of the purposes of marking and the methods of scoring to achieve those ends. These vary between subjects. For example in the humanities many teachers use a 13-point (or so) letter scale (using either Greek or Roman letters), whereas in the sciences teachers use numbers before conversion to the final grade, be it a number or a letter (Thomas, 1984). I have seen one attempt to get teachers in the humanities to use numbers and try to mark to the normal curve in the hope that the number of firsts would be increased. However, when the conversions were made their marks and distributions came out as in the past. It seems that in their memories there was always that student who did well – the super-first – who never somehow appears again. Vernon (1965) put it another way: those teachers who claim this year to have had exceptional students, seem strangely enough to have had them every year, and presumably vice versa. It has probably as much to do with the disposition of teachers as with their subjects although these dispositions may be related to the subjects they teach and the peer view of requirements. In the absence of data these remarks are however surmise.

One way in which inter-subject comparisons of the standards of subjects may be made is to use a technique adopted by the Joint Matriculation Board for studies of the

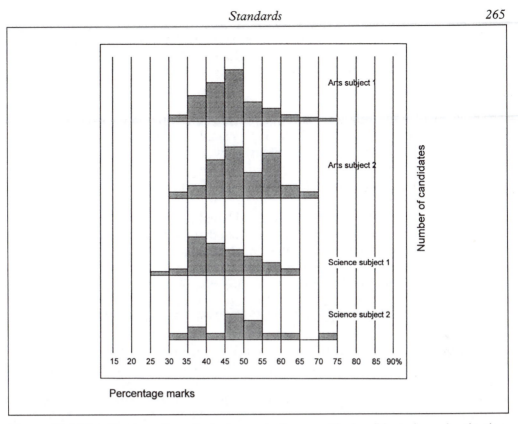

Figure 10.4 Distribution of marks in two arts (humanities) subjects in an institution of higher education in the UK.

Ordinary and Advanced levels of the General Certificate of Education (Forrest, Smith and Brown, 1970; Forrest and Smith, 1972). At the Ordinary level the criterion used was a standardized test of numerical and verbal skills. The average total reference test score of the candidates in each subject sample was compared with the average GCE grade of the same candidates in that subject. From a regression analysis the relative leniency or severity of subjects was determined. However, the authors pointed out, no reference test can take into account the influence on examination results of factors such as the length of course pursued by the candidates, the quality of teaching, and the motivation of students. For this reason, they investigated an alternative technique for comparing standards and found that it gave similar results. This method compared the average grades for all candidates offering a pair of subjects, so that the performance of a group of candidates in one subject is compared with their performance in an another. The number of pairs of subjects may be extended, and if one subject is made common to each pair, the performance of candidates in the common or basic subject can be compared with their performance in the others. This approach does not require a reference test (Forrest and Smith, 1972). Given the power of computers it would be possible to assemble a database for the analysis of inter-module standards within a degree programme using this approach. At the university level a not dissimilar approach was used by de Nevers in a study of grade inflation at the University of Utah (see below).

Grade inflation

The problem of grade inflation has concerned the authorities in Canada, the UK and the US. In Canada it was believed that high schools had inflated grades in order to help secure students admission to university. However, a study of results over a period of ten years found that there had only been a moderate increase in marks. Different trends in entering marks could largely be accounted for by demographic factors (Casas and Meaghan, 1995).

At the university level in the UK, Brown and Knight (1994) have drawn attention to the fact that Minister of Education had suggested that the reported increase in 2:1 and first-class degrees awarded (Tarsh, 1990) might be due to a relaxation of standards. Brown and Knight also noted that in the US Ewell and Jones (1991) had suggested that institutions might manipulate performance measures without reflecting any real difference in underlying performance. These are real and complex issues that are well illustrated by Tarsh (1990). He focused on the relationship between degree class and entry to employment and found that there had been a steady increase in the average degree class of entrants to the labour market. He suggested that if a degree class is an indicator of quality then employers should have noticed an improvement in the quality of the intake. However, there was no evidence that employers had observed such a change. At the same time employers might only have become vocal if they had seen a decline in quality of the intake. Alternatively the recruitment standards of employers could have risen, or the steady improvement could have passed them by.

Another possibility is that employers found the content of degrees acceptable but were concerned with what the degree studies did not contain. In which case any changes in performance related to content would have had to have been substantial for it to have been noticed. A shift from a 2.2 to a 2.1 may not then be as substantial a shift as is imagined especially when the standard error is taken into account. Some employers did indeed make a song about what was not in degree programmes, and in the UK the Enterprise in Higher Education Initiative was set up to remedy these perceived deficiencies. Its progenitors were adamant that it was not about changing content. A major study by Harvey, Moon and Geall (1997) would seem to give some support to these views (see GSP, 1997b). The Graduate Standards Programme suggested that one effect of the changing pattern of classified awards may have been to make students think that the only worthwhile degree is an upper-second (2.1) (Purcell and Pitcher, 1996). This, it is argued, may be one of the causes leading to the rise in the performances of these degrees over the last decade (GSP, 1997b).

Elton (1998) considers that the 'so-called' upward drift is an artefact due to the inclusion of coursework assessment and uses official data to support his claim. He argues that grade inflation is due to changing courses 'and unchanging examiners who lack and continue to lack professionalism'. A point that is more than supported by Warren Piper's (1994) study of professors and examinations.

Whatever the truth of the matter the universities found that they are in a no-win situation. First they are accused of not achieving high enough standards. Then when an improvement is reported they are accused of lowering standards. The press, politicians and public are ill informed about the matters which form the substance of this chapter and are in no position to judge. At the same time there may be something in the theory that both teachers and employers adapt to changing circumstances. For example, in the US, Milton, Pollio and Eison (1986) suggested a theory, subsequently tested, which throws further light on examiner behaviour. Between 1950 and 1965 grade deflation occurred. While the average SAT scores slightly increased, the GPA on leaving higher education slightly decreased. Higher ability students found it more difficult to get good grades. If it is assumed that SAT scores should correlate with GPA then from around 1965 there was substantial grade inflation. The SAT scores on entry declined substantially while the GPA increased as a mirror of the decline. Milton *et al.* explain these changes as a function of the view which society has of grades during a particular period.

Following Goldman and Hewitt, (1975, 1976), Milton and his colleagues used Helson's (1964) adaptation level theory to argue that teachers necessarily adapt to changing circumstances. They suggest that if college grades are considered as an adaptation level phenomenon, then the graders' standard for a given grade category will depend on the ability level of the students he or she teaches. For this type of analysis, grade inflation can be defined as the use of constant grade distribution in the face of lowered student ability levels, and grade deflation as the use of constant grade distribution in the face of raised ones. Similar arguments apply to subjects, and lead to the view that while some fields may not have intrinsically lower standards, students having low SAT scores seek out those fields if they are seen to give easy grading. In contrast, high ability students gravitate toward the hard grading classes. Milton *et al.* found that students with high adaptation levels had higher GPA's even when SAT and ACT scores were taken into account. They argued that for some students a Grade C is probably no less valued than a Grade A by others.

There is support for this theory from the University of Utah. De Nevers (1984) described how the engineering department in that university became aware of the problem from business recruiters. They asked why engineering students had an average GPA of 2.8 compared with other University of Utah students with average GPAs of 3.5 or more. Students below 3.5 were considered failures. Worse still, the students complained that, to earn their grade, they had to do much more work than their friends in other colleges with whom they had been at high school. When the engineers came to examine the problem they found evidence of grade inflation in other areas of the university. Moreover, this had had an effect on the number of summa cum laude awards offered.

They plotted the correlation of average ACT admission score with average grade given in all junior and senior level classes over a period of six years. This showed evidence of grade inflation (see Figure 10.5). For example the average grade given in education was 3.7. About 70 per cent of the class were given As and 30 per cent Bs. In nursing and fine art a similar situation pertained. In contrast, the engineers were at 2.8. Comparison with the ACT scores for the period showed that the best grades were not going to the best students, for there was a significant negative correlation. The least talented, as measured by ACT, were going to the high-level grading colleges while those with high ACT scores were going to low-level ones. In the first year studied a graduate with a GPA of 3.5 obtained magna cum laude and 3.1–3.49 cum laude; 30 per cent of the nursing graduates obtained magna cum laude, but only 19 per cent of the engineers were similarly rewarded. The engineers averaged 3.1 point higher on the ACT than nurses. As a result of these findings, the university recorded a new measure called the honours point scale that had the effect of determining the number of honours awarded by reference to the average score of the class. Consequently the percentage of those graduating magna cum laude in nursing fell from 30 per cent to 0.8 per cent over a six-year period. It was also clear that the academically able as measured by the ACT now get better grades. There is no reason to suppose that this does not happen in other parts of the world.

It may be objected that the Utah method would not work in the 'A' level system of selection used in England because it is not established that 'A' level subject exam-

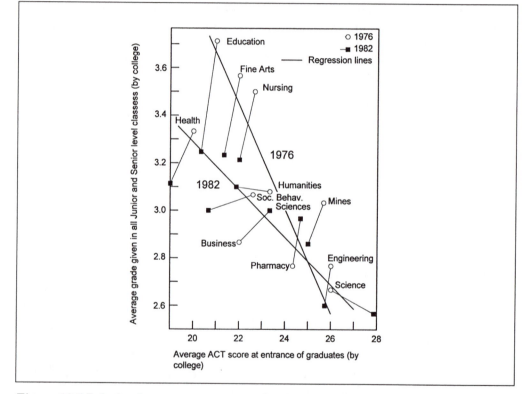

Figure 10.5 Relation between average grade given in upper division classes and ACT score at entrance of graduates, by college, University of Utah, 1976 and 1982. The 1976 regression has $R^2 = 0.64$, *P=0.0006; the 1982 regression has* R^2, *P= 0.0006. The 1976 grades are the sum of the autumn quarter grades in 1974 and 1975. The 1982 grades are for all of the academic year 1981–2.*

(Reproduced from de Nevers (1984) in Heywood 1989a (by kind permission of the editors of *Engineering Education*.)

inations are each of the same standard. But as Forrest (1991) has pointed out, with the increase in non-traditional students there is every reason to base entry on an independent test of the ACT/SAT type with content requirements based on 'A' levels.

The need for quantifiable data which supports or challenges the collective experience of assessors and moderators would seem to be self-evident. Whether or not this would improve practice is an open question. Given that Cross, Frary and Weber's (1993) American study of academic attitudes to and practice of grading is generalizable it will be a difficult task. They found that many faculty members' grading practices were inconsistent with their beliefs about the nature of test scores. It seemed that many were unaware of the basic premise in educational measurement that scores should measure achievement (Ebel, 1965). Perceptions of ability should not contaminate the scoring.

In so far as grade inflation is concerned they recommended that assessments should be developed which did not compress the results into the range 70 to 100. A more spread-out distribution would result in a more reliable assignment of letter grades which make it more comparable with the scales used in the British Isles, and all their attendant problems! Agreement should be reached with colleagues as to what is the minimum acceptable performance. This should determine the pass level not an arbitrary percentage. All of which would seem to suggest more specific statements of criteria.

Grade intervals, selection and threshold

Although the problem of comparability between subjects has been much discussed in Britain, the idea that there are other systems for reporting marks, or that the number of intervals in the awarding profile may be different, has been little considered except for the GCE 'A' level examination. Yet it is clear from experience in Canada and the United States that the number of intervals and where they are placed is not sacrosanct. In Canada the universities have had anything between 3 to 12 passing grades (Ratzlaff, 1980; Taylor, 1977). In Denmark a 13-point scale is used. In the United States a common practice is to relate a course grade, which may be as few as 2 and as many as 12 points for a particular course to a fine grade (300 points) for the overall cumulative GPA for all courses. It has not always been thus, and Milton *et al.*'s analysis of why this has been the case is salutary.

It seems that, in the 300 years for which records exist, there have been short (1–4), 9-point, 13-point and 20-point scales. At Yale in 1783 there was a class of award called 'perjores' which derived its name from an English class of 'unmentionables'(the British sometimes use the term unclassified today). One of the most interesting developments came from Meyer (1908) at the University of Missouri. Arising from the fact that he had dared to fail a whole class he investigated grading practices and found chaos. He suggested a ranking scheme which seems to have underpinned the A-B-C-D-E-F system then beginning to make itself felt. He suggested the following rank order:

3 per cent	Excellent	A
22 per cent	Superior	B
50 per cent	Medium	C
22 per cent	Inferior	D
3 per cent	Failure	F

Here we see the normal curve at work. It is evident that attitudes to grading and in consequence practices vary among faculty. This has been illustrated by Cross *et al.* (1993) who randomly selected over 800 staff at Virginia Polytechnic and State University. They found that nearly half of the teachers used more or less fixed percentage ranges (e.g. 60–70 = D; 71–80 = C). Another large group of teachers indicated that they assigned letter grades by taking into account the difficulty of the test questions, the performance of students with whose work they were familiar, and gaps, in the score distribution. About 6 per cent graded 'on the curve' i.e. awarded the same proportions of As, Bs, Cs etc. regardless of the scores.

Distributions can have a powerful influence on results, particularly in systems that are highly selective. For example, when the English initiated GCE 'A' level in 1951 they agreed the norms shown in Table 10.1. These were intended as no more than rough indicators. It will be seen that the shape of the distribution curve affects the distinctions made between candidates when the grade intervals are drawn (Figure 10.6).

Table 10.1 Recommended grade distributions against percentage of entry in the General Certificate of Education

Grade	Percentage of entry	Cumulative percentages
A	10	10
B	15	25
C	10	35
D	15	50
E	20	70
Ordinary Level		
Pass	20	90
Fail	10	100

Source: Ministry of Education (1960)

An important consideration that relates to the standard error of marks is the narrowness of the B–C and C–D intervals. A person whose actual score is D could have a true score in the C interval; the same might be true of a candidate in the C interval in respect of the B one. This can have profound consequences for candidates who are seeking admission to universities and require a C or a B in that subject. This point was also made in the discussion of Figure 10.1 where it will be seen that the intervals in the North American system are very much smaller than those used in Britain. The width of the intervals has therefore been the subject of much debate and statistical investigation. Two views have emerged. The first is that the intervals in a

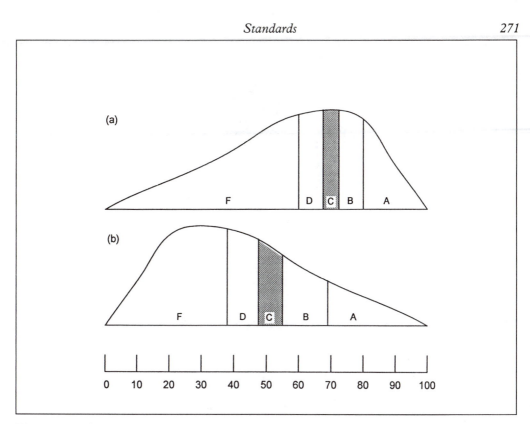

Figure 10.6 An illustration of the effects of the type of distribution on the marks (grades) of candidates to show that a given grade has different meanings in different distributions.
(adapted from Forrest and Whittaker (1983). In the original diagrams the distributions were related to the percentage mark scheme shown in Table 10.1, and included E, O and F grades (Heywood, 1989a)).

grading system should reflect the underlying reliability of the mark scale. Since there is an error this is best accommodated by a limited number of grades. The opposite view is based on the belief that if there are few grades there is a loss of information about the candidate. In a system of equal intervals the candidate stands less chance of moving outside the desired intervals when his number is small than when it is large. This point has been illustrated by Cresswell (1986b) (Figure 10.7) who argues that those who use examinations as selection systems are able to make finer distinctions between the candidates if there are more divisions. This may be necessary in selection procedures if there are more applicants than jobs or places at college. When broad bands are used some additional selecting mechanism may be necessary. With large intervals a greater proportion of candidates are likely to get true scores. However, those scores that are incorrect are subject to very large errors, whereas the errors are greatly reduce in a system which uses narrow intervals.

Those who take the broad interval view (Please, 1977; Mitchelmore, 1981) might argue that, since broad-band criteria lead to relatively poor predictions of perform-ance, additional criteria from, for example, the reports of school principals and

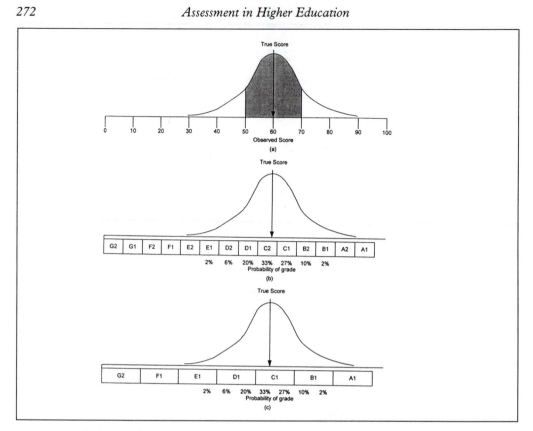

Figure 10.7 *The effects of grade intervals on true score and grading.*
(Slightly adapted from J. Cresswell (1986a) with his permission in Heywood (1989a). (a) For a candidate
with a true score of 60 marks how likely it is that he will actually obtain any particular mark; (b) for a
candidate with a true score of 60 marks how likely it is that he will actually obtain any particular one of a
large number of intervals; (c) for a candidate with a true score of 60 marks how likely it is that he will
actually obtain any particular one of a small number of intervals.)

interviews are desirable. In the United States Stanford University has made a
particular point of the value of variety in admissions procedures, even interviews,
although it is more costly. A Dean of Admissions wrote:

> Contrary to popular myth, test scores and grades, in and of themselves, while not
> insignificant, are nevertheless secondary. In short, an applicant with a high level of
> achievement in a first rate academic program and only modest test scores fares
> better in our process than a student with high test scores and high grades but only a
> modest academic program. (Hargaden, 1982)

One argument in favour of a large number of intervals is the motivational effect. It may
be far easier for a student to perceive an advance over a small interval than over a large
one. It has been demonstrated that the distance between B- and C+ is perceived
psychologically by students to be much larger than between any other pair of adjacent
categories (Stancato and Eizler, 1983).

The Educational Testing Service indicated that the standard error of the verbal portion of the Scholastic Aptitude Test (SAT) is 30 points in each direction. For this reason they should be seen as a band and not a point. However, as White (1985) who cited these figures in relation to the assessment of essays pointed out, 'almost everyone ignores this caution'. In the US this is extremely serious if, as is the case in some colleges, admission or rejection depends on a 10-point difference.

The inescapable conclusion is that the best approach is not to use intervals at all but to quote the mark obtained together with the standard error and leave the selectors with the problem! This view is supported by the contention that in the initial stages of marking examiners are simply not able to make fine distinctions. The alternative is to move toward some kind of criterion grading, an issue which will be discussed in the next chapter. The problem is no different at the level of the classroom.

Milton *et al.* (1986) argue that classroom grading is such a context-dependent phenomenon, subject to so many factors, that exactness is in doubt. To overcome this problem they argued that the US system should move to a less differentiated one in which the objective is learning and mastery rather than ranking (and by implication selection). They also argued for a credit/no credit system with an honours grade available to the select few. To accommodate such a system faculty members would have to state what an acceptable level knowledge was. In today's parlance they would have to state a threshold level. Support for this view has come from Walhout (1997) who described his 40-year experience of grading. He argued that grade inflation could be limited if the number of intervals were set at three, i.e. A, B, and C. A remains the grade for honours level but A- must be understood not to be cognisant of honours work. B means competent, satisfactory work but open to improvement. It absorbs the former C level that indicated the average student. 'It is now the middle range or mean average not a grade above the average. The C grade indicates sufficiently acceptable work to pass a course but suggests that considerable improvement is called for. The C grade is now the same as the former low C and D levels.' For inflation to be driven out of the system Cs would have to be used regularly and As rarely, and students and teachers would have to understand the system clearly. This is an attempt to describe threshold standards.

In Britain the Graduate Standards Programme (GSP, 1997b) considered that the concept of threshold standards was not reflected in the conceptual vocabulary or traditional practice within honours degrees. It felt that the introduction of modular degrees might change the situation since such systems require explicit definitions of learning outcomes. There is no reason why courses within unitized systems should not declare outcomes and design their assessment approaches accordingly. Indeed a multiple strategy approach to assessment and learning is more likely to be accommodated in such a system than in a modularized system. The problem with modular systems is that they can bring rigidities that do not sit well with learning or teaching for learning. It is significant that the Graduate Standards Programme (GSP, 1997b) does not consider the impact of modular systems on learning.

More generally some authorities have tried to move away from grading to alternative systems. In Britain the Graduate Standards Programme considered that the British system was dominated by honours programmes in which 'the attainment of many graduates is seen in terms of their relative deficiency rather then their positive achievement' (GSP, 1997b). The Programme thought the needs of an expanded system of higher education lay in the direction of many more ordinary degrees which, it seems, would make it more like the Scottish system. Others have argued the case for records of achievement (see Chapter 11). In the United States although there was a rapid growth in pass–fail systems (Wittich, 1972) they do not seem to have caused a significant movement in this direction. The purpose of these courses was to encourage students to take a broad range of courses without impediment to their Grade Point Averages. At the California Institute of Technology students in the first course of that kind undertook the reading which it was hoped they would do. However, by the third year, the improvements in learning that had been noticed in the first year had declined (Milton *et al.*, 1986). The experience in Britain and Ireland is that pressure in the culture causes students to take a higher rather than a course that is perceived to be 'lower'. In consequence students are pressed into honours programmes irrespective of their capability. While it is desirable for effective learning that students should perceive themselves to be successful, the social press drives them into a situation where only a few will be regarded as successful by society at large. This, in all probability means that much talent is wasted. Since there is little or no escape from the social press it would seem that a new approach to grading is necessary. From the point of view of employers the most useful approach must surely be that adopted by Alverno College which ensures the development of generic abilities within the courses taken, and these characterize the award given by the college (Alverno, 1994). This college has a very clear idea about what 'graduateness' means and it is stated as a profile not a grade.

Conclusion

Traditional examinations other than objective tests and grading systems have been shown to be relatively unreliable. Apart from the error that accompanies any score, assessors are not agreed on the purposes of testing or what they should be testing. For some more is tested than achievement and knowledge of the student is taken into account. Examining is treated as an art and not a science. Few assessors have any knowledge of the fundamentals of measurement, or if they do, they do not allow it to interfere with the processes developed and conducted by their peers. Little attention is paid to the way in which students learn and the idea that assessments should be designed to enhance learning remains a novelty. All avenues lead to the view that if the processes of examining and assessment are to be improved more explicit statements of criteria showing how these should influence learning will have to be made.

Chapter 11

Toward Outcomes Based Assessment

Summary

Much of the preceding chapter was concerned with the reliability of written assessments. The first objective of this chapter is to consider some of the outcomes based approaches to the assessment of writing that might improve both reliability and validity. The approach to writing across the curriculum in the US is contrasted with subject specific requirements in the UK.

The influence of the assessor's perceptions of marking is discussed and it is suggested that as an assessor marks they create an essay in much the same way as the writer. A discussion of the components of the academic critical essay begins with a note on the different perceptions that students have of the purposes of essays and in consequence the need for tutors to explain the purpose of learning, what they require, and how they will be assessed. Some general criteria for assessing essays as well as several ways of helping students to learn how to write essays are suggested. The advantages and disadvantages of two approaches to marking developed in the United States are discussed. These are holistic and primary trait.

Primary trait marking focuses on particular and restricted information about writing. Each domain is assessed by scales that describe relative outcomes against a specified performance. What constitutes 'good' and 'poor' performances is described. In this sense the scales are criterion referenced. The approach is therefore performance based, and by inference from the performance, competency based. When used across the curriculum the scales can be designed to meet the particular needs of subjects, and enhance learning in those subjects. A second objective is to demonstrate that problems and practice in performance based assessment apply equally in the sciences as they do in the humanities, and this point is reinforced in Chapter 12.

The third objective is to reinforce the principal that there is a need for a correspondence between course (instruction) and assessment objectives, and at the same time to consider some problems of question design.

The fourth objective is to examine the idea of tests of the outcomes of general education that are independent of the programme that is delivered. The COMP test developed by the American College Testing Programme is described. It is of interest beyond the US because of its focus on what are called key (or core, or personal transferable) skills elsewhere. The Alverno College programme, which seeks to assess general education, is in marked contrast to traditional courses and has stimulated developments in other colleges in the US.

The fifth objective is to discuss profiles and their relevance to reporting graduateness. The COMP tests, like the scales for primary traits, are profiles. Such profiles might be used to describe graduateness. An example of this potential is given from medicine. They may also be used to define thresholds or bench marks. Learning profiles lend support to those who seek an alternative to Grade Point Averages and Honours degree Classifications especially in vocational and professional subjects. This leads to the sixth objective, which is to discuss the attempts that have been made in Australia and Britain to establish highly valid criterion referenced systems to assess competences in vocational and professional subjects. These have been in the pursuit of national standards, and they and their potential and limitations are considered. It seems that their use may enhance learning in the traditional craft and professional studies. In Australia the professions have taken a user-friendly approach to the development of competences. Associated with these issues is the problem of assessing work experience for its contribution to a student's final grade.

A major problem with all these new schemes is that the use of raters to assess performance with relatively high inference will be likely to lower the reliability of the ratings. This is supported by such research as has been done on National Vocational Qualifications in the UK.

Finally, in the UK discussion about profiles has been inextricably linked to the idea of an acceptable record of achievement which the student would keep. It would be used to provide information to others about their capabilities and education and training needs. Examples of personal profiles used in higher education are discussed.

The chapter ends with a reinforcement of the view expressed in earlier chapters that changes in assessment practice necessitate a change in the role of teachers and programme teams since they have to become involved in the totality of the curriculum process.

Introduction

Intention

The intention of this chapter is to describe some of the attempts that have been made to define criteria for assessment, and to suggest alternative methods of reporting performance based and describing *graduateness* based on such criteria. It is offered as a source of ideas for teachers and programme designers for the design and evaluation of assessment. It should be appreciated, therefore, that many of the approaches to assessment described overlap with one another, and that it is possible to conceive of an assessment system which could be described by several of the sections. It may be helpful to conceive of the chapter as three overlapping sections. The first deals with the first three objectives outlined in the summary, the second with the fourth objective, and the third with the remaining objectives outlined in the summary.

Writing across the curriculum and its assessment

Nowhere are the differences between the systems of higher education in the British Isles and the United States highlighted more than in attitudes taken to writing by the academic community. In the United States it is expected that within the system of education students will continue to improve their writing skills within the courses they study. Very often there is collaboration between the subject tutor and writing specialists (Walvoord and McCarthy, 1990). Universities often have Writing Centers which 'attempt not so much to produce a good piece of writing as to give confidence and strategies to grow and improve' (Leahy, 1990). Some courses, as is also the case with mathematics, provide for remediations but there are many courses designed to enhance creativity and develop problem solving (thinking) skills within the subjects of the curriculum (e.g. Brent and Felder, 1992) as well as within English (Kloss, 1996). Skills are required to write technical reports and sometimes courses concerned with this dimension also attempt to achieve some of the other goals of general education (Olds, 1998) including skill in concept mapping and an understanding of how they (students) learn (see Chapter 8). Narrative may also help reflective practice (Kramp and Humphreys, 1993). Writing skills are also tested on entry both in state-wide and local proficiency tests (White, 1985). There is a voluminous literature on the topic and a subject association with its own journal.

The situation in the British Isles where students may have to write between 18 and 20 essays during the year as a whole is in stark contrast. Apart from a few complaints, especially from academics in the equivalent of the American Ivy League universities, that students cannot spell or present a piece that is grammatically correct, little attention has been paid to writing. It is assumed that by the age of 16 when traditional students have to choose the study direction they are going to take (i.e. crudely as between the humanities, social science, languages, and the sciences including technology) they will have acquired the necessary writing skills to take them through college. In the module that Hounsell (1984a, 1984b) investigated, three 2000–3000 word essays were handed in during the first two terms with an extended essay of between 3000 and 3500 words in the final term. The students spent between 13 and 15 hours on each essay. One student quoted by Hounsell said 'basically I am a full-time essay writer'. However, the view that students can write is coming to be contested partly because of changes in the school curriculum and partly because of research.

As the higher education systems expand and diversify in order to cater for the mass of the population, and as more non-traditional students enter programmes prevailing attitudes are likely to change probably in the direction of testing the intake for the purpose of providing remediation for those found to be in need. Only then is it likely that the possibilities of writing, enhancing problem solving and decision-making skills will be considered.

As things stand, in those subjects which require essays to be written in examinations or for coursework assignments, academics are likely to continue to expect a particular genre of essay which Whittock (1997) has called the Academic Critical Essay (ACE). In a written examination a student may have to write three such essays and each one could be as much 800–1000 words. Coursework assignment essays have tended to require even greater lengths. It is these Academic Critical Essays which have been the subject of many of the reliability and grading studies discussed in Chapter 10.

A position statement on writing in the US

One consequence of the American approach has been the positive attempt to develop a philosophy of writing across the curriculum. This means that tutors other than specialists in writing may be involved in its assessment. Such assessments are put to many diverse uses, as for example the awarding of grades, the placement of students in courses and the certification of proficiency. They may also tend to be overstructured, short and unauthentic, and may not be good expressions of course criteria. The Conference on College Composition and Communication in its position statement on writing assessment, argued that the 'primary purpose of the specific assessment should govern its design, its implementation and the generation and dissemination of results' (CCC, 1995). Tutors concerned with its assessment 'should elicit from student writers a variety of pieces, preferably over a period of time; should encourage and reinforce good teaching practices; and should be solidly grounded in the latest research on language learning'.

In this context the idea that writing should be assessed from a number of pieces of work is important. First, because it recognizes that there are many genre, and second that in order to test the range of skills many small pieces will be required during a semester. Such pieces are unlikely to test the skills involved in the Academic Critical Essay or an extended piece of creative work. Clearly if writing is to develop thinking both are required and with different contents.

The authors of the position statement make a number of assumptions. Not least among them is that '*assessment drives pedagogy*'. The consequences of this view have already been discussed in Chapter 2. The conference argues that classroom practices must 'harmonize with what practice and research have demonstrated to be effective ways of teaching writing and becoming a writer'. What is easiest to measure may not be what is wanted. For example, a multiple-choice test will not test skill in composition. At the same time essay tests can distort the notion of what writing is. An essay assessment has to allow students to reflect, to talk to others, to read on the subject and to revise. In other words the summative judgement has to allow for development through and completion of the exercise. The Conference reminded its readers that the 'means used to test students' writing ability shapes what they consider writing to be'. They can come to believe that grammar and style exist independently of the overall purpose of their discourse.

Behind this statement lies a conflict between the need to teach grammar and the desire to enhance creativity. This conflict was at the heart of the debate about the teaching of English in schools in Britain in the 1980s, and more especially as it related to the needs of low achieving children. It creates a problem for assessors in other subjects who are contributing to 'writing across the curriculum'. How much attention should they pay to poor grammar and spelling especially when the essay they are marking fulfils all the other requirements. Does the marker correct every mistake or is it sufficient to ensure that the student is able to 'control English grammar, usage and syntax. Spell English words and use them appropriately. Punctuate according to accepted conventions', and demonstrate these in the paragraphs they write. These outcomes, together with others on the organization of the essay, would be expected by Iyasere (1984), from a first term of instruction in composition. The problem as Schweibert (1996) and the Committee indicate is to prevent the student from assuming that the implementation of rules is writing.

Schwiebert (1996) argued that for too many students writing is reduced to a set of rules that inhibit thought and emotion at their source. 'It is as if students' sense of the "correct" way to write in an English class squeezes the life out of anything they want to say.' In order to enrich thinking students must be exposed to diverse forms of writing and this may accomplished by asking them to choose forms (of writing) and topics which they use most regularly and spontaneously in everyday life. He asks his students to draw grids (matrices). On one axis they list topics and on the other forms of writing appropriate to the topic for which the grid has been constructed. Thus a grid in public affairs included topics such as politics, health policy, congress and election campaigns. The forms included letter to the editor, press conference, obituary, editorial. A student interested in public affairs might have to prepare an oration, and public and popular talks. He also showed a grid for intensely personal writing. Students completing this grid might write a letter, complete a 'reminiscence' or draft a dramatic monologue. Apart from anything else his grids show the enormous diversity of genre and how, by completing the grids, students can learn to develop a range of styles relevant to their interests.

The argument for the submission of a variety of pieces is based on the assumption that 'an individual's writing "ability" is the sum of a variety of skills employed in a diversity of contexts, and individual ability fluctuates unevenly among these varieties' (CCC, 1995). This view has stimulated many programmes to adopt portfolio assessment. Related to this position is the view that in situations where there are 'high stakes', writing should be evaluated by more than one teacher.

One other assumption that the Conference's committee made could be called the 'authentic' assumption. It is that 'language is always learned and used most effectively in environments where it accomplishes something the user wants to accomplish for particular readers in that environment.' The consequences of this for the American system is that there is no one test which will satisfy all environments. Therefore, the best test may have to be locally designed. This may be by schools with common goals or similar student populations. It may even be by the tutor. This is the current situation on the other side of the Atlantic. However, the assessment of essays brings with it the same problems of setting and marking irrespective of the culture in which they are completed. That is, how can they be marked to achieve high standards. The trend has been to move from impression marking to marking governed by criteria of one kind or another the danger of which is too much impositioned structure.

Assessors' perception of marking

Diederich (1974) of the Educational Testing Service found that the assessors whose work he studied grouped essays into five categories according to what they valued. Some would assess against structure and others against style. Impression markers it seems may have entirely different perceptions of what it is they are marking. In these circumstances it is important that the assessors should be aware of their own prejudices and values. There has been newspaper criticism in the UK that the ideology of assessors can enter into the frame so that those who subscribe to the same ideology are more often rewarded than those who don't: but this was some years ago.

Related to this study is one by Branthwaite, Trueman and Berisford (1981) at the University of Keele in England who attempted to relate examiner-personality to marking. It led them to raise concerns about the nature of staff-student interactions as they are exposed in marking, especially when the candidates are known to the assessor. This finding lends support to the views of those who like the Educational Testing Service, advocate as many as three scorers for their writing assignments and such pieces of work. Multiple-judgements they believe are better than one, and like objective tests they believe that pre-testing is important, for it enables weaknesses in a topic to be spotted. A highly selective essay might find 20 minutes for its writing sufficient (Breland, 1983, 1987; ETS (undated); White, 1985). It presupposes markers are scoring against the same criteria. If they don't they may conclude like Bell (1980) that the differences between 13 social science assessors were such that the only action which could be taken would be to reduce the weighting of the award for essays. Norton (1990) found that there were differences between the perceptions of students and teachers as to what were the most important criteria. Students were more concerned with content whereas teachers were more concerned with argument. Norton found that the time spent on the essay, the number of books used and references quoted and the proportion of research-based work led to higher essay marks among the psychology students whose work he investigated.

Hake and Andrich (1975) assisted our understanding of the process of marking when they argued that *the grader is creating the essay in much the same way as its writer.* Their thesis about marking is based on this assumption as well as the view that the abstract generalization of the whole (in this case , the essay) generates it own parts.

> We assume that teachers or graders have a conceptualization of the essay as a whole; therefore, they, when reading an essay, expect an integrated whole with meaningful and logical connections in the writing, paragraphs, sentences, syntactical, and phonological structures. If the concept of the essay as a finished product suggests that the essay is made up of integrated parts, then the whole essay should have harmony among its parts. Because breaks in harmony stand out, flaws should be a conspicuous feature for the reader.

They argue that graders notice blocks or flaws in the communication from the students and correct them by fitting it to their view of what is correct.

> We must be aware that there are many ways to correct a flaw in language. The way the grader decides to correct the flaw will affect the way he classifies the flaw and even if or when he will perceive another flaw.

They suggest an observation scheme for graders which has four hierarchically ranked dimensions. They are:

(1) Essay continuity and organization, relationships independent of symbol. For example:

(a) The statement has a meaningless or ambiguous relationship among its components because (i) an incorrect or inconsistent definition is included, (ii) a term for which no definition has been offered or implied is included ... etc.

(b) An objective usage flaw because (i) an incorrect comparative or superlative, (ii) no comparative or superlative... etc.

(c) A semi-colon (i) used incorrectly, (ii) omitted ... etc.

(2) Statement or paragraph continuity; transformation to symbol.

(3) Mechanics and usage transformation among symbols.

(4) Punctuation inflectional or referential; signals among symbols.

The resultant scheme is very elaborate. Its advantage is that it should help students to construct better essays although the scheme was designed in the first place to assist the marker to recognize the components of the essay, their relationships and functions in respect of each other. It was also to assist the marker in the grading of flaws within those specific dimensions. According to their theory, the more flaws there are in dimension (1), the more there will be in the other three dimensions. When this scheme was proposed computers were unable to question flaws and the task of marking against such a scheme would have been difficult if not impossible. Such computer-assisted-marking is no longer out of the question. It may turn out to be a very useful aid to student learning provided it does not constrain the students to particular formulae. Hake and Andrich argue that their approach avoids this difficulty:

> If teaching composition is to be considered a professional activity, it must move closer to the concerns of rhetoric and language and away from excessive attention to correctness. We claim that if these concerns are taught, correctness will be a result and what is important is the sequence of invention, arrangement, organization and style.

Once again the need for a correspondence between course and assessment objectives is exemplified. These necessarily lead to criteria that can help student learning as well as aid assessment. There is no doubt that many students find the Academic Critical Essay difficult to write, otherwise why would so many C grades and below be given. Therefore, students need to know the purpose of learning, how to structure such essays within their particular subjects, and understand how assessors mark them.

The Academic Critical Essay

Hounsell (1984a) found three perceptions among the students he investigated of what the essay was for. These were the essay as argument, as viewpoint, and as, arrangement, i.e.

1. An ordered presentation of an argument well supported by evidence.

2. An ordered presentation of a distinctive viewpoint on a problem or issue.

3. An ordered presentation embracing facts and ideas.

Hounsell pointed out that those who see the essay as 'argument' are able to discuss the activity as they see it, and because it involves 'argument' they see themselves as 'makers of meaning'. There is a concern 'to abstract and construct meaning through an active engagement with subject matter'. An essay which is viewed as arrangement will depend on regurgitation. Those who take the perspective of the essay as 'viewpoint' will see it at as a medium for self-expression

Whittock, (1997) takes the view that academics require students to follow a particular formula. He points out that his dictionary, *The Collins Concise Dictionary of the English Language* (1978) gives two senses of the word *discursive,* an essay being defined as a *short piece of discursive prose presenting its author's views on a chosen topic.* These senses are 'wandering from one topic to another, rambling; digressive. (and) *Philos.* Going from premises to conclusions in a series of logical steps.' The Academic Critical Essay (and for that matter the extended assignment or dissertation) belongs to the second sense. It is, to quote Whittock, 'a truncated thesis in which within a small span a problem is investigated, hypotheses are formed and tested, evidence is adduced, and conclusions arrived at.' His more detailed list of the components, and these would be the components which would have to be assessed, is shown in Figure 11.1. It is a limited genre and many students do not take to it easily. Moreover, it limits self-expression. Thus it is that those concerned with the teaching of writing per se argue that students should be exposed to different genre during their college career. Nevertheless, the academic critical essay is the expression of a mode of critical thinking encouraged by study in the humanities. Therefore, its reliability and validity are of considerable concern to learners.

Figure 11.1 shows that it is very constrained. Some might argue that it inhibits creativity. It will also be seen that the criteria are open to interpretation. At the most general level it is still possible to vary style even though the constraints are considerable. As we have seen, style is something that affects assessors. Also, as has been shown above, different assessors may not attach the same degree of importance to each of the criteria and this could lead to a mark that is substantially at variance with a mark obtained from impression marking. What corresponds to an 'excellent' formulation for one assessor might not be so for another. To use this marking scheme, marks would have to be assigned for each component. As soon as this is done the task becomes more onerous. A less onerous scheme suggested by Iliffe (1966) for the British system of marking honours degree essays is shown in Figure 11.2.

An inspection of essays over a long period of time shows that one of the factors which distinguishes the low achieving from the high achieving student is the way in which they use the knowledge base. The low achiever is more likely to describe that base without any particular insight whereas the high achiever is able to take a reflective stance and offer a critique or, extend the ideas offered or bring them together in a new synthesis. Iliffe's scheme allows for these differences. It is interesting to evaluate Iliffe's scheme from the point of view of the student perspectives uncovered by Hounsell.

1. A Statement of a problem and a brief exposition of its nature and significance.
2. Clarifications of any terms or concepts which are relevant.
3. A noting of alternative solutions that have been (or could be) offered.
4. An indication of why they are to be considered inadequate and less satisfactory to what is now being proposed.
5. Objections to the hypothesis examined and shown to be weak in foundation.
6. Data selected to test the hypothesis by showing the merits or defects in application.
7. A justification for selection.
8. Interpretation of the data in the light of the hypothesis.
9. If necessary, provision of further grounds for the appropriateness of such interpretations (i.e giving warrants for making them thus).
10. Demonstration of the hypothesis's merits/and or deficiencies by application to test situations.
11. Acknowledgement of the strengths and weaknesses of the original hypothesis.
12. Qualifications of or amendments to the hypothesis in the light of the evidence.
13. A concise summary of what advance in knowledge or understanding has been successfully achieved by the whole process.

Figure 11.1 The principal features of the Academic Critical Essay (Whittock, 1997 unpublished. Communicated by John Cowan)).

80. Outstanding answer: shows independent reading and thinking.
70. Best possible organization of all expected points.
60. Well organized use of most major points.
50. Sensible use of some major points.
45. Clear signs of understanding, but material thin.
(pass)
40. Some relevant material but incomplete grasp.
30. Not an answer to the question set, but shows some understanding of the general field.
20. Very muddled, but shows some understanding of the general field.
10. Poorly organized and almost completely lacking in relevance.

Figure 11.2 Iliffe's (1966) guide for marking essays in the British university context.

Does it cover all three perceptions or does it cover one at the expense of the others? If his scheme, and for that matter Whittock's model, is criticized on the ground that it does not meet what a particular teacher wants, then it is up to that teacher to explain what he/she wants. In any case, this would seem to be necessary since Hounsell (1984b) also found five different strategies were used by students to plan their essays. These were related to the conception that the students had of essay writing but they also included no plan.

While I have found Iliffe's scheme a valuable aid, I have discovered that I tend to mark toward the centre of the scale. It seems as though there is always an answer which I saw last year (or the year before that) which was a little bit better in the present pile. Not withstanding the fact that I give students the criteria, one thing is clear; the good scripts stand out from the rest, as do the poor (Hall and Daglish, 1982). The problem as indicated in Chapter 10 is in the middle. Another difficulty with this scheme is that it does not take into account every eventuality. One procedure which I use is to select, say, ten scripts from the bundle of 140 or so, mark them and add notes to the scheme and then mark the remainder and revise the ten. An American study suggests that the ten should be re-assigned to the batch and re-marked. This means that no marks should be put on them when they are first marked (Mitchell and Anderson, 1986). I have also used content check lists alongside the Iliffe scheme. There is generally no time to use them in detail with every essay, but if they are regularly consulted they seem to provide both a check and a balance. My approach is impression backed up by criteria, and I suspect that that is what many of us do.

It is probable that we are also influenced in marking by the script that came before. It is also possible that we may be influenced by the first essay we mark in an answer book when marking an answer to a second question in the same book (Hales and Tokar, 1975). This suggests that we should mark all the answers to the same question before we mark answers to other questions. None of this is news, but it is good to be reminded of some of the things of which we are aware. In this respect, Brown, Bull and Pendelbury (1997) remind us that it is important to know when we are likely to feel irritable and tired. In the United States the trend has been to use either holistic or primary trait marking.

Holistic marking: toward outcomes based assessment

When a checklist is used and the assessor marks against the individual categories, the marking is said to be analytic. In contrast, impression marking could be described as synthetic in that the grade arises from the assessor's total impression. It is also holistic but this term has come to be used to describe a particular system developed for the large-scale essay scoring by the Educational Testing Service (ETS; Diederich, 1974).

Holistic scoring depends on a set of scales similar to, but somewhat more extensive than, those suggested by Iliffe. These descriptions when they are assigned a mark are called rubrics. Sometimes six-point scales are used and sometimes four. In a six-point scale described by Holt (1993) a score of four or above defines competency. So at one and the same time these scales are measures of competency or performance. This may be illustrated by a slightly different approach used at the University of Georgia to assess the essay writing competence of students wishing to enter that university. The assessors compare the answers with model answers that have been designed from a rubric to illustrate the type of performance required to meet the rubric's specification. In this scheme, as in others described by White (1985), the assessors were brought together to mark some 4500 scripts together at one session. The difference between this scheme and those employed by the school examination boards in England is that the examiners do not go home after they have received their instructions. Rather the essays are marked in a single sitting. Thompson and Rentz (1973) describe how model answers are used to illustrate the expected performance at three points on a four-point scale. They are written to obtain behavioural specifications of performance at the three levels. These descriptors are what would now be called rubrics. For example,

> The '4' (level) theme clearly and effectively states a thesis that relates directly to the assigned topic. The theme concentrates on this central idea and has a clear overall organization plan. The major points in the theme are developed logically and are supported by concrete specific evidence or detail that will arouse the reader's interest. The theme should reveal the writer's ability to select effective, appropriate words and phrases, to construct and organize sentences and paragraphs, to make careful use of effective transitional devices, and to maintain a consistent appropriate tone. The theme should also be free from mechanical errors.

The model answers were developed against this set of pre-specified characteristics (outcomes) of writing quality. Thompson and Rentz claim that a high degree of reliability was obtained. In this system 75 raters are located in seven centres, and mark 3000 essays per day. This means that if 10 per cent of all scripts were reviewed in a national system of moderation with more than 40,000 candidates the raters would not be involved in more than two days' work per subject. Working in groups the raters are:

> instructed to read each essay quickly to gain an overall impression of its quality in relation to the three model essays and to assign a rating based on that comparison. Three raters judge each essay independently to ensure reliable results. This approach to scoring does not require a rater to thoroughly evaluate a paper analytically but merely to compare the paper with selected models.

Holistic marking involves the judgement of the paper against the rubrics and is thus more thorough. Thompson and Rentz reported high reliabilities. 'For 91 per cent of the essays graded at least 2 out of the 3 raters agreed exactly on the score that the essay ought to have', which is approximately 60 per cent. Others have reported similar reliabilities for multiple assessments of this kind (Holt, 1993). The authors do not tell us whether the markers knew the previous rating. As we have seen, McVey (1975) (Chapter 10) suggests that where this is known the reliability of the second marker is influenced by this knowledge in such a way that he or she will tend to agree with the first score.

The scale was also limited to effectively three points and this would tend to increase the reliability because the area of potential agreement is widened (Cronbach and Gleser, 1965). Even so, research on multiple assessor rating by ETS was far from sanguine. Even with their methods of calibration, they did not think that reliability could be much improved because of the unpredictable habits of examiners (Braun, 1986). Nevertheless reported reliabilities of 0.85 must be regarded as excellent given the findings reported in Chapter 10. In Britain many would regard such a result as incredible. Model answers of this kind are not easy to prepare.

The Association of American Medical Colleges has evaluated the reliability of holistic scoring on the Medical College Admission Test (MCAT) (Mitchell and Anderson, 1986). This test was introduced to give examinees an opportunity to demonstrate skill in (1) developing a central idea, (2) synthesizing concepts and ideas, (3) separating relevant from irrelevant information, (4) developing alternative hypotheses, (5) presenting ideas cohesively and logically, and (6) writing clearly.

Twenty raters, who were trained by a method suggested by White (1985), participated in scoring sessions which marked a sample of 3117 papers. Each essay within a batch was rated on a six-point holistic scale by two raters. Papers that were more than one score point apart were read by a third rater. Such was the comparability that third readings were required on only 5.3 per cent of all the papers. The mean score of all the ratings was 3.4 and the standard deviation 0.94. The ratings took place over three days. The mean scores for day 2 were lower than those for days 1 and 3. The means for days 1 and 3 were closer to the theoretical mean for the six-point scale. During the scoring there were calibration exercises. However, these were more frequent on day 1 than on days 2 and 3. The investigators suggest that calibrations should be frequent, and that other activities should be introduced to reduce the effects of boredom and fatigue.

White (1985) considers that the development of holistic scoring helped the writing profession resist the pressures of 'pseudo-objectivism', and analytic reductionism with its 'supposedly immutable laws of usage and grammar'. As is evident from Hake and Andrich (1975), there has to be a balance between the two as they are related. White (1985), nevertheless., is conscious of the limitations of holistic scoring. He considers that it gives no meaningful diagnostic information beyond the comparative ranking it represents. One consequence has been the parallel attempt to obtain separate scores for sub-skills. The problem with this analytic scoring is that there is no agreement as to what the sub-skills are or, indeed whether they exist. Therefore, it is difficult to obtain reliable scores. It is also very slow to score. He confirms the position outlined in Chapter 10, namely that the reliabilities of holistic scoring may well be overestimated.

Holt (1993) has demonstrated how reflection on the criteria for grading may lead one to revise them. He gives an example of poor question design to illustrate his point. But this is a more general point relating to all assessment design, and will be considered next.

Question design

Apart from the fact that questions can be ambiguous, they can also be so vague as not to be understood. Edwards (1984) gave examples of two questions he would not want to set in a paper on systems analysis. The questions were:

1.   Discuss the importance of the evaluation phase in systems design. Describe a system which you have assessed and discuss your conclusions.

2.   Describe briefly the term systems design. Give a brief description of five different techniques which you feel are important in systems design, stating when they can be used to advantage.

He objected to these questions on the ground that he would find them difficult to answer. He wanted to test the students' ability to do rather than to describe. His first point illustrates the need to draft model answers or at least outlines at the time of drafting questions. The second point focuses on the value of coursework for determining what a student can do, although suitably posed questions can achieve this goal in specified circumstance. Sometimes the goal will be good but the institutional means for achieving it difficult.

It is well known in school education that teachers' questioning tends to focus on the lower level skills of *The Taxonomy*, i.e. knowledge and comprehension. It is surprising, however, to find that this happens in higher education. Laurillard (1984) reported that, while questions in the sciences are normally intended to test problem solving, many of the tasks faced by students in engineering and science did not call for much more than comprehension. Moreover, this influenced the style of learning they adopted. For many tasks they adopted a standard procedure and did not engage in thinking at a deeper level. She found that many questions did not demand hypothesis testing or explanations of theory. Marton and Säljö (1984) also found that the type of question set in social science influenced the learning strategy. They used questions that on the one hand, required a precise recollection of what was said and, on the other hand, questions devoted to major line of reasoning. In their answers the participants had to give evidence that they understood how the conclusions developed from the argument, and provide judgements as to whether the reasoning was correct and consistent. It is easy to see that surface learning should enable the student to accommodate the first type of question. However, as Gibbs, Habeshaw and Habeshaw (1986) point out, not all essays are of the same kind. For example, a design essay may benefit a person with a different orientation.

Not all those responding to the question set to produce a deep approach did so. Those who did not interpret the demands as intended focused on the conspicuous tasks which they would have to do after reading the material on which the question was set. This led them to summarize rather than understand. Thus to obtain understanding the question must be designed so as to elicit understanding Students may also be helped if they know how the marks will be allocated. The first point is illustrated by Holt (1993). His example relates to a question set in an economics course. It read:

> Carefully explain the difference between Gross Domestic Product and Gross National Product. Why has the United States switched to GDP?

Instead of leaving the question at this point a further instruction is given:

> Use accurate definitions and appropriate examples. Explain the US shift to GDP in terms of your examples. Your writing should be clear and credible.

Most teachers will be aware of these difficulties but it is as well to be reminded of them from time to time. Holt concluded that the students did not really understand the question. 'They wrote as though they were telegraphing information to the professor, someone who already knows the topic, rather than explaining it to someone with no background in the subject.' This analysis suggested how the question might be rewritten.

> Bob is a reasonably bright guy, but he's not had the advantage of a course in economics. He is confused by a report on US economics. 'Another term for Gross National Product?' he asks. Write a note to Bob explaining the difference between GNP and GDP.

As indicated above, we may expect to learn better how to write essay questions if we understand what students consider an essay to be within the context of our subject. We can learn about questioning from students themselves. Brent and Felder (1992) describe a 'problem definition exercise' in which students are asked to make up problems that could be used in homework assignments or tests. They note that this is not an easy task. Students may produce superficial problems if they are inclined to surface learning. They suggest that one way round this would be to require the students to relate their questions to the higher levels in *The Taxonomy*. Felder (1985) had asked a first-year graduate course in chemical reactor analysis to construct a final examination along these lines and found the response to be highly creative. They concluded, that 'Students are capable of a great deal more creativity than anyone thinks they are.'

In addition to designing questions that have the same facility (which is extremely difficult to do because logically identical questions may have psychologically different effects (Knight, private communication)), examiners also need to have information about the popularity or unpopularity of questions. When a question is particularly unpopular, choice is restricted. Morrison (1974) developed both choice and facility indices for essay examinations which take into account the ability of the candidates answering the questions (given in Glossary). These indices, together with a discrimination index, can provide useful feedback to examiners when relatively large numbers of students are involved. With small numbers the assumptions on which they are based are a useful reminder to examiners of what they should seek to obtain when designing questions.

Helping students write essays and answer other types of question; feedback

Many students find Exemplars very helpful. The GCE examining boards in the UK have made a practice of publishing candidate responses with examiner comments (Bryant, 1983; Ridd, 1983). It is increasingly common for teachers to provide students with the scheme of assessment as was the case in the project work and student teacher assignments described below.

Gibbs gave students two contrasting essays about the same topic. One was intended to require a deep approach and the other a surface approach. Each student assesses the answer and judges which is best. Then, in pairs and then in fours, the students compare their views and consider the intentions which underlies the two essays. In this way the students also learn skills of exploration and analysis and obtain a wider perception of the issues involved. One alternative would be to provide the students with a checklist of the kind shown in Figure 11.1. Another would be to provide them with holistic, or primary trait scales of a kind to be described. The same ideas apply to other types of question, as for example, those that might be asked in the sciences.

Many teachers in higher education underestimate the value of feedback as an aid to learning.

Primary trait marking: another step toward outcomes based assessment

In the United States primary trait scoring was developed by the National Assessment of Educational Progress. Conceptually it is the same as holistic scoring (White, 1985). The development of this approach to assessment in the US has been summarized by Cooper and Odell (1977). It arose from a criticism of holistic scoring which argues that the scoring guides are quite general and not specific to the question in hand. The purpose of primary trait scoring is to focus on particular and restricted information about the writing produced. White (1985) writes:

> For example, in order to measure what the team called 'imaginative expression of feeling through inventive elaboration of a point of view,' the students were shown a photograph of five children playing on an overturned rowboat. The writing assignment directed those taking the test to imagine that they were one of the children in the picture or someone standing nearby and then to tell a good friend what was going on 'in a way that expresses strong feelings.' The papers were scored only on the writer's ability to use dialogue, manage a point of view, and control tense structure, all as ways to discover the writer's ability 'to project him/herself into a situation, find a role and an appropriate audience, and then reveal an attitude toward the material in relation to the role.'

White considers that the great advantage of primary trait scoring is that it provides a narrow focus to holistic measurement. He also considers this method is of value because of the direct link that it has with classroom teaching. It applies to any subject in the curriculum and many rubrics have been published. It will also be noticed that they could apply at any level of education provided they are assessed at a level appropriate to the age of the students and course structure. For this reason the contributions from school literature are relevant as a source of ideas in many subjects of curriculum (e.g. Hibbard *et al.*, 1996; Marzano, Pickering and McTighe, 1993). Holt's (1993) objection to primary trait scoring is that it is 'cumbersome' to score.

Walvoord and McCarthy (1990) describe how they evaluated a biology course on two separate occasions, and how a primary trait scoring sheet devised and revised by the teacher was used. The course was in biological literature. The teacher, Virginia Anderson, expected the students to conduct original scientific research in which they compared two commercially available products to discover which was best. She expected the students also to report their findings in the same way as a scientist would. Inevitably her primary trait scoring schedule followed this heuristic the categories of which are listed in Figure 11.3. Each of these categories was allocated up to five points each point level being defined. The details of the category on 'Designing an Experiment' are shown.

It will be appreciated that the scoring of reports against such schedules is time consuming. It can also be rewarding if it is seen to produce gains in student performance, and in any event it will be of great help to those students who want to progress in science.

A study by the Educational Testing Service of the multiple-rating Test of English as a Foreign Language using a primary trait scale showed that while the readers differed in the degree of severity/leniency with which they administered the scale their impact on examinees' scores was relatively minor. However, the investigators noted that even

Categories

A. Title

B. Introduction

C. Scientific format demands

D. Methods and materials section

E. Non-experimental information

F. Designing an experiment

G. Defining operationally

H. Controlling variables

I. Collecting data and communicating results

J. Interpreting data: Drawing conclusions/implications.

Example of Category F 'Designing an Experiment'

5   Student selects experimental factors that are appropriate to the research purpose and audience; measures adequate aspects of these selected factors; establishes discrete sub-groups for which data significance may vary; student demonstrates an ability to eliminate bias from the design and bias-ridden statements from the research; student selects appropriate sample size, equivalent groups, and statistics; student designs a superior experiment.

4   As above, but student designs an adequate experiment.

3   Student selects experimental factors that are appropriate to the research purpose and audience; measures adequate aspects of these selected factors; establishes discrete sub-groups for which data significance may vary; research is weakened by bias or sample size of less than 10.

2   As above, but research is weakened by bias and inappropriate sample size.

1   Student designs a poor experiment.

Figure 11.3 Primary trait scoring sheet for biology due to Anderson (cited by Walvoord and McCarthy, 1990 and at the 1996 Assessment Forum of the American Association for Higher Education, Washington, DC). Principle categories and an example.

small adjustments could have important consequences for examinees whose scores were near decision-making points in the score distribution (Myford, Marr and Linacre, 1996).

Anderson's schedule may be compared with one used by the Joint Matriculation Board (JMB) for part of its assessment of course work in engineering science at 'A' level. During the two years of the programme students were required to submit from their journal two from a number of experimental investigations which they had completed during the two-year period of the course. Such investigations were usually of about 12 hours duration, and were chosen by the student. Favourites included the evaluation of washing-up liquids and automobile engine oils. Anderson's scheme could have been used for assessment. The scheme shown in Figure 11.4 that was actually used has many facets in common with Anderson's. It was based on the aims and objectives of the course that are shown in Figure 11.5. Both schemes impose a considerable workload on the assessor and a trade-off has to be made between what is desirable and what it is believed to be essential to test. The categories have to be chosen within that framework.

The origins of the JMB scheme are very different to those of primary trait analysis. The board had wanted to change its approach to the assessment of practical work in

		Grade
1	**Theoretical understanding**	
	In relation to his/her depth of understanding of the theoretical aspects of the problem the candidate has shown sufficient understanding of the problem to enable him/her to plan the approach competently	3
	Sufficient understanding of the problem to be seldom in need of help	2
	Limited understanding of the problem	1
	Little or no understanding of the problem	0
2	**Planning the investigation**	
	In determining the activities to be undertaken the candidate considered a range of appropriate possibilities with respect to the type and scope of measurements to be made and came to a reasoned conclusion	3
	Considered a range of possibilities and came to a less well-reasoned conclusion	2
	Considered an inadequate range of possibilities	1
	Exercised little or no judgement	0
3	**Procedures and equipment**	
	In selecting the experimental procedures and equipment to be used the candidate made a well reasoned assessment of the alternatives available and came to a well-argued conclusion	3
	Lacked depth in determining the final choice	2
	Made some attempt to consider alternative approaches	1
	Unthinkingly adopted standard procedures or relied entirely on the teacher's advice	0
4	**Errors**	
	The report included a statement of errors together with estimates of magnitudes and a discussion of their relative significance	3
	A statement of errors and estimates of the magnitude of each error	2
	A statement of errors (including the most important errors)	1
	No explicit statement of errors	0
5	**Critical review**	
	In considering the investigation in terms of the results obtained and the conclusions reached the candidate made a thorough appraisal including a thorough estimate of the effects of the assumptions made and including suggestions for improving the approach and/or taking the work further	3
	As above but with one of the features missing	2
	Some significant appraisal of the work done	1
	Made no significant appraisal of the work done	0
6	**Personal contribution. In planning and executing the investigation the candidate exercised**	
	Initiative and judgement throughout	3
	Lacked initiative and judgement at times	2
	made little personal contribution	1
	Relied entirely on external help	0

Figure 11.4 The scaled component of the schedule for the assessment of experimental investigations in Engineering Science at the Advanced level (JMB, Manchester).

engineering science. In the past there had been a practical examination at the end of the two-year period of the course. This was thought to be unsatisfactory because it did not reflect what engineers did in practice. It was decided to replace these examinations with coursework in which the students would complete a number of investigations together with a major project during the two-year period. Separate schemes of assessment were devised for the investigations and the project. The first attempts were criterion referenced for mastery (JMB, 1971). A candidate either could or could not perform a task. The assessor was required to answer 'yes' or 'no' to a question put about these abilities. Dissatisfaction with this strict criterion approach was expressed by the teacher assessors. Among the reasons given was the fact that in

---

(i) Technique
 (a) The development of the facility for making accurate observations and the ability to make reasonable estimates of the errors incurred in making such observations.
 (b) Familiarization with the use of scientific apparatus and equipment.

(ii) Originality
The development of the ability to:
 (c) Formulate hypotheses from given sets of observations
 (d) Formulate experiments to test hypotheses
 (e) Devise and improve upon experimental procedures
 (f) Appreciate the relative importance of errors in differing sitauations.

(iii) Analysis
The development of the ability to:
 (g) Discriminate between possible alternatives
 (h) Formulate problems in a form appropriate for investigation
 (i) Recognize assumptions made and assess their importance
 (j) Extrapolate.

(iv) Synthesis
The development of the ability to:
 (k) Produce a unique communication
 (l) Produce a plan or a proposed set of operations
 (m) Derive a set of abstract relations
 (n) Design and evaluate.

Figure 11.5 Aims of practical work in Engineering Science at the Advanced level (Carter, Heywood, and Kelly, 1986).

the major areas (categories) of the scheme it operated to the disadvantage of students perceived to be 'very good'. The final grade ought to be determined by distributions within the categories, and not be the sum of criterion-referenced scores, the mastery element of which was held to be minimalist. However, some criterion-referenced items were retained because they were considered essential to determine if the candidate had the minimum competence to proceed. They were also necessary to ascertain that all the objectives had been obtained. These questions were:

(1) Has the candidate made safe use of the apparatus involved? (2) Has the candidate succeeded in making accurate observations within the limits of the apparatus used? (3) Has the candidate presented the observations in a clear and workmanlike manner? (4) Are the findings of the investigation consistent with observations made? (5) Does the report contain an account of the essential features of the work?

A 'yes' answer was required to all of these questions for the candidate to be examined.

The scheme which emerged might be described as a grade semi-criterion referenced scale (JMB, 1972, 1974). It was the subject of continuing evaluation and modification although the principal categories remained the same. The candidates' reports were marked by their teachers and then re-marked by external moderators. Published data for a ten-year period showed that moderation produced reasonably consistent results from year to year, and that teacher marks were slightly higher than those of the moderators. The moderators had the marks of the teachers in front of them at the time of moderation (Carter *et al.*, 1986). However, it was very costly and the moderation exercise was subsequently simplified. Other organizations developed similar rubrics with some different categories. The rubrics are a restatement of the objectives. Many teachers and assessment experts now call them learning outcomes. They are of course intended outcomes until such time as they are assessed when they are actual outcomes.

One criticism of schedules such as these is that some of the individual items measure two qualities as opposed to one (see Figure 12.4 for example). Some would argue that each quality should be scaled separately. It is recommended that students should be instructed on how such schedules are used. Learning should be assessment led.

It is held by some assessment designers that the generic categories are transferable, i.e. if one learns analysis in one context they will be able to undertake analysis in another. This is contentious. It may be the case if the student is shown the possibility of transfer. Even the interpretation of what analysis is in one subject may differ from the interpretation of what it is in another.

Sources of primary traits (objectives/outcomes)

The literature contains many lists of outcomes and objectives. Mention has already been made of the value of the literature on high school education in North America and the enormous number of primary traits to be found in that literature. Various individuals, as we have seen, have produced their own taxonomies in Australia, the UK and the US (see Chapter 2). In the UK Otter directed a study in which small subject groups drew up outcomes for design, engineering, English, environmental science and social science (Otter, 1992) which have been widely quoted. The actual lists of outcomes are given in an earlier study (Otter, 1989). The groups approached the derivation of outcomes differently. The design and social science group made a statement of *general learning outcomes*. Within in each of five major design activities the design group listed the outcomes that contributed to the specific category. There were 69 in all. The environmental science group used a *subject specific learning outcomes approach*. They defined the syllabus (content) of the course under eight headings. Within those headings they listed learning outcomes. There were 11 practical outcomes and 7 personal outcomes. The English group produced plans for the assessment of critical thinking. The engineering group used the concept of a good graduate to develop a set of competences for inclusion in their learning outcomes. The overall study was aimed at determining what a degree really means (i.e. graduateness), and it included attempts to show how the learning outcomes could be assessed, how they were related to levels within the curriculum, and how they were related to the system of accreditation. Other sources include analyses of the work done by professionals such as those that will be described below.

There are, therefore, many sources of ideas. However, these ideas have to be internalized if they are to work. They have to have the same meaning for each member of the disciplinary community, and since these approaches require a considerable change in attitude it is likely that many members of a group may take a long time to internalize the new approach. Murphy (1976) has demonstrated this point in respect of a group of teachers who were asked to design assessments to meet specified objectives within a system of public examinations. They had no prior experience of this approach and it took two experimental examinations, set over a period of 18 months for most of them to internalize the new thinking demanded of them. For this reason the development of multiple-strategy approaches to assessment and learning is best undertaken at a departmental level in which everyone can be involved. Where institution wide objectives have to be achieved (e.g. core skills/abilities) it would be necessary only for the department to show how they would be achieved. The two illustrations below illustrate what is possible.

Focused (guided) impression marking

We are easily disposed to different systems of marking. Some will prefer holistic, some primary trait, and others impression marking (i.e. reading a script and assigning a mark without reference to any scale). I have used all three and have been involved in the design and evaluation of primary trait scales for public examinations in the high school sector, and I have explained how I use Iliffe's model. I use this for both written examinations and assignments and inform my students of the scale. However, together with my students I developed an assessment-led model for the marking of substantial exercises the results of which had to be presented in a report. The aim of the scheme was to help graduates who were learning to teach to relate theory to practice during their teaching practice (practicum) in schools. The process they were asked to follow is shown in Figure 11.6 (Heywood, 1991). Unfortunately a government regulation relating to the payment of teachers for qualifications required that the diploma to which this course contributed be awarded with honours (see Chapter 10). This meant that the marks for this particular course had to be norm-referenced. The first major assessment schedule is shown in Figure 11.7 (Heywood, 1992).

The idea was that the students would complete a number of exercises in which they would evaluate a particular model or strategy of instruction with the pupils they were teaching. During the first couple of years they were impression marked. Brief comments accompanied some returned work. Then, because I wanted to evaluate the communalities between the reports to see if anything could be learnt from them, I devised a loosely structured scheme of marking. This led to more instructions to the class. The students felt the instructions were not sufficient and this had a two-fold effect. On the one hand it led to the scheme shown in Figure 11.7, and on the other hand, it caused a considerable expansion in the work which the students had to do. Reports were now produced of some 5000 words and as many as 7000 words in some cases. The story of how the workload was contained has been told elsewhere (Heywood, 1999). The point of interest here is the effectiveness of the assessment schedule.

Inspection of the domains shows that each could have either a holistic or a primary trait scale. Each evaluates a skill involved in the pursuit of a particular model of research. They are, therefore, generic and in theory the schedule should be applicable to any of the activities. Each is assessed against a semi-primary trait. The marking scale allows room for manoeuvre.

1. Student preparation
- (a) read the literature on the topic
- (b) select a small topic from the literature for investigation.
    (This may replicate one of the studies reported in the literature)
    - (a) design a lesson to test the hypothesis shown in (b). (This to include the entering characteristics of the pupils, a statement of aims and objectives, the instructional procedures showing how they will test the hypothesis etc.)
    - (b) design a test of knowledge and skill which is directly related to the objectives of the lesson.

2. Student implementation
- (a) implement class as designed.
- (b) immediate evaluation
    What happened in the class?
    What happened to me?
    What have I learned about me?
    What have I learned about the class?

3. One week (or) so later
- (a) test students
- (b) substantive evaluation
- (c) How does what I have done relate to the theory which I set out to evaluate?
- (d) How, if at all, will this influence my teaching in the future?

4. Complete and submit report at the required time.

Figure 11.6 Scheme for the evaluation of a method of instruction by a student teacher.

The Assessment Checklist.

The marks are intended to be a guide to the relative importance of the sections in the calculation of the final mark.*

1. Statement of class details including entering characteristics (a) a brief statement (gender, number, age, achievement range (1) (b) show where they are in the subject (3); (c) (a) and (b) plus detailed description of the pupils (5). If you have given these details in a previous lesson plan enter this information at the top of this lesson plan. Note if there have been any changes in respect of particular individuals. (to a maximum of 5 for the section).

2. Adequate statement of theoretical background (a) as would be copied in a book (3); (b) showing additional insight (e.g. relationships with other theories (5); (c) showing linkage with lesson. Avoid duplication of this section with section 5 below (maximum of 7 for this section).

3. Statement of behavioural objectives (a) imprecise; (b) precise but wanting more than the lesson can give (2); (c)process objectives provided they can observed in respect of individuals in the class (2); (d) terminal objectives stating what the student will be able to do at the end of the class in terms of knowledge and learning skills (5) (to max of 5 for the section).

4. A test designed to assess that the objectives have been achieved (6) and that the instructional theory under evaluation has been tested (5) (to a maximum of 12 for the section).

5. Schema of lesson plan showing concepts, strategies and summary of content. Clearly showing how instructional strategies related to the problem established in the theoretical background (see section 2 above) Also see Heywood (1982) for outline of schema (to maximum of 18 for section).

6. Evaluation showing (a) what happened in the class (b) personal response to class (5); (c) test at a time distant from the class (see note 4); (d) simple statistics of the test(s) (i) mean scores (3); (ii) standard deviation(s) (3); (e) interpretation (3), and conclusions from the test(s) (5); (f) reservations and assumptions (5); (g) supporting illustrations from students' work in the class or test (4); NB if test is not used a full justification of the method of evaluation used must be given.

7. Evaluation of the theory in the light of this study and your other experience during the year (maximum of 18 for the section).

8. Presentation (a) formal according to regulations (i.e. A4 paper, on one side margins etc) (3); (b) general literacy (e.g. grammar explanations to the point (4). (to maximum of 7 for the section)

*NB This assessment should not be taken to mean that the subject matter content is necessarily correct.

Figure 11.7 Assessment schedule for the scheme outlined in Figure 11.6.

Three difficulties were experienced with the scheme. First, the spread of answers within each individual domain was wide and the small number of marks available did not always do justice to this spread. This was particularly true of domains 2 and 7. Domain 7 was given more prominence in later schedules and the marks for other domains were adjusted to take this into account. Second, the summed marks did not always reflect the quality of the report. Some were over-marked and some were under-marked. In order to get over this difficulty an impression mark was given after the scoring had been completed. This became the 'real' mark unless a student objected. Since there are problems with discretionary reconciliation, as Wiliam (1995) has pointed out, it was important to both justify the mark and allow negotiation. An independent evaluation of my impression marking showed the means and standard deviations to be consistent year in and year out. A written justification of the marks awarded accompanied each schedule. While the domains remained roughly the same during a seven-year period student requests for further explanation led to some topic specific statements in the trait domains. If this schedule had been designed around primary traits additional scales would have to have been introduced in some of the domains (e.g. domain 2). It may be argued that parts of the schedule (e.g. domains 1 and 3) would have been better presented in primary trait form and I am inclined to agree.

Both the primary trait and this scheme are much more time consuming than the holistic scheme. Yet the reading of the response to each domain was holistic in the sense that it was taken as whole and only then were marks awarded. At the end a general mark was given based on my evaluation (impression) of the report as compared with others in the sample. The time taken to mark each report ranged from 20 to 40 minutes. Thus work from 100 students would occupy between 30 and 50 hours marking time. Since the six exercises were combined about 150 hours per annum had to be set aside for marking. Considerable value-added has to be perceived to continue with such a scheme.

Four principles derive from this and the other work reported in the previous paragraphs. First, any improvement in assessment will not be accomplished easily. The cost is primarily in time. Put at its most simple even the design of questions has to be undertaken with great care and consideration. Second, it is important to listen to what students have to say orally and in their reports. They can help with the design of rubrics. Third, if at all possible develop the assessment schedule with colleagues. In any event, ensure the assigned marks are checked by a colleague or a student or, as I found, they may not add up. Fourth, new assessments may cause a tutor to question what he/she is doing and to redesign the course so that instructional procedures focus on the objectives (outcomes) to be achieved. In this case by the fifth year the original course had been abandoned in favour of lecture periods which discussed each activity prior to its being undertaken and after it had been completed. Fifth, do a benefit–cost analysis and if its costs outweigh its benefits, consider alternative approaches to assessment.

The results of this combination of holistic and trait marking support Wigdor and Garner's (1982) view that, few content domains are as clear cut as the word in a spelling book ... in practice, the distinction between 'norm referenced tests' and 'domain referenced tests' is not as sharp as much of the discussion has implied. The importance of the discussion about these different kinds of assessments is that it forces discussion on what the assessments are trying to measure.

Primary traits, and for that matter holistic scales, are profiles of performance. Primary traits present a profile of skills or qualities. The curriculum designer has to select those traits that are perceived to be important since there are clear limits as to what it is reasonable to assess with the time span available for assessment. Also the instructional strategies required to develop particular skills and qualities may require different time spans for their acquisition. The models described here are mini-replications of the Alverno model but they have been confined to a particular course within a programme. They do answer the criticism that the Alverno model is not transferable to large institutions. If it can be developed for a course it can be developed for a programme, and this appears to be the position of the Quality Assurance Agency in England. There is no reason why a department (programme) should not seek to develop key 'abilities'. Neither is there any reason why institutions should not require the development of such abilities as communication, problem solving, and critical thinking. How these would be achieved would be for the programmes to demonstrate.

In the schemes described above there was no generic assessment of problem solving although the students had to use problem solving skills to achieve the desired outcomes. More is always achieved than the outcomes specify. Neither is there a generic 'practical ability' although the completion of the activities being assessed required practical skills. This approach sometimes generates criticism because the role of content is not clear. These scales are primarily about how content is handled. Nevertheless, it is easy enough to include a scale for content.

Assessing the outcomes of general education

The purpose of this section is to consider the idea of tests of the outcomes of general education that are independent of the programme delivered (i.e. in the same way that 'A' level is to the curriculum delivered by schools in England. In this case the COMP test developed by ACT (1981, 1989, 1992) is of interest because its objectives include assessment of what have been called key (core, personal transferable) skills elsewhere.

The purpose of COMP (College Outcome Measures Program) was to help institutions evaluate their curricular and/or design learning activities which help students obtain knowledge, skills and attitudes necessary for functioning in adult roles after graduation. These aims go beyond education for work and take into account more general aspects of living. A distinction is made between content areas (functioning within social institutions and using science and technology), and process areas (communicating, solving problems, and clarifying values). The assessments covered six outcomes expected of general education. They were, to quote Forrest (1985):

> Communicating – can send and receive information in a variety of modes (written, graphic, oral numeric, and symbolic), within a variety of settings (one to one, in

small and large groups, and for a variety of purposes (to inform, to persuade, and to analyze).

Solving problems – can analyze a variety of problems (scientific, social and personal), and can select or create and implement solutions to problems.

Clarifying values – can identify personal values and the values of other individuals, can understand how values develop, and can analyze the implications of decisions made on the basis of personally held values.

Functioning within social institutions – can identify social institutions (religious, marital, and familial institutions; employment; and civic, volunteer, and recreational organizations), and can analyze own and other's functioning within social institutions.

Using science and technology – can identify those activities and products which constitute the scientific/technological aspects of culture (transportation, housing, clothing, health maintenance, entertainment and recreation, communication, health and data processing), can understand the impact of such entities on the individuals and the physical environment in a culture, and can analyze the uses of technological products in culture and personal use of such products.

Using the arts – can identify those activities and products which constitute the artistic aspects of a culture (music, drama, literature, dance film and architecture), and can analyze uses of works of art within a culture and personal uses of art.

Two kinds of assessment are used. The first comprises an objective test and an activity inventory. The former has as its goal the estimation of the group's ability to apply general education skills and knowledge to problems and issues commonly confronted by adults. The latter assesses the quality and quantity of involvement in key out-of-class activities in the six outcome areas. It is a self-report inventory in multiple-choice format. It may be completed at home or in groups. It asks students what they do, not what they think. ACT believes it can help determine if a non-traditional student could earn credits through portfolio assessment.

The second set of measures are called 'authentic'. There are four which may be measured individually or in groups. They are the composite examination, and assessment of reasoning and communication, speaking assessment and writing assessment. Questions in the composite examination are based on television documentaries, recent magazine articles, ads, short stories, art prints, music, discussions and newscasts that are presented in a variety of formats. The responses range through short and long answers to audio-taped response and what ACT regarded as innovative multiple choice questions.

Forrest and Steele (1982) claim that scores correlate strongly with instruments such as indicators of effective functioning as a job supervisor, and social economic status of job function. This suggests that the tests are valid insofar as they are representative of potential performance in adult functions.

Score gains, between entrance to college and graduation, were measured at 44 institutions. In four-year colleges the most gains were found in the first two years, and it is argued that this is to be expected (Forrest, 1985). These institutions varied considerably in their approaches to general education. At one end of the spectrum there was a group of 19 characterized by an individualized, practical instructional style. In these institutions the persistence to graduation rate was much higher than in others. Forrest concludes that it seems likely that persistence is related to the perceived relevance and practical skill building within the structure of the education programme.

In another study of alumni Forrest found that the extent to which college provided an orientation programme was related to graduate satisfaction. This would support the views of those who believe that university programmes should take account of the qualities required for work. Forrest suggests that institutions need to provide guidance to new students on how they can make the best use of what an institution has to offer. Technical reports of studies over a 15-year period support these and other findings (ACT, 1981, 1991).

The COMP tests provide a profile and as such a possible alternative to Grade Point Averages and honours degree levels. They have the potential to define thresholds and in consequence benchmarks. Some of the work done in American schools is instructive in this matter (Hibbard *et al.*, 1996). However, there are many teachers in the USA who would not accept that the best way of measuring the outcomes of general education was by a test like the COMPS. For example, some 17 institutions working with Alverno College reported 65 approaches to assessing general education outcomes that are of general interest. (Schulte and Loacker, 1994). More generally, and worldwide, the use of objective tests to evaluate general education outcomes is open to criticism (see Chapter 13).

Profiles

The term 'profile' has been used fairly loosely in education. It is sometimes synonymous with record of achievement and portfolio. A profile is a portrayal of the characteristics of a person or institution in relation to some kind of activity or another. Profiling is the task of drawing up a profile either by the person or institution concerned or by an external observer (assessor). Profiles have been used in industry for at least half a century for the purpose of appraisal (Fleishman, 1967). Hundreds of profile schemes have been produced (Law, 1984) but there has been very little evaluation of their reliability and validity. Within the last 25 years profiles have acquired some importance in education, especially in the school and further education systems in Australia and the UK (e.g. Hitchcock, 1990). As long ago as 1977 the Scottish headteachers carried out an investigation of profiles in their schools (SHTA, 1977). In Australia 'subject profiles' have been used in the State of Victoria since 1986. These chart the students' progress in the subjects of the curriculum, and at particular stages show where the student is at and where he/she has to go in terms of specified criterion statements. Brewer and Tomlinson (1981) described how in a nine-week course with seven modules in anatomy which used to complementary teaching techniques the students were tested on each module for recall, comprehension, application and short chain problem solving. The test results represented a learning curve which they called a *learning profile*. Using an anxiety test and the Banks Learning Styles Inventory they found five distinct profiles among the students of which two related to the same category. The type I students started with a high level of performance on entry to the course in all the behavioural areas. There was little change in their performance throughout the course and the investigators suggest that these were the best students. The test items were not particularly discriminative for this group. If more items had been introduced they would have been too demanding for the rest of the group. Again, with type II students there is relatively little change in performance in time. However, they differed from type I students in that they started at a lower level of entry behaviour. Their examination results conformed with predicted scores whereas those of the type I students exceeded expectations. Type IIIA students showed very substantial improvement in problem solving but there was a variation in their application. Type IIIB showed an improvement in the combined skills profile. Even so, within this category other subtypes were distinguishable. Type IV students deteriorated in all dimensions and never mastered the subject. The type III students obtained the most benefit from the course. From the analyses it seems that Types I and III gained most from the method. The investigators suggest that students of Types I, IIIA and IV probably utilized deep processing whereas types II and IIIb probably used a surface approaches to learning. Once again these results show just how complex any class is, even when the students in it are above average ability.

As has been shown repeatedly in this book many factors contribute to both achievement and potential. Success is obtained in many ways. For this reason, a single grade as a measure of a person's overall performance is regarded as unsatisfactory or, to use Jackson's (1985), term 'hazardous' or, as lawyers would say 'unsafe'. Profiles may therefore provide a means for overcoming this difficulty, and may also be used to give information about personal qualities and interests. Assiter and Fenwick (1992) who described developments in profiling in higher education in the UK defined a profile as 'a document that records student's achievements or outlines of what needs to be achieved'. It may of course do both, particularly if it is a student who is completing the profile.

Assiter and Fenwick (1992) distinguish between three types of profile that may overlap and are inter-linked. The first is the *prescribed learning outcome* profile, that is a summative assessment of what a student has achieved in terms of learning outcomes. It may be graded but the assessment criteria would have to describe what constitutes achievement of each grade. These are similar to, if not the same as, the criterion profiles that have long been used in technical and professional education. It is these that might be used to describe 'graduateness'. The second is the *negotiated outcomes profile*. This is similar to the first with the exception that the student would play a role in determining what educational objectives they wish to achieve. Assiter and Fenwick consider that such profiles would be appropriate for the work-based components of a programme. They would also be appropriate for a course of independent study negotiated by the student. The third is the *personal development profile* that is used for the formative development of students. Such profiles are often similar to diaries, journals and logbooks. Fazey (1993) describes how diaries were used with sport, health and physical education students. They necessarily involve the student in

Criterion 1: Information gathering
This criterion is concerned with the trainee's willingness, ability and skill in gathering information necessary for diagnosis and/or decisions.
Behavioural objectives

The unacceptable trainee:
1. Follows no routine of history taking.

2. Fails to identify or does not bother to develop salient leads.
3. Will not pursue alternative hypothesis.
4. Does not seek information on clinical, psychological and social factors.
5. Recording is sketchy and not systematic.
6. Tends to use investigations in a 'blunderbuss' fashion.

The acceptable trainee:
1. Takes a comprehensive history, when appropriate, including clinical, psychological and social factors.
2. Records his information carefully.

3. Uses previous and continuing records intelligently.
4. Plans investigations and uses diagnostic services intelligently.

Criterion 2: Problem-solving
This criterion is concerned with the trainee's ability and skill in using information gained to develop diagnosis and support clinical activity.
Behavioural objectives

The unacceptable trainee:
1. Does not fully realize the implications of the data which he collects.
2. Is unable to interpret the unexpected result which he may often ignore.
3. His thinking tends to be rigid and unimaginative and impedes his recognition of associated problems.
4. His general shortcomings – rigidity of thought and lack of capacity to range round flexibly, i.e. 'diverge' when thinking over a particular problem – have an inhibiting effect on his problem-solving skills.

The acceptable trainee:
1. Realizes the importance of unexpected findings and seeks to interpret them.
2. Understands the nature of probability and uses this to assist his diagnosis and decision-making.
3. Takes all data into account before making a decision and routinely tests alternative hypothesis.
4. Thinks effectively – he has the capacity to range flexibly, or 'diverge', in the search for relevant factors in connection with the particular problem in hand, and he has also the capacity to focus, or 'converge', in his thinking on whatever factors have been decided upon as relevant skills.

Criterion 3: Clinical judgement
This criterion is concerned with the trainee's ability to use sound judgement in planning for and carrying out treatment, and conveying his advice and opinion to patients.
Behavioural objectives

The unacceptable trainee:
1. Is concerned more with treatment than the overall welfare of his patient
2. Plans treatment when now familiar with the procedures or therapy selected.
3. Choice of treatment is rigid.

4. Tends to use set routine or 'favourite' prescriptions, whether appropriate to a particular patient or not.
5. Does not explain his proposals in terms understood by the patient.

The acceptable trainee:
1. Is familiar with the uses and limitations of the treatment he selected. He recognizes his or her own limitations.
2. Considers simple therapy or expectant measures first.
3. Shows regard for the individual patient's needs, wishes and total circumstances.
4. Is flexible and will modify treatment or decisions immediately the clinical situation requires he should do so.
5. Takes patient into his confidence and explains his proposals in terms appropriate to the individual patient.

Criterion 4: Relationship to patients
This criterion is concerned with the trainee's effectiveness in working with patients.
Behavioural objectives

The unacceptable trainee:
1. Does not relate well to patients either through aloofness, discourtesy, indifference or pressures of work.
2. Has difficulty in understanding his patient's needs.
3. Is unable to give patients confidence and may even unnecessarily alarm them.
4. Reacts poorly to a patient's hostile or emotional behaviour.
5. Does not Figure sympathy or compassion in dealing with patients.

The acceptable trainee:
1. Gives patients confidence, affords co-operation and relieves their anxiety.

2. While patients appreciate his interest in their well-being he does not become emotionally involved.
3. Is honest with the patient and his or her family.

4. Patients like the trainee and feel he is an easy person of whom to ask questions or with whom they may discuss problems.

Figure 11.8 Nine criterion measures required for the assessment of trainee general practitioners (Reproduced by kind permission of the authors J. Freeman and P. Byrne (1976) .)

Criterion 5: Continuing responsibility
This criterion is concerned with the trainee's willingness to accept and fulfil the responsibility for long-term patient care.
Behavioural objectives

The unacceptable trainee:
1. Either loses interest after initial treatment or does not spend time on follow-up care.
2. Becomes discouraged with slow progress and cannot cope with a poor prognosis.
3. Is unable to communicate hard facts to a patient or his relatives.
4. Uses ancillary personnel inadequately or demands greater assistance than they are competent to give him.
5. Fails to review a patient's case at suitable intervals.

The acceptable trainee:
1. Encourages patients to work for their own rehabilitation and shows that he too has the same objective.
2. Observes patient's progress and alters management and therapy as required.
3. Understands the roles of ancillary personnel and makes maximum effective use of their help.
4. Maintains a positive and persistent attitude to health and under proper circumstances to recovery

Criterion 6: Emergency care
This criterion is concerned with the trainee's ability to act effectively in emergency situations.
Behavioural objectives

The unacceptable trainee:
1. Panics easily and loses valuable time by ineffective action.
2. Becomes confused under pressure and has difficulty in establishing priorities.
3. Is unable to delegate appropriate aspects of care to others.
4. Is unable or unwilling to make and sustain decisions alone.

The acceptable trainee:
1. Quickly assesses a situation and establishes priorities with full regard to life-saving procedures.
2. Is aware of the consequences of delay.
3. Is able to obtain and organize the assistance of others.
4. Is able and willing to make and sustain decisions alone if necessary.

Criterion 7: Relationship with colleagues
This criterion is concerned with the trainee's ability to work effectively with his colleagues and members of the health team.
Behavioural objectives

The unacceptable trainee:
1. Has difficulty in personal relationships and lacks the ability to give and take instruction gracefully.
2. Tends to be tactless or inconsiderate.
3. Is unable to inspire the confidence or cooperation of those with whom he works.
4. Is unwilling to make referrals or seek consultation. Does not support colleagues in their contacts with patients.

The acceptable trainee:
1. Gets on well with other people. He is conscious of the need for teamwork and fits in well as a member or, on occasion as leader of a team.
2. Seeks consultation when appropriate and respects the views of others.
3. Acknowledges the contributions of others.
4. Creates an atmosphere of 'working with' not 'working for' in other people. Demonstrates self-control.

Criterion 8: Professional values
This criterion is concerned with the trainee's attitudes and standards as an individual member of the medical profession.
Behavioural objectives

The unacceptable trainee:
1. Attempts to cover up his errors from his colleagues.
2. Is difficult to locate in emergencies and absent when required without making deputizing arrangements.
3. Discusses medical mismanagement with patients.
4. Recognizes his own professional capabilities and limitations.

The acceptable trainee:
1. Is kind, courteous, honest and humble. Reports accurately, including his own errors.
2. Respects the confidences of colleagues and patients.
3. Places patient care above personal considerations.

Criterion 9
This criterion is concerned with the trainee's willingness, ability and skill in gathering information necessary for diagnosis and/or decisions.

Figure 11.8 Continued

self-assessment (see Chapter 14). Personal data may be incorporated in a portfolio so that it can be used for both formative and summative assessment.

Graduateness

A criterion or prescribed learning outcome profile may be used as an indicator of graduateness provided that the parameters are well defined. The licence to fly an aircraft is of this kind. Such licences are tests of competency and directly related to the job that has to be done. Profiles have been used in other professional fields, as for example, teacher education (Gibney and Wiersma, 1986). As indicated, the scores in the primary trait schedules shown above would, if published separately, form a profile. Carter *et al.* (1980) seem to think that there might be some value in providing students with a profile of that kind, irrespective of the grade awarded.. This would, it seems, be more appropriate for a personal development profile. In the US a list of descriptive statements designed to achieve such a goal was proposed by Hazeltine (1976) of Brown University. From the point of view of defining graduateness the profile developed by Freeman and Byrne (1976) for the assessment of trainee general practitioners is of contemporary relevance. It is shown in Figure 11.8. The assessors were asked to rate the performance of the trainee on each criterion on a 12-point scale. These scales, known as the Manchester Trainee Evaluation Scales, have their origins in work by McGuire (1967) in the United States on the assessment of performance in orthopaedic surgery. A similar scheme developed in the Department of General Practice at the University of Sheffield was stimulated by the NVQ (National Vocational Qualifications) and placed it in a wider context. The criteria are more specific and there are more of them. A nine-point scale is used and descriptions are provided for 'criterion not achieved', 'criterion achieved', and 'possible distinction' for each criterion (Challis, Usherwood and Joesbury, 1994). It is relatively easy to develop similar profiles in other subjects as Murphy (1976) has shown for student teaching and schools reports. In schemes of this kind it would be possible to relate the scale to degree class or threshold.

Freeman and Byrne found that when the profile ratings of the same trainees were compared for different tutors, there was a high degree of correlation among the tutors about the performance of the best trainees. However, discrepancies occurred in the middle range of performance, as well as in the rating given to the poorest students. Freeman *et al.* (1982) found that the best trainees had clearly defined goals in respect of the course, whereas the poorest did not. And when the personality ratings were correlated with the profile, the best trainees were found to be those who were less rigid and authoritarian. This suggests that profiling is subject to the same problems as formal examinations. As soon as an assessor is asked to scale, problems of reliability arise. This suggests that as with holistic scoring, students should be assessed by two examiners. They would have to agree the final award. Criterion profiles were not used by themselves for assessment but with other forms of assessment in this study (Freeman and Byrne, 1976).

Delandshere (1994) discussing new approaches to teacher assessment in the United States summarizes the situation thus:

Although the new assessment procedures differ in the type of performance they elicit (i.e. written, oral, behavioral, or any combinations of those) they all require a rating scheme that is based on analyzing the information provided according to specific criteria and on assigning ratings on a set of dimension scales (e.g. understanding of subject matter, knowledge of students, knowledge of instructional strategies, knowledge of professional debates. All ratings from different pieces of the assessment are eventually polled together and a certification decision is made at the end of the process. The complex nature of the performance produced by the candidates when responding to the new assessment procedures requires an equally complex rating scheme that relies on the assessors' professional judgement *[and this may be in respect of only one component of a course as my example, above, shows]*. Compared to multiple-choice tests from which highly reliable scores can be derived the new instruments are facing a reliability challenge. Indeed, the use of raters to assess performance with relatively high inference will be likely to lower the reliability of the ratings. This is a critical issue since the ultimate question when making a licensing decision is the accuracy and consistency of the final decision. In other words would the decision be the same if it had been made by different assessors, at a different time, or with different exercises? Since accuracy cannot be reached without consistency, reliability of the final decision is the main objective for licensure and certification examination. Consistency of the final decision however, can only be attained by ensuring the reliability of the individual ratings that are used to reach the final decision. (My comment in the italics).

In my own student teaching assessment activities (see above) one of the exercises which I set was re-assessed by an independent rater. Her task was to establish whether or not she agreed with the inferences I had made from an analysis of the reports of two separate year groups. My purpose had been to establish if general conclusions could be drawn from the scripts about the relative merits of expository versus discovery teaching. While there were some differences between us the level of agreement found was generally high (Heywood and Heywood, 1993).

Frameworks for the assessment of vocational and professional competences (competency based assessment)

In Australia, New Zealand and the UK specific attempts have been made to provide a system of competency standards that specify the requirements for particular jobs in terms of expected outcomes. Such a framework would lead to the specification (profile) of transferable skills that would enable workers to progress their careers within industries and occupational groups. In Britain in the early 1970s Thomas and Madigan (1974) drew attention to the fact that when there were major closures in manufacturing industry many skilled workers failed to find re-employment and were lost to jobs outside of industry. Part of the problem it seemed was that the skills which these workers had were not perceived either by them or other employers to be transferable. Thomas and Madigan suggested 'that a theory of labour arenas which reflects the "political" nature of job choice might provide a more adequate basis for the analysis of job search and job change'. Youngman *et al.* (1978) adapted this concept. They suggested that a labour arena comprises a group of skills which are already possessed or which may be readily acquired and crosses the divide of job perceptions derived from job titles which at that time were the primary information required by those concerned with personnel selection. They devised and evaluated a technique by which occupational families could be discovered within companies and across industries (see below).

The system of National Vocational Qualifications (NVQs) in England attempts to assess the skills learnt in particular jobs and to provide certification for that learning. It is derived from a culture which in vocational education and training values experience often at the expense of the theoretical as well as from the view that industry knows best. One consequence of this view was the need, to quote Wolf (1998), 'to unshackle assessment from the need to follow a course of study and to increase the degree to which qualifications provided substantive guarantees of performance'. It was strongly influenced by behaviourist approaches to education and in particular to outcomes models. Burke (1995) considers 'that the single most *efficient cause* contributing to this new emphasis was the publication in 1991 of Jessup's (1991) *Outcomes: NVQ's and the Emerging Model of Education and Training.*' Thus candidates had to present evidence of the outcomes being achieved.

In order to establish the system the then Employment Department was to establish recognized standards of competence relevant to work and it would do this by creating employer-led organizations which identify and establish these standards (so-called Lead Bodies) (Wolf, 1995, 1998). The standards had to take a very precise form and were based on functional analyses which determined the competence requirements in an industry, organization or occupation.

> Standards state in outcome terms what is expected of an individual performing a particular occupational role. They do not look at the underlying abilities or traits of the individual but describe the expectations which the individual is required to meet ... The process of functional analysis proceeds as follows (i) describe the key purpose of the occupational area; (ii) Ask, 'What needs to happen for this to be achieved?' (iii) Repeat the process until the functions being identified are at the unit level; (iv) Repeat the process for each unit until the functions are at element level. (DE).

The theory was that national standards could be met if the outcome specifications were specified in great detail. Therefore a candidate had to provide exhaustive evidence. The portfolio method was found to be the most sensible way of accommodating this approach (see Chapter 12 for discussion of portfolios). Sampling, as would be done in a public examination, was not seen to be feasible.

NVQs are assessed by internal and external verifiers. The internal verifier works in the organization where the NVQs are being assessed, and the external verifier acts rather in the same way as external examiners, and ensures that the assessment has been carried out to national standards. As indicated the principal vehicle for assessment is the portfolio. Wolf (1998) cites Eraut and his colleagues who wrote:

> NVQ assessment and quality assurance is dominated by paper work, NVQ's typically involve over a thousand separate assessment decisions ... The need to record

Level 4   competence in a broad range of complex, technical or professional work activities, performed in a variety of contexts and with a substantial degree of personal responsibility and autonomy. Responsibility for the work of others and allocating responsibility is often present.

Level 5   competence which involves the application of a significant range of fundamental principles and complex techniques across a wide and often unpredictable variety of contexts. Very substantial personal autonomy and often significant responsibility for the work of others and for the allocation of substantial resources features strongly, as do personal accountabilities for analysis and diagnosis, design, planning, execution and evaluation.

Figure 11.9 From the general guide to the NVQ Levels (Guide to National Vocational Qualifications, 1991), Employment Department, Sheffield.

Assessing Risk

In order to demonstrate this unit of competence candidates need to:

1. Demonstrate an understanding of the theories underlying the concept of risk and apply them to a particular practice situation.

2. Consider and interpret

   (a) the provisions of relevant legislation, statutes, policies, and codes of practice;
   (b) available resources; and
   (c) general social work theory, in relation to an analysis of clients' needs.

3. Collect and consider the multiplicity of factors (personal, situational and contextual) relevant to the risks of a particular practice situation.

4. Gain a detailed understanding of the client's interpretation of the situation.

5. Collect and analyse information concerning the resources and capabilities of the client and of others in the client's situation, and devise strategies to ensure that such personal resources are utilized and supported.

6. Consult other professionals in order to make and justify decisions arising from conflicting views as to priorities of risk and vulnerability.

7. Consult with clients and relevant members of the client's situation in order to analyse and balance the interests of the client and others.

8. Devise a 'risk plan' which summarizes the key decisions involving assessment and prioritization of risk in the situation, and the criteria whereby the effectiveness of those decisions will be evaluated.

9. Work with the emotions and ethical issues arising from the complexities and risks inherent in the client's situation.

Figure 11.10 A unit of competence (Assessing Risk) within the general module in the ASSET Competence-based training model leading to the award of an honours degree in professional practice in the social services (Anglia Polytechnic, Chelmsford, 1991).

all these decisions, together with some indication of the evidence on which they were based, helps to explain the almost universal adoption of the portfolio system for storing assessed information. (Eraut *et al.*, 1996).

Thus each National Vocational Qualification consists of a number of units which are made up from a group of standards (i.e. elements for which performance criteria are stated. The units according to the original code of practice should be packages which make sense and are valued in the context of employment. NVQs are classified by five levels.

Levels 4 and 5 shown in Figure 11.9 are intended to correspond to professional qualifications and therein lies their significance for higher education. For example, a joint project between the Employment Department, Essex County Council Social Services and Anglia Polytechnic used the NVQ approach to derive the standards in the assessment of the practical component of an honours degree in professional practice. In this scheme a functional analysis determined the competences used in the employment setting. Units (modules) of competence consisting of coherent sets of elements were established as shown in Figure 11.10. A learning contract is negotiated between the candidate, the tutor and the workplace supervisor. This states the elements of competence which have to be accomplished, as well as the criteria for assessment and how they are to be met. It included plans for the candidate's practice to be observed (Anglia Polytechnic, undated).

Such independent research as has been done on the assessment of NVQs has been summarized by Wolf (1998). She draws attention to conflicting investigations one of which was conducted for the government. This claimed that there was a large measure of agreement between assessors whereas the independent survey did not consider that this was a reasonable representation of the findings. Wolf's study of occupational assessors who had not received any training showed low levels of inter-assessor agreement. This is not surprising. It would seem that the only way to improve reliability would be for a large group cross-moderation exercise of the kind undertaken in the US. It also seems that there was an unwillingness to look at research in the school system which evaluated reports conducted as part of school assessment within the GCE 'A' level system, as for example, the engineering science programme referred to above. It seems to be a characteristic of innovation in curriculum and assessment that in the initial stages of development the designers expect far too much from students and teachers, a position from which they, the designers, have subsequently to withdraw (e.g. Carter, Heywood and Kelly, 1986).

NVQs came in for much criticism. Apart from complaints about the amount of paper work involved they were also criticized because they paid insufficient attention to the role of knowledge in determining outcomes. A similar criticism was made of the Enterprise in Higher Education Initiative (Heywood, 1994).

The introduction of the General National Vocational Qualifications (GNVQs) was described in detail in Chapter 5. The idea that they would be equivalent to the GCE 'A' level was controversial. They were also based on portfolios, and Wolf (1998) found that even where there was a relatively high level of agreement between the assessors, there was room for concern. However (and at the risk of oversimplification), the desire for parity of esteem has meant that from a pedagogy which could be described as 'progressive' (as in educational theory) they have become academicized. Whereas the intention was that the content should be related to practice in broad occupational areas, and encourage self-management in the direction and responsibility for learning, tightly prescribed outcomes have rendered these goals unattainable in many courses. Present government policy is to make GNVQs more like 'A' levels. Issue No. 2 of volume 11 (1998) of the *Journal of Education and Work* is devoted to this topic. While the authors of the various papers believe that the GNVQ has failed to deliver its progressive aims, and while its future is in doubt, they believe that it has provided a model on which future curriculum constructors could build.

In Australia a similar attempt has been made to create a standards framework. Like the system in the UK it became too complicated and resource intensive. It was too task-oriented, detailed and prescriptive. It had eight levels (as opposed to five in the British system). Curtain and Hayton (1995) who reviewed its development pointed out that if organizations were becoming more flat and requiring a greater degree of task variety from those working in teams, these eight levels might discourage participation in a national vocational and education system. This would support the view that organizations should undertake their own task analyses of the kind undertaken by Youngman *et al*. These also enable organizational structure to be evaluated, as well as to focus on the current and future requirements of the enterprise and its employees.

Youngman *et al*. (1978) analysed the jobs done by engineers in a company in the aircraft industry. Interviews with a representative sample yielded 434 operations (originally called abilities) which the engineers performed between them. These were put together in a rating schedule and each engineer in the organization was asked to say which ones they used. The results clustered into 14 segments called activities from which training programmes could be derived. Cluster analysis was also used to derive the skills used by particular groups of engineers and to relate these to the needs of the organization. The perceptions that the engineers had of their jobs and of themselves were also obtained. It was also possible to examine the structure of the organization in the light of these findings. Over and above the statistical analyses, a face validity analysis of the items was undertaken to yield a taxonomy similar in kind to that of *The Taxonomy of Educational Objectives*. This yielded five major categories (Application, Communication, Diagnosis, Evaluation and Management (direction and control)). A similar kind of study has been undertaken with dental technicians (Butler, 1978).

A criticism of this work, and of NVQs and GNVQs is that they do not take into account the knowledge required to perform these skills in the work situation. Youngman *et al*. (1978) had taken this point into account. They were aware of a study by Meuwese (1968) who had devised a technique which enabled an academic department to determine its objectives in outcomes form for the purpose of designing an individualized learning curriculum in industrial engineering based on the Keller plan (Meuwese, 1971). They had adapted the technique for their study, and believed it would not be difficult to marry the two together.

Meuwese (1968), of Eindhoven Technological University, used the categories of *The Taxonomy* to derive 300 behavioural statements from some 40 of his colleagues in the Department of Industrial Engineering. The same teachers then rated and classified them after which they were factor and cluster analysed. The factorial analysis yielded six main factors into which the objectives were gathered. These were:

i   The social system components of industrial engineering;

ii   Machine shop technology;

iii Systems analysis;

iv   Critical analysis and synthesis in industrial relations;

v   Organization and planning;

vi   The management of mechanical systems.

In Australia an 'integrated' approach has been taken to the development of competency based assessment in the professions (Gonczi, 1994). It is claimed that this approach overcomes all the objections to competency based assessment in the literature. It stems from the idea that competency is relational.

> It brings together disparate things – abilities of individuals (deriving from combinations of attributes) and the tasks that need to be performed in particular situations. Thus competence is conceived of as a complex structuring of attributes needed for intelligent performance in specific situations. Obviously it incorporates the idea of professional judgement ... It allows us to incorporate ethics and values as elements in competent performance, the need for reflective practice, the importance of context and the fact that there may more than one way of practising competently. (Gonzci, 1994)

This philosophy necessitates a multiple-strategy approach to assessment for competence to be inferred, and it allows that knowledge may need to be tested independently from performance. It sees assessment as being integrated. Gonczi cites the assessment of classroom assessment of teaching which could be used to assess among other things, classroom management skills, knowledge of subject matter being taught, ethical principles, lesson planning within one assessment event. My experience, as outlined above, is that this could be another example of over-assessment i.e. wanting too much from the same event. Nevertheless, he gives examples of practice in law and medicine, although in this paper no evaluations are presented. Such approaches necessarily profile the learner.

Profiling work experience

A desire to allow work-based experience to count toward the award of university degrees and diplomas caused questions about their validity and reliability to be asked. Benett (1993) applied classical test theory to the problem and concluded that under certain stated conditions it is possible to determine if work-based assessments are valid, reliable and comparable. He suggests that at the level of institutions and employment-based learning centres, assessments can be valid and reliable. He suggests also that those responsible for courses in cooperation with employers, should ensure that:

(a)   the learning process and the procedures for the assessment (and self assessment) of work based learning are well document and made public;

(b)   the most appropriate set of tasks in which to assess competences are identified; and

(c)   biases (personal, professional and theoretical) are discussed with employers, other course staff and students alike.

Solutions to this problem are only likely to come about if there is considerable collaboration between the college and those directly responsible in industry for training students. Just how complex this can be is illustrated by a study undertaken by Ford and Rennie (1999) who show how an objectives approach may go some way in solving the problem. They undertook a project of two year's duration to devise and evaluate employer and student self-assessor schedules, and at the same time to provide training for both the industrial tutors and the students. The students were pursuing a course in environmental science at the University of Salford and were required to undertake a professional placement of between 12 and 15 months between their second and the fourth year of academic studies.

A group of environmental health officers representing a large number of local government authorities met with the teaching staff to help develop the assessment schedule. They had all provided placements for students in the past. They began by specifying what they expected the students to achieve during their professional placement. Twelve of those present agreed to develop the schedule and provide notes for guidance. When these were completed, they were discussed by the whole group, and eventually agreement was reached. The domains developed were Comm-unications, Personal and Interpersonal Skills, Approach to Learning, Organizational Skills, and Investigative skills and Problem Solving.. In parallel with this activity students who were nearing the completion of their professional placement designed

---

Organizational Skills.

How do you review and prioritize your personal workload?

Tend to deal with things as they come up or as they are asked for. No personal appointments diary.
Keep an appointments diary and deal with things as they are asked for.
Keep an appointments diary and intermittent lists of targets when pressure of work demands organization.
Keep an appointments diary. Keep a checklist of short and long-term targets. Add/delete items as they arise/are dealt with.

Do you approach your work with active interest, seeking and accepting a level of responsibility you can handle?

Not always keen on some areas of work. Prefer to await instruction or take on tasks which prove difficult to handle.
Respond positively to interesting topics or staff who make an effort. Do not like to push self forward.
Willing and responsive approach to work. Accept manageable responsibility.
Willing and responsive approach to work. Seek and enjoy manageable responsibility.

How do you keep a (systematic) personal record of your experience?

Keep a haphazard daily diary of visits made and photocopies of all available material.
Keep a chronological record of training programme and copies of proformas and other interesting material.
Keep a subject indexed record of training with selected interesting material and proformas.
Keep a subject indexed record which includes a personal review of sample visits and relevant proformas.

Figure 11.11 Extract from a schedule for the student self-assessment of work experience. Section on organizational skills. (From Ford and Rennie (1999).)

the self-assessment schedule. The section on organizational skills is shown in Figure 11.11. They defined the learning aims of the period and then devised behavioural objectives against which students could monitor their own performance. The two schedules were almost identical although they had been developed separately. This convergence might not be as surprising as it seems since both groups received a similar 'how to do it' session and shown various taxonomies. However, it is more than probable that their recent and continuing experience weighed heavily in their discussions and there were differences between the performance indicators preferred by employer assessors who observe performance and the students who assess their own performance (see Chapter 14). Those who participated in the programme received prior training in the use of the schedule.

The students and assessors were interviewed toward the end of the placement by an independent investigator. Eighty-nine per cent of the assessors considered the scheme to be clear and understandable and most of these favoured the four-point scale which was used; however, 15 per cent thought that a six-point scale would allow more flexibility. One thought that the four-point scale would produce a tendency for assessors to give students the benefit of the doubt. In so far as validity is concerned only 12 per cent made negative comments about the schedule. However, 48 per cent felt some inappropriate material was included especially that which related to more complex professional competences. Students would not always be able to demonstrate capabilities in these areas.

> The main difficulty assessors found in applying the scheme occurred when the assessment criteria required them to evaluate students' understanding or appreciation of issues. These were contained in indicators addressing sensitivity to the influence of cultural and socio-economic factors; understanding of the structures and policies of local authorities and departments; and an interest in environmental concerns beyond the remit of the departments in which they worked. Such assessments were problematic because they necessitated assessment of something that could not be directly observed.

The assessors believed that the most significant strength of the scheme was the clear identification of criteria. It facilitated the identification of the students' strengths and weaknesses and this could lead to changes in training programmes. The major weakness was perceived to be the element of subjectivity in completion of the schedule; personal bias could influence judgement. It was also pointed out that to use the scheme properly considerable amounts of time were required and this was a disadvantage. One of the problems with schemes like this is that they have high validity but may not be as reliable as conventional examinations, a fact that is compounded by the relatively large number of assessors used. Ashworth and Saxton (1992) suggest that the primary purpose of such schemes should be to facilitate experiential learning rather than to worry about the final grade, and this is a view with which Ford and Rennie concur. They believed they had limited subjectivity by designing instruments that were seen to be valid by both assessors and students. Assessment criteria and performance indicators were closely defined to try to reduce personal bias and training officers and students were briefed about the content of the schedules and the operation of the scheme. A somewhat similar development in New Zealand has been described by Rainsbury *et al.* (1998). They used a standards based approach but it did not adequately describe the different levels of achievement obtained through the grade descriptors. They also found that students' negotiation skills needed to be developed before they attended the collaborative meeting with the other partners. Although the numbers in the sample were small they found that females out-performed males and were more realistic in their self-assessments.

As indicated in Chapter 5 The American College Testing Program's Work Keys assessment requires candidates to detail their attainments at work in a portfolio. The work keys assessment tests are each of one hour's duration. The results that are sent to

---

Introduction:

Your Personal Profile/Record of Achievement is a tool that you can use to monitor and record your development, both academically and personally while you are at Sheffield University, taking into account your experiences both in your course and outside of it. You will be required to complete the Profile during the year, agreeing written statements with a tutor twice a year. It is not, however, supposed to be another chance to satisfy your department.

'Why bother?' 'Isn't that what exams are supposed to do?'

Reflection on what you have learned and how you have learned is one of the most useful means of self-development. The Record of Achievement helps you focus your thoughts, providing you with space to write down a short summary of them, almost like a diary. Having this information written down helps you in a number of ways:

- it will assist your identification and development of your strengths and weaknesses
- you will be able to set your own personal objectives, specifically for your needs, to be achieved at your pace
- you will be able to use it when you need to prepare a CV.

It will also assist your relationship with your tutor, providing you with a useful framework for discussion. This will improve your tutor's knowledge of you and be beneficial when s/he comes to write a reference for you.

Although your tutor is involved at certain stages with your Record, it is important to remember that it belongs to you. Your thoughts, musings and notes are your own, to be shared with the people you choose. Only the mid and end of year statements need to be agreed between you and your tutor; everything else is your property. If, however, you want to use other parts of the Record in discussion with your tutor you should do so.

The notes and questions in the Record are only meant to guide your thinking process. They are not meant to tell you what to do or how to think, but are merely a starting point. You can discuss them with friends, tutors and other members of staff, or just think about them yourself. It is important to remember that there is no right answer to any of the questions and that what may be good for you may not necessarily be good for someone else.

Figure 11.12 The Introduction to the personal Profile/Record of Achievement developed by the Enterprise Unit, University of Sheffield (taken from the **Assessment of Enterprise Learning in Higher Education,** *Technical Report No. 20, 1994, Employment Department, Sheffield).*

the individual explain how the scores were obtained and detail how an individual might improve his/her scores (ACT, 1997).

Profiles and records of achievement

In the UK, discussion in schools about profiles has become inextricably linked with the concept of a National Record of Achievement. The intention was that students on leaving school would 'have a ready portfolio of evidence and a usable and acceptable summary of their achievements which can provide information to others and can be used as a basis for further development'. (Employment Department, 1991). The Department also believed that the solution of the problem of how to assess the personal transferable skills associated with enterprise education would be to record the students' development in these areas during the course of their studies (Heywood, 1994). In consequence the Department proposed that the National Record of Achievement should be kept throughout higher education. This did not happen but the idea is alive and well. The Dearing Committee (Dearing, 1997) called it a *Progress File* and suggested that it would have two elements (1) an official record of achievement or transcript, provided by institutions, and (2) a means by which students can monitor, build and reflect upon their own personal development. The transcript would also supply a standard set of information. It seems it would be similar to American transcripts because individual marks would be given for modules. The Committee of Vice-Chancellors and Principals is currently engaged with the Quality Assurance Agency in working out a sustainable policy on progress files.

The Enterprise Unit at the University of Sheffield developed a Personal Profile/ Record of Achievement. Figure 11.12 shows the introduction to the Sheffield Personal Profile. It is accompanied by a log book. The first-year booklet includes sections for written communication, information handling, working in groups, oral presentation, problem solving, using information technology, an academic section and study habits. Each of these takes one page. Space was provided for comments to be made in each of the three terms of the year. An example of the type of comment that may be made preceded each section. The log is intended to summarize current achievements and indicate future objectives. When the profile was designed note was taken of one of the findings of research on school records of achievement to the effect that children were bored with always being asked 'where they were at'. A different strategy was used and this was to identify areas that the tutors said were difficult. So the instructions in the Academic and Study habit sections read:

> Academic section: What part of your course is the most interesting? Why? What are you learning? What are you not learning? What ways of thinking are you developing through your academic study – analytical, reflective, conceptual? How do these apply to other areas of your life? What parts of your course do you like? What part of the course are you worst at? What can you do to improve? How do the other skills referred to in this Record relate to your academic work? What is scholarship – ability to find and deal with evidence, ability to conceptualise, information handling and processing, more?

Study habits: When you are unsure of something to do with your course or learning, what do you do? When have you approached lecturers, tutors, friends for guidance and help before? How do you organise your work? What sort of goals or objectives do you set yourself? How much close supervision do you need? How do you plan ahead for your study? How do you organise your study? How do you organise your course work to fit around your extra-curricular activities? What could you do to organise yourself better? If things aren't working out, what things can you do to help yourself? What services exist to help you – tutors, counselling services, Students Unions?

It will be seen that these were designed to encourage reflective thought. Clearly, the relationships that the student establishes with the academic organization as well as those with his/her tutors are important if personal profiles are to be effective. Assiter and Fenwick (1992) consider that tutors will require training if they are to participate in this kind of work. Such training is as much about attitudes as it is about knowledge, for the incorporation of learner-centred instruction into teaching is not always accomplished with ease. The implementation of a personal profile system of this kind requires the support of the central organization as well as considerable resources.

It is argued that the completion of a Record of Achievement makes the learner take responsibility for his/her learning provided the tutors allow this to happen. As such motivation is improved (Broadfoot, 1988), recording experience also develops the capacity for reflection since the learner has to reflect on what to say (Walker, 1985). And they may enable the accreditation of new kinds of curriculum in higher education (FEU, 1987). There is an effusive literature but little evaluation.

One very small-scale study set out to evaluate two approaches to the recording of experience in the education component of a sandwich (cooperative) degree prog-ramme in applied biology and education at the University of Bath (James and Denley, 1992). The authors wished to develop an alternative to checklist models of student teacher profiling which judged professional competence by aggregating narrowly defined and decontextualized competences. They pointed out, as have others, that the issue of student teacher profiling is complex. They compared two different models which were administered while the students were on the undergraduate certificate of education component of the course. Their purpose was to obtain a descriptive record of the student's experience so as to engage the student in reflection on that experience. The five components or areas of study on which the student was asked to reflect were, science (9), specialist science (5), the teacher's wider professional role (9), inform-ation technology (4), and economic and industrial understanding (3). These were sub-divided into further relatively broad categories the number of which are shown in parentheses. The students were provided with a large log book which was section-alized. At various times the entries were completed and discussed with their tutor. Among the difficulties exposed was the fact that the students found it daunting when faced with such a large book, and some had difficulty in completing it. It was observed that the students could only evaluate in a superficial way. The introduction of the record also influenced the structure of the course because the time available for discussion was reduced. On reflection the tutors felt they had made the activity too complex, and they had their view confirmed that checklists of 'narrow,' very detailed, and limited competences were unlikely to be successful. In their second model, with the same students, they arranged for the record to be built up over time so the students were not presented with a large book at the beginning. They also arranged for writing to be incorporated in an extended way because the students like writing about their experiences. They tried to make the document a more integral feature of the course and in this way to make it become a facilitator of learning. Therefore, the students were to describe the main features of their learning experience, say what they had learnt, analyse it in terms of improving their practice, and indicate what actions they propose to take. The students responded better to this model. However, the authors note that there is danger that students will become overloaded with reflection (reflection overload). Nevertheless, they conclude that the record does have the potential to provide a record of students' experience that is not only consistent with reflective practice, but facilitates it.

Another small-scale evaluation, by Trowler and Hinett (1994), offered some words of caution. They point out that for an innovation of this kind to be successful it has to be compatible with the institution. It may work very well in a small collegiate institution and they cite the example of such an institution where the students themselves had designed a personal development profile. They also reinforce the point made by Heywood (1994) that any scheme that is not accredited or fully integrated into course assessment and tutorial practice is unlikely to achieve the aims proposed for records of achievement in higher education. They would look with horror on the Dearing proposal in that a top-down fiat for their implementation is a recipe for failure as innovation theory would confirm. Any development should be accompanied by small-scale experimentation.

Implications for teaching

This chapter has described, from a number of different perspectives, the move toward outcomes or performance based assessment. Apart from the fact that accountability demanded clarity of objectives it was hoped that they would provide improved reliability and validity. There are many problems associated with their design and implementation to be overcome. There is the danger that so many outcomes are declared that the curriculum becomes overcrowded and learning is inhibited.

The art of assessment design in these circumstances is to choose a few key domain objectives for assessment and to design the curriculum to meet the key concepts and skills that those objectives embrace. This is not an easy task. Some assessment methodologies are time consuming and need to be subject to benefit–cost analysis, but this should take into account the advantages and disadvantages of the existing system. It is clear from previous chapters that this must not be done in isolation from student learning and development. This will require a substantial change in the role of teachers and teams.

Taken as a whole, the sections in this chapter suggest that a variety of systems are possible. However, several of the assessment strategies discussed, as for example profiles, are untried and untested. This discussion is continued in the next chapter which reviews developments in more practical areas (i.e. oral and aural examining and various kinds of coursework) as well as problem-based learning and portfolios.

Chapter 12

Practicals, Projects, Problem-based Learning and Portfolios

Aural and oral assessment

Aural assessment

Aural and oral skills are key communication skills yet by and large they have been ignored in higher education with the exception of foreign language learning, medicine and *viva voce* examinations in higher degrees. The ability to listen is greatly underestimated. In foreign languages, business oriented degrees pay especial attention to these skills (White, 1980).

The traditional aural test was a dictation administered in the examination room. Now it is very often a radio broadcast transmitted in a language laboratory. The students can play the tape backwards and forwards as many times as they like within a specified period (e.g. 40 minutes). White (1980) reported that students make as many as four times the errors they would make in a traditional test in this kind of comprehension test which, of course, will involve recall. It discriminates sharply between good and weak students.

In some higher education examinations the student listens to a text intended for speaking after which he/she answers questions on, or makes a summary of, the text. Such tests are scored by an error count. Some institutions complicate matters (as some do with objective tests) by weighting the errors according to the importance attached to the error.

Oral assessment

Oral examinations have two functions that may or may not be combined in the same assessment.

These are to test the candidate's command of: (1) an oral medium; (2) of content as demonstrated through the oral medium. We generally associate the first with testing capabilities in a modern language, and the second with the *viva voce* that accompanies many higher degrees or the medieval disputation. In all these instances there is an overlap between the functions.

In so far as language competence is concerned the school examination boards in England have completed a number of studies of the problems of assessing aurals and orals and precise regulations for the conduct of such assessments have been drawn up (for example AEB, 1982, 1985; Forrest, 1985). Oral tests in languages are of several kinds. For example, the 15 minute conversation is normal, but there may be translation-at-sight tests, and telephone tests. Another approach is to use role plays (see below). As with the aural, the trend is toward the real situation. Brown and Knight (1994) draw attention to the scenario where a student of German might have to prepare three topics, one of which would be chosen at random for an oral.

It is self-evident that oral examinations pose many problems not least among them the emotional disposition of the candidate during the examination. Nevertheless skills in communication are now regarded as core skills that everyone should possess, and in consequence oral examining is becoming more important. However, oral tests in, say, medicine, are quite different from those frequently used in modern foreign languages.

In regard to the second function, the ability to communicate cognitive knowledge and understanding Joughin (1998) distinguished between six dimensions of oral assessment that he had found in the literature which included references to orals in chemistry (Juhl, 1996), English (Dressel, 1991), geography (Church and Bull, 1995), the medical sciences, and psychology (Hill, 1984). First is *primary content type*. Assessments are made of knowledge and understanding, applied problem solving abilities, inter-personal and intra-personal competence. Not surprisingly the oral examination is used in the clinical situation in medicine. In the traditional oral the candidate was sent off to examine the patient and report back. Surprisingly, the examiner did not witness the examination of the patient. It was appreciated that this was unreliable, and simulations were introduced (see below).

Fabb and Marshall (1983) described The Formal Oral examination developed by the College of Family Physicians in Canada. It lasts for 25 minutes and constitutes 20 per cent of the total examination marks. A case is selected which represents a common condition in family practice: its solution is intended to require a stepwise approach to the evaluation of the problem and is made complex by the inclusion of inter-family relationships. The solution will involve a consultant physician and workers in the paramedical profession. A major goal of the technique is to cause the candidate to create options for action, which is in contrast to the situation in most written examinations in medicine, where the options are given and not created. Creative problem solving in this context is achieved by getting candidates to ask for data so that their problem solving abilities can be observed. It also allows the examiner to stimulate the candidates' thinking.

A comprehensive rating schedule is provided. Fabb and Marshall claim that, because of content validity, the method of scoring, and the training of examiners, it allows for the accurate assessment of the candidate. As part of examiner training videotapes were prepared to demonstrate good and poor techniques of diagnosis.

In New Zealand 40 final-year medical students were video recorded during an oral examination. At a later date these recordings were individually rated by six research psychiatrists who were also experienced examiners. Verbal and non-verbal behaviour was rated using visual analogue scales. The agreement between the assessors in the allocation of oral marks was found to be low but the score was found to be positively associated with student confidence but negatively with anxiety in men (Thomas, 1992).

Newble, Hoare and Sheldrake (1980) argued that the unreliability of clinical tests was due to the complexity of skills being assessed, the mix of patients being tested, and the variance of the examiners. They considered the last of these to be the most intractable. Therefore the problem was to select examiners who were consistent and to provide them with an objective rating form and training with simulated patients.

Mast and Davis (1994) argue that the advantages of oral examinations in medicine are that they are flexible, can assess long-term problems or evolving cases, and can use practical data. They cite an evaluation of the Canadian oral in support of the view that structured questions can improve reliability to acceptable levels. In the past there had been much criticism of clinical tests.

More generally, Lockyer and Harrison (1994) report two studies which used multiple measures to assess clinical performance. One of these studies concluded that oral examinations, standardized patients, and chart stimulated recall, were able to distinguish between groups of physicians and were valid methods of assessing competence.

Mast and Davis (1994) draw attention to the *triple jump* variation of the oral. This was developed as part of the McMaster problem-based curriculum (see below). As the title indicates, the exercise consists of three components. These are:

A vignette or clinical problem to test hypothesis generation, data gathering and interpretation, current knowledge, early problem formulation, and ability to define learning issues.

An intermediary step comprised of searching the literature, using either a personal or institutional library, or other learning resources.

A final component, permitting the learner to present final conclusions about the case and findings from the literature, thus permitting an assessment of information- retrieval or self-directed learning skills, and self-assessment ability.

Joughin points out that in clinical examinations personal skills, such as the ability to present information and be interviewed are assessed. But, because these are not an overall assessment of the skills possessed by the interviewee, but only of those observed at the time, these assessments could affect the judgement of the candidate. He also notes that an oral examination may test more than one of the categories within this dimension. In management in education, for example, experienced teachers who wish to become principals of schools need to be exposed to situations which draw out both the cognitive and affective dimensions of behaviour because many of the problems they will face will arise in conflict situations. To help experienced teachers learn about their behaviours in 'live' situations a series of role-playing exercises was devised. Each member of the course is given a role to play in a case study written by another member of the group. This case study is based on an actual school experience of the writer. The case study writer and the tutor act as observers. The role players invent their own scripts to complete the case study. The de-briefing followed this pattern:

1. The case study writer gives his or her impressions of the role play.

2. Each contributor describes their feelings during the role play.

3. Each contributor states the most significant thing they learnt from the role play.

4. The case study writer describes what actually happened in the situation on which the case was built.

5. The tutor reviews the case and draws attention to appropriate management practices and theory.

One of the objectives of the programme was to develop a high level skill of self-assessment. It is thought that such programmes cannot (or should not) be tutor assessed. To achieve credit on this course all the exercises had to be completed together with a three-hour written examination based on set-reading relevant to the course and prior-notice questions (FitzGibbon and Heywood, 1986).

Joughin's second dimension is *interaction*. This refers to the social interaction between the examiner and the candidate during the interview. *Interaction* is polarized between presentation without comment and a high level of dialogue. An intermediate position is when there is a presentation followed by questioning. In all cases there is a potential for bias. At the same time this interaction allows for follow-up questions particularly in the assessment of problem solving (Brown and Knight, 1994). However, this could distort assessment if there are no guide lines as to how this should be done and the awards made. If the candidate and the examiner have been in contact through teaching over a long period of time the interaction of their personalities may also have some effect on the performance of both the candidate and the examiner (Freeman *et al.*, 1982).

Within the interview situation it has been shown that shy students as well as those who are highly voluble can be disadvantaged. It has been observed that in such situations the highly anxious report a greater incidence of task-irrelevant thoughts than less anxious persons (Ganzer, 1968; Holloway *et al.*, 1967). Their preoccupation with the task may be accompanied by irrelevant comments of a self-deprecatory kind (Sarason and Stoops, 1978). In the examination setting interviewers may be influenced more by unfavourable information than favourable. It is also important to consider if the information could be obtained in another way. If large numbers of students are to be interviewed it is important to maintain the same cognitive structure, and in so far as possible affective environment. There is a danger that if the interview is unstructured the examiner will talk more than the candidate. Structuring interviews has been shown to increase inter-rater reliability. In any case the interview should be supported by other performance data (Holdsworth, 1981; Mayfield, 1964). It is possible that candidates may feel two examiners are preferable to one, and just as there is evidence to show that interviewers need training, so there is a need to train interviewees.

Joughin's third dimension relates to the degree of authenticity. It is clear from the examples above and some to follow that the medical profession seeks a high level of authenticity. The fourth dimension relates to the degree of *structure*. A *closed* structure follows a set of questions in a given order whereas an *open* structure follows a 'loosely structured agenda'. His fifth dimension is that of the examiner. The oral form of examination is open to assessment by multiple examiners. Joughin draws attention to the fact that students can be drawn into the process of examining through rating forms which could be used to indicate where improvements in oral examining might be made. It may also be used by peers to assess their colleagues in, say, project work. Most assessment is, however, summative and conducted by the teachers. Finally, Joughin distinguishes between degrees of orality; some forms of assessment are purely oral whereas some forms of oral assessment may be secondary to another form of examining.

In sum the content validity of oral examinations is considered to be high. The predictive validity is much more problematic and much debate about assessment in medical education has been concerned with this issue (Gonnella *et al.*, 1993). Kern *et al.* (1998) consider that there are still problems with inter- and intra-rater reliabilty. Attempts to improve reliability have been made by the introduction of rating schedules and many have been published. Brown, Bull and Pendelbury (1997) have published rating scales for assessing the management of discussion, and oral proficiency. Students should be given these scales in the interests of validity. The latter are based on criterion referenced grading scales for the measurement of foreign language proficiency. (Similar tests have been developed by the US State Department for the assessment of the language competences of college students (Frith, 1979).)

Kern *et al.* (1998) point out that orals are faculty intensive. Brown and Knight (1994) also note that they are time consuming, and can erode teaching time. They note that *vivas* are also used as quality checks of group work, and may indicate the level of input which particular students have made to the exercise. Their final point is that the resources have to be made available if presentations and *vivas* are to be relatively stress free (e.g. overhead projectors, powerpoint and other devices must work and be checked beforehand).

Simulations

Corley (1983) considered that 'role playing is the most versatile of all simulation formats, equally adaptable for teaching and evaluation'. Simulations are sometimes the only technique available for performance assessment as for example when determining interviewing skills.

Smit and van der Molen (1997) describe an advanced psychology course at the University of Groningen in which the students learn to lead interviews in organizations, selection interviews, and interviews involving the breaking of bad news. They use a simulation designed to test the students' ability in carrying out a selection interview with an applicant. The students were given a description of the job the applicant applies for together with the applicant's letter. They were to take the role of the selector and the interview was to last for 25 minutes. In version A the selector had to find out if the candidate fulfilled the requirement of being able to cooperate, and in version B if they could work independently. In both versions the selector has the task of finding out which useful skills the candidate has in relation to the job applied for.

Two standard case histories were developed. Two female students were employed as actors and they received some training including practice of the actor's role. A 15-item behavioural rating scale was developed (1=skill not applied or applied inadequately; 5=skill applied adequately). The quality of the simulations was invest-igated among two groups of advanced psychology students (one group had not participated in the course), and a group of personnel officers. The psychology students participated in simulations before and after the course. Half the students took version A and the other half version B. The interviews were videotaped and rated afterwards by three advanced students trained in the use of the rating list. The results were found to be reliable in terms of internal consistency and inter-rater reliability. It was found that the student's score was very dependent on the type of the interview. This is consistent with the view that scores on performance based tests are dependent on the task. While they considered that the simulation instrument is not efficient, its benefits were high. Teachers often find this to be true of some of the assessment 'gimmicks' they invent in the classroom. In this case the students were stimulated to do their best in practising for interviews, weaknesses in students' performance could be detected and remedial instruction could be provided. The administration took 30 minutes and the scoring 40 minutes per interview.

In another study at Hong Kong Polytechnic University students of hotel and tourism acted in turn as trainers and trainees in a simulated training session. The students worked in pairs and one was required to plan and conduct a training session with their partner as the trainee. This took place in front of an audience consisting of all the students in the group (17–20) and the tutor. All were rated on the trainer's checklist. It included the major categories for environment, equipment and material, professional and personal factors, attention, involvement, demonstration, explan-ation, activity, other checks, task analysis, prep sheet, and lesson plan which is, like many others, used for the evaluation of teaching and training (e.g. Heywood, 1982). Kwan and Leung (1996) who conducted this study found that there was some agreement between peer group and tutor markings. When the marks were converted to grades the level of agreement between them ran at about 47 per cent. The level of agreement between the two gradings was not statistically significant. It seemed that the peer ratings were more stringent than the tutors in the high mark range but less stringent than the tutor's in the low mark range. Kwan and Leung point out that this finding might be due to the fact that the students were not skilled in rating. The ability to judge the performance of peers requires some training. The fact that they were not involved in the design of the schedule may also have contributed to these differences. My own experience of trying to introduce self-assessment in similar circumstances would support their views.

White (1980) described how in the Royal Society of Arts Diploma for Bilingual Secretaries the candidates were put in role-playing situations in which, for example, a visitor to a firm requires help from a secretary linguist. A mark scheme is a provided and standardization procedures applied. This consists of a sample taped oral examin-ation with a commentary on the performance of both the candidate and the examiner. The marking scheme is biased against the candidate who does badly and includes a scale for language quality adjustment.

White reported that there was a debate about who should assess. Some said it should be the student's teacher. However, the Royal Society of Arts said that when teachers did assess, the pass rate became too high.

Simulations have been widely practised in medical education for many years. Some of them are now computer based in medicine (Christie and Jones, 1995) and other subjects (e.g. entrepreneurship, Wolfe and Bruton, 1994). One of the most important developments has been that of the *standardized patient*. McGuire (1993) distinguishes between the stimulus for the test, *standardized patient*, and the test situation, the *Simulated Clinical Encounter* (SCE). She describes an SCE which embraces the *Objective Structured Clinical Examination* (OSCE) developed by Harden and Gleeson (1979) at Dundee. The OSCE consists of between 10 and 20 'stations'. At each station the candidate is allowed a specified amount of time (usually a few minutes) to perform a standardized single task. It was designed so that it could be administered to very large classes. In the 20 to 50 minute SCE the examinee performs all of the initial work-up on a real or simulated patient.

At the University of Southern Illinois the post-clerkship examination has been based on standardized patients for many years. As described by Vu *et al.* (1993) a *standardized patient* is a person

> carefully coached by a specific training method to accurately portray an actual patient. With each problem the examinees are assessed directly on their interactions with, and workups of, the patient, namely, on their ability to perform a history and physical examination, to educate the patient, and/or to interact with and relate to the patient. In most testing situations, the examinees are also given a follow up written test to assess their skills in evaluating the patient's problems, in ordering relevant laboratory and diagnostic tests, in interpreting test results, and or in managing the patient.

In their evaluation study which was designed to determine the predictive value of the standardized patient test, Vu *et al.* (1993) found that it identified more correctly the candidates who received high ratings in their subsequent training (residency) than it did those with low ratings. However, when the details of the data were taken into consideration, Vu *et al.* (1993) concluded that the standardized patient was a relatively good predictor of the readiness of students for residency.

Other situations in which role playing has played a part include teaching. In micro-teaching the trainee is video-taped while teaching a small class of pupils. They are then able to observe what they did and have it critiqued by their tutor and sometimes their peers. The units are systematically arranged to cover a number of skills (e.g. questioning) (Brown, 1975; Brown and Atkins, 1996). In medicine Crijnen *et al.* (1990) reported that clinical interviewing skills can be helped by intensive small group teaching that includes expert and peer review of video-taped encounters with simulated patients. In the area of social skills role plays have been used to assess assertiveness, social competence among psychiatric in-patients, and a range of other skills (Ellis and Whittington, 1983). In management, role playing is at the heart of the Assessment Center technique.

The Assessment Center (technique)

The Assessment Center is a technique which has been widely used in industry for selection, identification of potential and self-development (Dale and Iles, 1992; Feltham, 1989). It has also been used for the selection of students and the sampling of learning in institutions of higher education (Thornton and Byham, 1982). In Scotland and Pennsylvania it has been used for the selection of student teachers. It is a multiple-strategy approach to assessment and has its origins in Germany in the 1930s in procedures to select officers for the military. Perhaps the most important 'seller' of the technique was the AT and T Management Progress Study. There, 422 personnel (mainly newly recruited college graduates and some younger personnel who had received early promotion) took part in a three-and-a-half-day assessment centre. The results had no bearing on their future career in the company and were used only for the purposes of subsequent research over a 25-year period. By 1965 42 per cent of the 103 predicted to make 'middle management' had done so (Feltham, 1989; Howard and Bray, 1988).

One of the most important studies of its use in higher education is the Outcome Measurement Project of the American Assembly of Collegiate Schools of Business (AACSB, 1987). As part of this study they commissioned the development of measures of non-subject matter characteristics which they had identified in another project. These were: leadership, oral communication and presentation skills, written communication, planning and organizing, information gathering and problem analysis, decision making, delegation and control, self-objectivity and disposition to lead. The simulations that were used to assess these characteristics were:

1. *In-Basket.* To simulate the responsibilities of a middle level manager in a manufacturing organization.

2. *Analysis/oral presentation exercise.* To role-play a manager who must make recommendations concerning expansion. To prepare a written statement and present an oral report.

3. *Unit Start Up Exercise.* To role-play a manager charged with establishing a word processing unit.

4. *Group Discussion Exercise.* To take the role of head of department and to conduct a meeting concerned with the allocation of funds.

5. *Edwards Personnel Preference Schedule.* Pencil and paper instrument used in this case to assess the disposition to lead.

These exercises can be changed according to the requirements of the project. Once the purpose of the assessment centre has been defined the first task is to determine the criteria to be assessed. In the language of the technique these criteria are called dimensions. They are often derived from occupational analysis. Each criterion may be broken down into component objectives and behaviours associated with those objectives indicated. This is very similar to primary trait analysis described in Chapter 11. The care with which these assessments have to be developed is no different to that required for any other approaches to performance assessment. Dale and Isles (1992) make the point that the exercises should reflect and not just simulate the job in terms of content and context.

Feltham (1989) makes the point that it is a mistake to assume the dimensions are stable and enduring traits. He cites the example of *persuasiveness*. A particular individual might appear to be more persuasive in a group problem solving task than in presentation. Skilled performance tends to be specific to the task and may not be transferable. Inter-personal skills utilized in a team task may not transfer to the skills required for one-to-one counselling. Thus, he argues that conclusions about individuals are likely to be more valid if they relate to tasks as well as to dimensions. This is an enduring problem for most types of assessment. Of course, it may be necessary to know about the candidate's persuasiveness in several different situations. Dale and Isles (1992) support this view. 'Assessment Centers were never designed nor should be used to measure stable personality traits, but situation specific skills.' Once the dimensions have been decided it is possible to design the simulations and develop the rating methods. Even though comparability is extremely difficult to ensure with group exercises, the simulations ought to be standardized so that they are the same for all participants. Both the simulations and rating scales should be trialled for validity and reliability. Each simulation enables the assessment of more than one skill. It can be adapted to assess both the process and products of learning. The much cited work of Alverno College is the best example of an adaptation of this approach.

The technique has the disadvantage that it requires a considerable investment in human resources and training. It is the most expensive of all assessment techniques. Commonly six assessees might be assessed by three assessors. The procedure could last for as long as three days. Costs can be reduced if some of the exercises are video-taped. The assessors can then view the tapes at times convenient to them – and their work schedule. British investigators have suggested that discussions between the assessors after the performance are not necessary and that the mechanical pooling of ratings would not lower the validity (Wingrove, Jones and Herriot, 1985). Feltham (1988) considers that the mechanical combination of the information is probably more valid than judgmental information. There seems little doubt that some assessors could be influenced in discussion. As we have seen, this happens when written papers are double marked and first-raters' remarks remain on the papers (see Chapter 10).

Laboratory practicals and projects

Laboratory practicals

Over the years many faculties have been concerned with the value of practical work and the quality of the assessments made (Boud, Dunn and Hegarty-Hazel, 1986; Kempa, 1986). Experiments were carried out to discover the merits of different kinds of laboratory work (Jordan and Carter, 1986), and enquiries were undertaken to determine the objectives of laboratory work (Lee, 1969).

Among the attempts made to describe different types of practical was the Joint Matriculation Board's definitions of the activities to be carried out for the practical component of assessment in engineering science ('A' level) (JMB, 1972). These are shown in Figure 12.1. It will be seen that the experimental investigations are a form of discovery learning. Lee (1969) used this classification to obtain the objectives of undergraduate practical work in engineering by obtaining the views of practising engineers. Jordan and Carter (1986) subsequently identified the 20 aims of laboratory work shown in Figure 12.2. They also identified behavioural objectives associated with these aims in both the cognitive and affective domains.

(i) *Controlled assignments*

Controlled assignments are of short duration and normally accomplished within a two hour period; they are intimately connected with the subject matter. Pupils may work singly or in groups. Such assignments will;

(a) Reinforce and illuminate lesson material.

(b) Familiarize students with the use of scientific equipment.

(c) Develop a reliable habit of faithful observation, confirmation and immediate record in a journal style.

(d) Introduce the techniques of critical review, analysis, deduction and evaluation.

(e) Promote good style and presentation in the formal technical report.

(ii) *Experimental investigations*

An experimental investigation poses an engineering or scientific problem and involves the student in an analysis of the situation and appropriate selection of procedures and techniques for solution. The end point of the particular investigation may or may not be known but the means for its achievement are comparatively discretionary.

The time needed for an investigation of this type should normally lie in the range 6 to 12 hours.

A record of an investigation should include;

(a) A clear account of the analysis of the problem.

(b) Brief report and comments on the work as the experiment proceeded.

(c) Comment upon the results.

(d) An appraisal of what has been achieved.

Projects

The project is a major undertaking for which it is suggested that 50 hours of laboratory time would be suitable. The pupil will be required to design a device or design and conduct an investigation to fulfil a specification and to evaluate the degree of fulfilment achieved.

Projects call for mental connective abilities rather than for craft skills and the time spent on construction or practical investigation should be kept at a minimum, the emphasis being on design and the formulation of problems, literature search in its widest sense and evaluation.

Figure 12.1 Definitions of controlled assignments, experimental investigations and projects for engineering science at GCE A level.
(Extracts reproduced by kind permission of the Joint Matriculation Board, Manchester from Carter, Heywood and Kelly, (1986.)

Aim	Behavioural objectives capable of being tested and being observed
1. To stimulate and maintain the student's interest in engineering.	Student likes working in the laboratory, is often to be seen there, arrives early, leaves late.
2. To illustrate, supplement and emphasize material taught in lectures.	Student uses lecture material, in laboratory problems and vice versa, has knowledge of methods learned.
3. To train the student to keep a continuous record of laboratory work.	Student keeps well laid out notebook for this purpose rather than loose sheets of paper.
4. To train the student in formal writing of the experimental procedures adopted in laboratory practicals, and the writing of technical reports.	Student hands in well-written reports on time, discusses them with tutors and attempts to improve them.
5. To teach the student how to plan an experiment so that he derives useful, meaningful data.	Student comes to laboratory having read necessary references and with prepared plan of operation.
6. To give the student training in the processing and interpretation of experimental data.	Student uses graphs and tables intelligently, draws fair conclusions from them and deals sensibly with errors.
7. To train the student to use particular apparatus, test procedures or standard techniques.	Student shows competence in handling common laboratory equipment and learns how to use new equipment quickly.
8. To improve the learning/teaching process by improving the communication and rapport between staff and students.	Student talks with the staff, initiating discussion on the experiment and other matters.
9. To strengthen the student's understanding of engineering design, by showing him that practical work and design work must be integrated to achieve viable solutions to design problems.	
10. To develop the student's skill in problem-solving in both single and multi-solution situations.	Student progresses from 'dashing off in all directions' methods to planned attacks on problems.
11. To provide each student with an opportunity to practise the role of a professional engineer so that he can learn to perform that role.	Student Figures responsible, truthful and reliable attitude towards the data, use of time, care of equipment, etc.
12. To provide the student with a valuable stimulant to independent thinking.	Student creates his own solution to problems, does not wait to be told what to do. In discussion student puts his own points clearly.
13. To show the use of practical work as a process of discovery.	
14. To demonstrate use of experimental work as an alternative to analytical methods of solving engineering problems.	
15. To help students understand that small models of plant or process can aid greatly in the understanding and improvement of such plant and process.	
16. To familiarize the student with the need to communicate technical concepts and situations to inform and persuade management to certain courses of action to disseminate technical knowledge and expertise for the benefit of all.	Student can explain clearly what he has done and why using proper technical concepts, using graphs, tables, sketches, etc. as seems most useful.
17. To help students bridge the gap between the unreality of the academic situation and the industrial scene, with its associated social, economic and other restraints which engineers encounter.	
18. To teach the student how accurate measurements made with laboratory equipment can be; to teach him how to devise methods that are precise when precision is required.	Student can determine and report errors correctly, can devise more accurate methods of measurement and demonstrate them. Student also guesses correctly and knows when to ignore errors and when to 'round-off' numbers.
19. To teach the student what 'Scientific Method' is and how it is applied in an Engineering laboratory.	
20. To give the student confidence in his ability to imagine a concept or hypothesis, to plan an experiment, to test it, to carry out that experiment and report its results to others.	Student acts confidently yet sensibly and safely in the laboratory.

Figure 12.2 The aims of laboratory work with corresponding behavioural objectives where appropriate. (Reproduced by kind permission of Jordan and Carter, 1986.)

Title
This should be a clear statement of the problem to be tackled. While the title should be brief, it must not be vague or so general that it does not convey the essence of the project.

Analysis of the problem
The problem to be dealt with in the project should be analysed as fully as possible. A general statement of the problem should be given, where possible, quantities laid down together with the limitations under which you will be working, such as restraints of size, cost, use and availability of workshop facilities and assistance. For example, if an engine test bed is to be constructed, the size and nature of the engine test bed and associated equipment should be stated, the use to which the engine is to be put should be given and the parameters to be measured should be listed. If the project is of a more investigatory nature a similar analysis is required. For example, if it is concerned with an investigation into atmospheric pollution, the nature of the variables to be measured, the periods over which measurements are to be made, the factors likely to affect these variables and the uses which might be made of the information gained should be stated.

Practical problems to be solved
Having considered the project in outline you will be able to recognize the major practical problems which need to be overcome. These may be the design and manufacture of a piece of equipment or the design of experimental procedures, or both.

Possible solutions
It should be possible at this stage to see your way to solving these major practical problems in order that success can be achieved. It is therefore important that you should offer likely solutions to these problems. It may be that one solution is so obviously the best that a lengthy consideration of alternative approaches is unnecessary. In most cases, however, a number of alternative solutions will occur to you or will arise as a result of consultation with your teacher or other people. The final choice of a solution will in most cases depend on further work and consultation, and the use of appropriate references. Your outline should give the main direction of your ideas at the time of submission.

Resources
The choice of the best solution will also depend upon the resources you have available. You should, therefore, list under the appropriate headings, equipment, manufacturing facilities, materials required, references, consultants, technical assistance available and the approximate cost involved. Such headings will not be equally important for all projects.

You will now be in a position to draw up an approximate timetable of operation. It does not help to make wild guesses about the number of hours you will need; it is better to work in weeks available and then split the period into component parts. Do not forget to list the time necessary for writing the final report. In planning your time always assume that any task will take you much longer than you imagine on a first consideration. It is also important to allow a certain degree of flexibility; if you draw a time sequence diagram, allow for a fair amount of variation.

References
In submitting your project outline, list the books and articles you have read in connection with planning and also the individuals whose advice you have sought.

Future work
You are strongly advised to read the appropriate sections of the Notes for the guidance of schools at all stages of the project, particularly during the planning period. When the moderators have studied you outlines they will forward their comments to your teacher. You are strongly advised to follow any recommendations made by your teacher or the moderator.

Figure 12.3 Guidance notes for the completion of the Project Outline to be submitted for validation by the Moderators prior to the commencement of the Project in Engineering Science (Carter, Heywood and Kelly, 1986).

	Mark (max.50)
A Historical information-located and recorded	
1 In relation to the data collected the information is:	
-inaccurate while the treatment of the topic is slight	1
-accurate while the treatment of the topic is slight	2
-accurate while the treatment of the topic is adequate	3
-accurate while the treatment of the topic is excellent	4
2 In respect of the available resources the candidate has made:	
-poor uses of the resources available	1
-some use of the resources available	3
-excellent use of the resources available	4
3 Two more marks may be made to candidates who use primary sources.	

B Comprehension, i.e. the use the candidate makes of the historical information to construct a coherent pattern.

	Mark (max.50)
4 The candidate's understanding of the historical content	
-shows little or no relevance to the topic	1
-shows some relevance to the topic	3
-shows a clear grasp of the material	4
5 The candidate's understanding of the historical content may be judged in part according to the degree to which he/she relies on direct transcription This candidate	
-relies totally on unacknowledged transcription	1
-uses some unacknowledged transcription but attempts to express the topic in his/her own words	3
-has written report in his/her own word acknowledging sources where necessary	4
6 Two additional marks may be awarded to a candidate whose total presentation shows a grasp of the historical setting of the topic (e.g. use of maps, diagrams, relevant illustrations, quotations)	

C Analysis and synthesis (analysis is a preliminary step to arranging the material collected in a coherent pattern. It involves the selection of the most important and relevant points from the information assembled. Synthesis is the expression of the pattern that emerges from the analysis of the subject matter).

	Mark (max.50)
7 This candidate	
-made no attempt at analysis	0
-fails to distinguish relevant from irrelevant material and issues and important from unimportant material	1
-distinguishes some important issues arising from his/her topic	3
-has isolated the important issues, factors or questions arising from his/her topic	4
8 This candidate	
-shows little attempt to organize the material collected	1
-has organized the material into a coherent pattern	3
-has organized the material so as to answer questions or describe issues, or to explain factors involved in the material	4
9 Two additional marks may be awarded to candidates who have imposed an original structure on the material collected	

D Evaluation (the candidate applies a standard of reasoning and judgement which leads him/her to assess causes and consequences and to distinguish between fact and opinion; history and legend. The project should have some form of conclusion in which the candidate is expected to explain his findings and/or opinions having taken into account different viewpoints and values).

	Mark (max.50)
10 This candidate:	
-made no attempt to distinguish fact from opinion; history from legend; causes from consequences	0
-fails to distinguish fact from opinion; history from legend; causes from consequences	1
-shows some ability to distinguish fact from opinion; history from legend; causes from consequences.	3
-assesses causes and consequences; distinguishes fact from opinion and history from legend	4

Figure 12.4 An assessment scheme for project work in history (Heywood 1977b).

	Mark (max.50)
11 This candidate	
-made no attempt to draw a conclusion	0
-fails to come to any conclusion or judgement	1
-accepts received opinion and judgement without comment	3
-critically examines (questions) received opinions and judgements and forms his own independent judgement	4
12 Two additional marks may be awarded to candidates who show a critical approach to the sources they have used	

Figure 12.4 continued

This movement to define the aims of laboratory work in behavioural terms also led to attempts to improve the quality of assessments and criterion and semi-criterion referenced measures began to be made. They are now said to be 'performance based'. Many grading schedules were developed. Most have similarities with the scheme for the experimental investigations in engineering science shown in Figure 11.4. Because there are so many aims the choice of which objectives to focus on will always be a matter of compromise.

An area of controversy is created by answers to the question, how much practical work and assessment? This can only be decided when the purposes for which it is desired are clear. Answers to this question may lead to the view, as they did in engineering science, that only certain activities should be assessed. However, the student was required to keep a journal in order to demonstrate that he or she had completed experimental work in other content and skill areas of the course.

A variety of techniques are used to assess practicals. For example, the engineering science assessment requires a written report with teacher comments on the assessment schedule. Pencil and paper tests using multiple-choice questions have also been used as have interviews and straightforward observation. The type of test should depend on the outcome desired. The same general principles of assessment outlined Chapters 10 and 11 apply.

Project work

The inclusion of 'the project' has a long and respectable history in education. However, like many educational ideas it has many interpretations. There is variety in both practice and assessment. Very early on the need to move to performance based schemes of assessment was perceived, and such a scheme appeared in the very first issue of *Assessment and Evaluation in Higher Education* (Black, 1975; see also Prosser and Oliver, 1983). The concept of the project as it was undertaken in engineering science (see Figure 12.1) illustrates the general principles. A student is asked to plan, specify, make, test, and evaluate an artefact or an idea. An artefact might, for example, be an electronically controlled device or a computer programme. An idea might be the evaluation of a traffic scheme. In the JMB scheme the students each choose the topic, prepare a plan, detail the method of evaluation, and cost that activity. At this stage they obtain the agreement of their teachers for their project outline (see Figure 12.3). It is submitted to an external moderator acting on behalf of the board for advice and approval. When the project is completed it is rated by the teacher first and then moderated. A scheme similar to that for the experimental investigations (see Figure 11.4) is used which mirrors the categories (primary traits) in the outline (i.e. Planning; Execution; Design activity (originality); Use of resources: Critical review (evaluation or self-assessment); and, personal contribution (determination of how much is due to candidate and teacher, and others).

In some project activities the teacher chooses the project. The project may be large and extended over a long period. Equally it may be small and extended over a short period. Sometimes they play a key role in the final year of study as for example capstone projects in engineering courses in the United States. Projects are sometimes undertaken by teams. Some post-war European universities and/or institutes were structured around interdisciplinary themes, and teaching was by the project/problem method (Heywood, 1973; see Cowan, 1998 on the University of Aalborg). Extensive projects have been undertaken individually and in teams during the industrial periods of sandwich (cooperative) courses and it is not unknown for students undertaking work experience during their vacation to be given projects. Extensive fieldwork in geography and the biological sciences, and large dissertations in the humanities are the equivalent of projects but there can be 'live' activities in these subjects. Kent, Gilbertson and Hunt (1997) have reviewed fieldwork in geography and emphasized the need for debriefing and feedback. Very often projects are mini-research exercises (Heywood, 1961), carried out by the students themselves or in collaboration with their teachers Howard and Sharp, 1983).

Projects may be used to provide a scaffold for interdisciplinary study on the basis that real life projects usually require knowledge from many sources, some of which may not be within a participant's specialization. Specialists can acquire help from other specialists and it is not uncommon for information specialists to assist. For example at Napier University a librarian supported the work of a biologist. The researchers asked students to complete three projects of increasing complexity. They required detailed literature searches. The purpose of the projects was to increase the student's ability and willingness to read scientific literature. McElroy and McNaughton (1979) reported that this goal was achieved among first-year students, and that the attitudes engendered persisted throughout the course.

Carter and Lee (1981) found among first-year students of electrical engineering that while there were those who would do well as practical engineers irrespective of the teaching method used, there were those who could not do project work. But there was a large group whose performance could be improved by carefully designed strategies and experimental studies. Subsequently a degree course was developed for persons who thought they would benefit from alternative instruction based on the project method.

The literature in the education journals of professional societies contains many reports of project activities, and problems relating to their implementation have been well documented over the years. In this respect it is of interest to find that the early experience of the Open University (a distance learning institution) was similar to that experienced by others in more traditional institutions (Bynner and Henry, 1984; Henry, 1977). For example, the amount of time required by tutor and student for guidance and work was problematic. The role of the supervisor in project work was equally problematic (Cook, 1980). It was found that some Open University students also required guidance in choosing a viable topic and in identifying, locating and collecting information. In the engineering science project those students who had difficulty in choosing a topic were sometimes those who could not focus on a small area of the topic they had chosen for development (Carter, Heywood, and Kelly, 1986).

The cost and organization of individual support is also problematic (Silk and Bowlby, 1981). For some departments it can be too costly (Harris and Bullock, 1981). There is no doubt that some project work can be expensive but very substantial work can be accomplished for very little cost.

The general impression is that many students like project work, and that they are highly motivated by it (Hiles and Heywood, 1972). Garvin *et al.*(1995) reported that students liked the ownership which project work gave. They had decided what to do, how to do it and who would do it. In the JMB projects many students spent too much time on them. This created problems for both the teacher assessors and moderators. How should a first-class project that took many more hours than was suggested by the regulations be rated? How should it be compared with a project completed within the time allowed, that was not so good? In these circumstances the moderators had to rely on teacher judgements about the way resources had been used, the help received, etc. How does an assessor judge if experts in the family have assisted the student? How much of the work is the student's own work? And, so on. Some teachers were put off project work because they felt questions like this could not be answered. One reason why team projects were discounted was the difficulty of assessing the work of individual students.

In a paper which showed that the same problems continue to be faced Tariq *et al.* (1998) show how the Schools of Biology and Biomedical Science at Queen's University, Belfast moved from relatively subjective schemes to semi-criterion referenced schemes of the type used in engineering science. The paper charts the history of the innovation and the problems faced by its developers. Their rationale was due rather more to their desire to change the focus of instruction from instructor to student centred learning. They did not seek to argue that the assessment strategy under discussion was the best or only assessment format possible.

They began with a pilot survey in which a new schedule was used. This included 20 items each of which was assessed on a six-point letter grade scale. They were able to undertake a limited statistical comparison of marks between the 'old' and 'new' systems. It was found that the new assessment strategy made no significant difference to the numerical outcome, and did not, therefore influence degree marks or classifications. So why change?

Tariq and her colleagues claim that

unlike the 'old' assessment strategies the new scheme breaks down the project into a large number of clearly defined explicit criteria. In doing so, it assists staff, particularly those assessing only the thesis, to perform their assessment more objectively than was previously possible, thus helping them to clarify and justify their conclusions not only to other examiners but to their students.

In this scheme formal provision was made for feedback to the students whereas in the past feedback had been informal and dependent on the tutor. A feedback component is added to the pro forma. In the event, the School of Biology retained the A to E scaling without detailed descriptors for the 17 criteria that were agreed. The School of Biomedical Sciences used a scheme similar to that of engineering science with seven letter grades in which each grade was explained. The principal categories for the honours project were:

Comprehension of concept and aims; background information; initiatives; motivation/application; appropriateness of methods and/or experimental design; organizational skills; competence and independence; ability to problem solve.

A new pro forma was introduced for the thesis that had the following principal categories:

Literature review; handling of findings/analysis; interpretation/critical assessment of findings; depth of understanding; conclusions; appreciation of relevance of findings to subject area; organisation of material; clarity of presentation; ideas for continuation and/or modification of the project.

The similarities between this scheme and those for engineering science, history, and the academic essay and the student teacher research project described in Chapter 11 show that what these schemes do is to explicate assumptions that are commonly held throughout the academic community.

Some of the skills belong in the category of personal transferable skills. In this respect Tariq and her colleagues report that when students were asked to rate the level of importance of each of the skills and criteria they attached more importance to subject specific criteria than to a range of personal transferable skills. Are students reluctant to acknowledge these skills, or are they playing the assessment game?

All of these schemes are open to the criticisms made of the schedule that assessed the student-teacher projects described in Chapter 11. They can too easily become checklists for some students who operate in strategic learning modes, they can impose a learning regime that some students will not find conducive either to their learning or creativity, and there is a tension between strict criterion referencing and setting difficulty levels. Nevertheless, it is my experience that the improvements in student work are overwhelming especially when the tutor was providing a single subjective grading without explanation.

These schemes cannot be free of ambiguities. In the case of the engineering science students were asked to volunteer to do an experiment in the presence of their teacher and two moderators. They were assessed by the published scheme and it was found that four items caused considerable difficulty. These were revised. In a later study a sample of students were asked to give an example, from their own experience, of the type of response they thought was required to gain an affirmative answer to the particular assessment question. Their teachers were asked to indicate agreement or disagreement with the candidates' examples. This also led to changes in the scheme. It was found that the distributions of marks were reasonably spread and consistent from one year to another. Such variations as occurred did so at the top end of the scale. Consistency was found in the differences between the marks of the moderators and the teachers. The ratings of the teacher assessors were more generous than the moderators. The average difference in scores was found to be of the order 12 per cent at the top of the range and 7 per cent at the bottom for which reason a standardizing procedure was adopted (Carter, Heywood and Kelly, 1986).

It was found that the ability to formulate a problem appeared to be a crucial skill: it separated out those who would be able to do the project from those who could not. The fact that it did this consistently lent support to those like McDonald (1968) who hold the view that problem finding and problem solving are different skills. Postgraduates, it seems, also find problem-definition difficult (Zuber-Skerritt and Knight, 1986), and the type of problem is likely to influence the approach to the problem definition finally adopted. For example, engineering projects are essentially of the 'think-up' type whereas the problems faced by a doctor are of the 'find out' type. Medical problem solving may be more akin to fault-finding in engineering. The other area of difficulty that the students experienced was in completing a satisfactory critical review. It was found to be a high level skill for which training would seem to be necessary. The other feature of the evaluation arose from the correlation that was obtained from the coursework mark and the written paper on project planning where the candidate had to prepare a design specification. It was thought that since they had done this in the project they would be able to do this in the pencil and paper examination. This was found not to be the case. A low correlation was found. At first it was thought that the teachers were not showing the relevance of coursework to this particular test, and this may well have been the case. Teachers were advised of this problem. Later it was suggested that different skills were involved in the two processes as a function of the time available. In planning the project the candidate had time to function at a strategic level. In the written examination there was no time to do this, and to use Sternberg's (1985a) terminology, candidates would have to use executive processing skills which are a function of the way in which knowledge is acquired and used, i.e. they have to use different information processing techniques (Heywood, 1989a).

A major area of controversy has been the weighting that should be applied to projects. In some cases this has been surprisingly small and students have complained because the amount of work generated is not reflected in the grade awarded. Boud (1986) and his colleagues concluded that one of the reasons for this was that the reliability of assessment was perceived to be low. Boud pointed out that some of the schemes did not take content into account. It is true that there was no specific mention of content in the engineering science scheme but it was assumed that the content would have to be 'correct' if high scores were to be obtained. This debate, is of course, a re-run of the process-product debate in education and the relative importance to be attached to these dimensions of learning.

This discussion may have been be misleading in that most of the project work discussed has been in science and technology. Projects can be done in any subject. A student who is asked to write a novel undertakes a project. A dissertation is a project.

The same problems in assessment arise. A scheme used for the assessment of projects in history is shown in Figure 12.4.

Problem-based learning

Projects are a specific case of problem-based learning. This approach to learning has been developed in medicine and in particular at McMaster University in Canada, the University of Limburg in the Netherlands (the Maastricht Medical School), and the University of Newcastle in Australia. It has been the subject of considerable evaluation in these institutions (Nooman, Schmidt and Ezzat, 1990). At McMaster the problem-solving course in chemical engineering (MPS) is partly problem based. Its architect has written an introduction to it for the general reader (Woods, 1994). Woods defines problem-based learning with the aid of an illustration:

> Professor Case asks: 'Here is a toaster that isn't working, fix it! Or better still improve it.'

> Professor English begins: 'Today we're going to study the flow of electricity through metals, then we'll look at...'

Woods goes on to say:

> Both approaches use problems but for two completely different reasons. Case uses problems to drive learning. English uses problems to illustrate how to use knowledge after you have learned it.

One approach is student centred, the other is teacher centred. The former approach places great responsibility on the student to undertaken his/her own learning. In both cases there is teacher involvement, and in both cases a knowledge base is required. However, the subject-based approach of Professor English concentrates on building up the base using problems to illustrate principles, whereas the approach of Professor Case is to develop the knowledge base by solving a range of problems. It is argued that its advantage is that it helps the learner comprehend new material far better than subject-based learning. Put in another way, the learner can claim ownership of the learning more readily, and this is much more likely to be the case when the Professor gives a problem area and leaves the students to find and define problems.

It has the advantage that it can provide a framework for interdisciplinary studies and thinking since the solutions to many of life's problems require data from many knowledge areas. Within the traditional disciplines problem-based learning is likely to trespass across the boundaries of the subjects which make up the programme, and it may be deliberately designed so to do by constructing the curriculum around themes. Indeed the approach at McMaster and other medical schools has been to organize it in a multidisciplinary, thematic and integrated way (Barrows, 1985). Whichever approach is used, teachers have to change their roles and lose some of their authority.

> Preparing teaching materials, teaching students, and assessing educational progress, usually done by one person, become the responsibility of a team of faculty members appointed for each unit of subject matter. Because one of the main objectives of problem-based learning is to increase students' autonomy and control over their own learning processes, teachers are not expected to continuously direct and

control students with respect to what they have to study and how. (Moust, De Grave and Gijselaers, 1990).

Gijselaers and Schmidt (1990) describe the system at Maastricht thus:

> Students meet twice a week in a tutorial group (consisting of 8 to 10 students) to discuss and analyse medical problems. The task set before the group is to analyse the problems, detect deficiencies in their knowledge, and consequently formulate learning goals and intended study activities. The tutorial group is guided by a staff member, whose task is to facilitate the learning process and stimulate optional functioning of the group. The problems are collected in a so called block-book. This book is a guide to the student's learning activities. A block is a period of six weeks devoted to and organized around specific medical themes such as traumata, pain in the chest, or cancer.

Problem-based learning can he highly motivational. Norman and Schmidt (1992), who reviewed studies which had compared problem-based learning with conventional curricula, concluded that students on problem-based learning courses found them more stimulating than students on conventional courses. Such courses can foster self-directed learning, increase retention of knowledge and create interest in clinical subject matter. Schwartz *et al.* (1997), reporting on the experience of problem-based learning in medicine at the University of Kentucky, found that PBL students performed significantly better in examinations designed to test the clinical application of knowledge. They also learnt important time management skills.

Patel and Kaufman (1995) examined the role of basic science knowledge in the clinical curriculum. They examined how medical students use basic science in both conventional and problem-based learning. They found that although basic science and clinical knowledge are 'spontaneously' integrated, the basic science 'is so tightly tied to the clinical experience that students appear to be unable to detach basic science even when the clinical situations demand it'. There was no transfer of learning between the two. They found the elaborations that students made when they were called on to 'think' about problem features using basic science led to a fragmentation of knowledge structures. These elaborations led to factual errors which, as with Clement's engineering students (Chapter 9), persisted from first to fourth year. From the reasoning, that well-organized coherent information is easier to remember than disjointed facts, and because the purpose of science is to make it possible to organize observations, Patel and Kaufman argue, that some core basic sciences should be taught at the beginning of the curriculum outside of problem-based learning (see McKenzie, 1995 below).

In a biomedical science degree not associated with a medical school, Shelton and Smith (1998) report that first-year students who experienced a problem-based course designed to teach analytical science and laboratory practice were very positive about the practical applications of PBL. They also felt they related theory to practice. However, they were negative about taking responsibility for their own learning and examination notes. This meant that as the examination drew near the students began to worry that they had not collected sufficient facts. The data suggested to Shelton and Smith that some students grasp subject material by PBL easily but others find it difficult. The success of group work was undermined by the need to perform as individuals in the examination. The great majority thought that PBL made the examination harder. Shelton and Smith argue that a component of PBL should be retained because there was 'immeasurable progress in developing transferable skills'. They also observed gains in confidence. In the future they intend to include a problem-based element in the examination. Taken together these investigations suggest a multiple-strategy approach to both assessment and instruction, in which the associated objectives are made clear to students.

Several investigators draw attention to the difficulties which students have in adjusting to student centred learning from teacher centred instruction (McKenzie, 1995; Thompson, 1990; Woods, 1994). Woods uses a model of bereavement to show how students can be helped to accommodate change. At La Trobe University in Australia the orthoptics programme is varied over its three years. It proceeds from a more teacher directed course to a more student centred course and is designed to foster the development of inquiry skills (McKenzie, 1995). This progression is intended to enable students to slip into problem-based learning and reduces the fears which students have to non-conventional approaches to teaching. Duke *et al.* (1998), also at La Trobe, found that nursing students had unsophisticated conceptions of and approaches to learning which were not linked to professional practice outcomes. However, by the time they completed their last PBL they had come to recognize the 'link between participation in the process and the development of knowledge and skills for professional practice'.

Although Woods *et al.* (1997) set out to develop problem-solving skills alongside a conventional engineering programme their model shows how conventional courses could be reorganized to include a component of problem-based learning. The problem-based component in their course is limited when compared with the engineering programme at Aalborg University in Denmark (Cowan, 1989; Kjersdam and Enemark, 1994), or the medical school in their own university.

Woods found that while his colleagues used many techniques to develop problem-solving skills (e.g. open-ended problems, working backwards from the goal, students showing how they worked out problems) students could not solve problems when the conditions were changed slightly. Like students in high school they continued to rely on sample solutions. Woods and his colleagues concluded from their investigations that there is a subject-independent skill of problem solving which they defined as 'the process used to obtain the best answer to an unknown, or a decision subject to some constraints'. They believed workshops to develop this skill had potential. Altogether, they identified '37 separate skills; 4 related to self-management; 14 related to problem solving skills for well defined ordinary homework; 5 for solving ill-defined problems; 7 for interpersonal and group skills; 2 skills for self assessment; one for change management; and 4 lifelong learning skills.' These skills are both cognitive and attitudinal, and they overlap.

To achieve development in these skills they developed some 57 units each ranging from 1–24 hrs (e.g. *what is problem solving?* 1 hr; *asking questions*, 4–8 hrs; *coping with ambiguity*, 10–15 hrs). There were 18 units available for a 48-contact-hour course in the second year to develop individual skill in solving traditional homework problems.

Which units are selected depend on student needs. In the third year a course in the first semester gives practice in applying these skills. In the second semester a course focuses on the development of inter-personal skills, lifelong learning and team problem solving for open-ended systems and people. In the fourth year the focus continues in the same vein but for ill-defined and open-ended technical and inter-personal problems.

The programme was established in 1982 and has been the subject of continuous evaluation. The McMaster Problem Solving course (MPS) and the evaluations are summarized in detail in Woods *et al.* (1997). There is some indication that suggests that participation in MPS improved marks obtained in another course. The Course Perception Questionnaire produced a significantly higher rating than that for a control group in another engineering department. The MPS programme was found to increase the students' confidence in problem-solving skills when compared with a control group.

In order to test students' skill in problem solving they devised questions that would enable students to display the processes they used to solve problems in chemical engineering. One of their examples is shown in Figure 12.5. It derives from the objectives listed in Figure 12.6. It is evident that such activities are subject- independent and that assessment activities can be devised as a function of the subject studied. If a skill is independent then a goal of higher education would be achieved if it were tested in unseen unrelated circumstances requiring the application of problem-solving skills.

They also made evaluations of attitude and skill toward lifelong learning, alumni recruiter and response, and faculty and student acceptance. Of importance to assessment in higher education is the emphasis that they placed on self-assessment. They found that the outcomes from the MPS programme were better than those reported elsewhere. 'About 78% of our students' self assessment marks are within +/- 5% of the benchmarks, with 9% underestimated and 13% overestimated relative to the benchmarks.' The issue of self- assessment is taken up in Chapter 14. The approach adopted by Woods *et al.* (1997) illustrates, once again, the value of a multiple-strategy approach to the assessment of student learning and evaluation.

In a study which used the Course Experience Questionnaire to evaluate occupational therapy students' attitudes to their courses Sadlo (1997) obtained data from students on traditional, problem- based and hybrid courses. He found that the enhancement of learning was directly related to the extent to which the philosophy of problem-based learning was implemented. However, because students reported a lack of clarity in the objectives, he was led to ask the question – 'Who really generated the objectives of the PBL course?'

The design of problem-based learning is complex and it should not be undertaken lightly. For example, it has been shown that the experience of problem-based learning with small groups in continuing education may not be enhanced if the experience is too short. In one day formats interventions may be inadequate, discussion unfocused, and there may not be time for the group to cohere (Davis, Lindsay and Maxmanian, 1994).

For the troubleshooting problem given (in Figure 1, *not reproduced here*):

(a) brainstorm 50 possible causes and write these down in ten minutes. (10 min).

(b) analyse your list, note the basis of classification, and divide your ideas into at least seven different categories. (13 min).

(c) Select four technically feasible ideas. (2 min).

(d) Select the 'craziest idea' and write about your thought processes as you use this idea as a trigger or a stepping stone to obtain a 'new' technically feasible idea. (15 min).

Figure 12.5 Example of an assessment task in the McMaster Problem Solving Program in Engineering relating to Creativity, Classification and Awareness (Woods et al., 1997).

Given a term listed under 'concepts introduced' you should be able to give a word definition, list pertinent characteristics and cite an example. You will be able to describe d-lines, the limitations of short-term memory, and rationalize the processes and procedures used in brainstorming.

Given an object or a situation, as an individual you will be able to generate at least 50 uses, attributes, or ideas in 5 minutes.

Given an object or a situation, as an individual you will be able to generate at least 50 ideas in five minutes (or write out 50 ideas in ten minutes) and the ideas will belong to at least 7 different categories and a group of three independent judges shall identify one idea that is 'unique'.

Given a crazy idea, you will be able to describe your mental processes used to convert that idea into a technically feasible idea by using the triggered idea as a 'stepping stone'.

You will be able to describe your preferred style of brainstorming and your preferred use of triggers.

Figure 12.6 Six of the ten learning objectives for the McMaster Problem Solving unit on Creativity as they relate to the assessment task shown in exhibit 69.(Woods et al., 1997).

In so far as the assessment of student learning in problem-based learning is concerned, a variety of strategies are likely to have to be used if all the goals of problem-based learning are to be realized. At Southern Illinois University (Springfield) some students expressed unease, 'because assessment of their own performance had become more difficult. General criticism was expressed of those departments that had attempted to provide teaching in a problem based way but used only factual recall for assessment' (Thompson, 1990). Vu and Black (1997) found that problem analysis questions were difficult to design. Only a third of their questions in the first year and 17 per cent in the second year of clinical practice were judged by students to be at the appropriate taxonomic level. They also found in another study that students with a higher mean performance in their examinations judged fewer of the questions to be at the levels of comprehension and memory than did those students who had a lower mean performance.

Learning journals

Learning journals provide opportunities for students to reflect on their learning processes during the course. Cowan (1998) has described how he has used them to develop this capability (see Chapter 14). In Australia McCrindle and Christensen (1995) conducted an investigation of their efficacy with first-year students of biology. Their students were randomly assigned to either a scientific report group (control) or a learning journal group (experimental). It was found that during learning tasks those who completed the learning journals employed more meta-cognitive strategies and more sophisticated cognitive strategies. They performed significantly better in the final examination of the course. In another study at Hong Kong Polytechnic University Kember *et al.* (1996) found among students in allied health areas that students needed an introduction to reflective writing, as well as feedback, as it differed from other kinds of writing on the course. Training would seem to be required when students perceive new methods of assessment to be a radically different from the 'familiar'. A progamme of instructions based on students' considered needs has been developed by Beveridge (1997) at the University of Luton.

FitzGibbon (1994) used a development of the Myers Briggs Indicator by Kiersey and Bates (1984) to see if there was a relationship between personality type and attitudes to an exercise designed to help graduate student teachers develop skill in self-knowledge, and awareness by the completion of a journal. The journal was to include the following components:

- an educational autobiography
- reports of a minimum of three observations of experienced teachers teaching, usually in the practice school
- 'space diagrams' (described below) for some taught classes and for the staff of the practice school
- a description of the practice school
- analyses of significant events

- a sociometric map of one class
- a personal construct exercise (optional)
- a reflection on each term, and on the year.

She found that the NT's (intuitive personality types) did not find the autobiography useful as an aid to their development as a teacher. She suggests that either they thought the exercise was too subjective or that it was insufficiently theoretical. It also accounts for the fact that nearly 50 per cent of them found the observations very useful. On reflective thinking the SJ's (sensing personality types) found the reflections useful. However, it did indicate a relationship between personality, learning style and preferred activities and supports, therefore, an approach suggested by Silver and Hanson (1995) in their design for teaching and learning was adopted (see Chapter 8).

It is also a reminder that student evaluations of courses need to take into account the learning styles and personality characteristics of their pupils. The purpose of the journal was not only to help the students develop skills in reflective thinking and self-awareness but to be aware of their teaching styles (as 74 per cent were) and not to make a decision about matching teaching to learning skills on the basis of experience alone. That is why teacher-training courses need to ensure that student teachers have the opportunity to consider a range of models and to evaluate classes designed on the basis of one or another learning styles models.

Portfolio assessment

Portfolios have long been used in art and architecture to assess student performance. They are being used increasingly in teacher education (e.g. NBPTS), and outcome-based standards have been produced (NASDEC, 1994). Their use in other higher education subjects (e.g. English, engineering, medicine) has also been reported. In the United States the Office of Educational Research and Improvement (OERI, 1993) reported that at school level portfolios are being used for 'accountability reporting, program evaluations, and for a variety of administrative decisions affecting the future of individual students'. (Moss *et al.*, 1992). Also in the United States and Canada (Centra, 1994) university teachers have been encouraged to keep portfolios of their work for purposes of promotion, and the American Association for Higher Education initiated an extensive programme on their use and published case studies (Edgerton, Hutchings and Quinlan, 1991; Seldin and associates, 1993). Portfolios became the main vehicle for assessment in the system of national vocational education (NVQ) in the UK. They also had an important role to play in records of achievement.

A profile approach to the assessment of portfolios is almost dictated by the need for reliabilty and validity (e.g. Storms *et al.*, 1998) except where the stakes are low or a different view is taken of reliability. One of the problems is to provide assessment systems that ensure that attention is paid to instructional and learning quality as well as to psychometric integrity (LeMahieu, Gitomer and Eresh, 1995).

A review of developments in portfolios and records of achievement will be found in issue 3, volume 5 (1998) of *Assessment in Education: Principles, Policy and Practice*. It is solely devoted to this topic. Unfortunately, apart from a paper on NVQs, these reviews are mainly concerned with school education although it will be shown that many lessons can be learned from that experience. An earlier review of portfolio development and adult learning that is of equal interest was edited by Mandell and Michelson (1990).

The concept is not a unitary one and portfolios appear in many guises. For example, a report of a substantial project in science or technology, as was the case in engineering science, might be regarded as a portfolio. In Canadian higher education the portfolio is often understood as the summary statement that fronts a collection of evidence. They also seem to serve a variety of purposes and Wolf (1998) has made the point that they might serve different purposes at the different levels of education (i.e. elementary, secondary and higher).

Apart from the research which has been done on the reliability and validity of NVQs (see Chapter 11), and a few isolated papers, little is known about the advantages and disadvantages of portfolios in higher education. Most research has been done at school level, more especially in the United States. Both of the major testing agencies ACT (Colton *et al.*, 1997) and ETS (Storms *et al.*,1998) have developed portfolio systems. In the States of Kentucky and Vermont portfolios are a compulsory part of school education and they have been subject to much scrutiny as has the Pittsburgh writing scheme. From these investigations we learn that concepts of portfolio and portfolio assessment are nebulous, and that there are variations in purposes and procedures. However, Stecher (1998) reports that the large-scale applications share some common features:

> They contain the diverse products of students' learning experience, including written materials (both draft and final versions), pictures, graphs, computer programmes, and other outcomes of students' work. Portfolios are usually cumulative. They contain work completed over periods of weeks or months. Portfolios are embedded in instruction, i.e. entries are drawn from on-going schoolwork. As a result portfolios are not standardised. Since assignments differ across teachers, so do collections of students' work. Moreover, within a single class students will choose different pieces to include in their portfolios. Portfolios also have a reflective component – either implicit in a letter to the reviewer or explaining the selection of materials. Finally, there is an external framework for scoring portfolios and the framework is general enough to apply to portfolios that contain different contents.(Stecher, 1998)

This was very much the situation that applied to the assessment of the engineering science coursework referred to above. Each report contained details of the students' chosen work. Primary trait analysis was the basis of the assessment. Novak, Herman and Gearhart (1996) found that different rubrics used for scoring writing portfolios had different effects on teachers' understanding of narrative and their methods of instruction. In one engineering course in the US, the tutor marked the one or two page reflective component which accompanied the portfolio and not the portfolio itself, an action which might be regarded as unfair by some students unless emphasis on the process was made clear (reported in a Conference discussion). As might be expected, portfolios are now being recorded on disc even at the elementary level (e.g. Clovis and others in issue No. 3, of volume 55 of *Educational Leadership* (1997) which is devoted to integrating technology into teaching).

The advocates of portfolios and other forms of alternative assessment hoped they would reduce score inflation and the curriculum narrowing associated with multiple-choice tests. Portfolios are seen as as a means of bringing changes in instructional practice toward a more student-centred form of instruction. As yet they have not been aligned with curriculum framework, explicit standards or content. Stecher (1998) reports that:

> The portfolio assessments and their associated scoring rubrics were more clearly defined than the existing curriculum. As a result, teachers attended to the outcomes explicit in the scoring rubrics rather than the broader domains of performance they were supposed to represent. This situation has been referred to as 'rubric driven' instruction.

One study, however, at elementary level found that neither the scale nor rating process replaced teachers' observations and reliance on portfolio documents as the primary form of evidence about student learning (Jones and Chittenden, 1995).

Teachers believe that if the students' performance is shown to have improved, then the new level of performance may be sustained. They also believe portfolios would provide more meaningful information about student performance that would help teachers monitor students and communicate with parents. However, like all course-work, one of the problems which has had to be faced is the extent to which the portfolio is a product of the student's own work. Gearhart *et al.* (1993) commenting on elementary teachers' portfolio assessments concluded that the 'quality of work appeared to be a function of substantial and uncontrolled support as well as student competence. While this is not a grave concern for classroom assessment where teachers can judge performance with knowledge of their context, the problem is troubling indeed for large-scale assessment purposes where comparability of data is an issue.' In the engineering science coursework it was hoped this would be overcome by teacher comments on the extent of help given. Trust was placed in the teachers; even so it could have been abused. In the British higher education system, the same would pertain. An external examiner would find it very difficult to judge the extent of help received unless the report resulted from group work that had been peer-assessed.

In higher education Renee Betz (private communication) draws attention to the fact that the type of entry depends on the purpose of the portfolio. For English she distinguishes between a *showcase* portfolio and a *developmental or growth* portfolio. With relation to self-assessment in the former she asks, 'How can one encourage students to decide what is their own best work, regardless of outside evaluation? And how can we know what criteria a major is using in deciding what is the best work?' In contrast the growth portfolio places the responsibility for selection on the students and necessarily encourages self-assessment. Choices have to be more thoughtful. In her approach to portfolios Betz suggests that reflective pieces should form a major part of the contents.

In engineering Ashworth *et al.* (1995) describe how a portfolio was embedded in an integrated engineering degree course at Sheffield Hallam University: 25 per cent of the final degree mark would be allocated for the presentation of a professional and personal portfolio in the final year of the programme that would provide evidence of performance in the role of a potential professional engineer. The students were encouraged to collect evidence from the beginning of their course which included a one-year placement in industry. In the first two years the students were provided with a Professional and Personal Development programme. An evaluation by two members of the course team, and two independent researchers focused on issues that a questionnaire survey would not have captured. It used an in-depth interview technique together with a group interview with a small number of students who were self-selected. Faculty views were also obtained. The investigators concluded that the two aims of the portfolio process, to assist significantly the development of professional and personal capabilities, and to integrate work-based learning into the degree had been met. The portfolio was found to encourage self-reflection. From being a task to be fulfilled, the students gained a strong feeling of ownership and relevance, and became emotionally committed to it.

There are a number of intrinsic dilemmas which won't go away; for example, the tension between the personal nature of the portfolio and the need for teachers to apply impersonal assessment criteria. Ashworth *et al.* (1995) argue that that although there are difficulties with summative assessment the disadvantages are far outweighed by the advantages as helping the development of personal and professional capabilities. They note that because the technique is resource intensive it works better with small groups of students. So long as formal examinations remain, they believe that it is unlikely there will be a large-scale implementation of portfolios.

In medicine at University College Cardiff portfolios have been used for some time. All students entering clinical studies were randomized into either a study or control group. Both groups followed the normal curriculum Each study group followed a patient with cancer for nine months, supported by bi-monthly small group tutorials. During this time a portfolio was kept in which students recorded 'triggers' to learning and other key items. This portfolio could be submitted for formative evaluation. In the Objective Structured Clinical Examination (see Chapter 13) it was found that the students in the study group gained higher factual knowledge of oncology and this was significant among the weaker students. Those submitting portfolios for formative assessment had higher overall marks than those in the study group who did not. Finlay, Maughan and Webster (1998) suggest that these students were more motivated

Naizer (1997) undertook a study of the reliability and validity of portfolio assessment of student teachers. He asked the following questions:

- Are performance portfolio scores consistent among course instructors and student-peer raters?

- Can a set of established strategic knowledge measures, the number of education courses taken, and total hours of prior teaching experience be used to confirm concurrent validity of performance-portfolio scores?

- Do traditional measures (short/answer/discussion final examination) correlate with performance-portfolio scores?

The subjects of the study were 35 senior-year female students who had completed an elementary teacher preparation programme. The specific course for which the portfolios were prepared was a team-taught problem-based integrated mathematics/science methods course. Four portfolios related to four problems were required for the experiment. They were scored independently by instructors and a group of students who, for the purpose of the exercise were taken to be the third rater. In response to the first question it was found that rater variance was a very small percentage of the total variance. With respect to the second question it was found that 69 per cent of the group were classified correctly, suggesting that the portfolio had reasonable concurrent validity. In response to the third question it was found that the correlation between the final examination and portfolio scores was very low. Naizer assumes they were measuring different qualities. The performance portfolios provided evidence of the pre-service teachers' abilities to plan, design, execute and assess lessons, along with reflection on their performance and the results of their instruction. In respect of the reports of my students on their classroom research Naizer argues that they are a valid way of assessing the desired abilities of teachers even though his validation results cannot be applied to other systems. In this regard the reports of my students on their classroom research (Chapter 11) were equally valid.

Both the main testing agencies in the United States have sought to develop portfolio systems and both agree that that they can augment existing assessment practices (Colton *et al.*, 1997; Storms *et al.*, 1998). ACT have developed the PASSPORT (Portfolio Assessment System in Language Arts, Science, and Mathematics). The findings of their research are relevant to developments in higher education.

ACT claim that the system is unique because it allows teachers and students to develop the portfolio. Its purpose is to augment existing assessments, improve instruction, and complement ongoing classroom activities. Teachers dialogue with students to agree goals and choose five work sample descriptions from the 10 or 11 provided for each subject by ACT. Both students and teachers are provided within an information sheet in each subject which takes the student through the portfolio process in a particular work sample description The students work with the teacher to select their five best samples for the portfolio. The portfolio and associated materials are sent to ACT for scoring. The procedures differ from the engineering science approach only in so far as the teacher in that approach was involved in the assessment as the first rater. Welch and Martinovich-Barhite (1997) in Colton *et al.* (1997) concluded that the successful implementation of a portfolio assessment system must include a refined set of rubrics that have been field-tested and piloted. The reliabilty of the results can be increased by the systematic exposure of the scoring rubric and assignments to the participating teachers. As with engineering science the students must be able to understand the rubric and the tie between the example of work selected and the scoring process.

> In a large-scale assessment environment there must be some constraints placed on the type of assignments and selection of student work to enhance the ability to evaluate the work reliably. A system that allows for student selection without these guidelines and constraints will lead to results that are generalizable beyond the specific assignment.

LeMahieu, Gitomer and Eresh (1995) undertook an evaluation of the Pittsburgh Writing Scheme. In this scheme the portfolios were scored by two raters on each of three dimensions. These were accomplishment in writing, use of processes and strategies for writing, and growth development and engagement as a writer. They found that judgement consistency was greater than that found in other large-scale assessment, and they regarded that as a promising result. They considered that in addition to reasonable structuring and scoring, four additional criteria must be in place.

> First, the purposes of assessment must be clear and the practices must be consistent with the goal... Second, there must be a shared interpretive framework within the community conducting and using the assessment. This shared understanding is achieved through a hermeneutic approach, and when carried out in a disciplined way can satisfy psychometric concerns as well. Third there must be coherence in the system, so that accountabilty goals are consistent with classroom goals... Fourth and finally, the development of this portfolio-based instructional and assessment system was dominated throughout by conversations designed to address issues of quality in both instructional and psychometric terms.

And much the same can be said about all approaches to assessment with the proviso that the designers take into account the benefit costs that accrue to learners in low stakes formative learning, and high stakes summative assessment. Grading portfolios is problematic and highly expensive in time.

Cheating and plagiarism

Cheating in classroom tests is alive and well so is plagiarism in coursework. Portfolios are open to plagiarism, and the advent of electronic assessment of coursework may make plagiarism more accessible. Most of the studies on cheating have been done in North America.

In Canada it was found that 83 per cent of the respondents to a self-report inventory had cheated in college. The two most common types of cheating were being given and getting examination questions (Genereux and McLeod, 1995).

In the United States one ten-year follow-up study reported that over a ten-year period (1984 to 1994), there had been an increase in the number of students saying they had cheated (54% to 61%). It was found that compared to non-cheaters, the cheaters are less mature, less reactive to observed cheating, less deterred by social stigma and guilt, less personally invested in their education and, more likely to be receiving scholarships, and not doing so well in their studies (Diekhoff *et al.*, 1996). The strongest deterrents were the embarrassment of being found out, and the fear of punishment.

In Britain Franklyn-Stokes and Newstead (1995) undertook two investigations in different institutions and found that 60 per cent of the students admitted to copying each other's work, plagiarism, and altering and inventing research data. Because the data from the two studies were so similar they claimed that they probably gave a realistic picture of the occurrence of cheating. They did not find any significant difference between male and female students. The principal reasons for cheating were the pressure of time and the desire to increase marks. They found that the most common reasons for not cheating were that it was unnecessary, and that it would be dishonest. This is in contrast to the American finding where fear played an important role in deterrence.

Ryan (1998) helped to teach an 'information security concepts' course for George Washington University. She was surprised when many of the papers that were returned (electronically) were so good. However, on close inspection she considered them to be so good that the students could not have done them. She searched the Internet using an Alta Vista Search engine to conduct a search for specific phrases (or strings) in one paper. She found an on-line journal article that corresponded exactly to the original. There were five substitutions of words. Having discovered this plagiarism she checked every other paper and found that seven out of 42 students had plagiarised almost all of their papers. The same thing happened in the following year. She reported that students try to camouflage the original by changing the context: they skip footnotes altogether and give false references. Her great concern was that these activities took place in the context of a course focused on the value and protection of information and copyright law among other relevant matters. Yet when faced with this students did not show any remorse. One responded: 'You can't do this to me – I'm on a scholarship!'

At Sheffield Hallam University a study of student attitudes to plagiarism revealed that the students were very unclear as to what plagiarism is. It also suggested that when students are alienated from the university through lack of contact, when they are in large classes and when they work in groups some students facilitate cheating and some may excuse cheating (Ashworth, Bannister and Thorne, 1997). Newton (1996) who suggested some ideas for helping students with their work takes the view that weak essay writing is part of the problem:

> Many of the students I spoke with were distressed when I pointed out they had to acknowledge their sources. A common puzzled response is: 'but my entire essay would all be quotations or paraphrases? Nothing comes from me.' These students are very frustrated because they know, on the one hand, they must do research, but on the other hand they have been asked to develop a thesis and an argument. They are often capable of the former but terrified of the latter. I am convinced that many students lacking confidence and the skills to develop their own analysis or argument, deliberately retreat to plagiarism in the desperate and naïve belief that other people's ideas will be mistaken for their own argument.

Diekhoff *et al.* (1996) end their paper with a quote from Welsh (1993) thus:

> Student academic dishonesty exists in a broader social and educational context which included accusations of faculty plagiarism, administrative misuse of institutional and government funds, insider trading, and accusations of plagiarism and other forms of dishonesty by national leaders.

They conclude, 'Academic dishonesty is only a reflection of the normative patterns of the society in which it occurs.'

Perhaps the last word should be left to the Irish Revenue Commissioners who give relief to creative novelists but not to academic book writers. Their work is regarded as plagiarism. Is it possible for the academic community, like the tax collectors who do something about missing taxes, to take steps to minimize cheating?

Chapter 13

Structured Questions and Objective Tests

Structured questions

Short-answer questions

The 'phrase' short answer has many meanings. Generally it describes a question for which the answer is no more than two or three lines. Sometimes the total problem is set in such a way that a series of short answers are generated. This technique is commonly employed in comprehension exercises, where the candidates have to read an article during the examination and answer specific questions relating to their understanding of it. Sometimes, in England, 'short-answer' is related to problem-solving exercises that are intended to be completed in 10–15 minutes. The 'short-answer' definition in this case derives from a comparison with long essay or problem-solving activities that may take between 30 and 60 minutes to complete.

Short-answer questions should have greater reliability than essays, although this may not be true if a simple grading system is used (for example, A, B and C). An investigation by Mowbray and Davies (1967) suggests that greater reliability in marking short-note answers is at the expense of examiners' time, which they suggest demands more concentration. Wakeford and Roberts (1984) found that while markers can agree about the rank order of candidates, consistent idiosyncratic behaviour leads to odd pass/fail and pass/distinction decisions.

The modified essay question

The *modified essay question* (MEQ) was developed in medicine to test clinical problem solving. The *sequential management problem* (SMP) is a similar device (Newble, van der Vleuten and Norman, 1995). Knox (1975) wrote of the MEQ that:

> In the developing situation of a given case, questions can be devised to explore, among other things, perceptions of salient factors influencing decision making and attitudes thereby demonstrating the candidate's stated behaviour in relation to his daily professional work. It is thus possible for a candidate to indicate not only the *outcome* in terms of his stated actions that he might take, but also some of the thought *processes* leading to these actions.

Freeman and Byrne (1976) show part of one of their questions to illustrate the technique. It begins:

> In 1957 Mrs A, a slightly built woman aged 32 with two girls (aged three and six), moved into your area and registered with your practice. She told you that as a child

she had (a) rheumatism, (b) valvular disease of the heart (no adequate records are available).

(1)   What further questions would you have put to the patient to elaborate these two facts?

(2)   You learn that the valvular disease may have occurred at five years old and she had raised blood pressure with both her pregnancies. She has reported because she is about to have a dental anaesthetic for the removal of ten teeth and is afraid she might still have raised blood pressure.

On examination you find pulse regular at 90, BP 150/90, a slight displacement of the apex beat to the left. One feature of the ausculation of the heart suggested she might have mitral stenosis. List three sounds you might have heard that would suggest this diagnosis … etc.

Subsequent items go on to evaluate other aspects of skill in patient management such as aftercare. occupational advice, etc.

Knox suggests that the best approach to the design of an MEQ is for the assessor to draw up an example which tests both content and skills. A matrix of the kind shown in Table 13.1 might be used. He also suggests that the draft question be circulated among a group of experienced professionals who would be asked to answer the questions. In this way a bank of responses is built up. When this is done the group should meet to determine the acceptable and unacceptable responses. Marks can then be allocated. There is no need for each sub-question to carry the same number of marks. Nowdays it is common practice to show the total number of possible marks on the printed paper.

Table 13.1. Matrix scheme for the design of modified essay questions (simplified from Knox, 1975).

Subject area	Abilities exercised				
	Recall	Formulation of hypothesis	Plan formation	Synthesis	Totals
1					
2					
3					
4					
Totals					

The advantages claimed for MEQs are that they avoid the cueing inherent in multiple-choice questions that are widely used in medicine. They can also provide an element of reality, and scores can be weighted if, for example, when answer Z is dependent on answer Y. Although MEQs would appear to focus on diagnosis little is known about what they test, yet they would seem to have reasonable face validity (Feletti, 1980; Neufeld and Norman, 1985). They also appear to have reasonable reliability. Fabb and Marshall (1983) reported that experienced doctors do better than trainees when answering MEQs and that sometimes one question is a better predictor of performance than others. At Belfast it was discovered that women did better than men in the MEQ but that it had poor correlations with other parts of the exam.

Freeman *et al.* (1982) who gave pre- and post-test multiple-choice questions and MEQs to trainee graduate practitioners, found an increase in performance on both measures. The performance on the MEQ was greater. They also showed that among practitioners that experience of the MEQ was likely to influence performance positively. They expressed concern that, in spite of revision of the questions, the examinees obtained an undue percentage of marks in terms of their attitudes toward patient management rather than from fundamental problem-solving skills. If such skills are related to certain attitudes and qualities of mind then the problem is acute. They report that, whereas the marks tended to be rather high on the pre-entry test, there was a fairly good overall scatter of scores. To offset a tendency toward high marks it was suggested that a greater degree of weighting was necessary at the lower end of the marking scale. In spite of these difficulties the MEQ seemed to be perfectly effective for measuring change in trainee performance during the course.

One of the criticisms levelled against the MEQ is that no chance is given to candidates to demonstrate individual approaches to hypothesis formation because the scheme is based on a consensus among the panel members who designed the question. Nevertheless, the same critics claim that the MEQ can be used as an aid to learning, and as a self-audit service when used in the study of cases. They can be used as aids to group discussion, to illustrate topics prior to a lecture, and diagnose student weaknesses (Feletti, 1980).

If the focus is on diagnosis and problem solving within diagnosis than there were would seem to be no reason why they should not be used in other scientific and technological subjects to simulate reality. Freeman advises that the MEQ is better used where there is a possibility of several sensible and considered alternatives, and that a number of such questions are essential if the technique is to be valid.

Structured Essay Examinations (SEQ)

In India Verma, Chhatwal and Singh (1997) carried out a comparative study between a traditional essay examination in which the candidates were expected to answer five equally weighted questions, and an examination in which the same questions were put in a structured format. 'These components were framed into questions requiring the student to provide a definite answer with minimal ambiguity. Differential weighting was given to questions depending on the length of the expected answer.' Teachers who were not involved in the study helped structure the questions. Sixty-two final year medical students were divided into two equal groups using odd and equal numbers. Seven teachers of paediatrics, five from one university and two from another evaluated the papers without the help of marking schemes, model answers or other guide line. It was found that the internal consistency for the traditional paper was 0.37, and for SEQ 0.69 (both at the 0.05 level of significance). The mean marks obtained by both groups were 30 +/- 8.4 and 36+/- 8.4. Verma and his colleagues were led to suggest that the traditional examination put the candidates at a disadvantage. They noted that it was possible that some element of artificiality could have been introduced into the results because the examiners would have known that their work was going to be subject to scrutiny.

Verma *et al.* also point out that the two forms of examination do not test knowledge in the same way. The traditional examination may have tapped analysis and synthesis whereas the SEQ was more likely to have tested facts. They suggest it would, in a future replication, be important to design the questions to meet the higher order categories of the *Taxonomy of Educational Objectives*. This might, of course, lead to an MEQ type structure. This illustrates the point that changing a technique of assessment is likely to produce different outcomes.

In engineering technology, structured problem solving questions designed so that they could be computer-assessed were evaluated in a controlled comparison with traditional examinations at Coventry University. The students found the method acceptable and the investigators report no loss in validity (Lloyd, Martin and McCaffery, 1996).

Objective tests

An objective test is one in which the testee selects one answer from a number of alternatives that are either correct or incorrect. In Britain they are commonly called multiple-choice tests and given the letters MCQ. These tests have been used for a major part of this century in the United States, and not just in schools. They are in everyday use in higher education both for classroom quizzes and tests that contribute to a student's Grade-Point-Average. Probably the best-known tests are the Scholastic Aptitude Test (SAT) of the Educational Testing Service and the ACT of the American College Testing Program. They are important criteria in admissions to many US institutions of higher education. It is relative changes in the averages of these tests that are sometimes used by politicians to evaluate the performance of American education. That the SAT is so highly valued for admissions is illustrated by an investigation by Bridgman (1991) who found that the predictive capacity of a short, holistically scored expository essay added nothing to that which could be predicted from scholastic aptitude test score, a multiple choice test of writing skills or high school grade point average in samples of incoming students entering both state and selective colleges. However, they have not been without their critics (e.g. Hoffman, 1982) and they have had considerable success as the movement toward authentic and performance based testing indicates. The two-volume report of the National Research Council on ability testing discusses many of the issues associated with their use (Wigdor and Garner, 1982).

Within higher education such tests are given as quizzes in class, and used to determine class grade point averages. They come in many forms ranging from the MCQ to true/false. They are not always used with the psychometric precision that might be thought desirable. Entry to graduate school and various other kinds of further study is often conditional on passing a national standardized test, as for example, the Graduate Record Examination. Like the SAT and ACT, these have also been used to study the performance of American education over time (Adelman, 1983, 1994, 1998; Morgan, 1990). The Graduate Standards Project (1997) in the UK recommended that the role of these graduate examinations should be evaluated after they heard from some of the witnesses that they would like to see such tests introduced.

Many teachers of professional subjects outside of the United States use objective tests in their courses and a small body of experience is to be found in the literature in science and technology subjects. However, by far the most extensive use of objective tests on a worldwide basis is to be found in medicine and its ancillary professions. There has been much concern with the predictive value of examinations in medicine and while the traditional essay has been abandoned the objective test format has been retained. At the same time there has been a drive to develop assessment procedures which have the potential to predict subsequent performance (McGuire, 1993). The retention of the objective format in medicine is a reminder of the importance of knowledge and the need for general practitioners (and indeed all those engaged in medicine) to be able to recall a wide range of knowledge at relatively short notice. For this reason the objective examinations they take are very substantial indeed. Case and Swanson (1993) describe the examination of the American Board of Orthopaedic Surgery thus:

> The six hour examination included 277 multiple choice questions (MCQs). The examination assessed examinees' application of knowledge through the use of clinical vignettes combined with more than 150 radiographs, histosections, or other pictorial material that required the examinees to interpret the information and formulate a diagnosis or management plan.

Case and Swanson's project was to evaluate whether scores from the National Board of Medical Examiners (Parts I and II) predicted criterion measures of success in residency training. They related scores obtained in this examination to subsequent performance in the certifying areas of three examinations including the one in orthopaedic surgery described above. They found that candidates falling below a certain score in either part of the exam were at risk of failing. It was not therefore unreasonable to use this examination for selection for residency. However, they counselled that it should not be the sole determinant of selection, for many traits are important to success in residency and should all be considered. This reflects a more general view that multiple-choice tests are but one of a number of vehicles which may contribute to the overall performance of assessment.

Multiple choice tests have long been used in science subjects in the 'A' level of the General Certificate of Education in England (Wood, 1993). As the entry population to universities becomes more diverse departments and subject areas are likely to use them to determine the knowledge students have when they enter courses.. In modular courses of short time duration they may be a useful source of testing knowledge provided they are not used at the expense of other modes of assessment more likely to test higher order skills.

While it is commonly held that they only test knowledge of recall this is far from the case as the experience of medicine shows. Neither is it necessarily the case that the test should comprise items that can be answered with speed. Very telling items can be set in the area of diagnosis in engineering which require the candidate to spend time examining diagrams. There exist a whole variety of possibilities. However, it is undoubtedly true that they are the fairest way of testing knowledge of a wide-ranging syllabus.

The advent of the personal computer and the development of computer assisted learning ensures that their use is likely to be widespread. Optical mark readers have become very cheap and the ease with which they can be interfaced with PCs means that item analysis need not be done by hand. In its turn it will enable teachers to develop their own item banks. They can be used for both formative and summative evaluation (Zakrzewski and Bull, 1998). In the UK, Stephens, Bull and Wade (1998) have suggested guidelines for institutional strategies for computer assisted assessment.

In computer-assisted testing the issue of whether the mode of administration influences performance is important. Among 300 military recruits aged 18–25 it was found that those assigned to the computer mode from a random sample obtained lower mean scores in a test of arithmetic reasoning than those assigned to the traditional paper and pencil mode (Lee *et al.*, 1986). However, among a group of undergraduate students Lee showed that past computer experience significantly affected performance on a computerized test, a result that might have been anticipated. Computerized testing may therefore discriminate against those who have not had experience of that kind of testing for which reason test administrators need to take into account the candidates' previous test experience. There remains a great deal of research to be done on computer-assisted assessment.

With these points in mind the purpose of the remainder of this chapter is to outline the basic principles of objective testing as applied by examination boards and testing agencies, but it also includes a simplified method of item analysis for classroom testing. It excludes discussion of latent-trait theory on the ground that it is beyond the scope of that required by teachers in higher education. (For an introductory note see Heywood, 1989a; for a complete discussion see, Lord and Novick, 1968; Lumsden, 1977, 1978; Messick, Beaton and Lord, 1983; Smith, 1986: Weiss, 1983.)

The language of objective testing

The most commonly used form is the so-called multiple choice question, in which the candidate is asked to choose the correct answer from among four or five responses. Other types are multiple-completion and assertion-reason. Examples of these different types of question are shown in Figures 13.1 and 13.2. The terminology associated with objective items is shown in Figure 13.1. The questions are generally designed so that they each can be answered very quickly. True/false items are also used quite widely. The term 'item' is more generally used than 'question' although MCQ is often used in higher education.

Gibbs and his colleagues (1986) say that it is difficult to write best-answer questions, and that the most useful approach is to devise correct but poor answers for the distractors. One study has reported that high school students in the United States

Which of the following graphs represents a Normal (or Gaussian) distribution?

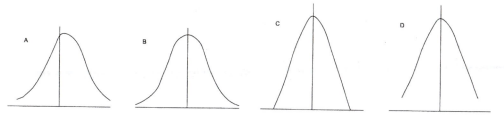

(An equally objective approach would be to request the candidates to label the diagrams.)

Terminology of objective items

Initial statement (stem)
A, B, C, and D, (options)
Correct answer (Key in this case, B)
Options other than correct answer (distractors)

Figure 13.1 A multiple-choice question illustrating the terminology used for objective items.

(A)   Example of a multiple-completion item
      Which two of the following were grievances of the American colonists in the eighteenth century:
      A.   The presence of British troops;
      B.   The laws restricting the importation of tea;
      C.   The threat to abolish slavery;
      D.   The debts of the British East India Company.
              1. A and D only   **2. A and C only**
              3. B and D only   **4. A and B only**

(B)   Example of a matching pairs item
      Which person in column 1 is correctly matched with the statement opposite his name in column 2?

1		2
A.	Brunelleschi	wrote of his ideal state in a book called Utopia
B.	Michelangelo	designed the dome of the cathedral in Florence
C.	Thomas More	sculpted the Pieta in St Peter's Rome.
D.	Harvey	discovered the circulation of blood.

(C)   Example of a best-answer item
      A manual for an aptitude test reports a Kuder-Richardson reliability of +0.95 for 25,000 children. Which of the following conclusions about the test is most appropriate?

A	**It is highly reliable**	B	**It is highly valid**
C	**It is highly internally consistent**	D	**It is suitable for selection purposes**

(D)   Example of an assertion-reason item

Assertion	*Reason*
The monarch rules Britain	The law assumes that the monarch can do no wrong

A	**The assertion and reason are correct statements and the reason correctly explains the assertion.**
B	**The assertion and reason are corret statements but the reason does not explain the assertion.**
C	**The assertion is correct but the reason is incorrect.**
D	**The assertion is incorrect but the reason is correct.**
E	**Both the assertion and reason are incorrect.**

Figure 13.2 Examples of objective items. C and D are reproduced from Gibbs et al. (1986) with the kind permission of the authors.

preferred matching items to multiple choice. They showed less test anxiety and scored better on them (Shaha, 1984).

Agutter (1979) has designed a precision test in which a student has to identify correct, imprecise and incorrect biochemistry statements which can be compiled from lectures (type 1), the student's own previous work (type 2), and the work of another student (type 3). He found that the greatest improvement in examination performance came when all three types were used in the order types 1, 2 and 3.

A *long menu extended-matching question* was developed by Case, Swanson and Stillman (1988) as a pattern recognition test Each item is constructed around a theme. In the example given by Newble, van der Vleuten and Norman (1995) that theme is shortness of breath. That theme is accompanied by about 20 options (e.g. anaemia, asthma). This is then followed by a lead-in, e.g. for each patient with shortness of breath select the most likely diagnosis. There are then a series of short statements describing a patient's symptoms for which the candidate has to select one of the options.

Newble *et al.* suggest that an alternative approach is required for deductive reasoning in addition to pattern recognition. Norman *et al.* (1994) had found that when examinees were presented with complex written clinical situations in which there was a minimum of clinical and laboratory information that it distinguished clearly between, first- and second-year residents and specialists. The experts were more likely to use physiological concepts to explain abnormal patterns of laboratory data and were less likely to rely on pattern recognition in complex atypical situations. Experience, it seems, provides them with additional schema which they can bring to bear on the problem (see Chapter 9).

Analysing objective tests

The traditional method of analysing objective tests uses the biserial method. The illustrations that follow all refer to items that have four options (A–D), the correct option in each table being placed within a square.

In Figure 13.3 the top line (headed Facility) gives the percentage response to each option: 3.8 per cent did not attempt an answer; 51.75 per cent (or half the population) got the question right, i.e. answered B. The group is then split into three sub-groups according to the total scores that they obtained on the entire test. Sub-group I is therefore the 'good' sub-group; II the 'average', and III the poor or low-achieving sub-group. In this test the maximum score was 39. Those in the 'good' sub-group scored in the range 18–31, those in the 'average' 13–17, and those in the 'poor' sub-group 2–12. Since the highest score was of the order 31, it is apparent that the test was difficult.

The item analysis asks the question: How many in each sub-group obtained the correct answer? It calculates this as a proportion of the sub-group. Thus 75 per cent of the 'good' sub-group got the answer right, as did 47 per cent of the 'average', and 21 per cent of the 'poor' sub-group. The item is said to discriminate well. More of the first sub-group as a proportion of that group got the answer right than the corresponding proportion of the third group. Contrast this with the analysis of the item in Figure 13.4, where there is very little discrimination between Groups I and II. Approximately the same proportion in each sub-group gets the answer right. There is some discrimination between the second and third sub-groups.

Some analysts prefer to have more than three sub-groups. There is some value in such an approach when the population being tested is large.

Facility (%)	A	B	C	D	Omits
	19.01	51.75	13.45	11.99	3.8

Group	Number	Number Correct	Proportion Correct
I	129	97	0.7519
II	133	63	O.4737
III	80	17	O.2125

Options	A	B	C	D
I	12	97	7	11
II	27	63	19	19
III	26	17	20	11

Point biserial correlation—0.4602.   Biserial correlation—0.6590

Figure 13.3 Item analysis of a 'good' multiple-choice question (40 item test)

Facility (%)	A	B	C	D	Omits
	8.48	24.07	28.2	37.75	1.5

Group	Number	Number Correct	Proportion Correct
I	143	45	0.3147
II	181	55	0.3039
III	136	13	0.0956

Options	A	B	C	D
I	2	45	46	50
II	12	55	56	55
III	25	13	30	65

Point biserial correlation—0.1029.   Biserial correlation—0.1144

Figure 13.4 Item analysis of a 'poor' multiple-choice question (40 item test)

The measure of discrimination is expressed as a biserial correlation, i.e.

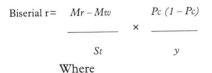

Where

Mr	=	mean score on the test as a whole for students who choose the correct answer to the item
Mw	=	mean score on the test as a whole for students who choose an incorrect answer to the item
St	=	standard deviation of the total test scores for all students
Pc	=	proportion of students choosing the right answer
(1-Pc)	=	proportion of students choosing the wrong answer
y	=	ordinate in the unit normal distribution, which divides the area under the curve in the proportions P and 1-P.

All that is necessary for an examiner to know is that it is common practice not to accept items which give a value below 0.28 for biserial *r*. This value is a function of sample size. Some latitude is allowable as the sample falls in numbers. It is also possible to show that point biserial *r* should be separated from biserail *r* on the lower side by about one-quarter of the value of biserial *r*, when the facility of the item is around 50 per cent. The proportional difference between the two decreases when the facility (the number giving the correct response) decreases well below 50 per cent and increases when it is well above 50 per cent.

Of the criteria so far described, the item in Figure 13.4 would be rejected whereas that in Figure 13.3 is very acceptable. We can learn more from such tabulations.

Item writers try to design the question so that each of the distractors appears to be a reasonable answer. If one is 'way out' the student will not give it second consideration. If it appears reasonably correct then some students should respond to each option. In Figure 13.3 some students have been attracted to each option, and given all the data, this must be regarded as a good item, especially as the most reliable tests are constructed of items with similar characteristics. The item in Figure 13.4 is deceptive: at first sight, the options would appear to be working well. Closer inspection shows that the item was very difficult even for the best group. In these circumstances it is possible that there was a lot of guessing, a view which is supported by the large numbers opting for the distractors C and D.

It will be appreciated that when many students give only the correct answer, the item is very easy. It would not be used in a test that seeks to differentiate between students, although it might be appropriate in mastery-learning. An item in which three of the options are used while the fourth is left alone is equally unsatisfactory. A very difficult item will discriminate badly and, in all probability, cause guessing.

A simple technique for the item analysis of a small group of students

The technique that follows is suitable for use in the classroom. The class is divided into two sub-groups (i.e. above and below average) and their performance compared. If the number of correct responses in the top 27 per cent of the pupils is denoted H and that of correct responses in the bottom 27 per cent denoted L then:

$$\text{Discrimination } (D) = \frac{H - L}{M}$$

Where

M =   the number of candidates in each of the subg-roups, i.e. those who make up 27 per cent. Fraser and Gillam (1972) suggest that the value of D should not fall below 0.3.

Reliability of objective tests

The problem of error in the marking of essay examinations has been discussed, and it was shown that individual scores are not 'absolute' values. This is as true of an objective test as it is of an essay. In all MCQ scores there is error, and teachers often ascribe this error to guessing. However, the contributory factors to error, even in an objective test, are complex. Diederich (1960) has calculated the standard error for multiple-choice items, and has found it to be 3 for between 24 and 47 items and 4 for between 48 and 89.

The definition (or, more correctly, description) of reliability as commonly applied to objective tests differs from that given in Chapter 10. The measurement is usually undertaken on one administration of objective tests and not on comparisons of the test taken on a different number of occasions. It stems from the assumption that the candidate's behaviour in responding to the test should be similar in respect of each item. For example, if the test were to be divided into two halves we would expect the candidate to perform equally well in both. If the candidate performs badly on the second half of the test but well on the first then the test is not reliable if all the items are of equal difficulty and measuring the same thing. A better measure would be to compare a candidate's performance on the odd-numbered items with his responses to the even numbered ones. The measure of reliability is the coefficient of correlation between the two halves of the test.

Unfortunately, there could be bias in the items in each half: for example, if the test is of work done during a semester and the first half of the test relates to the first half of the semester and the second part to the last half of the semester. To counteract bias, the equation commonly used for reliability is the Kuder-Richardson, i.e.

$$r_n = \frac{n}{n-1} \cdot \frac{s^2 + \Sigma p_i q_i}{S^2}$$

Where

n =   number of items in the test

st =   standard deviation of the test

p_i =   proportion of candidates responding correctly to item i,

q_i =   1-p_i

This equation looks at every possible split in the arrangement of the items and is therefore a better measure of the internal consistency, as reliability is sometimes called.

The assumptions on which this measure is based are first, that all the items in the test measure the same thing, and second, that maximum reliability is obtained when all the items in the test are of average difficulty. Inspection of the formula shows that it depends on the number of candidates with correct responses and those with incorrect ones (i.e. p_i and q_i.) Moreover, it depends on the product of p_i and q_i. The maximum value of this product occurs when half the candidates get the item wrong and half get it right (i.e. $0.5 \times 0.5 = 0.25$). Any other proportion produces a lower product, as, for example, when three-quarters get the item right and one-quarter get it wrong (i.e. $0.72 \times 0.25 = 0.1875$, which is much less than 0.25). This is a major reason for the view that tests should be constructed of discriminating items that have a facility of around 50 per cent. It is also clear that the longer the test, the greater will be its reliability. Similarly, the more difficult the test, the less its reliability. Thus reliability depends on the range of scores in the group tested.

To summarize, reliability explains the proportion of variance in the test that is non-error variance. It depends on the spread of scores and is a function of test length.

Test length and test structure

Such are the objections (fears, perhaps) of those involved in public examinations in British Isles of objective tests that odd stratagems are often adopted. Many examinations incorporate short and long answer questions together with objective items. One test I have seen began with 15 items and then changed to short answer questions, after which it was completed by another 15 objective items. It is difficult to object to the separation of the tests on grounds that they are 'separate' tests. However, since they were incorporated into the same examination, they should have been grouped together not only for the purpose of rhythm but for the reason that the separation of the two 15 sets of items might produce less reliability than when they are taken together. Of course, if the two sections are meant to measure different things then the argument changes, because the reliability equation assumes that all the items measure the same thing.

The National Foundation for Educational Research claims correlation coefficients of 0.95 with well-evaluated 50-item tests. My own work with teacher-made tests suggests that the comparisons we should make should be with a target value of around 0.8.

A question that arises is whether it is sensible to offer a small number of items as part of an examination? The answer to this question can be found by submitting the reliability obtained from a short test to the Spearman-Brown formula. This tells us what the reliability of a longer test would be if it were composed of items similar to those in the test for which the reliability has been obtained, i.e.

$$r_u = \frac{n r_{it}^{-2}}{1 + (n-1)\, r_{it}^{-2}}$$

Where

$n =$ the number of items in the test,

$r_{it} =$ the original reliability, and

$r_{it} =$ the reliability of the test n times as long.

In order to predict the reliability of a test that has 20 items to replace a 10-item sub-test of knowledge substitute 2n for n. The calculation is then for a test twice as long; for a test which is six times as long (i.e. 60 items) substitute 6n for n. What about an examination which includes 10 or 15 items as part of a test in which there are both long and short answers? While it is possible to calculate the reliability of the different components it is nevertheless difficult. We calculated the biserial, facility and reliability of a 10-item objective test which was included as part of a sample paper for a public examination, and found it to be 0.39, which, when recalculated, came to 0.72 for 40 items. This value is below that required for public examination. In general, the biserial correlations were reasonable, and this suggested that if some of the items were improved this short test would have had a better fit (see Heywood, 1977b).

Criticisms of this test rest rather more on examination structure than on length. In this particular examination the objective items followed a series of short answers, and this meant that the candidate had to change his or her response style. Having got used to one style of answering he or she had to make a sudden change to another. It is held to be important to maintain rhythm, although there is very little research on personal tempo (Nevo and Spector, 1979). This means retaining the same technique for a reasonable period of test time.

Cronbach and Gleser (1965) have pointed out that it is the degree of risk that can be tolerated which has to be ascertained. For example, in the classroom situation where one wishes to identify those who are below and above average a reliability of 0.5 will suffice. However, where the stakes are high, as for example in an examination that contributes to a degree grade, the test should conform to accepted standards of reliability. In my own work I have used between 40 and 80 items (Heywood, 1977b).

A key issue in objective tests that are seeking semi-mastery is where to draw the cut-off. Pokrajac and Culo (1994) investigated this problem at the University of Zagreb. They found, using a particular method of statistical analysis, that getting assessors to set a minimum pass level was useful in setting objective standards for the decision 'pass or fail,' even when there were large differences between the examiners.

Sometimes an objective test can replace short-answer questions requiring at least a sentence for their completion (Heywood, McGuinness and Murphy, 1980). This is not to argue that short answers involving sentences have no role. In engineering science we found it easier to design comprehension exercises with short-sentence answer questions than we did with multiple-choice items when testing the understanding of material in a technical item. The short-sentence technique was retained (Carter, Heywood and Kelly, 1986). (See Chapter 2).

Unusual responses: guessing

If there is one thing that unites critics of objective tests it is the risk of guessing. They conveniently forget that it can be argued with some confidence that it is the 'fudge factor' in essays which leads to the low inter-marker reliabilities so often reported. For some reason, examiners find it difficult to accept that the proportion of questions in an objective test that a candidate can answer correctly by blind guesswork is very unlikely to exceed 20–30 per cent. Yet, in an essay examination, wrote Iliffe (1966), many examiners are prepared to give marks based on impressions of answers composed largely of indifferent ideas and irrelevant material.

Nevertheless, much interest is centred on the equation used to correct a test score for guessing:

Score corrected for guessing = $R - \dfrac{W}{(K-1)}$

where

$R =$ number of correct responses
$W =$ number of incorrect responses
$K =$ number of choices offered in the item.

This equation illustrates the point that, as the number of options increase (for example, from four to five), the effects of guessing decrease. This is why many examiners prefer to write five options. However, all the items in my experimental examinations were written with four because we found it difficult to write attractive fifth options as distractors, and preferred to include a realistic one rather than 'none of these'. This does not mean that the total test score could be made up to 25 per cent by guessing because there is a one in four chance of correctly guessing in a single item. The assumption made by those who criticize objective tests is that students can randomize their guessing, but this is a highly sophisticated mental operation that would be beyond most students in the time allowed.

Lord and Novick (1968) wrote:

> Examinees who have partial information about an item do not respond at random nor do examinees with misinformation about that item. In these situations wrong answers cannot be equally attractive to the examinee.
>
>   No simple correction formula is appropriate in these cases...and elsewhere...
>
> The simple knowledge or random guessing model is used extensively despite its several weaknesses. One such weakness is that it ignores possible day-to-day variations in examinee performance which experience has taught us cannot be neglected. An equally serious weakness is that the model assumes that if the examinee is unable to pin-point the correct response then he is completely ignorant in this situation and has no basis for choosing among the possible responses. This second assumption can seldom be seriously entertained.

That unusual events are not just due to guessing may be illustrated by the person–response curves in Figure 13.5, the idea for which comes from Trabin and Weiss (1983). In Figure 13.5(a) the response of a candidate to a particular set of items is shown: 50 per cent of the items were answered correctly. The steep slope of the curve suggests that the candidate was answering the test in the way that would be predicated for a person of average ability. A good performance was returned on the relatively easy items whereas a poor one was seen on the relatively difficult.

Figure 13.5(b) shows another candidate who took the same test and whose performance was uneven across the range of items to the point that some more difficult items were answered well. Given that the candidate was also of average ability, we conclude that there is more error in the final score of 50 per cent obtained by the testee. The same is true of the candidate in Figure 13.5(c), who also obtained 50 per cent from the same test. Since these two candidates obtained correct answers to some

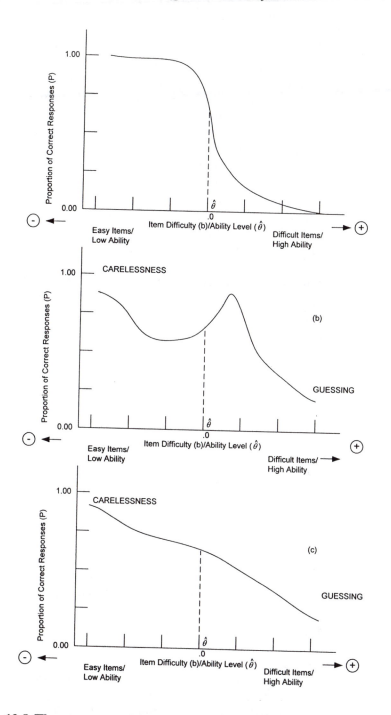

Figure 13.5. Three person–response curves for individuals with the same ability level (=).
(Adapted from Trabin and Weiss (1983).

very difficult questions whereas the first candidate did not, it is probable that these candidates were guessing. The lower performance of these two candidates on the easy items suggests that they might have been careless. The peak in the response to the more difficult items by the second candidate implies that the examiner might have had some special knowledge with which to improve his or her performance.

Single summated scores do not give us any information about the way in which the examiner approached the test. The paradox is that while we know this to be the case and while we accept that anxiety, motivation and prior knowledge all influence performance, we tend only to correct norm-referenced tests for guessing.

A major problem with the guessing equation is that it overcorrects for guessing when the distractors in the item do not prove attractive to weak students, and undercorrects when students are able to eliminate the distractors with ease. It may be concluded that the extent to which students resort to guessing largely depends on the quality of the item-writing. While most of the able students should choose the correct response, distractors incorporating popular errors or fallacies should appear correct to students with misinformation, while others should appear superficially correct to students with little information or skill relevant to the item. Indeed, the purpose of carrying out an item analysis is to ensure that items do discriminate between better and weaker students, and that the distractors are plausible.

As Iliffe (1966) has pointed out, guessing can be further eliminated by more complex item design. For example,

> Check three of the statements below which express best the function which education should serve in our society.
>
> 1...
> 2...
> 3...
> 4...
> 5...
> 6...
> 7...
> 8...

In this case there are 56 different possible answers. If credit is given only for choosing the three correct statements, the probability of gaining a mark by guessing is less than 0.2. However, as soon as the design becomes complex all sorts of other problems arise. As Cowan (private communication) points out it is a bit rough if a candidate gets no marks for getting two right and one wrong. Gulliksen (1950) makes the point that when there is a sufficiently long list of choices at the beginning of a test section the task of item writing is made easier.

Another method which has been used with students of approximately freshman level in England employs a complex statement about a given subject in the stem. A series of questions is then asked about the statement which demand one of the following responses against each item:

A- is true; B- is possibly true; C- contains insufficient evidence to justify itself; D- is false

Youngman and Heywood (1981) confounded traditional guessing theory when they asked 300 students aged 14+ to use a rating scale to describe how they answered each item in a multiple-choice test in mathematics. Among the scales were 'I guessed the answer to this question – completely/partly/not at all.' Other scales related to difficulty, interest, method of calculation, recall, and their prediction of the correctness of their answer. A number of criterion measures were also obtained including data from a multiple-aptitude test. When the data were analysed it was found that there was one group of pupils who guessed. They had some difficulty in answering the items and relied on recall. In addition to making the wrong prediction about the correctness of their answers they also failed to guess correctly.

This suggests that the guessing issue is much more complicated than has been previously thought. There are, it seems, groups of students who guess and groups who do not.

Perhaps the most important result for further investigation among larger samples is the finding that the 'guessers' guess wrongly. This supports the view of those authorities who do not feel there is any need to make a correction for guessing in the objective tests, but it also throws some light on the dispositions (response) sets of examinees.

Strategies in solving objective items and learning

An investigation by Scouller and Prosser (1994) of a small sample of first- and second-year students in Australia sought to establish a relationship between their orientation to learning, the skills they thought were being tested by MCQ examinations, and the study strategies they would use to prepare for forthcoming MCQ examinations. They found that students with surface general orientations toward study had a confused perception of MCQ examination and no strategies to prepare for them. In contrast a positive association between achievement and deep and/or achieving was found.

There are many other problems that need to be solved. Wigdor and Garner (1982), in their report to the National Research Council in the United States, point out that test developers have not made much of an effort to study the effect of test items on internal mental processes. As we have seen above, it would be useful to know much more about the problem-solving skills that students bring to the solution of problems set in the objective format Are there some students who work backwards from the answers, and, in any case, does this matter? If they do, is students' understanding of mathematics adequate?

One promising way forward would be to see how the solving of objective items helps develop skills in semi-automatization. Many of the tasks which examinees have to undertake in examinations are executive skills that are pursued over a long period of time. Yet much of life is concerned with semi-automatized problem solving. Problem-solving objective items might contribute significantly to the development of information-processing skills.

Intelligent guessing

In real life we are often called upon to guess, and there is a substantial case to be made for tests which develop the ability of 'intelligent guessing'. Billing (1973) writes about a student that:

> After graduation, he is likely to be called upon to venture opinions and interpretations, make decisions and carry designs on the basis of incomplete information. One aid to success in such situations could well be an ability to make intelligent 'guesses' and this factor should not perhaps be regarded as a superfluous and undesirable feature which merely complicates the interpretation of test results.

Billing suggested the model which follows for testing intelligent guessing:

> Four suggested answers are provided for each question below. Cross out those answers that you know or can deduce to be incorrect. In crossing out incorrect answers do not guess – there will be a penalty for this. Then indicate the correct answer by writing A, B, C or D against the question number in the right hand margin. If you don't know or cannot deduce the correct answer, use an intelligent guess. There will be no penalty for incorrect answers, so answer all questions. This system allows the paper to be marked in two ways. Firstly, a score is assigned on the basis of incorrect answers crossed out. Secondly, a score is given by the correct answer in the right hand margin. Your overall mark for the test will be the higher of the two scores.

Billing's analysis of data from a small sample of students exposed to such a test led him to conclude that knowledge and intelligent guessing may be two separate abilities which do not correlate.

Bligh (1973), in a more simple procedure, introduced a 'don't know' category into the true/false test and scaled thus:

Correct	Don't know	Incorrect
2	1	0

His purpose in developing what he called truth-functional tests was to:

> Objectively assess students' thought processes during lectures or other presentation methods of teaching ... Truth-functional tests are tests in which the student is asked to agree, disagree, or say he does not know whether a certain statement is true.

Bligh's particular tests were designed to exemplify the categories in *The Taxonomy of Educational Objectives*. He claimed that these tests are a direct measure of teaching effectiveness in terms of objectives achieved, that they have high reliability and construct validity, and that guessing can be correct.

In medical education Essex (1976) found that a partial-credit scoring schema was favoured by students when compared with a dichotomous approach. The variance of the dichotomously scored scheme was greater but not significantly more so than the partial credit scheme. He suggested that partial-credit schemes are useful if it is important to reward partial knowledge.

Ebel (1958) has gone so far as to argue that:

True/false questions can be thought provoking, unambiguous, and highly discriminating. The fact they are often not is more the fault of the writer of the item than of the form of the item.

At school level it has been shown that the introduction of deliberately flawed items has little effect on valididy and reliability, although the items become easier for the student (McMorris *et al.*, 1972). However, another experiment among political science students found that the concurrent validity and internal consistency were weakened by flawed items although the item difficulty was not flawed (Board and Whitney, 1972).

In a carefully designed experiment among first-year educational psychology students Owen and Freeman (1987) compared the efficacy of three and five option objective items. They did not find any significant difference between them, the major variation being in the time spent per item. The students preferred the shorter items and 97 per cent balloted for three-option item tests. Their findings supported previous work in Australia (Straton and Catts, 1980) and the United States (Tversky, 1964).

Tollefson (1987) evaluated the use of three formats (each written for 12 items): (1) one correct answer; (2) 'none of the above' as a foil; and (3) 'none of the above' as correct answers, in a college statistics examination. Students found that (3) was the most difficult of the formats, although no consistent differences in the item discriminations statistics were found. The most reliable test was the multiple- choice with one correct answer. The use of 'none of above' did not increase discriminations, as some authorities held it might do. A similar study by Oosterhof and Coats (1984) in a different content area supports these findings.

The question of triviality

Apart from the issue of guessing, the most often-used objection to objective items is that they only test recall of knowledge. To put it in another, more cogent, way – they do not test reasoning. If this is the case, it is argued, they have no potential in higher education because higher education is concerned with the development of reason.

Ebel (1965), an American authority on objective test, considered the differences between factual and reasoning questions thus:

> There are several important differences between factual and reasoning questions. Factual questions tend to be simpler to state, easier to answer, and less controversial when correct answers are announced. Reasoning questions, since they are designed to provoke though, sometimes also provoke arguments. Critics of objective test, including students who have just taken one, frequently find flaws such as these: (a) the best answer is not a completely correct answer; (b) some of the distractors provoke answers just as good as the 'correct answer'; (c) the problem situation is not described fully enough to prevent diverse interpretations leading to different answers.

The best answer to these criticisms is to present evidence that competent experts have agreed that the correct answer is clearly better than any other alternative offered, and that when the item is scored with this as the correct answer it discriminates clearly between students of high and low achievement. This evidence should not be used by a writer of test items as grounds for opposing changes in wording which improves the item by making the problem situation clearer, the best answer more nearly correct, or the distractors more clearly wrong – without destroying the ability of the item to discriminate. But this evidence can be used to defend thought-provoking items which require the examinee to make reasonable inferences about complex but concisely described problem situations. Loopholes for unwarranted assumptions and unconventional interpretations exist in almost all reasoning items. It is practically impossible to eliminate them without making the item excessively verbose. So long as experts can agree on a best answer, and so long as the item discriminates well between good and poor students, these alleged flaws in reasoning items need not be regarded as serious. They make the item somewhat less objective but more valid as an indication of important achievement. Objectivity is highly desirable, but it is not the most important quality of a test item. Validity should never be sacrificed to gain objectivity.

Assertion-reason and multiple-completion items have the positive value of being able to tolerate ambiguity. In England Iliffe (1966) attempted to dispel the fear that objective tests will encourage students only to amass isolated scraps of knowledge with two examples. The first said:

Tick any of the following statements which are not held to be true by Plato:

A.   The soul survives the body.

B.   All knowledge of 'right' and 'wrong' comes through the soul's encounter with the absolute.

C.   The world of the senses is a hindrance to the philosopher.

D.   The mind at birth is blank, and all ideas come from experience.

E.   Suicide is immoral.

According to Iliffe:

Clearly this question will be answered correctly only by a student who has studied and understood Plato's philosophy with some thoroughness. The form of the question requires a candidate to look careful at each of the five statements and to make a separate decision in each case: it is not enough to spot one of the five statements which fits the instructions and to ignore the rest.

In the next example the correct answer can be identified only by a candidate who is capable of making careful distinctions and of ranging in his mind over a number of instances of a constitution:

Which of these statements most adequately defines a constitution?

A.   All of the laws and customs of a people.

B.   That portion of the pattern of government which is legal rather than customary or political in nature.

C.   The formal written document under which a government functions.

D.   The basic functional pattern and powers of government, whatever their derivation.

In regard to the teaching of English literature Iliffe wrote that, 'the cry which commonly goes up from teachers of literature that these tests cannot tell us what we want to know about our students, cannot be answered in any way until the teachers are prepared to say clearly what it is they want to know about their students.' Once that is done, it is possible that some of the qualities or achievements with which they are concerned can be assessed by objective tests while others cannot. In the first category falls the ability to describe a work of literature in terms of its content, structure, form, style, etc.; also the ability to assess its place in the larger phenomenon called literature. In the second category (not susceptible to objective testing) must fall the students' own responses to the work of its characters, the way in which they relate what they have read to their own experiences, and where they interpret the work in such terms as mimetic, symbolic or moral. Purves (1961), in a careful analysis of this issue, concluded that good objective questions can be devised to deal with interpretation and evaluation. They measure 'the ability to reason about a work of literature more than they do a strictly literary skill; they measure the ability to justify conclusions from the evidence given.'

The problem is solved to the extent that the item writer can write appropriate items. Whether it is worth solving the problem in a particular assessment context is another matter, but that reasoning items in the humanities cannot be produced for particular groups of students is not confirmed by the evidence.

It is much easier to see that problem-solving skills are used in objective tests in mathematics, science, and technology, and this has been demonstrated repeatedly, even with respect to the construction of true-false tests (Avital and Shettleworth, 1968).

Hoare and Revans (1969) designed questions to test the skills of knowledge comprehension and application after students had read instructional programmes in chemistry for their first medical examinations. The programmes were pre- and post-tested in comparison with the published tests for the programmes. The improvement on the published tests was better than that of the tests designed from educational objectives. Nevertheless, consistent differences between students suggested that the knowledge and application questions were testing different abilities. The authors claimed that the investigation showed that programmed learning teaches students to apply, as well as remember, facts, theories and formulae. This study emphasized the importance of question design and the significance in obtaining a match between the materials, learning experiences and the assessment procedures.

Having said all this, it is important not to underestimate the value of recall in objective tests. Many professionals (for example, doctors and engineers) have to have a very wide range of knowledge at their disposal. Success in objective tests at what we suppose might be the level of recall might give weak students confidence. What they and we perceive to be recall may involve two different skills.

Lottery techniques

Diagnosis is clearly a skill that requires more than knowledge of recall. I have shown elsewhere how objective items can be used to test this skill but my items might take up to 15 minutes to answer (Heywood, 1974). Objective tests can be used to test this skill in a series format that leads the respondent through a case history. It is a challenge to design such tests. One formula that has been adopted might be called the lottery technique because the answer has to be uncovered as in a scratch card. This has been used to assess skill in fault diagnosis in electronic circuitry.

A similar technique has been devised for medical examinations by Barber Meller at McMaster University (cited by Fabb and Marshall, 1983). The answers (correct or incorrect) are given for each option but are covered up. As in the previous case, the candidate uncovers the information in the boxes and continues doing this until the answer is obtained. If the questions are set as simple multiple-choice items in which there is only one right answer, then in a 40-item test with four options there will be a possibility of 120 (3 x 40) negative answers. The score is the number of negative choices and the maximum score is zero negative marks, in which case the candidate will have scored all the items correctly. The least score is 120 and so on. Fabb and Marshall (1983) suggest that items regarded as important could be given a high weighing whereas those of least importance could be given a low weight. Such tests are now easily administered with the aid of personal computers.

In modern languages C-tests are sometimes used to diagnose language proficiency. In these approximately every seventh word is deleted from a passage. These tests can be set for any level and can test comprehension, grammar and voabulary (Coleman, 1999).

Test and item construction

If objective tests are to work well the evidence is that the items have to be well designed. This applies as much to classroom tests as it does to standardized tests. The rules are very simple, and of these the most important are:

1. Remember that what you think the examinee sees (reads into) the question may not in fact be what he or she actually reads and sees.

2. Write the items so that they are easy to read and, to achieve this, make sure they have rhythm.

It follows from these two principles that an item or series of items should be related to the objectives of the course. As we have seen, the majority of questions should be set at the difficulty level experienced by the average student. In order to obtain rhythm ensure that the stem and the options are grammatically correct. Do not bring the rhythm to a halt by the use of unnecessary subordinate phrases or double negatives, even when substantial time is allowed for the answer. The distractors should appear to be potentially real answers. In many instances their order is important. In 'number or equivalent questions' the numbers should be presented in descending or ascending order of magnitude. The terminology used in items should always be precise.

One of the great advantages of objective tests is that they can be pre-tested even in the classroom, although some would argue that appropriate sample populations among university students do not exist. Over a period of time a pool of items can be established (Wood and Skurnik, 1969) and this can be done relatively cheaply by groups of universities (Chelvu and Elton, 1977).

Leary and Dorans (1982), of the Educational Testing Service, have shown that in time-limited tests students usually score more highly if the items are arranged with the easier at the beginning and the most difficult at the end.

Lane *et al.* (1987) came to the conclusion that the idea of beginning tests with easy items was oversimplified. The performance of students was shown to be highest when statistical and cognitive difficulty (as measured by the categories of the *Taxonomy of Educational Objectives*) increased together and least when statistical and cognitive item difficulty changed in opposite directions. Since labelling affected performance positively it could be that it negates the effects of item order. The use of labels may cause students to employ more appropriate response sets.

Ebel (1965) devised three tests, each of 16 items, which were taken from another test of 61 items. In the first he chose items with difficulty values around the middle of the distribution of all the items. A mean score of 9.22 was obtained with a reliability of 0.485. When the level of difficulty of items distributed across the whole range of difficulty values the mean mark fell to 8.02 and the reliability to 0.416. Both distributions were reasonably bell-shaped, with the peak of the former above the median mark for the test (i.e. 8) and that of the latter below. The range of the latter was reduced. When he set a third test that included the eight most difficult items and the eight easiest from the 61, a sharp cut-off on either side of the median was produced. The mean score was 8.01 and most of the candidates were grouped in the band 6–9, the range being considerably reduced even when compared with the second test. The reliability fell to 0.13.

There is no compelling reason why all test score distributions should approximate to the normal curve. Rummel used a college-level mathematics test to exempt some entering freshmen (about 50%) from a course in basic mathematical skills. He found that item revisions which flattened the distribution of scores also reduced the errors made in exempting some freshmen and not others (quoted by Ebel, 1965).

The best guidance would seem to be that in the absence of detailed information about the students, or the characteristics of the subject (for example, mathematics), the examiner should try to produce a normal distribution. The results should be spread evenly and not bias the marking towards either end of the distribution.

The safest approach, therefore, is to begin by selecting items in the middle range of difficulty and checking these for discrimination, content and skill. A detailed knowledge of the candidates will give some of the degree of flexibility with which the teacher can approach this task.

Some of the difficulties in accommodating both weak and poor students might be overcome by using different examination structures. One of these is the partly tailored examination, a term which is apparently due to Bedard (1974).[1] He describes it as an examination in which there is both a compulsory and choice component. This is normal in many examinations in Britain and Ireland, where the facility to choose questions is part of the philosophy of examining. However, the structure of partly tailored tests is very different and more reliable and systematic. The maximum number of marks a student obtains is determined by the number of questions answered. The student's score is the ratio of marks he would have obtained if he had answered all the questions correctly plus the 'free' ones he chose to answer. Bedard's goals were:

1.   To try to provide an examination in the category of power tests for all examiners.

2.   To allow the examinee to adjust the examination of his individual differences.

3.   To keep the testing duties of teachers to a minimum.

A variation on this approach is the 'power test'. This is an 'open book' examination with extended time with opportunities for interaction. Baillie and Tookey (1997) used this type of examination in a materials science course for engineers. The examination answers were classified by the SOLO Taxonomy (Biggs and Collis, 1982). Comparisons were made with the results from students who took the same examination but with closed books in the previous year. It was found that more students adopted deeper approaches to learning. However, some students were not happy with the new approach and may have continued to surface learn. Baillie and Tookey point out that great care has to be taken in introducing innovations of this kind if all the students are to be relatively happy with the new procedure. They experimented with control groups taking examinations in algebra and calculus at secondary grade 12. They claimed that students benefited from this type of examination, particularly in respect of short-answer questions, and they felt that they offered opportunities for increasing the class average.

Weber, Frary and Cross (1995) have challenged the view that students should not be allowed choice in objective examinations. In their small-scale experiment graduate students were permitted to choose questions in examination which required them to select the best (better) answer from a list of responses that were supplied by the instructor. The test was taken under open-book conditions: 43 of the 50 items were judged to be above the knowledge level of the *Taxonomy of Educational Objectives*. None of the items were directly related to information given in class lectures or the text. 'Thus, the testing skills that were measured did not include how adept students were at locating correct responses from the materials they were permitted to bring to the examination.' The students were required to complete the 50 items and then select ten they would like to eliminate. The investigators computed the scores for the 50 item and 40 item tests and recorded the best grade for recording. They found that the reduction in test length did not affect the mean reliability even though the students tended to eliminate the more difficult items on the test. The investigators felt that one (from several) explanations of this might be that there was less guessing in the shorter test. If students eliminate the items over which they have most doubt then their tendency to guess will also be reduced. Since very high correlations were found between the two papers the authors argue that there is a case for the practice of optional choice. They also argue that it is possible to ensure that content validity standards are not violated.

Test-wiseness and test preparation

Sarnacki (1979) defined test-wiseness as a cognitive ability or set of skills which a test-taker can use to improve a test score independently of the content area of the test. For example, Smith (1982) devised a strategy that involved the student in examining the relationship of the four options to each other and found that when the testees were trained in this technique not only did they improve their test scores but they also acquired more self-confidence. Using the same strategy, Dolly and Williams (1983) were unable to detect a significant difference between undergraduates in an experimental group and a control group both taking classroom tests. However, in a subsequent investigation with 54 undergraduate education students they used four strategies. These included training students in how to maximize the chance of selecting a correct option when the test-taker was forced to guess because of a lack of information concerning the content of an item. This time, on all measures of test-wiseness they found that the experimental group did better than the control one. There was no significant difference between the experimental and control groups on the non-susceptible items. The training strategy, based on the view that test-wiseness is not a transferable skill but cue-specific (Diamond and Evans, 1972), was also investigated. The subjects were taught to respond to cues of length of option, middle value, similarity or oppositeness of options and cues from stem to option (deduction). Both groups produced similar performances when the cues were not present but the experimental group did better when they were. Dolly and Williams (1986) concluded that an efficient programme for test-wiseness would increase the accuracy of academic skills measurement and in support of this, like so many others, they referred to Ebel (1965), who had written: 'More error in measurement is likely to originate from students who have too little rather than too much, skill in test taking'.

Related to this is the problem of test preparation. Does it help or hinder the learner? Should the tests used in public examinations be published? The JMB has always published its tests. It is now a legal requirement in New York State that students who take the SAT have a right to a copy of the questions. Lockheed *et al.* (1982) found that out of 113,000 students only about 5000 asked for the questions, and those who applied were more able and ambitious students from wealthier and better educated families. Once again the power of tests to influence learning is shown.

Finally, McLeod and Snell (1996) report that students benefit from being involved in the evaluation process. In their study, because they had found it difficult to obtain a secure bank of items they asked students in the junior medicine clerkship to design multiple-choice questions. After a year the students' questions were compared with those of the faculty. They found that the average facility index and validity of the questions were comparable except that the students' questions were less frequently based on a clinical case scenario.

Notes

1. This is not the same as a tailored test which requires that each candidate is presented with items of 50 per cent difficulty for them (i.e. they should get one out of every two items correct). Wood (1986) does not believe that tailored tests of this kind would be optimal for the student psychologically because we do not know how motivation, task difficulty and immediate past experience work on each other.

Chapter 14

Reflective Practice
Peer and Self-Assessment and the Aims of Higher Education

The aims of higher education and their assessment

The purpose of assessment is to establish if the aims of higher education as expressed in such statements as those given in Chapter 2 are being met. These aims while being ideals are intended to be within reach. Some are more easily attained than others, especially those that pertain to the acquisition of knowledge. Others appear to be less tangible. Take the last purpose in the Rockfish Gap report of 1818 which led to the foundation of the University of Virginia, the first modern university in the United States. It reads:

> And, generally, to form them to habits of reflection and correct action, rendering them examples of virtue to others, and of happiness within themselves. (Attributed by McGrath (1962) to Jefferson)

McGrath quotes this in a discussion of Newman's views of the ends of higher education. Newman certainly held similar views and he saw the tutorial function as having a moral as well as an educational purpose. So strongly did he hold this view that he divided the Fellows of Oriel on this matter where he was tutor of the college (Culler, 1955). He believed that the outcome of higher education should be a philosphical habit of mind.

> A habit of mind is formed which lasts through life, of which the attributes, equitableness, calmness, moderation, and wisdom; or what in a former discourse I have ventured to call a philosophical habit. (Newman, 1852, 1947)

As McGrath explains using Newman's words:

> 'Any knowledge, if it really be such,' adds thus to the perfection of mind, but more particularly that 'comprehensive view of truth in all its branches, of the relations of science to science, of their mutual bearings and their respective values' which he calls "philosophy".

In practice the general education provided in higher education in the United States is more likely to attain that goal when there is an integrating mechanism that enables students to obtain a 'comprehensive view'. A student should grow toward this view propelled by the knowledge required. The fragmented system of assessment (i.e. course by course) would seem to operate directly against the acquisition of such a view. By contrast in Britain students specialize in one or two subjects, and it is assumed that a 'comprehensive view' will be obtained through osmosis.

An assessment of how well institutions of higher education achieve the goals of higher education would find many of them wanting. Evidence has been educed in previous chapters which shows that few of them relate development, academic and personal, to models of intellectual growth when they structure their courses. Evidence was also educed to show that many students leave higher education without acquiring higher order thinking skills in the subjects studied. The fact that in Britain the government felt it necessary to implement the Enterprise in Higher Education Initiative is indicative of a perceived failure by the institutions of higher education to meet the goals inherent in preparing graduates for work. That it should want to foster the development of personal transferable skills suggests more should be done, generally, to prepare students for life.

Similar developments took place in Australia and the United States. In Australia Boud (1995) promoted peer and self-assessment. In the United States some colleges designed courses to develop reflective judgement (see Chapter 8). There was a drive toward reflective practice. For many faculty the solution was to be found in learning journals and portfolios. Many wanted to try non-conventional methods of assessment that they believed would enhance learning. Among them were peer and self- assessment.

Peer assessment

In relation to laboratory work, Boud (1986) pointed out that when the aim of assessment is feedback, students themselves can provide each other with useful feedback and reinforcement. While this often happens in the laboratory it does not do so universally and he argued that peer assessment should be formalized in the laboratory. In this way, students begin to take responsibility for their own learning and gain insight into their own performance through having to judge the work of others. They are therefore a useful adjunct to assessment by staff. Another reason for interest in peer assessment is that it is possibly the only satisfactory way of obtaining information about the contributions of the individuals within a team to the work of the team. One of the reasons why many curricula shy away from team projects is that teachers believe that it is impossible to assess them; yet the ability to work with others and in teams is a skill highly prized in the outside world. Politicians are interested in group work for the reason that large lecture classes, which are the consequence of expansion, might be conducted by small group methods and thereby facilitate the development of problem solving and teamwork skills. Group work with peer assessment might reduce the amount of marking and, where feedback is quick, allow time for the counselling of students (Turner, 1983; see also Strachan and Wilcox, 1996). Earl (1986) in the context of developing communication skills within a course in mathematical modelling wrote:

> Students who have to embark on a consultancy role after graduating, should be trained to work in a team. They should be trained to listen and to translate, in this case from lay language to mathematical language and vice-versa; they may even have to be trained to translate from their own disciplinary dialect into more general mathematical language for their peers. They should be trained to distinguish between the stated constraints in a situation and the actual constraints. Importantly,

they should also be able to undertake team research, to be able to give effective oral presentation and be able to collaborate in the production of clear written reports. Group communication is thus central to the whole situation.

Earl went on to describe a scheme for this approach in which 10 per cent of the marks are awarded by peers. Another scheme in a politics course also incorporated peer marking but with the addition of cross-marking (Denscombe and Roberts, 1980). In a course in manufacturing technology:

> The students work in groups of five on various projects. They are assessed by staff for a group report, a group presentation and their individual contribution. The students fill in their form, whereby they quantify their contribution to the group and, on the reverse side, they comment on their team members regarding their relative level of performance and make any other relevant comments. The students' self assessment scores are then compared to the staff assessment. Where they vary wildly (only occasionally) it is usually due to personality clashes in the group. This is resolved by selectively interviewing group members to find out who did what etc. I have found that, in most cases, the student ranking within the group is similar to staff assessment, although they usually score higher than staff ... we haven't got it right yet, as we still get students complaining. However, the students do like it, as students who do not pull their weight are identified and thus the groups tend to work better. (J.E. Sharp, private communication)

In addition to published reports on peer assessment in such subjects as architecture (Fineman, 1980); English (Flynn, 1982; Schuster, 1983); mechanical engineering (Fry, 1990); medicine including surgery (Burnett and Cavaye, 1980; Laing and Nixon, 1990); music (Searby and Ewers, 1997); and theology (Collier, 1989); there are also reports of its relevance and validity in personnel selection (Dobson, 1989). In this context peer assessments, with appropriate criteria, have been made of performance, promotion, training and wages. From an analysis of 39 studies Dobson concluded that peer nominations and peer rankings are more valid than peer ratings. In peer nomination, each member of the group is asked to nominate and place in rank order a specified number of members of the group as being high or low on some performance parameter. In peer ranking, each member of the group ranks all the other members of the group, from high to low, on a scale in some performance characteristic. In peer rating, each member of the group rates all the other members of the group on some performance parameter. This essentially is the technique used in higher education to obtain peer grades.

Dobson suggests that peer rankings are the most discriminating of the three methods although, he noted, one study that found that peer nominations made during the third week of military officer training correlated 0.4 with success three years later. In respect of one day assessment centres, provided the appropriate behaviours have been elicited, peer group assessment should be relatively valid 'because peers assess each other, rather than themselves, questions with relatively high face validity can be asked directly with relatively little fear of faked response'.

It has been argued that friendship might bias the results but there is little evidence to suggest that this is the case. One study has found that racial prejudice may be found in peer evaluations, and for this reason it is suggested that groups should be homogenous.

Goldfinch and Raeside (1980) have warned against peer assessments that are arrived at as a result of group discussion about the contribution that each member made to the activity. While it may be seen to be 'fairer', it could lead to marks which reflect the personalities of the students, and not their actual contributions. In their study, the students privately rated the other members of the group. Marks were then calculated from these ratings by the tutors. The group project submission was given a group mark. A peer assessment factor was then calculated from the individual submissions. An individual's mark was the product of the peer assessment factor and the group mark. Students who contributed less than average were given a relatively small percentage of the group mark, while those who contributed more were given larger percentages. They felt that this method achieved the aim of rewarding individual students according to the percentage of the group's success that they contributed. One of the problems with a scheme like this is the large amount of subjectivity that is likely to be present in reporting.

Goldfinch and Raeside object to traditional rating scales used for peer group assessment because the students found them difficult to complete. Students also found it difficult to remember what had happened so they designed a different schema like those for primary trait analysis described in Chapter 11. This approach has been used with a large class of 200 students working in groups of three, four or five, on a realistic problem. Orsmond, Merry and Reiling (1996) also draw attention to the difficulty students might have with traditional rating scales. They asked students and tutors to rate posters against five criteria on a 0–4 scale. The categories, which were further defined, were self-explanatory, clear purpose (hypothesis), clear and justified conclusions, visually effective and attractive, and helpful level of detail. They wanted to examine the marking of individual criteria because in the past peer assessment studies had compared the mean tutor grade and that of the student for a given item of work. Their overall findings were that the overall agreement between tutors and students was 18 per cent, with 56 per cent of the students overmarking and 26 per cent undermarking. However, they found that these masked what was happening within the categories. A significant number of students undermarked 'clear and justified conclusion' whereas a significant number overmarked 'visually effective and helpful level of detail' when compared with the tutor. Various explanations for these differences are offered. One of them was that the students did not have a developed sense of criteria. Was it a lack of ability or a failure to understand the meaning of the criteria? Two studies referred to above found that students did not understand some of the criteria. It is an open question as to whether the results would have changed had a primary trait scale been used. Orsmond *et al.* make the point that peer assessment is not only a grading tool but an instructional technique. Thus while there might be doubt about the reliability of peer assessment in the summative mode, it does have a role to play in the formative mode. However, this finding can be criticized on the grounds that the students were in their first year. Such assessment should be regarded as training for subsequent peer assessment in later years. The students in this study felt they had benefited from the exercise: they believed they had been challenged, learnt to be more critical, as well as to work in a more structured way. Orsmond and his colleagues note that when marking against clear criteria, disagreements between tutor and student can easily be identified, and the tutor could be challenged as was the case in the student-teacher practice scheme described in Chapter 11.

Rafiq and Fullerton (1996) modified Goldfinch and Raeside's model for use in civil engineering. In the original model the students completed a two-part questionnaire. The first part related to skills involved in project tasks; the second part summarized a list of process skills related to group activities. When this was trialled, Rafiq and Fullerton found that the groups were reluctant to mark each other's work. The tutor monitoring the work also felt that bias crept into some of the assessments, and students had difficulty in remembering who did what. Rafiq and Fullerton, therefore, changed part one. Now the students were asked to keep a project diary. The tutor then allocated the marks on the basis of the project report 'in which the specific tasks that have been carried out are clearly identified by the students themselves, who have signed their own pieces of work.' The diaries are then used to confirm the tutor's own assessment. They are also a check against cheating. Because the project begins with a detailed brief that includes a time schedule another indicator is available of the work carried out by individual members of the group. The students were carefully briefed on the process. In the second part the student peer marking was carried in a classroom situation under examination conditions. This was partly to underline the seriousness of the exercise, and partly to avoid 'mark-fixing cartels'. It was found that the marks reflected the variation in contributions within a normal distribution.

Butcher, Stefani and Tariq (1995), some of whose work was described earlier, are much more confident about the performance of students in the biosciences. They arranged for self (A), and peer (B) assessment of project work by other group members, self-assessment (C) of contribution to the poster, peer assessment (D) of contribution to the poster by other group members, peer assessment of posters by students from other groups (E), staff assessment (F) of posters. They found that self-assessment marks were higher than those awarded by the peers. However, these differences were not statistically different but the discrimination of students with different abilities was achieved. The strongest assessor driven variation was found among staff. Butcher and his colleagues go so far as to argue that students 'could be assessed solely by one another to yield a useful complementary grade which might be used in conjunction with other forms of assessment in their courses'.

The marks derived from these projects contributed 10 per cent. The formula which they used to derive the individual's mark from the group mark was:

Individual's final percentage mark
= ¼ (mean of A and B) + ¼(mean of C and D) + ½ (F)

E was not included because it was not known how efficiently it had been carried out. (See Lejk, Wyvill and Farrow (1996) for a survey of methods in use in the UK.)

At Manchester Metropolitan University it was found that half of a group of students who had experienced peer assessment in marking felt that assessment was the role of the tutor. Apart from criticisms about the potential for bias and the interpretation of criteria students felt that peer assessment could increase motivation because of their involvement in the assessment process. It gave them an opportunity to compare and discuss the assignment with consequent gains in knowledge. Brindley and Scoffield (1998) concluded that it helped students to better understand the assessment process – although it was time consuming for the tutors.

In geography Pain and Mowl (1996) have reported how, with training in a workshop, peer and self-assessment can be used to improve performance in essay writing. Also in geography Stanier (1997) reported on the introduction of two student-centred techniques of learning, one of which was peer assessment the other group work. There was more resistance to group work than to peer assessment once it had been explained and justified.

At the University of Gezira in the Sudan the reliability, validity and acceptability of an instrument for use by medical student peers in a community setting was invest-igated because of the complexity of undertaking such assessments. The model was found to be reliable, reasonably valid, and acceptable to the students (Magzoub *et al.*, 1998).

In Australia Freeman (1995) addressed the problem of large classes: 210 students were divided into 41 teams during a course for a business degree. One of the assessable tasks was an oral class presentation worth 25 per cent of the students overall grade; 10 per cent of the marks were allocated to peer assessment. Two members of staff assigned to assess the operation of the groups also awarded the other 15 per cent of the marks. Teams of peers rated the presentations using a 22-point guide which they were given during the first week of the course. It was found that while there was little difference in the scores for the average presentation between staff and student scores that the deviations were considerable for any presentation. Students tended to downgrade good presentations as marked by staff and upgrade poor presentations. Freeman concluded that students could not be expected to undertake reliably the marking that would normally be undertaken by tutors without further controls. He suggested that students might be trained by using videos of previous presentations to indicate what was wanted.

The results obtained from the limited number of reported peer assessment exercises undertaken in several areas of the curriculum are encouraging. As Freeman (1995) suggests there needs to be much more research. In making their comments none of the investigators have drawn attention to the weaknesses of conventional assessment techniques. Neither have they mentioned that as things stand new and young teachers are thrown in at the deep end. Would a meta-analysis of the data show that peer assessment is no more and no less reliable than those obtained with traditional examinations? The way forward would seem to be through training.

It would also seem that the assessment of one's peers should lead to reflection on one's own capabilities. For this reason there is much interest in self-assessment since if one can reflect on one's own performance the learner ought to be able to direct that performance and take responsibility for it. As with most initiatives in education the 'terms' used were subject to a variety of interpretations. The purpose of the next section is to describe the usages to which the terms self-assessment and self-evaluation have been put.

Self-assessment versus self-evaluation

'Assessment' is sometimes substituted by 'evaluation'. Sometimes the commentator intends it to mean the same thing as self-assessment. Sometimes self-assessment is taken to mean self-grading and self- evaluation is taken to be a broader concept. As Taylor (1994) says 'the variety of terms reflects the different perspectives of self-evaluation'.

Klenowski (1995) defines student evaluation 'as the evaluation or judgement of the worth of one's performance and the identification of one's strengths and weaknesses with a view to improving one's learning outcomes'. Some would say there is no difference between this and self-assessment. However, Klenowski argues that it is broader than self-assessment which is the assigning of a grade because 'it refers to ascribing value to a learning experience: first in the identification of criteria used; second by what is considered meritorious: and third, by outlining the implications for future action'. Some would say of the first two criteria that that is what happens when a person assigns a grade to themselves. Cowan (1998) takes a similar view to Klenowski but it is not the view of Boud (1995) with whom Cowan takes issue. Cowan argues that when Boud writes that self-assessment 'has the self as agent and audience'. and 'is essentially formative and not absolute, although it can be used for summative purposes' he (Boud) is writing about self-evaluation. Cowan argues that evaluation 'is a process in which judgements are made by comparing performance with criteria or standards'. He says that assessment is concerned with *outcomes* whereas evaluation is concerned with *process*. But surely, by definition any comparison against standards is a grading or assessment.

A process is a complex flow of outcomes that lead to a solution or proposition. In respect of the engineering science projects described in Chapter 12 the student was asked to engage in a critical review. The rubric read:

> In comparing the final product with the original specification the candidate has produced a thorough and objective discussion in which consideration has been given to all major aspects of the work including suggestions for further development and a critical appraisal of the conduct of the projects with a clear indication of the lessons learnt, etc.

It was intended that this should have engaged the candidate in an evaluation of the processes which led to the final solution, and the lessons learnt should have inspired the growth in knowledge required for Newman's philosophical habit of mind.

This critical review had its origins in the category of evaluation in *The Taxonomy of Educational Objectives*.

> Evaluation is defined as the making of judgement about the value for some purpose, of ideas, works, solutions, methods, material, etc. It involves the use of criteria as well as standards for appraising the extent to which particulars are accurate, effective, economical, or satisfying. The judgements may be either quantitative or qualitative, and the criteria may be either those determined by the student or those which are given him ... it is not necessarily the last step in thinking or problem solving. It is quite possible that the evaluative process will in some case be the prelude

to the acquisition of new knowledge, a new attempt at comprehension or application, or a new analysis or synthesis.

Irrespective of this argument students find self-assessment or self-evaluation difficult. Some treat it as a superficial exercise, others find it difficult to get beyond superficiality, and only a few are able at first to function at a deep level. When they do there is evidence of reflective capability. This is why self-assessment or self-evaluation is so important.

There is not much point in pursuing this discussion further. Evaluation and assessment will continue to be used inter-changeably. Therefore, as Loacker of Alverno College (private communication) says, it is up to each writer to define the terms as they use them. Those writers referred to in this section did just that! The next section, as a prelude to a review of studies of self-assessment in industry and higher education, will consider the issue of reflective thinking primarily from the perspective of the teacher even though many of the reports on self-assessment relate their findings to the ability to reflect.

Self-accountability in teaching and reflective practice

As long ago as 1976 Elliott urged the school teaching community to engage in reflection. He was anxious that they should not be subjected to evaluation by the results of standardized tests. He believed that professionalism demanded that teachers should become accountable for themselves, and in this way meet the requirements for accountability in society. George Carter of Salford University has argued that had university teachers in Britain adopted this attitude toward their teaching they would not now be faced with the bureaucracy of external assessment (private communication). Elliott (1976) wrote:

> If teacher education is to prepare students or experienced teachers for accountability then it must be concerned with their ability to reflect on classroom situations. By 'practical reflections' I mean reflection with a view to action. This involves identifying and diagnosing those practical problems which exist for the teacher in his situation and deciding on those strategies for resolving them. The view of accountability which I have outlined with its emphasis on the right of the teacher to evaluate his own moral agency, assumes that teachers are capable of identifying and diagnosing their practical problems with some degree of objectivity. It implies that the teacher is able to identify a discrepancy between what he in fact brings about in the classroom and his responsibilities to foster and prevent certain circumstances. If he cannot do this he is unable to assess whether or not he is obliged to. I believe that being plunged into a context where outsiders evaluated their moral agency would be self-defeating since the anxiety generated would render the achievement of an objective attitude at any of these levels extremely difficult.

To accomplish this end he suggested that discrepancies could be found in a number of ways. These included the audio-recording of lessons and consultation with colleagues. Nowadays, he would presumably include video-recording. Reflection is the key generic skill. The teacher has to make a 'judgement' about whether or not to take action, and if action is required what sort of action to take. In medical education the discrepancy and the actions taken to remedy the discrepancy have been called 'proficieny theory' (Davis and Fox, 1994 on Knox, 1990). The reason why teacher educators have taken so much interest in the use of diaries, learning journals and portfolios is that they are thought to be a means of developing the reflective capability required for professional behaviour. It is also the reason why university teachers in the US are being encouraged to keep portfolios.

Like evaluation the term reflective practice means different things to different people, and depends on the theoretical base from which they started. LaBoskey (1994) as a result of a study of reflective practice among pre-service teachers concluded that what we believe about reflection influences our behaviour as reflective practitioners. I can illustrate these points from my own experience. I wanted my pre-service teachers whose instructional research project was described in Chapter 11 to evaluate what they had done. To me the term evaluation was taken from the Bloom *Taxonomy*. It meant a qualitative judgement immediately after the lesson to reflect on what had happened to themselves and their students during the lesson, a subsequent test on the matter of the lesson designed to meet the theory being examined, followed by an analysis and further qualitative judgement. In order to develop skill in the post-lesson evaluation, I commended Eisner's (1979) idea of connoisseurship, and asked them to become educational connoisseurs. Elton (1998) has suggested that university examiners in the UK should seek to develop this skill.

Eisner (1979) promoted the concept of educational criticism. He suggested that in order to evaluate their teaching teachers had to develop skills akin to those possessed by art connoisseurs.

> The consequence of using educational criticism to perceive educational objects and events is the development of educational connoisseurship. As one learns to look at educational phenomena, as one ceases using stock responses to educational situations and develops habits of perceptual exploration, the ability to experience qualities and their relationship increases.

Reflective thinking was required for the evaluations these pre-service teachers had to do. According to Eisner such thinking leads to theory and it is the base for curriculum planning.

> Prior to actual teaching: planning at home reflecting on what has occurred during a particular class session, and discussing in groups ways to organize a program. Theory sophisticates personal reflection and group deliberation. In so far as a theory suggests consequences flowing from particular circumstances, it enables those who understand the theory to take those circumstances into account when planning.

My analysis of some 5000 reports of student-teachers lessons confirmed that it takes a long time to develop skill in reflective practice. Had more time been available, more training could have been given. As it was, the reports showed many different levels of reflective capability. Some could undoubtedly reflect in depth. More time is needed to help the majority, although it seemed to me that some would never make it. LaBoskey reports similar sentiments. They confirm King and Kitchener's (1994) point that different individuals operate from different base levels, and that performance may vary across situations. Optimal performance in reflective judgement may be influenced by environmental factors. In higher education these would include course structure, type of instuction, and method of assessment.

Surprisingly Eisner's approach does not seem to have infiltrated teacher training in any large way. It was Schon's (1983) *The Reflective Practitioner* and subsequent books that triggered off interest in reflective practice not only in education but in other subjects as well (e.g. engineering, law, medicine).

Schon's idea of reflective practice is based on a five-stage model of experiential learning. Fox and Craig (1994) have slightly adapted his model to show how it relates to clinical practice in medicine. Thus in the first stage *knowing-in-action* the embedded knowledge we possess is brought into play. This knowledge is routine and automatic. It is the kind of knowledge represented by the first category of *The Taxonomy of Educational Objectives*. When we have a consultation with a physician the doctor searches through his/her bank of knowledge to see if there are recognizable symptoms that can be diagnosed. The same thing happens when we diagnose anything. Like the physician we can often be surprised when the evidence is contradictory and/or ambiguous. This is the stage of *surprises*. These may be something odd in a case history or laboratory report. Surprise causes us to review what has gone before to see how it differs from previous cases. Schon calls this the stage of *reflection-in-action*.

The next stage is to *experiment*. In the case of medicine this does not mean experiment for the sake of experiment. It may simply mean changing a prescription. 'These experiments are ad hoc in nature. They reflect the ability of the physician to reconstruct the information, knowledge and skills needed to accommodate the unusual features of the case' (Fox and Craig, 1994).

The final stage is *reflection-on-action*. This is necessary if what has been learnt is to be accommodated in the bank of knowledge.

Cowan (1998) argues that there is a third stage of reflection which was named for him by Ray McAleese as *reflection-for-action*. He was led to this view when he observed Open University students during a study weekend. At the beginning they:

> reflected on the difficulties which they encountered in their studies, and tried to extract examples of that, and to make some classification of these examples. At that time they were, in effect, defining their aspirations for the workshop activity which lay ahead. They were reflecting on types of problem which they hoped to be able to resolve more effectively in the future than in the past. I suggest that this reflection, being anticipatory, is aptly titled *reflection-for-action*.

Everyday experience would seem to confirm this point of view. The important contribution of Cowan's reflective dialogue is that he shows, how by merging the ideas of Kolb (see Chapter 8) and Schon, even though the reliance on reflection in the two models is for different purposes, it is possible to construct learning experiences for students during the course of their daily studies. This poses a challenge for assessment both in the design of questions and the methods to be used.

Cowan says that he knows when he deliberately reflects when:

I have *committed myself* to reflect, and know how and when I intend to prompt myself to do so. I *notice something* which perturbs me, and reflect in order to find improvement, explanation or understanding. I am *asked a question* which I cannot answer without reflecting; or I am given a task which makes a similar demand. An *intervention* by someone, not necessarily my tutor, requires me to think reflectively. *Dialogue* with a peer prompts me to engage in reflection, which may be shared. *I decide that I should reflect* on my processes of reflection, and determine my own outcomes and my desired standards in that reflection about reflection.

These would seem to meet the requirements for the practical reflection Elliott (1976) thought every teacher should undertake.

Self-assessment in industry and higher education

Self-assessment is used widely in management training programmes and personnel selection. In training rating forms of the kind shown in Figure 14.1 are used for the self-assessment of the contribution that one has made to the work of a group. This particular form was designed for the users to rate their contribution to a 'negotiation' having seen themselves perform on video.

Similar kinds of form can be used for the self and peer assessment of cooperative learning. Johnson and Johnson (1996) suggest the following parameters be rated on a four-point scale:

- On time for class.
- Arrives prepared for class.
- Reliably completes all assigned work on time.
- Work is high quality.
- Contributes to groupmates' learning daily.
- Asks for academic help and assistance when it is needed.
- Gives careful step-by-step explanations (not just tell answers).
- Builds on others reasoning.
- Relates what is being learned to previous knowledge.
- Helps draw a visual presentation of what is being learned.
- Voluntarily extends a project.

Of course there are other items which could be asked. There is, however, a broader picture. Research on assessment centres has shown that self-assessment can help individuals obtain a more objective picture of their strengths and weaknesses in relation to the purposes of assessment (e.g. personal development, selection for a job) (Schmitt, Ford and Stults, 1986). This, among other things, is one of the advantages claimed for self-assessment in higher education (Jarvinen and Kohonen, 1995; Woodward, 1998). Just as in industrial organizations, self-assessment can play a role in career development, as for example in teacher preparation (Sumsion and Fleet, 1996; Woodward, 1998), and the identification of training needs (Dobson, 1989), so

SELF-APPRAISAL – BEHAVIOUR IN DISCUSSION

Please study your performance from the video playback. This is a private assessment so be perfectly frank in answering the questions – otherwise you are only fooling yourself.

In this discussion I tended to:

	YES	NO
ask specific questions about the topic discussion	☐	☐
try to score debating points	☐	☐
get irritated with an opponent	☐	☐
ask for clarification/facts about a point made by the other side	☐	☐
contribute helpful suggestions	☐	☐
admit I was misinformed/wrong	☐	☐
interrupt before a speaker has finished	☐	☐
opt out of answering an opponent's question on the grounds that I would appear to give way	☐	☐
criticise when I had not really got a real point to make	☐	☐
close the door top further argument	☐	☐
change my mind when my assumptions were shown to be faulty	☐	☐
keep quiet when I had nothing constructive to say	☐	☐
overrule the chairman/leader	☐	☐
prepare my case before the meeting	☐	☐
not listen to an opponent's argument because I disagreed with his or her case	☐	☐

Now compare your results and consider whether your contribution to the meeting was:

Potentially destructive to your case						Potentially helpful to your case
	-3	-2	-1	0	+1	+2	+3

Because I was:

Bloody-minded							Co-operative
Quarrelsome							Benign
Rigid							Flexible
Intolerant							Tolerant
Close-minded							Open-minded
Talkative							Silent
Dependent							Independent
Lacking in Information/knowledge							Well-informed

| | -3 | -2 | -1 | 0 | +1 | +2 | +3 |

Now compare what you have written with your original score

    - points   + points

Now attempt to define ways in which training could help you improve your performance in discussion

Figure 14.1 Example of a self-assessment schedule for evaluating self-performance in a group conducting negotiations.

it can also help students identify their curriculum and learning needs as part of a more general self-monitoring of performance (Boyd and Cowan, 1985). The same applies to faculty (Taylor, 1994; Cowan, 1998). Schroeder (1989), in his study of high performing managers concluded that they have more accurate awareness of the competences they possess as strengths and as limitations and emphasize contributions based on their strengths. By implication all high performing persons might be supposed to have high levels of self-awareness.

In the process of reflection involved in self-assessment, an individual learns to distinguish between self-knowledge, that is, what we believe to be true about ourselves and, self-disclosure, that is, what we are prepared to tell other people about ourselves. Many academics object to self-assessment on the grounds that individuals will not disclose the truth about themselves or that certain patterns will emerge. For example, 'the best students would be hypercritical and thus would downgrade their work severely; the not-so-good students would be unable to recognise deficiencies in their work and would see my (the teacher's) ploy as an opportunity to grade themselves up'. (Liotts, 1990). Self-assessment should therefore help the student 'to develop self-confidence without developing over-confidence and bragadoccio' and in this way the more valid and reliable their personal judgements will become (Woods, Haymark and Marshall, 1988). This confidence should be accompanied by self-inspired learning.

Herriot (1989) argues that the selection process should be a matching process between candidates' occupational self-concept and the objectives which the organization has for the task. Applied to the selection of professional people, Makin (1989) argues that this matching process is the 'crucial criterion for selection'. The trouble is that it can all too often disguise sentiment. Just as in higher education examinations, candidates for selection to a job bring with them attitudes toward selection procedures. After all, a selection process is a test and just as tests (examinations) influence decisions about learning, so to does the selection procedure influence the decisions which the candidate makes (Herriot, 1989). But the outcomes of the process can also influence the applicants, either positively or negatively, particularly if the application was for internal promotion. Negative outcomes could lead to a lowering of self-esteem (Warr, 1987) but equally they could lead to a more realistic view of their talents. These are also the experience of some examinees, as Malleson (1965) pointed out in his discussion of identity (see Chapter 6).

In a study sponsored by the British Employment Department Connor and Warr (1990) describe the development and evaluation of a Personal Effectiveness Measure for use by the providers of training. They distinguish between intellectual effectiveness and non-intellectual effectiveness and the items in the instrument reflect these two factors. Within the non-intellectual dimension they assessed self-efficacy, social avoidance tendency and learning difficulties. Among 1000 trainees in hotel and catering, they found that high levels of personal effectiveness were linked to self-belief in the ability to carry out tasks and solve problems. Low social avoidance tendency scores and low learning difficulty scores were associated with high levels of personal effectiveness. These need to be related to confidence, for as Murray (1990) has pointed out personal development schemes can lead to overconfidence and unjustified personal expectations which, if they are not met, might create a negative self-concept. For example, one study of physicians showed that physicians who are either excessively overconfident or underconfident about their knowledge may have impaired clinical judgement (Hausmann *et al.*, 1990). While the principle of self-assessment is good of itself, factors such as these need to be taken into account, and for this reason other measures, which might be of value to the student, might be obtained. They also suggest that self-assessment should be a process of development in which the student is weaned from the tutor. Given the complexity of the issue, tutors are likely to need training since they are effectively put in the role of counsellor.

Self-assessment for grading

An important issue in self-assessment is the degree of teacher control over the process. Falchikov (1986) distinguishes between three types of control. These are: (1) self-assessment in which the learner judges her or his own performance against her or his own assessment criteria; (2) peer group assessment, where peers assess the learner with or without prior discussion of criteria (see Chapter 12); and (3) collaborative assessment where the tutor and the learner negotiate the assessment criteria and the final assessment grade. Fazey (1993) has argued that the skill of self-assessment cannot be taken for granted and that it must be treated as a skill that can be acquired. Penny and Grover (1996) affirm this view and argue that students do not readily reflect on their experiences. They found their students were highly pragmatic and technical, with a 'good' study (that which they were asked to self-assess) being defined in terms of criteria related to style, clarity and presentation. Fazey demonstrates two possible approaches to developing this skill with students in education courses and argues that structured approaches can lead to a situation where students will take responsibility for their learning.

Penny and Grover (1996) point out that the contribution which self-assessment makes to the overall degree classification in teacher education can be very small. Therefore, why should students take it seriously? Yet, 'these same students, once they graduate as teachers will make informal and formal assessments of their pupils work' for which they have received little or no training. The same applies to the new university teacher.

Self-assessment is something we do all the time. We all make judgements about our competence and efficacy in relation to jobs that have to be done and people with whom we are forced, for one reason or another, to compare. Sometimes these judgements are hasty and arrived at without rationale, and sometimes they are the result of due reflection. Students often privately predict their performance in comparison with others in their groups and, in the end, most of us, argues Rokeach (1960) desire to know the truth about ourselves in such terms. There is a tendency in human behaviour to want our judgements to be reliable and valid. Nevertheless, there is, as Dobson (1989) points out, a tendency among the majority of people to slightly distort these self-evaluations in order to maintain positive self-knowledge. Dobson says of job selection that 'it can be inferred that the probability of an inflated self-assessment increases when honesty is not valued; it is believed that an inflated self-assessment increases the probability of being selected (for a job); the job concerned is highly valued; or there are no alternative jobs available.' The converse applies in the case of accurate self-disclosure.

We can see at once how this relates to the reliability and validity of marking. If self-assessments are to be valid, then educators will have to take into account the potential conflict between the need for accurate self-knowledge on one hand and positive self-knowledge on the other, for the way in which learners resolve this conflict influences their motivation. Educators will not be able to divorce self-assessment from the context of learning (Boyd and Cowan, 1986).

Mabe and West's (1982) meta-analysis of 55 studies of self-assessment on the measurement of skills abilities and knowledge, and Falchikov's (1986) ten studies in education, as well as a continuing but small flow of papers (Somervell, 1993; Fazey, 1993; Jarvinen and Kohonen, 1995; Oldfield and MacAlpine, 1995; Sumsion and Fleet, 1996; Penny and Grover; 1996;Woodward, 1998), are encouraging. According to Mabe and West, among the conditions which will improve the accuracy of self-assessment are that it will be validated, that it will be anonymous, and that the candidates have experience of self-assessment. They also note that high intelligence, high achievement status and internal locus of control are associated with more accurate evaluations (see also Dobson, 1989). Educationalists involved in self-assessment consistently report the need for well-defined criteria. One might suppose that the more the scheme used for self-assessment is criterion referenced, the greater the validity and reliability that it might have. It may also be supposed that self-assessments in the cognitive domain are likely to be more accurate than those in the personal domain, since so many other factors enter into the making of personal judgements.

Earl (1986) took an opposite view of the need to state criteria. In the context of peer assessment, the staff involved in her study questioned how explicit the criteria should be. They felt that the degree of explanation depended on what the staff wanted the peer assessment to do. So they agreed to minimize the instructor imposed criteria and opted for general guidelines. An alternative that might have got over this difficulty was to have allowed the students to work out their own criteria, and then to have negotiated it them with staff. Students may have to be trained in self-assessment and they may be helped in this if the approach is via criterion-referenced schemes. A workshop in self-assessment has been developed for the McMaster problem-solving course (Woods *et al.*, 1988; also summarized in Heywood, 1994; see also Fazey (1993)for an alternative).

Falchikov (1986) made the point that when criterion-referenced schemes are used there is likely to be a higher rate of agreement between faculty and student. As indicated above, Penny and Grover (1996) found their students were more concerned with lower order criteria than with higher levels of theoretical and conceptual understanding. Falchikov noted that age and experience may be a cause of disagreement among markers and students. If criteria are agreed this should reduce the difference. Falchikov found that the differences in marks between tutor and student were acceptably low in 74 per cent of the cases. There was a slight tendency to undermark than overmark. She also found a tendency among the younger students to overgrade.

Sumsion and Fleet (1996) used a simple instrument to rate pieces of work submitted by final year student teachers in an Australian university. The dimensions were highly reflective, more than moderately reflective, moderately reflective, less than moderately reflective, and not reflective. Each of these was rated on a five-point scale from outstanding to pass. They found a low level of inter-coder reliability. They were led to ask the question as to whether reflection was suited to quantitative measurement. The scales may be too simplistic and may not provide insights into the complex nature of reflection. They found that students who were not academically able could reflect. It is, however, a questionable assumption that the ability to reflect and achievement are correlated. Nevertheless the point they make that reliance on written expression to judge reflection will operate against those who have not acquired an appropriate reflective writing genre.

Claxton (1995) is of the view that involvement in grading causes reflection:

> If a group of students selects a band of marks that is either significantly narrower or higher than the teachers would have chosen it seems that here too the exercise of critical reflection on what it is that one has produced cannot but help the development of learning acumen. Instead of becoming dependent on external authority for correction and evaluation, those functions are internalised by the student. And again this fosters the vital distinction between the 'informative' and the 'emotive' functions of evaluation. Being able to turn a critical eye on one's own product, while at the same time retaining equanimity towards self, is the vital factor in the development of resilience...

For Claxton intelligence is 'knowing what to do when you don't know what to do', and this requires resilience, resourcefulness, reflectivity and responsibility all of which the Alverno curriculum would claim to achieve.

Collaborative or negotiated assessment

One outstanding example of collaborative assessment that has been published is due to Boyd (a student) and Cowan (her tutor). In a course in design in civil engineering, Cowan gave the students responsibility for their own assessment. He established a contract with the class that they would set their goals week-by-week. He would not provide advice or direction.

> In lieu of examinations, each learner would prepare self-assessment in the form of a criteria list of her desired goals, a description of her actual learning and a reconciliation of these (in relation to agreed bench marks), leading to the choice of mark. Each stage in this process of assessment would be open to questioning, and discussion; but the ultimate decision would remain completely within the jurisdiction of the learner.

Their short paper is a dialogue about what happened (Boyd and Cowan, 1986). Boyd was shown the Perry model of intellectual development (Chapter 8) in order for her to gain an understanding of the psychological roots of learning. She wrote of her third-year experience with Cowan when he had placed the responsibility for learning and assessment on the students that:

In accepting responsibility for setting my own criteria. I clearly made a firm commitment to my eventual choice. Hence my learning must be rated at one of the higher levels of Perry's scale. Surface processing, which is encouraged by cue-consciousness, was absent – because I had chosen my aims and criteria and directed my learning accordingly. And deep processing was positively encouraged – because I was subject to no pressures other than those which were self imposed.

They met again after Boyd had completed four months of her final year, when both instruction and the assessment were conventional. Their comments on the more recent situation are in stark contrast for they concluded that:

There was no commitment at the higher level on Perry's scale, except in part of the final year project, where she had opted to work to her own criteria, rather than those of her supervisor.

Hard won habits of deep-processing and, in particular, of rigorously searching for key points and issues persisted to some extent in her private reading and even in attendance at lectures, although there was a marked regression compared with the working style in third year design.

At the same time, cue-seeking and cue-conscious activity were more frequent, more deliberate and more purposeful.

They continued.

These highly subjective and presumably biased impressions prompt us to wonder if it is possible to generate higher level commitment without involving the learners in setting goals and criteria; and also if the habit of deep processing, once developed, is likely to persist to some extent, even when circumstances actively encourage surface processing.

It is evident that if students are to make the most of their experience, they must reflect on it both at the time and in retrospect. Such reflections should not be ad hoc and it is for this reason that diaries, learning journals and portfolios are used. An investigation at Sheffield University reported that students showed marked individual differences in their ability to reflect. In relation to the immediate context engineering students found this most difficult. They were not used 'to talking in terms of feelings, nor could they see the relevance of such reflection to learning about engineering problems!' This was in contrast to students in health-related courses who found it helped them understand the feelings of their patients (Allen, 1991).

Boyd and Cowan (1986) are led to question 'if it is possible to generate higher Perry level of commitment, without involving learners in setting their own goals and criteria' which is why they argue self-assessment should replace examinations.

Curriculum-integrated self-assessment across an institution

Brief reference has been made to the curriculum at Alverno College in Chapter 2 and other chapters. By the mid-1980s the college had learnt from the self-assessments the students had conducted that self-assessment was an ability to be learned (Loacker and Jensen, 1988) so they aim to include some component of self-assessment in every assessment that the student makes. The students progress from a beginning stage through an intermediate stage to an advanced stage (Alverno, 1999). There are five components to this assessment. Observing, Interpreting/Analyzing, Judging, and Planning. Examples of each of these components are given in Figure 14.2.

A number of academic colleagues from the British Isles, including myself, have spent time at Alverno and some of us have been able to join in classes and interview students. Two of them spent several weeks following the programme. One of them, Judith George (who is deputy director of the Scottish Region of the Open University), summed up her experience thus:

Observing (Intermediate)

In observing self in action an intermediate student uses explicit ability or discipline frameworks to help organize her reflections (even though the application of framework to performance might be somewhat mechanical). She shows that aspects of the ability or discipline that have influenced her by meaningfully relating concepts to her performance.
Criteria.
Begins to apply disciplinary and/or ability frameworks to own performance: Communicates observations using disciplinary and/or ability language: -Stands back at critical points to reflect on performance.

Interpreting/Analyzing (advanced).

In interpreting/analyzing own performance an advanced student articulates how her performance is uniquely her own and uses her imagination to project how she might extend and refine it.
Criteria.
Explains components of performance that make it unique and distinctive and are part of student's style or voice: Uses frameworks in a way that reflects, extends, or recreates them: Synthesizes patterns of behaviours and processes over time and in varied contexts.

Judging (Beginning)

In judging own performance a beginning student uses her knowledge of the criteria to explain how her performance gives evidence of the behaviours inherent in the criteria. She uses paraphrasing to explore meaning implied in the criteria.
Criterion.
Makes connections between criteria and behaviours and performance.

Planning (Advanced)

In planning for further development an advanced student is aware of herself as a life-long-learner. She shapes her future performance by considering her past work, her intellectual processes, and a variety of discipline models and frameworks with attention to her own style and creativity.
Criterion.
Uses multiple models of performance to set and continue to refine goals for future ongoing development.

Figure 14.2 Extracts from the Framework for Development of Self Assessment at Alverno College (Alverno, 1999). Reproduced by kind permission of the College. (By criteria is meant the explicit public criteria as defined by the abilities – 'In order to show they can convince others of the credibility of there historical interpretation, for example, our students are told that they need to learn to present sufficient evidence, along with a number of other skills like using clear, concrete expression or structuring ideas into a connected whole. Once students are able to articulate criteria themselves they internalized their understanding of performance.' (Alverno, 1994))

It is important to appreciate that assessment at Alverno is not something which happens at the end of a course, or periodically during it. The very first commitment of each student entering Alverno is to go through the self-assessment programme; in this, she undertakes a number of diagnostic exercises – in reading, writing, listening, computing, public-speaking and maths. The object of these exercises is for her to come to an understanding, based upon the evidence she has gathered of what her starting point is, of where she is at present in relation to the development of these skills. *She* assesses her performance, and comes to a jointly negotiated agreement with an assessor on the outcome. The emphasis, stressed in an initial workshop on the subject and carried through all classes, is on judgement against declared criteria, and on observed and declared data.

Formative assessment, underpinning the college's philosophy of 'not yet' rather than 'failure', is constantly present; space is created in every class, and in assignments, to step aside from the work and to reflect critically on how, and how well, work is being done.

Here the sense of community of learning comes into play. Peer support and insight is regarded as one of the most valuable learning resources of a student. The skills of social interaction are explicitly fostered. Group work is not only a marked feature of every class; if a group is baffled, the instructor – or even another group – will help them to look first for flaws in their ability to use each other to tease out ideas, rather than look, as we would, to the material they are working on as the source of the problem.

Such support implies openness and security in a group. Group identity – especially among hard-pressed weekend part-timers – is very noticeable. Within this context, the affective aspects of learning, as well as the cognitive ones, are addressed deliberately and overtly in course design and presentation. The emotions aroused in the consideration of the moral dilemmas posed by technological advances, for example, are centrally addressed as legitimate and vital aspects of the subject; the process of balancing feeling against thought in decision making is observed and reflected upon, with no flagging of academic rigour.

And George concludes:

A curriculum and culture which can produce such highly motivated learners, the reflective, autonomous, deep-processing learners we would all love to teach, can but repay generously the time and effort devoted to its study. (From *A Learner's View of Alverno* – unpublished)

Toward multiple-strategy assessment and evaluation

Alverno College provides a curriculum that is assessment-led, for the purpose of enhancing learning within a liberal education. The college uses a multiple-strategy approach to assessment with the emphasis on positive formative assessment that is seen as the best way of promoting academic and personal development. These assessments lead to the mastery of the abilities that are the public outcomes of the programme, and academic facility in the subjects studied to major and minor levels. At the same time it also takes a multiple-strategy approach to the evaluation of its practices. For example, it has tried to establish the effects of the college experience on the subsequent career performance of its graduates (Mentkowski and Doherty, 1983). Evaluation is ongoing.

The work which led to the author's concept of multiple-strategy assessment was also based on the principle that assessments can influence student learning for the better. However, it was undertaken in the context of public examinations and was less comprehensive than the approach adopted by Alverno. It would have been more complete had the evaluation taken into account entering characteristics of the students such as interest, personality and problem-solving ability and followed them through into their subsequent careers. However, while this was understood, it was not possible. Nevertheless, the combination of examination and coursework were designed to focus on key abilities that had many similarities with the Alverno model.

These experiences suggest that there is no reason in principle why multiple-strategy assessment and evaluation cannot be developed in departments, or areas responsible for the teaching of specific subjects. In the case of the problem-based student teacher as researcher of instruction programme (see Chapter 12) the tutor focused on the key abilities thought to be important in the evaluation of instruction by teachers in their classrooms. It is, therefore, possible to adopt a small-scale approach to multiple-strategy assessment in a course or unit offered by a single teacher provided that the class is of a reasonable size. Otherwise the teacher will become overburdened with assessment if adequate feedback is to be provided.

There are many ways in which a multiple-strategy approach to assessment can be achieved. The one chosen has to emerge from the culture in which it is to be set. The criticism that it can only be achieved within small private colleges (2000+ day and weekend students) is without foundation. At the same time the Alverno model is resource intensive. Classes are small and the teachers are dedicated to achieving the goals of the programme. More importantly, they are not required to do research. The conflict between research and teaching, present in many universities, does not exist. So long as funding and promotion depend on research, the effort required to make radical and time-consuming changes in curriculum, assessment and instruction will not be found. Faculty will concentrate on obtaining good ratings for traditional methods of teaching spiced with the new technologies.

A multiple-strategy approach to assessment and evaluation is feasible at the department level but it will not work if there is not a whole-hearted commitment to the exercise. It requires that teachers collaborate in teams, and that each teacher offers what they feel they can do best. It will require a total rethink of a department's approach to teaching and learning, especially if it wishes, as in the case of Alverno, to track and provide for student development. Modular systems may promote difficulties but these are not insurmountable, as experience at the Colorado School of Mines shows (Chapter 8). If attention focuses on formative rather than summative assessment, the requirement for terminal assessments at the end of every semester may disappear, and where course structure is coherent, a summative examination focusing on specific key abilities that takes into account the knowledge dimension might be set at the end of the year.

The teaching Goals Inventory (TGI) is a self-assessment of instructional goals. Its purpose is threefold: (1) to help college teachers become more aware of what they want to accomplish in individual courses; (2) to help faculty locate Classroom Assessment Techniques they can adapt and use to assess how well they are achieving their teaching and learning goals; and (3) to provide a starting point for discussions of teaching and learning goals among colleagues.

In relation to the course you are focusing on, indicate whether each goal you rate is

Essential	A goal you always/nearly always try to achieve
Very important	A goal you often try to achieve
Important	A goal you sometimes try to achieve
Unimportant	A goal you rarely try to achieve
Not applicable	A goal you never try to achieve

There are no 'right' or 'wrong' answers; only personally more or less accurate ones.

1. Develop ability to apply principles and generalizations already learned to new problems and situations
2. Develop analytic skills
3. Develop problem-solving skills
4. Develop ability to draw reasonable inferences from observations
5. Develop ability to synthesize and integrate information and ideas
6. Develop ability to think holistically: to see the whole as well as the parts
7. Develop ability to think creatively
8. Develop ability to distinguish between fact and opinion
9. Improve skill at paying attention
10. Develop ability to concentrate
11. Improve memory skills
12. Improve listening skills
13. Improve speaking skills
14. Improve reading skills
15. Improve writing skills
16. Develop appropriate study skills, strategies, and habits
17. Improve mathematical skills
18. Learn terms and facts of this subject
19. Learn concepts and theories in this subject
20. Develop skill in using materials, tools, and/or technology central to this subject
21. Learn to understand perspective and values of this subject
22. Prepare for transfer or graduate study
23. Learning techniques and methods used to gain new knowledge in this subject
24. Learn to evaluate methods and materials in this subject
25. Learn to appreciate important contributions to this subject
26. Develop an appreciation of the liberal arts and sciences
27. Develop an openness to new ideas
28. Develop an informed concern about contemporary social issues
29. Develop a commitment to exercise the rights and responsibilities of citizenship
30. Develop a lifelong love of learning
31. Develop aesthetic appreciations
32. Develop an informed historical perspective
33. Develop an informed understanding of the role of science and technology
34. Develop an informed appreciation of other cultures
35. Develop capacity to make informed ethical choices
36. Develop ability to work productively with others
37. Develop management skills
38. Develop leadership skills
39. Develop a commitment to accurate work
40. Improve ability to follow directions, instructions and plans
41. Improve ability to organize and use time effectively
42. develop a commitment to personal achievement
43. Develop ability to perform skillfully
44. Cultivate a sense of responsibility for one's own behaviour
45. Improve self-esteem/self-confidence
46. Develop a commitment to one's own values
47. Develop respect for others
48. Cultivate emotional health and well-being
49. Cultivate an active commitment to honesty
50. Develop capacity to think for one's self
51. Develop capacity to make wise decisions
52. In general, how do you see your primary role as a teacher? (Although more than one statement may apply, please circle only one.)

Teaching students facts and principles of the subject matter

1. Providing a role model for students
2. Helping student develop higher-order thinking skills
3. Preparing student for jobs/careers
4. Fostering student development and personal growth
5. Helping students develop basic learning skills

Figure 14.3 *Teaching Goals Inventory, Self-Scorable Version.*
From the Teaching Goals Inventory, Self- Scorable Version In Classroom Assessment Techniques by T. A. Angelo and K. P.Cross (1993- Jossey Bass, San Fransisco). Reproduced by kind permission of the authors.

Classroom assessment and personal accountability

Elliott (1976) argued that if teachers were to be professionals they should engage in reflective behaviour. Cowan (1998) showed how he had developed this skill in a profound way but some teachers may be frightened by his approach. However, in spite of the pessimism of earlier paragraphs there is much that can be done which is relatively simple to improve conventional teaching and assessment. For example Gibbs, Habeshaw and Habeshaw (1993) have suggested 53 techniques of assessment. In other books they have suggested 53 ways of helping students to learn and 53 things that can be done in lectures. Angelo and Cross (1993) have suggested 50 classroom assessment techniques (CATs). These have the purpose of collecting data on student learning in order to improve it. One of them, the one-minute question, was referred to in Chapter 9. Another, concept mapping, was also described in Chapter 9. Their book describes how teachers have used each of them in their classrooms. They assume that classroom assessment is context-specific. 'What works well in one classroom will not necessarily work in another.'

Angelo and Cross (1993) and others developed a Teaching Goals Inventory (TGI). The purpose of this inventory was to 'help teachers become more aware of what they wanted to accomplish in individual courses, help faculty locate classroom assessment techniques they can adapt and use to assess how well they are achieving their teaching and learning goals, and provide a starting point for discussions of teaching and learning goals among colleagues.' This inventory is shown in Figure 14.3.

Fitt and Heverly (1994) have described how the Angelo and Cross approach to classroom assessment can meet the requirements of the continuous quality improvement philosophy. In a graduate course on research design, students were provided with a form which enabled them to define their skills in relation to the global competences they were expected to master as a result of the course. When the course is finished the tutor relates the level of coverage given to each competency and the students rate their skills on each concept or procedure. Performance can then be related to coverage and adjustments to the course made if necessary. Fitt and Heverly argue that such a model could encourage students to become active partners in classroom learning, and promote reflective practice.

In a later project Cross and Steadman (1996) expanded the concept to the idea of classroom research. This has many similarities with the student teacher as researcher programmer described in Chapter 12. Inspection of the literature shows that there are many examples of teachers undertaking research in their own classrooms and even in their own departments in Australia, the UK and the US. Some of the investigations have been quite sophisticated, and some have used consultants supplied by the university (Heywood, Sharp and Hides 1999). Aptitude treatment studies often show that things may not be as they seem in the classroom, and that what happens in classrooms is more complex than teachers perceive (e.g. Freeman, Lynn and Baker, 1999)

Some of the assumptions which Angelo and Cross (1993) made about classroom assessment provide a more than satisfactory ending to this text. They are:

To improve their effectiveness, teachers need first to make their goals and objectives explicit and then to get specific, comprehensible feedback on the extent to which they are achieving these goals.

To improve learning, students need to receive appropriate and focused feedback early and often: they also need to know how to assess their own learning.

The type of assessment most likely to improve teaching and learning is that conducted by faculty to answer questions they themselves have formulated in response to issues or problems in their own teaching.

Systematic inquiry and intellectual challenge are powerful sources of motivation, growth, and renewal for college teachers, and classroom assessment can provide such a challenge.

Classroom assessment does not require specialized training: it can be carried out by dedicated teachers from all disciplines.

Starting from the well established principal that assessment is a powerful influence on learning, this text has explored the complexity of the relations between assessment, learning and instruction. It has argued that the effective delivery of the curriculum depends on multiple-strategy approaches to curriculum and instruction, as well as to the evaluation of institutions and programmes. While there is much that individuals can do through classroom assessment and research, the overall effectiveness of programmes depends on the support of institutions and the structures they create for this purpose.

Glossary

Appraisal
Not used until recently in educational settings. In industry it is employed to describe the formative (annual) assessment of personnel. Sometimes called performance appraisal. It usually involves the person and his or her managers establishing objectives for the future as well as evaluating performance in the past. This term is also used of departments and institutions, and in this sense is similar to evaluation. The appraisal of students using similar approaches that involve the students is likely to become important.

Aptitude
The potential to perform. The term is often confused with 'ability'. Batteries of standardized ability and aptitude tests, in addition to measuring specific abilities, also measure overall learning ability. A test like the Wechsler measures performance in specific abilities which, taken together, are also indications of future potential.

Arithmetic mean (average)
The result of adding all the scores together and dividing by the number of cases.

Backwash effect
Used to describe the effect of an examination or test on both learning and teaching.

Borderline review
Used to describe the procedure employed by test agencies or examiners to review the performance of those candidates who are a mark or so on either side of borderline between two grades.

Bunching
Description of a cluster of marks which has a low standard deviation and are clustered within a limited range. This shows that the examination is not discriminating. In mastery tests scores should bunch around the mastery level.

Chi-squared test
A test of significance. Its purpose is to determine if the observed frequencies (for example, of a test or survey) differ from expected or theoretically predicted frequencies:

$$\chi^2 = \quad \Sigma \quad \frac{(O-E)^2}{E}$$

where O = observed frequencies and E = expected frequencies. When $\chi^2 = 0$ the observed and expected frequencies agree exactly: when $\chi^2 > 0$ they do not agree and the larger the value, the greater the discrepancy. χ^2 tables are available for various levels of significance, particularly for 5 per cent and 1 per cent. They are tabulated against degrees of freedom. The degrees of freedom are one less than the number of items in the sample. The chi-squared test should not be used when the expected frequency of a cell is less than 5.

Confidence limits
These limits reflect the accuracy or inaccuracy of test scores. They are expressed as a percentage (for example, we may be 95 per cent confident that a candidate's score does not vary above x or below y). There are various methods for calculating confidence limits (Glutting *et al.*, 1987), of which the standard error of measurement is the best known. (See below and Chapter 3)

Correlation
The coefficient of correlation expresses the degree of relationship either for the same group of individuals or for paired individuals such as twins. Correlations supply evidence of a statistical association between variables. Two measures of correlation are commonly used in educational measurement.

(1)   *Spearman-Rank Difference Coefficient of Correlation*. This expresses the relationship between rank orders of individuals as, for example, when a group of candidates take two tests. In Example 1 there is little or no correlation, whereas in Example 2 there is a one-to-one correlation.

	EXAMPLE 1			EXAMPLE 2			EXAMPLE 3	
	Test A	Test B		Test A	Test B		Test A	Test B
	1	10		1	1		1	2
	2	9		2	2		4	6
Candidate's	3	8	Candidate's	3	3	Candidate's	6	3
number in rank	4	7	number in rank	4	4	number in rank	3	1
order of scores	5	6	order of scores	5	5	order of scores	2	4
	6	5		6	6		7	7
	7	4		7	7		8	5
	8	3		8	8		9	6
	9	2		9	9			9
	10	1		10	10		10	10

The more interesting cases are those of the kind shown in Example 3.
The formula for the coefficient is:

$$r = 1 - \frac{6(\Sigma d^2)}{n(n^2 - 1)}$$

where d = difference between a pair of ranks and n = number of ranks.

(2)   *Pearson Product Moment Correlation Coefficient.* This coefficient expresses the correlation between scores as opposed to ranks:

$$r = \frac{\Sigma Z x Z y}{n}$$

where Σ = sum of
Zx = any individual score expressed in standard form,
Zy = any individual's score on the related measure also expressed in standard form,
n = number of individuals.

Criterion error
The error in judgements made by different examiners about the criteria in an examiner's script.

Criterion-referenced grading
Grades are awarded for specified performance in which the criteria are described in detail in mastery terms. (See Criterion-referenced testing).

Criterion-referenced testing
Tests designed to check that a student has obtained mastery in an area of knowledge or skill. Formative assessment is based on criterion rather than norm-referenced tests.

Decile
(See Quantile.)

Discriminant analysis
A statistical technique which enables the differences between two or more groups of objects with respect to several variables to be studied simultaneously. (See Klecka, 1980.)

Discrimination index
(D). For choice type essay and problem-solving type tests. D is the product-moment correlation between the marks for a question and the corresponding total marks gained by the candidates on the other questions. When a candidate's mark is x_q on a question and xt is his or her total mark the discrimination index is given by the product-moment correlation between x_q and $(xt - x_q)$. Morrison (1974) says that D should preferably be greater than 0.4.

Facility index *(F)*

For choice type essay and problem-solving type tests:

$$F = 50 + (M_q - M_t) \text{ per cent}$$

where M_q is the mean percentage mark obtained for the question and Mt the mean total percentage mark obtained in the test for the sub-group answering the question (i.e. mean ability index). Morrison (1974) states that $(M_q - M_t)$ is reasonably independent of the leniency or severity of marking, and that M is a close approximation to the ability of the sub-group answering the question.

Factorial analysis

A method of testing hypotheses about the relationship between variables which are correlated. In educational and psychological testing it seeks to establish what is common between two or more tests (communality) and what is specific to each (specificity). The presence of specific components in tests reduces the correlation between them. The factors produced by factorial analysis are not 'actual' factors of the mind because test scores derive from complex mental processes. They are categories which aid the classification of the abilities (aptitudes–skills) tested, and as such contribute to the evaluation of test validity. The results of factor analysis are often difficult to interpret. They are greatly influenced by the size of the sample as well as its heterogeneity or homogeneity. Curvilinear relationships between variables should be treated with caution. Factor analysis is closely related to the concept of variance. Thus communality is related to the common variance between tests and unique variance to the specificity. The unique variance contains two components, one due to error and the other to the specific component. There are two kinds of common factor, i.e. general factors, which 'load' significantly on all the tests in the analysis, and groups ones, which load on a few of the tests in the same factor. There are several techniques of factor analysis, and the one adopted influences, the interpretation made. (See Child,1970; Kim Jae-On and Mueller, 1978; Vernon, 1956). (See also Scattergram.)

Hurdle

A component of assessment which has to be passed before either the next section of a course can be begun (for example, in mastery learning) or the next component or an examination or test marked. For example, in the Engineering Science Examination described in Chapter 13 a pass in coursework is required if the candidate is to pass his or her examination.

Incline of difficulty

A term used to describe a series of items (questions) designed to become progressively more difficult.

Median

The middle score in a distribution or the point between two middle scores.

Mode

The score made by the most number of persons.

Moderation

Has the same meaning as scaling when two components of a test are brought into alignment. This may be achieved statistically or by an examiner who inspects samples of a candidate's work. In public examinations such persons are sometimes called moderators. They may or may not also vet the questions which are set in examinations.

Norm-referenced testing

Describes those tests which are used to discriminate between students, i.e. to show how particular students stand in relation to their peers. Terminal tests and examinations in higher education are most often norm-referenced.

Percentiles – percentile score Percentile rank:

The percentile score is the percentage of persons who fall below a given raw score. The 40th percentile is the point above which 60 per cent of the scores fall and below which 40 per cent fall. The ninetieth percentile is the point above which 10 per cent of the scores fall and below which 90 per cent fall. The percentile rank indicates the percentage of scores falling below a given score. Given a normal distribution, t scores and z scores can be converted to percentile ranks. (See Quantile.)

Profile reporting

Method of describing the performance of a candidate by reference to specified criteria. (See Chapter 11.)

Quantile

Generic term used to describe decile, percentile and quartile. Deciles divide a frequency distribution into ten parts, percentiles 100 parts and quartiles four parts. The 90th percentile corresponds to 90 per cent of the total frequency.

Quartile

(See Quantile.)

Range

The difference between the highest and lowest scores. It is an indication of variability. Unfortunately, it emphasizes extreme cases, for which reason the standard deviation is preferred.

Raw score

The unadjusted score obtained by a candidate on a test.

Regression analysis

A technique for discovering the nature of the association between variables. Given that sufficient information is known about one variable (the independent variable x axis), it may be used to predict the dependent variable (y axis). The equation describes the line of best fit (regression line) through a series of points on a scattergram.

Reliability

An expression of the extent to which a test can be repeated on an identical population and obtain the same distribution. Usually expressed as a coefficient of correlation.

Methods of determining Reliability

1. Split Halves Method: Normally it will not be possible to repeat a test. This method enables the internal consistency of a single test to be determined. Consider a multiple-choice test. Its reliability is calculated by correlating the results obtained by the candidates from the odd-numbered items with those of their scores from the even-numbered ones. The Spearman-Brown formula is used for this calculation:

$$r_{tt} = \frac{nr_{it}^{-2}}{1 + (n-1)r_{tt}^{-2}}$$

when n is the number of items in the test r_{it} is the average item-test correlation in the test and r_{tt} is the reliability of the test (or part-test)

2. Kuder-Richardson Method: In this method the test does not have to be split into two halves and restored for the calculation of the correlation coefficients. It assumes that all the items in the test measure the same ability, are of the same difficulty and that the correlations between them are equal. Following Thorndike's notation the formula is

$$r_n = \frac{n}{n-1} \left[\frac{s^2 + \Sigma p_i q_i}{s^2} \right]$$

where n is the number of items in the test,
s is the standard deviation of the test,
pi is the proportion of candidates responding correctly to item I

$$q_i = 1 - p_i$$

(3) Test-Rates: The same instrument is used on the same group of students in similar circumstances.

(4) Equivalent Forms: Equivalent forms of the same test are made as similar as possible in respect of content, mental processes, level of difficulty, etc. The two forms of the test are taken one after the other. For example, in an experiment with Modern Mathematics, the Southern Regional Examinations Board rewrote an objective test into short answers. They obtained a higher reliability with the short answers.

The reliability of an objective test may be increased by increasing its length, although there is a limit where the practical increase in reliability does not justify an increase in the number of items. It will be clear that the standard error and the reliability are related and that in short tests the standard error proportionately more effect. Thus in tests (particularly public examinations) which are measuring achievement through a variety of measures the inclusion of a single set of measures among others (for example, an objective test among short and long responses) should be treated in terms of its effect on the total examination. The question is sometimes asked, how short can an objective test be to give good reliability? Because of the complexity of this subject the reader should refer to the treatise on this topic in the books listed above (see Chapter 13).

Scaling (See also Standard score).

A Procedure for Scaling

This particular example was derived by a group of teachers who were given several textbooks in which were contained a variety of procedures. They chose this particular method to illustrate the problem which they subsequently built into the script of a videotape.

(A)   Inspection of Table 1 shows two tests and the distribution of scores.

(B)   Purpose of exercise: to determine that 8 out of 10 in Test One is the better mark.

(C)   Obtain the Mean Mark for each Test

Test 1

1 received 2 = 2
4 received 2 = 12
6 received 4 = 24
8 received 5 = 40
6 received 6 = 36
7 received 4 = 28
8 received 1 = 8

Total marks = 150
Mean = 150/30 = 5

Table 1			
Test One		*Test Two*	
X	F	X	F
0	0	0	0
1	0	1	0
2	1	2	0
3	4	3	7
4	6	4	5
5	8	5	2
6	6	6	2
7	4	7	2
8	1	8	5
9	0	9	7
10	0	10	0

$X =$ marks

$F =$ frequency of a given score awarded among two classes each of 30 students in the same subject taught and assessed by different teachers.

Test 2

Total marks = 180

Mean = 30/6 =

To establish how each student in Class 1 did in relation to the students, it is necessary to find out how each set of marks deviates from the mean.

X M d

0- 5 = − 5
1- 5 = − 4
2- 5 = − 3
3 − 5 = − 3
4 − 5 = − 1
5 − 5 = − 5
6 − 5 = − 5
7 − 5 = − 2
8 − 5 = − 3
9 − 5 = − 4
10- 5 = − 5

(d = deviation of possible marks (X) from the mean for Test 1)

The next step is to establish how often each deviation occurs. Each deviation is multiplied by the number of times it appears thus:

f	d	fd
0	-5 =	0
0	-4 =	0
1	-3 =	-3
4	-2 =	-8
6	-1 =	-6
8	0 =	0
6	1 =	6
4	2 =	8
1	3 =	3
0	4 =	0
0	4 =	0

Next, the average deviation fd^2 is found:

d	fd	
-5	0 =	0
-4	0 =	0
-3	-3 =	9
-2	-8 =	16
-1	-6 =	-6
0	0 =	0
1	6 =	6
2	8 =	16
3	3 =	9
4	0 =	0
5	0	0

Next calculate the standard deviation.
The standard deviation is then calculated for Test 2. It is 2.37.

(d)   The z score (standard score) is now calculated. For example:

$$\frac{\text{Actual Score} - \text{mean}}{\text{Standard deviation}} \qquad \text{e.g.} \; \frac{8 - 5 = 2.1}{1.4}$$

(e)   The standard scores are converted into t scores as follows:

Z scores $10 + 50$ or $t = 10\% + 50$

Therefore the scaled scores for the highest values in the two tests are:
Test 1: $t = 50 + 10(2.1)$ $50 + 21 = 71\%$
Test 2: $t = 50 + 10(1.3) = 50 + 13 = 63\%$

Therefore the eight out of ten score in Test 1 is better than the nine out of ten score in Test 2.

Scattergram
It is possible to get some idea of the degree of correlation between two measures from the scattergram of the scores. The candidates's scores are plotted for each test on the same graph, thus

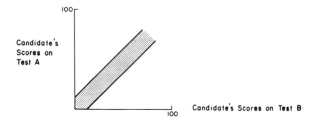

The plots below indicate when a relationship between the tests may be expected. Scores are distributed throughout each of the bands

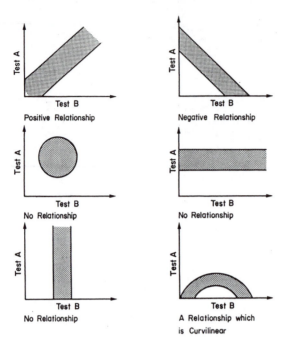

The majority of scores lie within the shaded bands

Youngman has shown how simple correlation plotting can be used to provide a quick representation of variable intercorrelations, and thus provide an introduction to factor analysis. (Youngman, M. B. (1980). Correlation scatter plotting as a quick substitute for factor analysis. *Research in Education*, 25, 13–18).

Significance

When it is assumed that data obtained by measurement should conform to the normal distribution departures from the distribution may or may not be significant. Statistical tests of significance compare the found distribution with the normal one. When a sample is taken from a known population assumptions are made about it which are expressed in the form of hypotheses. More often than not a full hypotheses (Ho) is formed which can be accepted or rejected.

For example, when setting a hurdle (pass level) for a test we may wish to relate the score to the proportion of candidates obtaining that score. So we test the assumption that the mean value of all the scores in a test is S1. We reject that mean only if it is clearly rejected by the mean score of the sample.

$$\therefore H_0 : = \mu S_1$$

The alternative hypothesis is

$$H_1: \mu \neq S_1$$

$$(\text{mean of population}) = \frac{\bar{x} - \mu}{\sigma/\sqrt{n}}$$

where n = sample size

σ = standard deviation,

$\bar{x}$ = arithmetic mean.

The level of significance is the maximum probability with which we risk rejecting the null hypothesis. The two levels most commonly used are 0.05 (5%) and 0.01 (1%), which tell us the level of 'chance' by which a sample differs from a true distribution. A 'one-tailed test' of significance considers the critical region where a distribution might depart from the normal in the area of one of the tails of the normal curve. A 'two-tailed test' takes account of both tails. (See also Chi-squared test and Confidence limits.)

Spread
(See Standard deviation and Variability.)

Standard deviation (SD.s()
Very often we wish to compare the performance of a group of students on similar tests or two groups of students on the same test. The simplest way to do this would be to quote the average of mean marks of the group(s) on the different tests. The mean mark should be accompanied by some measure of the spread or scatter of the scores, i.e. the extent to which the individuals in the group depart from the mean. Thus the mean should be accompanied by a statement of the range (one plus the difference between highest and lowest scores of the group) of marks. Taken together, these two items give some idea of the variability between the groups. They are, however, unsatisfactory measures. The usual measure of variability is the standard deviation. This is the square root of the mean of the squared deviations of the scores from the arithmetic mean:

Standard deviation = $\Sigma x^2/N$

Where Σ = the sum and x = the deviation of each score from the arithmetic mean. When the standard deviation is small the scores will be clustering about the mean. One standard deviation accounts for approximately 68 per cent of the area under the normal curve (i.e. 34% on either side of the mean).

Standard error (or a score)

(1)   Calculation:

$$\text{Standard error of a score} = \sqrt{\frac{\text{Standard deviation of the scores on the test}}{\left(\begin{array}{c}\text{Reliability of the scores on coefficient of the test}\end{array}\right)}}$$

(2)   Diederich (1960) gives the following table for objective tests (i.e. for answers which can be scored 1 or 0), which are intended to measure performance within a reasonably generous time limit. (Such tests are sometimes called Power tests as opposed to Speed Tests, in which the speed of response is considered an important variable.)

(Number of items (e.g. multiple-choice questions) in the test	*Standard error*
Less than 24	2
24–47	3
48–89	4
90–109	5
110–129	6
130–150	7

Thus in objective tests of 60 items (which are increasingly common at GCE 'A' and 'O' levels) the score band for a candidate with a score of 30 would be within the range 26–34. As the test becomes longer the proportion of error becomes smaller.

(3)   Note that, in addition to the standard error of a score, there are many other standard errors (averages, differences, correlations, etc.). These are arrived at in different ways but all have the same meaning. The standard error of a single score is usually larger than that of an average. Similarly, the standard errors of each of two scores will be smaller than that of the difference between them. To be sure that two scores present differences in ability the difference between them would be at least twice the standard error of that difference.

Standard score
See also Scaling. The standard score is derived from a raw score to enable the relative performance of a student in different subjects to be calculated. There are various methods used to achieve this goal.

(1) z scores: this is the method used in the illustration for sealing. A z score is the deviation of a score from the arithmetic mean in standard deviation units. They are useful in a simple situation where it is of interest to find out how well a candidate did in respect of two or more subjects.

For subject A $z = \dfrac{X - \bar{x}}{\sigma}$

For subject B $z = \dfrac{X_B - \bar{x}_B}{\sigma_B}$

Where $\bar{X}$ = the near mark of the subject under consideration,

$\quad\quad X$ = raw score of the subject under consideration,

Where σ = standard deviation.

The standardized score indicates in which subject the candidate did best. Often it will not be that for which the highest raw mark was given.

(2) t scores: while z scores may be positive or negative, t scores are always positive, and for this reason are often used. They are adjusted to an arbitrary scale with a given mean standard deviation. These are often set at 50 and 10, respectively:

$$t = \bar{X} + \frac{\sigma A}{\sigma}(X - \bar{x})$$

where t = the score in the arbitrary scale,

(σ = standard deviation in the original distribution,

(A = standard deviation in the arbitrary scale,

$\bar{X}$ = the arithmetic means in the original scale,

$\bar{X}A$ = the arithmetic means in the arbitrary scale,

X = the score in the original scale.

Standardization

Has two meanings. In the first it relates to standardized tests and is the process of administration. Standardization is to ensure that the tests are always administered in the same way. In the second it is the process of aligning the marks of a group of examiners responsible for the tests and examinations in a particular subject.

Variability

Describes the distribution of a score. (See also Range and Standard deviation.)

Variance

A central value for calculating the average deviation of a dispersion (range). It is the average of the square of the deviations:

$$\text{Variance} = \frac{\Sigma\,(x - \bar{x}^2)}{n}$$

Because it is measured in units of the square of the deviations it is more usual to quote the standard deviation which is the square root of the deviations (see above). The concept of variance is very important in assessment because we often wish to known if the scores in a test can be explained by the action of another variable (for example, intelligence, personality trait, sex), i.e. we ask, how much do the variations in x contribute to the variations in y? When several variables are involved a technique called analysis of variance (abbreviated to ANOVA) is used.

Weighting

Defines the contribution which a component or sub-test makes to the total mark of the test.

References

AACSB (1987) *Outcome Measurement Project. Phase III Report*. St Louis, MO: American Assembly of Collegiate Schools of Business.

AAU (1992) *Annual Report of the Director of the Academic Audit Unit*. London: Committee of Vice Chancellors and Principals.

Abercrombie, M.L.J. (1960) *The Anatomy of Judgement*. Harmonsdworth: Penguin.

Abouserie, R. (1994) 'Sources and levels of stress in relation to locus of control and self-esteem in University Students.' *Educational Psychology 14*, 3, 323–330.

Abouserie, R. (1995) 'Self esteem and achievement motivation as determinants of students' approaches to studying.' *Studies in Higher Education 20*, 1, 19–26.

Abrami, P., d'Appollonia, S. and Cohen, P.A. (1990) 'Validity of student ratings of instruction: What we know and what we do not.' *Journal of Educational Psychology 82*, 219–231.

Abrami, P., d'Appollonia, S. and Rosenfield, S. (1994) 'The dimensionality of student ratings: What we know and what we do not know.' In J. Smart (ed.) *Higher Education. Handbook of Theory and Practice*. New York: Agathon Press.

Abrami, P., Leventhal, L. and Perry, R.P. (1982) 'Educational education.' *Review of Educational Research 52*, 446–464.

ACT (1981) *Defining and Measuring General Education, Knowledge and Skills*. Comp Technical Report 1976–1981. Iowa City, IA: American College Testing Program.

ACT (1989) 'Using today's knowledge to build a brighter future.' *College Outcome Measures Project*. Iowa City, IA: American College Testing Program.

ACT (1992) *Clarifying and Assessing General Education Outcomes*. Comp Technical Report 1982–1991. *Iowa City, IA: American College Testing Program*.

ACT (1997) *Work Keys Preliminary Technical Handbook*. Iowa City, IA: American College Testing Program.

Adelman, C. (1983) *The Standardized Test Scores of College Graduation 1964–1982*. Washington, DC: National Institute of Education.

Adelman, C. (1994) *Lessons of a Generation; Education and Work in the Lives of the High School Class of 1972*. San Francisco: Jossey-Bass.

Adelman, C. (1998) *Women and Men of the Engineering Path. A Model for Analyses of Undergraduate Careers*. Washington, DC: US Department of Education and National Institute for Science Education.

Adey, P. and Shayer, M. (1994) *Cognitive Intervention and Academic Achievement*. London: Routledge.

AEB (1982) *Marking Procedures in Modern Languages at Ordinary Level*. Guildford: Associated Examinations Board.

AEB (1985) *How AEB Sets and Marks Examinations*. Guildford: Associated Examinations Board.

AERA (1985) *Standards for Educational and Psychological Testing*. Washington, DC: American Educational Research Association.

Agutter, P.S. (1979) 'Precision testing: A method for improving students' written work in biochemistry.' *Journal of Biological Education 13*, 1, 25–31.

Ainley, P. (1994) *Degrees of Difference. Higher Education in the 1990's*. London: Lawrence and Wishart.

Alexander, C.N. and Langer, E.J. (1990) *Higher Stages of Human Development*. Oxford: Oxford University Press.

Alexander, K.L. and Pallas, A.M. (1984) 'Curriculum reform and school performance: an evaluation of the "new basics".' *American Journal of Education 92*, 391–420.

Allen, M. (1991) *Issues in Assessment*. Report of the Personal Skills Unit. Sheffield: University of Sheffield.

Allport, F.H. (1955) *Theories of Perception and the Concept of Structure*. New York: Wiley.

Allwood, C.M. and Montgomery, H. (1979) *The Pedagogics of Problem Solving. R and D for Higher Education*. Stockholm: National Board of Universities and Colleges.

Alpert, R. and Haber, R.N. (1960) 'The achievement anxiety test.' *Journal of Abnormal and Social Psychology 61*, 207–215.

Alverno College (1994) *Student Assessment-as-Learning at Alverno College*. Milwaukee, WI: Alverno College Institute.

Alverno College (1999) *Self-Assessment at Alverno College*, Milwaukee, WI: Alverno College Institute.

Amin, M.E. (1993) 'University of Yaounde (Cameroon): correlates of course evaluation.' *Assessment and Evaluation in Higher Education 18*, 2, 135–139.

Anastasi, A. (1980) 'Abilities and the measurement of achievement.' In *New Directions for Testing and Measurement*. San Francisco: Jossey-Bass.

Anderson, C.W. and Roth, K.J. (1989) 'Teaching for meaningful and self-regulating learning of science.' In J. Brophy (ed.) *Advances in Research on Teaching 1*, 265–309.

Anderson, L.W. (1996) 'Rethinking Bloom's Taxonomy: implications for testing and assessment.' Cyclostyled. Columbia, SC: University of South Carolina.

Anderson, L.W. and Sosniak, L.A. (eds) (1994a) *Bloom's Taxonomy. A Forty Year Retrospective*. Ninety Third Year Book of the National Society for the Study of Education. Chicago: University of Chicago Press.

Anderson, L.W. and Sosniak, L.A. (1994b) Excerpts from the *Taxonomy of Educational Objectives*, Handbook 1, Cognitive Domain. In L.W. Anderson and L.A. Sosniak (eds) *Bloom's Taxonomy. A Forty Year Retrospective*. Chicago: University of Chicago Press.

Anderson, S. and Percival, F. (1997) 'Developing HE Staff to appreciate the needs of flexible learning for Access students–developing flexible learning access students to appreciate the needs of HE'. In S. Armstrong, G. Thompson and S. Brown (eds) *Facing Up to Radical Changes in Universities and Colleges*. London: Kogan Page.

Ang, C.H. and Noble, P.J. (1993) *Incremental Validity of ACT Assessment Scores and High School Course Information for Freshman Course Placement*. Research Report 93–5. Iowa City, IA: American College Testing Program.

Angelo, T.A. and Cross, K.P. (1993) *Classroom Assessment Techniques*. San Francisco: Jossey-Bass.

Anglia Polytechnic (undated) *The ASSET Model of Professional Development*. Accreditation and Support for Specified Expertise from Employment Experience and Training. Chelmsford: Anglia Polytechnic, Department of Health, Nursing and Social Work.

Anglin, J.M. (1977) *Word, Object and Conceptual Development*. New York: Norton.

Armstrong, S., Allinson, C.W. and Hayes, J. (1997) 'The implications of cognitive style for the management of supervisor relationships.' *Educational Psychology 17*, 1–2, 209–217.

Ashcroft, K. and Palacio, D. (1996) *Researching into Assessment and Evaluation in Colleges and Universities*. London: Kogan Page.

Ashworth, P., Bannister, P. and Thorne, P. (1997) 'Guilty in whose eyes? University students' perceptions of cheating and plagiarism in academic work and assessment.' *Studies in Higher Education 22*, 2, 187–203.

Ashworth, P. and Saxton, J. (1992) *Managing Work Experience*. London: Routledge.

Ashworth, P. *et al.* (1996) Unpublished conference report of an evaluation of the use of portfolios in engineering which were described in R.N. Payne, M.D. Bramhall, J.S. Lawson, I. Robinson and C. Short (1993) 'Portfolio assessment in practice in engineering.' *International Journal of Technology and Design Education 3*, 3, 37–42. (Contact M.D. Bramhall for information.)

Assiter, A. and Fenwick, A. (1992) *Profiling in Higher Education: An Interim Report*. CNAA Project Report 35. London: Council for National Academic Awards/Employment Department.

Astin, A.W. (1973) 'Measurement of determinants of the outputs of higher education.' In L. Solomon and P. Taubman (eds) *Does College Matter? Some Impacts of Higher Education*. New York: Academic Press.

Astin, A.W. (1974) 'Measuring the outcomes of higher education.' In H.R. Bowen (ed.) *Evaluating Institutions for Accountability*. San Francisco: Jossey-Bass.

Astin, A.W. (1977) *Four Critical Years* San Francisco: Jossey-Bass.

Astin, A.W. (1985) *Achieving Educational Excellence*. San Francisco: Jossey-Bass.

Astin, A.W. (1994, 1997a) *What Matters in College. Four Critical Years Revisited*. San Francisco: Jossey-Bass.

Astin, A.W. (1997b) 'How good is your institutions retention rate.' *Research in Higher Education 38*, 6, 647–657.

Ausubel, D.P. (1968) *Educational Psychology: A Cognitive View*. New York: Holt, Rinehart and Winston.

Avital, S.M. and Shettleworth, J.S. (1968) *Objectives for Mathematics Learning. Some Ideas for Teacher*. Bulletin No 3. Ontario, Canada: Ontario Institute for Studies in Education.

Baggaley, J., Ferguson, M. and Brooks, P. (1980) *Psychology of the TV Image*. Aldershot: Gower.

Baillie, C. and Tookey, S. (1997) 'The "power test": its impact on student learning in a materials science course for engineering students.' *Assessment and Evaluation in Higher Education 22*, 1, 33–38.

Baird, L.L. (1988) 'Diverse and subtle arts: assessing the generic academic outcomes of higher education.' In C. Adelman (ed.) *Performance and Judgement. Essays in the Assessment of College Student Learning*. Washington, DC: US Department of Education, Office of Research and Improvement.

Banta, T.W., Lund, J.P., Black, K. and Oblander, F.W. (1996) *Assessment in Practice. Putting Principles to Work on College Campuses*. San Francisco: Jossey-Bass.

Barger, G.W. (1982) 'Classroom testing procedures and classroom anxiety.' *Improving College and University Teaching 31*, 1, 25–26.

Barnes, L.B., Christensen, C.R and Hansen, A.J. (1994) *Teaching and the Case Method* (3rd edn) Boston, MA: Harvard Business School Press.

Barnett, R. (1990) *The Idea of Higher Education*. Buckingham: Society for Research into Higher Education/Open University Press.

Barnett, R. (1992) *Improving Higher Education: Total Quality Care*. Buckingham: Society for Research into Higher Education/Open University Press.

Barnett, R. (1994) *The Limits of Competence*. Buckingham: Society for Research into Higher Education/Open University Press.

Barrows, H.S. (1985) *How to Design a Problem-Based Curriculum for the Preclinical Years*. New York: Springer.

Barry, P. (1982) Interview: A talk with A. Bartlett Giamatii. *College Record Review, 123*, 1–7.

Bartlett, F.C. (1932) *Remembering. A Study in Experimental and Social Psychology*. Cambridge: Cambridge University Press.

Bartlett, F.C. (1958) *Thinking. An Experimental and Social Study*. New York: Basic Books.

Baume, C. and Baume, D. (1992) *Course Design for Active Learning*. CVCP Staff Development and Training Unit. Sheffield: University of Sheffield.

Baumrind, D. (1978) 'A dialectical materialist's perspective on knowing social reality.' In W. Damon (ed.) *New Directions in Child Development: Moral development*. San Francisco: Jossey-Bass.

Baxter-Magolda, M.B. (1987) 'Comparing open-ended interview and standardized measures of intellectual development.' *Journal of College Student Personnel 28*, 443–448.

Bean, J. (1980) 'Dropouts and turnover: the synthesis and test of a causal model of student-attrition.' *Research in Higher Education 12*, 155–187.

Becker, H., Greer, E. and Hughes, E. (1968) *Making the Grade: The Academic Side of College Life*. New York: Wiley.

Bedard, R. (1974) 'Partly tailored examinations.' *Alberta Journal of Educational Research 20*, 1, 15–23.

Belenky, M.F., Clinchy, B.M., Goldberger, N.R. and Carule, J.M. (1986) *Women's Ways of Knowing*. New York: Basic Books.

Bell, R.C. (1980) 'Problems in improving the reliability of essay marks.' *Assessment and Evaluation in Higher Education 5*, 3, 254–263.

Benett, Y. (1993) 'The validity and reliability of assessments and self-assessments of work based learning.' *Assessment and Evaluation in Higher Education 18*, 2, 83–94.

Benjamin, M., McKeachie, W.J., Lin, Y.G. and Holinger, D.P. (1981) *Journal of Educational Psychology 73*, 6, 816–824.

Bennett, C., Foreman-Peck, L. and Higgins, C. (1996) *Researching into Teaching Methods in Colleges and Universities.* London: Kogan Page.

Bennett, N., Desforges, C., Cockburn, A. and Wilkinson, B. (1984) *The Quality of Pupil Learning Experiences.* London: Laurence Erlbaum.

Bennett, S.J., Bigger, S.W., Ngeh, L.N., Orbell, J.D and Yuriev, E. (1995) 'HELPA: a rapid means of student evaluation of lecturing performance in higher education.' *Assessment and Evaluation in Higher Education 20*, 2, 191–202.

Bennett, S.K. (1982) 'Students perceptions and expectations for male and female instructors: evidence relating to the question of gender bear on teacher education.' *Journal of Educational Psychology 73*, 6, 816–824.

Berliner, D.C. and Biddle, B.J. (1995) *The Manufactured Crisis. Myths, Fraud, and the Attack on America's Public Schools.* Reading, MA: Addison Wesley.

Beveridge, I. (1997) 'Teaching your students to think reflectively; the case for reflective journals.' *Teaching in Higher Education 2*, 1, 33–43.

Bey, C. (1961) 'A social theory of intellectual development.' In N. Sanford (ed.) *The American College.* New York: Wiley.

Biggs, J.B. (1987) *Student Approaches to Studying and Learning.* Hawthorne, Vic: Australian Council for Educational Research.

Biggs, J.B. (1990) 'Teaching. Design for Learning.' Keynote paper. Annual Conference, Higher Education Research and Development Society of Australasia.

Biggs, J.B. and Collis, K.F. (1982) *Evaluating the Quality of Learning. The SOLO Taxonomy.* New York: Academic Press.

Billing, D.E. (1973) 'The effects of guessing on the results of objective tests: A novel approach.' In D.E. Billing (ed.) *Research into Tertiary Science Education.* London: Society for Research into Higher Education.

Bishop, S. and Carpenter, J. (1993) 'Constructivism: an introduction and critique.' *Spectrum (Education and Christian Belief) 25*, 2, 147–158.

Black, J. (1975) 'Allocation and assessment of project work in the final year of the engineering degree course at the University of Bath.' *Assessment and Evaluation in Higher Education 1*, 1, 35–53.

Blair, P. (1977) 'Cost efficiency of self-paced education. An experiment with Keller PSI.' *Engineering Education 8*, 67, 763–764.

Blanc, R.A., De Buhr, L.E. and Martin, D.C. (1982) 'Breaking the attrition cycle: the effects of supplemental instruction on undergraduate performance and attrition.' *Journal of Higher Education 54*, 1, 80–90.

Bligh, D. (1973) 'Truth functional tests.' In D.E. Billing (ed.) *Research into Tertiary Science Education.* London: Society for Research into Higher Education.

Bloom, A. (1987) *The Closing of the American Mind. How Higher Education has Failed Democracy and Impoverished the Minds of Today's Students.* New York: Simon and Schuster.

Bloom, B.S. (1976) *Human Characteristics and School Learning.* New York: McGraw-Hill.

Bloom, B.S. (1994) 'Reflections on the development and use of the Taxonomy.' In L.W. Anderson and L.A. Sosniak (eds) *Bloom's Taxonomy. A Forty Year Retrospective.* Chicago: University of Chicago Press.

Bloom, B.S. *et al.* (1956) *The Taxonomy of Educational Objectives, Vol. 1 Cognitive Domain.* David McKay, New York (published in the UK in 1964 by Longmans Green).

Bloom, B.S., Hastings J.T. and Madaus, G. (1971) *Handbook on Formative and Summative Evaluation of Student Learning.* New York: McGraw-Hill.

Blundell, R., Dearden, L., Goodman, A. and Reed, H. (1997) *Higher Education Employment and Earnings in Great Britain.* London: Institute of Fiscal Studies.

Blyth, W.A.L., Derricott, R., Elliott, G.F., Sumner, H.M. and Waplington, A. (1973) *History, Geography and Social Science 8–13.* An interim Report. Liverpool: Schools Council Project, University of Liverpool.

Board, C. and Whitney, D.R. (1972) 'The effect of selected poor item-writing practices on test difficulty, reliability and validity.' *Journal of Educational Measurement 9*, 3, 225–233.

Bojar, S. (1971) 'Psychiatric problems of medical students.' In G.B. Blaine and C.C. McArthur (eds) *Emotional Problems of the Students.* New York: Appleton, Century Crofts.

Bok, B. (1986) *Higher Learning.* Cambridge, MA: Harvard University Press.

Boli, J., Katchadourian, H. and Mahony, S. (1988) 'Analyzing academic records for informed adminstration: the Stanford curriculum study.' *Journal of Higher Education 59*, 1, 54–68.

Bom Mo Chung (1994) 'The Taxonomy in the Republic of Korea.' In L. W. Anderson and L.A. Sosniak (eds) *Bloom's Taxonomy. A Forty Year Retrospective.* Chicago: University of Chicago Press.

Boniface, D. (1985) 'Candidates' use of notes and textbooks during an open-book examination.' *Educational Research 27*, 201–209.

Boud, D. (1986) *Implementing Student-Staff Assessment.* Higher Education Research and Development Society in Australasia, University of New South Wales.

Boud, D. (1995) *Enhancing Learning Through Self Assessment.* London: Kogan Page.

Boud, D., Dunn, J. and Hegarty-Hazel, E. (1986) *Teaching in Laboratories.* London: Society for Research into Higher Education.

Bowen, H. (1977) *Investment in Learning. The Individual and the Social Value of Higher Education.* San Francisco: Jossey-Bass.

Boyd, H. and Cowan, J. (1985) 'A case for self-assessment based on recent studies of student learning.' *Assessment and Evaluation in Higher Education 10*, 3, 225–235.

Boyle, B. and Christie, T. (eds) (1996) *Issues in Setting Standards. Establishing Comparabilities.* London: Falmer Press.

Boyle, B.P. and Combs, R.H. (1971) 'Personality profiles related to emotional stress in the initial year of medical training.' *Journal of Medical Education 46*, 882–887.

Branthwaite, E., Trueman, M. and Berrisford, T. (1981) 'Unreliability of marking: Further evidence and possible explanation.' *Educational Review 33*, 1, 41–46.

Braun, H.I. (1986) *Calibration of Essays. Final Report*. Princeton, NJ: Educational Testing Service.

Braxton, J.M., Sullivan, A.V. and Johnson, R.M. (1997) 'Appraising Tinto's theory of college student departure.' In *Higher Education: Handbook of Theory and Research*. New York: Agathon Press.

Braxton, J.M., Vesper, N. and Hosseler, D. (1996) 'Expectations for college student persistence.' *Research in Higher Education 36*, 5, 595–612.

Breland, H.M. (1983) *The Direct Assessment of Writing Skill*. New York: College Entrance Examination Board.

Breland, H.M. (1987) *Assessing Writing Skill*. New York: College Entrance Examination Board.

Brent, R. and Felder, R.M. (1992) 'Writing assignments. Pathways to connections, clarity, creativity.' *College Teaching 40*, 2, 43–47.

Brewer, I.M. and Tomlinson, J.D. (1981) 'Unreliability of marking: further evidence and a possible explanation.' *Educational Review 13*, 1, 41–46.

Bridges, D. (1992) 'Enterprise and liberal education.' *Journal of Philosophy of Education 26*, 1, 91–98.

Bridges, D. (1996) 'Competency-based education and training: progress or villainy?' *Journal of the Philosophy of Education 30*, 3, 361–376.

Bridgman, B. (1991) 'Essays and multiple choice tests as predictors of college freshman GPA.' *Research in Higher Education 32*, 3, 319–332.

Brindley, C. and Scoffield, S. (1998) 'Peer assessment in undergraduate programmes.' *Teaching in Higher Education 3*, 1, 79–89.

Broadfoot, P. (1988) 'Profiles and records of achievement: a real alternative.' *Educational Psychology 8*, 4, 291–297.

Brockbank, P. (1968) 'Examining exams.' *Times Literary Supplement 3465*.

Brophy, J. (1987) 'Synthesis of research on motivating students to learn.' *Educational Leadership 45*, 40–48.

Brown, G. (1975) *Microteaching: A Programme of Teaching Skills*. London: Methuen.

Brown, G. and Atkins, M. (1996) 'Explaining.' In O. Hargie (ed.) *Handbook of Communication Skills*. London: Routledge.

Brown, G., Bull, J. and Pendelbury, M. (1997) *Assessing Student Learning in Higher Education*. London: Routledge.

Brown, G. and Pendelbury, M. (1992) *Assessing Active Learning*. CVCP Staff Development and Training Unit. Sheffield: University of Sheffield.

Brown, R.W. (1998) 'Tough assessor or Santa Claus: Rationalizing the assessment process.' *Proceedings 28th Frontiers in Education Conference 1*, 654–652. New York: IEEE.

Brown, S. and Knight, P. (1994) *Assessing Learners in Higher Education*. London: Kogan Page.

Brown, W.F. and Holtzman, W.H. (1966) *Manual of the Survey of Study Habits and Attitudes*. New York: Psychological Corporation.

Brown, V.A. and Caton, H. (1983) 'The theory of biology and the education of biologists: A case study.' *Studies in Higher Education 8*, 1, 23–32.

Bruffee, K.A. (1995) *Collaborative Learning. Higher Education, Interdependence and the Authority of Knowledge*. Baltimore, MD: The Johns Hopkins University Press.

Brumby, M. (1979) 'Problems in the concept of natural selection.' *Journal of Biological Education 13*, 2, 119–122.

Bruner, J., Goodnow, J. and Austin, G.A. (1956) *A Study of Thinking*. New York: Wiley.

Bryant, F.J. (1983) *Marking 'A' Level Physics*. Manchester: Joint Matriculation Board.

Burke, J. (1995) 'Introduction.' In J. Burke (ed.) *Outcomes Learning and the Curriculum. Implications for NVQ's, GNVQ's and other Qualifications*. London: Falmer Press.

Burman, E. (1994) *Deconstructing Developmental Psychology*. London: Routledge.

Burnett, W. and Cavaye, G. (1980) 'Peer assessment by fifth year students of surgery.' *Assessment and Evaluation in Higher Education 5*, 3, 273–278.

Burns, T. and Stalker, G. (1961) *The Management of Innovation*. London: Tavistock.

Busato, V.V., Prins, F.J., Elshout, J.J and Hamaker, C. (1998) 'Learning styles: A cross-sectional and longitudinal study in higher education.' *British Journal of Educational Psychology 68*, 427–441.

Butcher, A.C., Stefani, L.A.J. and Tariq, V.N. (1995) 'Analysis of peer-, self- and staff assessment in group project work.' *Assessment in Education: Principles, Policy and Practice 2*, 2, 165–186.

Butler, N.P. (1978) 'Job titles and job specifications of operating dental auxiliaries. An attempt at rationalization by means of a frequency distribution.' *Journal of the Irish Dental Association 24*, 3, 3–10.

Bynner, J. and Henry, J. (1984) 'Advanced project work in distance teaching.' *Higher Education 13*, 4, 413–421.

Cabrera, A.F., Castaneda, M.B., Nora, A. and Hengstler, D. (1992) 'The convergence between two theories of college persistence.' *Journal of Higher Education 63*, 2, 143–164.

Cameron, L.A. (1984) 'Standardisation techniques in the aggregation of marks.' *Studies in Education 2*, 2, 56–64.

Cameron, L.A. and Heywood, J. (1985) 'Better testing: Give them the questions first.' *College Teaching 33*, 2, 76–77.

Candy, P.C. (1997) 'Some issues impacting on university teaching and learning: Implications for academic developers.' In S. Armstrong, G. Thompson and S. Brown (eds) *Facing Up to Radical Change in Universities and Colleges*. London: Kogan Page.

Canter, F.M. and Meisels, M. (1971) 'Cognitive dissonance and course evaluation.' *Improving College and University Teaching 19*, 2, 111–113.

CAPIOA (1993) *Report of the Committee on Accountability, Performance Indicators and Outcomes Assessment to the Minister's Task force on university accountability*. Toronto, Canada: CAPIOA.

Carroll, J.B. (1985) 'Words, meanings and concepts.' In L.W. Anderson (ed.) *Perspectives on School Learning: Selected writings of John B. Carroll*. Hillsdale, NJ: Lawrence Erlbaum Associates.

Carter, G., Armour, D.G., Lee, L.S. and Sharples, R. (1980) 'Assessment of undergraduate electrical engineering laboratory studies.' *Institution of Electrical Engineers Proceedings 127*, A7, 460–474.

Carter, G. and Heywood, J. (1992) 'The Value Added Performance of Electrical Engineering Students in a British University.' *International Journal of Technology and Design Education 2*, 1, 4–15.

Carter, G., Heywood J. and Kelly, D.T. (1986a) *A Case Study in Curriculum Assessment. GCE Engineering Science (Advanced)*. Manchester: Roundthorn.

Carter, G. and Lee, L.S. (1974) 'University first year electrical engineering examinations.' *International Journal of Electrical Engineering Education 11*, 149.

Carter, G. and Lee, L.S. (1981) 'Project work in undergraduate studies.' *Programmed Learning and Educational Technology 26*, 48.

Casas, F.R. and Meaghan, D.E. (1995) 'Grade inflation and university admissions in Ontario: separating fact from perception.' *Canadian Journal of Higher Education 25*, 3, 49–70.

Case, R. (1985) *Intellectual Development*. New York: Academic Press.

Case, S.M. and Swanson, D.B. (1993) 'Validity of NBME Part I and Part II scores for selection of residents in Orthopaedic Surgery, Dermatology, and Preventive Medicine.' In J.S. Gonnella, M. Hojat, J.B. Erdman and J.J. Veloski (eds) *Assessment Measures in Medical School, Residency and Practice*. New York: Springer.

Case, S.M., Swanson, D.B. and Stillman, P.S. (1988) 'Evaluating diagnostic pattern recognition: The psychometric characteristics of a new item format.' In *Proceedings of the 27th Conference on Research in Medical Education*. Washington, DC: Association of American Medical Colleges.

Cashin, W.E. and Downey, R.G. (1992) 'Using global student rating items for summative evaluations.' *Journal of Educational Psychology 84*, 563–572.

Cassidy, S. (1999) *Using a Self-Report Measure of Student Proficiency to Evaluate Teaching and Learning in Higher Education*. Salford: Teaching and Learning Committee, University of Salford.

Cattell, R.B. and Kline, P. (1967) *The Scientific Analysis of Personality and Motivation*. New York: Academic Press.

Cattell, R.B. and Warburton, F.W. (1967) *Objective Personality and Motivation Tests*. Urbana, IL: University of Illinois Press.

Cave, M., Hanney, S. and Kogan, M. (1988) *The Use of Performance Indicators in Higher Education. A Critical Analysis of Developing Practice*. London: Jessica Kingsley Publishers.

CCC (1995) 'Writing Assessment: A position statement.' *CCC 46*, 3, 430–437. Conference on College Composition and Communication.

CDP (1987) 'Performance Indicators: A position Statement.' Mimeo. London: Committee of Polytechnic Directors.

Centra, J.A. (1975) 'Colleagues as raters of classroom instruction.' *Journal of Higher Education 46*, 327–337.

Centra, J.A. (1994) 'The use of the teaching portfolio and student evaluations for summative evaluation.' *Journal of Higher Education 65*, 5, 555–570.

Challis, M., Usherwood, T. and Joesbury, H. (1994) *Assessment of Specified Competences in Undergraduate General Practice Medical Training*. Issue no. 25, Competence and Assessment. Sheffield: Employment Department.

Champagne, A.N., Gunstone, R.F. and Klopfer, L.E. (1983) 'Naïve knowledge and science learning.' *Research in Science and Technological Education 1*, 2, 173–183.

Chapman, K. (1996a) 'Entry qualifications, degree results and value-added in the UK.' *Oxford Review of Education 22*, 3, 251–264.

Chapman, K. (1996b) 'An analysis of degree results in geography by gender.' *Assessment and Evaluation in Higher Education 21*, 4, 293–311.

Chapple, M. and Murphy, R. (1996) 'The nominal group technique: Extending the evaluation of students' teaching and learning experiences.' *Assessment and Evaluation in Higher Education 21*, 2, 147–160.

Chau, C. (1997) 'A bootstrap experiment on the statistical properties of students' ratings of teaching effectiveness.' *Research in Higher Education 38*, 4, 497–517.

Chelvu, C.J. and Elton, L.R.B. (1977) 'An item bank for multiple choice questions.' *Physics Education 12*, 4, 263–266.

Chi, M., Glaser, R. and Farr, M. (eds) (1988) *The Nature of Expertise*. Hillsdale, NJ: Lawrence Erlbaum.

Chickering, A. (1969) *Education and Identity*. San Francisco: Jossey-Bass.

Child, D. (1970) *The Essentials of Factor Analysis*. London: Holt, Rinehart and Winston.

Choppin, B.L. (1973) *The Prediction of Academic Success*. Slough: National Foundation for Educational Research.

Christenson, H. (1979) 'Test anxiety and academic achievement in high school students.' *Perceptual and Motor Skills 49*, 648.

Christie, A. and Jones, M. (1995) 'Educational technology in the teaching of clinical reasoning and access to knowledge resources.' In J. Higgs and M. Jones (eds) *Clinical Reasoning in the Health Professions*. Oxford: Butterworth-Heinemann.

Church, A. and Bull, S. (1995) 'Evaluating and assessing oral presentations: a limited but effective role for employers in the geography curriculum.' *Journal of Geography in Higher Education*, 196–202.

Church, C.H. (1983) 'Course Control in the University Sector.' In C.H. Church (ed.) *Practice and Perspective in Validation*. London: Society for Research into Higher Education.

Church, C.H. and Murray, R. (1983) 'Of Definitions, Debates and Dimensions.' In C.H. Church (ed.) *Practice and Perspective in Validation*. London: Society for Research into Higher Education.

Cinquepalmi, R., Fogli-Muciaccia, M.T. and Picciarelli, V. (1983). 'Piaget-type questionnaire scores: A quantitative analysis and its implications for teaching science freshmen.' *European Journal of Science Education 5*, 1, 87–95.

Clack, G.B. (1994) 'Medical graduates evaluate the effectiveness of their education.' *Medical Education 28*, 5, 418–431.

Clarke, W., Lang, M. and Rechnitzer, E. (1986) *The Class of 82. Report on the findings of the 1984 national survey of graduates 1982*. Ottawa, Canada: Minister for Supply and Services.

Clarke, B.R. (1960) 'The cooling-out function of higher education.' *American Journal of Sociology 65*, 569.

Claxton, G. (1995) 'What kind of learning does self-assessment drive? Developing a 'nose' for quality; comments on Klenowski.' *Assessment in Education; Principles, Policy and Practice 2*, 3, 339–344.

Clement, J. (1981) 'Solving problems with formulas.' *Engineering Education, 72*, 158–161.

Clement, J. (1982) 'Students' preconceptions of introductory mechanics.' *American Journal of Physics 50*, 1, 66–70.

CNAA (1992) *The External Examiner and Curriculum Change.* Discussion Document No. 7. London: Council for National Academic Awards.

Cobb, S. (1976) 'Social support as a moderator of life stress.' *Psychosomatic Medicine 38*, 300–314.

Coelho, S.M. and Sere, M.G. (1998) 'Pupils' reasoning and practice during hands-on-activities in the measurement phase.' *Research in Science and Technological Education 16*, 1, 79–96.

Cohen, P.A. (1980) 'Effectiveness of student-rating feedback for improving college instruction: a meta-analysis.' *Research in Higher Education 13*, 321–341.

Cohen, P.A. (1981) 'Student ratings of instruction and student achievement: A meta-analysis of multi section validity studies.' *Review of Educational Research 51*, 281–309.

Cohen, P.A. (1987) 'A critical analysis and reanalysis of the multisection validity analysis.' Paper presented to the American Educational Research Association, San Francisco.

Coleman, J.A. (1999) *University Language Testing and the C-Test.* Portsmouth: University of Portsmouth Occasional Paper.

Coles, M. (1998) 'Do advanced science qualifications prepare students for employment and higher education?' *Research in Science and Technological Education 16*, 1, 53–66.

Collier, G. (ed.) (1983) *The Management of Peer Group Learning. Syndicate methods in Higher Education.* London: Society for Research into Higher Education.

Collier, G. (1989) *A New Teaching: A New Learning.* London: SPCK.

Collier, G. (1993) 'Learning moral judgement in higher education.' *Studies in Higher Education 18*, 3, 287–297.

Collier, G. (1997) 'Learning moral commitment in higher education.' *Journal of Moral Education 26*, 1, 73–83.

Collinge, J.N. (1994) 'Some fundamental questions about scientific thinking.' *Research in Science and Technological Education 12*, 2, 161–174.

Colton, D.A. *et al.* (1997) *Reliability Issues with Performance Assessments: A Collection of Papers.* ACT Research Report Series 97–3. Iowa City, IA: American College Testing Program.

Connor, M. and Warr, P.B. (1990) *The development of Personal Effectiveness Measures for use by Training Providers.* Final report. MRC/ESRC. Sheffield: University of Sheffield.

Cook, M.C.F. (1980) 'The role of the academic supervisor for undergraduate dissertations in science and science related subjects.' *Studies in Higher Education 5*, 2, 175–179.

Coombs, R.H. and Virshup, B.B. (1990) 'Enhancing the psychological health of medical students: the student well-being committee.' *Medical Education 28*, 1, 47–54.

Cooper, C. and Odell, L. (eds) (1977) *Evaluating Writing: Describing, Measuring, Judging.* Urbana, IL: National Council of Teachers of English.

Cooper, S.E. and Miller, J.A. (1991) 'MBTI learning style–teaching style discongruencies.' *Educational and Psychological Measurement 51*, 3, 699–706.

Corley, J.B. (1983) 'Role playing simulations.' In W.E. Fabb and J.R. Marshall (eds) *The Assessment of General Practice.* Lancaster: MTP Press.

Cowan, J. (1983) 'How engineers understand: an experiment for author and reader.' *Engineering Education 73*, 4, 301–303.

Cowan, J. (1998) *On Becoming an Innovative University Teacher: Reflection in Action.* Buckingham: SRHE/Open University Press.

Cowan, J. and George, J. (1997) *Formative Evaluation-Bordering Action.* Research Report 97/5. Edinburgh: Open University in Scotland.

Cowan, J., Pottinger, I., Weedon, E. and Wood, H. (1994) 'Development through researching your own practice.' Mimeo. Edinburgh: Open University in Scotland.

Crain, W. (1992) *Theories of Development: Concepts and Applications.* 3rd edn. Englewood Cliffs, NJ: Prentice Hall.

Cresswell, M.J. (1986a) 'Examination grades. How many should there be?' *British Educational Research Journal 12*, 1, 37–54.

Cresswell, M.J. (1986b) 'A review of borderline reviewing.' *Educational Studies 12*, 2, 175–190.

Crijnen, A.M., Kraan, H.F. and Zuidweg, J. (1990) 'Evaluating growth in interviewing skills during medical school.' In Z.M. Nooman, H.G. Schmidt and E.S. Ezzat (eds) *Innovation in Medical Education. An Evaluation of its Present Status.* New York: Springer.

Cromwell, L.S. (ed.) (1986) *Teaching Critical Thinking in the Arts and Humanities.* Milwaukee, WI: Alverno Productions.

Cronbach, L.J. (1971) 'Test Validation.' In R.L. Thorndike (ed.) *Educational Measurement.* 2nd edn. Washington, DC: American Council on Education.

Cronbach, L.J. (1980) 'Validity on Parole; How can we go Straight?' In *New Directions for Testing and Measurement.* San Francisco: Jossey-Bass.

Cronbach, L.J. (1984) *Essentials of Psychological Testing.* 4th edn. New York: Harper and Row.

Cronbach, L.J. and Gleser, G.C. (1965) 'Interpretation of reliability and validity coefficients. Remarks on a paper by Lord.' In L.J. Cronbach and G.C. Gleser (eds) *Psychological Tests and Personnel Decisions* 3rd Edition. New York: Harper and Row.

Cronbach, L.J. and Snow, R.E. (1977) *Aptitudes and Instructional Methods.* New York: Irvington.

Crooks, T.J. (1988) *Assessing Student Performance.* Green Guide 8. Sydney: Higher Education Research and Development Society of Australasia.

Crooks, T.J., Kane, M.T. and Cohen, A.S. (1996) 'Threats to the valid use of assessments.' *Assessment in Education, Principles, Policy and Practice 3*, 3, 265–285.

Crosier, D. and Woodrow, M. (1997) 'Don't call it "drop-out;" The danger of the discourse of deficiency.' In *Beyond Access: Diversity and Opportunity in Higher Education*. Utrecht: Expertise Centrum Allochtonen Hoger Onderjwis.

Cross, K.P. (1986) 'A proposal to improve teaching.' *AAHE Bulletin*, Sept, 9–15.

Cross, K.P. and Steadman, M. (1996) *Classroom Research. Implementing the Scholarship of Teaching*. San Francisco: Jossey-Bass.

Cross, L.H., Frary, R.B. and Weber, L.J. (1993) 'College grading. Achievement, attitudes, and effort.' *College Teaching 41*, 4, 143–148.

Crouse, J. and Trusheim, D. (1988) *The Case Against the SAT*. Chicago: University of Chicago Press.

Crowther, Lord (Chairman of a Committee) (1959) *15–18*. (Two volumes) Central Advisory Council for Education. London: HMSO.

Crum, R. and Parikh, A. (1983) 'Headmaster's reports, admissions and performance in social science.' *Educational Studies 9*, 3, 169–184.

Cuban, L. (1984) 'Policy and research dilemmas in the teaching of reasoning: Unplanned designs.' *Review of Educational Research 54*, 655–681.

Culler, A.D. (1955) *The Imperial Intellect. A Study of Newman's Educational Ideal*. Newhaven, CT: Yale University Press.

Culver, R.S., Cox, P., Sharp, J. and FitzGibbon, A. (1994) 'Student learning profiles in two innovative honours degree engineering programmes.' *International Journal of Technology and Design Education* 4, 257–287.

Culver, R.S. and Hackos, J.T. (1982) 'Perry's model of intellectual development.' *Engineering Education 73*, 2, 221–226.

Culver, R.S. and Olds, B. (1986) 'EPICS: An integrated program for the first two years.' *Proceedings ASEE St Lawrence Section Conference*, 1986. New York: Troy.

Culver, R.S. and Sackman, N. (1988) 'Learning with meaning through marker events.' *Proceedings Frontiers in Education Conference*. Santa Barbara, NY: IEEE.

Curtain, R. and Hayton, G. (1995) 'The use and abuse of competency standards framework in Australia: A comparative perspective.' *Assessment in Education: Principles, Policy and Practice 2*, 2, 205–224.

CVCP (1969) *The Assessment of Undergraduate Performance*. London: Committee of Vice Chancellors and Principals.

CVCP (1985) 'Report of a Steering Committee for Efficiency Studies in the Universities.' (The Jarratt Report). London: Committee of Vice Chancellors and Principals.

CVCP (1987) *Academic Standards in the Universities*. (Responses to the Reynolds Report) London: Committee of Vice-Chancellors and Principals.

Czuchry, M. and Danserau, D.F. (1998) 'Node link mapping as an alternative to traditional writing assignments in undergraduate psychology.' *Teaching Psychology*, in press.

Dale, M. and Isles, P. (1992) *Assessing Management Skills. A Guide to Competencies and Evaluation Techniques*. London: Kogan Page.

Dalziel, J. (1998) 'Using marks to assess student performance: some problems and alternatives.' *Assessment and Evaluation in Higher Education 23*, 4, 351–366.

Danserau, D.F. and Newbern, D. (1997) 'Using knowledge maps to enhance excellence.' In W.E. Campbell and K.A. Smith (eds) *New Paradigms for College Teaching*. Edina, MI: Interaction Book Co.

Davidow, W.H. and Malone, M.S. (1992) *The Virtual Corporation; Structuring and Revitalising the Corporation for the 21st Century*. New York: HarperCollins.

Davis, D. and Fox, R.D. (1994) 'The place of research in CME.' In D.A. Davis and R.D. Fox (eds) *The Physician as Learner. Linking Research to Practice*. Chicago: American Medical Association.

Davis, D., Lindsay, E. and Mazmanian, P. (1994) 'The effectiveness of CME interventions.' In D. Davis and R.D. Fox (eds) *The Physician as Learner. Linking Research to Practice*. Chicago: American Medical Association.

Davis, M. (1980) 'The CNAA as a Validating Agency.' In D.A. Billing (ed.) *Indicators of Performance*. Guildford: Society for Research into Higher Education.

Dearing, R. (1977) *Higher Education in the Learning Society*. Report of a National Committee. National Committee of Enquiry into Higher Education, Norwich: HMSO.

De Cecco, J.P. and Crawford, W.R. (1974) *The Psychology of Learning and Instruction*. Englewood Cliffs, NJ: Prentice Hall.

De Nevers, N. (1984) 'An engineering solution to grade inflation.' *Engineering Education*, April, 661–663.

DeBord (1993) 'Promoting reflective judgement in counseling psychology graduate education.' Thesis. University of Missouri Columbia. Cited by P.K. Wood.

Delandshere, G. (1994) 'The assessment of teachers in the United States.' *Assessment in Education; Principles, Policy and Practice 1*, 1, 95–114.

Dember, W. (1965) 'The new look in motivation.' *American Scientist* 53, 409–427.

Denscombe, M. and Roberts, L. (1980) 'Participating in assessment; the political dimensions of student self-grading.' *Teaching Politics 9*, 2, 134–144.

Derricott, R. (1985) *Curriculum Continuity. Primary to Secondary*. Slough: National Foundation for Educational Research.

Dertouzos, M., Lester, M.L. and Solow, R.M. (1989) *Made in America. Regaining the Productive Edge*. Cambridge, MA: MIT Press.

Diamond, J.J. and Evans, W.J. (1972) 'An investigation of the cognitive-correlation of test wiseness.' *Journal of Educational Measurement* 9, 145–150.

Diederich, P.B. (1960) *Short Cut Statistics for Teacher Made Tests*. Princeton, NJ: Educational Testing Service.

Diederich, P.B. (1974) *Measuring Growth in English*. Urbana, IL: National Council of Teachers of English.

Diekhoff, G.M. *et al.* (1996) 'College cheating: ten years later.' *Research in Higher Education 37*, 4, 487–502.

Diez, M. (ed.) (1988) *Changing the Practice of Teacher Education. Standards and Assessment as a Lever for Change*. Washington, DC: American Association of Colleges of Teacher Education.

Dillon, J.T. (1990) *The Practice of Questioning.* London: Routledge.

Dinkelspiel, J.R. (1972) 'A teachable subject.' *Journal of Higher Education 42*, 1, 42.

Dobson, P. (1989) 'Self and Peer assessment.' In P. Herriott (ed.) *Assessment and Selection in Organizations: Methods and Practice for Recruitment and Appraisal.* Chichester: Wiley.

Doherty, G. (1993) 'Towards total quality management in higher education.' *Higher Education 25*, 321–339.

Dolly, J.P. and Williams, K.S. (1983) 'Teaching testwiseness.' Paper presented at the annual meeting of the Northern Rocky Mountain educational Research Association, Jackson, New York.

Dolly, J.P. and Williams, K.S. (1986) 'Using test taking strategies to maximise multiple choice test scores.' *Educational and Psychological Measurement 46*, 3, 619–625.

Donald, J.G. (1982) 'Knowledge structures; methods for exploring course content.' *Journal of Higher Education 54*, 1, 31–41.

Donald, J.G. and Denison, D.B. (1996) 'Evaluating undergraduate education: The use of broad indicators.' *Assessment and Evaluation in Higher Education 21*, 1 23–40.

Drake, S. (1974) 'Translation of G. Galilei.' *Two New Sciences.* Madison, WI: University of Wisconsin.

Dressel, P.L. (1971) 'Values, cognitive and affective.' *Journal of Higher Education 42*, 5, 400.

Dressel, P.L. (1976) *Handbook of Academic Evaluation.* San Francisco: Jossey-Bass.

Dressel, J.H. (1991) 'The formal oral group exam: challenges and possibilities–the oral exam and critical thinking.' Paper presented at the annual meeting of the National Council of Teachers of English, Seattle, 22–27 November (ED 347 527).

Drew, T.L. and Work, G.G. (1998) 'Gender-based differences in perception of experience in higher education: Gaining a broader perspective.' *Journal of Higher Education 69*, 5, 542–555.

Driver, R.P. (1973) Ph.D dissertation. University of Illinois, Urbana-Champagne.

Driver, R.P. (1983) *The Pupil as Scientist.* Milton Keynes: Open University Press.

Driver, R.P. and Bell, B. (1986) 'Students' thinking and the learning of science: a constructivist approach.' *School Science Review 67*, 444.

Driver, R.P. and Easley, J. (1978) 'Pupils and paradigms: a review of literature related to concept development in adolescent science studies.' *Studies in Science Education 5*, 61–84.

Duff, A. and Cotgrove, S. (1982) 'Social values and the choice of careers in industry.' *Journal of Occupational Psychology 55*, 5, 97–107.

Duit, R. (1995) 'The constructivist view: a fashionable fruitful paradigm for science education research and practice.' In L.P. Steffe and J. Gale (eds) *Constructivism in Education.* Hillsdale, NJ: Lawrence Erlbaum.

Duke, M., Forbes, H., Hunter, S. and Prosser, M. (1998) 'Problem based learning (PBL): conceptions and approaches of undergraduate students of nursing.' *Advances in Health Science Education 3*, 1, 59–70.

Dunkin, M.J. (1990) 'Willingness to obtain student evaluations as a criterion of academic staff performance.' *Higher Education Research and Development 9*, 51–60.

Dunkin, M.J. and Barnes, J. (1986) 'Research on teaching in higher education.' In M.C. Wittrock (ed.) *Handbook of Research on Teaching.* New York: American Educational Research Association, MacMillan.

Dunleavy, P. (1986) *Studying for a Degree in Humanities and Social Sciences.* London: MacMillan.

Eachus, P. and Cassidy, S. (1997a) 'Self-efficacy, locus of control and styles of learning as contributing factors in the academic performance of student health professionals.' *Proceedings of the First Regional Congress of Psychology for Professionals in the Americas.* Mexico City, Mexico.

Eachus, P. and Cassidy, S. (1997b) 'The health student locus of control scale.' *Perceptual and Motor Skills 85*, 997.

Earl, S.E. (1986) 'Staff and peer assessment: measuring an individual's contribution to group performance.' *Assessment and Evaluation in Higher Education 11*, 1, 60–69.

Ebel, R.L. (1958) 'Using examinations to promote learning.' In R.M. Cooper (ed.) *Two Ends of the Log.* Minneapolis: University of Minnesota Press.

Ebel, R.L. (1965) *Measurements and Educational Achievement.* Englewood Cliffs, NJ: Prentice Hall.

Edgerton, R., Hutchings, P. and Quinlan, K. (1991) *The Teaching Portfolio; Capturing the Scholarship of Teaching.* Washington, DC: American Association of Higher Education.

Edwards, R.M. (1984) 'A case study in the examination of systems analysis.' *Assessment and Evaluation in Higher Education 9*, 1, 31–39.

Eisner, E.W. (1979) *The Educational Imagination: On the Design and Evaluation of School Programs* New York: Macmillan.

Eizler, C. (1983) 'The meaning of college grades in three grading systems.' *Educational Research Quarterly 8*, 12–30.

El-Khawas, E. (1986) *Campus Trends.* Higher Education Panel Reports, No. 73, August. Washington, DC: American Council on Education.

Elkind, D. (1988) *The Hurried Child. Growing up too Fast too Soon.* Reading, MA: Addison-Wesley.

Ellinwood, S., Mayerson, N. and Paul, S.C. (1983) 'An Assessment of Stress Among Law Students at the University of Utah.' Salt Lake City, UT: University of Utah.

Elliott, J. (1976) 'Preparing teachers for classroom accountability.' *College Teaching, 100*, 49–71.

Elliott, J. (1990) 'Educational research in crisis: performance indicators and the decline of excellence.' *British Educational Research Journal 16*, 1, 3–18.

Ellis, R. and Whittington, D. (eds) (1983) *New Directions in Social Skill Training.* London: Croom Helm.

Ellis, W. (1995) *The Oxbridge Conspiracy.* Harmondsworth: Penguin.

Elton, C.F. and Rose, H.A. (1974) 'Students who leave engineering.' *Engineering Education 62*, 1, 30–32.

Elton, C.F. and Rose, H.A. (1996) 'Within university transfer. It's relation to personality characteristics.' *Journal of Applied Psychology 50*, 6, 539.

Elton, L. (1996) 'Strategies to enhance student motivation: a conceptual analysis.' *Studies in Higher Education 21*, 1, 57–68.

Elton, L. (1998) 'Are UK degrees going up, down or sideways?' *Studies in Higher Education 23*, 1, 35–42.

Employment Department (1986) White Paper. Employment Department. London: HMSO.

Employment Department (undated) 'Assessable Standards for National Certification.' Guidance Note 2. *Developing Standards by Reference to Functions.* Sheffield: Employment Department.

Employment Department (1991) *The National Record of Achievement: A Business Guide.* Sheffield: Employment Department.

Engelkemeyer, S.W. (1998) 'Institutional performance measures.' *AAHE Bulletin 31*, 4.

Engler, B. (1979) *Personality Theories. An Introduction.* Boston, MA: Houghton Mifflin.

Ennis, R.H. (1981) 'Eight fallacies in Bloom's taxonomy.' In C.J.B. Macmillan (ed.) *Philosophy of Education 1980.* Bloomington, IL: Philosophy of Education Society.

Ennis, R.H. (1992) 'The degree to which critical thinking is subject specific: clarification and needed research.' In S.P. Norris (ed.) *The Generalisability of Critical Thinking.* New York: Teachers College Press.

Ennis, R.H. (1993) 'Critical thinking assessment.' *Theory into Practice 32*, 3, 179–186.

Entwistle, A. and Entwistle, N. (1992) 'Experiences of understanding in revising for degree examinations.' *Learning and Instruction 2*, 1–22.

Entwistle, N.J. (1981) *Styles of Learning and Teaching.* Chichester: Wiley.

Entwistle, N.J. (1988) 'Motivational factors in students' approaches to learning.' In R.R. Schmeck (ed.) *Learning Strategies and Learning Styles.* New York: Plenum Press.

Entwistle, N.J., Hanley, M. and Ratcliffe, G. (1979) 'Approaches to learning and levels of understanding.' *British Educational Research Journal 5*, 99–114.

Entwistle, N.J. and Kozeki, B. (1985) 'Relationships between school motivation, approaches to studying, and attainment among British and Hungarian adolescents.' *British Journal of Educational Psychology 55*, 124–137.

Entwistle, N.J. and Ramsden, P. (1983) *Understanding Student Learning.* London: Croom Helm.

Entwistle, N.J. and Wilson, J.D. (1977) *Degrees of Excellence. The Academic Achievement Game.* London: Hodder and Stoughton.

Enyeart, M.A., Baker, D. and Vanharlingen, D. (1980) 'Correlation of inductive and deductive logical reasoning to college physics achievement.' *Journal of Research in Science Teaching 17*, 3, 263–267.

Eppler, M.A. and Harty, B.L. (1997) 'Achievement motivation goals in relation to academic performance in traditional and non-traditional college students.' *Research in Higher Education 38*, 5, 557–573.

Ericksen, S.C. (1984) *The Essence of Good Teaching.* San Francisco: Jossey-Bass.

Ericsson, K.A. and Simon, H.A. (1984) *Protocol Analysis.* Cambridge, MA: MIT Press/Bradford.

Erwin, D. (1997) 'Developing strategies and policies for changing universities.' In S. Armstrong, G. Thompson and S. Brown (eds) *Facing up to Radical Change in Universities and Colleges.* London: Kogan Page.

Essex, D.L. (1976) 'A comparison of two item scoring procedure.' *Journal of Medical Education 51*, 565–572.

Ethington, C.A. (1997) 'A hierarchical linear modelling approach to studying college effects.' In J. Smart (ed.) *Higher Education. Handbook of Theory and Research.* Vol 12. New York: Agathon Press.

ETS (undated) Brief from ETS on the work of G. Conland and M. Fowles. *Test Development Manual for the Testing of Writing Ability.* Princeton, NJ: Educational Testing Service.

ETS (1980) *An Approach for Identifying and Minimizing Bias in Standardized Tests: A Set of Guidelines.* Princeton, NJ: Educational Testing Service.

ETS (1986) *Standards for Quality and Fairness.* Princeton, NJ: Educational Testing Service.

Ewell, P. (1988) 'Outcomes, Assessment and Academic Improvement.' In 'Search of usable knowledge.' In J. Smart (ed.) *Higher Education: Handbook of Theory and Research Vol 5.* New York: Agathon Press.

Ewell, P. (1993) *A Preliminary Study of the Feasibility and Utility for National Policy of Instructional 'Good Practice' Indicators in Undergraduate Education.* Mimeo. National Center for Education Statistics. Boulder, CO: NCHEMS.

Ewell, P. (1996) 'The current pattern of state level assessment: Results of a national inventory.' in G.H. Gaither (ed.) *Performance Indicators in Higher Education: What works, What Doesn't and What's Next?.* Proceedings. Symposium. Washington, DC: American Association for Higher Education.

Ewell, P. (1997) 'Identifying indicators of curricular quality' In J.G. Gaff *et al.* (eds) *Handbook of the Undergraduate Curriculum.* San Fransico, CA: Jossey-Bass.

Ewell, P. and Jones, D.P. (1991) *Action Matters: The Case for Indirect Measures in Assessing Higher Education's Progress in National Education Goals.* Boulder, CO: National Center for Higher Education Management.

Fabb, W.E. and Marshall, J.E. (1983) *The Assessment of Clinical Competence in General Family Practice.* Lancaster: MTP Press.

Falchikov, N. (1986) 'Product comparisons and process benefits of peer group and self-assessments.' *Assessment and Evaluation in Higher Education 11*, 2, 146–186.

Fassinger, P.A. (1995) 'Understanding classroom interaction: students' and professors' contributions to student silence.' *Journal of Higher Education 66*, 1, 82–96.

Fazey, D.M.A. (1993) 'Self-assessment as a generic skill for enterprising students; the learning process.' *Assessment and Evaluation in Higher Education 18*, 3, 221–234.

Felder, R.M. (1985) 'The generic quiz.' *Chemical Engineering Education 19*, 4, 176–214.

Felder, R.M. (1995) 'A longitudinal study of engineering student performance and retention. IV instructional methods and student responses to them.' *Journal of Engineering Education 84*, 4, 361–367.

Felder, R.M., Felder, G.M. and Dietz, E.J. (1997) 'A longitudinal study of alternative approaches to engineering education: Survey assessment of results.' *Proceedings of the Frontiers in Education Conference,* Vol 3, 1284–1289, ASEE. New York: IEEE.

Feldman, K.A. (1976a) 'Grades and college students' evaluations of their courses and teachers.' *Research in Higher Education 4*, 69–111

Feldman, K.A. (1976b) 'The superior college teacher from the student's view.' *Research in Higher Education 5*, 243–288.

Feldman, K.A. (1998) 'Reflections on the study of effective college teaching and student ratings. One continuing quest and unresolved issues.' In J. Smart (ed.) *Higher Education. Handbook of Theory and Practice 13.* New York: Agathon Press.

Feldman, K.A. and Newcomb, T. (1969) *The Impact of College on Students.* San Francisco: Jossey-Bass.

Feletti, G.I. (1980) 'Reliability and validity studies on modified essay questions.' *Journal of Medical Education 51,* 565–567.

Feletti, G.I. and Neame, R.L.B. (1981) 'Curricular strategies for reducing examination anxiety.' *Higher Education 10,* 6, 675–686.

Feltham, R. (1988) 'Assessment Center decision making: Judgemental versus mechanical.' *Journal of Occupational Psychology 61,* 237–241.

Feltham, R. (1989) 'Assessment centres.' In P. Herriot (ed.) *Assessment and Selection in Organizations.* Chichester: Wiley.

Fernandez Prieto, C. and Marsh, M. (1999) 'Learning through text: A Spanish CALL course.' in J. Heywood, J. Sharp and M. Hides (eds) *Improving Teaching in Higher Education.* Salford: Teaching and Learning Committee, University of Salford.

Festinger, L. (1957) *A Theory of Cognitive Dissonance.* Stanford, CA: Stanford University Press.

FEU (1987) *Profiles in Context.* London: Further Education Unit, Department of Education and Science.

Fincher, C. (1985) 'Learning theory and research.' In J. Smart (ed.) *Higher Education. Handbook of Theory and Research 1.* New York: Agathon Press.

Fincher, R.M.E., Lewis, L.L. and Kuske, T.T. (1993) 'Relationships of interns' performances to their self-assessments of their preparedness for internship and to their academic performance in medical school.' In J.S. Gonnella, M. Hojat, J.B. Erdman and J.J. Veloski (eds) *Assessment Measures in Medical School, Residency and Practice.* New York: Springer.

Fineman, S. (1980) 'Reflections on peer teaching and assessment- an undergraduate experience.' *Assessment and Evaluation in Higher Education 6,* 1, 82–93.

Finlay, I.G., Maughan, T.S. and Webster, D.J.T. (1998) 'A randomized controlled study of portfolio learning in undergraduate cancer education.' *Medical Education 32,* 2, 172–176.

Fischer, C.F. and King, R.M. (1995) *Authentic Assessment. A Guide to Implementation.* Thousand Oaks, CA: Corwin Press.

Fischer, K.W., Kenny, S.L. and Pipp, S.L.(1990) 'How cognitive processes and environmental conditions organize discontinuities in the development of abstractions.' In C.N. Alexamder and E.J. Langer (eds) *Higher Stages of Human Development.* Oxford: Oxford University Press.

Fisher, S. (1994) *Stress in Academic Life: The Mental Assembly Line.* Buckingham: Society for Research into Higher Education, Open University Press.

Fitt, D.X. and Heverly, M.A. (1994) 'Classroom assessment of student competencies.' *Assessment and Evaluation in Higher Education 19,* 3, 215–224.

Fitzgerald, M. (1994) 'Assessment and Audit in Disrepute' *The Times Education Supplement 1147.*

FitzGibbon, A. (1987) 'Kolb's experiential learning model as a model for supervision of classrooms teaching for student teachers.' *European Journal of Teacher Education 10,* 2, 163–178.

FitzGibbon, A. (1994) 'Self-evaluation exercises in initial teacher education.' *Irish Educational Studies 13,* 145–164.

FitzGibbon, A. and Heywood, J. (1986) 'The recognition of conjunctive and identity needs in teacher development. Their implications for the planning of in-service training.' *European Journal of Teacher Education 10,* 2, 163–178.

FitzGibbon, C.T., Tymms, P.B. and Vincent, L. (1994) *Comparing Examination Boards and Syllabuses at 'A' Level: Students' Grade, Attitudes and Perceptions of Classroom Processes: A-Level Information System.* Newcastle upon Tyne: University of newcastle upon Tyne.

Fleishman, E.A. (ed.) (1967) *Studies and Research in Industrial Psychology.* Homewood, IL: Dorsey Press.

Fleming, D. (1992) 'Meta Competence.' *Competence and Assessment 16,* 9–12. Sheffield: Employment Department.

Flynn, E. (1982) 'Freedom, Restraint and Peer Group Interaction.' Paper presented at annual meeting of the Conference on College Composition and Communication (33rd), San Francisco, CA.

Fogarty, G.J. and Taylor, J.A. (1997) 'Learning styles among mature-age students: some comments on the Approaches to Studying Inventory (ASI-S).' *Higher Education Research and Development 16,* 3, 321–330.

Fong, B. (1987) *The External Examiner Approach to Assessment.* Commissioned paper, AAHE Assessment Forum. Washington, DC: American Association for Higher Education.

Ford, N.J. and Rennie, D.M. (1999) 'Development of an authentic assessment scheme for the professional placement period of a sandwich course.' In J. Heywood, J. Sharp and M. Hides (eds) *Improving Teaching in Higher Education.* Salford: University of Salford, Teaching and Learning Committee.

Fordyce, D. (1991) 'The nature of student learning in engineering.' *International Journal of Technology and Design Education 2,* 3, 22–40.

Forrest, A. (1982) *Increasing Student Competence and Persistence: The Best Case for General Education.* Iowa City, Iowa: American College Testing Program.

Forrest, A. (1985) 'Creating Conditions for Student Institutional Success.' in Nole *et al.* (eds) *Increasing Student Retention.* San Francisco: Jossey-Bass.

Forrest, A. and Steele, J.M. (1982) *Defining and Measuring General Education Knowledge and Skills.* Technical Report. American College Testing Program, Iowa City, Iowa.

Forrest, G.M. (1985) 'Oral assessment.' In T. Husen and T.N. Postlethwaite (eds) *The International Encyclopedia of Education.* Oxford: Pergamon Press.

Forrest, G.M. (1991) In a paper presented to the International Conference on Testing at St Patrick's College, Drumcondra, Dublin. July.

Forrest, G.M and D.J. Shoesmith (1985) *A Second Review of GCE Comparability Studies.* Manchester: Joint Matriculation Board.

Forrest, G.M., Smith, G.A. and Brown, M.H. (1970) *General Studies (Advanced) and Academic Aptitude.* Manchester: Joint matriculation Board.

Forrest, G.M. and Smith, G.A. (1972) Standards in Subjects at the Ordinary Level of the GCE June 1971. Manchester: Joint Matriculation Board.

Forrest, G.M. and Whittaker, R.J. (1983) *Problems of the GCE Advanced Level Grading Scheme.* Manchester: Joint Matriculation Board.

Fox, R. (1994) 'Validating lecture effectiveness questionnaires in accounting.' *Accounting Education 3*, 3, 249–258.

Fox, R. (1999 'From quantitative to qualitative assessment: evaluating student questionnaires of teaching effectiveness.' In J. Heywood, J. Sharp, and M. Hides *Improving Teaching in Higher Education.* Salford: Teaching and Learning Committee, University of Salford.

Fox, R and Craig, J. (1994) 'Future directions of research on physician learners.' in D.A. Davis and R. Fox (eds) The Physician as Learner. Linking Research to Practice. Chicago: American Medical Association.

Franklyn-Stokes, A. and Newstead, S.E. (1995) 'Undergraduate cheating: who does what and why?' *Studies in Higher Education 20*, 2, 159–172.

Fraser, W.J. and Gillam, J.N.(1972) *The Principles of Objective Testing in Mathematics.* Heinemann, London.

Freeling, N. (1991) *The Kitchen Book; The Cook Book.* Andre Deutsch, London

Freeman, M. (1995) 'Peer assessment by groups of group work.' *Assessment and Evaluation in Higher Education 20*, 3, 289–301.

Freeman, J. and Byrne, P. (1976) *Assessment of Post-Graduate Training in General Practice.* 2nd edn. London: Society for Research into Higher Education.

Freeman, J., Lynn, N. and Baker, R. (1999) 'The evaluation of a course for the development of enterprise skills.' In J. Heywood, Sharp, J. and Hides, M. (eds) *Improving Teaching in Higher Education.* Salford: Teaching and Learning Committee, The University of Salford.

Freeman, J., McComiskey, J.G. and Buttle, D. (1968) 'Research into divergent and convergent thinking.' *International Journal of Electrical Engineering Education 6*, 99–108.

Freeman, J., McComiskey, J.G. and Buttle, D. (1968) 'Student selection. A comparative study of student entrants to architecture and economics,' *International Journal of Educational Science 3*, 3, 189–197.

Freeman, J., Roberts, J., Metcalfe, D. and Hillier, V. (1982) *The Influence of Trainers on Trainees in General Practice.* Occassional paper No. 21. London: Royal College of General Practitioners.

Freeman, J. and Sharp, J. (1999) 'Group dynamics and the learning process.' In J. Heywood and J. Sharp (eds) *Improving Teaching in Higher Education.* Salford: Teaching and Learning Committee, University of Salford.

Freeman, J. and Thomas, E.(1999) 'Computer Literacy in Biological Science.' In J. Heywood, M. Hides and J. Sharp (ed.) *Improving Teaching in Higher Education.* Salford: Teaching and Learning Committee, University of Salford.

Frith, J.R. (1979) 'Testing the FSI Testing Kit.' *ADFL Bulletin 11*, 2, November cited by Fong, 1987.

Fry, S.A. (1990) 'Implementation and evaluation of peers marking in higher education.' *Assessment and Evaluation in Higher Education 15*, 3, 177–189.

Furneaux, W.D. (1962) 'The Psychologist and the University.' *Universities Quarterly 17*, 33.

Furst, E.J. (1958) *Constructing Evaluation Instruments.* New York: David Mckay.

Furst, E.J. (1994) 'Bloom's taxonomy: Philosophical and educational issues.' In L.W. Anderson and L.A. Sosniak (eds) *Bloom's Taxonomy. A Forty Year Retrospective.* Chicago: University of Chicago Press.

Fyfe, W. (1996) *Approaches to Learning: A Lifelong Perspective.* Project report 1995/3. Edinburgh: The Open University in Scotland.

Gaff, J.G. and Ratcliff, J.L. *et al.* (1996) *Handbook of the Undergraduate Curriculum.* San Fransisco: Jossey-Bass.

Gagné, R.N. (1965, 1977) *The Conditions of Learning.* Holt, Rinehart and Winston.

Gagné, R.N., Briggs, L.J. and Wager, W.W. (1992) *Principles of Instructional Design* (4th edn) Orlando, FL: Harcourt Brace Jovanovich.

Gainsbauer, T.J. and Mizner, G.L. (1980) 'Developmental stresses in medical education.' *Psychiatry 43*, 60–70.

Gaither, G.H. (ed.) (1995)'Assessing Performance in an Age of Accountability.' *Case Studies. New Directions for Higher Education 91.* San Francisco: Jossey-Bass.

Gaither, G.H. (ed.) (1996)*Performance Indicators in Higher Education. What Works, What Doesn't and What's Next? Proceedings of a Symposium.* Washington, DC: American Association for Higher Education.

Galassi, J.D., Frierson, H.T. and Sharer, R. (1981) 'Behaviour of high, moderate and low test anxious students during an actual test situation.' *Journal of Consulting and Clinical Psychology 49*, 1, 51–62.

Ganzer, V.J. (1968) 'Effects of audience presence and test anxiety on learning and retentions in a serial learning situation.' *Journal of Personality and Social Psychology 8*, 194–199.

Garvin, J.W. (1995) 'Group projects for first-year university students: an evaluation.' *Assessment and Evaluation in Higher Education 20*, 3, 301–306.

Gearhart, M., Herman, J.L., Baker, E.L. and Whittaker, A.K. (1993) *A Question for the Validity of Large-Scale Portfolio Assessment.* CRESST, Graduate School of Education (CSE Report 363, University of California, Los Angeles.

Geisinger, K.F. (1980) 'Who are giving all these 'A's.' *Journal of Teacher Education 31*, 2, 11–15.

Geisler-Brenstein, E., Schmeck, R.R. and Hetherington, J. (1996) 'An individual difference perspective on student diversity.' *Higher Education 31*, 1, 73–96.

Genereux, R.L. and McLeod, B.A. (1995) 'Circumstances surrounding cheating; a questionnaire study of college students.' *Research in Higher Education 36*, 6, 687–704.

Gerhardt, R.C. (1976) 'An alternative to grades.' *Improving College and University Teaching 14*, 2, 82–3, 86.

Gibbs, G. (1981) *Teaching Students to Learn. A Student Centred Approach.* Milton Keynes: Open University Press.

Gibbs, G. (1992) 'Improving the quality of student learning through course design.' In R. Barnett (ed.) *Learning to Effect.* Buckingham: SRHE/Open University Press.

Gibbs, G., Habeshaw, T. and Habeshaw, S. (1986, 1993) *53 Interesting Ways to Assess your Students.* Bristol: Technical and Educational Services.

Gibbs, G. and Lucas, L. (1995) *Using Research to Improve Student Learning in Large Classes.* Paper presented at the 3rd International Improving Student Learning Symposium, Exeter, Mimeo.

Gibbs, G., Lucas, L. and Simonite, V. (1996) 'Class size and student performance 1984–1994.' *Studies in Higher Education 21,* 3, 261–273.

Gibbs, G., Morgan, A. and Taylor, E. (1984) 'The world of the learner.' In F. Marton, D. Hounsell and N. Entwistle (eds) *The Experience of Learning.* Edinburgh: Scottish Academic Press.

Gibney, J. and Wiersma, W. (1986) 'Using profile analysis for student-teacher evaluation.' *Journal of Teacher Education 37,* 3, 41–45.

Gigliotti, R.J. and Buchtel, F.S. (1990) 'Attributional bias and course evaluations.' *Journal of Educational Psychology 82,* 341–351.

Gijselaers, W.H. and Schmidt, H.G.(1990) 'Development and evaluation of a causal model of problem-based learning.' In Z.M. Nooman, H.G. Schmidt and E.S. Ezzat (eds) *Innovation in Medical Education.* New York: Springer.

Gilbert, J.K., Watts, D.M. and Osborne, R.J. (1982) 'Students' conception of ideas in mechanics.' *Physical Education 17,* 42–46.

Gilligan, C. (1982) In a different voice: Women's conceptions of self and morality. *Harvard Educational Review, 47,* 481–517.

Gilligan, C., Murphy, J.M. and Tappan, M.B. (1990) 'Moral development beyond adolescence.' In C.N. Alexander and E.J. Langer (eds) *Higher Stages of Human Development.* Oxford: Oxford University Press.

Gipps, C.V. (1994) *Beyond Testing: Toward a Theory of Educational Assessment.* London: Falmer.

Gipps, C.V. and Murphy, P. (1994) *A Fair Test.* Buckingham: Open University Press.

Glaser, R. (1984) 'Learning and instruction: A letter for a time capsule.' In S.F. Chipman *et al.* (eds) *Thinking and Learning Skills.* Hillsdale, NJ: Erlbaum Associates.

Glenn, J. *et al.* (1997) 'Validation of a questionnaire to screen university students for learning disabilities.' *Advances in Health Science Education 2,* 3, 213–220.

Glutting, J.J. Mcdermott, P.A. and Stanley, J.C. (1987) 'Resolving differences among methods of establishing confidence limits for test scores.' *Educational and Psychological Measurement 47,* 3, 607–614.

Goldfinch, J. and Raeside, R. (1990) 'Development of peer assessment technique for obtaining individual marks on a group project.' *Assessment and Evaluation in Higher Education 15,* 3, 210–231.

Goldman, R.D. and Hewitt, B.N. (1975) 'Adapatation level as an explanation for differential standards in college grading.' *Journal of Educational Measurement 12,* 149–161.

Goldman, R.D. and Hewitt, B.N. (1976) 'Why college grade point average is difficult to predict.' *Journal of Educational Psychology 68,* 9–14.

Goleman, D. (1996) *Emotional Intelligence: Why it Can Matter More Than IQ.* London: Bloomsbury.

Gonczi, A. (1994) 'Competency based assessment in the professions in Australia.' *Assessment in Education: Principles, Policy and Practice 1,* 1, 27–44.

Gonnella, J.S., Hojat, M., Erdman, J.B. and Veloski, J.J. (1993) *Assessment Measures in Medical School, Residency and Practice.* New York: Springer.

Good, T.L. and Brophy, J.E. (1973) *Looking in Classrooms.* New York: Harper and Row.

Gowdy, A.A. (1996) 'Effective student focus groups; the bright and early approach.' *Assessment and Evaluation in Higher Education 21,* 2, 185, 190.

Graham, S.W. and Cockriel, J. (1990) 'An assessment of the perceived utility of various college majors.' *NACADA Journal 10,* 1, 8–17.

Granzin, K.L. and Painter, J.J. (1976) 'A second look at cognitive dissonance and course evaluation.' *Improving College and University Teaching 32,* 1, 46–53.

Grasha, A.F. (1984) 'Learning styles: The Journey from Greenwich Observatory (1796) to the college classroom (1984).' *Improving College and University Teaching 32,* 1, 46–53.

Grasha, A.F. (1990) 'The naturalistic approach to learning styles.' *College Teaching 38,* 3, 106–113.

Grayson, J.P. (1997) 'Academic achievement of first-generation students in a Canadian University.' *Research in Higher Education 38,* 6, 659–675.

Green, R.M. (1994) *The Ethical Manager.* New York: Macmillan.

Green, S. (1990) *Analysis of Personal Transferable Skills Requested by Employers in Graduate Recruitment Advertisements in June 1989.* mimeo. Sheffield: Personal Skills Unit: University of Sheffield.

Gregory, S. (1972) *Creativity in Engineering.* London: Butterworth.

GSP (1997a) *Final report of the Graduate Standards Programme.* Vol 1. London: Higher Education Quality Council.

GSP (1997b) *Final report of the Graduate Standards Programme.* Vol 2. London: Higher Education Quality Council.

Guilford, J.P. (1954) 'Three faces of intellect.' *American Psychologist 14,* 469.

Guilford, J.P. (1956) 'Traits in creativity.' In H. Anderson (ed.) *Creativity and its Cultivation.* New York: Harper and Row.

Gulliksen. H. (1950) *Theory of Mental Tests.* New York: Wiley.

Gur, R.C. and Sackheim, H.A.(1979) 'Self-deception: A concept in search of a phenomenon.' *Journal of Personality and Social Psychology 37,* 147–169.

Haberman, M. (1988) 'Minorities. Proposals for recruiting minority teachers. Promising practices and minority detours.' *Journal of Teacher Education, 39,* 38–44.

Hadwin, A.F. and Winne, P.M. (1996) 'Study strategies have meagre support: a review with recommendations for implementation.' *Journal of Higher Education 67,* 6, 692–715.

Hake, R. and Andrich, D. (1975) *The Ubiquitous Essay.* Chicago: Chicago University Press.

Hales, L.W and Tokar, E. (1975) 'The effect of quality preceding responses on the grades assigned and subsequent response to an essay question.' *Journal of Educational Measurement* 12, 2, 115–117.

Hall, C. and Fitzgerald C. (1995) Student summative evaluation of teaching: code of practice. *Assessment and Evaluation in Higher Education* 20, 3, 307– 314.

Hall, C.G.W. and Daglish, N.D. (1982) 'Length and quality: An exploratory study of inter-marker reliability.' *Assessment and Evaluation in Higher Education* 7, 2, 186–191.

Hall, W. and White, S. (1997) 'Developing strategies and policies for changing universities.' In S. Armstrong, G. Thompson and S. Brown (eds) *Facing up to Radical Changes in Universities and Colleges.* London: Kogan Page.

Halonen, J.S. (ed.) (1986) *Teaching Critical Thinking in Psychology.* Milwaukee, WI: Alverno Productions.

Harden, R.M. and Gleeson, F.A. (1979) *Assessment of Clinical Competence Using an Objective Structured Clinical Examination.* Booklet No 8. Dundee: Association for Medical Education.

Hargaden (1982) *From School to College.* Testimony to the National Commission on Excellence in Education. Chicago, 23rd June.

Hargeaves, D.J. (1996) 'How undergraduate students learn.' *European Journal of Engineering Education* 21, 4, 425–434.

Harris, N.D.C. and Bullock, K. (1981) 'What price projects?' *Journal of Biological Education* 6, 2, 151–152.

Harrow, A. (1972) *A Taxonomy of the Psychomotor Domain: A Guide for Developing Behavioural Objectives.* New York: David Mckay.

Hartle, T.W. (1986) 'The growing interest in measuring the educational achievement of college students.' In C. Adelman (ed.) *Assessment in Higher Education.* Washington, DC: US Department of Education.

Hartley, J. (1998) *Learning and Studying. A Research Perspective.* London: Routledge.

Hartley, J. and Greggs, M.A. (1997) 'Divergent thinking in arts and science students: contrary imaginations at Keele revisited.' *Studies in Higher Education* 22, 1, 93–97.

Hartog, P. and Rhodes, E.C. (1935) *An Examination of Examinations.* London: Macmillan.

Hartog, P. and Rhodes, E.C. (1936) *The Marks of Examiners.* London: Macmillan.

Harvey, L. and Knight, P. (1996) *Transforming Higher Education.* Buckingham: Open University Books.

Harvey, L., Moon, S. and Geall, V. (with Bower, R.) (1997) *Graduates' Work: Organizational Change and Student's Attributes.* Birmingham: Centre for Research in Quality, University of Central England.

Hausmann, C.L., Weiss, J.C., Lawrence, J.S. and Zeleznik, C. (1990) 'Confidence weighted answer technique in a group of pediatric residents.' *Medical Teacher* 12, 2, 163–168.

Hayes, J. and Allinson, C. (1996) 'The implications of learning styles for training and development: a discussion of the matching hypothesis.' *British Journal of Management* 7, 63–73.

Hazeltine, B. (1976) 'Student evaluation using lists of description statement.' *Research in Higher Education* 4, 1–22.

Heames, R. and Cox, S.(1997) 'Reducing stress in teaching and learning.' In S. Armstrong, G. Thompson and S. Brown (eds) *Facing up to Radical Changes in Universities and Colleges.* London: Kogan Page.

Hellige, J.B. (1993) *Hemispheric Asymmetry; What's Right and What's Left.* Cambridge, MA: Harvard University Press.

Helson, H. (1964) *Adaptation Level Theory.* New York: Harper and Row.

Henry, J. (1977) 'The courses' tutor and project work.' *Teaching at a Distance* 9, 1–12.

Henry, J. (1990) 'Enriching prior knowledge. Enhancing mature literacy in higher education.' *Journal of Higher Education* 61, 4, 425–447.

HEQC (1994) *Learning from Audit.* London: Higher Education Quality Council.

Herrnstein, R. and Murray, C. (1994) *The Bell Curve. Intelligence and Class Structure in American Life.* New York: Free Press.

Herzberg, F., Mausner, B. and Synderman, B. (1959) *The Motivation to Work.* New York: Wiley.

Herriot, P. (1989) 'Interactions with clients in personnel selection.' In P. Herriot (ed.) *Assessment and Selection in Organisations: Methods and Practice for Recruitment and Appraisal.* Chichester: Wiley.

Hesseling, P. (1966) *A Strategy for Evaluation Research.* Aassen: Van Gorcum.

Hewitt, C.R. (1971) Thesis. Lancaster: University of Lancaster Library.

Heywood, J. (1961) 'Research by sixth formers.' *Nature* 191, 860.

Heywood, J. (1969) 'An Evaluation of Certain Post-War Developments in Higher Technological Education.' Thesis. Lancaster: University of Lancaster Library.

Heywood, J. (1970) 'Qualities and their assessment in the education of technologists.' *International Bulletin of Electrical Engineering Education* 9, 15.

Heywood, J. (1971) 'A report on student wastage.' *Universities Quarterly* 25, 2, 189–237.

Heywood, J. (1973) 'New types of course and diplomas.' (summary of a report) *Education and Culture 23.* Council of Europe, Strasbourg.

Heywood, J. (1974) *Assessment in History (Twelve to Fifteen) Public Examinations Evaluation Project.* Report No. 1. School of Education. Dublin: University of Dublin.

Heywood, J. (1976) *Assessment in mathematics. Twelve to Fifteen.* Public examinations Evaluation project. Dublin: University of Dublin.

Heywood, J. (1977a) *Assessment in Higher Education.* 1st edn Chichester: Wiley.

Heywood, J. (1977b) *Examining in Second level Education.* Dublin: Association of Secondary teachers of Ireland.

Heywood, J. (1982) *Pitfalls and Planning in Student Teaching.* London: Kogan Page.

Heywood, J. (1983) 'Professional studies and validation.' In C.H. Church (ed.) *Practice and Perspective in Validation.* London: Society for Research into Higher Education.

Heywood, J. (1984) *Considering the Curriculum During Student Teaching.* London: Kogan Page.

Heywood, J. (1989a) *Assessment in Higher Education.* 2nd edn. Chichester: Wiley.

Heywood, J. (1989b) *Learning, Adaptability and Change. The Challenge for Education and Industry.* London: Paul Chapman.

Heywood, J. (1991) 'Leaving insularity behind: A European comment on the Lawler report.' in J. Coolahan (ed.) *Teacher Education in the Nineties: Toward a New Coherence*. Brussels: Association for Teacher Education in Europe.

Heywood, J. (1992) 'Student teachers as researchers of instruction.' In J.H.C. Vonk and H.J. van Helden (eds) *New Prospects for Teacher Education in Europe*. Brussels: Association for Teacher Education in Europe.

Heywood, J. (1994) *Enterprise Learning and its Assessment in Higher Education*. Technical Report No 20, Learning Methods Branch, Sheffield: Employment Department.

Heywood, J. (1995) 'Toward the improvement of quality in engineering education.' In D. Budny (ed.) *Proceedings Frontiers in Education Conference* pp 2a 3.8–13). New York: IEEE.

Heywood, J. (1996) 'Theory into practice through replication of research in student teaching practice. A partial evaluation of a course.' Paper presented at Association of Teacher Educators Annual Conference, St Louis, MO.

Heywood, J. (1997a) 'On the value of replicating forgotten research on the teaching of concepts during graduate student teaching practice.' *ATE Conference,* Washington. ERIC ED 406 332.

Heywood, J. (1997b) 'Outcomes Based Engineering Education II: The merits of continuous programme evaluation.' *Proceedings 27th Frontiers in Education Conference 1*, 567–575. New York: Institute of Electrical and Electronic Engineers.

Heywood, J. (1997c) 'An evaluation of Kolb's learning style theory by graduate student teachers during their teaching practice.' *Association of Teacher Educators Conference*, Washington, DC. ERIC ED 406 333.

Heywood, J. (1998) 'Pupils attitudes to technology: A review of studies which have a bearing on the attitudes which freshmen bring with them to engineering.' *Proceedings 1998 Frontiers in Education Conference 1*, 270–274. New York: IEEE.

Heywood, J. (1999) 'Appendix.' In *Professionalism and the Education and Training of Post Primary Teachers*. Submission to the Expert Advisory Group on the Content and Duration of Teacher Education Programmes for Post Primary Teachers of the Department of Education and Science. Dublin.

Heywood, J., Carter, G.C. and Kelly, D.T. (1997) 'The development of assessments and tests in a multiple-strategy approach to examining a course in engineering science in the United Kingdom.' Proceedings of a Symposium on best Assessment Processes in Engineering education, Rose-Hulman Institute of Technology, Terre Haute, In.

Heywood, J. and Heywood, S. (1993) 'The training of student teachers in discovery methods of learning.' In A.L. Leino, P. Hellgren and K. Hämäläinen (eds) *Integration of Technology and Reflection in Teaching: A Challenge for European Teacher Education*. Brussels: University of Helsinki/Association of teacher education in Europe.

Heywood, J. and Montagu-Pollock, H. (1977) *Science for Arts Students. A Case Study in Curriculum Design*. London: Society for Research into Higher Education.

Heywood, J., McGuinness, S. and Murphy, D.E.(1980) *Final Report of the Public Examination Evaluation Project*. Dublin: University of Dublin.

Heywood, J., Sharp, J. and Hides, M. (eds) (1999) *Improving Teaching in Higher Education*. Salford: Teaching and Learning Committee, University of Salford.

Hibbard, K.M *et al.* (1996) *A Teachers Guide to Performance Based Learning and Assessment*. Alexandria, VA: Association for Supervision and Curriculum Development.

Higgins, T. (1994) 'Applications procedures to higher education: an admission of failure?' In S. Haselgrove (ed.) *The Student Experience*. Buckingham: SRHE/Open University Books.

Highhouse, S. and Doverspike, D. (1987) 'The validity of the learning style inventory 1985 as a predictor of cognitive style and occupational preference.' *Educational and Psychological Measurement 47*, 3, 749–753.

Hildebrand, M. (1975) 'How to recommend promotion for a mediocre teacher without actually lying.' *Journal of Higher Education 43*, 44–62.

Hiles, D.A. and Heywood, J. (1972) 'Teacher attitudes to projects in A level engineering science.' *Nature 236*, 261–263.

Hill, D.S. (1984) 'Oral assessment: standards and strategies.' *Professional Practice of Psychology 5*, 2, 69–78.

Hill. M., Baker, S.R., Talley, L.J. and Hobday, M.D. (1980) 'Language preferences for freshmen chemistry students: an exploratory study.' *Journal of Research in Science Teaching 17*, 6, 571–576.

Hirsch, B. (1987) *Cultural Literacy*. New York: Macmillan.

Hirschfeld, L.A. and Gelman, S.A. (eds) (1994) *Mapping the Mind; Domain Specificity in Cognition and Culture*. Cambridge: Cambridge University Press.

Hirst, P.H. (1974) *Knowledge and the Curriculum. A Collection of Philosophical Papers*. London: Routledge and Kegan Paul.

Hitchcock, G. (1989) *Profiles and Profiling. A Practical Introduction*. 2nd ed. Harlow: Longman.

Hitchcock, G. (1990) 'Knowledge skills and curriculum change: Issues for Social Teaching.' *Journal of Further and Higher Education 14*, 3, 28–47.

Hoare, D.E. and Revans, M.M. (1969) 'Measuring attainment of educational objectives in Chemistry.' *Chemistry Education 6*, 3, 78.

Hoffman, B. (1982) *The Tyranny of Testing*. New York: Cromwell Collier Press.

Holdsworth, R. (1981) 'Improving the selective interview.' *Education and Training 23*, 2, 36–37.

Holland, J.L. (1978) *Manual for the Vocational Preference Inventory*. Palo Alto, CA: Consulting Psychologists Press.

Hollandsworth, J.G., Galazeski, R.C., Kirkland, K., Jones, G.E. and Van Norman, L.R. (1979) 'An analysis of the nature and effects of test anxiety: cognitive, behavioural and physiological components.' *Cognitive Therapy and Research 3*, 2, 165–180.

Holloway, P., Hardwick, J.L., Morris, J. and Start, K.B. (1967) 'The validity of essay and viva-voce examining techniques.' *British Dental Journal 123*, 8, 227–232

Holroyd, K.A. and Appel, M.A. (1980) 'Test anxiety and physiological responding.' In I. Sarason (ed.) *Test Anxiety: Therapy, Research and Application*. Hillsdale, NJ: Lawrence Erlbaum.

Holt, D.(1993) 'Holistic scoring in many disciplines.' *College Teaching 41*, 2, 71–74.

Holt, J. (1964) *How Children Fail*. New York: Dell.

Honey, P and Mumford, A. (1992) *The Manual of Learning Styles*. Maidenhead: Peter Honey.

Horn, J. and Donaldson, G. (1976) 'On the myth of intellectual decline in adulthood.' *American Psychologist 31*, 701–719.

Hounsell, D. (1984a) 'Learning and essay writing.' In F. Marton, D. Hounsell and N.J. Entwistle (eds) *The Experience of Learning*. Edinburgh: Scottish Academic Press.

Hounsell, D. (1984b) 'Essay planning and essay writing.' *Higher Education Research and Development 3*, 1, 13–30.

Houston, W.R. (1980) 'The status of competency based education: an American report.' *Journal of Education for Teaching 7*, 1, 17–23.

Howard, A. and Bray, D. (1988) *Managerial Lives in Transition. Advancing Age and Changing Times*. New York: Guilford Press.

Howard, G.S., Conway, C.G. and Maxwell, S.E. (1985) 'Construct validity measures of college teaching effectiveness.' *Journal of Educational Psychology 77*, 187–196.

Howard, J.R. and Henney, A.L. (1998) 'Student participation and instructor gender in the mixed age college classroom.' *Journal of Higher Education 69*, 4, 384–405.

Howard, K. and Sharp, J.A. (1983) *The Management of a Student Research Project*. Aldershot: Gower.

Howard, R.W. (1987) *Concepts and Schemata: An Introduction*. London: Cassell.

Hsi, S., Linn, M.C. and Bell, J.E. (1997) 'The role of spatial reasoning in engineering and the design of spatial instruction.' *Journal of Engineering Education 86*, 2, 151–158.

Hubbard, J. and Clemens, W. (1961) *Multiple Choice Examinations in Medicine*. London: Henry Kimpton.

Hudson, L. (1966) *Contrary Imaginations*. London: Methuen.

Husbands, C.T. and Fosh, P. (1993) 'Students' evaluations of teaching in higher education: experiences from four European countries.' *Assessment and Evaluation in Higher Education 18*, 2, 95–114.

Hutton, S.P. and Gerstl, J. (1969) *The Anatomy of a Profession*. London: Tavistock.

Hyerle, D. (1996) 'Thinking maps: Seeing and understanding.' *Educational Leadership 53*, 4, 85–89.

Hyland, T. (1996) 'Reconsidering competence.' *Journal of Philosophy of Education 31*, 3, 491–503.

ICE. (1974) *Final Report of the Committee on the Form and Function of the Intermediate Certificate Examination*. Dublin: Government Publications.

Iliffe, A.N. (1966) 'Objective Tests in Some Aspects of Testing for Academic Performance.' *Bulletin No. 1*. Lancaster: Department of Higher Education, University of Lancaster.

Imrie, B.W. (1984) 'In search of academic excellence: samples of experience.' *Proceedings of the Tenth International Conference on Improving University Experience*. University of Maryland, University College..

Imrie, B.W. (1995) 'Assessment for learning: Quality and taxonomies.' *Assessment and Evaluation in Higher Education 20*, 2, 175–189.

Imrie, B.W., Blithe, T.M. and Johnston, L.C. (1980) 'A review of Keller principles with reference to mathematics covering Australia.' *British Journal of Educational Technology 11*, 2, 105–121.

Isaacs, G. and Imrie, B.W. (1980) 'A case for professional judgement when combining marks.' *Assessment and Evaluation in Higher Education 6*, 1, 3–25.

Iyasere, M.M. (1984) 'Setting standards in multiple section courses.' *Improving College and University Teaching 32*, 4, 173–179.

Jackson, I. (1985) 'On detecting aptitude effects in undergraduate academic achievement scores.' *Assessment and Evaluation in Higher Education 6*, 1, 3–25.

Jacobi, M., Astin, A.W and Ayala, D.A. (1987) *College Student Outcomes Assessment; A Talent Development Perspective*. AHSE-ERIC Higher Education Report No 7. Washington, DC: Association for the Study of Higher Education,

Jahoda, M. (1964) *The Education of Technologists*. London: Tavistock.

James, C. (1977) 'The effect of question choice on the reliability of examinations.' *International Journal of Electrical Engineering Education 14*, 107–113.

James, C.R. and Denley, P. (1992) 'Using records of student experience in an undergraduate certificate in education course.' *Evaluation and Research in Education 6*, 1, 23–28.

James, P. (1996) 'The development of problem-solving skills in environmental education.' *Environmental Education and Information 16*, 4, 416–426.

James, P. (1999) 'Measuring the development of deep learning.' In J. Heywood, J. Sharp and M. Hides (eds) *Improving Teaching in Higher Education*. Salford: Teaching and Learning Committee, University of Salford.

Janis, I.L. (1972) *Victims of Group Think*. Boston, MA: Houghton Miflin.

Janis, I.L. (1982a) 'Decision making under stress.' In L. Goldberger and S. Bregritz (eds) *Handbook of Stress: Theoretical and Clinical Aspects*. New York: Free Press.

Janis, I.L. (1982b) *Stress, Attitudes and Decisions: Selected Papers*. New York: Praeger.

Jarvinen, A. and Kohonen, V. (1995) 'Promoting professional development in higher education through portfolio assessment.' *Assessment and Evaluation in Higher Education 20*, 1, 25–36.

Jessup, G. (1991) *Outcomes, NVQ's and the Emerging Model of Education and Training*. London: Falmer Press.

Jevons, F.R. (1972) Chapter 1 in F.R. Jevons and H.D. Turner (eds) *What Kind of Graduates do we Need?* Oxford: Oxford University Press.

Johnes, J. (1990) 'Determinants of student wastage in higher education.' *Studies in Higher Education 15*, 1, 87–99.

Johnes, J. and Taylor, J. (1990) *Performance Indicators in Higher Education*. Buckingham: Open University Press/Society for Research into Higher Education.

Johnson, D.W. and Johnson, R.T. (1996) *Meaningful and Manageable Assessment through Cooperative Learning*. Edina, MN: Interaction Book Co.

Johnson, D.W., Johnson, R.T. and Smith, K.A. (1991) *Active Learning: Cooperation in the Classroom*. Edina, MN: Interaction Book Co.

Johnson, G.M. and Buck, G.H. (1995) 'Students' personal and academic attributions of university withdrawal.' *Canadian Journal of Higher Education 25*, 2, 53–77.

JMB (1971, 1972, 1974) *Notes for the guidance of schools. Engineering Science Advanced.* Manchester: Joint Matriculation Board. (revised annually)

Jones, B. (1997) 'Comparing examinations standards: is a purely statistical approach adequate?' *Assessment in Education: Principles, Policy and Practice 4*, 2, 249–263.

Jones, B. and Ratcliffe, P. (1996) 'Comparing the standards of examining groups in the United Kingdom.' In B. Boyle and T. Christie (eds) *Issues in Setting Standards. Establishing Comparabilities.* London: Falmer Press.

Jones, E.S. (1993) *Comprehensive Examinations in American Colleges.* New York: Macmillan.

Jones, J. and Chittenden, E. (1995) *Teachers' Perceptions of Rating an Early Literacy Portfolio.* Princeton, NJ: Center for Educational Performance, E.T.S.

Jordan, T.A. and Carter, G. (1986) 'The determination of attitudes of students to their undergraduate courses.' *Assessment and Evaluation in Higher Education 11*, 1, 11–27.

Joughin, G. (1998) 'Dimensions of oral assessment.' *Assessment and Evaluation in Higher Education 23*, 4, 367–378.

JPIWG (1994a) *Management Statistics and Performance Indicators in Higher Education.* Report of the Joint Performance Indicators Working Group. mimeo. Bristol: Higher Education Funding Council for England.

JPIWG (1994b) Explanatory and Statistical Material to Accompany Consultative Report. mimeo. Bristol: Higher Education Funding Council for England.

Juhl, L. (1996) 'General chemistry in technical education.' *Journal of Chemical Education 73*, 1, 72–77.

Kagan, D.M. and Fasan, V. (1988) 'Stress and the instructional environment.' *College Teaching 36*, 2, 75–81.

Kaplan, L. (1978) *Developing Objectives in the Affective Domain.* San Diego, CA: Collegiate Publishing.

Karelis, C. (1996) 'Observations on the evolution of assessment.' In G.H. Gaither (ed.) *Performance Indicators in Higher Education: What Works, What Doesn't and What's Next.* Symposium. Washington, DC: American Association for Higher Education.

Karplus, R. (1974) *Science Curriculum Improvement Study: Teachers Handbook.* Berkeley, CA: Lawrence Hall of Science.

Keller, G. (1996) 'The great american assessment tussle.' In G.H. Gaither (ed.) *Performance Indicators in Higher Education: What Works, What Doesn't and What's Next?* Symposium. Washington, DC: American Association for Higher Education.

Keller, F.S. (1968) 'Goodbye teacher.' *Journal of Applied Behavioural Analysis 1*, 78–79.

Kells, H. (ed.) (1993) *The Development of Performance Indicators for Higher Education. A Compendium for Twelve Countries.* Paris: OECD.

Kelly, J.A. (1982) 'Stress management training in a medical school.' *Journal of Medical Education 57*, 2, 91–99.

Kember, D. *et al.* (1996) 'Developing curricula to encourage students to write reflective journals.' *Journal of Vocational Education and Training 4*, 3, 329–348.

Kember, D. and Gow, L. (1994) 'Orientations to teaching and their effect on the quality of student learning.' *Journal of Higher Education 65*, 1, 58–76.

Kember, D., Jamieson, Q.W., Pomfret, M. and Wong, E.T.T. (1995) 'Learning approaches, study time and academic performance.' *Higher Education 29*, 3, 329–343.

Kempa, R.F. (1986) *Assessment in Science.* Cambridge: Cambridge University Press.

Kent, D. and Towse, P. (1997) 'Students' perceptions of science and technology in Botswana and Lesotho.' *Research in Science and Technological Education 15*, 2, 149–160.

Kent, M., Gilbertson, D.D. and Hunt, C.O. (1997) 'Fieldwork in Geography teaching: a critical review of the literature and approaches.' *Journal of Geography in Higher Education 21*, 3, 313–332.

Kern, D.E., Thomas, P.A., Howard, D.M. and Bass, E.B. (1998) *Curriculum Development for Medical Education: A Six Step Approach.* Baltimore, MD: The Johns Hopkins University Press.

Kernan, M.C. and Howard, G.S. (1990) 'Computer anxiety and computer attitudes: an investigation of construct and predictive validity issues.' *Educational and Psychological Measurement 50*, 3, 681–690.

Kerridge, J.R. and Mathews, B.P. (1998) 'Student rating of courses in HE: Further challenges and opportunities.' *Assessment and Evaluation in Higher Education 23*, 1, 71–82.

Kidson, M. and Hornblow, A. (1982) 'Examination anxiety in medical students: Experience with visual analogue scale of anxiety.' *Medical Education 16*, 247–250.

Kiersey, D. and Bates, M. (1984) *Please Understand Me: An Essay in Temperament Styles.* Oxford: Oxford Psychologists Press.

Kim Jae-On and Muller, C.W. (1978) *Introduction to Factor Analysis.* Beverly Hills, CA: Sage.

King, J.B. (1986) 'The three faces of thinking.' *Journal of Higher Education 57*, 1, 78–92.

King, P.M. (1992) 'How do we know? Why do we believe? Learning to make reflective judgements.' *Liberal Education 78*, 1, 2–9.

King, P.M. and Kitchener, K.S. (1994) *Developing Reflective Practice.* San Francisco: Jossey-Bass.

Kirby, J.R. (1988) 'Style, strategy and skill in reading.' In R.R. Schmeck (ed.) *Learning Styles and Learning Strategies.* New York: Plenum Press.

Kitchener, K.S. (1983) 'Cognition, meta-cognition and epistemic cognition: A three-level model of cognitive processing.' *Human Development 4*, 222–232.

Kjersdam, F. and Enemark, S. (1994) *The Aarlborg Experiment.* Aalborg: Aalborg University Press.

Klecka, W.R. (1980) *Discriminant Analysis.* Beverly Hills, CA: Sage.

Klenowski, V. (1995) 'Student self-evaluation processes in student-centred teaching and learning contexts of Australia and England.' *Assessment in Education: Principles, Policy and Practice 2*, 2, 145–164.

Kline, P. (1983) *Personality: Measurement and Theory.* London: Hutchinson.

Kline, P. (1993) *The Handbook of Psychological Testing.* London: Routledge.

Kloss, R.J. (1993) 'Stay in touch won't you? Using the one minute paper.' *College Teaching 41*, 2, 60–63.

Kloss, R.J. (1994) 'A nudge is best: Helping students through the Perry scheme of intellectual development.' *College Teaching 42*, 4, 151–158.

Kloss, R.J. (1996) 'Writing things down versus writing things up: Are research papers valid?' *College Teaching 44*, 1, 3–7.

Kneale, P. (1997) 'The rise of the "strategic student": How can we adapt to cope?' In S. Armstrong, G. Thompson and S. Brown (eds) *Facing up to Radical Change in Universities and Colleges.* London: Kogan Page.

Knefelkamp, L.L. (1974) *Developmental Instruction: Fostering Intellectual and Personal Growth of College Students.* Doctoral Dissertation. University of Minnesota.

Knight, P. (1991) '"Value-added" and history in public sector higher education.' *Public Sector History Newsletter 3*, 1, 23–31.

Knight, P., Helsby, G. and Saunders, M. (1998) 'Independence and prescription in learning: researching the paradox of advanced GNVQs.' *British Journal of Educational Studies 46*, 1, 54–67.

Know, A.B. (1990) 'Influences on participation in continuing education.' *Journal of Continuing Education: Health Professionals 10*, 261–274.

Knox, J.D.E. (1975) *The Modified Essay Question.* ASME Booklet No 5. Dundee: Association for the Study of Medical Education.

Kogan, M. (1986) *Education Accountability. An Analytic Overview.* London: Hutchinson.

Kohlberg, L. (1990) 'Which postformal levels are stages?' *Adult Development 2.*

Kohlberg, L., Kauffman, K., Scharf, P. and Hickey, J. (1975) 'The just community approach to corrections: A theory.' *Journal of Moral Education 4*, 243–260.

Kohlberg, L. and Ryncarz, R.A. (1990) 'Beyond justice reasoning: Moral development and consideration of a seventh stage.' In C.N. Alexander and E.J. Langer (eds) *Higher Stages of Human Development.* Oxford: Oxford University Press.

Kohlberg, L. and Turiel, E. (1971) 'Moral development and moral education.' In G. Lesser (ed.) *Psychology and Educational Practice.* Chicago: Scott Freeman.

Kolb, D.A. (1984) *Experiential Learning: Experience as a Source of Learning.* Englewood Cliffs, NJ: Prentice-Hall.

Koon, J. and Murray, H.G. (1995) 'Using multiple outcomes to validate student ratings of overall teacher effectiveness.' *Journal of Higher Education 66*, 1, 61–81.

Kozma, R.B. (1982) 'Instructional design in a chemistry laboratory course: the impact of structure and aptitudes on performance and attitudes.' *Journal of Research in Science Teaching 18*, 3, 261–270.

Kraan, H.F. *et al.* (1990) 'To what extent are medical interviewing skills teachable?' *Medical Teacher 12*, 3/4, 315–327.

Krakower, J. (1985) *Assessing Organizational Effectiveness. Considerations and Procedures.* Boulder, CO: NCHEMS.

Kramp, M.K. and Lee Humphreys, W. (1993) 'Narrative self assessment and the reflective learner.' *College Teaching 41*, 3, 83–88.

Krathwohl, D. (1985) *Social and Behavioural Science Research.* San Francisco: Jossey-Bass.

Krathwohl, D. (1994) 'Reflections on the taxonomy: Its past present and future.' In L.W. Anderson and L.A. Sosniak (eds) *Bloom's Taxonomy: A Forty Year Retrospective.* Chicago: University of Chicago Press.

Krathwohl, D., Bloom, B. and Mersia, B.B. (1964) *Taxonomy of Educational Objectives. The Classification of Goals. Vol 2: Affective Domain.* New York: David Mckay. (Also published by Longmans Green in the UK in 1964)

Kropp, R.P. and Stoker, H.W. (1966) *The Construction and Validation of Tests of the Cognitive Processes as Described in the Taxonomy of Educational Objectives.* Cognitive Research Project No 2117. Tallahassee, FL: Institute of Human Learning and Department of Educational Research and Testing.

Kwan, K.-P. and Leung, R. (1996) 'Tutor versus peer group assessment of student performance in simulation training.' *Assessment and Evaluation in Higher Education 21*, 3, 205–214.

LaBoskey, V.K. (1994) *Development of Reflective Practice. A Study of Preservice Teachers.* New York: Teachers College Press.

Laing, L. and Nixon, M. (1990) 'How we teach Behavioural Science.' *Medical Teacher 12*, 2, 143–153.

Lam, Y.L.J. (1978) 'Anxiety reduction correlates of adult learners: A longitudinal study.' *Alberta Journal of Educational Research 24*, 2, 81–93.

Lane, D.S., Bull, K.S., Kundert, D.K. and Newman, D.L. (1987) 'The effects of knowledge item arrangement, gender and statistical item difficulty on test performance.' *Educational and Psychological Measurement 47*, 4, 865–880.

Larkin, J.H. and Rief, F. (1979) 'Understanding and teaching problem solving in physics.' *European Journal of Science Education 1*, 2, 191–203.

Laurillard, D.M. (1984) 'Learning from problem solving.' In F. Marton, D. Hounsell and N.J. Entwistle (eds) *The Experience of Learning.* Edinburgh: Scottish Academic Press.

Law, B. (1984) *Uses and Abuses of Profiling.* London: Harper and Row.

Laycock, M. (1997) 'QILT: A whole institution approach to Quality Improvement in Learning and Teaching.' In S. Armstrong, G. Thompson and S. Brown (eds) *Facing Up to Radical Change in Universities and Colleges.* London: Kogan Page.

Leahy, R. (1990) 'What the college writing center is – isn't.' *College Teaching 38*, 2, 43–48.

Leary, L.F. and Dorans, N.J. (1982) *The Effect of Item Re-arrangement on Test performance: A Review of the Literature.* Research report 82–30. Princeton, NJ: Educational Testing Service.

Lee, J.A., Moreno, K.E. and Sympson, J.B. (1986) 'The effect of mode of test operation on test performance.' *Educational and Psychological Measurement 46*, 2, 467–474.

Lee, L.S. (1969) 'Towards the classification of the objectives of undergraduate practical work in mechanical engineering.' Thesis. Lancaster: University of Lancaster Library.

Leiden, L.I., Crosby, R.D. and Follmer, R.D. (1990) 'Assessing learning style inventories and how well they predict academic performance.' *Academic Medicine 65*, 6, 395–401.

Lejk, M., Wyvill, M. and Farrow, S. (1996) 'A survey of methods of deriving individual grades from group assessment.' *Assessment and Evaluation in Higher Education 21*, 3, 267–280.

LeMahieu, P.G., Gitomer, D.H. and Eresh, J.T. (1995) *Portfolios Beyond the Classroom: Data Quality and Qualities.* Princeton, NJ: E.T.S. Center for Performance Assessment.

Lesh, R. and Lamon, S. (eds) (1992) *Assessment of Performance in School Mathematics.* Washington, DC: AAAS Press.

Levinson, D. (1978) *Seasons of a Man's Life.* New York: Knopf.

Levinson, R., Murphy, P. and McCormick, R. (1997) 'Science and technology concepts in a design and technology project: A pilot study.' *Research in Science and Technology Education* 15, 2, 235–256.

Levy, J. (1997) 'SARTOR. Why Change?' *Engineering Science and Education Journal* 6, 3, 91–92.

Levy, P. and Usherwood, R. (1991) *Interpersonal Skills for Library Information Work. Final Report to the British Library.* Sheffield: Department of Information Studies, University of Sheffield.

Lewis, A. and Smith, D. (1993) 'Defining higher order thinking.' *Theory into Practice* 32, 3, 131–137.

Lewis, R.G. and Smith, D.H. (1994) *Total Quality in Higher Education.* Delray Beach, FL: St Lucie Press.

Lewy, A. and Bathory, Z. (1994) 'The Taxonomy of Educational Objectives in Continental Europe and the Middle East.' In L.W. Anderson and L.A. Sosniak (eds) *Bloom's Taxonomy. A Forty Year Retrospective.* Chicago: University of Chicago Press.

L'Hommedieu, R., Menges, R.J. and Brinko, K.T. (1990) 'Methodological explanations for the modest effects of feedback.' *Journal of Educational Psychology* 82, 232–241.

Linke, R. (1991) *Performance Indicators in Higher Education.* Report of a trial evaluation study commissioned by the Commonwealth Department of Employment and Training. 2 Vols. Canberra: Australian Government Publishing Service.

Liotts, P.H. (1990) 'All my best students are flunking.' *College Teaching* 38, 3, 96–100.

Lloyd, D., Martin, J.G. and McCaffery, K. (1996) 'The introduction of computer based testing on an Engineering Technology course.' *Assessment and Evaluation in Higher Education* 21, 1, 83–90.

Loacker, G., Cromwell, L., Fry, J. and Rutherford, D. (1984) *Analysis and Communication: An Approach to Critical Thinking.* Milwaukee, WI: Alverno Publications.

Loacker, G., Cromwell, L. and O'Brien, K. (1986) 'Assessment in higher education: to serve the learner.' In C. Adelman (ed.) *Assessment in American Higher Education: Issues and Contexts.* Washington, DC: US Department of Education.

Loacker, G. and Jensen, P. (1988) 'The power of performance in developing problem solving and self assessment abilities.' *Assessment and Evaluation in Higher Education* 13, 2, 128–150.

Lockheed, M.E., Holland, P.W. and Nenceff, W.P. (1982) *Student Characteristics and the Use of SAT Test Disclosure Materials.* Princeton, NJ: Educational Testing Service.

Lockyer, J. and Harrison, V. (1994) 'Performance assessment: The role of chart review analysis and CME.' In D.A. Davis and R.D. Fox (eds) *The Physician as Learner. Linking Research to Practice.* Chicago: American Medical Association.

Lonergan, B. (1954) *Insight.* London: Darton, Longman and Todd.

Lonergan, B. (1972) *Method in Theology.* London: Darton, Longman and Todd.

Long, S. (1976) 'Sociopolitical ideology of students' perception of university.' *Higher Education* 5, 4, 423–435.

Lord, F.M. and Novick, M.R. (1968) *Statistical Theories of Mental Test Scores.* Reading, MA: Addison-Wesley.

Lord, T.R. (1985) 'Enhancing the visual spatial aptitude of students.' *Journal of Research in Science Teaching* 22, 395–405.

Loveluck, C. (1995) 'Ethical considerations of quality in higher education.' *Assessment and Evaluation in Higher Education* 20, 1, 9–14.

Low, G. (1995) '"Hallelujah verry!" Responding to "very" in survey questions.' *Evaluation and Research in Education* 9, 1, 15–28.

Luchins, A.S. (1942) 'Mechanisation in problem-solving: The effect of "Einstellung".' *Psychological Monographs* 248.

Lumsden, J. (1977) 'Person reliability.' *Applied Psychological Measurement* 1, 477–482.

Lumsden, J. (1978) 'Tests are perfectly reliable.' *British Journal of Mathematical and Statistical Psychology* 31, 19–26.

Lyddy, F. (1998) 'Its not what you do: What is the link between academic success and learning style?' *The Psychologist* 11, 11, 545.

Lyons, N. (1983) 'Two perspectives: On self, relationships and morality.' *Harvard Educational Review* 53, 125–145.

Mabe, P.A. and West, S.G. (1982) 'Validity of self-evaluation of ability: A review and meta-analysis.' *Journal of Applied Psychology* 66, 451–457.

McCarthy, B. (1990) 'Using the 4MAT system to bring learning styles to schools.' *Educational Leadership*, Oct, 31–37.

MacDonald, F. (1968) *Educational Psychology.* Belmont, CA: Wadsworth

MacFarlane Smith, I. (1964) *Spatial Ability.* London: University of London Press.

Mackie, K. (1981) *The application of learning theory to adult teaching.* Adults: Psychological and Educational Perspectives Series. Monograph No. 2. Nottingham: University of Nottingham.

Mackintosh, N.J. (1998) *IQ and Human Intelligence.* Cambridge: Cambridge University Press.

Magzoub, M.E.M.A., Schmidt, H.G., Dolmans, D.H.J.M. and Abdelhameed, A.A. (1998) 'Assessing students in community settings; the role of peer evaluation.' *Advances in Health Science Education* 3, 1, 3–13.

Makin, P. (1989) 'Selection of professional groups.' In P. Herriot (ed.) *Assessment and Selection in Organizations.* Chichester: Wiley.

Malleson, N. (1965) *A Handbook of British Student Health Services.* London: Pitman.

Mandell, A. and Michelson, E. (eds) (1990) *Portfolio Development and Adult Learning: Purposes and Strategies.* Chicago: National Council for Adult and Experiential Learning.

Mann, R., Ringwald, B.E., Arnold, S., Binder, J., Cytrynbaum, S. and Rosenwein, J.W. (1970) *Conflict and Style in the College Classroom.* New York: Wiley.

Marlin, J.W. (1987) 'Student perception of end-of-course evaluation.' *Journal of Higher Education* 58, 6, 704–716.

Marlin, M. (1997) 'Emotional and cognitive effects of examination proximity in female and male students.' *Oxford Review of Education* 23, 4, 479–486.

Marques, L. and Thompson, D. (1997) 'Misconceptions and conceptual changes concerning continental drift and plate tectonics among Portuguese students aged 16–17.' *Research in Science and Technological Education* 15, 2, 195–222.

Marris, P. (1964) *The Experience of Higher Education.* London: Routledge and Kegan Paul.

Marsh, H.W. (1982) 'The SEEQ: a reliable, valid and useful instrument for collecting students' evaluations of university teaching.' *British Journal of Educational Psychology 52*, 77–95.

Marsh, H.W (1987) 'Students' evaluations of university teaching: research findings, methodological issues and directions for future research.' *International Journal of Educational Research 11*, 253–388.

Marsh, H.W (1991) 'Multidimensional students' evaluations of teaching effectiveness: dimensionality, reliability, validity, potential biases, and utility.' *Journal of Educational Psychology 83*, 285–296.

Marsh, H.W. and Dunkin, M.J. (1992) 'Students' evaluation of university teaching: A multidimensional perspective.' In J. Smart (ed.) *Higher Education. Handbook of Theory and Practice.* Vol. 8. New York: Agathon Press.

Marsh, H.W. and Hocevar, D. (1984) 'The factorial invariance of student evaluations of college teaching.' *American Educational Research Journal 21*, 341–366.

Marshall, J. (1993) 'Assessment During Post Graduate Training.' In J.S. Gonella, M. Hojat, J.B. Erdman and J.J. Veloski (eds) *Assessment Measures in Medical School, Residency and Practice.* New York: Springer.

Marshall, S. (1980) 'Cognitive-affective dissonance in the classroom.' *Teaching Political Science 8*, 1, 111–117.

Marshall, T.H. (1939) 'Professionalism in relation to social structure and policy.' Reprinted in T.H. Marshall (1963) *Sociology at the Cross Roads and Other Essays.* London: Heinemann.

Martin, D.C. (1996) 'Developing indicators to monitor quality at Winona State University.' In T.W. Banta, J.P. Lund, K. Black and F.W. Oblander (eds) *Assessment in Practice.* San Francisco: Jossey-Bass.

Martin, M. (1997) 'Emotional and cognitive effects of examination proximity in female and male students.' *Oxford Review of Education 23*, 4, 479–486.

Marton, F. (1988) 'Describing and improving learning.' In R.R. Scmeck (ed.) *Learning Strategies and Learning Styles.* New York: Plenum Press.

Marton, F., Hounsell, D. and Entwistle, N.J. (1984) *The Experience of Learning.* Edinburgh: Scottish Academic Press.

Marton, F. and Säljö, R. (1976) 'On qualitative 1. Outcomes and process. 2 Outcomes as function of the learners task.' *British Journal of Educational Psychology 46*, 4–11 and 115–127.

Marton, F. and Säljö, R. (1984) 'Approaches to learning.' In F. Marton, D. Hounsell and N. Entwistle (eds) *The Experience of Learning.* Edinburgh: Scottish Academic Press.

Marzano, R.J., Pickering, D. and McTighe, J. (1993) *Assessing Student Outcomes.* Alexandria, VA: Association for Supervision and Curriculum Development.

Mast, T. and Davis, D.A. (1994) 'Concepts of Competence.' In D.A Davis and R.D. Fox (eds) *The Physician as Learner. Linking Research to Practice.* Chicago: American Medical Association.

Matt, G.E., Perchesky, B. and Cervantes, C. (1991) 'High school habits and early college achievement.' *Psychological Reports 69*, 91–96.

Matthews, G.B. (1980) *Philosophy and the Young Child.* Cambridge, MA: Harvard University Press.

Matthews, M.R. (1994) *Science Teaching.* London: Routledge.

Matthews, P.S.C. (1997) 'Problems with Piagetian constructivism.' *Science and Education 6*, 105–119.

Matthews, R.L., Brown, P.R. and Jackson, M.A. (1990) *Accounting in Higher Education: Report of the Review of the Accounting Discipline in Higher Education.* Canberra: Australian Government Publishing Service.

Mayfield, E.C. (1964) 'The selection interview – a revaluation of published research.' *Personnel Psychology 17*, 239–260.

McCagg, J.G. and Danserau, D.F. (1990) *A Convergent Paradigm for Examining Knowledge as a Learning Strategy.* Annual meeting. Boston, MA: American Educational Research Association,

McCarthy, P. and Schmeck, R.R. (1988) 'Students' self-concepts and the quality of learning in public schools and universities.' In R.R. Schmeck (ed.) *Learning Strategies and Learning Styles.* New York: Plenum.

McClelland, D.C. *et al.* (1958) *Talent and Society.* New York: Van Nosatrand.

McCrindle, A.R. and Christensen, C.A. (1995) 'The input of learning journals on metacognitive and cognitive processes and learning performance.' *Learning and Instruction 5*, 3, 167–185.

McDonald, M. and Hogg, T. (undated) *The Stressbuster's Guide: Coping with Stresses of OU Study and Exams.* Edinburgh: Open University in Scotland.

McDowell, L. (1995) 'Effective teaching and learning on foundation and access course in engineering, science and technology.' *European Journal of Engineering Education 20*, 4, 417–425.

McElroy, A.R. and McNaughton, F.C. (1979) 'A project based approach to the use of biological literature.' *Journal of Biological Education 13*, 1, 52–57.

McElwee, P.G. (1993) 'The conceptual understanding of scientific principles in home economics.' *Research in Science and Technological Education 11*, 3, 5–17.

McElwee, P.G. (1995) 'Personal to scientific understanding.' Ph.D. Thesis (2 vol) Dublin: University of Dublin Library.

McGaghie, W., Miller, G.E, Sajid, A.W. and Telder, T.V. (1978) *Competency-Based Curriculum Development in Medical Education: An Introduction.* Geneva: World Health Organization.

McGill, I. and Beaty, L. (1992) *Action Learning: A Practitioners Guide.* London: Kogan Page.

McGivney, V. (1996) *Staying or Leaving Course, Non-completion and Retention of Mature Students in Further and Higher Education.* Leicester: National Institute for Adult and Continuing Education.

McGrath, F. (1962) *The Consecration of Learning.* Dublin: Gill.

McGuire, C. (1967) *An Evaluation Model for Professional Education: Medical Education.* Chicago, Il: College of Medicine.

McGuire, C. (1993) 'Perspectives in assessment.' In J.S. Gonnella, M. Hojat, J.B. Erdmen and J.J. Veloski (eds) *Assessment Measures in Medical School, Residency and Practice.* New York: Springer.

McKenzie, L. (1995) 'Teaching clinical reasoning to orthoptics students using problem-based learning.' In J. Higgs and M. Jones (eds) *Clinical Reasoning in the Health Professions*. Oxford: Butterworth/Heinemann.

McKenzie, J., Sheely, S. and Trigwell, K. (1998) 'Drawing on experience: An holistic approach to the student evaluation of courses.' *Assessment and Evaluation in Higher Education 23*, 2, 153–164.

Mcleod, P.J. and Snell, L. (1996) 'Student-generated MCQs.' *Medical Teacher 18*, 1, 23–25.

McMorris, R.F., Brown, J.A., Snyder, G.W. and Pruzek, R.M. (1972) 'Effects of violating stem construction principles.' *Journal of Educational Measurement 9*, 4, 287–295.

McNabb, T. (1990) *Course Placement Practices of American Post-Secondary Institutions*. Research report 90–10. Iowa City, IA: American College Testing Program.

McPeck, J.E. (1981) *Critical Thinking and Education*. New York: St Martins Press.

McVey, P.J. (1975) 'The errors in marking examination scripts.' *International Journal of Electrical Engineering Education 12*, 3, 203.

McVey, P.J. (1976a) 'Standard error of the mark for an examination paper in electronic engineering.' *Proceedings Institution of Electrical Engineers 123*, 8, 843–844.

McVey, P.J. (1976b) 'The paper error of two examinations in electronic engineering.' *Physics Education 11*, 58–60.

Mentkowski, M. (1988) 'Paths to integrity: educating for personal growth and professional performance.' In S. Srivasta (ed.) *Executive Integrity: The Search for Human Values in Organizational Life*. San Francisco: Jossey-Bass.

Mentkowski, M. (1994) 'Institutional and Program Assessment at Alverno College. Symposium on Institutional Assessment Across the Educational Spectrum.' Annual meeting of the American Educational Research Association. Alverno College, Milwaukee, WI.

Mentkowski, M. and associates (forthcoming) *Learning that Lasts*. San Francisco: Jossey-Bass.

Mentkowski, M. and Doherty, A. (1983) *Careering After College: Establishing the Validity of Abilities Learned in College for later Careering and Professional Performance*. Final Report to the National Institute for Education. Milwaukee, WI: Alverno Productions.

Mentkowski, M., Much, N.C. and Giencke-Holl, L. (1983) *Careering after College. Perspectives on Lifelong Learning and Career Development*. Milwaukee, WI: Alverno Productions.

Mentkowski, M. and Strait, M. (1983) *A Longitudinal Study of Student Change in Cognitive Development, Learning Styles and Generic Abilities in an Outcome Centred Liberal Arts Curriculum*. Research Report No. 6 to the National Institute of Education. Milwaukee, WI: Alverno College.

Messick, S. (1989) 'Validity.' In R.L. Linn (ed.) *Educational Measurement*. 3rd edn. American Council on Education. New York: Macmillan.

Messick, S. (1992) *The Interplay of Evidence and Consequences in the Validation of Performance*. Princeton, NJ: Educational Testing Service.

Messick, S. (1994) 'The interplay of evidence and consequences in the validation of performance assessment.' *Educational Researcher 23*, 2, 13–23.

Messick, S. and associates. (1976) *Individuality in Learning. Implications of Cognitive Styles and Creativity for Human Development*. San Francisco: Jossey-Bass.

Messick, S., Beaton, A. and Lord, F. (1983) *A New design for a New Era*. Princeton, NJ: Educational Testing Service.

Meuwese, W. (1968) 'Measurement of Industrial Engineering Objectives.' 16th International Congress of Applied Psychology, Amsterdam.

Meuwese, W. (1971) 'Construction and Evaluation of a Course in Technical Mechanics.' Committee for Higher Education, Council of Europe, Strasbourg.

Meyer, D. (1993) 'Recognizing and changing students' misconceptions. An instructional perspective.' *College Teaching 41*, 3, 104–108.

Meyer, M. (1908) 'The grading of students.' *Science 28*, 712, 243–250.

Michaels, S. and Kieran, T.R. (1973) 'An investigation of open and closed book examinations in mathematics.' *Alberta Journal of Educational Research 19*, 3, 202–207.

Miller, G.A. (ed.) (1961) *Teaching and Learning in Medical School*. Cambridge, MA: Harvard University Press.

Miller, G.E. (1990) 'The assessment of clinical skills/competence/performance.' *Academic Medicine 65*, 563–567.

Miller, G.W. (1970) *Success, Failure and Wastage in Higher Education*. London: Harrap.

Miller, J.E., Wilkes, J. and Cheetham, R.D. (1993) 'Tradeoffs in student satisfaction: Is the "perfect" course an illusion?' *Journal of Excellence in College Teaching 4*, 27–47.

Milton, O. and Edgerley, J.W. (1976) 'The testing and grading of students.' *The Change Magazine*.

Milton, O., Pollio, H.R. and Eison, J.A. (1986) *Making Sense of College Grades*. San Fransisco: Jossey-Bass.

Mitchell, K. and Anderson, J. (1986) 'Reliability of scoring for the MCAT essay.' *Educational and Psychological Measurement 46*, 3, 771–775.

Mitchell, L. (1987) 'Assessing occupational competence: What does it mean in practice.' *Competence and Assessment 2*, 3–6.

Mitchelmore, M.C. (1981) 'Reporting student achievement: how many grades?' *British Journal of Educational Psychology 51*, 2, 218–227.

Monk, M. (1990) 'A genetic epistemological analysis of data on children's ideas about DC electrical circuits.' *Research in Science and Technological Education 8*, 2, 133–144.

Moore, W.S. (1988) *The Learning Environment: Preferences and Instruction Manual*. Olympia, WA: CSID.

Moran, A. (1991) 'What can learning styles research learn from cognitive psychology?' *Educational Psychology 11*, 3/4, 239–245.

Moran, G. (1984) *Religious Education Development: Images for the Future*. Minneapolis, MN: Winston Press.

Morgan, R. (1990) *Predictive Validity Within Categorisations of College Students: 1978, 1981*. Report RR–90–14. Princeton, NJ: Educational Testing Service.

Moreira, M.A. (1985) 'Concept mapping: an alternative strategy for evaluation.' *Assessment and Evaluation in Higher Education* 10, 2, 159–168.

Morris, L.W. and Liebert, R.M. (1969) 'Effects of anxiety on timed and untimed tests: Another look.' *Journal of Consulting and Clinical Psychology 37*, 1, 165–171.

Morrison, R.B. (1974) 'Item analysis and question validation.' In H.G. Macintosh (ed.) *Techniques and Problems of Assessment.* London: Edward Arnold.

Moss, P.A. *et al.* (1992) 'Portfolios, accountability and an interpretive approach to validity.' *Educational Measurement: Issues and Practices 11*, 3, 12–21.

MoSTEP (1998) Draft Document. Missouri Standards for Teacher Education programs.

Moust, J.H.C., de Grave, W.S. and Gijselaers, W.H. (1990) 'The tutor role a neglected variable in the implementation of problem-based learning.' In Nooman, H.G. Schmidt and E.S. Ezzat (eds) *Innovation in Medical Education.* New York: Springer.

Mowbray, R.M. and Davies, B.M. (1967) 'Short note and essay examinations.' *British Journal of Medical Education 1*, 356–358.

Murphy, D.E. (1976) Problems associated with a new national system of assessment. Thesis. University of Dublin, Dublin.

Murphy, P.S., Hill, S., Linke, R. and Aylward, D. (1994) *Quantitative Indicators of Australian Research.* Commissioned Report No. 27. Canberra: Australian Government Publishing Service.

Murphy, R. (1982) 'A further report into reliability of marking of GCE examinations.' *British Journal of Educational Psychology 52*, 1, 58–63.

Murphy, R. (1996) 'Firsts among equals: the case of British university degrees.' In B. Boyle and T. Christie (eds) *Issues in Setting Standards: Establishing Standards.* London: Falmer Press.

Murray, H.G. (1980) *Evaluating University Teaching. A Review of Research.* Toronto: Ontario Confederation of University Faculty Associations.

Murray, H.G. (1983) 'Low inference teaching behaviours and student ratings of college training effectiveness.' *Journal of Educational Psychology 71*, 856–865.

Murray, M. (1990) Doctoral Dissertation, Department of Education, University of Dublin, Dublin.

Muscatine Committee (1968) *Education at Berkeley: Report of a Select Committee on Education.* Berkeley, CA: University of California Press.

Myers, I. and McCaulley, M. (1985) *Manual: A Guide to the Development and Use of the Myers-Briggs Type Indicator.* Palo Alto: Consulting Psychologists Press.

Myford, C.M., Marr, D.B. and Linacre, J.M. (1996) *Reader Calibration and its Potential Role in Equating for the Test of Written English.* Center for Performance Assessment. Princeton, NJ: Educational Testing Service.

Naizer, G.L.(1997) 'Validity and reliability issues of performance-portfolio assessment.' *Action in Teacher Education 18*, 4, 1–9.

NASDEC (1994) *Outcome Based Standards and Portfolio Assessment. Outcome Based Standards for Teacher Education Standards for Elementary, Middle and High School Levels.* Washington, DC: National Association of State Directors of Teacher Education and Certification.

NBPTS (undated) *Teaching and Learning. School Site Portfolio. Early adolescence/Generalist Certification.* San Antonio, TX: National Board for Professional Teaching Standards.

NCES (1977) *State Indicators in Education 1997.* National Center for Education Statistics, Washington, DC: US Department of Education.

NCVQ (1991) *General National Vocational Qualifications: Proposals for the New Qualifications.* Consultation paper, NCVQ, London.

Nelms, V.C. and Thomas M.G. (1998) 'Assessment: A process.' In M. Diez (ed.) *Changing the Practice of Teacher Education.* Washington, DC: American Association of Colleges of Teacher Education.

NEPC (1977) *Student Outcomes Information for Policy Making.* Final Report of the NPEC Working Group on Student Outcomes from a Policy Perspective. Washington, DC: Council for the National Postsecondary Cooperative in Association with the National Center for Education Statistics.

Neufeld, V.R. and Norman, G.R. (1985) *Assessing Clinical Competence.* New York: Springer.

Nevo, B. and Sfez, J. (1985) 'Examiners' feedback questionnaire.' *Assessment and Evaluation in Higher Education 10*, 3, 236–249.

Nevo, B. and Spector, M. (1979) 'Personal tempo in taking tests of the multiple choice type.' *Journal of Educational Research 73*, 2, 236–249.

Newble, D., Hoare, J. and Sheldrake, P.F. (1980) 'The selection and training of examiners for clinical examinations.' *Medical Education 14*, 345–349.

Newble, D., van der Vleuten, C. and Norman, G. (1995) 'Assessing clinical reasoning.' In J. Higgs and M. Jones (eds) *Clinical Reasoning in the Health Professions.* Oxford: Butterworth-Heinemann.

Newman, J.H. (1852, 1947) *The Idea of a University.* London: Longmans Green.

Newport, J.F.(1996) 'Rating teaching in the ASA: Probing the qualifications of student raters and novice teachers.' *Assessment and Evaluation in Higher Education 21*, 1, 17–22.

Newton, J. (1996) 'Plagiarism and the challenge of essay writing: Learning from our students and using classroom assessment and classroom research to develop a pedagogy for plagiarism.' Conference on Assessment and Quality. American Association for Higher Education, June. Washington, DC.

NGA (1986) *The Governors 1991 Report on Education.* Washington, DC: National Governors' Association Centre for Policy Research and Analysis.

Nichols, J.O. (1991) *A Practitioner's Handbook for Institutional Effectiveness and Student Outcomes Assessment Implementation.* New York: Agathon Press.

Noble, J. (1991) *Predicting College Grades from ACT Assessment Scores and High School Coursework and Grade Information.* Research Report 91–3. Iowa City, IA: American College Testing Program.

Noble, J. and McNabb, T. (1989) *Differential Coursework and Grade in High School: Implications for Performance on ACT Assessment.* Research Report 89-5. Iowa City, IA: American College Testing Program.

Nooman, Z.M., Schmidt, H.G. and Ezzat, E.S. (eds) (1990) *Innovation in Medical Education. An Evaluation of its Present Status.* New York: Springer.

Nordvall, R.C. and Braxton, J.M. (1996) 'An alternative definition of the quality of education. Toward usable knowledge for improvement.' *Journal of Higher Education 67,* 5, 483–497.

Norman, G.R. (1985) 'Defining competence: A methodological review.' In V.R Neufeld and G.R. Norman (eds) *Assessing Clinical Competence.* New York: Springer.

Norman, G.R. and Schmidt, H.G. (1992) 'The psychological basis of problem based learning: a review of the evidence.' *Academic Medicine 67,* 557–568.

Norman, G.R., Trott, A.D., Brooks, L.P. and Smith, E.R.M. (1994) 'Cognitive differences in clinical reasoning related to postgraduate training.' *Teaching and Learning in Medicine 5,* 114–120.

Norris, S.P. (ed.) (1992) *The Generalizability of Critical Thinking: Multiple Perspectives on an Educational Ideal.* New York: Teachers College Press.

Norton, L.S. (1990) 'Essay-writing: What really counts?' *Higher Education 20,* 4, 411–442.

Novak, J.R., Herman J.L and Gearhart, M. (1996) *Issues in Portfolio Asssessment; the Scorability of Narrative Collections.* CRESST. CSE Report 410. Los Angeles: Graduate School of Education, University of California at Los Angeles.

Nulty, D.D. and Barrett, M.A. (1996) 'Transitions in students' learning styles.' *Studies in Higher Education 21,* 3, 333–345.

Nunn, C.E. (1996) 'Discussion in the classroom. Triangulating observational and survey results.' *Journal of Higher Education 67,* 3, 243–266.

NUS (1967) *Report on Student Wastage.* London: National Union of Students.

O'Brien, K. (1990) *Portfolio Assessment at Alverno College.* Milwaukee, WI: Alverno College Institute.

OERI (1993) *Student Portfolios: Administrative Uses.* Washington, DC: Office of Educational Research and Improvement.

Okebukola, P.A. (1992) 'Can good concept mappers be good problem solvers in science?' *Research in Science and Technological Education 10,* 2, 153–170.

Oldfield, K.A. and MacAlpine, J.M.K. (1995) 'Peer and self–assessment at tertiary level-an experiential report.' *Assessment and Evaluation in Higher Education 20,* 1, 125–132.

Olds, B.M. (1998) 'Technical writing across the curriculum: Process, problems and progress.' In *Proceedings of the 28th Annual Frontiers in Education Conference 1,* 518–522. New York: IEEE.

Oosterhof, A.C. and Coats, P.K. (1984) 'Comparison of difficulties and reliabilities of quantitative word problems in completion and multiple choice item formats.' *Applied Psychological Measurement 8,* 287–294.

Opacic, S. (1994) 'The student learning experience in the mid 1990's.' In S. Haselgrove (ed.) *The Student Experience.* Buckingham: Society for Research into Higher Education/Open University Press.

Ormell, C.P. (1974) 'Bloom's Taxonomy and the Objectives of Education.' *Educational Research 17,* 1, 3–15.

Orsmond, P., Merry, S. and Reiling, K. (1996) 'The importance of marking criteria in the use of peer assessment.' *Assessment and Evaluation in Higher Education 21,* 3, 239–250.

Otter, S. (1989) *Understanding Learning Outcomes.* UDACE. Sheffield: Employment Department.

Otter, S. (1991) *What Can Graduates do? A Consultative Document.* UDACE. Sheffield: Employment Department.

Otter, S. (1992) *Learning Outcomes in Higher Education.* Unit for Development of Adult Continuing Education: Employment Department. London: HMSO.

Owen, S.V. and Freeman, R.D. (1987) 'What's wrong with three-option multiple choice items.' *Educational and Psychological Measurement 47,* 2, 513–522.

Ozga, J. and Sukhnandan, L. (1998) 'Undergraduate non-completion.' In *Undergraduate Non-completion in Higher Education in England.* Bristol: Higher Education Funding Council.

Pablo, J.E., Subira, S., Martin, M.J., deFlores, T. and Valdes, M. (1990) 'Examination-associated anxiety in students of medicine.' *Academic Medicine 65,* 706–707.

Pace, C.R. (1984) *Measuring the Quality of Student Experiences.* Los Angeles: Higher Education Research Institute, University of California.

Pace, C.R. (1990) *College Student Experience Questionnaire.* (3rd edn) Bloomington, IN: Center for Postsecondary Research and Planning, Indiana University.

Pain, R. and Mowl, G. (1996) 'Improving geography essay writing using innovative assessment.' *Journal of Geography in Higher Education 20,* 1, 19–31.

Palmer, D.H. (1997) 'Investigating students' private perceptions of scientists and their work.' *Research in Science and Technological Education 15,* 2, 173–184.

Paris, S.G., Wixson, K.K. and Palinscar, A.S. (1986) 'Instructional approaches to reading comprehension.' In E.Z. Rothkof (ed.) *Review of Research in Education.* Washington, DC: American Educational Research Association.

Parkerson, G.R., Broadhead, W.E. and Tse, C-K. J. (1990) *Academic Medicine 65,* 9, 586–588.

Partington, P. (ed.) (1992) *Student Feedback: Context, Issues and Practice.* CVCP. Sheffield: The Universities and Colleges Staff Development Agency, Sheffield University.

Pascarella, E.T. (1985) 'College environmental influences on learning and cognitive development. A critical review and synthesis.' In J.C. Smart (ed.) *Higher Education Handbook of Theory and Research.* New York: Agathon Press.

Pascarella, E.T., Edison, M., Hagedorn, L.S., Nora, A. and Terenzeni, P.T. (1996) 'Influences on students' internal locus of attribution for academic success in the first year of college.' *Research in Higher Education 37,* 6, 731–756.

Pascarella, E.T. and Terenzeni, P.T. (1980) 'Predicting freshmen persistence and voluntary drop out decisions from a theoretical model.' *Journal of Higher Education 51*, 60–75.

Pascarella, E.T. and Terenzeni, P.T. (1991) *How College Affects Students*. San Francisco: Jossey-Bass,

Pask, G. (1988) 'Learning strategies, teaching strategies and conceptual or learning style.' In R.R. Schmeck (ed.) *Learning Strategies and Learning Styles*. New York: Plenum Press.

Passnau, R.O. and Stoessel, P. (1994) 'Mental health service for medical students.' *Medical Education 28*, 1, 38–39.

Patel, V.L. and Kaufman, D.R. (1995) 'Clinical reasoning and biomedical knowledge: Implications for teaching.' In J. Higgs and M. Jones (eds) *Clinical Reasoning in the Health Professions*. Oxford: Butterworth/Heinemann.

Pavelich, M.J. and Moore, W.S. (1996) 'Measuring the effect of experiential education using the Perry model.' *Journal of Engineering Education 85*, 287–292.

PCFC (1990) *Performance Indicators. Report of a Committee Of Enquiry*. (The Morris Report). London: Polytechnics and Colleges Funding Council.

Penn, W.Y. (1990) 'Teaching ethics: A direct approach.' *Journal of Moral Education 19*, 2, 124–138.

Penny, A.J. and Grover, C. (1996) 'An analysis of student grade expectations and marker consistency.' *Assessment and Evaluation in Higher Education 21*, 2, 173–184.

Perkins, D. (1995) *Outsmarting IQ. The Emerging Science of Learnable Intelligence*. New York: Free Press.

Perry, R.P. (1991) 'Perceived control in college students: implications for instruction.' In J.C. Smart (ed.) *Higher Education: Handbook of Theory and Research*. New York: Agathon Press.

Perry, R.P. and Penner, K. (1989) 'Academic Achievement in College Students through Attributional Retraining.' Paper presented at the meeting of the American Educational Research Association, San Francisco.

Perry, R.P. and Penner, K.S. (1990) 'Enhancing academic achievement in college students through additional retraining and instruction.' *Journal of Educational Psychology 82*, 262–271.

Perry, W.G. (1970) *Intellectual and Ethical Development in College Years. A Scheme*. New York: Holt, Rinehart and Winston.

Petter, A. (1982) 'A closet within the house: learning objectives and the law school curriculum.' In *Essays in Legal Education*. Toronto: Butterworth.

Pike, G.R. (1989) 'Background, college experience and the ACT–Comp Exam: Using construct validity to evaluate assessment instruments.' *Review of Higher Education 13*, 91–117.

Pike, G.R. (1994) 'The relationship between alumni satisfaction and work experiences.' *Research in Higher Education 35*, 1, 105–123.

Pinsky, S. and Weigel, R. (1983) 'Engineering: A stress management plan for advisers.' *Engineering Education 73*, 7, 742–745.

Please, N.W. (1977) 'Estimation of the proportion of candidates who are wrongly graded.' *British Journal of Mathematical and Statistical Psychology 24*, 2, 230–238.

Plovnick, M.A. (1971) *A Cognitive Theory of Occupational Roles*. Cambridge, MA: Sloan School of Management, Massachusetts Institute of Technology. Working paper 524–571.

Pokrajac, N. and Culo, F. (1994) 'Multiple choice question tests in physiology: a preliminary attempt to apply the minimum pass level.' *Medical Education 28*, 5, 409–417.

Powers, D.E. and Enright, M.K. (1987) 'Analytical reasoning skills in graduate study: perceptions of faculty in six fields.' *Journal of Higher Education 58*, 6, 658–682.

Pring, R. (1971) 'Bloom's Taxonomy: A philosophical critique.' *Cambridge Journal of Education 1*, 83–91.

Prosser, M.T. (1979) 'Tertiary science instructional materials: a cognitive analysis.' *Research and Developmental Higher Education 1*, 127–142.

Prosser, M.T. and Oliver, D.(1983) 'Making the process and criteria of tertiary science project assessments more explicit.' *Assessment and Evaluation in Higher Education 8*, 1, 29–41.

Pryor, J. and Torrance, H. (1997) 'Making sense of formative evaluation.' *International Studies in Educational Administration 25*, 2, 115–125.

Pulich, M.A. (1983) 'Student grade appeals can be reduced.' *Improving College and University Teaching 31*, 1, 9–12.

Purcell, K. and Pitcher, J. (1996) *Great Expectations: The New Diversity of Graduate Skills and Aspirations*. London: Higher Education Careers services Unit, Institute of Employment Research.

Purves, A.C. (1961) *Literary Criticism, Testing and the English Teacher*. Quoted by Iliffe (1966).

QAA (1997) *Subject Review Handbook: October 1998 to 2000*. Gloucester: Quality Assurance Agency.

Rae, J. (1998) 'Steely strategy beats silver spoons: The right school.' *The Times*, p.17, January 5.

Rafiq, Y. and Fullerton, H. (1996) 'Peer assessment of group projects in civil engineering.' *Assessment and Evaluation in Higher Education 21*, 1, 69–82.

Rainsbury, E., Hodges, D., Sutherland, J. and Barrow, M. (1998)'Academic, employer and student collaborative assessment in a work-based cooperative education course.' *Assessment and Evaluation in Higher Education 23*, 3, 313–324.

Ramsden, P. (1984) 'The context of learning.' In F. Marton, D. Hounsell and N.J. Entwistle (eds) *The Experience of Learning*. Edinburgh: Scottish Academic Press.

Ramsden, P. (1988) 'Context and strategy: situational influences on learning.' In R.R. Schmeck (ed.) *Learning Strategies and Learning Styles*. New York: Plenum Press.

Ramsden, P. (1991) 'A performance indicator of teaching quality in higher education: the Course Experience Questionnaire.' *Studies in Higher Education 16*, 2, 129–150.

Ramsden, P. (1992) *Learning and Teaching in Higher Education*. London: Routledge.

Ramsden, P. and Entwistle, N.J. (1981) 'Effects of academic departments on students' approaches to studying.' *British Journal of Educational Psychology 51*, 129–142.

Ratzlaff, H.C. (1980) 'Upgrading grading practices.' *Improving College and University Teaching 28*, 2, 81–84.

Renner, J.W. and Lawson, A.E. (1973) 'Piagetian theory and instruction in physics.' *The Physics Teacher 11*, 2, 138–145.

Resnick, D. and Goulden, M. (1987) Paper presented at the 2nd National Conference on Assessment in Higher Education, American Association for Higher Education. See also in D. Halpern (ed.) *Student Outcomes Assessment. A Tool for Improving Teaching and Learning*. San Francisco: Jossey-Bass.

Resnick, L.B.(1987) *Education and Learning to Think*. Washington, DC: National Academy Press.

Rest, J.R. (1983) 'Morality.' In P.H. Mussen (ed.) *Handbook of Child Psychology 3: Cognitive Development*. New York: Wiley.

Reynolds, P.A. (1986) *Academic Standards in the Universities*. London: Committee of Vice-Chancellors and Principals.

Reynolds, P.A. (1990) 'Is the external system an adequate guarantee of academic standards?' In C. Loder (ed.) *Quality Assurance and Accountability in Higher Education*. London: Kogan Page.

Richardson, J.T.E.(1994) 'Using questionnaires to evaluate student learning: Some health warnings.' In G. Gibbs (ed.) *Improving Student Learning: Theory and Practice*. Oxford: Centre for Staff Development, Oxford Brookes University.

Richardson, J.T.E.(1995) 'Mature students in higher education: An investigation of approaches to studying and academic performance.' *Studies in Higher Education 20*, 1, 5–17.

Richmond, K. (1963) *Culture and General Education*. London: Methuen.

Ridd, T. (1983) *Marking A-Level History Syllabus*. Manchester: Joint Matriculation Board.

Ridgeway, J. and Passey, D. (1992) 'An international view of mathematics assessment: Through the glass darkly.' In M. Niss (ed.) *Investigations into Assessment in Mathematics Education*. Kluwer, Dordrecht: ICMI.

Riding, R.J. (1991) *Cognitive Styles Analysis*. Birmingham: Learning and Training Technology.

Riding, R.J. (1996) *Learning Styles and Technology Based Training*. Sheffield: Department for Education and Employment.

Riding, R.J. and Staley, A. (1998) 'Self-perception as learner, cognitive style and business studies students' course.' *Assessment and Evaluation in Higher Education 23*, 1, 43–58.

Riding, R.J. and Wright, M. (1995) 'Cognitive style, personal characteristics and harmony in flats.' *Educational Psychology 15*, 3, 337–349.

Rinehart, S.D., Stahl, S.A. and Erickson, L.G. (1986) 'Some effects of summarization training on reading and studying.' *Reading Research Quarterly 21*, 422–437.

Robinson, P. (1997) *The Myth of Parity of Esteem. Earnings and Qualifications*. Discussion Paper No 354. London: Centre for Economic Performance, London School of Economics and Political Science.

Rochford, K. (1989) *Visual Learning Disabilities and Under-Achievement Among Engineering Students*. Proceedings of the World Conference on Engineering Education for Advanced Technology, Sydney, February.

Rodgers, R. (1989) 'Student development.' In U. Delworth and S. Komies (eds) *Student Services: A Handbook for the Profession*. San Francisco: Jossey-Bass.

Rogers, G. (1994) 'Measurement and judgement in curriculum assessment systems.' *Assessment Update 6*, 1, 6–7.

Rohwer, W.D. and Sloane, K. (1994) 'Psychological perspectives.' In L.W. Anderson and L.A. Sosniak (eds) *Bloom's Taxonomy: A Forty Year Retrospective*. Chicago: University of Chicago Press.

Rokeach, M. (1960) *The Open and Closed Mind*. New York: Basic Books.

Rollers, D.R., Giardina, R., Herman, G. and Woditsch, G. (1972) 'The first year of the first Little college.' *Journal of Higher Education 43*, 5, 337.

Rosati, P. (1997) 'Students' psychological type and success in different engineering programs.' *Proceedings Frontiers in Education Conference 2*, 781–784. New York: ASEE/IEEE.

Rosenshine, B. and Meister, C. (1992) 'The use of scaffolds for teaching higher level cognitive strategies.' *Educational Leadership 49*, 7, 26–33.

Ross, G.M., Parry, J. and Cohen, M. (1993) *Philosphy and Enterprise: The Implications for Philosophy of the Enterprise in Higher Education Initiative*. Leeds: Department of Philosophy, University of Leeds.

RSA (1989) *Education for Capability Manifesto*. London: Royal Society of Arts.

Rutsohn, J. (1978) 'Understanding personality types. Does it matter?' *Improving College and University Teaching 26*, 4, 249–254.

Rutter, M. and Smith, D.J. (eds) (1995) *Psychosocial Disorders in Young People*. Chichester: Wiley.

Ryan, J.J. (1998) 'Student Plagiarism in an Online World.' *ASEE Prism*, Dec, 21–24.

Ryle, A. (1969) *Student Casualties*. London: Allen Lane.

Ryle, A. and Lungi, M. (1968) 'A psychometric study of academic difficulty and psychometric illness.' *British Journal of Psychiatry 114*, 47.

Sadler-Smith, E. (1996) 'Approaches to studying: Age, gender and academic performance.' *Educational Studies 22*, 3, 367–380.

Sadlo, G. (1997) 'Problem-based learning enhances the educational experiences of occupational therapy students.' *Education for Health 10*, 1, 101–114.

Sambell, K. and McDowell, L. (1998) 'The construction of the hidden curriculum: messages and meanings in the assessment.' *Assessment and Evaluation in Higher Education 23*, 4, 391–402.

Sandler, B.R., Silverberg, L.A. and Hall, R.M. (1996) *The Chilly Classroom Climate: A Guide to Improve the Education of Women*. Washington, DC: National Association for Women in Education.

Sarason, I.G. and Stoops, R. (1978) 'Test anxiety and the passage of time.' *Journal of Consulting and Clinical Psychology 46*, 102–109.

Sarnacki, R.E. (1979) 'An examination of testwiseness in cognitive test domain.' *Review of Educational Research 2*, 252–279.

SCANS (1992) *Learning A Living: A Blue Print for High Performance*. A SCANS Report for America 2000. Washington DC: US Department of Labor.

Schlaefli, A., Rest, F. and Thoma, S. (1985) 'Does moral education improve moral judgement? A meta-analysis of intervention studies using the Defining Issues Test.' *Review of Educational Research 55*, 319–352.

Schmeck, R.R. (1993) 'Learning styles of college students.' In R. Dillon and R.R. Schmeck (eds) *Individual Differences in Cognition vol. 1*. New York: Academic Press.

Schmelkin, L.P., Spencer, K.J. and Gellman, E.S. (1997) 'Faculty perspectives on course and teacher evaluations.' *Research in Higher Education 38*, 5, 575–592.

Schmitt, N., Ford, J.K. and Stults, D. (1986) 'Changes in self-perceived ability as a function of performance in an assessment center.' *Journal of Occupational Psychology 59*, 327–336.

Schoenfield, A.H. (1985) *Mathematical Problem Solving*. New York: Academic Press.

Schon, D.A. (1983) *The Reflective Practitioner*. New York: Basic Books.

Schroder, H.M. (1989) *Managerial Competence: The Key to Excellence*. Columbus, Ohio: Ohio University Press, Kendal Hunt.

Schulte, J. and Loacker, G. (1994) *Assessing General Education Outcomes for the Individual Student: Part 1, Designing and Implementing Performance Assessment Instruments*. Milwaukee, WI: Alverno College Institute.

Schuster, C. (1983) *The Un-assignment: Writing groups for Advanced Expository Writing*. Paper presented at Annual meeting of Wyoming conference on Freshmen and sophomore English.

Schwartz, R.W., Burgett, J.E., Blue, A.V., Donnelly, M.B. and Sloan, D.A. (1997) 'Problem-based learning and performance-based testing; effective alternatives for undergraduate surgical education and assessment of student performance.' *Medical Teacher 19*, 1, 19–23.

Schweitzer, R.D. (1996) 'Problems and awareness of support services among students at an urban Australian university.' *Journal of American College Health 45*, 2, 73–77.

Schwiebert, J.E. (1996) 'The topic/form grid: diverse forms of writing enrich thinking.' *College Teaching 44*, 1, 8–12.

Scouller, K.M. and Prosser, M. (1994) 'Students' experiences in studying for multiple choice question examinations.' *Studies in Higher Education 19*, 3, 267–279.

Searby, M. and Ewers, T.(1997) 'An evaluation of the use of peer assessment in higher education; a case study in the school of music: Kingston University.' *Assessment and Evaluation in Higher Education 22*, 4, 371–383.

Seldin, P. *et al.* (1993) *Successful Use of Teaching Portfolios*. Bolton, MA: Anker.

Self, D.J., Baldwin, D.C. and Wolinsky, F. (1992) 'Evaluation of teaching medical ethics by an assessment of moral reasoning.' *Medical Education 26*, 3, 178–184.

Selmes, I.P. (1985) *Approaches to Learning at Secondary School: Their Identification and Facilitation*. Ph.D Thesis, Edinburgh: University of Edinburgh.

Severiens, S.G. and Ten Dam, G.T.M. (1994) 'Gender differences in learning styles: A narrative review and quantitative meta-analysis.' *Higher Education 27*, 4, 487–501.

Seymour, E. and Hewitt, N.M. (1997) *Talking about Leaving. Why Undergraduates Leave Science*. Boulder, CO: Westview Press.

Shaha, S.H. (1984) 'Matching tests: Reduced anxiety and increased test-effectiveness.' *Educational and Psychological Measurement 47*, 4, 469–481.

Shannon, D.M., Twale, D.J. and Hancock, G.R.(1996) 'Use of instructional feedback and modification methods among university faculty.' *Assessment and Evaluation in Higher Education 21*, 1, 41–54.

Sharp, J. and Culver, R. (1996) 'Cooperative learning in a manufacturing management course.' In *Proceedings 26th Annual Frontiers in Education Conference*, 161–171. New York: IEEE.

Sharp, J.E. (1998) 'Learning styles and technical communication: improving communication and teamwork skills.' *Proceedings 28th Frontiers in Education Conference 1*, 512–517. New York: IEEE.

Sharp, J.E., Harb, J.N. and Terry, R.E. (1997) 'Combining Kolb learning styles and writing to learn in engineering education.' *Journal of Engineering Education 86*, 2, 93–102.

Shayer, M. and Adey, P. (1981) *Towards a Science of Science Teaching: Cognitive Development and Curriculum Demand*. London: Heinemann.

Shelton, J.B. and Smith, R.F. (1998) 'Problem based learning in analytical science undergraduate teaching.' *Research in Science and Technological Education 16*, 1, 19–31.

SHTA (1977) *Pupils in Profile*. Scottish Headteachers Association. London: Hodder and Stoughton.

Shubbar, E. (1990) 'Learning the visualization of rotators in diagrams of three dimensional structures.' *Research in Science and Technological Education 8*, 2, 145–154.

Shulman, L. (1992) *Toward a Pedagogy of Cases: Case Methods in Teacher Education*. New York: Teachers College Press.

Sigman, E. and Oltman, P.K. (1976) *Field Dependence and the Role of Visual Framework in the Perception of Size*. Princeton, NJ: Educational Testing Service.

Silk, J. and Bowlby, S. (1981) 'The use of project work in undergraduate teaching.' *Journal of Geography in Higher Education 5*, 2, 155–162.

Silver, H. (1990) *A Higher Education. The Council for National Academic Awards and British Higher Education 1964–1989*. London: Falmer Press.

Silver, H. (1996) *External Examiners: Changing Roles*. London: Council for National Academic Awards.

Silver, H.F. and Hanson, R.J. (1995) *Learning Styles and Strategies*. Princeton, NJ: The Thoughtful Education Press.

Silver, L. (1968) 'Anxiety and first semester law school.' *Wisconsin Law Review 4*, 4, 1201–1218.

Simpson, E.J. (1966) 'The classification of objectives in the psychomotor domain.' *Illinois Teacher of Home Economics 10*, 4, 110–144.

Sims, R., Veres, J.G., Watson, P. and Buckner, K.E. (1986) 'The reliability and classification stability of the learning style inventory.' *Educational and Psychological Measurement 46*, 3, 743–760.

Skolnik, M.L. (1989) 'How academic program review can foster intellectual conformity and stifle diversity of thought and method.' *Journal of Higher Education 60*, 6, 619–643.

Sloboda, J.A. (1990) 'Combating examination stress among university students: action research in an institutional context.' *British Journal of Guidance and Counselling 18*, 2, 124–136.

Smit, G.N. and van der Molen, H.T. (1997) 'The construction and evaluation of simulations to assess professional interviewing skills.' *Assessment in Education: Principles, Policy and Practice 4*, 3, 353–364.

Smith, G.A. (1978) *JMB Experience of the Moderation of Internal Assessments.* Occasional Paper No. 38. Manchester: Joint Matriculation Board.

Smith, J.K. (1982) 'Converging on correct answers: a peculiarity of multiple choice items.' *Journal of Educational Measurement 3*, 211–220.

Smith, R.A. and Cranton, P.A. (1992) 'Students' perceptions of teaching skills and overall effectiveness across instructional settings.' *Research in Higher Education 33*, 747.

Smith, R.M. (1986) 'Reason fit in the Rasch model.' *Educational and Psychological Measurement 46*, 359–372.

Smyth, J. (1989) 'Collegiality as a counter discourse to the intrusion of corporate management in higher education.' *Journal of Tertiary Educational Administration 11*, 2, 145–149.

Sockett, H. (1971) 'Bloom's Taxonomy. A philosophical critique.' *Cambridge Journal of Education 1*, 16–25.

Somervell, H. (1993) 'Issues in assessment, enterprise and higher education: the case for self, peer and collaborative assessment.' *Assessment and Evaluation in Higher Education 18*, 3, 221–234.

Sperry, R.W., Gazzaniga, M.S. and Bogen, J.E. (1960) 'Inter-hemispheric relationships.' In P.J. Vinken and G.W. Bruyn (eds) *Handbook of Clinical Neurology 4.* Amsterdam: Elsevier.

Spielberger, C.D. (ed.) (1966) *Anxiety and Behaviour.* New York: Academic Press.

Spires, H.A. (1993) 'Learning from a lecture: Effects of comprehension monitoring.' *Reading Research and Instruction 32*, 19–30.

SSPEI (1991) *Education Counts. An Indicator System to Monitor the Nation's Educational Health.* Report of the Special Study panel on Education Indicators to the Acting Commissioner of Educational Statistics) Washington, DC: National Center for Education Statistics.

Stancanto, R.A. and Eizler, C.F. (1983) 'When "C" is not a "C": The psychological meaning of grades in educational psychology.' *Journal of Instructional Psychology 10*, 158–162.

Stanier, L. (1997) 'Peer assessment and group work as vehicles for student empowerment: A module evaluation.' *Journal of Geography in Higher Education 21*, 1, 95–98.

Stanton, H.E. (1988) 'Improving exam performance with the clenched fist technique.' *College Teaching 36*, 3, 107–109.

Starch, D. and Elliott, E.C. (1912) 'Reliability and grading high school work in English.' *School Review 20*, 442–457.

Starch, D. and Elliott, E.C. (1913a) 'Reliability of grading work in mathematics.' *School Review 21*, 254–259.

Starch, D. and Elliott, E.C. (1913b) 'Reliability of grading work in history.' *School Review 21*, 678–681.

Stearns, S.A. (1994) 'Steps for active learning of complex concepts.' *College Teaching 42*, 3, 107–108.

Stecher, B. (1998) 'The local benefits and burdens of large-scale portfolio assessment.' *Assessment in Education: Principles, Policy and Practice 5*, 3, 335–352.

Steffe, L.P. and Gale, J. (1995) *Constructivism in Education.* Hillsdale, NJ: Lawrence Erlbaum.

Stein, R.B. (1996) 'Performance reporting/funding program: Missouri's efforts to integrate state and campus strategic planning.' In G.H. Gaither (ed.) *Performance Indicators in Higher Education: What Works, What Doesn't and What's Next?* Washington, DC: Symposium, American Association for Higher Education.

Steinaker, N. and Bell, M.R. (1969) *An Experiential Taxonomy.* New York: Academic Press.

Stephens, D., Bull, J. and Wade, W. (1998) 'Computer-assisted assessment: suggested guidelines for an institutional strategy.' *Assessment and Evaluation in Higher Education 23*, 3, 283–294.

Stephenson, J. and Yorke, M. (eds) (1998) *Capability and Quality in Higher Education.* London: Kogan Page.

Sternberg, R.J. (1985a) *Beyond IQ: A Triarchic View of Intelligence.* Cambridge: Cambridge University Press.

Sternberg, R.J. (1985b) 'Critical thinking: Its nature measurement and improvement.' In F.R. Lincke (ed.) *Essays on the Intellect.* Alexandria, VA: Association for Supervision and Curriculum Development.

Stevens, R. (1973) 'Law school and law students.' *Virginia Law Review 59*, 551–707.

Stewart, A. (1977) *Analysis of Argument: An Empirically-Derived Measure of Intellectual Flexibility.* Boston, MA: McBer and Co.

Stice, J.E. (1979) 'PSI and Bloom's mastery model: A review and comparison.' *Engineering Education 70*, 175.

Stice, J.E. (1987) 'Using Kolb's learning cycle to improve student learning.' *Engineering Education 77*, 5, 291–296.

Storms, B.A., Sheingold, K., Nunez, A.M. and Heller, J.I. (1998) *The Feasibility, Comparability and Value of Local Scorings of Performance Assessments.* Princeton, NJ: Center for Performance Assessment, E.T.S.

Strachan, J.B. and Wilcox, S. (1996) 'Peer and self assessment of group work: developing an effective response to increased enrolment in a third-year course in microclimatology.' *Journal of Geography in Higher Education 20*, 3, 343–353.

Straton, R.G. and Catts, R.M. (1980) 'A comparison of two- three- and four-choice item tests given a fixed number of total choices.' *Educational and Psychological Measurement 40*, 357–365.

Sumsion, J. and Fleet, A. (1996) 'Reflection: Can we assess it? Should we assess it?' *Assessment and Evaluation in Higher Education 21*, 2, 121–130.

Supovitz, J.A. and Brennan, R.T. (1997) 'Mirror, mirror on the wall, which is the fairest test of all? An examination of the equitability of portfolio assessment relative to standardized tests.' *Harvard Educational Review 67*, 3, 472–506.

Sutherland, P. (1995) 'An investigation into Entwistlean adult learning styles in mature students.' *Educational Psychology 15*, 3, 257–270.

Svensson, L. (1976) *Study Skill and Learning.* Goteborg: Acta Universitatis Gothoburgensis.

Svinicki, M.D. and Dixon, N.M. (1987) 'The Kolb model modified for classroom activities.' *College Teaching 35*, 4, 357–365.

Swartz, R.J. (1987) 'Teaching for thinking: A developmental model for infusion of thinking skills into mainstream instruction.' In J.B. Baron and R.J. Sternberg (eds) *Teaching Thinking Skills: Theory and Practice.* New York: W.H. Freeman.

Szafran, R.F. (1981) 'Question pool study guides.' *Teaching Sociology 9*, 1, 31–43.

Taba, H. and Freeman, F.F. (1964) 'Teaching strategies and thought processes.' *Teachers' College Record 65*, 524–534.

Tait, H. and Entwistle, N. (1996) 'Identifying students at risk through ineffective study habits.' *Higher Education 31*, 1, 97–116.

Tariq, V.N., Stefani, L.A.J., Butcher, A.C. and Heylings, D.J.A. (1998) 'Developing a new approach to the assessment of project work.' *Assessment and Evaluation in Higher Education 23*, 3, 221–240.

Tarsh, J. (1990) 'Graduate employment and degree class.' *Employment Gazette 98*, 10, 489–500.

Taylor, H. (1977) 'Differences in grading systems among universities.' *The Canadian Journal of Higher Education 7*, 1, 47–54.

Taylor, L. (1994) 'Reflecting on teaching: The benefits of self evaluation.' *Assessment and Evaluation in Higher Education 19*, 2, 109–122.

Terenzini, P. and Wright, T. (1987) 'Influences on students' academic growth during four years of college.' *Research in Higher Education 26*, 161–179.

Terwilliger, J. (1997) 'Semantics, psychometrics and assessment reform. A close look at "authentic" assessment.' *Educational Researcher 26*, 8, 24–27.

Thomas, B. and Madigan, C. (1974) 'Strategy and job choice after redundancy: a case study in the aircraft industry.' *Sociological Review 22*, 83–102.

Thomas, C.S. (1992) 'The oral examination: a study of academic and non-academic factors.' *Medical Education 27*, 5, 433–439.

Thomas, P.R. and Bain, J.D. (1982) 'Consistency in learning strategies.' *Higher Education 11*, 3, 249–259.

Thomas, R. (1984) 'Examination of a formulae method for assigning letter grades.' *Engineering Education, 74*, 7, 673–675.

Thompson, D.G. (1990) 'Reactions to the introduction of problem-based learning into a medical school: faculty and student views.' In Z.M. Nooman, H.G. Schmidt and E.S. Ezzat (eds) *Innovation in Medical Education*. New York: Springer.

Thompson, D.J. and Rentz, R.R. (1973) *The Large Scale Essay Testing: Implications for Test Construction and Evaluation*. The Hague, Netherlands: Mineo. International Symposium on Educational Testing.

Thomson, K. and Falchikov, N. (1998) '"Full on until the sun comes out": the effects of assessment on student approaches to studying.' *Assessment and Evaluation in Higher Education 23*, 4, 379–390.

Thorndike, R.L. and Hagen, E.R. (1977) *Measurement and Evaluation in Psychology and Education*. New York: Wiley.

Thornton, G.C. and Byham, W.C. (1982) *Assessment Centers and Managerial Performance*. New York: Pergamon.

Tiberius, R.G., Dackin, H.D., Slingerland, J.M., Jubas, K., Bell, M. and Marlow A. (1989) 'The influence of student evaluative feedback on the improvement of clinical teaching.' *Journal of Higher Education 60*, 6, 665–681.

Timpson, W.W. and Andrew, D. (1997) 'Rethinking student evaluations and the improvement of teaching: instruments for change at the University of Queensland.' *Studies in Higher Education 22*, 1, 55.

Tinto, V. (1975) 'Dropout from higher education. A theoretical synthesis of research.' *Review of Educational Research 45*, 89–125.

Tinto, V. (1987) *Leaving College: Rethinking the Causes and Cures of Student Attrition*. Chicago: University of Chicago Press.

Togolini, J. and Andrich, D. (1995) 'Differential subject performance and the problems of selection.' *Assessment and Evaluation in Higher Education 20*, 2, 161–170.

Tollefson, N. (1987) 'A comparison of item difficulty and item discrimination of multiple choice items using the "none of the above" and one correct response options.' *Educational and Psychological Measurement 47*, 2, 377–383.

Tomlinson, P. and Towell, R. (1999) 'Redesigning and testing the effectiveness of the final year syllabus in French.' In J. Heywood, J. Sharp and M. Hides (eds) *Improving Teaching in Higher Education*. Salford: Teaching and Learning Committee, University of Salford.

Tooth, D., Tonge, K. and McManus, I.C. (1989) 'Anxiety and study methods in preclinical students: Causal relation to examination performance.' *Medical Education 23*, 5, 416–427.

Toppins, A.D. (1987) 'Teaching students to teach themselves.' *College Teaching 35*, 95–99.

Torrance, H. (ed.) (1995) *Evaluating Authentic Assessment*. Buckingham: Open University Press.

Tough, A. (1979) *The Adult's Learning Projects*. Austin, TX: Learning Concepts.

Trabin, T.E. and Weiss, D.J. (1983) 'The person response curve: fitness in individuals to item response theory models.' In D.J. Weiss (ed.) *New Horizons in Testing*. New York: Academic Press.

Travers, R.M. (1980) 'Taxonomies of educational objectives and theories of classification.' *Educational and Policy Analysis 2*, 5–23.

Trigwell, K.(1987) 'The crib card examination system.' *Assessment and Evaluation in Higher Education 12*, 1, 56–65.

Trost, G., Klieme, E. and Nauels, H.U. (1998) 'The relationship between different criteria for admission to medical school and student success.' *Assessment in Education: Principles, Policy and Practice 5*, 2, 247–254.

Trowler, P. and Hinett, K. (1994) 'Implementing the recording of achievement in higher education.' *Capability 1*, 1, 53–61.

Trumper, R. and Gorsky, P. (1997) 'A survey of biology students' conceptions of force in pre-service training for high school teachers.' *Research in Science and Technological Education 15*, 2, 133–147.

Turner, C. (1983) *Developing Interpersonal Skills*. Bristol: Further Education Staff College, Blagdon.

Turow, S. (1977) *One L*. New York: Penguin.

Tversky, A. (1964) 'On the number of alternatives of a choice point.' *Journal of Mathematical Psychology 1*, 368–391.

Tyler, L.E. (1978) *Individuality: Human Possibilities and Personal choice in the Psychological Development of Men and Women*. San Francisco: Jossey-Bass.

UCAS (1996) *GNVQ/GSVQs and Offer Making: Information for Higher Education Selectors*. Cheltenham: Universities and Colleges Admission Service.

Underbakke, M., Borg, J.M. and Peterson, D. (1993) 'Researching and developing the knowledge base for teaching higher order thinking.' *Theory into Practice 32*, 3, 138–146.

Van Overwalle, F. (1989) 'Success and failure of freshmen at university: a search for determinants.' *Higher Education 18*, 3, 287–308.

Vaughan, K. (1982) 'University first year chemistry by the Keller plan (PSI).' *Programmed Learning and Educational Technology* 19, 2, 125–134.

Vazquez-Abad, J., Winer, L.R. and Derome, J.R. (1997) 'Why some stay: a study of factors contributing to undergraduate physics.' *McGill Journal of Education* 32, 3, 209–229.

Verma, V., Chhatwal, J. and Singh, T. (1997) 'Reliability of Essay type questions – effect of structuring.' *Assessment in Education: Principles, Policy and Practice* 4, 2, 265–270.

Vernon, P. (1956) *The Measurement of Human Abilities.* London: University of London Press.

Von Almen, T.K., Fawcett, J.M., Randall, H.M. and Franklin, F.A. (1991) 'Psychosocial changes during the first year of medical school.' *Medical Education* 25, 3, 174–181.

Vu, N.V. and Black, R. (1997) 'Problem analysis questions for assessment in problem-based learning: development and difficulties.' *Education for Health* 10, 1, 79–89.

Vu, N.V., Distlehorst, L.H., Verhulst, S.J. and Colliver, J.A. (1993) 'Clinical performance-based test sensitivity and specificity in predicting first year residency performance.' In J.S. Gonnella, M. Hojat, J.B. Erdman and J.J. Veloski (eds) *Assessment Measures in Medical School, Residency and Practice.* New York: Springer.

Wachtel, H.K. (1998) 'Student evaluation of college teaching effectiveness: A brief review.' *Assessment and Evaluation in Higher Education* 23, 92, 191–212.

Wakeford, R.E. and Roberts, S. (1984) 'Short answer questions in an undergraduate qualifying examination: a study of examiner variability.' *Medical Education* 18, 168–173.

Walhout, D. (1997) 'Grading across a career.' *College Teaching* 45, 3, 83–87.

Walker, D. (1985) 'Writing and reflection.' In D. Boud (ed.) *Reflection: Turning Experience into Learning.* London: Kogan Page.

Walvoord, B.E. and McCarthy, L.P. (1990) *Thinking and Writing in College. A Naturalistic Study of Students in Four Disciplines.* Urbana, IL: National Council of Teachers of English. Circulated by B.E. Walvoord at the Assessment Forum (annual conference) of the American Association for Higher Education, 1996. Washington, DC.

Wankowski, J.A. (1969) 'Some aspects of motivation in success and failure at university.' *Report of the 1968 Annual Conference of SHRE.* London: Society for Research into Higher Education.

Wankowski, J.A. (1973) 'Disenchanted élite in motivation.' *Report of the 1972 Annual Conference of SRHE.* London: Society for Research into Higher Education.

Ware, J.E. and Williams, R.G. (1980) 'A reanalysis of Dr Fox experiments.' *Instructional Evaluation* 4, 15–18.

Warr, P.B. (1987) 'Workers without a job.' In P.B. Warr (ed.) *Psychology at Work.* 3rd edn. Harmondsworth: Penguin.

Warren, J. (1976) *Evaluation of the Office of Education Criteria for the Recognition of Accrediting and State Approval Agencies.* Cyclostyled. Berkeley, CA: Educational Testing Service.

Warren Piper, D. (1993) *Quality Management in the Universities.* Canberra: Department of Employment, Education and Training, Australian Government Printing Service.

Warren Piper, D. (1994) *Are Professors Professional? The Organisation of University Examinations.* London: Jessica Kingsley Publishers.

Warrington, E.K., James, M. and Hinsbourne, M. (1966) 'Drawing disability in relation to laterality of cerebral lesion.' *Brain* 89, 53–82.

Watkins, D. (1981) 'Identifying the study process dimensions of Australian university students.' *Australian Journal of Education* 26, 1, 76–85.

Watson, D.E.R., Hallett, R.F. and Diamond, N.T. (1995) 'Promoting a Collegial approach in a Multidisciplinary Environment for a Total Quality Improvement Process in Higher Education.' *Assessment and Evaluation in Higher Education* 20, 1, 77–88.

Watson, G. and Glaser, E.M. (1964) *Watson-Glaser Critical Thinking Appraisal Manual.* Orlando, FL: Harcourt Brace Jovanovich.

Weber, L.J., Frary, R.B. and Cross, L.H. (1995) 'Allowing Students a choice of items in objective examinations.' *Assessment and Evaluation in Higher Education* 20, 3, 301–306.

Weber, P. and Weber, F. (1990) 'Using 4MAT to improve student performance.' *Educational Leadership* 48, 2, 41–46.

Weidman, J. (1989) 'Undergraduate socialization. A conceptual approach.' In J. Smart (ed.) *Higher Education: Handbook of Theory and Research.* Vol 5. New York: Agathon Press.

Weiss, D.J. (ed.) (1983) *New Horizons in Testing Latent: Trait Theory and Computerized Adaptive Testing.* New York: Academic Press.

Welsh, J.F. (1993) 'Student academic dishonesty in higher education: social context and institutional response.' Unpublished report. Kansas Board of Regents, Topeka, Kansas.

Westerheijden, D.F. and van Vught, F. (1995) 'Assessment of quality in Western Europe.' *Assessment Update* 7, 2, 1–11.

Weston, C. and Cranton, P.A. (1986) 'Selecting instructional strategies.' *Journal of Higher Education* 57, 3, 259–288.

White, E.M. (1985) *Teaching and Assessing Writing.* San Francisco: Jossey-Bass.

White, J.E.G. (1980) 'Trends in examinations and assessment in modern languages.' *Assessment and Evaluation in Higher Education* 6, 57–81

Whitfield, P.R. (1975) *Creativity in Industry.* Harmondsworth: Penguin.

Whitman, N.E., Spendlove, D.C. and Clark, C.H. (1984) *Student Stress: Effects and Solutions.* Washington, DC: ASHE-ERIC Higher Education Research Report, No. 2.

Whittock, T. (undated) *The Academic Critical Essay (ACE).* Unpublished. Communicated by J.Cowan.

Wigdor, A.K. and Garner, W.R. (eds) (1982) *Ability Testing: Uses, Consequences and Controversies* (2 vols). Washington, DC: National Academic Press.

Wiggins, G. (1989) 'A true test: Toward more authentic and equitable assessment.' *Phi Delta Kappan* 20, 703–713.

Wiggins, G. (1993) *Assessing Student Performance.* San Fransisco: Jossey-Bass.

Wilhoyte, R.L. (1965) Problems of meaning and reference in Bloom's Taxonomy; Cognitive Domain. Doctoral Thesis, Indiana University. Cited by Furst (1994).

Wiliam, D. (1995) 'Combination, aggregation and reconciliation: evidential and consequential bases.' *Assessment in Education: Principles, Policy and Practice 2*, 1, 53–73.

Williford, A.M. and Moden, G.O. (1996) 'Assessing Student Involvement. Case 57 Ohio University.' In T. Banta, J.P. Lund, K. Black and F.W. Oblander (eds) *Assessment in Practice*. San Fransisco: Jossey-Bass.

Wilmot, A.S. and Nuttall, D.L. (1974) *The Reliability of Examinations at 16+*. Basingstoke: Macmillan.

Wilson, K.L., Lizzio, A. and Ramsden, P. (1997) 'The development, validation and application of the course experience questionnaire.' *Studies in Higher Education 22*, 1, 33–53.

Wilson, J.D. (1981) *Student Learning in Higher Education*. Beckenham: Croom Helm.

Wilson, P.R.D. (1986) 'The forecasting of economics finals results – a case of *post hoc ergo propter hoc*.' *Assessment and Evaluation in Higher Education 11*, 1, 28–42.

Wilson, R.C. (1986) 'Improving faculty teaching: effective use of student evaluations and consultants.' *Journal of Higher Education 68*, 48–56.

Wine, J.D. (1982) 'Evaluation anxiety: A cognitive-attentional construct.' In H.W. Krohne and L. Laux (eds) *Achievement, Stress and Anxiety*. Washington, DC: Hemisphere.

Wingrove, J., Jones, A. and Herriot, P.(1985) 'The predictive validity of pre and post discussion assessment centre ratings.' *Journal of Occupational Psychology 58*, 189–192.

Winne, P.H. (1995) 'Inherent details in self-regulated learning.' *Educational Psychologist 30*, 173–187.

Winter, D., McClelland, D.C. and Stewart, A. (1981) *A New Case for Liberal Arts: Assessing Institutional Goals and Student Development*. San Francisco: Jossey-Bass.

Wiseman, H., Guttfreund, D.G. and Lurie, I. (1995) 'Gender differences in loneliness and depression of students seeking counselling.' *British Journal of Guidance and Counselling 23*, 2, 231–243.

Witkin, H.A. (1976) 'Cognitive styles in academic performance and in teacher student relations.' In S. Messick *et al.* (eds) *Individuality in Learning*. San Francisco: Jossey-Bass.

Witkin, H.A. and Goodenough, D.R. (1981) *Cognitive Styles*. New York: International Universities Press.

Witkin, H.A., Moore, C.A., Oltman, P.K., Goodenough, D.R., Friedman, F. and Owen, D.R. (1977) *A Longitudinal Study of the Role of Cognitive Styles in Academic Evaluation in College Years*. GRE Research report 76-10. Princeton, NJ: Educational Testing Service.

Witkin, H.A., Ottman, D.R., Raskin, E. and Karp, S.A. (1971) *A Manual for the Embedded Figures Test*. Palo Alto, CA: Consulting Psychologists Press.

Wittich, B. von (1972) 'The impact of pass fail systems upon the achievement of college students.' *Journal of Higher Education 43*, 499.

Wolf, A. (1995) *Competence-Based Assessment*. Buckingham: Open University Press.

Wolf, A. (1998) 'Portfolio assessment as national policy: The National Council for Vocational Qualifications and its quest for pedagogical revolution.' *Assessment in Education: Principles, Policy and Practice 5*, 3, 413–446.

Wolfe, J. and Bruton, G. (1994) 'On the use of computerized simulations for entrepreneurship education.' *Simulation and Gaming 25*, 3, 402–415.

Wong, Y.L. and Jones, W. (1982) 'Increasing meta-comprehension in learning disabled and normally achieving students through self-questioning training.' *Learning Disability Quarterly 51*, 228–239.

Wood, P.K. (1997) 'A secondary analysis of claims regarding the reflective judgement interview: Internal consistency, sequentiality and intra-individual differences in ill-structured problem solving.' In J. Smart (ed.) *Higher Education. Handbook Of Theory and Research*. New York: Agathon Press.

Wood, R. (1986) 'Agenda for educational measurement.' In D. Nuttall (ed.) *Assessing Educational Achievement*. Lewes: Falmer Press.

Wood, R. (1993) *Assessment and Testing*. Cambridge: Cambridge University Press.

Wood, R. and Skurnik, L.S. (1969) *Item Banking*. Slough: National Foundation for Educational Research.

Woods, D.R. (1994) *Problem-Based Learning: How to Gain the Most from PBL*. Hamilton, Ontario: McMaster University Bookshop.

Woods, D.R., Haymark, A.N. and Marshall, R.R. (1988) Self-assessment in the context of the McMaster problem solving program. *Assessment and Evaluation in Higher Education 13*, 2, 107-127.

Woods, D.R. *et al.* (1997) 'Developing problem solving skills: The McMaster problem solving program.' *Journal of Engineering Education 86*, 2, 75–92.

Woodward, C. and Woodward, N. (1998) 'Welsh primary school leavers' perecptions of science.' *Research in Science and Technological Education 16*, 1, 43–52.

Woodward, H. (1998) 'Reflective journals and portfolios: learning through assessment.' *Assessment and Evaluation in Higher Education 23*, 4, 415–424.

Work Keys (1995) *Work Keys*. Iowa City, IA: American College Testing program.

Wright, W.A. and Knight, P.T. (1999) Portfolio People: teaching and learning dossiers and the future of higher education. *Innovation in Higher Education*.

Yerkes, R.M. and Dodson, J.D. (1908) 'The relation of strength of stimulus to rapidity of habit formation.' *Journal of Comparative and Neurological Psychology 18*, 459–482.

Yorke, M. (1991) *Performance Indicators. Observations on their use in the Assurance of Course Quality*. Project Report 30. London: Council for National Academic Awards.

Yorke, M. (1996) *Indicators of Programme Quality*. London: Higher Education Quality Council.

Yorke, M. (1998) 'Performance indicators relating to student development: can they be trusted?' *Quality in Higher Education 4*, 1, 45–61.

Yorke, M. *et al.* (1998) 'Undergraduate non-completion in England.' In *Undergraduate Non-completion in Higher Education in England*. Bristol: Higher Education Funding Council.

Yost, M. (1991) 'Developing the expanded statement of institutional purpose.' In J.O. Nichols (ed.) *A Practitioners Handbook for Institutional Effectiveness and Student Outcomes Assessment Implementation*. New York: Agathon Press.

Youngman, M.B. (1980) 'A comparison of item-total point biserial correlation, Rasch and Alpha-beta item analysis procedures.' *Educational and Psychological Measurement 40*, 1, 80–82.

Youngman, M.B. and Heywood, J. (1981) 'Pupil's reactions to multiple choice questions items in mathematics.' *Educational Research 23*, 3, 228–229.

Youngman, M.B., Oxtoby, R., Monk, J.D. and Heywood, J. (1978) *Analysing Jobs*. Aldershot: Gower Press.

Zakrzewski, S. and Bull, J. (1998) 'The mass implementation and evaluation of computer-based systems.' *Assessment and Evaluation in Higher Education 23*, 2, 141–152.

Zangwill, O.L. (1961) 'Asymmetry of cerebral hemisphere function.' In H. Garland (ed.) *Scientific Aspects of Neurology*. London: E and S Livingstone.

Zeller, R.A. and Wells, J.J. (1990) 'Enhancing study skills in an introductory sociology course.' *Teaching Sociology 18*, 1, 46–51.

Zocolotti, P. and Oltman, P.K. (1976) *Field Dependence and Lateralization of Verbal and Configurational Processing*. Princeton, NJ: Educational Testing Service.

Zuber-Skerritt, O.J. and Knight, N. (1986) 'Problem definition and thesis writing: Workshops for post-graduate students.' *Higher Education 15*, 1/2, 89–103.

Subject Index

Author Index